AF710077

Fiduciaries of Humanity

Fiduciaries of Humanity

How International Law Constitutes Authority

EVAN J. CRIDDLE

AND

EVAN FOX-DECENT

OXFORD
UNIVERSITY PRESS

OXFORD
UNIVERSITY PRESS

Oxford University Press is a department of the University of Oxford. It furthers the University's objective of excellence in research, scholarship, and education by publishing worldwide. Oxford is a registered trademark of Oxford University Press in the UK and certain other countries.

Published in the United States of America by Oxford University Press
198 Madison Avenue, New York, NY 10016, United States of America.

© Oxford University Press 2016

All rights reserved. No part of this publication may be reproduced, stored in a retrieval system, or transmitted, in any form or by any means, without the prior permission in writing of Oxford University Press, or as expressly permitted by law, by license, or under terms agreed with the appropriate reproduction rights organization. Inquiries concerning reproduction outside the scope of the above should be sent to the Rights Department, Oxford University Press, at the address above.

You must not circulate this work in any other form
and you must impose this same condition on any acquirer.

Library of Congress Cataloging-in-Publication Data

Names: Criddle, Evan J., author. | Fox-Decent, Evan, author.
Title: Fiduciaries of humanity : how international law constitutes authority /
Evan J. Criddle and Evan Fox-Decent.
Description: New York : Oxford University Press, 2016. | Includes bibliographical
references and index.
Identifiers: LCCN 2016008310 | ISBN 9780199397921 ((hardback) : alk. paper)
Subjects: LCSH: International law. | Authority. | Sovereignty.
Classification: LCC KZ3410 .C74 2016 | DDC 341.01—dc23 LC record available at
http://lccn.loc.gov/2016008310

9 8 7 6 5 4 3 2 1

Printed by Edwards Brothers Malloy, United States of America.

Note to Readers

This publication is designed to provide accurate and authoritative information in regard to the subject matter covered. It is based upon sources believed to be accurate and reliable and is intended to be current as of the time it was written. It is sold with the understanding that the publisher is not engaged in rendering legal, accounting, or other professional services. If legal advice or other expert assistance is required, the services of a competent professional person should be sought. Also, to confirm that the information has not been affected or changed by recent developments, traditional legal research techniques should be used, including checking primary sources where appropriate.

(Based on the Declaration of Principles jointly adopted by a Committee of the American Bar Association and a Committee of Publishers and Associations.)

You may order this or any other Oxford University Press publication by visiting the Oxford University Press website at www.oup.com.

For Anika, my Joy

—EJC

For my soul mate, Adriana

—EFD

CONTENTS

ACKNOWLEDGMENTS

This book is the product of an eight-year collaboration spanning two countries, and we have incurred far too many intellectual and personal debts along the way to hold out hope of repaying them all here. We are especially grateful to three extraordinary deans—Hannah Arterian, Davison Douglas, and Daniel Jutras—and to our brilliant colleagues at McGill University, Syracuse University, and the College of William and Mary, for their steadfast support of this project. We have been fortunate to present early drafts of the chapters in this book to audiences at the annual meetings of the American Society of International Law, the European Society of International Law, the Canadian Political Science Association, the Junior International Law Scholars Association, the Law and Society Association, and the World Summit on Counterterrorism; as well as at conferences, workshops, and colloquia convened at Arizona State University, DePaul University, the University of Georgia, McGill University, the University of Notre Dame, the Royal Melbourne Institute of Technology, Syracuse University, Tel Aviv University, and the College of William and Mary. Additionally, our work on this book has benefitted from generous research grants awarded by the Canadian Social Science and Humanities Research Council.

Although we cannot recognize all of the friends and colleagues who have contributed to this project by name, we would be remiss if we failed to acknowledge the encouragement and illuminating comments we have received from Rakesh Anand, Arash Abizadeh, Bill Banks, Eyal Benvenisti, Kristen Boon, Keith Bybee, Trey Childress, Harlan Cohen, Anthony Colangelo, Nancy Combs, Geoffrey Corn, Tucker Culbertson, Ian Dahlman, Ashley Deeks, David Dyzenhaus, Stephen Galoob, Andrew Gold, Adil Haque, Tara Helfman, Florian Hoffman, Richard Janda, Chimène Keitner, Karen Knop, Robert Leckey, Ethan Leib, Jacob Levy, Eliav Lieblich, Clark Lombardi, Armand de Mestral, Patrick Macklem, Audrey Macklin, Frédéric Mégret, Timothy Meyer, Paul Miller, Saira Mohamed, Julian Mortenson, Victor Muñiz-Fraticelli, Donna Nagy, James Nickel, Rose Parfitt, René Provost, Teddy Rave, Bill Scheuerman, Christa Scholtz, Gordon Smith, Lionel Smith, Stephen Smith, Malcolm Thorburn, Cora True-Frost, Daniel Weinstock, Laurel Weldon, and Yves Winter. Many talented students also contributed their time and insights to the development of this manuscript, including Jonathan Berman, Amanda Campbell, Timothy Dené, Emily Edler, Greg Donaldson, Kaylee Gum, Kenneth Hunt, Claire Hunter, Carlos Iván Fuentes, Brandon Kaufman, Michaël Lessard, Andrew Lizotte, Scott Loong, Nelcy López-Cuéllar, Philip Mutton, Jayne

Olm-Shipman, Amanda Orcutt, Krishana Patel, Leonard Simmons, Kevin Smith, Drucilla Tigner, and Laura Zubler.

Some of the ideas that we develop in this book have appeared previously in articles and essays published in the *Cornell Law Review, German Law Journal, Human Rights Quarterly, Law and Philosophy, Legal Theory,* the *Notre Dame Law Review,* the *Queen's Law Journal, Theoretical Inquiries in Law,* and the *Yale Journal of International Law.* We are grateful to editors and anonymous peer reviewers at these journals for their assistance in refining the arguments presented here. Special thanks are due, as well, to Blake Ratcliff and the editorial team at Oxford University Press for their patience and professionalism.

Last, we express our love to Adriana and Anika for their devoted loyalty and care, and to Isaac, Andrew, Elin, Claire, Lucie, Maya, and Ronin—our intrepid "citizens of the world," who have grown up alongside this text.

1

The Fiduciary Character of Sovereignty

I. INTRODUCTION

In his classic treatise on the law of nations, the eminent Swiss jurist Emerich de Vattel asserted that "sovereign authority" is "established only for the common good of all citizens."[1] Therefore, any monarch who claimed sovereign privileges:

> ought to have his mind impressed with this great truth, that the sovereign power is solely intrusted to him for the safety of the state, and the happiness of the people; that he is not permitted to consider himself as the principal object in the administration of affairs, to seek his own satisfaction, or his private advantage; but that he ought to direct all his views, all his steps, to the greatest advantage of the state and people who have submitted to him.[2]

Having framed sovereignty as an entrusted power, Vattel reasoned that the law of nations would not permit a monarch to treat the idea of sovereignty as a license to oppress his own people. "When a sovereign does injury to any one" of his subjects, Vattel suggested, he "acts without real authority" and, "having lost all the sentiments of a sovereign, . . . no longer retains the prerogatives attached to that exalted rank."[3] Thus, a monarch's sovereign "*right* is derived from *duty*"—a legal obligation to exercise public powers solely for and on behalf of the people as a whole.[4]

Nearly three-and-a-half centuries later, in a very different context, U.N. Secretary-General Kofi Annan invoked a similar theory of sovereignty in his 1999 Annual Address to the U.N. General Assembly. Citing humanitarian tragedies in Kosovo and East Timor, the Secretary-General asserted that the international community shared responsibility with states to safeguard humanity from mass violence

1. Emmerich de Vattel, The Law of Nations: Or Principles of the Law of Nature Applied to the Conduct and Affairs of Nations and Sovereigns 13 (1758) (transl. 1876).

2. *Id.*

3. *Id.* at 21–22.

4. *Id.* at lv.

and oppression, and he linked these "new responsibilities" to a relational conception of sovereignty under international law:

> State sovereignty, in its most basic sense, is being redefined—not least by the forces of globalisation and international co-operation. States are now widely understood to be instruments at the service of their peoples, and not vice versa. At the same time individual sovereignty—by which I mean the fundamental freedom of each individual, enshrined in the charter of the UN and subsequent international treaties—has been enhanced by a renewed and spreading consciousness of individual rights. When we read the charter today, we are more than ever conscious that its aim is to protect individual human beings, not to protect those who abuse them.[5]

Although these two reflections on the character of sovereignty represent distinct epochs in the history of international law, they offer strikingly similar accounts of international legal order. Both Vattel and Annan suggest that public powers are entrusted to states for the benefit of their people. Under both accounts, states forfeit their authority to rule if they abandon the public-regarding "sentiments of a sovereign" by disregarding their fiduciary obligations to their people. These complementary visions of states as agents or trustees for their people distinguish Vattel and Annan as participants in a republican tradition that dates back to antiquity.

This book takes up the idea that states serve as fiduciaries for their people and, collectively, for humanity at large. Indeed, we shall see that in many contexts states are fiduciaries of humanity generally,[6] as well as discrete agents of the people within their territorial jurisdiction. As fiduciaries of humanity, states owe various context-specific duties to foreign nationals, including, in some cases, extraterritorial foreign nationals. Likewise, international institutions are also, we argue, fiduciaries of humanity. International institutions sometimes engage in a form of direct fiduciary governance akin to the fiduciary relationship between a sovereign state and its people, as occurred in Kosovo and East Timor. More generally, international institutions act as indirect fiduciaries by delegating public powers to states, monitoring state performance, and arbitrating international disputes within the framework of

5. Kofi Annan, Annual Address to the General Assembly, SG/SM/7136, Sept. 20, 1999, http://www.un.org/News/Press/docs/1999/19990920.sgsm7136.html (last visited Dec. 1, 2015).

6. In previous writings, we have referred to this cosmopolitan aspect of states' fiduciary role as a form of "joint trusteeship" for the benefit of humanity. *E.g.*, Evan Fox-Decent & Ian Dahlman, *Sovereignty as Trusteeship and Indigenous Peoples*, 16 THEORETICAL INQUIRIES L. 507 (2015); Evan Fox-Decent, *From Fiduciary States to Joint Trusteeship of the Atmosphere: The Right to a Healthy Environment through a Fiduciary Prism*, *in* FIDUCIARY DUTY AND THE ATMOSPHERIC TRUST 253 (Ken Coghill, Charles Sampford & Tim Smith eds., 2012); *see also* Eyal Benvenisti, *Sovereigns as Trustees of Humanity: On the Accountability of States to Foreign Stakeholders*, 107 AM. J. INT'L L. 295 (2013) (developing historical and theoretical grounds for viewing states as trustees of humanity as well as their people). We use the more general term "fiduciaries of humanity" in this work, however, in recognition of the fact that the juridical status and fiduciary obligations associated with statehood—although analogous to trusteeship—are not fully captured in the law of trust. The term 'fiduciaries of humanity' is also capacious enough to incorporate the idea that international institutions, subnational actors, and even some nonstate actors serve as fiduciaries of humanity under international law. *See infra* Chapter 8.

an international legal order that is intended to benefit humanity. The chapters in this book examine the theoretical and practical implications of these insights for public international law.

Arguably the most important of these implications is that the time has come to retire the traditional, but increasingly embattled, conception of state sovereignty as exclusive jurisdiction. In its place, we propose a new relational model that views sovereignty as emanating from a fiduciary relationship between states and the people subject to their jurisdiction. Adumbrating and defending this conception of sovereignty from the standpoint of public international law is this book's principal burden. The fiduciary model we develop is a "relational theory" in the sense that it conceptualizes state sovereignty under international law as arising from, and being defined and constrained by, features of the distinctive juridical relationship that international law constitutes between states and their people. Contemporary international law entrusts states with authority to exercise sovereign powers, but only in the name and for the benefit of the people subject to those powers (including, in some cases, foreign nationals). This idea is the criterion of legitimacy that flows from the fiduciary theory, and in subsequent chapters we shall see that it plays a central role in the assessment of the legality and scope of international law.

Fiduciary concepts have furnished a conceptual foundation of international legal relationships for centuries, from colonial encounters that sparked the emergence of international law as a discipline[7] to the contemporary law of occupation.[8] Until recently, however, the fiduciary character of state sovereignty has not received sustained attention as a normative theory of international law. This book suggests that the fiduciary model of state sovereignty merits further examination and elaboration because it offers a compelling philosophical account of contemporary international law's focus on human security and human rights as the central concerns of state sovereignty. Under the fiduciary model, sovereignty serves people rather than states. Consequently, a state's claim to exercise sovereign authority is derived from, and wholly dependent upon, the satisfaction of its relational duties to the people subject to its legal powers. At a general level, states must provide the people subject to their powers a regime of secure and equal freedom. More concretely, this means that states must treat their people always as ends rather than mere means (the Kantian principle of non-instrumentalization), and they must refrain from assuming arbitrary power over the legal and practical interests of their people (the republican principle of non-domination). We argue that these general obligations are constitutive of state sovereignty under international law.

A variety of more specific legal proscriptions and affirmative duties emanate from these general fiduciary obligations, including the prohibitions against genocide and

7. *See* Antony Anghie, Imperialism, Sovereignty, and the Making of International Law (2004) (critiquing the application of fiduciary concepts throughout the colonial era).

8. *See* Ralph Wilde, International Territorial Administration: How Trusteeship and the Civilizing Mission Never Went Away 322–26 (2008) (discussing this trustee conception); Eyal Benvenisti, The International Law of Occupation 6 (2004) (observing that an "occupant's status is conceived to be that of a trustee"); Adam Roberts, *What Is Military Occupation?*, 55 Brit. Y.B. Int'l L. 249, 259 (1984) (stating that "the idea of 'trusteeship' is implicit in all occupation law . . . all occupants are in some vague and general sense trustees").

torture; civil and political rights of due process, freedom of expression, freedom of religion, and legal equality; progressively implemented socioeconomic rights to food, housing, education, and health care; and obligations to provide refuge to foreign nationals fleeing persecution. The fiduciary character of a state's legal authority thus finds expression in a vast array of norms recognized under international law, ranging from the law governing recognition of emerging states and international human rights law (IHRL) to other areas such as international humanitarian law (IHL) and international refugee law (IRL). In contrast to traditional accounts of sovereignty, which posit a tension between a state's autonomy and principles of state responsibility, the emerging fiduciary model envisions a state's sovereign authority and its international legal obligations as inextricably connected. A state's sovereign authority to rule and its duty to serve the people entrusted to its care are mutually dependent features of the fiduciary constitution of sovereignty under international law.

The fiduciary model of sovereignty developed in this book is both a conceptual and normative theory of the philosophical foundations of state authority and a positive or interpretive theory of the juridical structure that already exists under international law of the relationship between the state and each person subject to its jurisdiction. The relationship between a state and its people is distinctively fiduciary because it shares constitutive features common to all fiduciary relationships, including trust, discretionary power, and vulnerability. In recognition of these features, international law regulates the distribution and exercise of sovereign powers, much as private law regulates the powers of other fiduciaries to protect the integrity of relations in which trust is reposed. Although international institutions rarely refer to fiduciary obligations when they assess state compliance with international law, they enforce states' obligations by applying legal norms that safeguard the dignity of persons subject to IHRL, as well as the status and standing of others who are subject to IHL, a status and standing that recognizes the individual as a proper subject and beneficiary of international legal order. Viewed from this perspective, we argue, the fiduciary model captures the essential normative foundations and legal structure of state sovereignty under contemporary international law. The fiduciary theory thus illuminates the implicit presuppositions of contemporary international law.

The book's methodology is a blend of inference to the best explanation and Rawls's idea of "reflective equilibrium."[9] In subsequent chapters we take as provisionally given core elements of different domains of international law—for example, the prohibition against torture within IHRL or the duty of non-refoulement under IRL—and show how those elements can be explained by the fiduciary theory. We infer the plausibility of the fiduciary theory from the explanation it supplies of the central precepts of multiple domains of international law. The fiduciary view is thus an *interpretive* theory of international law. But as noted, the fiduciary account is also a *prescriptive* theory, as it has conceptual and normative resources that enable a constructive critique of various aspects of international law, including pieces generally thought to lie at the core, such as the purported jus cogens or peremptory status of the prohibition against piracy. This critical appraisal occurs through a process of reflective equilibrium under which the specific particulars of international law are

9. John Rawls, A Theory of Justice 20 (1971).

tested against the general requirements of the fiduciary theory, which at this stage of analysis is a theory enriched and strengthened by inclusion of the core elements of international law well-suited to a fiduciary explanation.

More concretely, we will show that the fiduciary model has normative implications that should inform efforts to strengthen international legal frameworks through the principles of non-instrumentalization and non-domination. For example, the fiduciary principle's relational conception of sovereignty aids in identifying which international norms merit induction into the canon of international "human rights," and it clarifies the circumstances under which states, during emergencies, may derogate from their international obligations to respect human rights. Additionally, the fiduciary model offers resources for refining international law on the use of force, mediating tensions between IHRL and IHL, and refining the international norms that govern administrative detention during armed conflict and refugee crises. In these and many other respects, the fiduciary model outlines an agenda for reform that should guide international law's progressive development.

II. THE CLASSICAL MODEL OF SOVEREIGNTY

Historically, the fiduciary conception of state sovereignty has been overshadowed by a second model that emphasizes a state's autonomy to the exclusion of all other considerations. This "classical model" of sovereignty views states as having authority to govern and represent their people on strictly their own terms, and that states possess this authority as an absolute (or near absolute) legal entitlement. Conventional accounts trace the classical model to French philosopher Jean Bodin, who famously defined "sovereignty" in the sixteenth century as a "power absolute and perpetual," "supreme," and "subject to no law."[10] For Bodin, the term "sovereignty" reflected a state's "absolute authority" to govern its people "without the consent of any superior, equal, or inferior being necessary."[11] This account of state sovereignty as absolute and exclusive authority did not map particularly well onto the governing institutions of Europe during Bodin's lifetime, when the idea of a pan-European Christian commonwealth supported multilayered political authorities, obligations, and interdependencies. With the dissolution of the Holy Roman Empire in the seventeenth century, however, Bodin's account of sovereignty gained greater appeal as a practical roadmap for moving Europe beyond the civil and religious strife of the Thirty Years' War. The idea of unitary, territorially defined sovereign states vested with absolute power, interacting with one another based on principles of comity and reciprocity, held out the promise of a more stable geopolitical order. The Treaty of Westphalia gave formal recognition to these principles in 1648, inaugurating a new era in which

10. Jean Bodin, Les Six Livres de la République 179–228, 295–310 (1986) (1576) (quoted in Paul Gordon Lauren, The Evolution of International Human Rights: Visions Seen 26 (1998)).

11. *Id.* But for an important corrective to the "absolutist" reading of Bodin, see Daniel Lee, *"Office Is a Thing Borrowed": Jean Bodin on Offices and Seigneurial Government*, 41 Pol. Theory 409, 411 (2013) (arguing that Bodin distinguished sharply between "lawful government" and "*seigneurial* government," advocating for the former and against the latter).

the sovereign autonomy of nation-states emerged as the primary constitutive doctrine of international law.

During the late nineteenth century, the classical model reached its high-water mark with the rise of international legal positivism. Consistent with the classical model, international legal positivism defined states as the sole legitimate sources of all executive, legislative, and judicial power within their respective jurisdictions. States thus enjoyed exclusive political power, unfettered regulatory discretion, and a monopoly on the lawful use of force within their borders. Although some theorists believed that heads of state might be held accountable in the hereafter for the discharge of their duties, the classical model insisted that there was no higher power on earth to which states might legitimately be called to account. In the absence of a global sovereign, states by default were the ultimate judges of the legality of their own domestic conduct. States' de facto control over their territory was thought, therefore, to confer exclusive de jure authority to rule their people.

In contrast to states' exclusive jurisdiction and mutual independence as regards their internal affairs, international relations were thought to be characterized by the expansive freedom that individuals would share in a Hobbesian pre-political "state of nature." Although states could adopt international legal norms voluntarily by international custom or treaty, they were not legally bound by norms to which they had withheld their consent. Moreover, when states failed to honor their international legal obligations, the burden fell upon other states to enforce international agreements by seeking reparation and the cessation of ongoing illegal conduct through reciprocal reprisals or countermeasures. Under the classical model, states alone possessed legal personality and could use international law to pursue whatever ends they chose; individuals and other private entities lacked legal standing to contest the form, content, and implementation of international law. The concept of absolute territorial sovereignty thus generated the subjects of international law, laid the theoretical foundation for international legal obligations, and furnished decentralized (if somewhat crude and underdeveloped) institutional mechanisms for enforcing those obligations.

Elements of the classical model feature prominently in the works of leading publicists from before Westphalia to the present. Hugo Grotius, the seventeenth-century Dutch jurist widely considered the founder of modern international law, famously defined "sovereignty" in classical terms as a state's power to act without being "subject to the legal control of another."[12] Although Vattel departed from the classical model in some respects, he likewise asserted that every state "possesses an absolute independence on all the others," and treated states as the only legitimate subjects of international law.[13] Some publicists, such as Samuel Pufendorf and his followers, devoted such energy to defending the state's sovereign independence from external constraint that they rejected the notion that a state could be legally bound even by its own treaty obligations to other states.[14]

12. Hugo Grotius, The Law of War and Peace 102 (Francis W. Kelsey transl., 1925).

13. Vattel, *supra* note 1, at xiii.

14. *See* Wilhelm G. Grewe, The Epochs of International Law 354 (2000) (Michael Byers, transl. 2000); Arthur Nussbaum, A Concise History of the Law of Nations 148 (1962).

The classical model had a profound impact on international society for centuries. Within Europe, the model's foundational principle of nonintervention had the virtue of (imperfectly) suppressing the types of religious and ethnic conflict that had engulfed the continent in the decades leading up to Westphalia. Outside Europe, the classical model served initially to enable European imperialism. Because European powers declined to recognize non-European powers as sovereign states, the classical model led, in Jean Cohen's words, to rampant "domination and exploitation of non-sovereign territories (the rest of the world)," such that the very concept of "[s]overeignty has been associated with arbitrary and rapacious power politics ever since."[15] Eventually, "fierce competition among sovereign states construed as self-contained, self-interested entities, undermined the rudimentary mechanisms enabling coexistence within European international society."[16] Nonetheless, the decline of Western imperialism in the late nineteenth and twentieth centuries did not lead ultimately to the classical model's demise, but rather to the replication of Western-style statehood throughout the world, with former colonies laying claim to the same sovereign rights of territorial integrity, political independence, and nonintervention.[17]

Although the classical model of sovereignty dominated international legal and political theory after Westphalia, relatively few theorists accepted the model in its purest form. For example, although Grotius characterized state sovereignty as independent jurisdiction, he famously tempered his endorsement of the classical model by emphasizing the demands of natural law as the "dictate of right reason," and affirming that some international norms would bind states regardless of their consent (*ius scriptum*).[18] Vattel likewise developed a concept of "necessary law" that would operate as a side-constraint on state voluntarism, and he described a state's sovereignty in terms of duty-based powers "to provide for the Necessities of the Nation," to "procure the true Happiness of the Nation," and to "fortify . . . against External Attacks."[19] Thus, despite the classical model's dominance, the notion that states necessarily enjoy absolute discretion in their exercise of public powers never achieved universal acceptance among legal and political theorists.

Over the course of the late nineteenth and twentieth centuries, several developments in public international law further weakened the Westphalian paradigm. The classical conception of states interacting with one another as independent agents in a perpetually pre-political state of nature became less and less tenable as newly recognized states in Eastern Europe submitted to international oversight of their treatment of ethnic and religious minorities. As a descriptive theory of public authority, the classical model became even less plausible with the development of regional governance regimes such as the European Union, which assumed regulatory powers traditionally associated with autonomous states, and the emergence of the U.N. Security Council as a global guarantor of "international peace and

15. Jean L. Cohen, Globalization and Sovereignty: Rethinking Legality, Legitimacy, and Constitutionalism 29 (2012).

16. *Id.*

17. *See* Daniel Philpott, Revolutions in Sovereignty: How Ideas Shaped Modern International Relations (2001).

18. Grotius, *supra* note 12, at 38–39.

19. Vattel, *supra* note 1, at lviii (table of contents).

security."[20] The proliferation of other international regulatory organizations such as the World Trade Organization, international tribunals such as the International Court of Justice and International Tribunal for the Law of the Sea, and an ever-growing cadre of international peacekeeping forces and human rights monitors offered further confirmation that international society had evolved beyond the Westphalian paradigm.

At the same time, the modern human rights movement eroded the classical model of sovereignty by introducing enhanced scrutiny of states' internal policies and emphasizing state accountability to the international community. International criminal prosecutions in Nuremburg and Tokyo in the 1940s, followed by comparable initiatives in Arusha and The Hague in the 1990s, demonstrated that the "organized hypocrisy" of state sovereignty would no longer afford state officials a blanket immunity to oppress their people.[21] Moreover, by the end of the twentieth century, many observers concluded that the political, economic, technological, and cultural forces of globalization had diminished the importance of states vis-à-vis other transnational actors to such an extent that states could no longer claim to be the exclusive legitimate subjects of international lawmaking. Collectively, these developments have generated increasing demand for a more nuanced and inclusive theory of international authority that would recognize a diversity of actors as legitimate stakeholders and would subject states to meaningful accountability in accordance with an international rule of law.

III. FROM CLASSICAL SOVEREIGNTY TO RELATIONAL SOVEREIGNTY

What these developments mean for the future of sovereignty remains uncertain. Some legal scholars, such as Louis Henkin and Sir Elihu Lauterpacht, have argued that the very idea of state sovereignty undermines popular sovereignty and human rights. In their view, international law should abandon the concept of state sovereignty as it is an outdated relic of seventeenth-century political theory.[22] Other scholars, such as Jeremy Rabkin, have risen to the defense of sovereignty, insisting that states require independence from external interference to enable their people to exercise their right to self-determination effectively through their elected representatives.[23] Most courts and commentators have staked out an intermediate position between these extremes: a state need not enjoy wholly unfettered autonomy to qualify as "sovereign," they argue, because a state's sovereignty includes the power to enter binding agreements and delegate powers to international institutions. Rather than jettison the classical model of sovereignty entirely, the conventional

20. U.N. Charter ch. VII; *see also* PHILPOTT, *supra* note 17, at 36–43 (characterizing these developments as "revolutions" in the constitution of international society).

21. STEPHEN D. KRASNER, SOVEREIGNTY: ORGANIZED HYPOCRISY (1999).

22. *See* Louis Henkin, *That S-word: Sovereignty, Human Rights, and Globalization, Et Cetera*, 68 FORDHAM L. REV. 1 (1999); Elihu Lauterpacht, *Sovereignty—Myth or Reality*, 73 INT'L AFF. 137 (1997).

23. JEREMY A. RABKIN, THE CASE FOR SOVEREIGNTY: WHY THE WORLD SHOULD WELCOME AMERICAN INDEPENDENCE (2004).

wisdom today seems to be that the classical model can be redeemed by unbundling the privileges traditionally associated with sovereignty. According to this view, sovereignty is best understood not as an indivisible and inalienable entitlement, but rather as a bundle of rights, privileges, powers, and immunities that a state is free to exercise, delegate, or waive at its discretion.[24] States may limit their own discretionary power via delegation without forfeiting their sovereignty, the theory goes, provided that their independence from external constraint remains sufficiently robust to allow them to regulate the life of their community effectively.[25]

However laudable these efforts to rehabilitate the classical model may be, they have failed to resolve the model's shortcomings and have spawned new problems of their own. The primary problem is that under the classical model a state's sovereignty is linked, by definition, to the state's independence from external constraint. Once sovereignty has been divided into a bundle of alienable rights, privileges, powers, and immunities, however, the classical model of sovereignty loses its coherence. Does a state forfeit part of its "sovereignty" if it submits to international legal norms and institutions, for example, by committing to respect human rights, by submitting to international inspections of its nuclear facilities, or by delegating monetary policy to regional organizations? Are some states therefore more sovereign than others? How many sticks may a state delegate before it ceases to qualify as a "sovereign" subject of international law? The classical model is ill-equipped to answer such questions because under its absolutist approach to state autonomy, even the slightest encroachment by international legal norms or institutions on a state's ultimate authority over its internal affairs undercuts the state's sovereignty.[26] Given these problems, it is unsurprising that some international legal scholars would express skepticism about whether sovereignty is worth retaining as a framing concept for international legal order.

Equally problematic, both the traditional classical model and the new bundle-of-rights approach are poorly equipped to explain why contemporary international law treats some international norms such as the prohibitions against military aggression and torture as jus cogens—peremptory norms that sovereign states may never abrogate by mutual agreement or derogate from during public emergencies.[27] If states truly wield absolute and exclusive authority with respect to their internal affairs, then it is unclear why states are considered to be legally obligated to respect jus cogens norms such as the prohibitions against slavery, torture, and prolonged

24. *See, e.g.*, J.L. Brierly, The Law of Nations: An Introduction to the International Law of Peace 48–49 (4th ed. 1949) (describing sovereignty as "an aggregate of particular and very extensive claims that states habitually make for themselves in their relations with other states").

25. Timothy Endicott, *The Logic of Freedom and Power*, *in* The Philosophy of International Law 245, 252–55 (Samantha Besson & John Tasioulas eds., 2010) (arguing that "the content of sovereignty" for Hart "is determined by the powers and forms of independence that a state needs *in order to be a good state*"). *Cf.* Henry Sumner Maine, International Law: A Series of Lectures Delivered Before the University of Cambridge, 1887, at 58 (1888) ("The powers of sovereigns are a bundle or collection of powers and they may be separated one from another.").

26. *See* R.P. Anand, Confrontation or Cooperation? International Law and the Developing Countries 95 (1987) (observing that for this reason the concept of "absolute sovereignty is sheer nonsense").

27. *See* Vienna Convention on the Law of Treaties, art. 53.

arbitrary detention—irrespective of their consent to these norms.[28] Indeed, if we take the classical model of sovereignty seriously, any delegation of authority by the state from its bundle of rights, privileges, powers, and immunities would always be subject to rescission, with the consequence that all international obligations would be purely discretionary. If international law is to be taken seriously, the international community needs a more sophisticated account of state sovereignty.

The most promising efforts to reconceptualize sovereignty have defined state authority in relational terms, with human dignity taking center stage as sovereignty's raison d'être. In the seventeenth century, the classical model of sovereignty plausibly advanced the cause of human dignity by protecting individuals from the kind of religiously motivated violence that ravaged Europe during the Thirty Years War. Pufendorf apparently saw no irony in defending absolute state sovereignty while simultaneously defining the "general law for supreme sovereigns" in relational terms: " 'Let the people's welfare be the supreme law.' "[29] By the mid-twentieth century, however, the classical model had fallen out of favor as it became painfully apparent that the model had enabled states to victimize their own people with impunity. Legal scholars, such as Hersch Lauterpacht, contended that international law could not achieve its humanitarian purposes without redefining sovereignty as a legal relation sensitive to principles of self-determination and human rights.[30] Adherents of this approach came to view international law and international institutions not simply as value-neutral frameworks for resolving inter-state disputes, but rather as purposive regimes designed "to reaffirm faith in fundamental human rights, in the dignity and worth of the human person," and "in the equal rights of men and women and of nations large and small."[31] Although some human rights advocates favored jettisoning the concept of state sovereignty entirely in the aftermath of World War II, many leading theorists embraced the relational conception of sovereignty, developing nuanced legal frameworks for integrating concepts of state sovereignty and human rights within an international public order dedicated to human dignity.[32]

In the late 1960s and 1970s, the United Nations operationalized the relational conception of sovereignty in response to racial discrimination in postcolonial Africa. When the government of Southern Rhodesia unilaterally declared independence in 1965, both the General Assembly and the Security Council refused to accept the declaration, based on the government's exclusion of the black majority from political participation,[33] and the Security Council ultimately called on other states to likewise

28. *See* Restatement (Third) of Foreign Relations of the United States § 702 cmts. d–i, § 102 cmt. k (1987).

29. Samuel Pufendorf, *On the Law of Nature and of Nations, in* Political Writings 242 (Craig Carr & Michael Seidel eds., 1994).

30. *See* Hersch Lauterpacht, International Law and Human Rights 68 (1968) ("The purpose of the State is to safeguard the interests of the individual human being and to render possible the fulfillment, through freedom, of his wider duty to man and society.").

31. U.N. Charter, pmbl.

32. *See, e.g.*, Myers S. McDougal, Harold D. Lasswell & Lung-Chu Chen, Human Rights and World Public Order: The Basic Policies of an International Law of Human Dignity (1980).

33. *See* GA Res. 1747 (XVI), 28 June 1962, A/RES/1747; SC Res. 202, 6 May 1965, S/RES/202; and GA Res. 2022 (XX), 5 Nov. 1965, A/RES/2022.

withhold recognition.[34] In December 1966, the Security Council took the unprecedented step of calling on all states to impose a mandatory embargo on certain goods from Southern Rhodesia.[35] A decade later, the Security Council once again interceded in the domestic affairs of a member-state by imposing a mandatory arms embargo and other measures against South Africa to pressure the ruling regime to abandon its policy of apartheid.[36] Although the Security Council rationalized its actions as falling within its Chapter VII authority to maintain "international peace and security,"[37] critics contended that the Security Council had exceeded its mandate and undermined state sovereignty by interceding in what were quintessentially "matters . . . within the domestic jurisdiction" of the target states.[38] Such calls to preserve states' exclusive sovereign jurisdiction over their internal affairs proved unavailing. Over the next three decades, the Security Council's resolutions against Southern Rhodesia and South Africa paved the way for international sanctions against dozens of other countries that had engaged in human rights abuses against their people. By piercing the veil of state sovereignty in this manner, the United Nations undermined the classical model of state sovereignty and implicitly endorsed a relational vision of international legal order.

Relational accounts of state sovereignty gained additional momentum at the close of the Cold War as new democracies took root in Central and Eastern Europe, and institutions such as the Security Council, international criminal tribunals, and regional security organizations became more active in ensuring state accountability for human rights obligations. Some legal scholars such as James Crawford, Gregory Fox, Thomas Franck, and Michael Reisman greeted the fall of the Berlin Wall with calls to abandon the classical model in favor of "popular sovereignty" and a "right to democratic governance."[39] Human rights advocates continued to emphasize the need for effective external checks on state power to prevent states and nonstate actors from systematically violating human rights. Writing in this vein, Francis Deng and several coauthors argued in the early 1990s that international law should re-conceptualize sovereignty as a "responsibility for promoting citizens' welfare and liberty."[40] A state's sovereign authority to govern its people internally entailed a concomitant "responsibility for failed policies and their disastrous humanitarian consequences," they asserted; states were therefore accountable "both to the national body politic and the international community" for their use and abuse of public powers.[41] When states transgressed their obligations to respect, protect, and

34. *See* S.C. Res. 277, S/RES/277, 18 Mar. 1970, ¶ 2.

35. *See* S.C. Res. 232, S/Res/232, 16 Dec. 1966.

36. S.C. Res. 418, S/Res/418, 4 Nov. 1977; S.C. Res. 919, S/Res/919, 25 May 1994.

37. U.N. Charter, Ch. VII, art. 39.

38. UN Charter, Ch. I, art. 2(7).

39. *See* James Crawford, Democracy and International Law (1993); W. Michael Reisman, *Sovereignty and Human Rights in Contemporary International Law*, 84 Am. J. Int'l L. 866 (1990); Thomas Franck, *The Emerging Right to Democratic Governance*, 86 Am. J. Int'l L. 46 (1992); Gregory H. Fox, *The Right to Political Participation in International Law*, 17 Yale J. Int'l L. 539 (1992).

40. Francis M. Deng et al., Sovereignty as Responsibility: Conflict Management in Africa, at xi (1996).

41. *Id.* at xii, 211.

fulfill human rights, the international community as a whole bore a residual responsibility to take steps necessary to safeguard human dignity—including, potentially, through humanitarian military intervention.

In the years that followed, this conception of the international community's "responsibility to protect" would capture the imagination of the international community, informing Secretary-General Annan's approach to humanitarian crises[42] and inspiring an influential report by the International Committee on Intervention and State Sovereignty.[43] The General Assembly likewise endorsed the basic outlines of the "responsibility to protect" idea in its 2005 World Summit Outcome,[44] as did the Security Council in resolutions responding to crimes against humanity in Libya.[45] Collectively, these developments heralded the emergence of a new model of sovereignty in which states could no longer wield sovereignty as a shield to deflect international scrutiny of their human rights practices.

Although these transformations to the concept of sovereignty have not gone unnoticed, international legal theory has struggled to keep pace with these developments. A number of scholars have emphasized the relational structure of state sovereignty.[46] Most have been content, however, to document the features of contemporary international law that reflect the turn to relational sovereignty, without providing a rigorous theoretical account of it.[47] There are problems with this approach. As Allen Buchanan has observed, principles such as sovereignty must be "embedded in the structure of a moral philosophy of law" to avoid becoming "opportunistic tools for rationalizing failure to act or for wrongful action, [or] rhetorical veils to mask the unrestrained pursuit of narrow self-interest or the lack of will to follow through on basic moral commitments."[48] With the classical model's collapse and the rise of relational sovereignty, there is a pressing need for a rigorous

42. *See* Kofi A. Annan, We the Peoples: The Role of the United Nations in the Twenty-First Century, Report of U.N. Secretary-General to the General Assembly, U.N. Doc. A/54/2000, ¶ 219 (2000) (arguing that "no legal principle—not even sovereignty—can ever shield crimes against humanity" from international intervention); Annan, *supra* note 5.

43. INT'L COMM'N ON INTERVENTION AND STATE SOVEREIGNTY, THE RESPONSIBILITY TO PROTECT (Dec. 2001), http://www.responsibilitytoprotect.org/ICISS%20Report.pdf (last visited Dec. 1, 2015).

44. 2005 World Summit Outcome, G.A. Res. 60/1, A/RES/60/1, 24 Oct. 2005, ¶¶ 138–39 [hereinafter World Summit Outcome].

45. S.C. Res. 1970, S/Res/1970, 26 Feb. 2011; S.C. Res. 1973, S/Res/1973, 17 Mar. 2011.

46. *See, e.g.*, RUTI TEITEL, HUMANITY'S LAW (2011); HELEN STACY, HUMAN RIGHTS FOR THE 21ST CENTURY: SOVEREIGNTY, CIVIL SOCIETY, CULTURE (2009); ALLEN BUCHANAN, JUSTICE, LEGITIMACY, AND SELF-DETERMINATION: MORAL FOUNDATIONS FOR INTERNATIONAL LAW (2004); Anne Peters, *Humanity as the A and Ω of Sovereignty*, 20 EUR. J. INT'L L. 513 (2009); Helen Stacy, *Relational Sovereignty*, 55 STAN. L. REV. 2029 (2003).

47. Noteworthy exceptions include FERNANDO TESÒN, A PHILOSOPHY OF INTERNATIONAL LAW (1998), and BUCHANAN, *supra* note 46.

48. BUCHANAN, *supra* note 46, at 16; *see also* Andreas Paulus, *International Adjudication*, *in* THE PHILOSOPHY OF INTERNATIONAL LAW, *supra* note 25, at 223 (marking the need for a "Dworkinian examination of the foundational principles of an international legal order allowing for legal decisions standing on principle").

philosophical theory of the moral foundations of relational sovereignty, one that is capable of specifying the source, structure, and scope of state authority under international law.

IV. THE FIDUCIARY MODEL OF SOVEREIGNTY

We argue that the relational character of state sovereignty is best understood as a fiduciary relationship between a state and the nationals and non-nationals amenable to its jurisdiction.[49] We are not the first, of course, to assert that the relationship between a state and its legal subjects bears a fiduciary character. The fiduciary conception of state authority can be traced back to the writings of Plato and Aristotle, who each characterized public officials as "guardians" charged with promoting the public good.[50] Cicero similarly argued that "the administration of the government, like the office of a trustee, must be conducted for the benefit of those entrusted to one's care, not those to whom it is entrusted."[51] Polemical tracts from the Puritan Revolution in Britain drew upon these ideas to justify constraining the authority of the king. For example, Henry Parker's *Observations* of 1642 rejected royal claims to absolute power, by asserting that "all rule is but fiduciarie" and that it would be "unnaturall for any Nation . . . to subject it selfe to a condition of servilitie."[52] A generation later, these ideas resurfaced in Locke's famous description of the

49. Legal and political theorists have vigorously debated the so-called "democratic boundary problem," which concerns the criteria that states should use (if any) to define membership in their political community. *See, e.g.*, Rainer Bauböck, *Morphing the Demos into the Right Shape: Normative Principles for Enfranchising Resident Aliens and Expatriate Citizens*, 22 Democratization 820 (2015); Sarah Song, *The Boundary Problem in Democratic Theory: Why the Demos Should Be Bounded by the State*, 4 Int'l Theory 39 (2012). Under contemporary international law, individuals have a "right to nationality" within a state. *See, e.g.*, Universal Declaration of Human Rights art. 15, G.A. Res. 217(A)(III), U.N. GAOR, 3d Sess., U.N. Doc. A/810 (1948) ("Everyone has a right to a nationality."). The contours of this right are contested, and it is unclear to what extent international law establishes a concomitant right to citizenship. *See, e.g.*, Peter J. Spiro, *A New International Law of Citizenship*, 105 Am. J. Int'l L. 694, 695 (2011). We do not address the democratic boundary problem in this book aside from a brief discussion in Chapter 7 of refugee status as a potential pathway to citizenship, and some concluding remarks at the end of Chapter 8 on the idea of an unbounded demos. We defend, however, the proposition that international law requires states to guarantee fundamental security under the rule of law for foreign nationals who are subject to their jurisdiction. Moreover, we claim in Chapter 8 that noncitizens have a special call on international law in their dealings with foreign states, as international law alone can legitimate a state's claim to authority over noncitizens.

50. *See* Plato, The Republic (H.D.P. Lee transl., 1961) (1955); Aristotle, The Ethics of Aristotle (D. P. Chase transl., E.P. Dutton & Co. 1950); Aristotle, Politics (H. Rackham, M.A. transl., Loeb ed., 1932); *see generally* Robert E. Natelson, *The Constitution and the Public Trust*, 52 Buff. L. Rev. 1077, 1097–98 (2004).

51. Cicero, *Moral Goodness*, *in* De Officiis, I.XXV.85, at 87 (Walter Miller transl., 1997) (1913).

52. Richard Tuck, Natural Rights Theories: Their Origin and Development 146 (1979).

legislative power as "only a Fiduciary power to act for certain ends."[53] These ideas laid the foundation for subsequent challenges to monarchical sovereignty in the late eighteenth century. While Edmund Burke and others defended the status quo by asserting that the king, the parliament, and the judiciary held public power in an irrevocable trust,[54] American revolutionaries such as the authors of *The Federalist Papers* invoked the fiduciary conception of state authority in support of republican democracy, insisting that all public institutions and public officials must be subject to meaningful public accountability for their discharge of public powers.[55] The Pennsylvania Constitution of 1776 expressed this idea by declaring that "all power" is "derived from, the people; therefore all officers of government, whether legislative or executive, are their trustees and servants, and at all times accountable to them."[56] For republicans of the American founding and the early nineteenth century, this fiduciary conception of public power grounded a new conception of popular sovereignty based upon the idea that sovereign powers belonged ultimately to the people, with public institutions and officials holding those powers in trust solely to use on the people's behalf.[57] Although the fiduciary model received only sporadic attention in legal and political theory during the late nineteenth and twentieth centuries, leading public intellectuals such as Frederick Maitland, John Stuart Mill, and John Rawls referenced the fiduciary conception of public powers,[58] as did national courts in a host of jurisdictions.[59]

53. John Locke, Second Treatise of Civil Government § 149, at 367 (Peter Laslett ed., 1988) (1690).

54. Edmund Burke, *Discontents in the Kingdom, in* Burke's Politics: Selected Writings and Speeches of Edmund Burke on Reform, Revolution, and War 3, 28 (Ross J.S. Hoffman & Paul Levack eds., 1949) (1770).

55. *See, e.g.,* The Federalist No. 46, at 294 (James Madison), (New American Library 1961) (1788) ("The federal and State governments are in fact but different agents and trustees of the people, constituted with different powers and designed for different purposes."); The Federalist No. 65 (Alexander Hamilton), *supra* note 60, at 397 ("The delicacy and magnitude of a trust which so deeply concerns the political reputation and existence of every man engaged in the administration of public affairs speak for themselves.")

56. Pa. Const. of 1776, art. IV.

57. *See* Jedediah Purdy, A Tolerable Anarchy: Rebels, Reactionaries, and the Making of American Freedom 10 (2009) (observing that "[this] idea that power flowed from the whole political community to the government, which held it in 'trust,' was central to American political language in the nineteenth century.").

58. *See* Frederick William Maitland, *Trust and Corporation, in* Selected Essays 151, 220 (H.D. Hazeltine et al. eds., 1936) ("[W]hen new organs of local government are being developed, . . . it is natural . . . that their governmental powers should be regarded as being held in trust."); John Stuart Mill, *Representative Government, in* Utilitarianism, Liberty and Representative Government 230, 321 (1947) (describing public power as a "trust" that must be "fulfill[ed]"); John Rawls, The Law of Peoples (1999) (arguing that "an important role of government . . . is to be the effective agent of a people as they take responsibility for their territory").

59. *See, e.g.,* Stone v. Mississippi, 101 U.S. 814, 820 (1879) ("The power of governing is a trust committed by the people to the government."); Black River Regulating Dist. v. Adirondack League Club, 121 N.E.2d 428, 433 (N.Y. 1984) (characterizing the legislative power as "akin

The fiduciary model also influenced the development of public international law. With the Peace of Westphalia and the emergence of autonomous states in the seventeenth century, the prevailing view of international order, at least between European powers, was that states interacted with one another in a pre-political state of nature. Nonetheless, for over four centuries, these powers pressed the fiduciary model of the state into ideological service as they sought to extend European sovereignty over foreign lands. Spanish theologian Francisco de Vitoria, who generally defended the interests of indigenous peoples against Spanish conquest, claimed that indigenous peoples were essentially children incapable of self-government. Indigenous peoples were therefore susceptible to a purportedly civilizing European trusteeship, albeit one that could exist only provisionally, and for the benefit of the colonized peoples.[60] With a like sympathy for Indians subject to British rule, Burke argued that the East India Company had breached the trust-like authority Parliament had given it over colonial India. As a consequence of this breach of fiduciary obligation, Burke contended, the governing powers that had been entrusted to the Company reverted back to Parliament (not to India).[61]

Even when European powers recognized non-European powers as independent states, they often perpetuated trustee-like relationships through unequal treaties. Under the protectorate system of the eighteenth and nineteenth centuries, European powers promised to defend weak nations from external attack in exchange for the right to exercise special privileges within the state.[62] Protectorates maintained formal independence internally, which relieved colonial powers of the burden of day-to-day administration, but they ceded control over their external relations to powerful protector-states. Some protector states also reserved the right to intervene in the protectorate to quell civil unrest and restore legal order.[63] European powers rationalized the protectorate system as a fiduciary relationship that benefitted newly independent states that were not yet prepared to assume the full burdens of sovereignty.[64]

During the interwar period, the mandate system established by the League of Nations further entrenched the colonial trusteeship ideas championed by Vitoria and Burke. Article 22 of the Covenant of the League of Nations stipulated in

to that of a public trust to be exercised not for the benefit or at the will of the trustee but for the common good.").

60. *See* FRANCISCO DE VITORIA, POLITICAL WRITINGS (Anthony Pagden & Jeremy Lawrance eds., 1991); *see generally* ANGHIE, *supra* note 7, at 23–27, 144–45; Jedediah Purdy & Kimberly Fielding, *Sovereigns, Trustees, Guardians: Private-Law Concepts and the Limits of Legitimate State Power*, 70 LAW & CONTEMP. PROBS. 165, 180–210 (2007).

61. *See* David Bromwich, *Introduction to* EDMUND BURKE, ON EMPIRE, LIBERTY, AND REFORM: SPEECHES AND LETTERS 1–39 (David Bromwich ed., 2000) [hereinafter ON EMPIRE]; Edmund Burke, *Speech on Fox's East India Bill* (1783), *in* ON EMPIRE, *supra*.

62. *See* VATTEL, *supra* note 1, pt. 1, ch. 1, § 6.

63. *See* ANGHIE, *supra* note 7, at 78–88.

64. *See, e.g.*, Berlin Conference, General Act, art 6 (Feb. 26, 1885) ("All the Powers exercising sovereign rights or influence in the [Basin of the Congo] bind themselves to watch over the preservation of the native tribes, and to care for the improvement of the conditions of their moral and material well-being, and to help in suppressing slavery and especially the slave trade.").

part that mandate states, comprised of the former territories of Germany and the Ottoman Empire, were "not yet able to stand by themselves," and that their well-being therefore fell to the League as a "sacred trust of civilization."[65] The mandatories owed duties of good governance to both the international community through the League of Nations and their subject wards, which in theory were to be groomed for self-rule. Although the League of Nations eventually dissolved, the mandate regime continued in diminished form after World War II under the United Nations Trusteeship System, and has occasionally offered redress to trust territories.[66]

On balance, the historical record suggests that fiduciary concepts enabled colonialism by lending it a veneer of legality. Although European powers framed their relationships with colonized nations as benevolent "trusteeships" or "wardships," in practice, European paternalism infantilized non-Europeans, forcing them to accept a distinctly Western model of political and legal order while entrenching economic and political inequities between colonial and colonized peoples.[67] Nonetheless, the wrongfulness of colonialism arguably did not lie in the trust-like structure of colonial rule per se, but in colonialism itself, which denied colonized peoples' opportunity for self-government. In a postcolonial world in which fiduciary concepts are wedded inextricably to popular sovereignty, the fiduciary model has the potential to strengthen, rather than subvert, the idea that public power ultimately belongs to the people. Disabused of its colonialist ideology and already open to a relational vision of public authority, international law may now be ready to realize the promise of popular sovereignty envisioned by the fiduciary conception of the state.

Some recent developments suggest that the international community may be primed to embrace a fiduciary model of sovereignty. The past two decades have witnessed an increased emphasis on principles of popular sovereignty and state accountability for human rights violations, underscoring the relational character of sovereignty as a right belonging to the people that the state may exercise solely for their benefit. Concurrently, many political theorists have returned to the republican tradition, exploring how principles of popular sovereignty and non-domination

65. League of Nations Covenant art. 22, ¶ 1; *see also* HERSCH LAUTERPACHT, PRIVATE LAW SOURCES AND ANALOGIES OF INTERNATIONAL LAW 191–200 (1970) (discussing the fiduciary structure of the mandate system as a "trust" or "guardianship," and concluding that the "general and fundamental principles are the relation of derivation of powers or delegation on one hand, and of trust, duty, and confidence on the other"); DUNCAN CAMPBELL LEE, THE MANDATE FOR MESOPOTAMIA AND THE PRINCIPLE OF TRUSTEESHIP IN ENGLISH LAW (1921) (tracing the mandate concept to Roman fiduciary law and describing the British Mandate for Mesopotamia as "the very child of English law—the English law of Trust").

66. In 1989, Nauru, a Micronesian island and trust territory under Australia's administration, claimed before the ICJ that Australia had engaged in self-dealing by managing the island's phosphate deposits for the benefit of Australia rather than Nauru. Australia eventually settled with Nauru, paying an amount that included Nauru's claim to the loss it suffered as a consequence of Australia's self-dealing. *See* Ramon E. Reyes Jr., Nauru v. Australia: *The International Fiduciary Duty and the Settlement of Nauru's Claims for Rehabilitation of Its Phosphate Lands*, 16 N.Y.L. SCH. J. INT'L & COMP. L. 1 (1996).

67. ANGHIE, *supra* note 7, at 145–46; *see also* HANS J. MORGENTHAU, POLITICS AMONG NATIONS: THE STRUGGLE FOR POWER AND PEACE 65 (1948) (characterizing the "sacred trust" concept as "a ready instrument of ideological disguise").

(i.e., a conception of individual liberty as freedom from arbitrary power) might inform international law and international relations.[68] A growing body of legal scholarship has employed the fiduciary model as a conceptual framework for rethinking the purpose and structure of public law.[69] Scholars have applied the fiduciary model to issues such as constitutional interpretation,[70] justification defenses in criminal law,[71] judicial deference to administrative agencies,[72] legislative redistricting,[73] odious debt in international finance,[74] environmental protection,[75] and principles of judicial and congressional ethics.[76] From the perspective of international law, however, the fiduciary character of sovereignty remains under-theorized, and its practical implications require further development.[77]

The following discussion outlines a new philosophical theory of relational sovereignty based on the argument that states stand in a fiduciary relationship with the nationals and non-nationals subject to their authority. We begin by sketching the

68. *See, e.g.*, PHILIP PETTIT, REPUBLICANISM: A THEORY OF FREEDOM AND GOVERNMENT (1999); QUENTIN SKINNER, LIBERTY BEFORE LIBERALISM (1998); MORTIMER SELLERS, REPUBLICAN PRINCIPLES IN INTERNATIONAL LAW: THE FUNDAMENTAL REQUIREMENTS OF A JUST WORLD ORDER (2006).

69. *See, e.g.*, EVAN FOX-DECENT, SOVEREIGNTY'S PROMISE: THE STATE AS FIDUCIARY (2011); Andrew Gold, *Reflections on the State as Fiduciary*, 63 U. TORONTO L.J. 655 (2013); David L. Ponet & Ethan J. Leib, *Fiduciary Law's Lessons for Deliberative Democracy*, 91 B.U. L. REV. 1249 (2011); Evan Fox-Decent, *The Fiduciary Nature of State Legal Authority*, 31 QUEEN'S L.J. 259 (2005).

70. *See, e.g.*, Gary Lawson et al., *The Fiduciary Foundations of Federal Equal Protection*, 94 B.U. L. REV. 415 (2014); Natelson, *supra* note 50.

71. *See* Malcolm Thorburn, *Justifications, Powers, and Authority*, 117 YALE L.J. 1078 (2008).

72. *See, e.g.*, Evan J. Criddle, *Mending Holes in the Rule of (Administrative) Law*, 104 NW. U. L. REV. 1271 (2010); Evan J. Criddle, *Fiduciary Administration: Rethinking Popular Representation in Agency Rulemaking*, 88 TEXAS L. REV. 441 (2010); Evan J. Criddle, *Fiduciary Foundations of Administrative Law*, 54 UCLA L. REV. 117 (2006).

73. *See* Ethan J. Leib et al., *Translating Fiduciary Principles into Public Law*, 126 HARV. L. REV. F. 91 (2013); D. Theodore Rave, *Politicians as Fiduciaries*, 126 HARV. L. REV. 671 (2013).

74. *See* Mitu Gulati & Lee Buchheit, *Responsible Lending and Borrowing*, United Nations Conference on Trade & Dev., No. 198, Apr. 2010).

75. *See* FIDUCIARY STATES AND THE ATMOSPHERIC TRUST (Ken Coghill et al., eds., 2012).

76. *See* Sung Hui Kim, *The Last Temptation of Congress: Legislator Insider Trading and the Fiduciary Norm Against Corruption*, 98 CORNELL L. REV. 845 (2013); Ethan J. Leib, *Fiduciary Principles and the Jury*, 55 WM. & MARY L. REV. 1109 (2014); Ethan J. Leib et al., *A Fiduciary Theory of Judging*, 101 CAL. L. REV. 699 (2013); Donna Nagy, *Owning Stock While Making Law: A Fiduciary Solution to an Agency Problem in Politics*, 47 WAKE FOREST L. REV. 845 (2013). Other legal and political theorists have made passing references to the fiduciary character of public authority. *See, e.g.*, BUCHANAN, *supra* note 46, at 104 (noting public officials' "role-defined obligations as public fiduciaries").

77. In addition to our previous writings, Eyal Benvenisti's "GlobalTrust" Project has explored the practical implications of conceptualizing "sovereigns as trustees of humanity." *See* http://globaltrust.tau.ac.il/publications/ (last visited Mar. 17, 2016) (providing links to relevant articles and working papers).

juridical structure of fiduciary relations in private law. Next, we briefly discuss several popular, but ultimately unconvincing, theories of the moral basis for fiduciary duties. In their place, we offer a Kantian theory under which the fiduciary state owes its legal subjects an overarching duty to establish a regime of secure and equal freedom. We draw on this Kantian theory throughout the book to show how the relational character of sovereignty can explain core areas of public international law, such as IHRL, IHL, and IRL. We pause in this chapter, however, to outline two alternative accounts of the state's fiduciary role. The first is a Lockean account that, like the Kantian articulation of the fiduciary model, involves a substantive theory of law and legal order. The second alternative is based on Joseph Raz's "service conception" of practical authority.[78] This is a conceptual account of authority intended to be consistent with a wide range of substantive theories of law and public authority, including the Kantian and Lockean accounts. Last, we introduce our thesis that the fiduciary model of state sovereignty operates as an emerging "constitution" for international society by providing a legal framework for evaluating claims to sovereign authority.

V. THE LEGAL STRUCTURE OF FIDUCIARY RELATIONSHIPS

To appreciate why state sovereignty can be characterized as the outgrowth of a fiduciary relationship between a state and its people, we must begin by identifying the distinguishing characteristics of fiduciary relationships generally. Familiar fiduciary relationships include trustee-beneficiary, agent-principal, director/officer-corporation, lawyer-client, doctor-patient, partner-partnership, joint venturer-joint venture, parent-child, and guardian-ward. All fiduciary relationships share a common structure: the law entrusts one party (the fiduciary) with discretionary power over the legal or practical interests of another party (the beneficiary). A fiduciary's discretionary power is a form of authority that entitles the fiduciary to exercise judgment on the beneficiary's behalf in relation to her legal or practical interests.[79] A fiduciary's power is *discretionary* insofar as a fiduciary is authorized to make choices on the beneficiary's behalf in the absence of specific instructions that would eliminate the need for a fiduciary to exercise independent judgment.

By definition, fiduciary power is also other-regarding, purposive, and institutional. It is *other-regarding* in the strictly factual sense that the fiduciary may exercise this power only for the benefit of the beneficiary. Fiduciary power is *purposive* in that it is held for limited purposes, such as an agent's power to contract on behalf of her principal, or an attorney's power to present legal claims and defenses on behalf of her client. Last, fiduciary power is *institutional* in that it must be situated within a legally permissible institution, such as the family or the corporation, but not, for example, within a kidnapping ring.[80] In all fiduciary relationships, it is the

78. *See* Joseph Raz, Ethics in the Public Domain: Essays in the Morality of Law and Politics 211, 341 (rev'd ed. 1994).

79. *See* Evan J. Criddle, Liberty in Loyalty: A Republican Theory of Fiduciary Law (manuscript on file with the author); Fox-Decent, *supra* note 69, at 93–94, 101; Paul B. Miller, *Justifying Fiduciary Duties*, 58 McGill L.J. 969, 969 (2013).

80. The law seeks to extinguish rather than regulate kidnapping because kidnapping always constitutes wrongful interference and domination.

institutional entrustment of discretionary authority for a prescribed purpose that defines and circumscribes a fiduciary's power to manage another's legal or practical interests.

Within the scope of the fiduciary's discretionary power, the beneficiary is vulnerable to an abuse of fiduciary power precisely because the fiduciary is authorized to exercise that power on the beneficiary's behalf. Even if the beneficiary were able to monitor the fiduciary strictly, and with a proverbial gun to his head, the fiduciary could in principle abuse the power entrusted to him merely because, by definition, it has been entrusted to him such that he is authorized to exercise it.[81] The beneficiary can categorically avoid this vulnerability only by ending the fiduciary relation by withdrawing the fiduciary's authorization. If the beneficiary is not entitled to withdraw the fiduciary's authorization, as is common with trusts, someone else must withdraw the fiduciary authorization to end the beneficiary's vulnerability. Notice that even if the beneficiary retains authority to exercise the *type* of authority conferred on the fiduciary, the simple fact that the fiduciary and beneficiary are separate persons renders the beneficiary incapable of exercising the *token* or instance of power entrusted to the fiduciary, and thereby makes her vulnerable to its abuse.[82]

In many private-law fiduciary relationships (e.g., lawyer-client, doctor-patient, agent-principal), the fiduciary is a person to whom the beneficiary has turned for professional services or expert advice. The fiduciary is empowered to act on the beneficiary's behalf to do things that the beneficiary is legally entitled to do for herself, such as defend a suit, tend an injury, or sign a contract. In other types of fiduciary relationships, however, the beneficiary's vulnerability is qualitatively different because the beneficiary lacks the legal or practical capacity to exercise the power entrusted to the fiduciary. Children and wards of guardians, for example, lack legal capacity to act as autonomous adults. Similarly, artificial persons, such as corporations, cannot act except through their agents or representatives; they have legal capacity but no practical capacity to use it without others acting for them. Most interesting for present purposes, however, are circumstances in which multiple beneficiaries are subject to a common fiduciary power, such as pension fund claimants with competing demands on the same fund. In these contexts, the contending beneficiaries are not entitled to exercise the fiduciary's power to distribute assets among beneficiaries with rivalrous claims because no person can be judge and party to the same cause. As we shall see, mutatis mutandis, the same principle applies to private parties vis-à-vis the state and its sovereign powers.

81. One could imagine fanciful scenarios in which a beneficiary imprisons or otherwise physically restrains an authorized fiduciary, and thereby avoids vulnerability, but these measures would not *categorically* end the beneficiary's vulnerability, because the reprieve from vulnerability depends on the contingent success of the restraint. Furthermore, such restraint arguably extinguishes the fiduciary relationship by eliminating the basic fact situation to which fiduciary principles respond; namely, one party acting on behalf of another.

82. Cases of boards of directors and other collectively administered fiduciary offices present complications, as it may appear that the beneficiary is not vulnerable to any one director (she is vulnerable to the board), yet every director owes fiduciary duties. It is enough that the beneficiary is vulnerable to the discretionary power of an office, the integrity of which depends on the subjection of its co-fiduciaries to fiduciary duties.

At its most general, the fiduciary's obligation is to act solely for the purpose for which the fiduciary's power is authorized. Implicit in this general obligation of fidelity to purpose is a requirement of self-abnegation; the fiduciary cannot let her duty conflict with her interest (the "no-conflict rule"),[83] nor can she take unauthorized profits (the "no- profit rule").[84] The hallmark fiduciary duty of loyalty in private law is largely enforced through application of the no-conflict and no-profit rules, and consists in a duty to exercise entrusted power with exclusive and due regard for the beneficiary's interests subject to the fiduciary's power. Fiduciaries are bound by the duty of loyalty under the common law of fiduciary relationships, even if they have not expressly negotiated for the application of this rule. The content of the fiduciary's duty expands beyond the prohibitions against self-dealing when the legal or practical interests of multiple classes of beneficiaries are subject to a single fiduciary's discretionary power. Here, the fiduciary's duty consists in an obligation of fairness or even-handedness as between the different classes of beneficiaries, as well as an obligation of reasonableness in the sense that the fiduciary must accord due regard to the respective interests of each beneficiary class. These duties are implicit in the grant of any discretionary power over a varied constituency, because without the requirement that the fiduciary fulfill the purpose of her office impartially and reasonably, her power could not credibly be interpreted as a power held and exercised on behalf of all who are subject to it.

Commonly paired with the fiduciary duty of loyalty is a fiduciary's duty to exercise care in exercising her entrusted discretionary authority. Although legal scholars have debated whether the duty of care is better classified as a distinctive fiduciary duty or a more generic duty sounding in tort,[85] the fact remains that all fiduciaries are bound by law to employ their entrusted discretion through a deliberative decision-making process that reflects solicitude toward beneficiaries' best interests. At a minimum, a fiduciary is expected to investigate the nature of a problem or opportunity, discern the range of permissible actions, evaluate the pros and cons of each alternative, and develop an objectively reasonable rationale for the action taken. The fiduciary representative must give due consideration to relevant experience or expertise, be it the fiduciary's own expert judgment or the consultation of other specialists. The fiduciary may not arbitrarily neglect or ignore readily accessible sources of information that may be important to her decision. In some fiduciary relationships, such as principal-agent or doctor-patient, a fiduciary's deliberative responsibilities entail an obligation to consult the beneficiary before taking actions that would substantially impact the beneficiary's legal or practical interests.

83. *See, e.g.*, Guth v. Loft, 5 A.2d 503, 510 (Del. 1939) (explaining that the duty of loyalty "demands that there shall be no conflict between duty and self-interest").

84. *See, e.g.*, Chan v. Zacharia (1983–84) 154 C.L.R. 178, 198–99 (Aus.) (Deane, J.) (holding that the no-profit rule "requires the fiduciary to account for any benefit or gain obtained or received by reason of or by use of his fiduciary position"); Ultraframe (U.K.) Ltd. v. Fielding [2005] EWHC 1638 (Ch.), ¶¶ 1318–22 (U.K.) (describing the no-profit rule as a prohibition against corporate directors retaining unauthorized profits).

85. *See* Miller, *supra* note 79, at 976 ("It is likewise unclear whether the duty of care, which requires fiduciaries to act reasonably in fulfilling their mandates, is a fiduciary duty"); Kelli Alces, *Debunking the Corporate Fiduciary Myth*, 35 J. Corp. L. 239, 250 (2009) ("There is some debate about whether the duty of care is a fiduciary obligation at all.").

In short, a fiduciary's exercise of discretionary power must follow a course of prudent and rational deliberation. Whether or not there exists a distinctive fiduciary duty of care, the key point is that in fiduciary cases, the duty of care requires the fiduciary to take affirmative steps to exercise her discretionary power in a manner that is calculated to advance the beneficiary's legal and practical interests. The duty of care thus establishes requirements of affirmative prudence and diligence to insulate a beneficiary from domination at the hands of her fiduciary.

The duties of loyalty and care operate along two distinct dimensions. First, the duties of loyalty and care furnish "conduct rules" that provide direction to fiduciaries, communicating the legal system's expectations regarding a fiduciary's performance. Second, the duties offer "decision rules" that tell judges and other authorities how they should review a fiduciary's conduct.[86]

Many areas of private fiduciary law reflect significant "acoustic separation"[87] between fiduciary conduct rules and decision rules. Although courts have held that fiduciaries are subject to the highest standards of diligence, deliberation, conscientiousness, and solicitude when they exercise discretionary power on behalf of their beneficiaries,[88] these robustly demanding[89] conduct rules are not directly enforceable in a court of law.[90] Instead, courts apply more constrained decision rules, which render the duties of loyalty and care tractable to judicial enforcement. For example, rather than require a fiduciary to demonstrate her subjective commitment to pursue her beneficiary's interest with affirmative diligence, courts apply an "objective" decision rule for duty of care claims. In most contexts, this decision rule asks courts to consider what "a reasonable or prudent person in like circumstances" would do.[91]

86. For an enlightening introduction to the distinction between "conduct rules" and "decision rules," see Meir Dan-Cohen, *Decision Rules and Conduct Rules: On Acoustic Separation in Criminal Law*, 97 Harv. L. Rev. 625 (1983).

87. *Id.*

88. *See, e.g., Guth*, 5 A.2d at 510 (describing the duty of loyalty as a "rule that demands of a corporate officer or director, peremptorily and inexorably, the most scrupulous observance of his duty, . . . affirmatively to protect the interests of the corporation" with "undivided and unselfish loyalty"); Grossberg v. Haffenberg, 11 N.E.2d 359, 360 (Ill. 1937) (asserting that partners are required to practice "utmost good faith," observing "the highest standards of honor and honesty").

89. Philip Pettit offers an illuminating account of "robustly demanding" norms, which contemplate fidelity to others' interests amidst shifting circumstances, in Philip Pettit, The Robust Demands of the Good: Ethics with Attachment, Virtue and Respect (2015).

90. *See* Lionel D. Smith, *Can We Be Obliged to Be Selfless?*, *in* Philosophical Foundations, *supra* note 74, at 141, 142 (characterizing a fiduciary's duty to pursue beneficiaries' best interests as a legal "requirement" but not an enforceable legal "duty"); Arthur B. Laby, *Resolving Conflicts of Duty in Fiduciary Relationships*, 54 Am. U. L. Rev. 75, 123 (2004) (characterizing the duty of care as a "legally enforceable imperfect duty"). *But see* Ethan Leib & Stephen Galoob, *Fiduciary Legal and Political Theory: A Critique*, 125 Yale L.J. (forthcoming 2016) (mistakenly suggesting that fiduciary norms enforced by courts are always "robustly demanding").

91. Robert H. Sitkoff, *The Economic Structure of Fiduciary Law*, 91 B.U. L. Rev 1039, 1043 (2011); (citing Restatement (Third) of Trusts § 77 (2007); Restatement (Third) of Agency § 8.08 (2006); Principles of Corporate Governance: Analysis and Recommendations § 4.01(a) (1994)). When a trustee is retained for his or her special skills, the applicable

In American corporate law, courts apply an even less rigorous decision rule for some duty of care claims, overturning corporate business judgments only upon a showing of "gross negligence."[92] Thus, despite the fact that fiduciaries bear legal obligations to pursue the best interests of their beneficiaries vigorously and selflessly, fiduciary law's decision rules generally permit courts to enforce the duties of loyalty and care only in settings where a fiduciary's behavior reflects an obvious breach of trust.

To facilitate adherence to a fiduciary's duties of loyalty and care, private law also contains information-forcing rules that are designed to promote transparency and facilitate monitoring and enforcement. Fiduciaries are required to keep clear and accurate records and give their beneficiaries a comprehensive accounting for their performance upon request. Fiduciaries must comply with these requirements whether or not their beneficiaries can demonstrate that they have suffered a distinct injury. These ancillary duties of disclosure and accounting enable beneficiaries to police fiduciaries' compliance with their primary fiduciary duties.

VI. THE MORAL FOUNDATIONS OF FIDUCIARY OBLIGATION

Why does private law impose fiduciary duties on trustees, agents, guardians, corporate directors, and others who have assumed discretionary power over their beneficiaries' legal or practical interests?

Legal scholars have proposed a variety of theories to explain the normative basis for fiduciary obligations in private law. Some scholars argue that the moral foundation of fiduciary obligations is consent. According to this theory, fiduciary duties represent implied contractual terms that arise whenever one party contracts for another party to exercise expert judgment for their benefit or the benefit of a third party.[93] Other scholars suggest that fiduciary obligations are morally justified under the law of property to protect parties who entrust property or other "critical resources" to another's care.[94] Still other scholars contend that the moral foundation for fiduciary obligations is the moral virtues or public goods that these obligations promote, including enhanced trust and trustworthiness, utility-maximizing social cooperation, and more robust compliance with other legal obligations.[95] Each of

standard is a reasonable person in possession of those skills. *See id.* at 1043–44 (citing UNIFORM PRUDENT INVESTOR ACT § 2(f) (1994); RESTATEMENT (THIRD) OF TRUSTS § 77(3) (2007); RESTATEMENT (THIRD) OF AGENCY § 8.08 (2006)); Laby, *supra* note 90, at 123 ("Courts typically have applied the doctrine of negligence to establish when an action (or inaction) of a fiduciary results in breach.").

92. *See, e.g.*, Smith v. Van Gorkom, 488 A.2d 858, 873 (Del. 1985); Aronson v. Lewis, 473 A.2d 805, 812 (Del. 1984).

93. *See, e.g.*, Sitkoff, *supra* note 90; John H. Langbein, *The Contractarian Basis of the Law of Trusts*, 105 YALE L.J. 625 (1995); Frank H. Easterbrook & Daniel R. Fischel, *Contract and Fiduciary Duty*, 36 J.L. & ECON. 425 (1993).

94. *See, e.g.*, Larry E. Ribstein, *Are Partners Fiduciaries?*, 1 U. ILL. L. REV. 209 (2005); D. Gordon Smith, *The Critical Resource Theory of Fiduciary Duty*, 55 VAND. L. REV. 1399 (2002).

95. *See, e.g.*, TAMAR FRANKEL, FIDUCIARY LAW: ANALYSIS, DEFINITIONS, DUTIES, REMEDIES OVER HISTORY AND CULTURES 317 (2008); Matthew Conaglen, *The Nature and Function of Fiduciary Loyalty*, 121 L.Q. REV. 452 (2005); Lawrence E. Mitchell, *The Naked*

these theories of fiduciary obligation suffers from descriptive and normative shortcomings, which have been well documented elsewhere.[96]

The best justification for fiduciary duties, we believe, is that these legal obligations are necessary to provide for the beneficiary's secure and equal freedom vis-à-vis the fiduciary. To the extent that the fiduciary holds discretionary power over the beneficiary's legal or practical interests, private law denies the fiduciary the right to hold or exercise this power in a manner that would subject the beneficiary to domination or instrumentalization.[97] As Paul Miller has shown, the formal juridical structure of the fiduciary relationship reflects these principles: because private law authorizes the fiduciary to exercise the beneficiary's legal rights exclusively for and on behalf of the beneficiary, the fiduciary lacks a legal right to pursue opportunities or appropriate resources that arise within the scope of the fiduciary relationship for the fiduciary's personal gain.[98] Hence, any profits obtained by the fiduciary through the misappropriation of the beneficiary's opportunities or resources belong as a matter of right to the beneficiary.[99] Private law also protects the beneficiary from domination by directing the fiduciary to exercise reasonable care in her administration of the beneficiary's legal and practical interests. Fiduciary obligations such as the duties of loyalty and care are justified, in short, to ensure that private law does not enable the fiduciary to wield despotic power over the legal and practical interests of the beneficiary.[100]

Immanuel Kant provides a complementary account of the moral basis of fiduciary obligations in an argument concerning the duties that parents owe their children. According to Kant, parents' duties to care for their children arise as a consequence of the parents' unilateral act of procreation:

> [C]hildren, as persons, have by their procreation an original innate (not acquired) right to the care of their parents until they are able to look after themselves, and they have this right directly on the basis of principle (*lege*), that is, without any special act being required to establish this right.
>
> For the offspring is a *person* . . . [I]t is quite correct and even necessary Idea to regard the act of procreation as one by which we have brought a person into the world without his consent and on our own initiative, for which deed the parents incur an obligation to make the child content with his condition so far as they can. They cannot destroy their child . . . since they have brought not

Emperor: A Corporate Lawyer Looks at RUPA's Fiduciary Provisions, 54 WASH. & LEE L. REV. 465, 480 (1997); Robert Flannigan, *Fiduciary Obligation in the Supreme Court*, 54 SASK. L. REV. 45, 46 (1990); P.D. Finn, *The Fiduciary Principle, in* EQUITY, FIDUCIARIES AND TRUSTS (T.G. Youdan ed., 1989).

96. For a helpful introduction to (and refutation of) these and other prevailing justificatory theories of fiduciary obligations, see Miller, *Justifying Fiduciary Duties*, *supra* note 79.

97. *See* FOX-DECENT, *supra* note 69, at 42–47; Criddle, *supra* note 79.

98. *See* Miller, *Justifying Fiduciary Duties*, *supra* note 66.

99. *See* Paul B. Miller, *Justifying Fiduciary Remedies*, 63 U. TORONTO L.J. 570 (2013).

100. *See generally* Criddle, *supra* note 79.

> merely a worldly being but a citizen of the world into a condition which cannot now be indifferent to them even just according to concepts of Right.[101]

To understand Kant's argument, we must review briefly his theory of right, or legality, which entails a very specific conception of the idea of innate right. For Kant, legal rights embody our moral capacity for putting others under legal obligations, and are either acquired or innate.[102] Property and contractual entitlements are acquired rights because some act is required on the part of the right-holder for him to acquire them. An innate right, on the other hand, "is that which belongs to everyone by nature, independently of any act that would establish a right."[103] Persons have one, and only one, innate right, which all possess equally by virtue of their shared humanity: the right to as much freedom as can coexist with the same freedom of everyone else. Freedom, Kant explains, is simply "independence from being constrained by another's choice."[104] It follows that in a world where interaction with others is unavoidable, law must enshrine and secure rights within a regime of equal freedom in which no party can unilaterally impose terms of interaction on another.[105]

Rights under Kant's theory protect the freedom and dignity of agents, rather than their welfare or interests.[106] Correlative duties arise from rights because their absence would signal a deprivation of freedom or an insult to dignity. That a breach of duty might set back interests is irrelevant to whether there is a duty in the first place. Under Kant's theory, inquiry into liability addresses whether there has been a breach of duty, and this inquiry is categorically distinct from the subsequent inquiry into damages that tracks the effect of the breach on the relevant

101. *See* IMMANUEL KANT, THE METAPHYSICS OF MORALS 98–99 (Mary Gregor transl., 1991) (1797) (emphasis in original) (footnote omitted). It is settled law in Canada that parents owe their children fiduciary duties. *See* M.(K.) v. M.(H.), [1992] 3 S.C.R 6 (Can.). For an argument that U.S. family law should follow suit, see Elizabeth S. Scott & Robert E. Scott, *Parents as Fiduciaries*, 81 VA. L. REV. 2401 (1995).

102. KANT, *supra* note 100, at 63. The summary of Kant's discussion of rights in the text refers exclusively to coercively enforceable legal rights and their correlative legal obligations. Kant is not referring to unenforceable ethical duties arising from the categorical imperative under his doctrine of virtue, such as the duty of beneficence. For a discussion of the intimate relationship in Kant between legality and coercion, see Arthur Ripstein, *Authority and Coercion*, 32 PHIL. & PUB. AFF. 2 (2004).

103. KANT, *supra* note 101, at 63.

104. *Id.*

105. Hobbes's theory of law similarly deploys a prohibition on unilateralism as a central organizing idea, a theme we will develop throughout the course of this book, and in particular in Chapter 8. THOMAS HOBBES, LEVIATHAN WITH SELECTED VARIANTS FROM THE LATIN EDITION OF 1668 (Edwin Curley ed. 1994) (1651); *see also* Evan Fox-Decent, *Unseating Unilateralism*, *in* PRIVATE LAW AND THE RULE OF LAW (Lisa Austin & Dennis Klimchuk eds., 2014).

106. *See* L.W. SUMNER, THE MORAL FOUNDATION OF RIGHTS 1–14 (1987) (arguing that rights are best conceived as protected choices, but grounded on consequentialist considerations); JOSEPH RAZ, THE MORALITY OF FREEDOM 165–92 (1986) (defending the interest theory under which rights protect interests). For subsequent defense of the interest theory, see Andrei Marmor, *On the Limits of Rights*, 16 LAW & PHIL. 1 (1997).

interests. The distinction between harms and wrongs expresses the same distinction. An actor can wrong without harming, such as when she invades your privacy by reading your junk mail without permission. And she can harm without wronging, as might occur if she launched a business to compete with yours. Although it is true that many rights, including human rights, protect important interests, for Kant they are properly designated as rights only if their infringement would constitute a breach of duty, which is understood as a deprivation of freedom or an insult to dignity, regardless of whether the purported breach leads to a setting back of interests.

Consider now Kant's claim that children have an innate and legal right to their parents' care. When parents unilaterally create a person who cannot survive without their support, the child's innate moral capacity to place the parents under obligation is triggered to ensure the child's security. As persons, children cannot be treated as mere means or objects of their parents' freedom to procreate. The parents' freedom to procreate can coexist with the child's right to security from the perils of a condition to which she never consented only if the child is treated as a person worthy of respect, and not as an object the parents can destroy or abandon. Because the child cannot negotiate the terms of her relationship with her parents, and because the parents cannot set those terms unilaterally, the law intercedes to provide a framework for interaction that guarantees the secure and equal freedom of the child vis-à-vis her parents. Moreover, as long as the child lacks legal or practical capacity to make autonomous decisions, the parents bear an obligation to exercise their fiduciary power—entrusted to them by operation of law—in furtherance of the child's best interests.

Legal personality and its intrinsic dignity supplies the moral basis of the beneficiary's right to the fiduciary obligation in other fiduciary relationships. A relationship in which the fiduciary has discretionary power over the beneficiary's legal or practical interests can be understood as a relation mediated by law only if the fiduciary, like the parent, is precluded from exploiting her position. Fiduciary law prevents the fiduciary from unilaterally setting the terms of her relationship with the beneficiary. The beneficiary's entrusted interests are immune to the fiduciary's appropriation because those interests and the means of pursuing them made available by the fiduciary relationship belong to the beneficiary rather than the fiduciary. The fiduciary principle thus permits the fiduciary to exercise power on the beneficiary's behalf, but subject to strict limitations arising from the beneficiary's vulnerability to the fiduciary's power and her intrinsic worth as a person.

VII. A KANTIAN THEORY OF FIDUCIARY SOVEREIGNTY

Bearing in mind the constitutive features of fiduciary relations and Kant's theory of right, we are now in a position to explain how the state and its institutions stand in a fiduciary relationship to their people.

The idea that public officials and public institutions serve as fiduciaries for their people comports with the constitutive features of fiduciary relationships generally. All agents and instrumentalities of the state—including the primary legislative, executive, and judicial institutions—are vested by law with discretionary power to make, interpret, or enforce laws on behalf of their people. The legislative, executive, and judicial powers entailed by sovereignty are discretionary in the sense that public officials must exercise discretion in determining how to exercise their powers. Even with precise instructions from their people, as might occur through a referendum, in practice there will always be discretion regarding the means, timing, and implementation of a legal initiative. Moreover, public powers are each, in their own familiar ways, institutional, purpose-laden, and other-regarding. As we will discuss further in Chapter 2, public powers are institutional in the sense that international law confers these powers on legally designated institutions—typically states—to be exercised through their constitutive agencies and instrumentalities. Public powers are other-regarding and purpose-laden in that they are to be exercised for the benefit of a state's people, and relate to the construction of a legal order that makes equal freedom possible, but which the state's people, in their separate and individual capacities, cannot provide.

The Kantian account of fiduciary relations offers a framework to explain, in non-instrumental terms, the juridical and moral purpose for which international law authorizes states to wield non-consensual coercive power. Under Kant's legal theory, individuals have one innate right: the right to as much freedom as can be reconciled with the equal freedom of others. Public institutions are necessary to vindicate this right because in their absence individuals would be subject to the continual threat of unilateral and arbitrary interference from others. The fiduciary principle entrusts public powers to the state in order to secure them against unilateralism and thereby provide for their equal freedom. International law honors this principle by entrusting each state with authority to establish the conditions necessary to protect individuals' innate right to equal freedom. International law thus charges states with creating legal institutions to ensure that all persons subject to their jurisdiction enjoy equal freedom, a civil condition wherein no individual is able to instrumentalize or dominate others with impunity.

Although the relationship between the state and its people is distinctive in a variety of respects, it bears important similarities to other fiduciary relationships where beneficiaries are not entitled to exercise the power held by the fiduciary. Just as individual beneficiaries of a pension fund are not entitled to set unilaterally the terms of the management or disposition of fund investments, individuals within a state may not exercise public powers in their individual capacities. Only through the intermediation of public institutions such as the state can a people constitute itself collectively as an organized polity for the purpose of guaranteeing equal freedom under the rule of law for its individual members.

The state-subject fiduciary relationship also bears important similarities to Kant's account of the parent-child fiduciary relationship. Just as parents have the power to bring a person into the world without his consent, the creation of a new state has the consequence of bringing a new "people" into international legal order as a legal person endowed with collective rights of self-determination. And just as a child's inherent dignity supports the law imposing affirmative obligations of loyalty and care on his parents, the inherent dignity of a state's people supports international law imposing affirmative obligations of a fiduciary nature on the state.[107] For

107. To be clear, we do not argue that states are entitled to exercise sovereign power simply by virtue of their unilateral assumption of power. When a state gains control over a foreign people through an act of aggression, for example, its relationship to that people more closely resembles that of a kidnapper to his captive than a parent to her child. Although a people's right to self-determination may demand public institutions such as states, the relationship between a state and its people must be established in a legally authorized way. We will have more to say in

states, these affirmative obligations are encompassed in their charge as fiduciaries to establish a regime of secure and equal freedom for their people.[108] Because public powers are entrusted by law to the state and cannot be exercised by private parties without legal authorization, the public depends on the state to exercise its powers in the public interest, and the public is uniquely vulnerable to the abuse of public power. Despite their ability within democracies to participate in public elections, popular referenda, and other democratic processes, individuals remain vulnerable to the threat of arbitrary state action. It follows that the state's assumption of sovereign powers—public powers that private parties lack capacity to exercise—triggers fiduciary obligations owed to the nationals and non-nationals subject to the state's jurisdiction.[109]

To satisfy the fiduciary principle, the state must respect the Kantian principle of non-instrumentalization, ensuring that public officials and private parties treat others always as ends and never as mere means. The state must also secure persons against domination radiating from the threat of arbitrary interference. A state that guarantees legal order by preventing public officials and private parties from instrumentalizing and dominating others with impunity fulfills its fiduciary purpose to establish the conditions necessary for individuals to enjoy equal freedom.[110]

These features of the fiduciary character of sovereignty dictate that states bear robust fiduciary obligations to protect and care for their people, and to labor diligently to establish and maintain the rule of law. Accordingly, international law subjects states to affirmative obligations, which are premised on the expectation that states will vigorously pursue the well-being of their people. These robustly demanding obligations include states' sovereign responsibility to proactively protect and fulfill civil and political rights within their jurisdictions,[111] including by protecting

Chapter 2 about how international law's power-conferring rules for state recognition reflect a fiduciary conception of sovereignty.

108. Of course, analogies between the state-subject relationship and other fiduciary relationships such as corporation-shareholder, trustee-beneficiary, and parent-child should be used circumspectly with a healthy appreciation of their limits. As Judge Cardozo observed in another context, we must take care in legal analysis to ensure that such analogies, "starting as devices to liberate thought," do not "end . . . by enslaving it." Berkey v. Third Ave. Rye Co., 155 N.E. 58, 61 (N.Y. 1926) (Cardozo, J.). For example, although the parent-child analogy is useful for illuminating the moral basis of a state's fiduciary obligations to protect and establish legal order for its people, a state is not entitled to treat its people as children who lack the practical capacity to make autonomous decisions.

109. *Cf.* John Finnis, Aquinas: Moral, Political, and Legal Theory 283 (1998) ("[P]ublic authority is not merely a moral liberty but essentially a responsibility (a liberty coupled with, and ancillary to, a duty."). For insightful discussion of Finnis's "duty to govern" and its relationship to authority (the right to govern) and legal obligation (the duty to obey the law), see Leslie Green, *The Duty to Govern*, 13 Legal Theory 165 (2007).

110. For further discussion of Kant's theory of public law, see B. Sharon Byrd & Joachim Hruschka, Kant's Doctrine of Right (2010); Arthur Ripstein, Force and Freedom: Kant's Legal and Political Theory (2009); and Mary J. Gregor, Laws of Freedom (1963).

111. *See* U.N. Office of the High Commissioner for Human Rights, *International Human Rights Law*, http://www.ohchr.org/EN/ProfessionalInterest/Pages/InternationalLaw.aspx (last visited Nov. 13, 2015) ("The obligation to protect requires States to protect individuals and groups

their people from violence;[112] and to work progressively, "to the maximum of [their] available resources," toward the "full realization" of economic, social, and cultural rights, such as "just and favourable conditions of work," "continuous improvement of living conditions," and "the highest attainable standard of physical and mental health."[113] Under international law, all states are obligated to exercise discretionary judgment in charting a course toward the progressive achievement of these objectives for their people, pursuant to their overarching fiduciary obligation to establish a regime of secure and equal freedom under the rule of law.

Although we recognize the importance of states' affirmative fiduciary obligations, the chapters that follow devote less attention to these obligations in order to concentrate on other norms that comprise the firm juridical core of international law's fiduciary constitution. As we shall argue in subsequent chapters, a state's fiduciary duties include peremptory (jus cogens) norms such as the prohibitions against slavery, aggression, and torture; due process protections such as judicial review of national security detention; and international refugee law's requirement of non-refoulement. These peremptory norms reflect the limits of sovereign authority under international law, because their violation could never be consistent with a state's fiduciary obligation to treat its people as coequal beneficiaries of a regime of equal freedom. Nonperemptory human rights such as freedom of expression, association, and movement also reflect the fiduciary character of sovereignty under international law. Because departures from these norms are sometimes consistent with a state's fiduciary duties, IHRL properly recognizes that states may impose some general limitations on the exercise of these nonperemptory rights, and may sometimes derogate from these norms to address temporary national crises, without violating their fiduciary obligations to their people. Collectively, these norms confirm that states are not entitled to set unilaterally the terms of their relationship with their people.

In the coming chapters we shall see that the fiduciary model provides a solid theoretical foundation for specifying the meaning of norms, such as the prohibition against torture, which have been subject to conflicting interpretations. In particular, the model furnishes a set of principles (e.g., integrity, formal moral equality, and solicitude) that may inform public deliberation as lawmakers and adjudicators determine the best approach for securing legal order within a particular context. Although these principles do not fit neatly into international law's conventional

against human rights abuses. The obligation to fulfil means that States must take positive action to facilitate the enjoyment of basic human rights.").

112. *See, e.g.*, U.N. Secretary-General, *Implementing the Responsibility to Protect*, U.N. Doc. A/63/677 ¶ 10(a) (2009) (asserting that "the responsibility to protect is an ally of sovereignty, not an adversary," and "grows from the positive and affirmative notion of sovereignty as responsibility"); World Summit Outcome, *supra* note 44, ¶ 138 ("Each individual State has the responsibility to protect its populations from genocide, war crimes, ethnic cleansing and crimes against humanity."); *see generally* David Louis Attanasio, The State Obligation to Protect (2015) (unpublished Ph.D. dissertation, University of California, Los Angeles) (on file with the author) (arguing that a state's responsibility to protect reflects the fiduciary character of its relationship with its people).

113. International Covenant on Economic, Social and Cultural Rights arts. 2.1, 7, 11.1, Dec. 16, 1966, 993 U.N.T.S.23.

doctrine of sources,[114] they carry the force of international law as "elementary considerations of humanity"[115] that are constitutive of state sovereignty. The fiduciary theory thus affirms the foundational commitments of international law and offers resources for clarifying and progressively developing the law in areas where theory and doctrine remain in flux.

Who are the "people" to whom a state owes fiduciary obligations? As discussed previously, fiduciary relationships arise whenever a party is entrusted with discretionary power to act on behalf of a beneficiary. International law entrusts states with authority to exercise public powers on behalf, and for the benefit, of all individuals within their jurisdiction. Although a state's sovereign jurisdiction is defined primarily according to its territory, jurisdiction also extends extraterritorially via enduring status-based relationships such as nationality and, to a more limited extent, through temporary jurisdictional contacts such as occupation of foreign territory. It follows, therefore, that all individuals within a state's jurisdiction—adults and children, nationals and non-nationals, loyalists and revolutionaries—are people entitled to be treated as beneficiaries of the state's fiduciary power. Nonetheless, as we shall argue in Chapter 8, the state's nationals have a special relationship to the state, and conversely, foreign nationals subject to a state's authority have a special call on international law.

A core purpose of international law and international institutions, we argue, is to mediate the fiduciary relationship between a state and its people by conditioning a state's claim to sovereign authority on its fidelity to its fiduciary obligations. Just as the state is necessary to emancipate individuals from unilateralism on the part of private parties, we argue that international law and international institutions are necessary to prevent the state from holding power that would expose its people to domination. To the extent that international law vests the state with sovereign authority, the fiduciary principle dictates that the state must be accountable to international law and international institutions for its performance in establishing a regime of secure and equal freedom for its people.

The fiduciary model we propose therefore endorses Hobbes's important insight regarding the need for a state to serve as an impartial arbiter to mediate the relationships among its people, and it extends this insight to explain the role of international law in mediating not only the relationship between states, but also between a state and its own people. Consistent with the spirit of normative individualism that pervades international human rights discourse, the fiduciary model shares Kant's

114. *See* Statute of the International Court of Justice art. 38 (identifying five sources for rules of decision: international conventions, international custom, general principles of law recognized by civilized nations, and, as subsidiary means, judicial decisions and scholarly commentary). For a penetrating critique and reformulation of the doctrine of sources, see Harlan Grant Cohen, *Finding International Law: Rethinking the Doctrine of Sources*, 93 Iowa L. Rev. 65 (2007).

115. The Corfu Channel Case (United Kingdom v. Albania), [1949] ICJ Rep. 4, ¶ 22; Case Concerning Military and Paramilitary Activities in and Against Nicaragua (Nicaragua v. United States), [1986] ICJ Rep. 14, ¶ 218; *see also* Barcelona Traction, Light and Power Co., Ltd. (Belg. v. Spain) 1970 ICJ Rep. 4, 32 (Feb. 5) (asserting that "basic rights of the human person" qualify as obligations *erga omnes*); Bruno Simma & Philip Alston, *The Sources of Human Rights Law: Custom, Jus Cogens, and General Principles*, 12 Aust. Y.B. Int'l L. 82 (1988) (arguing that such principles may constitute "general principles of law recognized by civilized nations").

commitment to normative individualism rather than Grotius's vision of the state as fiduciary for its people collectively.[116] Under international law today, a state must respect the legal and practical interests of each of its subjects individually; it may not treat any of its subjects as mere instruments for advancing the "greater good." The fiduciary principle thus reconciles the state's coercive public powers with principles of individual moral agency and popular sovereignty, while also explaining the authority of international legal norms and international institutions that regulate the relationship between the state and its people.

As we will explain further in Chapter 5, the fiduciary theory also places constraints on a state's authority to exercise power abroad. Because international law entrusts states with authority to serve as fiduciaries primarily for their own nationals and others within their jurisdiction, states do not owe the same set of robust fiduciary obligations to foreign nationals abroad. Hence, although states are responsible for establishing a regime of secure and equal freedom within their jurisdiction, they do not bear a comparable responsibility under the fiduciary model to protect or fulfill human rights for all people everywhere in the world. Nonetheless, to the extent that states derive their sovereign authority by entrustment from an international legal order that is designed to guarantee equal freedom for all humanity, states bear an obligation to refrain from taking actions abroad such as the indiscriminate use of force within armed conflict that are inimical to the fiduciary constitution of international legal order. Such limits on states' authority to exercise power abroad reflect the fact that states collectively administer international legal order and, accordingly, bear fiduciary obligations as joint fiduciaries of humanity to respect the dignity and rights of foreign nationals. The idea that states are joint fiduciaries of humanity is central to our fiduciary interpretation of IRL in Chapter 7. In Chapter 8 we extend the idea to suggest that international institutions are likewise fiduciaries of humanity, and that their authority can be explained and justified on this basis.

The fiduciary model respects the demands of popular sovereignty by acknowledging the people's entitlement to the proper exercise of the state's sovereign powers, and the resulting fiduciary position of the state vis-à-vis the people. Just as private-law fiduciaries wield discretionary power over the legal and practical interests of their beneficiaries, international law authorizes states to exercise discretionary power over sovereign rights and interests that reside ultimately with their people.[117] A plausible political implication of combining the fiduciary model with popular sovereignty is democracy, as democracy permits the people to elect and dismiss those who wield state power. The novelty of the theory we propose, however, is that the state-subject fiduciary relationship, properly understood, is also a distinctively legal relationship. Under the fiduciary model, a state's sovereign authority to govern its people domestically and represent its people internationally is held in a fiduciary capacity for its people. As a consequence, a state is obligated under international law to work toward the establishment of a regime of secure and equal freedom for its

116. *See* GROTIUS, *supra* note 12, bk. 2, ch. 25, §§ 1–3.

117. Although he rejected the concept of popular sovereignty within established states, Grotius likewise distinguished the "right of sovereignty" from "exercise of the right," observing that although an infant, insane, or captive king possesses the right of sovereignty, the exercise of sovereignty in such cases may fall to a guardian or regent. GROTIUS, *supra* note 12, at 137.

people (the purpose for which international law entrusts the state with sovereignty), and it must respect, protect, and fulfill human rights (its core substantive fiduciary duties) to qualify for the rights and privileges associated with sovereignty. These legal features of the fiduciary relationship between a state and its people are constitutive of a new conception of popular sovereignty that yields specific legal obligations to which all states are subject strictly by virtue of the sovereign powers they possess.

The fiduciary model's distinctly legal conception of popular sovereignty underscores international law's vital role in regulating claims to sovereignty. Under the fiduciary model, all states derive their authority to exercise sovereign powers—powers that belong to their people collectively—from both national and international law. Within an established state, national law commits legislative, executive, and adjudicative powers to particular institutions and officials. National law may constrain the power of public institutions and officials by placing them under fiduciary duties. But national law is ill-positioned to address disputes involving rival claims to state sovereignty. As Patrick Macklem has observed, international law alone can "shape an international political reality into an international legal order by determining the legality of multiple claims of sovereign power."[118] Likewise, only international law stands in the impartial position necessary to specify the content of international human rights, thereby ensuring that the relationship between a state and its people is consistent with the fiduciary principle. Consequently, international law plays a critical role in regulating claims to sovereign authority and addressing states' breach of their fiduciary duties to respect, protect, and fulfill human rights.

VIII. LOCKEAN AND RAZIAN THEORIES OF FIDUCIARY SOVEREIGNTY

Although we find the Kantian account of sovereignty most persuasive, and will rely on it throughout this book, Lockean and Razian theories of fiduciary sovereignty are also conceivable, and to some readers one or both of these may be more plausible than the theory we draw from Kant. We emphasize that the theories we now sketch do not attempt anything like a close interpretation of Locke or Raz, but rather adopt key elements of their legal and political theory (the Lockean theory) or the conceptual structure they attribute to authority (the Razian theory). In this sense, we hope the following accounts are Lockean and Razian enough to be congenial to scholars sympathetic to Locke or Raz. And although the question of whether such theories can explain the core content of international law is well beyond our remit, the conceivability of these theories suggests that the fiduciary conception of sovereignty is a big tent, one that in principle is available to a plurality of legal and political theories.

Locke is probably the modern thinker best known for defending a fiduciary account of authority, an account in which, as we have seen, legislative power is understood as "only a Fiduciary power to act for certain ends." But as noted above, the fiduciary view of public authority had attracted adherents in Britain, such as Henry Parker, well before Locke penned his *Second Treatise of Civil Government*. Richard Overton, writing in 1647, foreshadowed Locke when he wrote that public

118. Patrick Macklem, *What Is International Human Rights Law? Three Applications of a Distributive Account*, 52 McGill L.J. 575, 587–88 (2007).

authority "always is either in the hands of the *Betrusted* or of the *Betrustees*," and that if "the *Betrusted* betray and forfeit their *Trust*, . . . it returneth from whence it came . . .: For all iust *humane powers* are but betrusted, confer'd and conveyed by ioynt and common consent" for the protection of the people's "*owne safety and weale*."[119]

Like many writers of his day, Locke's theory of political authority begins in the state of nature, and with a particular account of law and natural rights. Locke thought that the "Law of Nature," while we are in the state of nature, endows us with various natural claim rights of non-interference derived from the Law-of-Nature injunction that "no one ought to harm another in his Life, Health, Liberty, or Possessions."[120] Furthermore, if the Law of Nature is not to be "in vain," Locke said, it must be enforceable, and so "the Execution of the Law of Nature is . . . put into every Man's hands, whereby every one has a right to punish transgressors of that Law to such a Degree, as may hinder its Violation."[121] Locke asserted that "every one" has a natural right of enforcement because in the state of nature we are all equal, so if anyone has the right, all must have it.[122] And, he wrote, as every individual has a natural right "to preserve mankind in general," everyone also has a general right to punish, even where others are the victims.[123]

Locke recognized that private enforcers are likely to be partial to their own causes and swayed by their passions. The "proper remedy" for this and other "inconveniences" of the state of nature is civil society.[124] On the institution of civil society, its members transfer their natural executive right to the state, which then possesses a natural right of punishment with a monopoly on enforcement. Locke believed that the state could not have rights or powers other than those transferred to it from its members, and so the private right of punishment in the state of nature lets him explain, via the transfer theory, the state's right of punishment.[125]

For Locke, however, the transfer of such authority is always conditional on the state respecting the terms on which it is transferred:

> there remains still *in the People a Supream Power* to remove or *alter the Legislative*, when they find the Legislative act contrary to the trust reposed in them. For all *Power given with trust* for the attaining an *end*, being limited by that end, whenever that *end* is manifestly neglected, or opposed, the *trust* must necessarily be *forfeited*, and the Power devolve into the hands of those that gave it, who may place it anew where they shall think best for their safety and security.[126]

119. Tuck, *supra* note 52, at 149 (quoting Leveller, Manifestoes of the Puritan Revolution (D.M. Wolfe ed., 1944)).

120. Locke, *supra* note 53, § 6, at 271.

121. *Id.* § 7, at 271. Locke also defended a private right of reparation for civil wrongs, but we will limit our brief discussion to his better-known theory of punishment. Grotius also defended a private right of punishment. *See* Grotius, *supra* note 12, bk. 2, ch. 20.

122. Locke, *supra* note 53, § 7, at 272.

123. *Id.* § 8, at 272.

124. *Id.* § 13, at 276.

125. *Id.* § 135, at 357.

126. *Id.* § 149, at 367 (emphasis in original).

On the surface, it seems one could hardly ask for a more supportive historical endorsement for the fiduciary view of sovereignty. Locke expressly views public power as authority held in trust for the benefit of the people. And his view that the people retain a "Supream Power" to remove the government resonates with the conception of popular sovereignty under which sovereignty itself ultimately resides in the people.

For scholars who adopt what we describe in Chapter 3 as the orthodox conception of human rights—the view that human rights are universal, natural, and timeless endowments arising from our common humanity—Locke's theory of natural rights may be particularly attractive. In Chapter 3 we defend a relational conception of human rights that, we argue, explains better than the orthodox view the wide range of rights recognized by IHRL. These rights include entitlements designed specifically to deal with threats to freedom and security found in modern societies, such as the right to unionize and due process rights. A further concern is that Locke's sovereign acquires public authority through a consensual transfer from the people who form the relevant demos. In cosmopolitan contexts involving non-nationals who are not part of the demos, the Lockean sovereign's authority over them is hard to explain.

Our larger concern with the Lockean account, however, is that its insistence on natural and unilateral executive rights, such as the natural right of punishment, is in tension with international law's claim to authority. That claim to authority, we will suggest, rests on international law's capacity to establish an international legal order that protects states and individuals from the unilateral actions of others. The threat of unilateralism is particularly salient in international affairs, where legal institutions are relatively weak. Of course, it may be possible to overcome the tension between natural executive rights and international law's anti-unilateralist claim to authority, and it may likewise be possible to explain why the tension is not objectionable. Alternatively, it may be possible to construct a Lockean account of fiduciary sovereignty that eschews natural executive rights, but affirms natural substantive rights in support of the orthodox conception of human rights. We cannot pursue this or other Lockean interpretations of fiduciary sovereignty, nor need we, as the success of our project will depend on the plausibility and normative attractiveness of its own rendering of international law, a criterion that is fully consistent with the possibility of other fiduciary accounts of international law.

The fiduciary conceptual model of authority is also compatible with Joseph Raz's well-known "service conception" of practical authority. The centerpiece of Raz's theory is the normal justification thesis (NJT), which supplies the (main) test for distinguishing legitimate from merely de facto authorities. Whereas de facto authorities, according to Raz, effectively *claim* an entitlement to direct others by imposing their will on them, legitimate authorities *are* entitled to direct others, and those others have a duty to obey.[127] Under the NJT, the way to establish that A is an authority for B is to show that B's compliance with A's directives would help B comply better with reasons that apply to her than she would if she were to follow her

127. Raz, *supra* note 78, at 341.

own judgment directly.[128] For example, drivers have prudential and moral reasons to drive safely, and they are more likely to comply better with those reasons if they regard traffic laws as authoritative and obey them rather than decide on every occasion whether to stop at an intersection, drive on a particular side of the street, and so on. The NJT purports to explain state authority by pointing to how the law helps people comply better with reasons that apply to them already (e.g., reasons associated with public safety); comply better, that is, than they would if they were left to follow their own independent judgment.

A well-documented problem with Raz's account is that it fails to explain the standing of authorities to impose coercible duties on their subjects. Although in some circumstances people may have a moral obligation to heed a directive that would help them comply better with reasons that apply to them, it does not follow that the failure to follow this directive would breach a duty to obey.[129] After all, such a directive may flow from a variety of sources such as a friend or an informational website that do not even purport to be authoritative. For example, an individual's moral obligations to obey directives that establish traffic rules does not automatically imply the existence of any particular putative authority that possesses the power to set and enforce these standards. To show that a putative authority possesses actual authority, Raz needs to establish that states and other authorities enjoy standing to impose duties on the people who are subject to them.

One way to rescue Raz's service conception from the standing problem is to locate the NJT within an interpersonal framework that can explain the standing of authorities to impose duties on others. We suggest that the fiduciary framework supplies such a structure.[130] Under the Razian account we propose, a state's authority arises from the combination of the state's de facto power over its subjects and the prohibition on unilateralism, the principle according to which private parties are not entitled to dictate terms or enforce justice claims unilaterally against one another. Implicit to the prohibition on unilateralism is the idea that private parties are moral equals, which precludes them from arrogating to themselves unilateral authority. In the sphere of public law, the prohibition on unilateralism has two major implications.

The first is that the law must authorize *someone* to exercise public power for the purpose of protecting individuals from unilateralism.[131] To the extent that international law authorizes states to perform this role, the prohibition on unilateralism

128. For some of Raz's formulations of the NJT over the years, see RAZ, *supra* note 106, at 53; RAZ, *supra* note 77, at 214; Joseph Raz, *The Problem of Authority: Revisiting the Service Conception*, 90 MINN. L. REV. 1003, 1014 (2005).

129. *See* Stephen Darwall, *Authority and Second-Personal Reasons for Acting*, *in* REASONS FOR ACTION 150 (David Sobel & Steven Wall eds., 2009); Stephen Perry, *Political Authority and Political Obligation*, *in* II OXFORD STUDIES IN PHILOSOPHY OF LAW (Leslie Green & Brian Leiter eds., 2013).

130. *See* Evan Fox-Decent, *Fiduciary Authority and the Service Conception*, *in* PHILOSOPHICAL FOUNDATIONS OF FIDUCIARY LAW (Andrew Gold & Paul Miller eds., 2014).

131. For this reason, Hobbes claims that guardianship is possible in civil society only, where a public authority can specify the guardian. HOBBES, *supra* note 105, ch xvi, ¶ 10, at 103. The law's authorization of guardianship eliminates the possible problem of children having conflicting

has a second implication: state authority carries with it the requirement that public powers be exercised in ways that are likely to help subjects comply better with reason.[132] Properly elaborated, this requirement warrants that exercises of public power will be regulated by legal standards that serve the state's people. Accordingly, state sovereignty can respect the prohibition on unilateralism because an individual's subjection to the state's authority is permissible only to the extent that such subjection conforms to legal standards that serve the individual's publicly avowable and legitimate interests. Although private advisers may be better suited in some settings to advise people as to reasons that apply to them, the state nonetheless may claim authority that private advisers lack because the state bears a special legal obligation to exercise public power for the benefit of its people. In sum, state sovereignty is consistent with the prohibition on unilateralism precisely because the law sets the terms of the relationship between a state and its people.

Assuming that the relationship between a state and its people is fiduciary in nature, we can specify more precisely international law's regulated authorization of state power. State sovereignty is structured by a fiduciary principle that authorizes state power subject to context-sensitive requirements derived from the prohibition on unilateralism. The Razian theory here developed, in other words, sets aside Kant's innate right of humanity, but adopts one of its requirements—the prohibition on unilateralism—as a context-sensitive juridical principle to which authority relations must conform. In regulating the relationship between a state and its people, the prohibition on unilateralism subjects the state to fiduciary requirements grafted from the NJT, thereby tying conceptually the legitimacy of the state's authority to the normative requirements that regulate its exercise.

Understood as a conceptual model, the Razian construal of the state's general fiduciary duty can accommodate the Kantian interpretation of it. On this NJT-informed construal, the state's general duty is to announce and enforce law in a way that helps its subjects comply better with the reasons that apply to them for having a state at all. The Kantian interpretation is one account of those reasons. But in theory, Lockean, fair play, natural duty, and other accounts of state legitimacy could operate as the substantive content of the Razian duty, should any of those theories happen to specify the reasons that apply to subjects for having a state. For theorists suspicious of the Kantian account of state legitimacy, or who consider it incomplete, the Razian approach offers a bigger conceptual tent within which distinctive or additional substantive grounds of legitimacy may be housed. Properly situated within an interpersonal fiduciary framework, therefore, the NJT supplies a complementary or alternative theoretical account of the moral basis for state sovereignty.

duties to other purported fiduciaries (aside from intra-parental conflicts, an issue with which all plausible accounts of parental authority are saddled).

132. Lionel Smith has argued that a fiduciary's purported duty is best understood as a required way of exercising powers, as there is tension between the fiduciary's possession of a discretionary power and a duty to act in a particular way. *See* Smith, *supra* note 90. The theory we develop, under a Kantian or Razian interpretation, is intended to be consistent with both Smith's view and the conventional view that purported fiduciary duties are actual duties.

IX. THE FIDUCIARY CONSTITUTION OF INTERNATIONAL LAW

In subsequent chapters of this book, we consider some of the fiduciary model's normative implications for international law, with particular emphasis on a state's fiduciary duty to respect, protect, and fulfill human rights. We argue that the fiduciary model brings into view the moral foundations of state sovereignty and offers a principled roadmap for bringing greater coherence to the progressive development of international law. The fiduciary model thus offers a compelling account of international law's constitutive legal structure. As Daniel Philpott has helpfully explained, the "constitution of international society" is comprised of:

> a set of norms, mutually agreed upon by polities who are members of the society, that define the holders of authority and their prerogatives, specifically in answer to three questions: Who are the legitimate polities? What are the rules for becoming one of these polities? And, what are the basic prerogatives of these polities?[133]

In the chapters that follow, we show that the fiduciary model answers each of these questions by specifying and clarifying the norms that govern how sovereign authority is defined, distributed, and regulated in contemporary international law.

As we explore these features of the fiduciary model, our analysis draws liberally upon Lon Fuller's explication of the "internal morality of law,"[134] a set of eight desiderata that positivists and anti-positivists alike have accepted as the starting point for inquiry into the rule of law.[135] Most of the desiderata are formal and bear on lawmaking, requiring the lawgiver to govern through general rules that are public, clear, prospective, possible to comply with, internally consistent, and stable over time. Fuller's last principle bears on the interpretation and administration of law, requiring congruence between legal norms as publicized and their practical application. Fuller characterized these formal criteria as a "morality of aspiration" rather than a strict legal duty, because their achievement would always be a matter of degree in practice.[136] Nonetheless, these criteria establish necessary conditions for international legal order in the sense that a manifest violation of any of the eight desiderata undermines international law's authority to impose morally binding obligations.

Fuller's account of the internal morality of law fits congenially within the fiduciary model's conception of the moral foundations of legal order. Under the fiduciary model, a state's flagrant failure to satisfy any of Fuller's eight formal criteria when promulgating and enforcing national law would transgress the principle of

133. PHILPOTT, *supra* note 17, at 12 (italics omitted).

134. LON L. FULLER, THE MORALITY OF LAW (rev'd ed. 1969).

135. *See, e.g.*, T.R.S. ALLAN, CONSTITUTIONAL JUSTICE: A LIBERAL THEORY OF THE RULE OF LAW (2001); JOSEPH RAZ, *The Rule of Law and Its Virtue*, *in* THE AUTHORITY OF LAW: ESSAYS ON LAW AND MORALITY 210 (1979); N.E. SIMMONDS, LAW AS A MORAL IDEA (2007); Paul Craig, *Formal and Substantive Conceptions of the Rule or Law: An Analytical Framework*, 1997 PUB. L. 467; Evan Fox-Decent, *Is the Rule of Law Really Indifferent to Human Rights?*, 27 LAW & PHIL. 533 (2008); Andrei Marmor, *The Rule of Law and Its Limits*, 23 LAW & PHIL. 1 (2004).

136. FULLER, *supra* note 134, at 41.

non-domination, calling into question the state's authority to exercise coercive public powers. The moral authority of international legal norms likewise depends upon their generality, publicity, feasibility, clarity, consistency, prospectivity, stability, and congruent application. Norms that violate one or more of these criteria lack the authority necessary to impose binding legal obligations on international actors.[137] Hence, human rights norms arguably require incorporation into international conventions, well-established custom, national legislation, judicial decisions, or other readily accessible formats before they can best satisfy Fuller's requirements of publicity and clarity. Although human rights derive their moral authority primarily from the fiduciary relationship between states and their people rather than from state consent per se,[138] the legal authority of human rights may be compromised by their unduly vague or inconsistent articulation. Accordingly, emerging human rights norms typically require refinement and formalization through positive international lawmaking processes before they are ready to be deployed in the service of international legal order.

If we borrow further from Fuller's terminology, it should be apparent that the fiduciary model of state sovereignty encompasses both a "morality of duty" and a "morality of aspiration." Under the morality of duty, a state bears affirmative legal duties toward its legal subjects, the content of which are prescribed by reference to the fiduciary character of sovereignty. As reflected in positive law, these duties include the obligation to refrain from practices such as slavery, corruption, and arbitrary discrimination, which treat persons as mere means to the state's ends. These duties are akin to the duty of loyalty's "no-conflict" and "no-profit" rules in private law because they represent minimum standards of integrity, formal moral equality, and solicitude that are central to the integrity of the state-subject fiduciary relationship.

State sovereignty is also subject to a morality of aspiration: the state's institutional purpose to establish a regime of secure and equal freedom for its people. Although no state has fully realized Kant's ideal of legal order, every state bears a responsibility to apply its executive, legislative, and judicial powers in pursuit of this goal. Ordinarily, international law accords states a generous margin of appreciation in determining how best to use their resources to achieve legal order, just as private law accords similar deference to trustees and corporate officers when analyzing their performance under the duty of care. At a minimum, however, the fiduciary model suggests that states are obligated to make a reasonably diligent and prudent effort to establish a regime of secure and equal freedom for their people. A state that blatantly neglects this duty through gross negligence such as systematic public corruption or waste, arbitrary violence against minority groups, or the failure to establish institutions necessary for the rule of law, compromises its sovereign authority

137. *See* Jutta Brunnée & Stephen J. Toope, Legitimacy and Legality in International Law 6 (2010) (drawing on Fuller's criteria to develop an "interactional theory" of international legal order).

138. *Cf.* Eyal Benvenisti & Alon Harel, Embracing the Tension Between National and International Human Rights Law: The Case for Parity, http://papers.ssrn.com/sol3/papers.cfm?abstract_id=2592869 (last visited Dec. 4, 2015) (arguing that "[t]he international order consisting of binding global directives facilitates a clear differentiation between duty-based decisions and discretionary decisions which depend on the good will of the state").

under international law. Hence, a state's sovereign duties to respect, protect, and fulfill human rights are, in Fuller's words, "basic rules without which an ordered society is impossible, or without which an ordered society directed toward certain specific goals must fail of its mark [*sic*]."[139] Beyond these concrete legal duties, the "primary appeal" of the fiduciary model, like Fuller's internal morality of law, "must be to a sense of trusteeship and to the pride of the craftsman."[140]

The fiduciary model thus resonates with Martti Koskenniemi's account of global constitutionalism as a "mindset" or "practice of professional judgment."[141] The fiduciary model may inform the development of international law as participants in international lawmaking processes draw upon its relational vision of international legal order when designing new international treaties and generating new norms of customary international law. The fiduciary model may also inform the work of judges in international, regional, and national courts, enabling them to better preserve international law's integrity against the centrifugal forces of fragmentation.[142] Sovereign states, international organizations, and other international actors should also take precautions to honor their fiduciary duties and internalize their sovereign mission to establish a regime of secure and equal freedom for their people. Viewed from this perspective, the constitutionalization of international law becomes, in Koskenniemi's words, less "an architectural project" than "a programme of moral and political regeneration"[143] that aspires to achieve the emancipation of all humankind. Thus, the fiduciary model of state sovereignty supplies not only an interpretive theory of international law that explains its core components, but also an agenda for reform that may support political mobilization for the progressive development of international norms and institutions.

The fiduciary model may strike some scholars as naively formalist and utopian. Such criticisms are nothing new, of course, as any effort to develop a normative theory of international law inevitably encounters resistance from political and legal realists who view such projects as "based on a false—too optimistic—conception of human nature."[144] Political realists may argue that the fiduciary theory's focus on the juridical structure of sovereignty obscures the role of power in global governance, and that it may perpetuate global inequities by erecting a façade of formal legal equality behind which powerful states and private firms will continue to practice political, economic, and cultural domination over disenfranchised peoples of the Third World.[145] Critical legal scholars may contend that the fiduciary theory

139. Fuller, *supra* note 134, at 5–6.

140. *Id.* at 43.

141. Martti Koskenniemi, *Constitutionalism as Mindset: Reflection on Kantian Themes About International Law and Globalization*, 8 Theoretical Inq. L. 9, 18 (2007).

142. *See* Ronald Dworkin, Law's Empire 176 (1986) (describing the principle of integrity as an effort to make the total set of laws coherent through purposive design (legislative integrity) or constructive interpretation (judicial integrity)).

143. Koskenniemi, *supra* note 141, at 5–6.

144. Hans J. Morgenthau, Scientific Man vs. Power Politics 14–16 (1947).

145. *See* Sundhya Pahuja, Decolonizing International Law: Economic Growth and the Politics of Universality (2013); Evgeny Pashkunis, Pashkunis: Selected Writings on Marxism and Law 169 (1980); Rose Parfitt, *Theorizing Recognition and International Personality*, *in* The Oxford Handbook of International Legal Theory

of sovereignty is too thoroughly tainted by its historical association with Western colonialism to be redeployed as a fresh basis for emancipatory critique.[146] Legal pluralists may argue that the international community is too diverse, with philosophical, religious, and cultural commitments and legal traditions that are far too varied, for satisfactory reconciliation under a singular moral theory of international law. For present purposes, we will limit ourselves to two brief anticipatory responses.

First, regarding the realist critique, we note that the purpose of this book is not to defend the effectiveness of particular international legal norms or institutions such as the U.N. Security Council, the U.N. Human Rights Council, or the International Criminal Court. A vigorous debate is currently underway in international law and international relations scholarship concerning the (im)potency of international law and international institutions in influencing state behavior.[147] No doubt many of the institutions that administer international law today are still in an embryonic stage of their development and will require further structural and procedural reform before they will be prepared to make a significant contribution to international legal order. The fiduciary model of sovereignty is not insensitive to the weaknesses of the current international system, and in subsequent chapters we identify and address some of these weaknesses. Our primary objective in this text, however, is not to assess the efficacy of international law in practice, but instead to expound international law's core purpose and thereby explain its main features while offering some prescriptions on how international law's efficacy should be measured.

Second, although we recognize that some might be tempted to reject the fiduciary theory on the grounds that it is draws upon a parochial, Western account of international legal order, we believe this objection has less merit than may at first appear. That fiduciary concepts have been associated historically with paternalistic Western attitudes toward the Third World is undoubtedly true. In contemporary discourse, however, the idea that states are bound by relational obligations toward their people is espoused by virtually every government around the world. Moreover,

(Florian Hoffman & Anne Orford eds., forthcoming); B.S. Chimni, *Third World Approaches to International Law: A Manifesto*, 8 INT'L COMMUNITY L. REV. 3 (2006); *Makau Mutua, Critical Race Theory and International Law: The View of an Insider-Outsider*, 45 VILL. L. REV. 841 (2000).

146. *See* NATHANIEL BERMAN, PASSION AND AMBIVALENCE: COLONIALISM, NATIONALISM, AND INTERNATIONAL LAW 69 (2012) (arguing that international law's "history of subordination" is "fundamentally irredeemable," although it may offer "a possible terrain of emancipatory struggle"); CHINA MIÉVILLE, BETWEEN EQUAL RIGHTS: A MARXIST THEORY OF INTERNATIONAL LAW 3 (2005) (suggesting that international law is "fundamentally unreformable"); Onuma Yasuaki, *When Was the Law of International Society Born?—An Inquiry of the History of International Law from an Intercivilizational Perspective*, 2 J. HIST. INT'L L. 1, 64 (2000) (describing alternatives to the Westphalian state system in China and the Middle East, and observing that international law embraced state sovereignty as its fundamental organizing principle only "as a result of the triumph of the imperial and colonial policies of the Western powers and the submission of non-Western peoples to them").

147. *See, e.g.*, ANDREW T. GUZMAN, HOW INTERNATIONAL LAW WORKS: A RATIONAL CHOICE THEORY (2010); BETH A. SIMMONS, MOBILIZING FOR HUMAN RIGHTS: INTERNATIONAL LAW IN DOMESTIC POLITICS (2009); JACK L. GOLDSMITH & ERIC A. POSNER, THE LIMITS OF INTERNATIONAL LAW (2006); Oona A. Hathaway, *Do Human Rights Treaties Make a Difference?*, 111 YALE L.J. 1935 (2002).

the foundational instruments of contemporary international law—including the U.N. Charter, the International Covenant on Civil and Political Rights, and the International Covenant on Economic, Social, and Cultural Rights—all reflect the international community's shared aspiration through the establishment of international legal order to protect humanity from state abuse of power. Moreover, the General Assembly's unanimous endorsement of the "responsibility to protect" concept strongly suggests that the relational theory of sovereignty, with its emphasis on the need for international supervision of state action, enjoys greater support internationally than the classical model ever did. To the extent that critics may object to the fiduciary model's Kantian formulation, it is worth underscoring that Kant's legal theory derives from an ideal of freedom that is by no means limited to Western traditions. As Amartya Sen has shown in his groundbreaking work *Development as Freedom*, "[t]he valuing of freedom is not confined to one culture only, and the Western traditions are not the only ones that prepare us for a freedom-based approach to social understanding."[148] By drawing on the logical implications of this common ideal of personal freedom, the fiduciary theory mutes pluralists' concerns about Western legal imperialism, and offers a promising foundation on which to construct a more robust global consensus regarding the legal character of sovereignty.

Although much more could be said to anticipate potential objections, our purpose is not to resolve the ongoing debate over international law's efficacy or to show that the fiduciary model is consistent with all legal, philosophical, political, or cultural traditions. Rather, we advance the fiduciary model here because we believe its core insight—that a state's sovereign "*right* is derived from *duty*"[149]—offers an historically grounded and normatively attractive theory of sovereignty under international law.

X. SUMMARY OF THE ARGUMENT

A fiduciary conception of sovereignty shapes the way international law distributes, constitutes and regulates the exercise of sovereign power. The primary bearers of sovereign power are states, but as we shall argue in the final chapter, the authority of international institutions is also fiduciary or trust-like in nature. We argue that the fiduciary model offers a normatively attractive account of international legal order, and we survey current international legal doctrines to explore the extent to which international law already reflects the fiduciary model. Although we claim that the fiduciary model offers a plausible interpretive account of international law's core normative commitments, we do not claim that this theory offers the only plausible interpretive account of international legal order. Nor do we claim that contemporary international law fully embraces the fiduciary model at present. Subsequent chapters therefore seek both to demonstrate the fiduciary model's virtues vis-à-vis other accounts of international law and to offer proposals for the progressive development of particular international legal regimes, so as to bring practice into greater conformity with the fiduciary constitution of sovereignty and international law. Through a variety of examples across diverse international legal regimes, we will

148. Amartya Sen, Development as Freedom 240 (1999).

149. Vattel, *supra* note 1, at lv.

show how attention to the fiduciary constitution of sovereignty could lend greater coherence and integrity to the international legal system as a whole. The purpose of the project is to chart a path toward greater convergence between "the moral ideal" of sovereignty as a "sacred trust" and "the legal rules intended to give it effect."[150]

In Chapter 2, we consider how the fiduciary character of sovereignty distinguishes states from other representative entities in the global arena, and we examine how the fiduciary model should inform the international community's legal recognition of emerging states. In Chapters 3 and 4, we explain how the fiduciary model of sovereignty offers a sound theoretical grounding for a distinctly legal conception of international human rights, including the full range of civil, political, economic, social, and cultural rights that are traditionally associated with internal self-determination. IHRL is primarily responsible for ensuring that states exercise their powers in a manner consistent with the other-regarding and purposeful character of their entrusted sovereign authority. Although human rights discourse obviously has profound political, social, and cultural resonances, the content and character of international human rights cannot be fully apprehended in these terms. We argue that international human rights are first and foremost *legal* rights because they are inextricably linked to the juridical character of sovereignty under international law. Although in some respects international law's formal incorporation of human rights norms is a relatively recent historical development,[151] the rise of IHRL during the latter half of the twentieth century represents a logical extension of fiduciary concepts that have been present in international legal discourse for centuries.

After reviewing IHRL's contributions to the fiduciary model of sovereignty, we consider how other fields of international law lend further support for international law's fiduciary constitution. Chapter 5 focuses on the law of armed conflict. We show that the fiduciary relationship between a state and its people underwrites the state's affirmative responsibility to protect its people from grave security threats that originate at home and abroad. Further, we argue that the fiduciary character of sovereignty has a cosmopolitan aspect, in that states must refrain from treating foreign nationals abroad as mere objects that they are at liberty to harm or destroy without justification. Prescriptively, these features of the fiduciary theory support duties to minimize human suffering during armed conflict, including by extending IHRL standards for the use of force to internal armed conflict, belligerent occupation, and humanitarian intervention, and embracing the controversial "least-harmful-means" test for the use of force in international armed conflict.

Chapters 6 and 7 address two contexts of cosmopolitan law that are especially relevant to the fiduciary model: the treatment of detained foreign nationals and persons seeking asylum. International law has long recognized that states bear duties toward foreign nationals within their jurisdictions. These include a duty to accord

150. South West Africa (Eth. v. S. Afr.; Liber. v. S. Afr.), Judgment, 1966 I.C.J. 6, 34–35 (July 18) (observing that because "the principle of the sacred trust has as its sole juridical expression the mandates system . . . it is necessary not to confuse the moral ideal with the legal rules intended to give it effect").

151. *See* Samuel Moyn, The Last Utopia: Human Rights in History (2011).

foreign investors "fair and equitable treatment,"[152] as well as a duty to practice "due diligence" in exercising police powers in order to protect foreign nationals on their soil from harm.[153] In Chapter 6, we demonstrate further that the fiduciary model explains and justifies core features of IHL's prisoner-of-war regime, as well as provides resources to assist legislators, policymakers, and judges in determining how due process standards apply to detention in other settings such as internal armed conflict and transnational counterterrorism. Chapter 7 argues that IRL also reflects a fiduciary relationship between states and foreign nationals subject to their jurisdiction, providing a form of surrogate fiduciary protection for foreign nationals who are rendered effectively stateless by threats arising within their country of origin. IRL's duty of non-refoulement flows naturally from the confluence of the state's position as a joint fiduciary of the earth's surface on behalf of humanity, on the one hand, and its position as a local fiduciary that international law entrusts with sovereignty over its territory and the people within it, on the other. Although these aspects of IHL and IRL are by no means the only ways in which the fiduciary model of sovereignty informs states' obligations to foreign nationals under international law, they are suggestive of the degree to which the fiduciary model's cosmopolitan features have become embedded in many fields of international law.

States bear primary responsibility for ensuring that their exercise of public powers is consistent with their fiduciary obligations toward their people. When disputes arise between states, or between a state and individuals, the rule of law requires that these disputes be referred to independent institutions. In Chapter 8, we consider how international institutions such as international courts and the U.N. Security Council perform this role today. We argue that international institutions serve as fiduciaries for humanity. Just as private law requires functioning courts and other public institutions to establish legal order between private fiduciaries and their beneficiaries, international law requires international institutions to ensure that states respect the internationally recognized rights of their own nationals and foreign nationals, as well as other states.

Our thesis, in short, is that international law's emerging fiduciary constitution is giving new meaning to the ancient maxim that "the good of the people is the supreme law" (*salus populi suprema lex esto*).[154] Over the past century, the classical model of sovereignty has been dismantled piece by piece in favor of a new model that conceives of states as fiduciaries of humanity. The transition between these distinctive constitutional visions of international legal order has been far from smooth. The shock waves generated by this tectonic shift continue to reverberate,

152. *See Fair and Equitable Treatment Standard in International Investment Law* (OECD Working Papers on International Investment 2004/03), http://dx.doi.org/10.1787/675702255435 (last visited Dec. 4, 2015).

153. *See* Dinah L. Shelton, *Private Violence, Public Wrongs, and the Responsibility of States*, 13 Fordham Int'l L.J. 1, 21–23 (1990).

154. *See* Thomas Hobbes, De Cive ch. XIII, pt. II (1651) ("*The safety of the people is the supreme Law* . . . .") (emphasis in the original); Marcus Tullius Cicero, *De Legibus* bk. III, pt. 3, § 8, *in* 2 The Political Works of Marcus Tullius Cicero (Francis Barham ed. & transl., 1842) (proposing the appointment of magistrates entrusted with "absolute authority over the army, for the safety of the people is the supreme law").

toppling old legal orthodoxies and catalyzing the development of new norms and institutions. Dissonance between the retreating classical model and the ascendant fiduciary model, coupled with increasing institutional specialization across the international legal system, has led to doctrinal fragmentation within and across the various sub-disciplines of international law. These dynamics, in turn, have undermined the international community's confidence in the coherence and integrity of the international legal system as a whole. Adumbrating the fiduciary constitution of sovereignty—its juridical structure and implicit jurisprudential commitments—thus represents an important first step toward understanding the grounds of international law's possible legitimacy.

2

Creating Fiduciary States

I. INTRODUCTION

In this chapter, we explore the role of international law in constructing the legal personality, jurisdiction, discretionary powers, and duties of states. We argue that international law conceives of states as fiduciaries for their people, and we explain how this conception informs the rights and duties associated with states' international legal personality.

Our emphasis on the state as the fundamental unit of global governance might strike some readers as shortsighted. Since the early 1990s, many international lawyers and political theorists have celebrated "the withering away of the state," as political, economic, technological, and cultural forces have led to the creation of new international organizations, transnational regulatory networks, and nongovernmental organizations (NGOs).[1] Ethnic violence in newly independent states has hastened the development of international tribunals and territorial administrations such as the International Criminal Tribunal for the Former Yugoslavia (ICTY) and the U.N. Interim Administration Mission in Kosovo (UNMIK). Increasing economic interdependence has elevated critical questions of public policy to the international level to be decided by entities such as the World Trade Organization (WTO) and the World Bank. Spurred partly by an increasingly dense network of transnational human rights NGOs, the past several decades have witnessed treaty bodies such as the European Court of Human Rights (ECHR), the Inter-American Court of Human Rights (Inter-American Court), and the U.N. Committee Against Torture become more actively involved in supervising state compliance with international human rights. Many international lawyers have hailed these developments as marking a transition away from Westphalia toward a more just and cosmopolitan world order in which states play a less prominent role.

Despite these significant changes to international order, the reality is that states are unlikely to exit the global stage anytime soon. For more than four centuries, international law has divided up the earth's surface among states claiming mutually exclusive territorial jurisdiction, making states the primary units of public governance throughout the world. Indeed, in most areas of the world, states are the only institutions with the practical capacity to establish legal order. States also continue to serve as the primary participants in the progressive development and global enforcement of international law. Although the state is by no means the only

1. Martti Koskenniemi, *The Wonderful Artificiality of States*, 88 ASIL Proc. 22, 23 (1994).

institution through which international law might conceivably establish secure and equal freedom for peoples of the world,[2] the fact remains that international law continues to rely upon states as the primary fiduciaries for humanity.

We argue that the state's durably privileged position in international law reflects the fiduciary character of its international legal personality. Much like the legal authority of agents and trustees in private law, the international legal authority of a state is grounded in a juridical relationship between the state and its beneficiaries—the people subject to its sovereign jurisdiction. Although other international institutions, such as the various organs of the United Nations, share the other-regarding and purposive characteristics of states, international law relies upon states to serve as the primary institutional vehicles for establishing secure and equal freedom for humanity. To ensure that states do not abuse this authority, international law requires states to exercise their powers in a manner that is consistent with their other-regarding purpose to establish secure and equal freedom under the rule of law. Thus, a state's international legal authority to exercise public powers is contingent on its fidelity to its fiduciary mission.

In many respects, international law's regulation of states mirrors the regulation of agents, trustees, guardians, and other fiduciaries under private law. Our argument, however, is not that the international law of statehood is merely analogous to private fiduciary law; rather, we contend that the juridical structure of statehood under international law should be understood as a fiduciary relationship between the state and its people. Three dimensions of the fiduciary constitution of state sovereignty merit special attention. First, international law *constitutes* the state as an international juridical institution and defines its legal capacity (i.e., sovereignty) to exercise rights, assume liabilities, and assert immunities as a fiduciary representative for its beneficiaries. Second, international law *distributes* sovereignty among states by identifying which persons and territory are subject to a state's administrative authority (i.e., jurisdiction). Third, international law *regulates* the exercise of public power by placing states under fiduciary obligations to exercise that power in a manner that is consistent with the other-regarding purposes of their entrusted authority (e.g., international human rights). This chapter focuses principally on the first two of these dimensions—the constitutive and distributive functions of international law—to demonstrate how these features have been shaped by the fiduciary character of state sovereignty.

Although this chapter focuses on states, the fiduciary model developed here has significant implications for other institutions. As we will discuss further in Chapter 8, international and regional organizations that serve as secondary guarantors of international legal order likewise stand in a fiduciary relationship with people whose legal or practical interests are subject to the organizations' discretionary powers. Other nonstate actors, such as private military contractors and insurgent groups, may also assume fiduciary obligations when they wield public powers either by delegation from states, international organizations, or regional organizations, or by unilateral assertion of authority over people or territory. To the extent that the international legal frameworks governing these fiduciary relationships are less developed than those governing states, the legal and normative frameworks

2. History suggests a variety of possible alternatives to the contemporary juridical state, including clan, city-state, and empire. *See generally* PHILIP BOBBITT, THE SHIELD OF ACHILLES: WAR, PEACE, AND THE COURSE OF HISTORY (2002).

discussed in this chapter provide a valuable template for designing legal standards to deal with a much wider range of international institutions.

II. CONSTITUTING FIDUCIARY STATES

Like other fiduciary institutions such as corporations or trusts, states live multiple lives. Viewed from a sociological perspective, the concept of the state structures the political and cultural life of a community by defining roles and relationships among members of society. But states are also creatures of law. Their legal personality—the juridical status that entitles them as artificial persons to be treated as subjects capable of claiming legal rights and assuming legal obligations—is established by rules of recognition under international law. Just as private law defines the legal capacity of corporations or trusts by specifying the type of transactions they may consummate on behalf of their beneficiaries, international law defines the legal capacity of states to act on behalf of their people. States may, for example, enter international agreements, participate in the formation and development of customary international law, become parties to international organizations, and claim immunity from suit in foreign courts. They may represent their people in disputes with foreign states and defend their people from external aggression. They are entitled to legislate, adjudicate, and enforce their domestic law autonomously. These rights to rule and represent a people flow from international law's constitution of the state as a juridical institution entrusted with public powers. International law thus transforms the raw power of the sociological state into a form of legal authority that is exercised by the juridical state. The collection of rights and duties associated with this institutionally defined legal personality comprises a state's "sovereignty."

A. What Is a State?

Because it is international law that confers legal personality upon states, the status of "statehood" is a legal conclusion that turns upon legal criteria. H.L.A. Hart underscored this point when he observed that "'a state' is not the name of some person or thing inherently or 'by nature' outside the law." Instead, "we can only know which states are sovereign, and what the extent of their sovereignty is, when we know what the rules are."[3]

Much hinges upon the rules international law employs to define the state. Depending upon how these rules are designed, the law of state recognition may facilitate self-determination as a principle of inclusion, emancipating and empowering peoples to participate as formally equal partners on the world stage.[4] Alternatively, it may operate as a principle of exclusion, consigning some peoples to a marginal legal status at the periphery of international society.[5] Whether international law

3. H.L.A. Hart, The Concept of Law 216, 218 (1951).

4. *See* Christine Chinkin, *The End of Sovereignty?*, 88 ASIL Proc. 72, 73–74 (1994).

5. *See* Jutta Brunnee & Stephen J. Toope, Legitimacy and Legality in International Law: An Interactional Account 78 (2010); R.P. Anand, Confrontation or Cooperation? International Law and the Developing Countries 23 (1987); Rose Parfitt, *Theorizing Recognition and International Personality*, *in* The Oxford Handbook of International Legal Theory (Florian Hoffman & Anne Orford eds., forthcoming).

includes or excludes particular aspiring states will profoundly impact not only political communities' international rights and duties, but also how international law itself develops over time by expanding or contracting the circle of participants in international lawmaking.

Given the central role of states in the international legal order, one might expect that the legal criteria for statehood would be relatively clear and uncontroversial. Yet this is hardly the case. Although some general standards are widely accepted, the prerequisites for statehood remain underspecified and controversial in many respects.

According to Article 1 of the 1933 Montevideo Convention on Rights and Duties of States, the traditional starting point for state recognition, an aspiring state must satisfy four requirements: "(a) a permanent population; (b) a defined territory; (c) government; and (d) [the practical] capacity to enter into relations with other states."[6] Critics have argued persuasively that these criteria are both overinclusive and under-inclusive. For example, some political communities have contested borders yet enjoy broad recognition as sovereign states. Other putative states satisfy all four of the Montevideo Convention's criteria but are not accepted as sovereign states. Thus, although the Montevideo Convention continues to serve as an influential statement on the criteria for statehood, few experts today consider the Convention's framework to represent either an empirically accurate or normatively satisfying account of the legal criteria for statehood.[7]

Over time, many scholars have proposed strategies for refining the Montevideo Convention's four criteria, but so far the literature has not yielded a universally accepted alternative. Arguably the most ambitious and comprehensive contribution to this field is John Crawford's magisterial study, *The Creation of States in International Law*.[8] Crawford sifts through centuries of state recognition practice, seeking to distill general customary criteria for the recognition of new states. He concludes that in order to qualify as a state an entity must be capable of extending powers of governance over persons and territory.[9] Like most contemporary scholars, however, he argues that a state's borders need not be clearly defined, nor need a state's population manifest permanent residence within a state. Instead, Crawford posits "independence" as "the central criterion of statehood."[10] According to Crawford, a state's independence has two dimensions: (1) "the separate existence of an entity within reasonably coherent frontiers"; and (2) "its not being 'subject to the authority of any other State or group of States,' which is to say that it has over it 'no other authority than that of international law.' "[11] Crawford rejects other potential criteria such as an entity's willingness to obey international law, the existence

6. 164 L.N.T.S. 19, USTS 881 (1934).

7. *See, e.g.*, HILARY CHARLESWORTH & CHRISTINE CHINKIN, THE BOUNDARIES OF INTERNATIONAL LAW: A FEMINIST ANALYSIS 125–37 (2000); Thomas D. Grant, *Defining Statehood: The Montevideo Convention and Its Discontents*, 37 COLUM. J. TRANSNAT'L L. 403, 453 (1999).

8. JAMES CRAWFORD, THE CREATION OF STATES IN INTERNATIONAL LAW (2006).

9. *Id.* at 59 (citing Island of Palmas Case, (1928) 2 R.I.A.A. 829, 838 ("Sovereignty in the relations between States signifies independence.")).

10. *Id.* at 62.

11. *Id.* at 66.

of a functioning legal system, and recognition by other states. These and other features may be relevant to the creation of juridical states, he argues, but they are not required.

Crawford's proposed independence criterion has not escaped criticism. Some scholars have observed that Crawford's primary contribution—the independence criterion—suffers from conceptual difficulties similar to those that have bedeviled the Montevideo Convention's criteria. The principal problem is that by positing independence from foreign control as the distinguishing criterion for statehood, Crawford conflates the legal privileges of statehood with the criteria necessary to identify a state. From a legal perspective, a state's independence from foreign interference is a legal entitlement that flows from its juridical personality as a state, not the reverse. As Jeremy Waldron has observed, a state's

> sovereignty is something made, not assumed, and it is made for the benefit of those whose interests it protects. In its international aspect, the sovereignty and sovereign freedom of the individual state are equally an artifact of [international law]. What its sovereignty is and what it amounts to is not given as a matter of the intrinsic value of its individuality, but determined by the rules of the international order.[12]

Although some degree of political and military independence might plausibly be necessary before an aspiring state could qualify for international recognition, Crawford's theory is unclear about how much independence is required. For example, must communities emerging from colonial domination achieve full political independence before they may claim the sovereign rights associated with statehood? May a political community qualify as a state if it has agreed to entrust its national defense to another state? What if an aspiring state relies on international financial and administrative assistance to maintain public order and basic public services? Once we take into consideration the myriad ways in which an aspiring state's de facto independence may be compromised, it becomes apparent that few states are fully "independent." Political and military independence are normative ideals linked to the principle of self-determination of peoples rather than minimal prerequisites for statehood. Accordingly, the international community has rejected bids for statehood notwithstanding the fact that aspiring states were functionally independent,[13] and it has recognized states that were heavily dependent on foreign assistance.[14] Like many scholars who have endeavored to clarify the criteria for statehood, Crawford purports to derive his "independence" criterion from state

12. Jeremy Waldron, *Are Sovereigns Entitled to the Benefit of the Rule of Law?*, 22 Eur. J. Int'l L. 315, 328 (2011); Jeremy Waldron, *The Rule of International Law*, 30 Harv. J. L. & Pub. Pol'y 15, 21 (2005).

13. *See, e.g.*, Benjamin R. Farley, *Calling a State a State: Somaliland and International Recognition*, 24 Emory Int'l L. Rev. 777 (2010) (noting that Somaliland is functionally independent and satisfies other traditional criteria for statehood but has not received recognition).

14. *See, e.g.*, Elena A. Baylis, *Beyond Rights: Legal Process in Ethnic Conflicts*, 25 Mich. J. Int'l L. 529, 544 n.50 (2004) (characterizing Ethiopia as "a classic example of a donor economy" that relies upon "foreign aid as a primary resource for public and private development").

practice and *opinio juris*, but his putatively "descriptive account" of statehood is better understood, in reality, as an under-theorized normative account of the legal entitlements associated with state sovereignty.

B. The Fiduciary Theory of Statehood

The fiduciary theory approaches the legal personality of states from a fresh perspective by taking as its point of departure the overarching juridical character of the state as a normative institution constituted by international law. Just as private law constitutes fiduciary relations by conferring authority on one party (the fiduciary) to exercise discretionary powers over the legal interests of another (the beneficiary), international law constitutes states by conferring authority on the representative institutions of a political community to exercise public powers on behalf of their people. In private law, fiduciary relationships often arise when a beneficiary affirmatively consents to allow a fiduciary to take her place in exercising her legal rights for her benefit (e.g., principal-agent relationships). In other fiduciary relationships, the law entrusts fiduciaries with authority to represent beneficiaries without requiring the beneficiaries' effective consent (e.g., parent-child and guardian-ward relationships). Legal and political theorists have debated whether a state's authority comes into existence through the coordinated consent of its people, or through the unilateral but effective assumption of public power by political elites. Regardless of how states arise in practice, the fiduciary theory suggests that their legal authority under international law derives from their fiduciary relationship with their people. International law entrusts states with authority based upon their assumption of public powers held for the benefit of their people. From a juridical perspective, therefore, the sovereignty of states constitutes a form of international legal authority that is anchored in the state's fiduciary relationship to the people subject to its public powers.

Under international law, a state's sovereign authority is, by definition, institutional, other-regarding, and purposive. State sovereignty is institutional in the sense that public powers may be exercised only by a state or another institution entrusted by the state to exercise authority in a fiduciary capacity.[15] Sovereignty is other-regarding in the sense that states are authorized to serve as representatives for the benefit of their people, performing governance functions that their people lack the legal capacity to undertake as private parties. Because the legal authority of states is defined and circumscribed by their representative role, states cannot use their entrusted public powers for purposes other than to benefit the people subject to them. The principle that states must use public powers for the public's benefit constitutes, in Samuel Pufendorf's words, the "general law for supreme sovereigns."[16] Just as private-law fiduciaries bear obligations of loyalty and care, the juridical character of a state's legal authority under international law entails an obligation to refrain from exploiting entrusted public powers for the benefit of public officials. This other-regarding character of a state's public powers mirrors the duty of loyalty

15. We address the role of international institutions as fiduciaries in Chapter 8.

16. Samuel Pufendorf, *On the Law of Nature and of Nations*, *in* POLITICAL WRITINGS 242 (Craig Carr & Michael Seidl eds., 1994).

in private law.[17] A state's legal authority is also purposive because international law entrusts public powers to the state only for limited purposes: to establish for their people secure and equal freedom under the rule of law.

The idea that international law recognizes states as institutional vehicles for limited purposes has been a recurring theme in legal and political theory for centuries. Thomas Hobbes, for example, famously framed state sovereignty in purposive terms as a vehicle for establishing human security, defining the "office of the sovereign" as none other than "the end for which he was trusted with the sovereign power, namely, the procuration of *the safety of the people*," where "by safety here is not meant bare preservation, but also all other contentments of life, which every man by lawful industry, without danger or hurt to the commonwealth, shall acquire to himself."[18] Kant claimed that the very point of the state is to provide a regime of equal freedom such that no person is subject to the will or another—unilateralism—but rather is subject to a publicly enforced framework of reciprocal limits.[19] Vattel devoted much of his influential treatise on the law of nations to the internationally prescribed purposes of states, including "to provide for the Necessities of the Nation," "procure the true Happiness of the Nation," and "fortify . . . against External Attacks."[20]

Over the past decade, the purposive conception of state authority has attracted renewed attention as the international community has embraced the idea that states bear a "responsibility to protect" their people from genocide, war crimes, ethnic cleansing, and crimes against humanity.[21] Nonetheless, the purpose of states as institutions constituted by international law is not merely to protect humanity from mass atrocities. On a more basic level, international law entrusts states with the responsibility to establish and maintain legislative, executive, and judicial institutions to provide basic public security, social services, and the rule of law for their people. States that decline to serve these functions undermine their own international legal authority to exercise public powers. International law thus constitutes states as purposeful institutions deployed in the service of humanity.[22]

17. *See* Paul B. Miller, *Justifying Fiduciary Duties*, 58 McGill L.J. 969 (2013).

18. Thomas Hobbes, Leviathan with Selected Variants from the Latin Edition of 1668 ch 30, ¶ 1, 219 (Edwin Curley ed., 1994) (emphasis in original).

19. Immanuel Kant, The Metaphysics of Morals 125 (Mary Gregor transl., 1991) (1797) (identifying the three branches of government—the legislative, judicial, and executive—which together can remedy unilateralism by providing for the public and authoritative specification, interpretation, and enforcement of law); *see also* Arthur Ripstein, Force and Freedom: Kant's Legal and Political Philosophy 145–81 (2009) (explicating the problem of unilateralism and Kant's institutional solution to it).

20. Emmerich de Vattel, The Law of Nations: Or Principles of the Law of Nature Applied to the Conduct and Affairs of Nations and Sovereigns (1758) (transl. 1876) (table of contents); *see also* Samuel Pufendorf, *On the Law of Nature and of Nations, in* Political Writings 242 (Craig Carr & Michael Seidel eds., 1994) (arguing that "[t]he general law for supreme sovereigns" could be encompassed in the maxim: "Let the people's welfare be the supreme law.")

21. 2005 World Summit Outcome, G.A. Res. 60/1, A/RES/60/1, 24 Oct. 2005, ¶ 138.

22. *See* Ruti Teitel, Humanity's Law 4 (2011).

The domestic purpose for which international law constitutes states is to establish municipal legal orders within which individuals can interact with one another and the state as legal equals under the rule of law, whereas the international purpose is to constitute an international legal order within which states themselves, as their people's representatives, can interact as legal equals under an international rule of law.[23] International law accomplishes these purposes by authorizing states to represent their people in a fiduciary capacity: states are clothed with authority to exercise discretionary administrative powers over the practical interests of their people, but they may do so only in a manner that is consistent with their institutional purpose and exclusively for the benefit of their people. Although contemporary international law gives states considerable latitude to determine how best to advance the interests of their people, opening a space for institutional pluralism among states,[24] the basic juridical structure and purpose of all states is the same: states are entrusted with authority in a fiduciary capacity to establish a regime of secure and equal freedom for their people. The fiduciary constitution of international legal order thus transforms the brute power of (some) de facto governments into states with sovereignty—the legal authority possessed by juridical states to exercise public powers on behalf of their people.

III. DISTRIBUTING SOVEREIGNTY

In addition to its role in defining states as juridical institutions, the international law of statehood is necessary to regulate the distribution of sovereignty among existing states and determine when the sovereign jurisdiction of an existing state should be limited to accommodate the creation of a new state. As Patrick Macklem puts it, international law alone can "shape an international political reality into an international legal order by determining the legality of multiple claims of sovereign power."[25]

International law distributes sovereignty primarily by dividing dominion over the earth's surface geographically among states. States are charged with establishing municipal legal order for those who reside or travel within their territory. Outside their territorial jurisdiction, states serve chiefly as agents for their people in international relations. From this perspective, people and territory are not properly understood as "qualifications" for statehood, as the Montevideo Convention suggests, but rather as structural features that are common to all state-subject relationships. People and territory are integral to the juridical structure of the state-subject fiduciary relationship as currently constructed because a state's sovereignty entails an entrustment of authority to govern within a territory for the benefit of a state's people. By regulating states' claims to territorial jurisdiction and the governance of peoples within their territories, international law allocates fiduciary responsibility

23. A juridical consequence of this state-centric system is the production of a cosmopolitan legal order to govern relations between states and noncitizens, as discussed in Chapters 5, 6, and 7.

24. *See, e.g.*, Gerry Simpson, *Two Liberalisms*, 12 Eur. J. Int'l L. 537 (2001).

25. Patrick Macklem, *What Is International Human Rights Law? Three Applications of a Distributive Account*, 52 McGill L.J. 575, 587–88 (2007); *see also* Patrick Macklem, The Sovereignty of Human Rights 29 (2015) (arguing that "[i]nternational law shapes global politics into legal order . . . by legally validating some claims of sovereign power and refusing to validate others" and by effecting the "distribution of sovereign power among [states]").

to states collectively for the protection and care of humanity. In Chapters 5–8, we explore some of the contexts in which states and international institutions serve not only as fiduciaries for their people, but also as fiduciaries of humanity generally.[26]

A. International Law's Distribution of Sovereignty over Time

Since its inception, international law has embraced the idea that all people are entitled to the security and legal order that a sovereign state (or empire) provides, and that public powers must be exercised in a manner that is consistent with the fiduciary principle. International law distributes sovereignty by territory to clarify which states stand in a fiduciary relation with which people, both to prevent states from overstepping their authority and to ensure that states can be held responsible for shirking their responsibilities to protect their people. As arbitrator Max Huber explained in the renowned *Island of Palmas* case, "[t]erritorial sovereignty . . . serves to divide between the nations the space upon which human activities are employed, in order to assure them at all points the minimum protection of which international law is the guardian."[27]

The idea that states serve as fiduciaries under international law can be traced back to the writings of Francisco de Vitoria, a Spanish theologian and Dominican friar at the University of Salamanca who is often described as an early "forerunner"[28] or "father"[29] of international law. In his seminal 1532 lecture "On the Indians Lately Discovered,"[30] Vitoria argued that indigenous peoples of the Americas, being endowed with reason and moral agency, possessed the same natural rights as Europeans, including the right to hold property.[31] According to Vitoria, Spain's conquest of the Americas could be justified only if strictly necessary to guarantee respect for natural rights. Vitoria observed that some indigenous communities in the New World had refused to respect the natural rights of Spanish citizens "to travel into the lands in question and to sojourn there,"[32] "carry on trade among the native Indians,"[33] "preach the Gospel,"[34] use wild plants and animals for sustenance, extract minerals, and exploit other natural resources.[35] If indigenous peoples violated their

26. *See* Eyal Benvenisti, *Sovereigns as Trustees of Humanity: On the Accountability of States to Foreign Stakeholders*, 107 Am. J. Int'l L. 295 (2013).

27. Island of Palmas Case, 2 R.I.A.A. 829, 839 (1928) (Huber J.).

28. 1 Lassa Oppenheim, International Law 83–84 (2d ed. 1912); David Kennedy, *Primitive Legal Scholarship*, 27 Harv. Int'l L.J. 1 (1986).

29. Christopher R. Rossi, Broken Chain of Being: James Brown Scott and the Origins of Modern International Law 5 (1998).

30. Francisco de Vitoria, *On the Indians Lately Discovered* (1532), *published in* Franciscus de Victoria, De Indis et de Ivre Belli Relectiones 115 (Classics of International Law ed. 1917) (translation based on Boyer ed. 1557; Muñoz ed. 1565; and Simon ed. 1696).

31. *Id.* at 128

32. *Id.* at 151.

33. *Id.* at 152.

34. *Id.* at 157.

35. *Id.* at 153.

duties under the law of nations to respect these natural rights of their Spanish visitors, and if they could not be persuaded to change course through peaceful means, Spain could lawfully intervene militarily to ensure respect for its own citizens' natural rights.[36] Spanish intervention would also be justified, Vitoria argued, to protect indigenous people from the "tyrannical and oppressive acts" of their own rulers, including human sacrifice and cannibalism.[37] According to this account, the law of nations entrusted Spain with authority to establish basic security and guarantee fundamental rights in the New World, subject to a fiduciary obligation to use the power thus conferred for the benefit of all people residing within the relevant territory.

Although Vitoria did not expressly characterize the relationship between a state and its own people in fiduciary terms, his account of indigenous communities' right to self-government suggests a fiduciary conception of public authority. Under Vitoria's account of natural law, indigenous people could claim a variety of rights vis-à-vis authorities within their own communities, including rights to travel, proselytize, hold property, engage in commerce, and to be free from human sacrifice and cannibalism. The violation of these rights would undermine an indigenous community's right to political independence and could justify foreign conquest. At the core of this account was an implicit theory about the nature of public authority under the law of nations—namely, that a political community's right to self-government depended upon its commitment to respect and protect individual rights.

Prior to the twentieth century, Vitoria's fiduciary conception of state sovereignty was exploited to lend an aura of respectability to the expansion of Western powers through colonial conquest. "Once the initial determination had been made and accepted that the colonial world was not sovereign," observes Antony Anghie, "the discipline [of international law] could then create for itself, and present as inevitable and natural, the grand redeeming project of bringing the marginalized into the realm of sovereignty, civilizing the uncivilized, and developing the juridical techniques and institutions necessary for this great mission."[38] Within two decades of Vitoria's lecture, the Spanish crown formally embraced Vitoria's theory, while largely ignoring its radical implications for the natural rights of indigenous peoples. Other colonial powers were also drawn to Vitoria's fiduciary theory and invoked it regularly (albeit not uniformly[39]) as justification for their own exercises in empire-building. For example, King James I of England invoked the principle of civilizing guardianship when he authorized the Virginia Company to establish what would become the Jamestown Colony for the purpose of "propagating of Christian religion," and to "bring the Infidels and Savages, living in those Parts, to human Civility, and to a settled and quiet Government."[40] Territories that lacked what Western observers recognized as a unitary government capable of establishing public security and legal order came to be viewed

36. *Id.* at 155.

37. *Id.* at 159.

38. Anthony Anghie, Imperialism, Sovereignty, and the Making of International Law 30 (2004).

39. *See* Johnson v. McIntosh, 21 U.S. (8 Wheat) 543 (1823).

40. Robert A. Williams, Jr, The American Indian in Western Legal Thought: The Discourses of Conquest 201 (1990) [hereinafter Williams, American Indian] (citing The

as *terra nullius*—land governed by none—and thus subject to the civilizing mission of Western colonial governance.[41] The international legal order that developed during the colonial period thus defined governance powers in fiduciary terms, and regulated claims to sovereignty over particular people and territory according to Western states' demonstrated capacity to establish security and legal order for the benefit of humanity.

By enabling European conquest in this fashion, international law purported to emancipate all of humanity from the state of nature by establishing governance structures that would guarantee security under the rule of law. The reality was, of course, very different. Whereas Vitoria had emphasized that Spain should seek every opportunity to promote security and individual rights abroad through persuasion rather than the sword, European statesmen invoked Vitoria's guardianship theory as a mandate for military conquest and imperialist exploitation.[42] As Robert Williams has observed, the legacy of Vitoria's guardianship account of state sovereignty was to "provide[] Western legal discourse with its first secularly oriented, systematized elaboration of the superior rights of civilized Europeans to invade and conquer normatively divergent peoples."[43]

As Western empires began to crumble in the nineteenth and twentieth centuries, Vitoria's fiduciary account of state authority shaped the pathway to international recognition for new, postcolonial states. International lawyers during this period continued to insist that "uncivilized" peoples could not qualify for full recognition and membership in the international society of states until they guaranteed basic rights and freedoms for their people and foreign nationals within their borders.[44] Although the international community never defined the legal standards of "civilization" with great precision, the standards were refined over time as established states developed demanding conditions for recognizing new entrants into the international society of states.[45] According to Gerrit Gong, these legal requirements included the following guarantees:

- "basic rights" such as "life, dignity, and property; freedom to travel, commerce, and religion";
- "an organized political bureaucracy with some efficiency in running the state machinery, and with some capacity to organize for self-defence";
- "adhere[nce] to generally accepted international law, including the laws of war;"

First Charter of Virginia, *in* DOCUMENTS OF AMERICAN HISTORY 8–10 (H.S. Commager ed., 8th ed. 1968)). In tension with the fiduciary theory was a competing vision of Native Americans as perpetual enemies (*perpetui inimici*) who could not be induced to civilized governance and must be destroyed. *See* ROBERT A. WILLIAMS, JR., SAVAGE ANXIETIES 192–96 (2012).

41. Vitoria rejected the concept of *terra nullius*, yet still accepted colonialism based on the fiduciary concept of benevolent guardianship.

42. WILLIAMS, AMERICAN INDIAN, *supra* note 40, at 93.

43. *Id.* at 106.

44. HERSCH LAUTERPACHT, RECOGNITION IN INTERNATIONAL LAW 31–32 (1947).

45. GERRIT W. GONG, THE STANDARD OF "CIVILIZATION" IN INTERNATIONAL SOCIETY (1984).

- "a domestic system of courts, codes, and published laws which guarantee legal justice for all within its jurisdiction, foreigners and native citizens alike;"
- "adequate and permanent avenues for diplomatic interchange and communication"; and
- discontinuance of practices considered "unacceptable" such as "suttee, polygamy, and slavery."[46]

The legal standards associated with the standard of "civilization" guided the introduction of new states into full juridical status and membership in the international community. For example, at the Congress of Berlin in 1878, Western states recognized Bulgaria, Serbia, Romania, and Montenegro in exchange for their commitment to observe the rule of law, including safeguards for religious freedom.[47] When Latin American republics sought international recognition in the early nineteenth century, the British Foreign Minister, Lord Canning, stated that his country's recognition would depend upon the republics demonstrating "reasonable consistency and stability" and abolishing the slave trade.[48] International recognition of China, Japan, Siam, and the Ottoman Empire likewise proceeded through conditional agreements—the so-called "unequal treaties" or "capitulations"—that provided protections for foreign nationals and, in some cases, established expectations for the reform or reconstruction of public institutions.[49] Japan made harmonization with the standard of "civilization" a national priority, studiously working toward this goal throughout the late nineteenth century until it "became the first non-European country to gain full international status and full recognition."[50] Although the specific conditions imposed upon new states varied in some respects, the overarching civilizing rationale for these conditions was broadly premised on the idea that aspiring states must demonstrate the requisite capacity and commitment to fulfill the purposes of a civilized "state" under international law, as defined by the dominant European powers.

With the founding of the League of Nations, the international community assumed a more formal role in preparing emerging states for statehood. Article 22 of the League Covenant asserted that some "colonies and territories" in the Middle East, Africa, and the Pacific, which were no longer under the control of Germany or the Ottoman Empire, were "inhabited by peoples not yet able to stand by themselves under the strenuous conditions of the modern world." For such peoples, the Covenant concluded "there should be applied the principle that the well-being

46. *Id.* at 15.

47. *See* Rose Sydney Parfitt, The Unequal Equality of Sovereigns: A Brief History of "Peripheral Personality," Jean Monnet Working Paper Series 20/13, at 22, http://jeanmonnetprogram.org/paper/the-unequal-equality-of-sovereigns-a-brief-history-of-peripheral-personality/ [last visited Mar. 4, 2016].

48. William G. Grewe, The Epochs of International Law 489–99 (Michael Byers, transl. 2000) (1984).

49. Gong, *supra* note 45, at 66–69.

50. *Id.* at 29–30.

and development of such peoples form a sacred trust of civilization." The resulting Mandate System was modeled expressly on private fiduciary law; according to General Smuts of South Africa, who proposed the creation of the Mandate System, the holdings of Germany and the Ottoman Empire after World War I were to be "liquidated," with the League of Nations becoming a trustee or executor for "this great estate."[51] In contexts where newly liberated peoples lacked either the institutional capacity or commitment to establish an independent state, the international community would assume responsibility for the affected peoples through the League. "The best method of giving practical effect to this principle," the Covenant proclaimed, was

> that the tutelage of such peoples should be entrusted to advanced nations who, by reason of their resources, their experience, or their geographic position, can best undertake the responsibility and who are willing to accept it, and that this tutelage should be exercised by them as Mandatories on behalf of the League.[52]

Thus, individual states would be appointed to administer the "sacred trust" reposed in the international community by providing interim governance, while preparing the former colony or territory to assume the full fiduciary obligations associated with sovereign statehood. Unlike previous iterations of colonial guardianship in which each colonial power was "answerable [only] to his own conscience,"[53] the Covenant "embodied" "securities for the performance of this trust" by holding mandatories accountable to a permanent commission, which received annual reports and supervised mandatories' fidelity to their fiduciary obligations.

By the conclusion of World War II, the formal distinction between "civilized" and "uncivilized" states faded from international law,[54] but many Western states continued to question the readiness of former colonies to assume the mantle of sovereignty. In response to these concerns, the League of Nations Mandate System was replaced by a new Trusteeship System supervised by the United Nations.[55] Eleven trusteeships were created from ten former mandates and one territory, Somalia, which previously had been under the control of Italy.[56] U.N. trusteeships aimed "to promote the political, economic, social, and educational advancement of the inhabitants of the trust territories, and their progressive development towards self-government or

51. ANGHIE, *supra* note 38, at 119 (quoting J.C. Smuts, *The League of Nations: A Practical Suggestion, reprinted in* 2 DAVID HUNTER MILLER, THE DRAFTING OF THE COVENANT 26 (1971) (1928)).

52. League of Nations Covenant, art. 22, ¶¶ 1–2.

53. GEORGE THULLEN, PROBLEMS OF THE TRUSTEESHIP SYSTEM: A STUDY OF POLITICAL BEHAVIOR IN THE UNITED NATIONS 11 (1964).

54. *See* GONG, *supra* note 45, at 86–87 (suggesting that "the period around 1937 is clearly the beginning of its end—at least by that name"); LAUTERPACHT, *supra* note 44, at 31 ("Modern international law knows of no distinction for the purpose of recognition, between civilized and uncivilized States within and outside the international community of civilized states.").

55. UN Charter art. 77(1).

56. *See* EUGENE PARKER CHASE, THE UNITED NATIONS IN ACTION 284–315 (1950).

independence as may be appropriate to the particular circumstances of each territory and its peoples and the freely expressed wishes of the peoples concerned."[57] Efforts were made to ensure that the institutional structures for supervising trusteeships would be "wider and more effective" under the U.N. Charter than they had been under the Charter of the League of Nations.[58] Mirroring the mandate system that preceded it, the U.N. trusteeship system cast Western powers in the role of secondary fiduciaries for foreign peoples, with the aim of helping local public authorities develop the institutional capacities necessary to qualify for full sovereignty.

In a series of decisions beginning in the 1950s, the International Court of Justice (ICJ) affirmed the fiduciary character of the Mandate and Trusteeship Systems. Its 1950 advisory opinion on South-West Africa, for example, stressed that the mandate system "was created, in the interest of the inhabitants of the territory, and of humanity in general, as an international institution with an international object—a sacred trust of civilization."[59] The ICJ emphasized this principle two decades later in another advisory opinion on South-West Africa. Speaking of the international community's "sacred trust" toward the mandate territories, the ICJ explained:

> It is self-evident that the "trust" had to be exercised for the benefit of the peoples concerned, who were admitted to have interests of their own and to possess a potentiality for independent existence on the attainment of a certain stage of development: the mandates system was designed to provide peoples "not yet" able to manage their own affairs with the help and guidance necessary to enable them to arrive at the stage where they would be "able to stand by themselves."[60]

According to the Court, fidelity to the other-regarding and purposeful character of the relationship was a constitutive legal constraint on the authority of an international mandatory or trustee to exercise public powers over a foreign power. "One of the fundamental principles governing the international relationship thus established," the Court explained, "is that a party which disowns or does not fulfill its own obligations cannot be recognized as retaining the rights which it claims to derive from the relationship."[61]

On the strength of these fiduciary principles, Nauru, a Micronesian island and trust territory under Australia's administration, later brought a claim against Australia before the ICJ. Nauru claimed that Australia had engaged in self-dealing by managing the island's phosphate deposits for the benefit of Australia rather than Nauru. In its 1989 decision dealing with preliminary objections, the ICJ emphasized Australia's obligation to administer Nauru's resources as a "sacred trust" for

57. *Id.* art. 76(b).

58. Legal Consequences for States of the Continued Presence of South Africa in Namibia (South West Africa) Notwithstanding Security Council Resolution 276 (1970), 1971 ICJ Rep. 16, 33 ¶ 56 (June 21) [hereinafter *South West Africa*].

59. South-West Africa (International Status) Case, 1950 ICJ Rep. 128, 132.

60. *South West Africa*, 1971 ICJ Rep. at 28, ¶ 46.

61. *Id.* at 46, ¶ 96.

the exclusive benefit of the people of Nauru.[62] Australia eventually settled with Nauru, paying an amount that included Nauru's claim to the loss it suffered as a consequence of Australia's self-dealing.[63]

Despite their formal fiduciary structure, both the mandate and trusteeship systems have been criticized justly as tools for veiled neocolonial exploitation. Anghie, in particular, has argued that "the universalizing mission of international law, by embracing the idea of trusteeship," was able to "continue its task of ensuring that the Western model of law and behavior would be seen as natural, inevitable and inescapable," while entrenching social and economic inequality between established and emerging states.[64] By insisting that the state was the only acceptable form of governance, colonial powers failed to recognize how tribal systems and other forms of small-scale political organization achieved security and legal order within indigenous communities. For many indigenous societies, the international community's expectation that all political communities must be organized as states with specialized public bureaucracies and defined territorial borders ran contrary to deeply engrained institutions of social organization. Colonial powers' paternalistic prejudices toward foreign peoples also prevented mandates and trusteeships from becoming effective vehicles for promoting political self-determination. One tract by a British legal expert on the Mandate for Mesopotamia, for example, noted that the Middle East needed the United Kingdom's benevolent trusteeship, with all of the legal authority and correlative obligations that this relationship entailed, because "the Arabs" were "wild, turbulent men," who were "not accustomed to self-government."[65] "Full sovereignty will come in due time to the territory," the author suggested, "but only when its people assume the dignity of an independent State."[66] By imposing Western models for self-government and then treating foreign peoples as culturally incompetent to assume the responsibilities associated with it, European powers used the Mandate and the Trusteeship Systems as tools for political and cultural imperialism.

B. Self-Determination and Fiduciary Representation

Over the past half-century, the framing of state sovereignty in fiduciary terms has acquired a new resonance as it has been redirected against great-power domination of developing nations, serving to underscore rather than undermine the idea that public power belongs ultimately to the people. Consistent with the fiduciary model,

62. *See* Case Concerning Certain Phosphate Lands in Nauru (Nauru v. Australia) (Preliminary Objections), 1992 ICJ Rep. 240, ¶¶ 41–44.

63. *See* Ramon E. Reyes, Jr., Nauru v. Australia: *The International Fiduciary Duty and the Settlement of Nauru's Claims for Rehabilitation of Its Phosphate Lands,* 16 N.Y.L. Sch. J. Int'l & Comp. L. 1 (1996).

64. Anghie, *supra* note 38, at 146.

65. Duncan Campbell Lee, The Mandate for Mesopotamia and the Principle of Trusteeship in English Law 19, 22 (1921).

66. *Id.; cf.* 1 James Lorimer, Institutes of the Law of Nations 123 (1883) (arguing against statehood for peoples governed by "religious creeds whose doctrine renders impossible the presumption of reciprocating will, e.g. the Mohammedan religion").

international law today recognizes the right of all peoples to full political participation and cultural identity within an independent and autonomous state that honors their fundamental rights and freedoms.[67] This "principle of equal rights and self-determination of peoples," as enshrined in the UN Charter,[68] has two dimensions: "external" self-determination and "internal" self-determination.[69] External self-determination provides that national groups have a right to freedom from colonial domination, that is, to "freely determine their political status and freely pursue their economic, social and cultural development."[70] When subnational groups are unable to break away from existing states, they may still claim a right to internal self-determination, which requires, at a minimum, that they enjoy full and equal participation in the processes of representative self-governance. Through these two dimensions of self-determination, international law seeks to redress the practical consequences of its requirement that indigenous peoples submit to the political organization of a state and territorially defined distribution of sovereign power among states.[71]

The right to external self-determination flows naturally from the fiduciary model of state sovereignty. A state may not subject a foreign people to its governing power unilaterally when international law has entrusted sovereignty to another state. Under international law, the authority associated with statehood is circumscribed along jurisdictional lines; it is not a license to subjugate other peoples. Hence, a state that assumes administrative control over a foreign people without international authorization violates international law, casting itself in the role of an unlawful occupier, a position analogous to a kidnapper, rather than a fiduciary state. Guided by these principles, the international community repeatedly has refused to recognize the extraterritorial authority of states that have asserted control over foreign territory through unauthorized military intervention.[72] Under the fiduciary model, the principle of external self-determination safeguards the liberty of peoples to self-organize into political communities governed by laws responsive to their interests, affirming the legal equality of all persons as equal beneficiaries of international legal order.

67. *See* International Covenant on Civil and Political Rights art. 1(1), Dec. 16, 1966, S. Exec. Doc. E, 95-2 (1978), 999 U.N.T.S. 171 [hereinafter ICCPR]; Declaration on Principles of International Law Concerning Friendly Relations and Cooperation Among States in Accordance with the Charter of the United Nations, G.A. Res. 2625, Annex, U.N. GAOR, 25th Sess., Supp. No. 28, at 122, U.N. Doc. A/8028 (1970); Convention Concerning Indigenous and Tribal Peoples in Independent Countries, International Labor Organization, Convention No. 169, June 27, 1989, ILO Official Bull. 59 (1989) (entered into force Sept. 5, 1991).

68. U.N. Charter art. 1, ¶ 2.

69. *See* Antonio Cassese, Self-determination of Peoples: A Legal Appraisal 67–140 (1995).

70. ICCPR, *supra* note 67, art. 1(1).

71. *See* Macklem, *supra* note 25, at 162 (arguing that the purpose of international indigenous rights "is to mitigate injustices produced by the way the international legal order conceives of sovereignty as a legal entitlement that it distributes to some collectivities it recognizes as States").

72. *See, e.g.*, S.C. Res. 360, S/RES/360 (Aug. 16, 1974) (declining to recognize the authority of Turkey in Northern Cyprus).

If external self-determination seeks to advance human dignity by reinforcing international law's distribution of sovereignty among states, internal self-determination seeks to mitigate the historical injustices for which international law is partially to blame, such as the denial of sovereignty to indigenous peoples.[73] Although international law does not recognize every plausible claim to sovereignty, such as the claims of indigenous peoples, it affirms that a state's authority to govern its people depends upon whether it "represents the whole of its population within its territory consistent with principles of equality, nondiscrimination, and self-determination."[74] States must honor the cultural and linguistic identities of ethnic minorities, as well as provide them an opportunity for equal participation in public affairs and an "equitable share" of public funds.[75] States must also provide credible institutional mechanisms for the vindication of minority rights.

Some municipal courts have held that states' fiduciary relationship with indigenous peoples entails an obligation to consult those peoples and seek to accommodate their concerns if a proposed state action will infringe their rights.[76] International law supports this principle of indigenous self-determination and states' duty to consult.[77] The Inter-American Court has gone so far as to hold that when states undertake large-scale development projects in indigenous territory, states must obtain the consent of the indigenous people, in effect making the indigenous people coauthors of the projects.[78] Violation of these autonomy-enabling principles would breach obligations that many states now recognize as fiduciary in character.

More controversially, under some circumstances the principle of internal self-determination may support independent statehood for substate groups that have

73. *See* Patrick Macklem, *Minority Rights in International Law*, 6 INT'L J. CON. L. 531 (2008) (developing a distributional account of minority rights).

74. Macklem, *supra* note 25, at 587–88.

75. *See* BRAD R. ROTH, GOVERNMENTAL ILLEGITIMACY IN INTERNATIONAL LAW 206–07 (1999) (citing the minority treaties of the League of Nations era).

76. *See, e.g.*, Seminole Nation v. United States, 316 U.S. 286, 297 (1942) ("In carrying out its treaty obligations with the Indian tribes the Government .... has charged itself with moral obligations of the highest responsibility and trust. Its conduct ... should therefore be judged by the most exacting fiduciary standards."); British Columbia v. Haida Nation (Minister of Forests), [2004] 3 S.C.R. 511 (Can.) (finding that the Crown's duty to consult indigenous peoples includes a duty to seek an accommodation of their interests); R. v. Sparrow, [1990] 1 S.C.R. 1075, 1077 (Can.) (declaring that the Crown is in a fiduciary relationship with aboriginal peoples and owes them a duty of consultation); New Zealand Maori Council v. Attorney-General, [1987] 1 N.Z.L.R. 641 (H.C.) (asserting that the Crown and the Maori are in a fiduciary relationship).

77. *See* Convention Concerning Indigenous and Tribal Peoples in Independent Countries art. 6, June 27, 1989, 28 I.L.M. 1382 (supporting duty to consult); Declaration on the Rights of Indigenous Peoples arts. 3–5, G.A. Res. 61/295, U.N. Doc. A/RES/61/295 (Sept. 13, 2007) (supporting self-determination); *id.* art. 18 (supporting general participatory rights); *id.* arts. 15, 17, 19, 30, 32, 36, 38 (supporting duties to consult).

78. Case of the Saramaka People v. Suriname, Judgment, 28 Nov. 2007 (Ser. C), No 172 (2007).

suffered systematic oppression at the hands of their state.[79] This implication of internal self-determination has been invoked in support of diverse subnational and transnational independence movements.[80] We need not canvass all of the possible conceptions or applications of self-determination, however, to recognize that a state cannot arbitrarily deny some of its nationals the opportunity to participate in national politics or withhold other critical rights or privileges of nationality. A state that established such a policy could not reasonably claim to be acting on behalf of the people prejudiced by it.

C. Objections to the Emerging Fiduciary Model of Sovereignty

Some powerful objections may be leveled against the fiduciary conception of state recognition. Although few would argue today that states may exercise their powers however they please, without regard to the needs of their people, some might object that to speak of states as fiduciaries threatens to mask their extraordinary capacity for mischief. As we have seen, Western powers historically imposed the state on foreign peoples as a form of alien political organization that displaced indigenous groups' traditional forms of self-government.[81] Even today, the idea that peoples might have to "earn" their sovereignty by satisfying the international community that they have the capacity and commitment to function as states could disenfranchise peoples seeking self-determination. Moreover, once states come into existence, they often become vehicles for oppression. The same trust that grounds a state's international legal authority, enabling the state to provide security and legal order for a people, may be exploited all too easily by political elites for their own ends. Experience teaches that such concerns are not merely hypothetical; by all accounts, the gravest atrocities of the past several centuries have been perpetrated by or with the assistance of states, including the genocide, enslavement, and forcible subjugation of peoples throughout the world. If a fiduciary model of the state has enabled these abuses by encouraging a paternalistic vision of the relationship between states and their people, as well as the colonial domination of foreign peoples, we might well ask whether the fiduciary model itself should be discarded in favor of some alternative vision of the state.

79. *Compare* Accordance with International Law of the Unilateral Declaration of Independence in Respect of Kosovo, Advisory Opinion, 2010 ICJ Rep. 141, 206, ¶ 205 (July 22) (separate opinion of Judge Cançado Trindade) (contending that a state that systematically "perpetrates ... grave breaches [of human rights] acts criminally, loses its legitimacy, and ceases to be a State for the victimized population"), *with id.* at 475–76, ¶¶ 21–22 (dissenting opinion of Judge Koroma) (arguing that territorial integrity trumps "the principles of equal rights and self-determination of peoples as precepts of international law").

80. *See* Morton H. Halperin & David J. Scheffer with Patricia L. Small, Self-Determination in the New World Order 49–51 (1992) (discussing these and other contexts where internal self-determination has been invoked); Allan Rosas, *Internal Self-Determination*, *in* Modern Law of Self-Determination 225, 228 (Christian Tomuschat ed., 1993) (noting disagreement over the concept of internal self-determination).

81. *See* Onuma Yasuaki, *When Was the Law of International Society Born?—An Inquiry of the History of International Law from an Intercivilizational Perspective*, 2 J. Hist. Int'l L. 1 (2000).

These weighty objections merit an equally sober response. To be sure, states have been the cause of incalculable suffering over the course of human history, and much of this suffering has been generated by states that have claimed to be acting in the best interest of humanity. If states have been the agents of human suffering, however, it is not *because* they have justified their authority in fiduciary terms, but *in spite of* this fact. Too often, states have relied on the fiduciary model to justify their exercise of sovereign power, while neglecting the obligations associated with this entrusted authority. Hence, an enduring practical challenge for international law has been to narrow the gap between the rhetoric and reality of states' fiduciary obligations, ensuring that international law is not merely a "sorry comforter" but a vantage point for clear-eyed critique of state practice and a meaningful practical constraint on state power.[82] Abandoning the fiduciary model's juridical conception of the state will not solve international law's well-documented "compliance problem,"[83] however, and it could make things worse by eliminating the conceptual and normative foundations of sovereignty under international law. Take away the fiduciary model's relational conception of sovereignty, and international law will lose much of its power as a critical framework for mobilizing the international community against state oppression. The better course, therefore, is to reaffirm the fiduciary character of sovereignty, clarify how the fiduciary principle constrains state power, and focus on developing the legal institutions necessary to enhance states' compliance with their fiduciary obligations.

IV. RECOGNIZING FIDUCIARY STATES

By outlining how international law distributes sovereignty among states, the fiduciary model sheds new light on a debate that has divided international legal theorists for generations: whether aspiring states need to obtain the recognition of other states and international organizations to qualify for juridical statehood under international law (the "constitutive theory"), or whether international recognition merely confirms a state's objective legal status (the "declaratory theory").[84] Most legal scholars have gravitated toward the declaratory theory, arguing that international law does not give established states unfettered discretionary authority to grant or withhold recognition of an aspiring state. If members of the international community deny recognition to a political community that meets the traditional criteria for statehood, they argue, this denial must be considered a political

82. IMMANUEL KANT, PERPETUAL PEACE: A PHILOSOPHICAL SKETCH (1795).

83. *See, e.g.*, ANDREW GUZMAN, HOW INTERNATIONAL LAW WORKS: A RATIONAL CHOICE THEORY (2008); Ryan Goodman, *Incomplete Internalization and Compliance with International Human Rights Law*, 19 EUR. J. INT'L L. 725 (2008); Harold Hongju Koh, *Why Do Nations Obey International Law?*, 106 YALE L.J. 2599 (1997).

84. This distinction between the declaratory and constitutive theories of state recognition closely tracks J.L. Austin's famous distinction between "constative utterances" (i.e., those that describe the world) and "performative utterances" (i.e., those that bring a state of affairs into existence via the utterance itself). *See* J.L. AUSTIN, HOW TO DO THINGS WITH WORDS (2d ed. 1975). Although Austin's terminology may be more precise, we will use the traditional legal terminology.

act, not one that carries the force of law.[85] Defenders of the constitutive theory have responded that the declaratory theory cannot be squared with state practice and is normatively unsatisfying. They observe that states have always treated their recognition decisions as having the force of law. Moreover, the international community's intermediating role in state recognition is indispensable to the community's healthy development, constitutivists argue, ensuring that bestowing sovereignty on an aspiring state does not negatively impact global peace and security. The persistence of this debate between supporters of the declaratory and constitutive theories, combined with perennial anxiety about the authority of the Montevideo Convention's four criteria, has prompted some scholars such as John Dugard to criticize state recognition as international law's "weakest link."[86]

The fiduciary model invites reconsideration of both the declaratory and constitutive theories, suggesting that neither offers an entirely satisfying account of state recognition. A brief reflection on the role of courts in private fiduciary law reveals why this is so.

In private law, a court's determination that parties occupy a fiduciary relationship with one another may be more or less "declaratory" or "constitutive" in character, depending on the context. Many fiduciary relationships form without the involvement of courts: principals hire agents, parents have children, investors entrust assets to investment managers. Fiduciary duties apply to these relationships long before courts are ever called on to recognize them. When courts recognize these relationships, their decisions are "declaratory" in the sense that they affirm a preexisting relationship, but they are "constitutive" to the extent that they have legal, rather than merely political, effect.

In other private-law contexts, however, judicial recognition is necessary to confer authority upon a fiduciary; until a court acts, no fiduciary relationship exists between the parties. For example, when an individual dies without leaving a will, a court must appoint an administrator to settle the estate and a guardian to care for the decedent's minor children. Pending court approval, no party is legally authorized to assume these fiduciary roles. Judicial recognition is also necessary in many contexts to transfer authority from one fiduciary to another—for instance, when stripping authority from a trustee or terminating parental rights. A court order is needed to terminate the existing fiduciary relationship and confer authority on a new trustee, guardian, or adoptive parent. Judicial intervention is also necessary in some contexts to effectuate a fiduciary's removal when multiple beneficiaries are subject to a single fiduciary power, such as pension fund claimants with competing demands on the same fund. In these settings, no beneficiary or group of beneficiaries is entitled to dismiss their fiduciary without a court order, because no person can be judge and party to the same cause. Hence, judicial recognition of a new fiduciary relationship is "constitutive" of the authority of these fiduciaries in two senses: (1) it is treated as a legal act, not a political act; and (2) it generates a legally recognized fiduciary relationship where none existed before.

In sum, a court's recognition of private fiduciary relationships is always "constitutive" in the sense that it is a performative act that carries legal consequences.

85. *See* CRAWFORD, *supra* note 8, at 22–26.

86. JOHN DUGARD, RECOGNITION AND THE UNITED NATIONS 1 (1987).

Nonetheless, determining whether judicial recognition has the effect of creating or merely affirming a new fiduciary relationship is context-dependent.

The fiduciary model of state sovereignty suggests that the international law of state recognition reflects a similar dynamic. In the current international legal system, the primary institutional mechanism for recognizing new states is not a single court but the collective judgment of the international community. Each state and international organization decides for itself whether an aspiring state qualifies for recognition, and each treats its decision as bearing legal consequences. In some contexts, the international community's collective recognition of a new state might plausibly be considered "declaratory" in the sense that it affirms a state's preexisting legal status. Following the rapid withdrawal of a foreign colonial power or the balkanization of a collapsed federal state, for example, the international community's decision to recognize a former colony or fully autonomous region as a new state could be viewed as a declaratory act analogous to judicial recognition of a principal-agent or parent-child relationship.[87] In the absence of conflicting claims to sovereignty over the people and territory of an aspiring state, the question would simply be whether the aspiring state meets the threshold requirements for state recognition. If so, the new state's sovereign status would date back to the point when it assumed responsibility for its own self-government rather than the point when it later achieved formal recognition from other members of the international community. International recognition in these settings would be "constitutive" only in the limited sense that the act of recognition would formalize retroactively the legal consequences of statehood between the state that is recognized and the state or international organization that recognizes it.

The separation of the Republic of South Sudan (South Sudan) from the Republic of Sudan offers an illustration of this weak constitutive mode of state recognition. Following decades of strife, warring factions in northern and southern Sudan concluded a Comprehensive Peace Agreement (CPA) in 2005, laying the foundation for a peaceful end to the country's civil war.[88] A key provision of the CPA authorized a popular referendum to decide whether to partition the country. In January 2011, 98.8 percent of the people of South Sudan cast their votes in favor of independence. Sudanese president Omer Hassan Al-Bashir accepted the result, and South Sudan became formally independent from the Republic of Sudan the following July.[89] Other states and international organizations quickly recognized South Sudan as a new state. From the perspective of international law, however, these formal acts of recognition were best viewed as "constitutive" only in the limited sense that they

87. *See* Matthew Craven, *Statehood, Self-Determination and Recognition*, *in* International Law 203, 218 (3d ed., Malcolm D. Evans ed., 2010) (observing that "the predominant means by which new States have emerged since 1945" has been renunciation of statehood over territory by a sovereign authority that cedes authority to a new regime).

88. At the time of this writing, however, South Sudan continues to experience sporadic internal violence between rival factions led, respectively, by President Salva Kiir and rebel leader (and former vice president) Riek Machar. *See* James Copnall, *South Sudan: Obstacles to a Lasting Peace*, BBC News, Aug. 26, 2015, *available at* http://www.bbc.com/news/world-africa-33912156.

89. *See* Jack McNeily, Comment, *A Condominium Approach to Abyei*, 13 Chi. J. Int'l L. 265, 266–75 (2012).

applied a formal seal of approval to South Sudan's international legal status as a new state. Because South Sudan's independence had been established previously by mutual agreement with the Republic of Sudan, no action of the international community was necessary to strip sovereignty from the Republic of Sudan and confer sovereign authority upon South Sudan.

In many contexts where disputes over statehood arise, however, the situation is markedly different. Most aspiring states today seek international recognition at the expense of an existing state's continuing claim to sovereignty. Such is the case, for example, when indigenous groups seek independence from colonial powers or substate entities attempt to secede from larger functioning states. Granting recognition to a new state under these circumstances is comparable to removing a trustee or terminating parental rights; in both contexts, beneficiaries lack legal authority to remove the fiduciary themselves, though they have the right to initiate removal proceedings.[90] Instead, the law entrusts an independent institution with the responsibility to withdraw authority from an errant fiduciary and entrust it to a new fiduciary.[91] In the international realm, the international community as a whole performs this quasi-adjudicatory function through the cumulative recognition decisions of individual states and international organizations. By recognizing a new state, the international community effectively withdraws recognition from an existing state with respect to their state's sovereignty over a part of its people and territory. The existing state's sovereignty over the affected territory thus terminates, along with its fiduciary relationship with the people associated with that territory. Examples include the international community's recognition of the People's Republic of Bangladesh in 1971 (stripping Pakistan's sovereignty over this territory) and, more recently, the growing recognition of Kosovo and Palestine as sovereign states (at the expense of Serbia and Israel, respectively). In these settings, state recognition is best understood as a fully "constitutive" act—one that transforms the legal status of a substate entity into that of a fully independent, sovereign state.

The decision to recognize a transfer of sovereignty from an existing state to a new state is not a step to be taken lightly. As in parental termination proceedings, international law applies a strong presumption that a people's best interests will be advanced by preserving the status quo—here, the territorial integrity of existing states (*uti possidetis juris*). International law's default assumption is that minority groups will be able to enjoy full political and cultural self-determination within their current states.[92] This assumption may be rebutted only where a substate entity

90. *Cf.* Accordance with International Law of the Unilateral Declaration of Independence in Respect of Kosovo, Advisory Opinion, 2010 ICJ Rep. at 38, ¶ 84 (22 July) ("[G]eneral international law contains no applicable prohibition of declarations of independence."). Whether a state's people possess a legal right to remove a corrupt or tyrannical *government* is, of course, a separate question. *See, e.g.*, Jordan J. Paust, *The Human Right to Participate in Armed Revolution and Related Forms of Social Violence: Testing the Limits of Permissibility*, 32 Emory L.J. 545, 560–69 (1983) (arguing in the affirmative).

91. *See* Christian Hillgruber, *The Admission of New States into the International Community*, 9 Eur. J. Int'l L. 491, 492 (1998) ("In this sense, a (new) state is not born, but chosen as a subject of international law.").

92. The Aaland Islands Question: Report of the Committee of Jurists, League of Nations Official Journal, Special Supp. 3 (Oct. 1920).

produces compelling evidence that their state has flagrantly violated its fiduciary obligations—for example, by systematically denying political rights to persons within part of its territory or engaging in ethnic cleansing. Even here, however, the proper remedy will not always be to recognize a new state. Guided by the international legal principles of self-determination, territorial integrity, and fiduciary obligation, the international community must consider a range of possible remedies for a state's breach of its fiduciary obligations. Ultimately, the global community will decide whether the human rights of a foreign people will be best served by the formal partition of an existing state, federative autonomy for the affected region, enhanced constitutional protections for minority groups, or other solutions. In making such decisions, individual states and international organizations are not charged with merely "declaring" the preexisting juridical status of new states. Instead, their role is to decide whether the principle of self-determination and other applicable norms of international law require sovereign authority to shift prospectively from an existing state to a new state that will more faithfully discharge its fiduciary obligations.

One implication of the fiduciary model is that a political community seeking independence from an existing state will not ordinarily qualify for recognition if it lacks the capacity for effective governance. To establish a decent legal order, an aspiring state must have a functioning government that is able to legislate, adjudicate, and enforce the law internally, as well as to engage in relations with other states. From this perspective, the Montevideo Convention's four "qualifications" come into sharper focus; to borrow from Brad Roth, an aspiring state must be able to unite people and territory within a "common and distinguishing pattern of effective governance"—one that may take a variety of forms in accordance with the principle of internal self-determination.[93] An aspiring state's capacity to carry out its role as fiduciary for its people is partly a function of its readiness to assert "effective control," in the sense of preventing private parties within its jurisdiction from instrumentalizing or dominating others with impunity. As noted in the International Committee of Jurists' 1920 *Report on the Status of Finland*, a political community generally will not be ready for independent statehood "until a stable political organization has been created and until the public authorities had become strong enough to assert themselves throughout the territories of the State without the assistance of foreign troops."[94] Strength to stand alone is not enough, however, to satisfy the requirement of governing capacity. A state's institutions also must have the institutional differentiation and functional expertise necessary to represent their people in making law, provide essential public services, and guarantee fidelity to the rule of law. In short, to qualify for statehood, an aspiring state ordinarily must develop the institutional capacity to meet its sovereign obligations for effective governance.

Of course, determining whether a state possesses the requisite capacity for effective governance is hardly a simple matter. States vary dramatically in their ability to guarantee public security under the rule of law. Even the most highly developed countries have mixed track records, and no state has demonstrated the capacity to

93. Brad R. Roth, *The Entity That Dare Not Speak Its Name: Unrecognized Taiwan as a Right-Bearer in the International Legal Order*, 4 E. Asia L. Rev. 91, 97 (2009).

94. Rebecca M.M. Wallace & Olga Martin-Ortega, International Law 66 (6th ed. 2009) (quoting the report).

secure legal order effectively for all of its people in all of its territory all of the time. In some contexts, newly created states have relied on international assistance to fulfill their fiduciary role for their people. In other contexts, states have been unable to gain effective control over their entire territory due to limited public resources or the counter-pressure of military insurgencies or violent criminal networks. Setting the bar for statehood too high could undermine the principles of popular sovereignty and self-determination by excluding some peoples from the benefits of membership in a sovereign state.

Occasionally, the international community has recognized states despite the fact that the states were ill-prepared at the time to guarantee their people's security under the rule of law. Generally speaking, these episodes have fallen squarely within the "declaratory" mode of state recognition—situations where the withdrawal of a foreign colonial power or state dissolution left a power vacuum that an aspiring state was best equipped to fill. In 1960, for example, states recognized the Congo (now the Democratic Republic of Congo) as an independent state, despite concerns that its central government had splintered into rival groups, each claiming to be the legitimate government; despite serious threats to the government from various secessionist movements; and despite the fact that the government was propped up by an ad hoc coalition of United Nations and Belgian forces, other foreign military and paramilitary personnel, and private mercenaries. "Anything less like effective government," observes Crawford, "would be hard to imagine."[95] Nonetheless, the international community concluded that recognition was necessary because Belgium had already formally withdrawn and renounced its claim to sovereignty, leaving its former colony to fend for itself. Denying recognition to the Congo, based upon its relatively weak capacity to secure public order, would have rendered its people stateless and invited foreign intervention. Ready or not, the international community gave Congo's struggling government the benefit of the doubt and concluded that the Congo qualified for recognition as a sovereign state.[96] From the perspective of the fiduciary model, the recognition of a state with limited governing capacity may be preferable to the legal black hole that would be generated by the absence of an internationally recognized state.

Conversely, even if an aspiring state has the raw capacity for effective governance, the fiduciary model suggests that it will not qualify for recognition if it lacks the requisite commitment to fulfill the other-regarding fiduciary purposes of juridical statehood. Support for this view is found in the conditions placed on the recognition of new states following World War II. States created from the collapse of the Austro-Hungarian, German, and Russian empires (e.g., Czechoslovakia, Poland, Romania, Yugoslavia) were admitted into the society of nations on the condition that they commit to principles of self-government, self-determination, respect for religious and

95. Crawford, *supra* note 8, at 56–57.

96. Another example of international recognition preceding full governing capacity is the creation of Croatia and Bosnia-Herzegovina in the early 1990s. In the absence of a central government capable of maintaining Yugoslavia's integrity as a unified state, members of the European Union recognized both Croatia and Bosnia-Herzegovina as independent states, despite the fact that much of their territories at the time was controlled by nongovernment forces. *See* Wallace & Martin-Ortega, *supra* note 94, at 67.

ethnic minorities, and other basic human rights.[97] Aspiring states that rejected these principles faced the prospect of nonrecognition. A particularly striking example is the former British Colony of Southern Rhodesia, which declared its independence in 1965. By all accounts, Southern Rhodesia maintained effective control within its borders and was capable of engaging in international relations. Nonetheless, the international community roundly condemned Southern Rhodesia's declaration of independence because its white-minority government held to a policy of racial apartheid.[98] The Security Council "call[ed] upon all States not to recognize this illegal racist minority regime,"[99] characterizing the government as an "illegal authority."[100] The international community thus served notice that political communities would not qualify for statehood if they refused to treat their people as equal beneficiaries under the rule of law. As Michael Reisman would later explain, "[t]he Rhodesia case confirmed that international law's prerequisites for the status and privileges of statehood extend well beyond effective control by the local territorial elite; the prerequisites now include, to some extent, establishing an expectation of present and probable future conformity with minimum standards of human rights."[101] Commitment to the fiduciary character of state sovereignty thus became a nonnegotiable prerequisite for state recognition.

Over time, the United Nations and other international institutions have assumed responsibility for overseeing "the conditional and progressive devolution of sovereign powers" to substate entities, often postponing international recognition until after an aspiring state has established the requisite capacity and commitment to serve as a capable fiduciary for its people.[102] Paul Williams, Michael Scharf, and various coauthors have characterized this developmental approach to state creation as "earned sovereignty."[103] Under the earned sovereignty paradigm, international institutions establish clear benchmark requirements for substate entities to achieve in preparation for recognition as sovereign states. Typically, these conditions involve a mix of institutional development, democratic reform, and commitments

97. *See* Parfitt, *supra* note 47, at 31; *e.g.*, Declaration on Yugoslavia, Extraordinary EPC Ministerial Meeting, Brussels, Dec. 16, 1991 (declaring that new states would be recognized following the disintegration of the former Yugoslavia only if they accepted "the rule of law, democracy and human rights" and provided "guarantees for the rights of ethnic and national groups and minorities").

98. *See* S.C. Res. 216, S/RES/216, 12 Nov. 1965; G.A. Res. 2024 (XX), 11 Nov. 1965.

99. *Id.* ¶ 2.

100. S.C. Res. 217, S/RES/217, 20 Nov. 1965, ¶; *see generally* Crawford, *supra* note 8, at 127–31.

101. W. Michael Reisman, *Private Armies in a Global War System: Prologue to Decision*, 14 VA. J. INT'L L. 1, 4 (1973).

102. Paul R. Williams & Frencesca Jannotti Pecci, *Earned Sovereignty: Bridging the Gap Between Sovereignty and Self-Determination*, 40 STAN. J. INT'L L. 347, 350 (2004); *see also* Hillgruber, *supra* note 91, 492–93 (noting that European Community member-states have conditioned recognition upon candidates assuming "international obligations and political duties as cumulative criteria").

103. *See, e.g.*, Williams & Pecci, *supra* note 102; James R. Hooper & Paul R. Williams, *Earned Sovereignty: The Political Dimension*, 31 DENV. J. INT'L L. & POL'Y 355 (2003); Michael P. Scharf, *Earned Sovereignty: Juridical Underpinnings*, 31 DENV. J. INT'L L. & POL'Y 373 (2003).

to observe human rights and the rule of law.[104] Once the conditions for statehood have been clearly articulated, the burden falls upon aspiring states to meet the qualifying conditions with the international community's assistance. This earned sovereignty paradigm resonates with the developmental approach of the earlier mandate and trusteeship systems, but it offers a more focused and transparent roadmap to statehood that is arguably less susceptible to foreign exploitation.

Kosovo's transition to independence vividly illustrates the earned-sovereignty approach at work. In 1999, the Security Council placed Kosovo under the interim territorial administration of UNMIK, with security provided by a NATO-led force, pending settlement of Kosovo's final status.[105] During the years that followed, the international community supported Kosovo's efforts to develop the political and administrative institutions necessary for effective governance. These efforts focused on "four pillars" essential to effective self-government: "interim civil administration, humanitarian affairs, institution building and reconstruction."[106] As Kosovo's institution-building process came to fruition, additional legal reform was necessary to ensure that an independent state would respect the rights of ethnic and religious minorities. Proclaiming "standards before status," U.N. Special Envoy Martti Ahtisaari declared that Kosovo would not qualify for "supervised independence" until it committed to being a "multi-ethnic society, which shall govern itself democratically and with full respect for the rule of law through its legislative, executive, and judicial institutions," and "to protecting the highest levels of human rights."[107] Upon declaring independence in February 2008, Kosovo formalized these standards as constitutional commitments and attained widespread (albeit not universal) recognition as a sovereign state.

The earned-sovereignty paradigm has informed the international community's approach to state-building in many other contexts as well. The Israeli-Palestinian Roadmap prepared by the United Nations, the United States, the European Union, and Russia provides a phased plan for creation of an independent Palestinian state, beginning with the development of Palestine's institutional capacity for self-government, democratization, and the cessation and renunciation of violence and terrorism.[108] Similar conditions have been incorporated into U.N.-sponsored agreements for the phased independence of Western Sahara (the Baker Plans) and Northern Ireland (Good Friday Accords).[109] In short, the international community has focused on preparing political communities to meet the fiduciary obligations associated with juridical statehood prior to their international recognition as

104. *See, e.g.*, Joanna Weschler, *Human Rights, in* THE UN SECURITY COUNCIL: FROM THE COLD WAR TO THE 21ST CENTURY 55, 56 (David M. Malone ed., 2004) (noting that human rights was part of the mandate of the U.N. Transitional Authority in Cambodia).

105. S.C. Res. 1244, S/RES/1244 (June 10, 1999).

106. Accordance with International Law of the Unilateral Declaration of Independence in Respect of Kosovo, Advisory Opinion, 2010 ICJ Rep. 141 (July 22).

107. Letter dated Mar. 26, 2007 from the Secretary General Addressed to the President of the Security Council, S/2007/168, Mar. 26, 2007 (enclosing Ahtisaari's report on Kosovo's future status).

108. *See* Hooper & Williams, *supra* note 103, at 358.

109. *Id.* at 359.

independent sovereign states. Under contemporary international law it is an aspiring state's capacity and commitment to establish basic security under the rule of law for the benefit of its people that constitutes the defining criterion for state recognition, not (pace Crawford) a state's de facto independence from foreign control.[110]

V. A DELIBERATIVE THEORY OF STATE RECOGNITION

The earned-sovereignty paradigm will have greatest appeal when there is consensus across the international community that a group is entitled to independent statehood. Such consensus is often elusive, however. States and international institutions sometimes find it difficult to discern whether an aspiring state has the capacity to maintain effective control over its territory and a firm commitment to respect the human rights of all its people. Reasonable minds frequently disagree about whether the principle of self-determination justifies the partitioning of an existing state, rather than a less intrusive remedy such as federative autonomy or enhanced legal protections for minorities. Some states apply the presumption in favor of an existing state's territorial integrity more strictly than others. Even when there is consensus about the need to create a pathway to formal statehood for a particular group, the international community does not always agree about what concrete steps an aspiring state must take to qualify. Partly as a result of these complexities, the international community has struggled to address the claims of self-proclaimed states such as Abkhazia, Eastern Ukraine, Kosovo, Palestine, Somaliland, South Ossetia, Taiwan, and Transnistria.

The fiduciary model of state sovereignty does not offer an escape from these challenging questions of legal judgment. On the contrary, it affirms the inescapably context-sensitive nature of state recognition. Just as private law relies on judges to make complex decisions about the best interests of a fiduciary's beneficiaries, states and international organizations must exercise judgment in deciding whether recognition of a new state is warranted to safeguard the practical interests of a people. Hence, Hersch Lauterpacht's observation rings true that state recognition "cannot be automatic" because "there must be someone to perform that task":

> In the absence of a preferable solution, such as the setting up of an impartial international organ to perform that function [of determining whether recognition of statehood is justified], the latter must be fulfilled by States already

110. Critical legal scholars have questioned whether "audacious experiments like UNMIK [that] purport to implement the most advanced internationalist principles" may "actually represent the continuation or resurrection of colonial power in contemporary form." NATHANIEL BERMAN, PASSION AND AMBIVALENCE: COLONIALISM, NATIONALISM, AND INTERNATIONAL LAW 111 (2012); *see also* Rose Parfitt, Book Review: *Brad R. Roth. Sovereign Equality and Moral Disagreement: Premises of a Pluralist International Legal Order*, 23 EUR. J. INT'L L. 1184, 1186 (2012) (hypothesizing "that the objective of the institutional pre-programming inherent in the concept of statehood" may operate principally "to ensure that the economies of new states remain open to transnational capital or face disciplinary action"). Even if the earned sovereignty paradigm is susceptible to abuse, and therefore may require further refinement, it is unlikely that eliminating prerequisites for state recognition such as legal protections for minorities, the renunciation of terrorist violence, and respect for the rule of law would better protect a vulnerable people against domination.

> existing. The valid objection is not against the fact of their discharging it, but against their carrying it out as a matter of arbitrary policy as distinguished from legal duty.[111]

In effect, international legal order enlists states and international organizations as joint fiduciaries of humanity to decide whether recognizing an aspiring state will best guarantee fiduciary governance for the people located within its territory.

Although the decision to grant or deny recognition to an aspiring state may be complex, it need not be unprincipled. Deciding whether to recognize a new state is a legal judgment that states and international organizations must justify according to established legal norms, including the principles of internal and external self-determination and the presumption favoring the territorial integrity of existing states (*uti possidetis*). The broader geopolitical landscape may be relevant to this legal judgment insofar as it illuminates whether recognition will promote secure and equal freedom under the rule of law. Under the fiduciary model, states and international organizations may decline to recognize an aspiring state if there is a reasonable basis for concluding that recognition would seriously threaten international peace and security (e.g., Somaliland, Taiwan). The fiduciary theory suggests that members of the international community may not withhold recognition to new states, however, based on matters properly within the domain of national self-determination such as a people's preferred model for political or economic organization (e.g., parliamentary democracy, a more or less free-market economy).[112] Nor may states use recognition as an opportunity to extract self-serving concessions such as robust protections for foreign investment. Denying recognition under these conditions would be inconsistent with the fiduciary character of state recognition.

Individual states and international organizations will sometimes disagree in good faith about how these principles apply to particular aspiring states, and it would be naïve to suppose that legal principle will always prevail over raw political calculation in practice. Nonetheless, the fiduciary model underscores that states are not entitled to grant or deny recognition in a conclusory or irrational manner, or based on arbitrary considerations of political convenience. As fiduciaries of humanity jointly entrusted with international legal authority over state recognition, all states and international organizations are required, in David Dyzenhaus's words, to "subscribe to the principles of interpretation that permit them to consider themselves free and equal participants."[113] A recognition decision has international legal effect, in other words, only if a state or international organization is prepared to justify the decision based on the relevant legal criteria. Hence, "when one state [or international organization] raises a question about the legality of another's action or proposed action, [the latter] must accept the onus of justifying its action as having a warrant

111. LAUTERPACHT, *supra* note 44, at 55.

112. *Cf.* Antony Anghie, *Colonialism and the Birth of International Institutions: Sovereignty, Economy, and the Mandate System of the League of Nations*, 34 NYU J. INT'L L. & POL. 513, 570 (2002) (observing that the mandate system "implicitly repudiated the idea that different societies had devised different forms of political organization that should command some degree of respect and validity in international law").

113. David Dyzenhaus, *Hobbes on the International Rule of Law*, 28 ETHICS & INT'L AFFS. 53, 61 (2014).

in a reasonable interpretation of the law."[114] An unreasoned or arbitrary decision to grant or deny recognition to a new state cannot properly be understood as an exercise of international legal authority, and thus would lack legal validity under the constitutive principles of international law's decentralized recognition regime.[115]

The fiduciary character of state sovereignty thus introduces a new deliberative theory of state recognition, one that draws out the best insights of both the declaratory theory and the constitutive theory while attending to these theories' respective weaknesses. The deliberative theory supports the idea that states must take the legal criteria for statehood seriously; they may not grant or deny recognition based on purely political concerns (contrary to some versions of the constitutive theory). When an aspiring state's claim to sovereignty over a given people and territory is not subject to competing claims (e.g., after the withdrawal of a colonial power), the international community's role is limited to ascertaining whether the aspiring state is willing and able to serve as fiduciary for its people, as informed by the Montevideo criteria and concerns for human rights, the protection of ethnic and religious minorities, and respect for the rule of law. Recognition in this setting is "declaratory" in the sense that it reflects an assessment that a political community satisfies the basic requirements for statehood under international law. Conversely, if an aspiring state seeks to break away from an existing state without that state's consent, it is insufficient for the aspiring state to show that it has the commitment and capacity to serve as a fiduciary for its people. To decide whether to grant recognition, the international community must determine whether partitioning an existing state will better secure equal freedom under the rule of law for the aspiring state's people, while applying a strong presumption in favor of preserving the territorial integrity of an existing state. Because recognizing a new state in this context means stripping sovereign authority from an existing state, these acts of recognition are "constitutive" of statehood in the same sense that a court decision terminating parental rights and transferring these rights to an adoptive parent is "constitutive" of parental authority. In both settings, recognition does not *declare* an authority's independently verifiable legal status so much as it *performs* the reassignment of status-based authority from one fiduciary to another.[116] Regardless of whether state recognition is primarily declaratory or constitutive in a particular context, members of the international community are under the same obligation to justify their recognition decisions, ensuring that the entrustment of authority to a new state is consistent with the principle that all people are entitled to membership within a state that guarantees their secure and equal freedom.

The deliberative theory overcomes long-standing objections to the declaratory and constitutive theories. For example, Crawford has criticized the constitutive

114. *Id.*

115. *See* Patrick Macklem, *Humanitarian Intervention and the Distribution of Sovereignty in International Law*, 22 ETHICS & INT'L AFF. 369, 375–80 (2008) (arguing that to have legal validity Security Council members' votes must be based on intelligible reasons). The political and popular implications of such a decision are a separate matter. *See* Robert D. Sloane, *The Changing Face of Recognition in International Law: A Case Study of Tibet*, 16 EMORY INT'L L. REV. 107, 110 (2002) (distinguishing legal, political, and popular recognition).

116. *See* AUSTIN, *supra* note 84, at 6–7.

theory on the ground that, from its perspective, it is "impossible to conceive of [an act of recognition] which is invalid or void. Yet the nullity of certain acts of recognition has been accepted in practice."[117] This chapter has shown Crawford's objection to be unfounded; it is, in fact, possible to endorse a constitutive approach to state recognition in some contexts while also accepting that some acts of recognition or nonrecognition lack legal effect. Under the fiduciary model of state recognition, any decision to grant or deny recognition without reasoned justification, or based on purely political considerations rather than legal criteria, would lack legal validity.[118] In addition, state recognition would be invalid under the fiduciary model if it transgressed a peremptory norm (jus cogens), such as the prohibitions against military aggression and apartheid, because the recognition of a state that violated such norms would always be inconsistent with the fiduciary character of state sovereignty under international law. Although states and international organizations necessarily exercise judgment when deciding whether to recognize an aspiring state, not all acts of recognition will qualify as legally valid.

Observing that states frequently disagree about whether aspiring states qualify for recognition, Crawford suggests that the constitutive theory suffers from a pathological "relativism."[119] The fiduciary model's context-sensitivity, however, is not the type of radical skepticism that denies the possibility of principled legal reasoning. Instead, it reflects an appreciation that the application of general principles of international law to complex global phenomena does not always yield straightforward answers. Legal principles provide a framework for reasoned deliberation that attends to the particularities of context—a framework we call the domain of legal judgment. In domestic law, this domain of legal judgment is entrusted largely to judges, who sometimes disagree about the law's proper application to particular cases. For better or worse, in matters of state recognition, international law entrusts legal judgment to the decentralized collegium of sovereign states and international organizations as fiduciaries for humanity generally. The potential for principled disagreement is an inescapable feature of state recognition. Although the fiduciary model does not avoid these challenges, it is superior to previous theories of state recognition, because it illuminates the context-sensitive character of the international legal principles that govern these decisions. The fiduciary model thus invites states and international organizations to address disagreements over state recognition on the basis of legal principle through a collective process of reasoned deliberation.

Crawford argues further that state recognition cannot track the constitutive theory because members of the international community "do not in practice regard unrecognized States as exempt from international law," and sometimes allow "unrecognized States" to exercise powers traditionally associated with statehood

117. Crawford, *supra* note 8, at 21.

118. Conceptualizing state recognition as an exercise of international legal authority does not necessitate turning a blind eye to the political process that generates recognition decisions. *See* Macklem, *supra* note 25, at 18–20 (distinguishing the "international legal validity" of a human rights norm, which turns on whether a norm's enactment comports with general positivist rules for the creation of legal rights and obligations, from "the politics behind [the norm's] legal production").

119. *Id.*

such as participation in international organizations.[120] This objection relies on an outdated conception of the legal status of nonstate actors. Contemporary international law recognizes the legal personality of many nonstate entities such as religious organizations, organized advocacy groups, insurgent armies, and corporations. International law requires these entities to observe generally applicable norms of international law, even if it does not entrust them with sovereign authority to wield public powers.[121] The fact that Southern Rhodesia did not qualify for statehood, for instance, did not absolve it of international responsibility for human rights violations. Furthermore, states are not the only institutions that international law entrusts with fiduciary responsibility. International organizations that undertake interim territorial administration (e.g., UNMIK) also serve as fiduciaries for the people subject to their governing power, a topic to which we return in Chapter 8. Under the law of occupation, forces that occupy enemy territory during armed conflict likewise bear limited fiduciary obligations toward foreign nationals. Subnational governments, although not endowed with independent international legal personality, are nonetheless bound by their parent-states' fiduciary obligations to wield public powers exclusively for the benefit of their people. Thus, the fact that unrecognized public authorities may bear international legal obligations does not suggest that recognition is merely a political act without legal significance.

VI. CONCLUSION

We have argued in this chapter that the fiduciary concept provides a unifying theoretical framework for state sovereignty that is congenial to the constitutive, distributive, and power-regulating projects of international human rights law. Just as the fiduciary principle governs the domestic exercise of sovereign power, it also underlies the authority of international law to regulate the constitution and distribution of state sovereignty, for in all of these dimensions international law's delegation of sovereign power to the state is made on behalf of every person subject to it.[122] The fiduciary model explains the leading criterion that Macklem identifies as regulating the distribution of sovereignty—namely, the principle that a government must represent "the whole of its population within its territory consistent with principles of equality, nondiscrimination, and self-determination."[123] Having entrusted

120. *Id.* at 26.

121. *See* Grant, *supra* note 7, at 405–06.

122. In an otherwise insightful dissertation on the fiduciary character of a state's obligation to protect its people, David Louis Attanasio suggests that our previous writings on the fiduciary character of sovereignty conflate a state's compliance with fiduciary obligations, on the one hand, with its authorization to assume fiduciary power, on the other. *See* David Louis Attanasio, The State Obligation to Protect 222, n.537 & 229, n.554 (2015) (unpublished Ph.D. dissertation, University of California, Los Angeles) (on file with the author). Although we argue that compliance with fiduciary obligations is a necessary condition for state authority, we do not take the position that a state's compliance with fiduciary obligations is *sufficient* to entitle a state to exercise sovereign authority over particular people or territory. As this chapter demonstrates, however, the fiduciary character of sovereignty does play a constitutive role both in defining statehood as a legal institution and in regulating the distribution of sovereign authority among states.

123. Macklem, *supra* note 25, at 586–87.

sovereignty to states, international law regulates the exercise of state power by preventing states from exploiting their people for factional ends. Just as private law requires fiduciaries to exercise their power in a manner that is consistent with the other-regarding, purposive character of fiduciary authority, public international law obligates states to use their public powers for the benefit of their people. As juridical institutions constituted by international law, states have no authority to use their sovereign powers for any purpose other than to advance the well-being of their people by establishing a regime of equal freedom under the rule of law. The fiduciary conception of the state thus provides a unified standard of authorization that permits critical scrutiny and regulation of both the international distribution and domestic exercise of sovereign powers.

Of course, the fiduciary model's appeal also depends upon whether it is capable of specifying discrete rules, standards, and principles to guide state practice and facilitate international accountability. In the next chapter, we begin to reclaim the fiduciary model from its troubled history by explaining how it provides a sound theoretical foundation for the jus cogens doctrine and the rise of international human rights.

3

Human Rights and Jus Cogens

I. INTRODUCTION

Among political theorists and philosophers, conventional wisdom holds that human rights are moral rights that all human beings share simply by virtue of their common humanity.[1] Since World War II, public international law has embraced the concept of human rights, accepting a wide range of international norms as full-bodied legal constraints on state action. Nonetheless, international law has yet to develop a robust theory capable of supplying a philosophical account of human rights as distinctively legal obligations. Although moral and political philosophers have endeavored to explain the theoretical basis of human rights construed as moral rights, none of the leading theories offers a persuasive justification for international human rights law (IHRL) as it has been understood and practiced for the past six decades.[2] Uncertainty regarding the philosophical basis of human rights has impeded efforts to clarify the scope, justiciability, and cross-cultural relevance of IHRL.

This is especially true of human rights that international law treats as peremptory. These rights belong to a class of norms called "jus cogens" (literally, "compelling law"). Jus cogens norms are considered peremptory in the sense that they are mandatory, do not admit derogation, and can be modified only by general international norms of equivalent authority.[3] The influential *Restatement on Foreign Relations of the United States* (*Restatement*) defines jus cogens to include, at a minimum, the prohibitions against genocide; slavery or slave trade; murder or disappearance of

1. *See, e.g.*, Jack Donnelly, International Human Rights 18 (1998); Alan Gewirth, Human Rights: Essays on Justification and Applications 1 (1982) [hereinafter Gewirth, Justifications and Applications]; H.L.A. Hart, *Are There Any Natural Rights?*, 64 Phil. Rev. 175 (1955); A. John Simmons, *Human Rights and World Citizenship*, *in* Justification and Legitimacy: Essays on Rights and Obligations 185 (2001).

2. There are two recent and important exceptions that explicitly attempt to explain international human rights as international legal rights: Allen Buchanan, The Heart of Human Rights 274 (2013) (defending a pluralist justification that envisions IHRL as requiring states to protect "basic equal status for all" and to provide "the conditions for leading a decent or minimally good life"); Patrick Macklem, The Sovereignty of Human Rights (2015) (arguing that IHRL serves to mitigate the adverse effects of international law's creation of international legal order through its distribution of sovereignty to states).

3. *See* Vienna Convention on the Law of Treaties art. 53, *opened for signature* May 23, 1969, 1155 U.N.T.S. 331, 8 I.L.M. 679 [hereinafter VCLT].

individuals; torture or other cruel, inhuman, or degrading treatment or punishment; prolonged arbitrary detention; systematic racial discrimination; and "the principles of the United Nations Charter prohibiting the use of force."[4] The concept of jus cogens has been widely perceived to establish a normative hierarchy within international law, endowing certain fundamental norms such as the prohibitions against slavery and genocide with a quasi-constitutional status vis-à-vis ordinary conventional and customary norms.[5]

There is considerable overlap between jus cogens and IHRL, but the two sets are not fully coextensive. Jus cogens is narrower than IHRL because not all human rights are absolute; limitations on freedom of expression and assembly, for example, are at times permissible. But jus cogens is also wider than IHRL because some peremptory norms, such as the prohibition on military aggression, are not part of IHRL. These sets of norms have distinctive histories in international law, though here too there is significant overlap. More significant for present purposes than their partially shared content and history, however, is the forceful challenge that both present to the classical conception of sovereignty according to which states enjoy plenary and exclusive jurisdiction within their territory. Under IHRL and jus cogens alike, states and their agents are held accountable to international legal standards protective of vulnerable parties subject to state power.

We argue that the fiduciary model offers a persuasive and unified account of IHRL and jus cogens because it brings them together within a relational conception of sovereignty that treats states (and state-like entities)[6] as fiduciaries of the people amenable to their jurisdiction. The basic idea is that the norms of IHRL and jus cogens emanate from a fiduciary relationship between the state and persons subject to its powers. The state's fundamental duty is to provide a regime of secure and equal freedom. It fulfills this duty, in part, by governing through norms that conform to two intermediate regulative principles. The two principles are *intermediate* because they fall between, on the one hand, secure and equal freedom, and on the other, concrete norms of international law. They are *regulative* because they help specify particular normative requirements of secure and equal freedom. The first principle is the Kantian maxim of non-instrumentalization that requires agents to be treated as ends always; the second is the republican principle of non-domination that proscribes the subjection of individuals to arbitrary power. Both reflect an ideal of independent agency. Independent agency is the capacity of an agent to exercise her powers of self-determination without wrongful interference (instrumentalization) or the threat of such interference (domination). For ease of reference,

4. RESTATEMENT (THIRD) OF FOREIGN RELATIONS OF THE UNITED STATES § 702 cmts. d–i, § 102 cmt. k (1987) [hereinafter THIRD RESTATEMENT].

5. *See, e.g.*, Martti Koskenniemi, *Hierarchy in International Law: A Sketch*, 8 EUR. J. INT'L L. 566, 566 (1997) (asserting that "*jus cogens* or imperative norms . . . presuppose relationships of normative hierarchy"); Dinah Shelton, *Normative Hierarchy in International Law*, 100 AM. J. INT'L L. 291, 323 (2006) (describing "universal norms" in international law as "a matter of necessity").

6. In this chapter we will generally refer to states as the bearers of fiduciary authority and obligation, as they are the primary bearers of sovereign authority under international law. But as discussed in Part IV of this chapter, and as we shall discuss in some detail in Chapter 8, certain international institutions and substate or nonstate entities may also hold public powers, and so the fiduciary theory is available to explain their authority and obligations, too.

we will sometimes refer to the conjunction of non-instrumentalization and non-domination as simply "independence," though at various points we will treat the two ideas separately.

The norms of IHRL and jus cogens are all justifiable as concrete specifications of these two principles. The fiduciary theory thus explains the relevant international norms as aspects of the state's fiduciary duty to guarantee a regime of secure and equal freedom. We shall see that the identification of such norms is further aided by indicia supplied by features of the state-subject fiduciary relationship as well as by Lon Fuller's internal morality of law.

As an interpretive theory, the fiduciary model explains the presence and juridical character of the norms that lie at the core of IHRL and jus cogens respectively. As a prescriptive theory, the fiduciary model supplies valuable guidelines for distinguishing peremptory human rights from others that are appropriately subject to limitation or derogation. Additionally, the prescriptive side of the fiduciary model specifies some norms as jus cogens that are not typically viewed as such (e.g., the prohibition on corruption), while casting doubt on the commonly alleged peremptory status of others (e.g., the prohibition on piracy).

By reframing human rights and peremptory norms as legal entitlements grounded in the state-subject fiduciary relationship, the fiduciary theory provides a fresh perspective. These norms are *relational* and *institutional* because they respond to threats that typically arise from relational interactions between public institutions and the people they serve. They are *legal* and *nonpositivist* because they constitute necessary conditions of legal order under a Fullerian and Kantian theory of right. They are *republican* because they answer to the ideal of non-domination. They are *practical* in that they take seriously the rights enshrined in the leading international conventions. Because human rights and peremptory norms under the fiduciary theory are necessary to guarantee every moral person's enjoyment of secure and equal freedom, they are *aspirational* and *universal* in scope. But they are also *deliberative* in that they are amenable to refinement and the principle of subsidiarity through democratic deliberation.

This chapter develops the fiduciary theory of IHRL and jus cogens in several stages. We begin by reviewing briefly the historical development of peremptory norms and the emergence of IHRL during the postwar era. We explain how the international community's failure to adopt a unifying theory has undermined efforts to specify determinate, justiciable, and cross-cultural international norms. We then suggest that leading contemporary accounts of human rights and peremptory norms do not provide satisfactory answers to central questions pertaining to human rights and jus cogens. As an alternative to these accounts, we defend the fiduciary theory by showing how it can explicate the character, scope, and content of IHRL and jus cogens.

II. DEVELOPING JUS COGENS AND INTERNATIONAL HUMAN RIGHTS LAW

Although the term "jus cogens" did not take root in international legal discourse until the twentieth century,[7] the principle that certain fundamental norms merit peremptory authority within international law bears a much older pedigree.

7. For early applications of the term "jus cogens" to international law, see Friedrich von der Heydte, *Die Erscheinungsformen des zwischenstaatlichen Rechts; Jus cogens und* jus dispositivum

Classical publicists such as Grotius, Vattel, and Christian Wolff drew upon the Roman law distinction between *jus dispositivum* (voluntary law) and *jus scriptum* (obligatory law) to differentiate consensual agreements between states from the "necessary" principles of international law that bind all states regardless of consent.[8]

Even after natural law conceptions of international law fell into disrepute in the nineteenth century with the rise of legal positivism, the classical notion of peremptory law continued to influence international legal theory well into the modern era. Early twentieth-century publicists such as Lassa Oppenheim and William Hall asserted confidently that states could not abrogate certain "universally recognized principles" by mutual agreement.[9] Outside the academy, judges on the Permanent Court of International Justice (PCIJ) affirmed the existence of peremptory norms in international law by referencing the concept in a series of individual concurring and dissenting opinions.[10] Collectively, these authorities affirmed the classical understanding that certain imperative norms are of such importance that they supersede conflicting consensual agreements between states.

Peremptory norms began to attract greater scholarly attention with the publication of Alfred von Verdross's influential 1937 article, "Forbidden Treaties in International Law."[11] Verdross argued that certain discrete rules of international custom had come to be recognized as having a compulsory character notwithstanding contrary state agreements. He defined peremptory law as the "*ethical minimum* recognized by all the states of the international community."[12] To illustrate the phenomenon of international jus cogens, Verdross argued that states bore an imperative duty under international law to undertake certain "moral tasks," including the "maintenance of law and order within states, defense against external attacks, care for the bodily and spiritual welfare of citizens at home, [and] protection of citizens abroad."[13] According to Verdross, examples of international treaties inconsistent with jus cogens would

im Völkerrecht [Manifestations of Law Between Nations; Jus Cogens and Jus Dispositivum *in International Law], in* 16 ZEITSCHRIFT FÜR VÖLKERRECHT 461 (Max Fleischmann, Walther Schücking & Karl Strupp eds., 1932).

8. *See* HUGO GROTIUS, DE JURE BELLI ET PACIS [ON THE LAW OF WAR AND PEACE] (William Whewell ed. & trans., The Law Book Exchange 2009) (1625); EMER DE VATTEL, LE DROIT DES GENS OU PRINCIPES DE LA LOI NATURELLE [THE LAW OF NATIONS OR PRINCIPLES OF NATURAL LAW] §§ 9, 27 (1758) (distinguishing "le Droit des Gens *Naturel*, ou *Nécessaire*" from "le Droit *Volontaire*"); CHRISTIAN WOLFF, *JUS GENTIUM* METHODO SCIENTIFICA PERTRACTORUM [A SCIENTIFIC METHOD FOR UNDERSTANDING THE LAW OF NATIONS] ¶ 5 (James Brown Scott ed., Joseph H. Drake trans., Clarendon Press 1934) (1764).

9. WILLIAM HALL, A TREATISE ON INTERNATIONAL LAW 382 (8th ed. 1924) (asserting that "fundamental principles of international law" "invalidate [], or at least render voidable," conflicting international agreements); 1 LASSA OPPENHEIM, INTERNATIONAL LAW 528 (1905).

10. For example, in the 1934 *Oscar Chinn Case*, Judge Walter Schücking's influential dissent stated that neither an international court nor an arbitral tribunal should apply a treaty provision in contradiction to *bonos mores*. Oscar Chinn Case, 1934 P.C.I.J. (ser. A/B) No. 63, at 149–50.

11. Alfred von Verdross, *Forbidden Treaties in International Law*, 31 AM. J. INT'L L. 571 (1937).

12. *Id.* at 574.

13. *Id.*

include those "binding a state to reduce its police or its organization of courts in such a way that it is no longer able to protect at all or in an adequate manner, the life, the liberty, the honor, or the property of men on its territory."[14] Treaties might also violate jus cogens if they obligated "a state to close its hospitals or schools, to extradite or sterilize its women, to kill its children, to close its factories, to leave its fields unploughed, or in other ways to expose its population to distress."[15]

Jus cogens and the idea of human rights as law gained enhanced recognition and credibility following the Second World War. For a generation of international lawyers, the prosecution of Axis leaders at Nuremburg and Tokyo offered compelling evidence that international law did, indeed, impose substantive limits on the invocation of state sovereignty as a shield for officials accused of crimes against humanity.[16] Anxious to move beyond the humanitarian calamities of World War II, state parties to the United Nations committed to work together to achieve "universal respect for, and observance of, human rights and fundamental freedoms."[17] Under the direction of the U.N. General Assembly, the Human Rights Commission endeavored to generate an international consensus regarding human rights through the preparation of the Universal Declaration of Human Rights (UDHR).[18] Although the UDHR affirmed "the inherent dignity and the equal and inalienable rights of all members of the human family,"[19] it did not propose a philosophical justification for human rights. Instead, the UDHR cataloged particular rights accepted throughout the world in an attempt to establish "a common standard of achievement for all peoples and all nations."[20]

Even during the UDHR's drafting process, human rights advocates recognized that the declaration's moral consensus regarding human rights was only a first step. For human rights to be meaningful in practice, states would also have to accept and implement these rights as genuine legal obligations. International and regional organizations set out to craft multilateral human rights conventions and design complementary institutional frameworks to bridge the gap between moral consensus and domestic implementation. At the international level, these efforts generated an impressive series of international agreements, including the International Covenant on Civil and Political Rights (ICCPR);[21] the International Covenant on Economic, Social and Cultural

14. *Id.*

15. *Id.* at 575.

16. *See* LAURI HANNIKAINEN, PEREMPTORY NORMS (JUS COGENS) IN INTERNATIONAL LAW: HISTORICAL DEVELOPMENT, CRITERIA, PRESENT STATUS 150 (1988) (surveying legal scholarship during the period 1945–1969 and reporting that "about eighty per cent [of scholars] held the opinion that there are peremptory norms existing in international law").

17. U.N. Charter arts. 55(c), 56.

18. Universal Declaration of Human Rights, G.A. Res. 217A, U.N. GAOR, 3d Sess., 1st plen. mtg., U.N. Doc. A/810 (Dec. 10, 1948) [hereinafter UDHR].

19. *Id.* at pmbl.

20. *Id.*

21. International Covenant on Civil and Political Rights, Dec. 16, 1966, S. Exec. Doc. E, 95-2 (1978), 999 U.N.T.S. 171 [hereinafter ICCPR].

Rights (ICESCR);[22] and the Convention Against Torture and Other Cruel, Inhuman, or Degrading Treatment or Punishment (CAT).[23] International agencies such as the U.N. Human Rights Commission, the U.N. High Commissioner for Human Rights, and the U.N. High Commissioner for Refugees began monitoring state compliance with these and other agreements. Regional bodies such as the Organization of American States, the Organization of African Unity, and the Council of Europe adopted additional regional human rights agreements, complemented by their own investigatory commissions and judicial tribunals.[24] This wave of convention drafting, ratification, and institutionalization strengthened human rights as binding legal norms, but without clarifying the philosophical basis for human rights' legal authority.

During the same period when states were pledging allegiance to the UDHR and the development of IHRL, international judges and scholars were declaring unequivocally that universal norms such as the prohibition against genocide would bind states irrespective of state consent.[25] These two strands of the postwar human rights movement—multilateral conventions and peremptory norms—converged in a remarkable way during the 1950s and 1960s with the United Nations International Law Commission's (ILC) preparation of the Vienna Convention on the Law of Treaties.[26] Early in the VCLT's drafting process, advocates for jus cogens found a powerful ally in the ILC's Special Rapporteur, Sir Hersch Lauterpacht. Acknowledging uncertainty over the scope and content of jus cogens, Lauterpacht asserted that peremptory norms derived their unique legal authority from two interrelated sources—international morality and general principles of state practice. In Lauterpacht's view, "overriding principles of international law" such as the suppression of slavery "may be regarded as constituting principles of international public policy (*ordre international public*). These principles . . . may be expressive of rules of international morality so cogent that an international tribunal would consider them forming a part of those principles of law generally recognized by civilized nations which the International Court of Justice is bound to apply [under] its Statute."[27] By

22. International Covenant on Economic, Social and Cultural Rights, Dec. 16, 1966, 993 U.N.T.S.23 [hereinafter ICESCR].

23. Convention Against Torture and Other Cruel, Inhuman or Degrading Treatment or Punishment, Dec. 10, 1984, S. Treaty Doc. No. 100–20 (1988), 1465 U.N.T.S. 85 [hereinafter CAT].

24. *See* Organization of American States, American Convention on Human Rights, Nov. 22, 1969, O.A.S. Treaty Series No. 36, 1144 U.N.T.S. 123; Organization of African Unity, African [Banjul] Charter on Human and Peoples' Rights, June 27, 1981, OAU Doc. CAB/LEG/67/3 rev. 5, 21 I.L.M. 58; Council of Europe, Convention for the Protection of Human Rights and Fundamental Freedoms, Nov. 4, 1950, ETS 5.

25. *See, e.g.*, Reservations to the Convention on the Prevention and Punishment of the Crime of Genocide, Advisory Opinion, 1951 ICJ Rep. 15, 23 (May 28) (asserting that "the principles underlying the [Genocide] Convention are principles which are recognized by civilized nations as binding on States, even without any conventional obligations").

26. VCLT, *supra* note 3.

27. *Id.* at 155; *see also* Application of the Convention on the Prevention and Punishment of the Crime of Genocide, 1993 ICJ Rep. 325, 440 (separate opinion of Judge Lauterpacht) ("The concept of *jus cogens* operates as a concept superior to both customary international law and treaty.").

identifying jus cogens with public policy and general principles of municipal law, Lauterpacht hewed closely to Verdross's original concern for "immoral" treaties contrary to international public policy.

Lauterpacht's colleagues on the ILC generally accepted his assessment that certain international norms had attained the status of jus cogens.[28] Yet despite general agreement over the existence of international jus cogens, the ILC was unable to reach a consensus regarding either the theoretical basis for peremptory norms' legal authority or the proper criteria for their identification. In the end, the ILC chose to open the VCLT for ratification without defining with specificity either the theoretical basis of jus cogens or the precise criteria for identifying particular peremptory norms. Article 53 recognized the existence of international jus cogens by declaring that "[a] treaty is void if, at the time of its conclusion, it conflicts with a peremptory norm of general international law."[29] In commentary accompanying the draft convention, the ILC indicated that "the prudent course seems to . . . leave the full content of this rule to be worked out in State practice and in the jurisprudence of international tribunals."[30] To this end, Article 53 stated by way of definition that "a peremptory norm of general international law is a norm accepted and recognized by the international community of States as a whole as a norm from which no derogation is permitted and which can be modified only by a subsequent norm of general international law having the same character."[31] In short, although Article 53 affirmed the existence of jus cogens as a corpus of non-derogable international norms, it did not expressly ground these norms in principles of natural law, state consent, public order, or any other theory of legal obligation.

The basic terms of the debate over peremptory norms have changed little since the VCLT entered into force in 1980. As then, the concept of international jus cogens today enjoys widespread acceptance among international publicists, and has been discussed with approval by numerous international, regional, and municipal courts.[32] However, scholarly debates over the nature, scope, and content of

28. *See* HANNIKAINEN, *supra* note 16, at 160–61 (noting that none of the twenty-five members of the ILC in 1963 denied the existence of jus cogens or contested the inclusion of an article on jus cogens in the VCLT); *see, e.g., Summary Records of the 877th Meeting,* [1966] 1 Y.B. Int'l L. Comm'n 227, 230–31, U.N. Doc. A/CN.4/188 (noting that the "emergence of a rule of jus cogens banning aggressive war as an international crime" was evidence that international law contains "minimum requirement[s] for safeguarding the existence of the international community").

29. VCLT, *supra* note 3, art. 53; *see also id.* art. 64 ("If a new peremptory norm of general international law emerges, any existing treaty which is in conflict with the norm becomes void and terminates.").

30. *Second Report on the Law of Treaties,*[1963] 2 Y.B. Int'l L. Comm'n 1, 53, U.N. Doc. A/CN.4/156.

31. VCLT, *supra* note 3, art. 53.

32. *See, e.g.,* Siderman v. Republic of Argentina, 965 F.2d 699 (9th Cir. 1992) (recognizing torture as a jus cogens violation); Armed Activities on the Territory of the Congo, Jurisdiction of the Court and Admissibility of the Application (Dem. Rep. Congo v. Rwanda) (Judgment of Feb. 3, 2006), http://www.icj-cij.org/docket/files/126/10435.pdf (recognizing genocide as a violation of jus cogens).

peremptory norms—questions deferred during the ILC's deliberations—remain equally contentious today.

International law's perennial anxiety over jus cogens has real-world costs. Over time, legal scholars have generated conflicting catalogs of peremptory norms, fueling skepticism about the jus cogens concept itself.[33] As Dinah Shelton has observed, concerns about jus cogens's uncertain basis and uneasy coexistence with state sovereignty have diminished the concept's influence in transnational dispute resolution.[34] In some municipal cases, courts have accepted international norms as peremptory, but have hesitated to enforce these norms for fear that they might thereby compromise state sovereignty.[35] In short, although the jus cogens concept has achieved widespread acceptance across the international community, its unsettled theoretical foundation has impeded its implementation and development. For jus cogens to achieve full legal standing, it needs to be reframed in a way that both illuminates its normative basis and explains its relationship to sovereignty.

The same is true of IHRL. In the absence of an underlying theory of human rights, basic questions regarding the scope and content of IHRL have proven to be deeply controversial, raising doubts about the juridical character of human rights while subverting the modern human rights movement's universalist ambitions.[36] Until recently, for example, the prohibition against state-sponsored torture was widely viewed as one of the most well-established and least controversial principles of IHRL, having been incorporated in the UDHR, ICCPR, and CAT, as well as in a host of regional agreements and municipal laws. The international community has defined the prohibition against torture with unusual specificity by spelling out several discrete elements in the CAT.[37] Yet notwithstanding these apparent advantages, the torture prohibition's definition, universality, and legal authority remain controversial. After the 9/11 terrorist attacks, the U.S. government challenged the prohibition against torture by employing and later defending "enhanced" interrogation techniques such as waterboarding, prolonged sleep deprivation, and hanging by the wrists.[38] Critics of enhanced interrogation techniques have struggled to explain why these practices should be considered human rights violations when the CAT fails to provide straightforward answers to many important questions regarding

33. *See generally* A. Mark Weisburd, *American Judges and International Law*, 36 VAND. J. TRANSNAT'L L. 1475, 1493 (2003) (noting that state delegations at the Vienna Conference "offered widely differing lists of rules meeting the requirements of *jus cogens*; of the twenty-six delegations . . . no more than thirteen agreed with respect to any one rule").

34. Shelton, *supra* note 5, at 305–17.

35. *See, e.g.*, Bouzari v. Iran, [2004] 71 O.R.3d 675, ¶ 93 (Can.) (holding that the prohibition against torture does not entail a right to a civil remedy enforceable in a foreign court).

36. *See* Charles Beitz, *What Human Rights Mean*, 132 DAEDELUS 36, 37 (2003); Allen Buchanan, *Human Rights and the Legitimacy of the International Order*, 14 LEGAL THEORY 39, 40–41 (2008).

37. CAT, *supra* note 23, art. 1(1) (defining torture to mean "any act by which severe pain and suffering, whether physical or mental, is intentionally inflicted on a person for [various] purposes . . . when such pain or suffering is inflicted by or at the instigation or with the consent or acquiescence of a public official or other person acting in an official capacity").

38. *See* Jeremy Waldron, *Torture, Necessity, and Existential Politics*, 95 CALIF. L. REV. 235, 235–36 & n.3 (2007).

the torture prohibition's scope. For example, how should the international community determine whether an individual's "pain and suffering" are sufficiently "severe" to constitute "torture"?[39] Are states prohibited from employing torture under circumstances of perceived necessity?[40] Judicial efforts to define human rights norms with precision are likely to remain highly controversial, unless those efforts can be grounded in a broader theory of human rights amenable to judicial inquiry.

As we look to the future, the legal and political legitimacy of IHRL will depend in no small part upon the principled specification of human rights norms. To achieve this objective, IHRL must develop a more rigorous theory of human rights—one capable of distinguishing authentic human rights, determining who may claim human rights violations against whom, and making human rights effective as justiciable legal rights. Indeed, after decades of relative neglect, there is a growing awareness within the human rights community that international law cannot achieve all three elements of its human rights agenda—transnational application, binding legal effect, and specification—without re-engaging the fundamental philosophical questions of human rights theory.[41]

III. IN SEARCH OF A THEORY

To be credible, a general theory of human rights and jus cogens must offer principled answers (or at least guidance) to certain fundamental questions regarding the basis, content, character, and scope of human rights and peremptory norms. Some of these questions are specific to human rights (including peremptory human rights), others relate to the combined sets of human rights and jus cogens, while some relate to the special character of jus cogens norms (some but not all of which are also human rights). These questions include:

- In what sense are human rights *rights*?
- Do human rights constitute *legal* rights, as distinguished from moral or political rights?
- How does the theory provide guidance for identifying international norms, distinguishing peremptory from nonperemptory norms, and clarifying their scope?
- What is the relationship between international norms and state lawmaking authority?
- Do international norms generate *positive* duties, such as a duty to provide education, in addition to negative duties of non-interference?

39. CAT, *supra* note 23, art. 1(1).

40. *See* John T. Parry, *Escalation and Necessity: Defining Torture at Home and Abroad, in* TORTURE 145, 158 (Sanford Levinson ed., 2004) ("If torture provides the last remaining chance to save lives in imminent peril, the necessity defense should be available to justify the interrogators' conduct.").

41. *See, e.g.*, CHARLES R. BEITZ, THE IDEA OF HUMAN RIGHTS xi–xii (2009); JAMES W. NICKEL, MAKING SENSE OF HUMAN RIGHTS 53 (2d ed. 2007); L.W. SUMNER, THE MORAL FOUNDATION OF RIGHTS 1–14 (1987); Joseph Raz, *Human Rights Without Foundations, in* THE PHILOSOPHY OF INTERNATIONAL LAW (John Tasioulis & Samantha Besson eds., 2010); Buchanan, *supra* note 36, at 44; Michael Freeman, *The Philosophical Foundations of Human Rights*, 16 HUM. RTS. Q. 491, 491 (1994); Jerome J. Shestack, *The Philosophical Foundations of Human Rights*, 20 HUM. RTS. Q. 201 (1998).

- Do international norms generate duties for both state and nonstate actors?
- Are international norms culturally relative or universal?

These issues rank among the most pressing and vexing in contemporary theoretical debates concerning human rights and jus cogens. We argue now that the leading theories of human rights and jus cogens struggle to offer persuasive answers to these and other questions. We begin with accounts of jus cogens that also implicitly theorize peremptory human rights, and then discuss several influential theories of human rights proper.

A. Consent Theories

Most contemporary commentators continue to view jus cogens through the voluntarist prism of state consent. The requirement of state consent is justified on grounds that states are sovereign and autonomous, and therefore states cannot be bound by norms to which they have not consented.[42] The leading consent-based theory of jus cogens conceives of peremptory norms as customary law that has attained peremptory status through state practice and *opinio juris*.[43] The *Restatement* endorses this position, stating that jus cogens "is now widely accepted . . . as a principle of customary international law (albeit of higher status)."[44] For consent theorists, a custom-based conception of jus cogens bolsters international law's legitimacy by ensuring that states maintain firm control over the generation and evolution of peremptory norms. States, however, rarely (if ever) express an affirmative intent to transform ordinary customary norms into peremptory law, and it is unclear what forms of state practice (if any) would support an inference of implied intent. Indeed, critics of jus cogens are quick to point out that many human rights norms such as the prohibition against torture, which are widely accepted as jus cogens, are also widely violated in practice.[45] Even if state practice clearly supported recognizing peremptory norms as customary international law, the voluntarist approach is hard-pressed to explain why customary norms would bind persistent objectors or nullify subsequent conflicting treaties. It is difficult, therefore, to dispute the assessment that "calling peremptory norms customary distorts the concept beyond recognition."[46]

42. *See* Gennady M. Danilenko, *International Jus Cogens: Issues of Law-Making*, 2 Eur. J. Int'l L. 42, 47 (1991); Georg Schwarzenberger, *International Jus Cogens?*, 43 Tex. L. Rev. 455, 457–60 (1965).

43. *See, e.g.*, Michael Byers, *Conceptualizing the Relationship Between Jus Cogens and* Erga Omnes *Rules*, 66 Nordic J. Int'l L. 211, 212 (1997) (arguing "that jus cogens rules are derived from the 'process of customary international law' ").

44. Third Restatement, *supra* note 4, § 102 n.6.

45. *See* Alexander Orakhelashvili, Peremptory Norms in International Law 113 (2006) (asserting that noncompliance with the peremptory norms against military aggression, torture, genocide, and slavery is too widespread to support the custom theory).

46. Orakhelashvili, *supra* note 45, at 114 (summarizing N.G. Onuf & Richard K. Bierney, *Peremptory Norms of International Law: Their Source, Function, and Future*, 4 Denver J. Int'l L. & Pol'y 187, 193 (1974)); *see also* Sampson v. F.R.G., 250 F.3d 1145, 1149 (7th Cir.

Some scholars have suggested that the requirement of state consent might be satisfied if a representative supermajority of states accepted an emerging norm as peremptory. The ILC's Commentary to Article 53 appears to be sympathetic to this approach. Peremptory norms need not achieve universal acceptance to create a binding international consensus, the ILC opines; instead, international norms may claim a consensus of "the international community of States as a whole" if a "very large majority" of representative states accept the norms as non-derogable.[47] Circumventing actual state practice, advocates of this consensus theory typically presume that states signal their consent to peremptory norms through a variety of expressive acts, whether they be unilateral declarations by heads of state, diplomatic correspondence, or the simple failure to register a timely objection to emerging norms. Consensus theory thus envisions a new, autonomous mode of general international law formation—a quasi-customary source that is not beholden to state practice or individualized state consent.[48]

The primary advantage of consensus theory over other consent-based theories of jus cogens is that it liberates peremptory norms from customary international law's persistent objector rule. Yet to the extent that consensus theory continues to posit state consent as the foundation of jus cogens, it remains vulnerable to the same theoretical quandary that vexes consent-based approaches to jus cogens generally, namely: Why may a supermajority of states impose non-derogable duties on a dissenting minority? And even if states did consent to a consensus-based source of international lawmaking, the consent-based paradigm would be ill-equipped to explain why states that disapprove of emerging peremptory norms in the future could not withdraw their consent at will.[49] Thus, international consensus is not particularly well-suited to furnish the theoretical underpinnings of jus cogens.

As many consent theorists have recognized, the very concept of jus cogens—peremptory norms that bind states irrespective of state consent—is sharply at odds with the consent-based account of international lawmaking.[50] If peremptory norms

2001) ("'Customary international law . . . rests on the consent of states.' . . . In contrast, a state is bound by jus cogens norms even if it does not consent to their application.") (quoting Comm. of U.S. Citizens Living in Nicar. v. Reagan, 859 F.2d 929, 940 (D.C. Cir. 1988)).

47. *See* Third Restatement, *supra* note 4, § 102 n.6 (citing United Nations Conference on the Law of Treaties, Mar. 26–May 24, 1968, *Report of the Proceedings of the Committee of the Whole*, 471–72, U.N. Doc. A/CONF.39/11 (May 21, 1968) (comments of the chairman)).

48. *See* W. Michael Reisman, *Unilateral Action and the Transformations of the World Constitutive Process: The Special Problem of Humanitarian Intervention*, 11 Eur. J. Int'l L. 3, 15 n.29 (2000) ("In human rights discourse, jus cogens has . . . evolv[ed] into a type of super-custom, based on trans-empirical sources and hence not requiring demonstration of practice as proof of its validity.").

49. *See* Jerzy Sztucki, Jus Cogens and the Vienna Convention on the Law of Treaties: A Critical Reappraisal 97 (1974).

50. *See id.* at 64 ("[T]he introduction of a consensual ingredient into the concept of *jus cogens* leads inevitably, in the ultimate instance, to the very negation of that concept."); *see* Siderman v. Republic of Argentina, 965 F.2d 699 (9th Cir. 1992) (stating that jus cogens norms "transcend consent").

are to be taken seriously as a source of international obligation, their imperative force must derive from some principle other than state consent.

B. Natural Law Theories

One response to the inadequacy of positivist theories of jus cogens has been to embrace peremptory norms as remnants of the natural law tradition. Prominent human rights theorists such as Louis Henkin and Louis Sohn have suggested that jus cogens norms such as the prohibitions against slavery and military aggression derive their peremptory character from their inherent rational and moral authority rather than state consent; as such, treaties, custom, and general principles might recognize and incorporate peremptory norms, but they could not abrogate them.[51] Similar affirmations of jus cogens as natural law may be distilled from the jurisprudence of the ICJ[52] and the Inter-American Commission on Human Rights.[53] Although few international lawyers today share Vattel's confidence in a universal natural law of reason, many nonetheless agree that "[t]he character of certain norms makes it difficult to portray them as other than peremptory."[54]

The conceptual challenges associated with natural law theory are well-documented. Although some peremptory norms such as the prohibitions against genocide and slavery are relatively uncontroversial, it is by no means clear how natural law theory would resolve disputes over the scope or content of less well-defined norms, such as the prohibition against torture, once jus cogens is uncoupled from state consent. More troubling still, natural law theory, like consent theory, struggles to explain how peremptory norms can place substantive limits on state action without eviscerating the concept of state sovereignty.[55] For these and other reasons, most international courts and publicists of the last half-century have eschewed reliance on natural law in favor of other theories of jus cogens.

51. Louis Henkin, The International Bill of Rights: The Covenant on Civil and Political Rights 15 (1981); Louis B. Sohn, *The New International Law: Protection of the Rights of Individuals Rather than States*, 32 Am. U. L. Rev. 1 (1982) (citing the "natural law concept of rights, rights to which all human beings have been entitled since time immemorial and to which they will continue to be entitled as long as humanity survives").

52. *Nicaragua*, 1986 ICJ Rep. at 112 (describing certain norms of international humanitarian law as "elementary considerations of humanity" that "constitute intransgressible principles").

53. *See, e.g.*, Michael Domingues v. United States, Case 12.285, Inter-Am. C.H.R., Report No. 62/02, OEA/Ser.L/V/II.117, doc. 5 rev.1 ¶ 49 (2003), http://www.cidh.org/annualrep/2002eng/USA.12285.htm (describing jus cogens as a "superior order of legal norms, which the laws of man or nations may not contravene[,] . . . rules which have been accepted . . . as being necessary to protect the public morality recognized by them") (internal citation and quotation marks omitted).

54. Orakhelashvili, *supra* note 45, at 108.

55. *See* Anthony D'Amato, *Human Rights as Part of Customary International Law: A Plea for Change of Paradigms*, 25 Ga. J. Int'l & Comp. L. 47, 63–75 (1995–1996) (discussing this tension).

C. Public Order Theories

A third tradition in international legal theory defines jus cogens as public order norms essential to the integrity of international law as a legal system. According to this theory, international law recognizes certain imperative norms as hierarchically superior to ordinary conventional and customary law in order to promote the interests of the international community as a whole and preserve international law's core values against fragmentation. According to public order theories of jus cogens, all peremptory norms serve one of two functions: they either safeguard the peaceful coexistence of states as a community or honor the international system's core normative commitments.[56]

Insofar as public order theory envisions jus cogens violations as offenses against the international community as a whole, this approach places peremptory norms in close proximity to *erga omnes* rules—offenses that give rise to generalized state standing. The ICJ famously endorsed the *erga omnes* concept in *Barcelona Traction* when it affirmed states' responsibility to refrain from "acts of aggression, and of genocide," and to observe "the principles and rules concerning the basic rights of the human person, including protection from slavery and racial discrimination," and characterized these norms as "obligations of a State to the international community as a whole."[57] Although superficially appealing, the ICJ's attempt to frame peremptory norms as duties owed by states to the international community as a whole poses significant conceptual difficulties of its own: In what sense does the international community suffer an injury when a state subjects its own nationals to slavery or racial discrimination? It is unclear why the international community as a whole could claim a more particularized interest in intrastate human rights observance than either its constituent member-states or the people who reside within them.

Public order theory's best response to this dilemma has been to recast peremptory norms as principles integral to the normative objectives of international law and constitutive of the international community itself. Myers McDougal, Harold Lasswell, Michael Reisman, and others have argued persuasively that jus cogens norms such as the prohibitions against acts of aggression and racial discrimination reflect international law's transformation into a purposeful global community of conscience dedicated to promoting human rights and the peaceful coexistence of states.[58] As evidence of this normative agenda, public order theorists point to instruments such as the Charter of the United Nations, which defines the United Nations'

56. *See, e.g.*, Bundesverfassungsgericht [BVerfGE] [Federal Constitutional Court] Apr. 7, 1965 (F.R.G.) (characterizing peremptory norms as "legal rules . . . indispensable to the existence of the law of nations as an international legal order") (quoted in Stefan A. Riesenfeld, Jus Dispositivum *and Jus Cogens in International Law: In the Light of a Recent Decision of the German Supreme Constitutional Court*, 60 Am. J. Int'l L. 511, 513 (1966)); Orakhelashvili, *supra* note 45, at 46 ("The purpose of *jus cogens* is to safeguard the predominant and overriding interests and values of the international community as a whole . . . .").

57. Barcelona Traction, Light & Power Co. (Belg. v. Spain) 1970 ICJ Rep. 3, 33.

58. Myres S. McDougal, Harold D. Lasswell & Lung-Chu Chen, Human Rights and World Public Order: The Basic Policies of an International Law of Human Dignity 3–6 (1980); W. Michael Reisman, Siegfried Wiessner & Andrew R. Willard, *The New Haven School: A Brief Introduction*, 32 Yale J. Int'l L. 575, 576 (2007).

objectives to include the promotion of "international peace and security," "friendly relations among nations," "human rights," and "fundamental freedoms."[59]

At the same time, public order's insight that peremptory norms shape and define international law's normative agenda does not, in and of itself, yield a promising positive or prescriptive theory of jus cogens. Public order theory does not illuminate the normative basis of peremptory norms, nor does it clarify which particular international norms should be deemed peremptory. When confronting these critical questions concerning the nature and content of peremptory norms, advocates of public order theory either retreat to circular reasoning about peremptory norms' indispensability to international society or recycle arguments from consent or natural law theory. Equally disconcerting, public order theory—like consent and natural law theory—does not address the enduring paradox at the core of human rights discourse: international law's seemingly contradictory commitments to state sovereignty and individual dignity. And as we shall see now, leading human rights theories fare no better.

D. Human Rights Theories

As noted already, the UDHR and subsequent human rights conventions were never intended to provide a full-fledged philosophical justification for human rights. At most, human rights conventions offer a few scattered philosophical fragments. For example, the UDHR declares that "[a]ll human beings are born free and equal in dignity and rights."[60] The ICCPR and ICESCR similarly purport to "derive" their schedules of rights "from the inherent dignity of the human person."[61] To the extent that these instruments share a common vision of human rights (however imperfect and incomplete), it is one that emphasizes human beings' freedom and equal dignity as a basis for international legal obligation. None of the leading human rights conventions explains precisely what the "inherent dignity of the human person" means, however, nor do they explain how particular rights might be "derived" from any particular conception of human dignity. For answers to these and other important questions regarding human rights, international law must look beyond these agreements to the complementary insights of moral and political philosophy.

Most theorists have grounded human rights in common values or attributes of humanity, such as human dignity or universal human interests. Under this orthodox approach, human rights are a subset of natural moral rights. Critics have complained that such efforts to derive human rights from first principles rely on contestable assumptions regarding the essential character of human nature.[62] Nonetheless, many contemporary human rights theorists such as John Finnis, James Griffin, and

59. U.N. Charter art. 1, ¶¶ 1–3; *see also* HANNIKAINEN, *supra* note 16, at 5 (explaining that in discerning jus cogens, "at present it can be said that the United Nations . . . acts on behalf of 'the international community of States as a whole' ").

60. UDHR, *supra* note 18, art. 1.

61. ICCPR, *supra* note 21, pmbl.; ICESCR, *supra* note 22, pmbl.

62. *See, e.g.*, Freeman, *supra* note 41, at 494; Shestack, *supra* note 41, at 208.

Michael Perry continue to insist that human rights cannot be fully understood or specified without recourse to a foundationalist justification.[63]

One prominent foundationalist theory is Alan Gewirth's Principle of Generic Consistency. Drawing on the Kantian tradition, Gewirth argues that human rights follow analytically from the idea that human freedom provides "necessary conditions of human action."[64] Gewirth observes that the very concept of human freedom presupposes human purposiveness, which in turn presupposes an agent's capacity to set her own purposes and make judgments about the good (i.e., the moral, philosophical, or religious doctrine she wishes to affirm and pursue). Once an agent recognizes that she is able to set her own purposes and make judgments about the good, she must accept that her "freedom and well-being are necessary"[65] for purposive action, and that she has a right to these generic features of successful action.[66] Because others also possess agency, the agent "must admit, on pain of self-contradiction"[67] that others have rights to freedom and well-being.[68]

Gewirth's Principle of Generic Consistency has not escaped criticism. Joseph Raz disputes Gewirth's assertion that "freedom is a necessary condition of human purposeful action," noting that slaves act purposefully without enjoying freedom.[69] In addition, even if Gewirth's Principle of Generic Consistency were persuasive as a theory of moral obligation, it would remain incomplete because it fails to elucidate human rights' legal character. On Gewirth's account, human rights could conceivably bind agents morally without imposing any correlative legal duty.

The orthodox idea that human rights are natural and moral rights nonetheless continues to attract adherents, perhaps none more rigorous than John Tasioulas. Tasioulas defends an interest-based conception that is pluralistic in that it is sensitive to "the diverse elements of a flourishing human life."[70] His conception is also pluralistic in its incorporation of the idea of human dignity, understood as "the equal

63. *See* John Finnis, Natural Law and Natural Rights 198, 210–13 (1980); James Griffin, On Human Rights (2008); Michael J. Perry, The Idea of Human Rights: Four Inquiries (1998).

64. Gewirth, Justifications and Applications, *supra* note 1, at 20.

65. Alan Gewirth, *The Epistemology of Human Rights*, 1 Soc. Phil. & Pol'y 14, 15 (1984).

66. Alan Gewirth, Reason and Morality 63–64 (1978) [hereinafter Gewirth, Reason].

67. *Id.* at 26.

68. Gewirth, Reason, *supra* note 66, at 17.

69. Raz, *supra* note 41, at 324 (citing Gewirth, Justifications and Applications, *supra* note 1, at 15). For a more recent account that resembles Gewirth's in some respects by grounding human rights on autonomy, but expands the foundational grounds to include liberty and welfare, see Griffin, *supra* note 63. Against Griffin, Raz argues, in effect, that his position collapses into Gewirth's if it relies on an austere account of personhood (i.e., the bare capacity for intentional action), and so is susceptible to the same criticism as in the text. Alternatively, if Griffin relies on a thicker conception of agency and the material conditions necessary to its successful exercise, as he appears to do, then his theory lacks criteria for specifying human rights, leaving in place the indeterminacy it is supposed to resolve. Raz, *supra* note 41, at 326.

70. John Tasioulas, *Towards a Philosophy of Human Rights*, 65 Current Legal Probs. 1, 7 (2012).

intrinsic objective worth of all human beings."[71] Tasioulas claims that these "grounding values"—universal human interests and human dignity—are not morally distinctive, but rather underlie human rights conceived of as "moral rights possessed by all human beings simply in virtue of their humanity."[72] In staking out his view, Tasioulas seeks to distinguish it from the foundationalist idea that human rights track only distinctive values, such as those associated with freedom or agency or the status of moral personhood, values that in principle are indifferent to human interests. Likewise, he argues against what he calls the "functionalist" view that the nature of a human right is determined by the function it serves as a marker for the legitimacy of a state or government, and as a possible trigger for international response (e.g., humanitarian intervention).[73] Tasioulas recognizes that human rights *can* serve this function, but it is not intrinsic to their nature, he claims, that they do so.

Tasioulas ultimately characterizes the idea of human rights as consisting in an "ethical sensibility" rather than a system of principles, one that aims to capture "a wider culture of thought and practice" that reflects the grounding values of universal human interests and dignity.[74] As such, his approach to specifying human rights does not begin with the practice of IHRL, but rather with the abstract question of whether "in the case of all human beings, it is 'possible' to serve the underlying values [of interests and dignity] through a duty with the proposed content."[75] If such a duty is possible because there is no "internal" impediment to it (e.g., there can be no duty to love someone romantically, as such an endeavor cannot be an object of duty), then the inquiry turns to the burden the putative duty would impose on others.

One worry with this approach is that it is overinclusive. Arguably, all human beings have an interest in being treated with civility, and it is equally arguable that an individual may reasonably take his dignity to be affronted if someone unjustifiably and deliberately treats him in a way that is uncivil. Unlike the case of romantic love, civility can be the object of duty, even legal duty.[76] Moreover, compliance with a duty of civility need hardly be burdensome. Yet it would strain our ordinary understanding of human rights to think that there is a human right to quotidian civility. If a friend invites you for dinner, the civil thing for you to do is to thank her before leaving, and you behave badly if you fail to do so. But we would mischaracterize the nature of the wrong if we claimed that you violated your friend's human rights, even if we assume that your rudeness was an affront to both her dignity and her interest in being treated civilly.

Tasioulas attempts to explain the absence from IHRL of this sort of case on the grounds that "its enforcement exceeds the proper bounds of state authority."[77] If,

71. *Id.*

72. *Id.*

73. *Id.* at 18–24 (discussing the functional accounts found in John Rawls, The Law of Peoples (2001); Ronald Dworkin, Justice for Hedgehogs (2011); and Raz, *supra* note 41.

74. Tasioulas, *supra* note 70, at 4, 5.

75. *Id.* at 15.

76. Doré v. Barreau du Québec, 2012 SCC 12, [2012] 1 S.C.R. 395 (upholding a bar association's sanction of a lawyer who sent a judge a vitriolic private letter).

77. John Tasioulas, *Human Rights, Legitimacy and International Law*, 58 Am. J. Jur. 1, 12 (2013). He refers to "certain forms of personal betrayal." *Id.*

however, human rights in part constitute the "proper bounds of state authority," then this reply begs the question. It is plausible that the enforcement of everyday gratitude exceeds the bounds of state authority precisely because no one has a human right to gratitude. Furthermore, although practical considerations may act as side-constraints on the scope of a state's enforcement authority (e.g., considerations such as cost and effectiveness), those external considerations have nothing to do with universal interests and dignity, which are the concerns that Tasioulas claims support the existence of a human right in the first place. In the result, Tasioulas's method for the specification of human rights leads to the arresting conclusion that there is a (natural and moral) human right to gratitude, but due to considerations external to it, this inchoate right is absent from IHRL. The more plausible view, we contend, is simply that there is no human right to gratitude.

The overinclusiveness of Tasioulas's theory points to two further deficiencies, at least from the perspective of an inquiry that seeks to explain and justify IHRL. The first is that even if it succeeds as a moral theory of human rights, it remains unclear why such rights may (or must) take the form of legal rights. As with Gewirth's Principle of Generic Consistency, Tasioulas's account, and in particular his method for the specification of human rights, fails to explain why human rights have a legal as well as moral character. Tasioulas acknowledges the difficulty of moving from interests to duties, at one point saying that for human rights to be "effective, action-guiding standards" what is ultimately needed is "some form of social fiat, such as convention or positive law, to supplement the deliverances of natural reason."[78] But an appeal to "some form of social fiat," without more, cannot help specify the moral content that is appropriately subject to fiat. The resort to fiat does not resolve the problem so much as surrender to it, once the "deliverances of natural reason" have run out. A more promising approach, we argue below, is premised on a conception of legality that has moral deliverances of its own.

A second deficiency of Tasioulas's theory brought out by the problem of overinclusiveness is its insensitivity to a prominent feature of the practice of IHRL; namely, that ordinarily the duty-bearers of IHRL are public authorities. Because Tasioulas's account, like orthodox theories generally, develops the intrinsic moral content of human rights from the standpoint of the bearer of universal and natural moral rights, any kind of natural or artificial person, whether private or public, can stand in as the duty-bearer. According to Tasioulas, "human rights need be neither widely-credited nor actually embodied in any social practice or legal institution."[79] He is thus hard-pressed to offer an argument of principle to explain the dominant position of public authorities as the duty-bearers within the practice of IHRL, notwithstanding that his second desideratum for a theory of human rights is "*fidelity* to the human rights culture that has emerged post-1945, especially as it is crystallized in the International Bill of Human Rights."[80]

78. John Tasioulas, *Human Dignity and the Foundations of Human Rights*, *in* Understanding Human Dignity 291, 298 (Christopher McCrudden ed., 2013).

79. John Tasioulas, *On the Nature of Human Rights*, *in* The Philosophy of Human Rights: Contemporary Controversies 17, 17 (Gerhard Ernst & Jan-Cristoph Heilinger eds., 2012).

80. *Id.* at 18.

Another influential tradition in human rights theory, the one Tasioulas refers to as "functionalist," draws on John Rawls's practical political philosophy of human rights. Instead of seeking to deduce rights analytically from fundamental assumptions about human nature, Rawls argues that rights claims can be grounded in a political conception of justice based on an "overlapping consensus" among rival social, cultural, and religious traditions.[81] The representatives of peoples from behind the veil of ignorance will agree that certain minimum norms (including human rights) are constitutive of a decent or well-ordered political order, and so it is unnecessary to reach agreement on the particular social, cultural, or religious considerations that ground human rights. Many human rights theorists have found this political conception of human rights appealing not only because it mediates ideological conflict and addresses concerns about cultural relativism, but also because it furnishes a persuasive positive theory for the development of IHRL.

Efforts to ground human rights in political conceptions of justice or contingent social practices have foundered, however, on a common problem: the idea of an overlapping consensus alone does not specify the scope or legal implications of human rights, or even why they should be thought to have legal rather than moral or political implications. As the prohibition against torture illustrates, the mere fact that virtually all states have recognized a particular human right often tells us little about the scope or legal consequences of the right. For international courts and other institutions charged with interpreting human rights, it is not enough to identify some norms as human rights; they must also be able to define human rights' scope and explain their legal consequences. Moreover, focusing on the overlapping consensus among states tends to reduce human rights norms to the lowest common denominator. States with stronger human rights traditions may respond to the codification of consensus-based norms by reverting to the mean, diluting their more protective national safeguards.[82] What is needed, therefore, to avoid these potential pitfalls, is a theory of human rights that both explains the authority of human rights norms and clarifies the proper content of those norms. As presently constituted, the political conceptions of human rights defended by Rawls and others do not accomplish these objectives.

IV. FIDUCIARY STATES AND INTERNATIONAL NORMS

We argue now that human rights and jus cogens norms are best conceived as norms emanating from a fiduciary relationship that exists between the state and persons subject to its powers, including citizens, resident aliens, and nonresident aliens. These norms arise from the state's assumption of sovereign powers, and are constitutive of sovereignty's normative dimension, which is to say, they are constitutive of a state's authority to exercise sovereign powers domestically and claim sovereign status as an international legal actor. But human rights and jus cogens norms are

81. *See* John Rawls, *The Law of Peoples*, *in* On Human Rights 42, 46, 68 (Stephen Shute & Susan Hurley eds., 1993).

82. *See* Jason Mazzone, *The Rise and Fall of Human Rights: A Skeptical Account of Multilevel Governance*, 3 Cambr. J. Int'l & Comp. L. 929 (2014); Andrew T. Guzman & Katerina Linos, *Human Rights Backsliding*, 102 Calif. L. Rev. 603 (2014).

also regulative in that they impose duties on states. A state that fails to satisfy its fiduciary duty to respect human rights and jus cogens subverts its claim to govern and represent its people as a sovereign actor. Put slightly differently, international law's power-conferring fiduciary norm authorizes the state to secure legal order, but subject to fiduciary constraints that include human rights and jus cogens. Under this theory, the state's sovereignty to govern domestically and represent its people internationally consists in its fiduciary authorization to do so. And because this authorization is constrained and constituted by a duty to respect jus cogens and human rights, state sovereignty is likewise constrained and constituted.[83]

The idea of a state-subject fiduciary relationship thus reveals the relational character of the fiduciary conception of human rights and jus cogens. We now flesh out the other features of the fiduciary model mentioned in the introduction; that is, its institutional, legal, nonpositivist, practical, aspirational, universal, and deliberative characteristics.

A. An Institutional Conception

The fiduciary model is institutional in two senses. First, as we have seen in Chapter 1, it is institutional in the constitutive sense that fiduciary relations must arise within legal institutions such as the family or corporation—frameworks in which the relationship is not defined by domination or wrongful interference with the vulnerable party. Second, the fiduciary theory is institutional in that it does not rely on pre-institutional and timeless natural rights, which sometimes are said to ground human rights. A. John Simmons provides an especially clear account of the pre-institutional view:

> *[H]uman* rights are possessed by all human beings simply in virtue of their humanity . . . . Human rights are those natural rights that are innate and that cannot be lost (i.e., that cannot be given away, forfeited, or taken away). Human rights, then, will have the properties of universality, independence (from social and legal recognition), naturalness, inalienability, non-forfeitability, and imprescriptability. Only so understood will an account of human rights capture the central idea of rights that can always be claimed by any human being.[84]

83. The fiduciary theory therefore satisfies Jon Mahoney's criterion that "a liberal conception of human rights must . . . justify the claim that human rights (a) *limit* and (b) *authorize limited* exercises in *political power*." Jon Mahoney, *Liberalism and the Moral Basis for Human Rights*, 27 Law & Phil. 151, 152 (2008). An advantage of the fiduciary theory is that it demystifies the role of human rights within a framework of limited authorization. Human rights denote limits through the obligations they impose, but claim-rights do not typically imply authorization. A separate principle is required for purposes of a power-conferring authorization, and in contexts of non-consensual coercion, such as the state-subject context, the best candidate is the fiduciary principle.

84. A. John Simmons, Justification and Legitimacy: Essays on Rights and Obligations 185 (2001) (citing inter alia Alan Gewirth, *The Epistemology of Human Rights*, *in* Human Rights 1, 3 (E.F. Paul, J. Paul & F.D. Miller, Jr. eds., 1986)) (other citations omitted) (emphasis in original).

As both Simmons and critics such as Charles Beitz observe, this transhistorical account is inconsistent with a wide range of rights recognized by IHRL, as these rights require or presuppose legal institutions.[85] Consider, for example, rights enshrined in the ICCPR to due process (arts. 9, 14, 15), a minimum core of which, we argue below, are jus cogens. Rights found in the ICESCR are even less amenable to the orthodox view. The ICESCR includes entitlements to work under "just and favourable conditions" (arts. 6–8), social security (art. 9), an adequate standard of living (art. 11), health (art. 12), education (art. 13), and enjoyment of cultural life (art. 15). These rights cannot exist in a pre-political state of nature devoid of public institutions, nor is it plausible to think that they existed in premodern societies, when the institutions necessary for their realization did not exist.

Rather than denying, as some philosophers do, that these rights are human rights, the fiduciary theory takes their institutional preconditions to heart because, under the theory, such rights are viewed as normative demands arising from the subjection of persons to public institutions.[86] In modern industrial societies, these include the institutions of private property and markets as well as legislatures, courts, and administrative agencies. IHRL and jus cogens protect individuals against threats of instrumentalization and domination made possible by the existence of these institutions.[87] Because these and other institutions are liable to change over time and vary across jurisdictions, there is no reason to think that the present catalog of international norms is complete or invariant. The catalog may change because threats to agency and dignity may change, or because contemporary threats may be newly apprehended by available norms, as the proliferation of instruments protective of vulnerable groups attests.[88] What is provisionally fixed within the fiduciary theory, however, is a commitment affirmed on legal grounds to non-instrumentalization and non-domination.

85. Charles Beitz, *Human Rights and the Law of Peoples*, *in* THE ETHICS OF ASSISTANCE: MORALITY AND THE DISTANT NEEDY 193, 196 (Deen K. Chatterjee ed., 2004); *see also id.* at 197–98 (citing Maurice Cranston as a proponent of this view: MAURICE CRANSTON, WHAT ARE HUMAN RIGHTS? 65–71 (1973)).

86. *Cf.* Tasioulas, *supra* note 79, at 35–36. To avoid the tension between IHRL and "timeless" human rights, Tasioulas rejects timelessness. He claims that human rights must be understood within the context of the historical period in which they appear. In the case of the rights enshrined within IHRL, the relevant period is modernity. Part of the point of the fiduciary theory is to explain human rights by taking seriously the moral demands of the state-subject relationship implicit to modernity. To the extent the project succeeds, it can be read as offering a principled argument for Tasioulas's rejection of timelessness.

87. For discussion of rights as guarantees against "standard threats," see HENRY SHUE, BASIC RIGHTS (2d ed. 1996). *See also* THOMAS POGGE, WORLD POVERTY AND HUMAN RIGHTS 64 (2002) (arguing that human rights are "moral claims on the organization of one's society").

88. *See, e.g.*, Convention on the Elimination of All Forms of Discrimination Against Women, G.A. Res. 34/180, Annex, U.N. Doc. A/RES/34/180 (Dec. 18, 1979); Convention on the Rights of the Child, Nov. 20, 1989, 1577 U.N.T.S. 3; Declaration on the Rights of Indigenous Peoples, G.A. Res. 61/295, U.N. Doc. A/RES/61/295 (Sept. 13, 2007).

B. A Fullerian Legal Conception

The legal character of the Kantian interpretation of the fiduciary model derives from its reliance on Kant's theory of right and the form of fiduciary relations within Kant's legal theory.[89] The rights available under this theory are enforceable claim-rights, and in this context they correlate to the state's duty to guarantee human rights and respect the norms of jus cogens. Just as a child's right to parental care is correlative to the parent's duty to provide support, the legal subject's human right to *x* is correlative to the state's duty to guarantee *x*. In both cases the fiduciary principle triggers the duty. And in both cases the reason for imposing a duty on the power-holder is the same as the reason for acknowledging the beneficiary's right: recognition of the right and the duty are necessary to avoid subjecting the beneficiary to instrumentalizing or dominating power. Right and duty coalesce to protect the equal independence of all.

One of the advantages of relying on a legal conception of human rights and jus cogens is that it treats international law on its own terms, within its own self-image, as law rather than as merely the aspirational goals of liberal political morality. The fiduciary theory does so, in part, by offering a distinctively legal explanation of the state's duty to guarantee human rights and respect jus cogens, an explanation that trades on the legal form of fiduciary relations. But the fiduciary model also points to formal and substantive criteria of a legal nature for specifying human rights and jus cogens, and so in this sense too it treats international law as law.

We begin by sketching seven formal criteria borrowed directly from Lon Fuller's internal morality of law, a set of desiderata that legal norms should aspire to satisfy irrespective of their substantive aims.[90] First, international norms must embody general and universalizable principles as opposed to ad hoc and particularized commands. The fiduciary theory is a general theory of public authority, and thus its substantive principles have a general and potentially universal character.

Second, international norms must be public so that states, as fiduciary agents of their people, can know them and adjust their policies and actions accordingly. States cannot be expected to conform their behavior to secret norms.

Third, compliance with international norms must be feasible in the sense that they cannot demand the impossible. States with entrenched poverty, for example, cannot be expected to alleviate such conditions in the very near term. States that permit or enforce slavery, on the other hand, can be required to eliminate it immediately (or as soon as humanly possible), as a slave state cannot under any interpretation be construed as a faithful fiduciary of its slave population.

Fourth, the subject matter of the norm should be clear and unequivocal, as the point is to provide a public criterion of justice capable of guiding state action. The prohibition on slavery, for example, is clear and unequivocal, whereas a prohibition on exploitation, without more, is not. The fact that international standards such as the prohibitions against slavery, arbitrary killing, and torture require explication

89. *Cf.* Jurgen Habermas, Between Facts and Norms 104–11 (1996) (arguing for a "legal" conception of human rights, but where "legal" is intended to denote a positivist detachment from morality).

90. *See* Lon L. Fuller, The Morality of Law 33 (rev. ed. 1969).

as applied to particular state acts does not render such norms insufficiently clear to guide state action.[91]

Fifth, international norms should be internally consistent as well as consistent with the wider corpus of international law. An inconsistent norm, or a norm that contradicts another, provides no guidance to the fiduciary state entrusted with securing legal order on behalf of its people.

Sixth, such norms should be prospective rather than retroactive in nature, as states cannot go back in time to bring their actions into conformity with them. This does not exclude the emergence of a new and even peremptory norm that requires reparations for past wrongs, as the norm would still apply to the state prospectively by requiring it to provide a remedy at some point in the future.

Finally, the set of international norms should remain relatively stable over time so that states can plan their actions and implement policies within a relatively stable framework of international law. With respect to emerging norms, this means that attention should be paid to the effect their recognition would have on benevolent state policies that were innocently developed without taking the emerging norm into account. In practice, the stability criterion is unlikely to play a major role because international norms are immanent to the state's fiduciary obligation to secure legal order, and international law already recognizes a good number of them. But a concern for stability would rule out the theoretical possibility of replacing currently accepted IHRL and jus cogens with an entirely different set.

In summary, the formal criteria ensure that international norms assume the form of general principles that provide public, feasible, clear, consistent, prospective, and stable guidance to fiduciary states entrusted to govern and represent their people. These criteria flow from the fiduciary conception of the state because they enable the state to act as a faithful fiduciary. In other words, the formal criteria set out necessary conditions that human rights and jus cogens norms must generally satisfy.

The fiduciary model also points to three substantive conditions of international norms derived from the nature of fiduciary relations. The fiduciary principle's authorization of state power requires the state and its institutions to act for the good of the people rather than for the good of its officials or rulers. The first condition is therefore a principle of *integrity*: human rights must have as their object the good of the legal subject rather than the good of the state's officials. Second is a principle of *formal moral equality*: the fiduciary state owes a duty of fairness or even-handedness to legal subjects because they are separate persons subject to the same fiduciary power. Human rights and jus cogens, therefore, must regard individuals as equal co-beneficiaries of the fiduciary state. Third is a principle of *solicitude*: international norms must be solicitous of the legal subject's legitimate interests because those interests, like the interests of the child vis-à-vis the parent, are vulnerable to the state's non-consensual coercive power. These desiderata offer a substantive justification of IHRL and jus cogens norms, a justification that operates independently of whether states have ratified particular conventions.

91. *See id.* at 64 ("Sometimes the best way to achieve clarity is to take advantage of . . . common sense standards of judgment . . . . A specious clarity can be more damaging than an honest open-ended vagueness.").

Yet, like the formal criteria, the substantive criteria establish necessary rather than sufficient conditions of human rights and jus cogens. This poses at least two problems. First, even taken together, the criteria enumerated thus far do not distinguish human rights susceptible to limitation from peremptory norms from which no derogation is permitted. Freedom of expression and the right to work, for example, are nonperemptory norms subject to justifiable restriction. But they are also specifiable in accordance with the seven formal criteria, they have the good of the subject rather than the official as their object, and they are consistent with the principles of formal moral equality and solicitude. Thus, the formal and substantive criteria enumerated thus far, even when taken collectively, do not provide a basis for distinguishing peremptory from nonperemptory norms.

A second issue is that the formal and substantive criteria alone do not provide a means for distinguishing human rights from rights that are not protected by IHRL. Consider the rights that better-off persons have to the property they own in excess of the property to which they are entitled as a matter of IHRL (whatever amount that may be). Assuming the requirements of IHRL are met, property law that regulates holdings in excess of IHRL's demands may satisfy the formal and substantive criteria set out above, but by hypothesis this set of property-law norms is not part of IHRL.

To help guide inquiry on the scope of IHRL, the fiduciary model appeals to its two intermediate regulative principles: non-instrumentalization and non-domination. It appeals to these principles within the context of the state-subject fiduciary relationship, a context in which legitimate state action must always be interpretable as action taken in the name of or on behalf of every agent subject to the state's power. This is the fiduciary theory's overarching criterion of legitimacy. We shall see below how this criterion and the theory's intermediary principles can guide deliberation toward the delineation of even notoriously open-textured social rights, such as the right to education. Taken together, Fuller's formal desiderata, the fiduciary theory's substantive criteria (integrity, formal moral equality, and solicitude), its intermediary principles of non-instrumentalization and non-domination, and its criterion of legitimacy can clarify which international norms qualify as human rights, as well as which human rights qualify as jus cogens.

Returning to the problem of distinguishing jus cogens norms, we see under the fiduciary model that the state's most general duty to secure legal order has within it a narrower duty to guarantee basic or fundamental security under the rule of law. Practices that arbitrarily kill or systematically dominate a state's subjects, as well as practices that infringe key aspects of the rule of law (such as corrupt adjudication), are prohibited by jus cogens under the fiduciary theory. To see by way of illustration how jus cogens norms might flow from the fiduciary model of the state, consider the peremptory prohibition against slavery. Let us assume that there is a state-subject fiduciary relationship, and that the fiduciary principle governing this relationship authorizes the state to secure legal order on behalf of every agent subject to state power. At a minimum, establishing legal order on behalf of every agent entails that each must have the possibility of acquiring rights that can enshrine and protect their respective interests; otherwise, such interests would be entirely vulnerable to the power and caprice of others. In other words, each agent must be treated as a person because each agent is an equally valid subject of the fiduciary authorization of public authority. As a principle of legality, the fiduciary principle must treat like cases alike.[92] Thus, the fiduciary principle has no capacity to discriminate arbitrarily between agents who, in virtue of the state-subject fiduciary relationship, enjoy equal status vis-à-vis the state as co-beneficiaries of the fiduciary principle's authorization of public authority.

Because slaves are denied the capacity to possess legal rights, a state that enforces slavery cannot claim to have secured legal order for the purpose of guaranteeing rights on behalf of each agent. It follows that if a state supports slavery, it does so in contravention of its most basic fiduciary obligation to ensure that each agent subject to its powers is regarded equally as a person capable of possessing legal rights. In other words, such a state would fail to satisfy the fiduciary theory's criterion of legitimacy: its slave regime is unintelligible as a regime established on behalf of the slave population. Because the fiduciary principle necessarily treats like cases alike and therefore regards every individual as an equal co-beneficiary of legal order, the fiduciary state must provide for every individual's secure and equal freedom. As a consequence, the fiduciary state is duty-bound to protect every individual against all forms of arbitrary discrimination (such as apartheid), and not just slavery.

In *The Heart of Human Rights,* Allen Buchanan claims that an indispensable requirement of the justification of international legal human rights is that such rights must be shown to "constrain sovereignty for the purpose of affirming and promoting the equal basic status of all people (the status egalitarian function)."[93] The fiduciary theory supplies a persuasive argument for this requirement by showing how every individual must be treated as an equal co-beneficiary of legal order. Under the fiduciary model, however, the idea of equal basic status is not an assumption of liberal political morality that law can serve instrumentally, as it is in Buchanan's account, but is rather a constitutive aspect of the sovereign authority international law delegates to states. Under Buchanan's theory, the ideal of equal basic status constrains sovereignty. Under the fiduciary theory, equal basic status emerges from the fiduciary principle's authorization of sovereign power, as the terms of that authorization require public powers to be held and exercised in a way that treats all as equals.

The fiduciary theory's formal and substantive criteria reveal that, as a legal conception of international norms, it is normatively substantial but metaphysically thin. The theory is normatively substantial because principles such as integrity, formal moral equality, and solicitude each have content that facilitates the specification and justification of international norms. But the theory is metaphysically thin because it does not affirm or presuppose a comprehensive conception of the good.[94] Nor does the fiduciary theory affirm or imply that individuals are in fact moral equals. As a legal conception, the fiduciary theory merely insists that for public institutions to act legally, they must regard individuals *as if* they were moral equals, because public institutions must regard all individuals as equal co-beneficiaries of legal order.

92. As H.L.A. Hart affirmed: "If we attach to a legal system the minimum meaning that it must consist of general rules . . . [T]his meaning connotes the principle of treating like cases alike." H.L.A. Hart, *Positivism and the Separation of Law and Morals, in* Essays in Jurisprudence and Philosophy 49, 81 (1983).

93. Buchanan, *supra* note 2, at 68.

94. *See, e.g.,* John Rawls, *The Idea of an Overlapping Consensus, in* John Rawls: Collected Papers 421, 424–25 (Samuel Freeman ed., 1999).

Public institutions must adopt this attitude because the fiduciary principle authorizes the state to secure legal order on behalf of every agent subject to it. Each agent is an equally valid subject of the fiduciary authorization of public authority, and because the fiduciary principle is a principle of legality, it must treat like cases alike. The fiduciary principle therefore has no capacity to discriminate arbitrarily between agents who, by virtue of the state-subject fiduciary relationship, enjoy equal status vis-à-vis the state as co-beneficiaries of public authority. Slavery and arbitrary discrimination are ruled out simply because the fiduciary principle cannot authorize such practices, which are inconsistent with the fiduciary principle that all agents are entitled to be treated as equal under the law—none of which presupposes or implies that individuals actually possess equal moral worth or equal dignity.

C. A Kantian Nonpositivist Conception

The nonpositivist credentials and relative thinness of the Kantian articulation of the fiduciary theory can be brought into relief by comparing it to John Rawls's political conception of international law. Rawls claims that a "law of peoples" can embrace "hierarchal" as well as liberal societies, so long as the hierarchical societies are "well-ordered."[95] Hierarchical societies are nonliberal in that they are organized by comprehensive religious, moral, or philosophical doctrines. Rawls asserts that part of what it means for a hierarchical society to be well ordered is for it to have a legal system "that takes impartially into account what it sees not unreasonably as the fundamental interests of all members of society."[96] A well-ordered hierarchical society must also respect an abridged catalog of "basic" human rights, as its legal system must be capable of imposing enforceable moral duties on persons within its territory, and could not do so if it violated those rights.[97]

Rawls argues that the moral presuppositions of well-orderedness are sufficiently thin that some hierarchical societies would be willing to accept them. The point is to distinguish tyrannical regimes that cannot be accepted into the "reasonable society of peoples" from other nonliberal societies that can.[98] The result is that liberal and (well-ordered) hierarchical societies can relate to one another on the basis of a stable and overlapping consensus conducive to a law of peoples. Although it is beyond the scope of this chapter to assess Rawls's law of peoples, three points are worth underscoring. The first is that the fiduciary theory, as a legal conception, resembles Rawls's theory in that it relies on a Kantian account of the right rather than a comprehensive conception of the good. Second, the fiduciary theory *explains why* rather than *assumes that* a well-ordered society cannot discriminate arbitrarily between individuals: it cannot do so because its institutions are under a fiduciary obligation to treat people even-handedly, as equal co-beneficiaries of the fiduciary state. Rather than assuming impartiality as an entrance condition into the "reasonable society of

95. John Rawls, *The Law of Peoples*, 20 Critical Inquiry 36, 37 (1993). A law of peoples is a "political conception of right and justice that applies to the principles and norms of international society." *Id.*

96. *Id.* at 51.

97. *Id.* at 52.

98. *Id.* at 37.

peoples," the fiduciary theory explains why impartiality participates directly in the constitution of human rights and jus cogens.

The third point is perhaps the most important: both Rawls's theory and the fiduciary theory trade on a moral space between pre-institutional natural rights and conventional rights, a domain we might call the normative space of legal order. For Rawls, if a state wishes to belong to the "reasonable society of peoples," it must be well ordered. For a state to be well ordered it must have a legal system capable of imposing enforceable moral duties, and a necessary condition of such a system is that it respect basic human rights. The requirement to respect human rights flows from an assumption that a failure to respect them would subvert a legal system's capacity to impose moral duties. Such a failure would thereby undercut the society's claim to well-orderedness and membership in the reasonable society of peoples. But whereas for Rawls the idea that states must respect human rights is a hypothetical imperative (if a state wants to be well ordered, it must respect human rights), under the fiduciary theory the imperative is categorical: the state must respect human rights because it has a fiduciary duty to do so.

Many philosophers reject the idea that there is normative space between natural (moral) rights and conventional (legal) rights, because they take these two categories to represent watertight compartments exhaustive of the domains within which rights operate. The rejection is present in the consequentialist account of rights defended by Wayne Sumner, but it is also present in the work of a number of natural rights theorists, including Simmons.[99] What unites Sumner and Simmons, despite the chasm that separates their substantive moral theories, is a commitment to the positivist idea that there is no necessary connection between law and morality; law is viewed as purely conventional, with no necessary grounding in or connection to morality.

The Kantian interpretation of the fiduciary theory, by contrast, affirms a nonpositivist framework in which law is necessarily connected to morality precisely because law is necessarily institutional. Human rights and jus cogens are the normative consequence of law's institutional nature because all legal institutions stand in a fiduciary relation to the persons subject to them. This relation is intrinsically both moral and legal in nature because its legality is explained by its distinctive internal morality. International norms, therefore, both occupy and partially constitute the normative space of legal order, and thus are part of legality's intrinsic morality. Because positivists such as Sumner and Simmons work within a rights paradigm defined by a hard distinction between the moral and the legal (a paradigm that implicitly rejects the distinctively normative space of legal order), and because positivism such as theirs dominates contemporary legal scholarship, it is not surprising that the fiduciary theory has gone (largely) unnoticed.

Now, a positivist could contend that legitimate or rights-respecting law must embody moral requirements, and so the fiduciary theory is not committed to nonpositivism because it can be interpreted to inform the legitimacy or rights-respecting conditions of legitimate or rights-respecting law.[100] The positivist interpretation, however, misses the sense in which, under the Kantian view to which

99. SUMNER, *supra* note 41, at 90–91; SIMMONS, *supra* note 86, at 186–94.

100. We thank James Nickel for suggesting this interpretation. In recent years, some positivists have denied that positivism is committed to the view that there is no necessary connection between law and morality. *See, e.g.*, John Gardner, *Legal Positivism: 5 1/2 Myths*, 46 AM. J. JURIS.

we subscribe, the form and substantive principles of fiduciary relations are intrinsic to them and constitutive of the legitimacy of those kinds of relations. On this view, there are no relevant moral requirements or legitimacy conditions external to fiduciary relations,[101] including the fiduciary relations that obtain between public authorities and their subjects. Indeed, for Kant, asymmetrical power relations, such as the parent-child relationship, are legitimate *only if* they assume the juridical form of fiduciary relations.

D. A Republican Conception

Let us consider now the sense in which the fiduciary theory of international norms is republican. It is republican because the fiduciary principle applies exclusively to relationships, including the state-subject relationship, in which the threat of the powerful dominating the vulnerable is always present, and domination is the evil republicanism opposes. One person dominates another to the extent that she has the capacity to interfere on an arbitrary basis in certain choices the other is in a position to make.[102] Domination is exemplified by the master-slave relationship in which the master can interfere arbitrarily with the choices of the slave. The master dominates the slave because she can command the slave with impunity, with no regard for the interests or opinions of the slave. Crucially, she dominates the slave whether she interferes with the slave or not. A constitutional legal authority guided by the rule of law, on the other hand, does not dominate its subjects. Although law interferes with an individual's choices by threatening sanctions, the threat of sanctions is not made on an arbitrary basis. Subjection to the rule of law is thus consistent with the republican ideal of non-domination, and indeed contributes to it as the rule of law limits the ability of the powerful to dominate the weak.

Fiduciary relations possess the form that relations of non-domination must assume whenever one party holds power over another, as they require the power-holder to act with due regard for the best interests of the beneficiary, taking into account his views and opinions. Philip Pettit gestures in this direction when he writes that if someone is able to interfere in another's affairs but only on condition that she further the other's interests and take his opinions seriously, the power-holder relates to the other "not as a master, but more in the fashion of an agent who enjoys a power of attorney" over the affairs of the other.[103] Agents are fiduciaries, and as such they are subject to other-regarding fiduciary duties that make domination impossible from a legal point of view. The threat of de facto domination is controlled de jure by the fiduciary principle.

Pettit rightly observes that the "abuse of human rights, and the existence of a power of such abuse, epitomizes domination; it means that those who are subject

199 (2001). Yet none, so far as we know, has attempted to reconcile positivism with Kant's understanding of law.

101. For discussion of this point and its connection to Kant's regulative ideal of external freedom, see Arthur Ripstein, Force and Freedom: Kant's Legal and Political Philosophy 71–81 (2009).

102. Philip Pettit, Republicanism: A Theory of Freedom and Government 52 (1997).

103. *Id.* at 23.

to such abuse live at the mercy of their actual or potential abusers, and under their effective control."[104] Conditions of non-domination, then, denote conditions in which the vulnerable are not at the mercy of the powerful. Because the fiduciary theory requires respect for human rights and jus cogens, it supports a framework of non-domination in which individuals subject to public power are protected against abuse. And because the fiduciary theory explains how respect for human rights and jus cogens can be demanded as a matter of law, it likewise explains how non-domination can operate as a legal principle as well as a political ideal.

Under the fiduciary theory, non-domination complements Kant's principle of non-instrumentalization in the following way. Whereas non-instrumentalization prohibits the state from wrongfully interfering with its subjects, non-domination bars the state from holding arbitrary power that ipso facto would pose a wrongful threat because it could be exercised wrongfully at any time. In other words, non-instrumentalization controls the actual exercise of power, while non-domination controls the omnipresent threat of its wrongful exercise, which is to say, the terms on which power is held and can be used. An implication of the control non-domination asserts over the possession of public power is that public institutions cannot become sectional instruments for treating certain classes of people as mere means to others' ends. The principle of non-domination embodies institutionally the principle of non-instrumentalization, and shows again why the fiduciary state is under a legal obligation to treat individuals as moral equals. In sum, the fiduciary theory is republican because it envisions international norms as intermediary legal precepts that shield vulnerable persons from both instrumentalization and domination, thereby providing for their independent agency.[105]

E. A Practical, Universal, and Aspirational Conception

We can now set out the related senses in which the fiduciary theory is practical, universal, and aspirational. It is practical because it takes seriously the practice of IHRL and jus cogens on its own terms, finding a place for both dignity and the view that human rights, as Beitz puts it, "are standards appropriate to the institutions of modern or modernizing societies coexisting in a global political economy in which human beings face a series of predictable threats."[106] The normative grounds of such rights are universal in that they derive from the idea that public institutions must always relate to the people subject to them on a basis of non-domination and non-instrumentalization. Human rights and jus cogens norms are the concrete embodiments of these principles, and as such they promise the emancipation and independence of those who suffer oppression. The fiduciary theory thereby casts international norms as the aspirational demands of a political program in the service of the vulnerable.

104. Philip Pettit, *A Republican Law of Peoples*, 8 EUR. J. POL. THEORY 70, 88 (2010).

105. For an argument that republicans should "connect the idea of domination to a basic set of vulnerabilities," see Simon Hope, *Republicanism and Human Rights: A Plausible Combination?*, 21 CAMBRIDGE REV. INT'L AFF. 367, 379–81 (2008).

106. Beitz, *supra* note 36, at 44.

F. A Deliberative Conception

The final aspect of the theory we sketch is its deliberative character. Allen Buchanan, Rainer Forst, and Amartya Sen have each grounded human rights in deliberative practices of public reasoning.[107] Buchanan, for example, argues that international human rights institutions have important epistemic functions in that they contribute to the specification of the content of human rights norms by both fact-finding and providing a public deliberative forum for their ongoing development and interpretation.[108] These open and inclusive deliberative practices legitimate human rights in a way that mitigates the risk of human rights assuming parochial cultural biases. We endorse this view. Although it is well beyond the scope of this chapter to set out the appropriate relationship between democratic deliberation and human rights, we indicate briefly how and why the fiduciary model can bring democratic deliberation into its fold.

The idea of a state-subject fiduciary relationship requires open deliberation to the extent feasible because this relationship is the legal expression of popular sovereignty, the idea that the state's sovereignty belongs to the people subject to sovereign power. A state that facilitates inclusive public deliberation over human rights, soliciting public input and providing reasoned justifications for laws and policies, demonstrates an appropriate solicitude for the legitimate interests of citizens and noncitizens. Such a state acknowledges, as Forst puts it, that "there is at least *one* fundamental moral demand that no culture or society may reject: the unconditional claim to be respected as someone who deserves to be given justifying reasons for the actions, rules, or structures to which he or she is subject."[109] Conversely, a state that does not support or engage in public deliberation and reasoned justification ordinarily fails to take seriously the dignity of legal subjects by reserving for itself the capacity to treat citizens and noncitizens arbitrarily, raising the specter of domination. Thus, public deliberation performs an indispensable legitimating function within the state-subject fiduciary relation as an expression of the state's respect for its subjects' dignity and independent agency.[110]

Buchanan summarizes nicely the main procedural constraints under which deliberation over human rights ought to occur:

> [I]nstitutions that contribute to the articulation of human rights norms ought to provide venues for deliberation in which the authority of good reasons is recognized, in which credible efforts are made to reduce the risk that strategic

107. Rainer Forst, The Right to Justification (2011); Buchanan, *supra* note 36; Amartya Sen, *Elements of a Theory of Human Rights*, 32 Phil. & Pub. Aff. 315 (2004); *see also* Michael Ignatieff, Human Rights as Politics and Idolatry 84 (2001) ("The fundamental moral commitment entailed by rights is not to respect, and certainly not to worship. It is to deliberation.").

108. Buchanan, *supra* note 36, at 61–65.

109. Forst, *supra* note 107, at 209.

110. *See* Henry S. Richardson, Democratic Autonomy: Public Reasoning About the Ends of Policy 242–46 (2002). We recognize that public deliberation and justification may be constrained to some extent by limited public resources, and that national security and other compelling interests may necessitate a measure of governmental secrecy. To the extent that states rely on such constraints, however, the fiduciary principle dictates that they must justify

> bargaining or raw power will displace rational deliberation, in which principled contestation of alternative views is encouraged, in which no points of view are excluded on the basis of prejudicial attitudes toward those who voice them, and in which conclusions about human rights are consistent with the foundational idea that there are moral rights that human beings (now) have, independent of whether they are recognized by any legal system.[111]

Deliberation under the fiduciary theory would take IHRL as its provisional starting point because the rights enshrined therein are broadly conducive to independent agency. Deliberative inquiry would be guided prospectively by the substantive principles that are constitutive of the state-subject fiduciary relation itself. Perhaps the most basic of these principles is the idea that persons must be regarded as moral equals, and thus are entitled to institutions supportive of their secure and equal freedom. Other more specific principles include those we have canvassed above: integrity, formal moral equality, solicitude, and equal security under the rule of law. Each of these principles should inform both the substantive content and deliberative process of human rights development, helping to traverse the normative terrain that lies between dignity and specific human rights as applied in particular political communities, a terrain these principles share with the ideal of independence.[112]

V. THE QUESTIONS REVISITED

Earlier we listed several questions that any credible theory of human rights and jus cogens must be able to address in a principled way. As noted, some of these questions are specific to human rights (including peremptory human rights), and others relate to the combined sets of human rights and jus cogens norms, whereas others still are specific to jus cogens norms (some but not all of which are also human rights). In some cases the argument can be just sketched or put by way of illustration, but the fiduciary theory yields principled guidance to all of them.

A. In What Sense Are Human Rights *Rights*?

The fiduciary theory views human rights as the consequence of persons' moral capacity as self-determining agents to place public institutions under legal obligations. Human rights protect individuals against state domination and instrumentalization by entitling all persons to be treated in certain ways by public institutions as a matter of right. Human rights are thus claim-rights against public authorities. As a matter of international law, jus cogens norms are trumps, whereas derogable human rights have presumptive force in that an adequate public justification must be offered if a state wishes to restrict their exercise.

the limits of public deliberation and justification based on reasonable, public-regarding factors, thereby ensuring that citizens and noncitizens are not subject to domination.

111. Buchanan, *supra* note 36, at 62.

112. The fiduciary theory thus arguably supports efforts to synthesize substantive principles and deliberative procedure in democratic theory. *See* AMY GUTMANN & DENNIS THOMPSON, WHY DELIBERATIVE DEMOCRACY? 95–124 (2004) (reviewing and challenging arguments for separating deliberative procedures from substantive principles).

B. Do Human Rights Constitute Legal Rights, as Distinguished from Moral or Political Rights?

Human rights are legal rights because they are constitutive of the state's legal authority to provide security and legal order as a fiduciary of the people subject to its power. They are legal rights correlative to the state's fiduciary (and therefore legal) duty to establish legal order on behalf of those people. A state that fails to respect human rights transgresses international law's fiduciary authorization of state sovereignty, an authorization that flows from the fiduciary principle, which is itself a principle of legality.

C. How Does the Fiduciary Theory Provide Guidance for Identifying International Norms, Distinguishing Peremptory from Nonperemptory Norms, and Clarifying Their Scope?

The fiduciary theory aids in identifying international norms by prescribing formal and substantive principles as well as a criterion of legitimacy for distinguishing genuine international norms from counterfeits. According to the fiduciary theory, all such norms serve a common purpose: to protect persons subject to state authority from domination and instrumentalization. Norms may qualify as human rights or jus cogens if they further these objectives and satisfy the fiduciary theory's substantive criteria of integrity, formal moral equality, and solicitude. For norms to qualify further as non-derogable jus cogens, their infringement must always be inconsistent with the state's fiduciary duty to secure legal order on behalf of every person subject to it, which is to say, their infringement would necessarily compromise the entitlement of individuals to basic security under the rule of law.

These substantive criteria offer a practical, principled framework for clarifying the content and legal force of international norms. Human rights such as freedom of expression and the right to work satisfy the basic criteria for human rights because they are consistent with the principles of integrity, formal moral equality, and solicitude.[113] Other human rights such as the prohibitions against genocide and slavery likewise satisfy these three substantive criteria, but they also qualify as peremptory norms because their violation could never be consistent with the state's fiduciary obligation to safeguard individuals' fundamental security under the rule of law. As these examples attest, the fiduciary theory bolsters the determinacy of IHRL and enables states to specify genuine human rights while distinguishing peremptory norms from ordinary, derogable human rights.

The fiduciary theory also helps to elucidate the scope of particular human rights. Consider once again the much-debated prohibition against torture. In the leading judicial decision on the torture prohibition, *Ireland v. United Kingdom*,[114] the European Court of Human Rights (ECHR) has asserted that torture can be distinguished from cruel, inhuman, and degrading treatment (CIDT) and other

113. The ICCPR and ICESCR provide that freedom of expression, the right to work, and various other human rights are subject to state derogation under certain circumstances. *See* ICCPR, *supra* note 21, arts. 4 & 19(2)–(3); ICESCR, *supra* note 22, arts. 4 & 7.

114. Ireland v. United Kingdom, 25 Eur. Ct. H.R. (ser. A) at 66 (1978).

abusive acts based on the relative "intensity of the suffering inflicted."[115] According to the ECHR, the prohibition against torture captures only the most heinous acts of "cruelty"—those that impose mental or physical suffering of "particular intensity."[116] This vision of torture and CIDT as distinct zones of wrongfulness along an ascending scale of pain and suffering has dominated human rights discourse since the 1970s.[117] But states have found the ECHR's ascending-scale test to be extraordinarily difficult to apply in practice. There is little agreement among courts and publicists about how states should measure the pain or suffering caused by a particular practice, let alone where they should draw the lines between torture, CIDT, and other types of mistreatment.[118] As a consequence, human rights advocates have struggled to explain why the pain and suffering imposed by waterboarding, hanging by the wrists, sleep deprivation, and other enhanced interrogation practices should be considered sufficiently "severe" to trigger the prohibition against torture.

The fiduciary theory draws the prohibitions against torture and CIDT into sharper relief. According to the fiduciary theory's principle of non-instrumentalization, any use of physical or mental violence that treats the individual as a mere means to the state's ends qualifies as CIDT. Thus, enhanced interrogation techniques such as waterboarding, hanging by the wrists, and prolonged sleep deprivation all qualify as CIDT under the fiduciary theory. Before we may label such practices "torture," however, we must consider an additional inquiry. Whereas the CIDT prohibition addresses the principle of non-instrumentalization generally, the torture prohibition targets a critical subset of CIDT in which the state deliberately inflicts mental or physical suffering for the purpose of breaking a subject's will in order to conscript the subject as a means to accomplish an end the subject does not share with the state.[119] For example, public officials engage in torture when they use violence to extract intelligence or coerce confessions from detainees.[120] The torture prohibition is also triggered when public officials intentionally inflict pain and suffering to compel subjects to renounce human rights such as their freedoms of expression, association, or religion.[121] Whatever the state's purpose may be, the fiduciary theory suggests that torture is distinguishable

115. *Id.* ¶ 167.

116. *Id.*

117. *See, e.g.*, Prosecutor v. Brdanin, Case No. IT-99-36-T, Judgment (Sept. 1, 2004), ¶ 483 (ICTY) ("The seriousness of the pain or suffering sets torture apart from other forms of mistreatment.").

118. *See id.* ¶ 484 (considering objective factors such as the "nature, purpose, and consistency of the acts committed," and subjective factors such as "the physical or mental condition of the victim, the effect of the treatment," and "the victim's age, sex, state of health, and position of inferiority"); Gail H. Miller, Defining Torture 2, 8 (2005) (observing that it is "virtually impossible to quantify 'severe pain and suffering' or to define it in absolute terms").

119. *Cf.* David Sussman, *What's Wrong with Torture?*, 33 Phil. & Pub. Aff. 1, 4 (2004) (arguing that the unique harm of torture is that it "forces its victim into the position of colluding against himself through his own affects and emotions, so that he experiences himself as simultaneously powerless and yet actively complicit in his own violation").

120. CAT, *supra* note 23, art. 1(1).

121. *Id.; see also* David Luban, *Liberalism, Torture, and the Ticking Bomb*, 91 Va. L. Rev. 425, 433–36 (2005) (discussing these and other purposes).

from CIDT based on the state's means to achieve its purpose—the conscription of a subject against her will through the illicit use of violence—rather than the relative "severity" or "intensity" of the subject's pain and suffering.[122] One important consequence of this definition is that public officials who deliberately inflict pain or suffering in any degree for the purpose of extracting information from unwilling subjects (whether through waterboarding, prolonged sleep deprivation, or any other enhanced interrogation technique) violate the prohibition against torture.

Viewed in this light, the fiduciary theory confirms and clarifies much of the CAT's definition of torture, but disputes one element. Under the fiduciary theory, the intentional infliction of "pain and suffering, whether mental or physical," constitutes torture if it is intentionally inflicted "by or at the instigation of or with the consent or acquiescence of a public official" for the purpose of breaking a subject's will in order to conscript the subject as a means to the state's ends.[123] Consistent with the CAT, torture may involve physical or mental harm, and it must have a nexus to "the instigation of or the consent or acquiescence of a public official or other person acting in an official capacity."[124] As the ECHR observes in *Ireland*, however, the CAT stipulates that an act constitutes torture only if it results in "*severe* pain and suffering."[125] On the fiduciary theory, acts of torture are not to be defined by the *degree* of pain or suffering inflicted—whether measured objectively or subjectively—but instead by the torturer's illicit *purpose* for inflicting pain and suffering: the conscription of a victim's will.[126] The fiduciary theory thus offers a principled framework for clarifying and critiquing the scope and content of the international prohibition against torture.

The conception of torture we propose should not be misconstrued to diminish the importance of the prohibition against CIDT, which also qualifies as a peremptory norm under the fiduciary theory. Any treatment of a detainee that is cruel, inhuman, or degrading violates the fiduciary principles of non-instrumentalization and non-domination by communicating the victim's "total subordination" to his or her captor.[127] Under the CAT, states already bear obligations to prevent CIDT

122. This principle is reflected obliquely in CAT article 1(1), which provides that torture "does not include pain or suffering"—however intense—that is not purposeful but merely "incidental to lawful sanctions." CAT, *supra* note 23, art. 1(1).

123. *Id.*

124. *Id.*

125. *Id.* (emphasis added).

126. Article 1 of the CAT provides in part that at an act will count as torture if it consists in the intentional infliction of pain or suffering "on a person for such purposes as . . . punishing him for an act he or a third person has committed or is suspected of having committed." Admittedly, torture conducted for this purpose, or merely to satisfy the sadism of the abuser, does not conform neatly to the conscription theory, as the "punished" victim may be wholly passive, with nothing specifically asked of him. Nonetheless, to the extent that the wrongdoing official purports to be engaged in an act of lawful punishment, he implicitly conscripts the victim to be part of a sham, as torture is an infliction of lawless violence rather than punishment. In the case of the pure sadist, the victim is deliberately conscripted *to be a victim*, a conscription that remains salient even if the sadist seeks nothing more than his prisoner's victimization.

127. *See* David Luban, Torture, Power, and Law 128–36 (2014) (articulating a communicative theory of torture and arguing that most, if not all, CIDT qualifies as torture).

in territory under their jurisdiction.[128] The fiduciary theory suggests further that the international community should adopt more robust legal safeguards against CIDT—including, for example, extending the CAT's non-refoulement obligation to cover individuals who could face CIDT abroad.[129] Even if torture can be distinguished from CIDT based on the distinctive moral harm that torture entails—the infliction of pain and suffering to conscript the victim's will in service of the torturer's ends—the level of legal protection afforded to individuals under these peremptory prohibitions should be the same.

The fiduciary theory affirms that states cannot justify acts of torture by invoking state necessity or citing their failure to ratify human rights treaties. The prohibition on torture is peremptory because states are never authorized to torture their subjects—not even when other lives may hang in the balance—as the fiduciary principle entitles all subjects to be treated as coequal beneficiaries under the rule of law. To permit a state to instrumentalize any subject through violence for the benefit of others would eviscerate the fiduciary authorization of state legal authority. For this reason, the fiduciary theory dictates that torture can never be justified under the rule of law, irrespective of whether perceived state necessity or national lawmakers would dictate otherwise.

Whereas the catalog of human rights that are part of IHRL is relatively well defined on account of the many universal and regional treaties that enshrine them, as indicated above, the list of peremptory norms is much more controversial. The interpretive side of the fiduciary theory affirms as jus cogens the norms set out in the *Restatement* (the prohibitions against genocide, slavery, murder or disappearance, torture or CIDT, prolonged arbitrary detention, systematic racial discrimination, and military aggression). But perhaps more significant, its prescriptive side allows it both to pick out certain norms as jus cogens that are not usually qualified as such, and to disqualify others that typically figure in catalogs of peremptory norms.

The fiduciary theory challenges conventional wisdom by excluding the venerable norm against piracy from the ranks of jus cogens.[130] Article 15 of the Convention on the High Seas, which is widely recognized as customary international law, defines piracy in relevant part as "illegal acts of violence, detention or any act of depredation, committed for *private* ends by the crew or passengers of a *private* ship or *private* aircraft."[131] Although such private acts may be illegal under international law, they are not violations of jus cogens because they do not in and of themselves address the limits of sovereign authority in the state-subject fiduciary relationship. To merit recognition as a peremptory norm, the international norm against piracy would have to be repackaged as a constraint on state authority satisfying the fiduciary theory's

128. *See* CAT, *supra* note 23, art. 16.

129. *See id.* art. 3 ("No State Party shall expel, return ('refouler') or extradite a person to another State where there are substantial grounds for believing that he would be in danger of being subjected to torture."); *see also* LUBAN, *supra* note 127, at 128–36 (proposing a broader definition of torture that would encompass CIDT).

130. *See* IAN BROWNLIE, PRINCIPLES OF PUBLIC INTERNATIONAL LAW 489 (6th ed. 2003) (characterizing the rule prohibiting piracy as jus cogens).

131. Convention on the High Seas, art. 15, Apr. 29, 1958, 13 U.S.T. 2312, 450 U.N.T.S. 82 (emphasis added).

formal and substantive criteria. This might be accomplished, for example, by shifting the piracy prohibition's focus from pure private conduct to state-sponsored or state-condoned piracy—practices tantamount to aggression.[132] Absent a clear nexus to the state-subject fiduciary relationship, however, the prohibition against piracy is best classified as a common crime.

The fiduciary theory also challenges conventional wisdom by recognizing as peremptory basic rights of due process and the prohibition on corruption. Beginning with due process, the fiduciary conception of state sovereignty demands that states afford all individuals the fundamental procedural protections of due process. International instruments such as the Universal Declaration and the ICCPR have long recognized that states must employ certain minimal procedures to safeguard human life and liberty from arbitrary deprivation, including the right to notice of criminal charges, an opportunity to be heard and to present evidence, and adjudication by an independent and impartial tribunal.[133] As international criminal law has matured over the past two decades, these fundamental due process norms have been codified as mandatory procedural rules for international criminal tribunals,[134] and a few scholars have asserted that due process should be recognized as a peremptory norm.[135]

The fiduciary theory supports classifying due process as a peremptory norm. A state transgresses its general fiduciary duty of solicitude and the principle of non-instrumentalization when it deprives individuals of life or liberty without employing decision-making procedures that are sufficiently robust to minimize the risk of a biased, arbitrary, or otherwise unfair hearing. What due process demands in a particular proceeding will turn upon contextual factors,[136] though some basic features of a fair hearing are clearly indispensable in all cases, such as the need for an impartial adjudicator. The basic attributes of a fair hearing protect individuals against arbitrary or self-serving government action and are integral to the state's fiduciary obligation to secure the rule of law. As such, they cannot admit derogation even during national emergencies, lest the state abdicate its fundamental fiduciary role.[137]

132. Lord McNair, The Law of Treaties 214–15 (1961) ("Can there by any doubt that a treaty whereby two States agreed to permit piracy in a certain area, or against the merchant ships of a certain State, with impunity, would be null and void?").

133. *See, e.g.*, UDHR, *supra* note 18, art. 10 (proclaiming the right to a fair and public hearing in an independent and impartial tribunal).

134. *See* Gregory S. Gordon, *Toward an International Criminal Procedure: Due Process Aspirations and Limitations*, 45 Colum. J. Transnat'l L. 635, 641–70 (2007) (chronicling these developments).

135. *See, e.g.*, Orakhelashvili, *supra* note 45, at 60 (describing "due process" as a peremptory norm). *But see* Michael Byers, Book Review, 101 Am. J. Int'l L. 913, 916 (2007) (asserting that "due process guarantees and the right to a fair trial" are "derogable").

136. *See, e.g.*, Mathews v. Eldridge, 424 U.S. 319, 335 (1976) (defining due process under the U.S. Constitution to require a multifactor balancing test).

137. See Chapter 6 for discussion of the requirements of due process in the context of war-on-terror detention.

The international norm against state corruption has received even less attention as a candidate for peremptory status.[138] This oversight cannot be explained away on the ground that public corruption is a lesser evil than other grave abuses of state power. To cite but one example, human rights observers in Angola chronicled "the disappearance of over four billion dollars from the public coffers [between 1997 and 2002,] an amount 'roughly equal to the total amount spent on the humanitarian, social, health, and education needs of a population in severe distress.'"[139] Such brazen kleptocracy undermines the very governmental institutions that are charged with preserving legal order and jeopardizes the physical security and liberty of nationals who depend on government assistance for relief from violence, starvation, and disease.

Viewed from the fiduciary theory's perspective, the international norm against public corruption merits peremptory authority within international law. The prohibition against self-dealing meets the fiduciary theory's substantive criteria by advancing the best interests of the people rather than state officials (*integrity*), refusing to privilege certain private interests over others arbitrarily (*formal moral equality*), and manifesting due regard for the interests of its beneficiaries (*solicitude*). The anticorruption norm also satisfies the specific substantive criteria because it requires the state to treat its national patrimony (e.g., tax revenue, resources, public services) as a public good to which every national has an equal claim under the rule of law and relevant municipal legislation. Like the prohibitions against summary execution and torture, the prohibition against corruption is necessary to ensure that the state regards its nationals as ends in themselves and never merely as means for the ends of others. More broadly still, there can be no derogation from the norm against corruption because corruption is the antithesis of the other-regarding mandate the fiduciary state enjoys to secure legal order. For these reasons, the fiduciary theory elevates the international norm against public corruption to the status of non-derogable jus cogens.[140]

Recognizing the norm against public corruption as a peremptory norm illuminates an important feature of jus cogens itself; that is, that peremptory norms track a particular quality of wrong rather than a quantity of harm. Public corruption offends the state-subject fiduciary relation irrespective of whether the corrupt acts are large or small in scope: a low-level public official who steals a pittance or

138. A few scholars have argued that wide-scale public corruption should be considered an international crime against humanity, suggesting by implication that the norm should be treated as peremptory. *See, e.g.*, Sonja B. Starr, *Extraordinary Crimes at Ordinary Times: International Justice Beyond Crisis Situations*, 101 Nw. U. L. Rev. 1257, 1297 (2007) ("Given the massive suffering caused . . . grand corruption seems to amount to a paradigmatic example of what should be considered an international crime.").

139. Starr, *supra* note 138, at 1283 (quoting Human Rights Watch, Some Transparency, No Accountability: The Use of Oil Revenue in Angola and Its Impact on Human Rights (2004), http://www.hrw.org/en/reports/2004/01/12/some-transparency-no-accountability); *see also* Ndiva Kofele-Kale, *The Right to a Corruption-Free Society as an Individual and Collective Human Right: Elevating Official Corruption to a Crime Under International Law*, 34 Int'l Law. 149, 161–63 (2000) (reviewing comparable examples of public corruption in Nigeria and the former Republic of Zaire).

140. Note that recognition of public corruption as a peremptory norm arguably renders Article 50 of the VCLT superfluous, as "the corruption of [a State's] representative" under Article 50 would render a treaty provision invalid under Article 53. VCLT, *supra* note 3, art. 50.

accepts a petty bribe violates the peremptory norm against corruption, just as a head of state violates jus cogens by draining the state treasury for private gain. The prohibition against corruption thus illustrates that the scope of jus cogens is not limited to acts such as military aggression or genocide that inflict harm on a massive scale. Violations of peremptory norms such as the prohibitions against corruption and torture are necessarily wrongful and legally impermissible on any scale.

D. What Is the Relationship between International Norms and State Lawmaking Authority?

Because human rights and jus cogens constitute, as well as constrain, state legal authority, states must comply with these norms whether they consent to them or not. Deliberative inquiry under the fiduciary theory takes as its starting point the idea that a state may not wantonly disregard human rights and jus cogens through the exercise of its lawmaking authority, because to do so would violate its fiduciary obligation to treat subjects as equal co-beneficiaries under the rule of law. So under the fiduciary theory, states must comply with all jus cogens norms regardless of whether they have persistently objected to some (or all) of them. But state lawmaking authority is also constrained by derogable human rights, where applicable. Although all such norms are subject to local deliberation and adjustment so as to reconcile them with local cultural and legal traditions without compromise to principle, states qua sovereign entities must align their lawmaking with international norms as the authority implicit to their lawmaking power depends on them doing so with a reasonable degree of success. We discuss further the complex relationship between international and national law in Chapter 8.

E. Do Human Rights Generate Positive Duties, Such as a Duty to Provide Education, in Addition to Negative Duties of Non-Interference?

The controversy in moral and political philosophy over positive duties roughly tracks disputes in human rights law over economic, social, and cultural rights ("economic rights").[141] Positive duties are those that typically require positive action and impose costs or burdens on the duty-bearer. In moral and political philosophy, libertarians hold that individuals have rights to bodily integrity and property, but these are said to give rise to only negative duties of non-interference that impose no cost on their bearers. For Robert Nozick and others, contract is the only legitimate source of positive duties.[142] The imposition of non-contractual positive obligations

141. Economic rights are also frequently challenged on the grounds that the judiciary would have to enforce them, and that judges lack institutional competence and democratic authorization to assess economic and social policy. For discussion and replies to this argument, see, e.g., Nickel, *supra* note 41, at 142–44; Patrick Macklem, Indigenous Difference and the Constitution of Canada (2001).

142. *See* Robert Nozick, Anarchy, State and Utopia (1974); Richard Epstein, Takings: Private Property and the Power of Eminent Domain (1985); Loren Lomasky, Persons, Rights and the Moral Community (1987).

is alleged to violate the liberty or property rights of the duty-bearer, whereas negative duties are consistent with those rights because they require only that the duty-bearer refrain from interfering with others.

In human rights law, libertarians typically support civil and political rights because these rights protect bodily integrity, liberty, and property. Libertarians claim that the state can respect these rights through self-restraint alone and without imposing redistributive costs on others.[143] Economic rights, on the other hand, are seen as suspect because they require positive state action and do imply redistributive costs. Defenders of economic rights counter that civil and political rights, such as the right to due process, also require positive state action and may be just as expensive to secure as some economic rights.[144] Yet libertarians insist that positive state action to guarantee civil and political rights is distinguishable from measures that effectively require wealth transfers from the well-off to the disadvantaged: the well-off benefit directly from the presence of universal civil and political rights, whereas in the case of wealth transfers, they receive no direct benefit. It is not the cost per se that bothers the libertarian, but that the cost of economic rights is paid by one party in favor of another who is alleged to have no claim to the transferred resources.

The Kantian interpretation of the fiduciary theory offers a fresh, if surprising, rejoinder to the libertarian's concern. The rejoinder may be surprising because Kant's theory of right is coldly indifferent to needs and interests. Within Kant's theory there is no duty of easy rescue because the imposition of such as duty would let the need (even the urgent need) of the rescuee unilaterally set the terms of interaction with the rescuer. In the absence of a legal relationship capable of sustaining positive duties, the only duties that exist under Kant's theory are the negative ones of non-interference cherished by libertarians. These are the only general and reciprocal duties that can be owed equally by all so as to respect the bodily integrity and property of others; they are the only kinds of general and reciprocal duties that can let everyone enjoy an equal freedom in which no party can impose terms unilaterally on another. Libertarians happily concede that the state is entitled to enforce these duties as well as positive obligations arising from contract: both kinds of duties are necessary to respect the rights and equal freedom of separate persons. What libertarians have overlooked is that fiduciary relations, like contractual relations, give rise to positive duties, as demonstrated by the parent-child case. Although Kant's theory does not impose a duty of easy rescue on strangers, it does impose this obligation on parents, and it imposes on other fiduciaries positive duties of a similar nature.

As a fiduciary, the state is under an obligation to secure its subjects' independence. To the extent that the economic rights set out in the ICESCR are necessary to protect agents from instrumentalization and domination, the state is under an obligation to respect, protect and fulfill them. To see how such duties may arise under

143. *See, e.g.*, Cranston, *supra* note 85.

144. *See, e.g.*, Nickel, *supra* note 41, at 148–49; Donnelly, *supra* note 1, at 30–32. Proponents of economic rights also claim that these rights, like civil and political rights, have a negative dimension, though it is the redistributive effect of the positive side of economic rights that makes them so controversial. *See, e.g.*, Donnelly, *supra* note 1, at 30.

the fiduciary theory, consider the right to education.[145] Article 13 of the ICESCR provides for a universal right to education that includes compulsory and publicly funded primary education. Secondary and higher education is to be made available to all and accessible by the progressive introduction of free education. Within a modern state with complex rules of private law and public law, an individual lacking in literacy and civic education would depend on the grace of others to know her legal rights. Although those educated others, like the beneficent slave master, might never abuse their power, they would necessarily dominate anyone forced to depend on them for want of education. Furthermore, the illiterate would be unable to access public offices, participate in public debates, or otherwise engage democratic processes that presuppose literacy and civic education. Because the fiduciary conception of the state views its subjects as agents of coequal status, it must provide the resources necessary for them to be able to know their rights and participate in political life on an equal footing. A necessary feature of this capability is education, and so the fiduciary state is under an obligation to provide it.[146] The libertarian citizen can be asked to contribute a fair share because the state on which he relies for liberty and property can retain its legitimacy only by complying with its fiduciary duty to provide education.

To put the point within the human rights vocabulary of "respect, protect, and fulfill," it is not enough for states to respect the right to education by refusing to interfere with private education schemes. Nor is it enough for states to protect the right if this means only that states will prosecute third parties who interfere with others' enjoyment of the right to education. States must actually fulfill the right so as to provide subjects with coequal legal and political status, and to secure them against dependence on others. States must do this because all state action must be authorized by the fiduciary principle on behalf of everyone subject to the state's power, and the fiduciary principle cannot authorize states to create a kind of order in which some are entirely dependent on the choices of others.

The fiduciary theory's injunction against dependence or domination has implications that extend beyond the right to education. The theory supports a right to minimal resources broadly consistent with the right to "an adequate standard of living" enshrined in Article 11 of the ICESCR. The state's fulfillment of this right is necessary to ensure that the propertyless are not left to depend for their survival on the charity of others. The same rationale applies to the right to public healthcare (Article 12 of the ICESCR); fiduciary states must fulfill this right because a failure to do so would place the disadvantaged ill at the mercy of others.

145. Our discussion is indebted to Arthur Ripstein's analysis of how a right to publicly funded education and poverty relief flows from Kant's legal and political theory. *See* RIPSTEIN, *supra* note 101, ch. 9.

146. Although we do not explore the link here, the fiduciary theory is congenial to the "capabilities" approach to freedom defended by Amartya Sen and Martha Nussbaum, one that stresses the importance of persons' capabilities to "lead the kind of lives they value—and have reason to value." AMARTYA SEN, DEVELOPMENT AS FREEDOM 18 (1999); *see also* Martha Nussbaum, *Nature, Function and Capability: Aristotle on Political Distribution*, *in* OXFORD STUDIES IN ANCIENT PHILOSOPHY (1988). The relevant capabilities, under the fiduciary theory, are those necessary to lead lives free of domination and instrumentalization.

A skeptic might think that the fiduciary theory is too demanding. James Nickel, for example, affirms that economic rights are human rights, but suggests that their scope should "aim at preventing the terrible rather than achieving the best."[147] One might think that the idea of progressive realization set out under Article 2.1 of the ICESCR goes too far by requiring states to "take steps . . . to the maximum of available resources, with a view to achieving progressively the full realization of the rights recognized in the present Covenant."[148] The fiduciary theory, however, supplies a principled benchmark against which to assess whether economic rights have attained "full realization": such rights are fully realized if their enjoyment permits agents to lead lives marked by independence rather than domination. In the case of education in developed countries, this would mean, at a minimum, equal access to free primary and secondary education. The implication of this right is that the state is entitled to assess and collect taxes to pay for basic public education, because without such education many individuals would be dependent upon others in a manner that would violate the principle of non-domination. But because an individual need not become a professional to enjoy independence, students might properly be expected to contribute to professional post-secondary education, provided that such education remains accessible to all. The fiduciary theory is thus consistent with the prevailing view that human rights establish a minimal threshold rather than a complete theory of distributive justice, though the threshold is set comparatively high.

F. Do International Norms Generate Duties for Both State and Nonstate Actors?

Under the fiduciary theory, any entity that exercises public powers assumes a fiduciary obligation to respect human rights and jus cogens. States have special obligations because international law confers upon them the primary legal authority to establish security and legal order within their territory. But sovereign states are not the only entities that may exercise public administrative powers. In many areas of the world, nonstate actors exercise administrative powers comparable to those of conventional sovereign states. The fiduciary principle dictates that any entity exercising non-consensual administrative powers over individuals—whether it be an international body such as the U.N. Interim Administration for East Timor, a subnational government such as the State of New York, or a political/paramilitary group such as Hezbollah—bears a fiduciary obligation to honor human rights and jus cogens.

Implicit to this extension of the fiduciary principle, other things being equal, is recognition of the international legitimacy of nonstate actors that possess state-like powers and comply with international norms. Although by hypothesis such actors do not enjoy a state's territorial sovereignty, they nonetheless exercise sovereign-like powers over individuals, and thus are properly subject to international law. This reveals that although international law holds the distribution of territorial sovereignty within its purview, as discussed in Chapter 2, the fundamental conception of sovereignty it embodies is *personal* rather than territorial, a theme to which we return in Chapters 6 and 7.

147. Nickel, *supra* note 41, at 36, 140.

148. ICESCR, *supra* note 22, art. 2.1.

G. Are Human Rights and Jus Cogens Culturally Relative or Universal?

On the fiduciary theory, international norms are provisional legal norms of universal application within and across institutionalized societies. These norms are of "universal" application in that some of them, such as the torture prohibition, apply to every human being, whereas others apply to everyone falling within the stipulated class of right-holder, such as women and children. Yet others attach universally to certain kinds of groups, such as the right of all peoples to self-determination. Such norms are provisional because they are subject to ongoing amendment and refinement pursuant to democratic deliberation, a deliberative process both structured and guided by the ideal of independence.

Several features of this conception of international norms mitigate concerns about Western parochialism. First, the conception is limited to addressing threats of instrumentalization and domination, with a special emphasis on those posed by the salient and ubiquitous institutions found in every state today. It does not impose its more institutional norms on traditional societies that lack the relevant threat-posing institutions. For example, the fiduciary conception does not require traditional aboriginal societies that rely on restorative justice mechanisms to provide a public defender for what might be a criminal trial in a formal Western legal system. General fiduciary obligations can be institutionalized in very different ways in different contexts. The fiduciary theory universalizes agents' independence, but it is democratic and sensitive to local conditions at the point of interpretation and application.

The deliberative, democratic aspect of the fiduciary theory, as indicated earlier, also mitigates the threat of Western bias by inviting representatives of traditional or non-Western societies to participate in the development of human rights law. Relying on democratic deliberation necessarily raises the difficult issue of who is to decide controversial disputes when general norms appear to stand in tension with local tradition. Still, there is no obvious reason to think that this issue would prove any more intractable in international relations than in the democratic politics of multinational states; in both cases, minorities exist and are entitled to a fair opportunity to participate, one that includes protection from majoritarian domination. And in both, the participation of minorities lends (or would lend) legitimacy to the process and its outcomes.

Finally, the fiduciary concept resonates with analogous legal concepts found in non-Western societies. Legal scholars have traced the fiduciary concept as far back as the Code of Hammurabi in Ancient Mesopotamia (present-day Iraq), and have shown that the idea of fiduciary obligation informed Islamic law and the Jewish law of agency.[149] The modern Anglo-American law of trust owes a considerable debt to the *waqf* from Islamic law—a donor-created endowment under the administration of a trustee for use by designated beneficiaries. Franciscan friars returning from the Crusades in the thirteenth century introduced the *waqf* to England.[150] Moreover,

149. *See* TAMAR FRANKEL, FIDUCIARY LAW 80–83 (2011); Avisheh Avini, *The Origins of the Modern English Trust Revisited*, 70 TUL. L. REV. 1139 (1996); Robert G. Natelson, *The Government as Fiduciary: A Practical Demonstration from the Reign of Trajan*, 35 U. RICH. L. REV. 191 (2001).

150. *See* FRANKEL, *supra* note 149, at 84–86; Avini, *supra* note 149, at 1140–43.

scholars in non-Western societies that traditionally emphasize collective identities (e.g., family, clan, nation, religion) over individual freedom have observed likewise that implied fiduciary obligations structure public and private legal institutions.[151] For example, one contemporary Chinese philosopher has described "the ideal Confucian society as a 'fiduciary community' in which the corporate effort of the entire membership turned the group into 'a society of mutual trust instead of a mere aggregate of individuals.'"[152] Thus, although the debate over cultural relativism cannot be addressed here, the fiduciary theory's sensitivity to local conditions, its democratic aspect, and its resonance in non-Western societies all suggest that it is less vulnerable to complaints of Western bias than other theories.[153]

VI. OBJECTIONS TO THE FIDUCIARY THEORY

The fiduciary theory of jus cogens and human rights that we have outlined in this chapter has attracted some spirited critiques. Generally speaking, however, the objections raised against the theory reflect misconceptions about the juridical character of international human rights and fiduciary duties.

Some fiduciary law scholars have expressed skepticism about extending fiduciary concepts to international human rights based on features of either the state-subject relationship or human rights norms that they believe are incompatible with fiduciary obligations.[154] For example, in the most detailed critique of our theory, Ethan Leib and Stephen Galoob endorse the idea that "fiduciary principles can be fruitfully applied to many domains of public law," but assert that human rights norms cannot qualify as fiduciary in nature because fiduciary norms require deliberation, conscientiousness (i.e., acting for the right reasons), and robust fidelity to beneficiaries' interests amidst changing circumstances.[155] According to Leib and Galoob, human rights norms cannot be fiduciary obligations because they are not sensitive to deliberation, do not require conscientiousness, and are not robustly demanding in the same sense as fiduciary obligations.

151. *See, e.g.*, Teemu Ruskola, *Conceptualizing Corporations and Kinship: Comparative Law and Development Theory in a Chinese Perspective*, 52 STAN. L. REV. 1599, 1607–08 (2000); *see also* SEN, *supra* note 146, at 240 ("The valuing of freedom is not confined to one culture only, and the Western traditions are not the only ones that prepare us for a freedom-based approach to social understanding.").

152. Ruskola, *supra* note 151, at 1627 (quoting TU WEI-MING, CENTRALITY AND COMMONALITY: AN ESSAY ON CHUNG-YUNG 67, 81 (1976)).

153. We recognize that certain aspects of the fiduciary model may challenge traditional practices in some societies. For example, some public officials may persist in treating their subjects as resources of the state (or its ruling class) rather than as ends-in-themselves. We take comfort, however, in the fact that few states defend under the banner of cultural relativism practices of exploitation and arbitrary discrimination. And in any event, the fiduciary theory is a normative as well as interpretive theory of international law, so it is no failing that some state practices flagrantly violate its requirements.

154. *See, e.g.*, Ethan Leib & Stephen Galoob, *Fiduciary Legal and Political Theory: A Critique*, 125 YALE L.J. (forthcoming 2016).

155. *See id.*

Leib and Galoob's critique misses the mark for several reasons. First, their proposed criteria for identifying fiduciary norms are prodigiously under-inclusive. The most well-established and central fiduciary norms of private law do not meet their proposed criteria, including the cardinal duty to follow instructions and the venerable "no-conflict" and "no-profit" rules. If a fiduciary exercises her power in a manner that is ultra vires her power (e.g., a trustee spends trust assets to buy her beneficiary a luxury sports car, but her mandate specifies that trust monies are to be spent exclusively on the beneficiary's education), then her exercise of her fiduciary power is *void ab initio*. It makes no difference whether she exercised her power after due deliberation, for the right reasons, and after a "robust" consideration of her beneficiary's present circumstances and best interests. The same is true of violations of the rules proscribing conflicts and profits, the only difference being that a fiduciary's exercise of power in those cases is *voidable* at the request of the beneficiary rather than simply *void ab initio*. As these cases reveal, core norms at the center of the practice of fiduciary law are indifferent to deliberation, conscientiousness, and robustness. Human rights norms such as the prohibition against torture perform a function similar to the "no-conflict" and "no-profit" rules, marking the limits in both cases of a fiduciary power-holder's authority. Sovereigns cannot violate human rights norms without impugning their authority as sovereigns, just as fiduciaries cannot make conflicted decisions without sacrificing their authority to act legally for their beneficiaries. It should come as no surprise, therefore, that IHRL has features that focus on a state's actions without regard to the state's deliberation, conscientiousness, or robust fidelity over time.

Second, Leib and Galoob's critique reflects a common misperception about the supposedly limited ambitions of IHRL. Contrary to the Leib-Galoob view, many human rights norms do require deliberation, conscientiousness, and robustness. Indeed, prominent human rights theorists such as Buchanan, Forst, and Sen have emphasized precisely these features of deliberation, conscientiousness, and robustness as defining characteristics of human rights norms.[156] To take but one example, although international scrutiny understandably tends to focus on states' negative duty to refrain from committing torture, states also bear affirmative obligations to use their best efforts, within the limits of their available resources, to establish laws, policies, and practices that will protect their people from the threat of torture. As the U.N. Committee Against Torture has explained, this affirmative "obligation to take effective preventive measures [to prevent torture] transcends the items enumerated specifically in the Convention,"[157] and entails a requirement of "[c]ontinual evaluation" to ensure that state laws, policies, and practices against torture are fully "effective" over time.[158]

Like the robust aspects of the duties of loyalty and care in private law, the deliberative and programmatic features of the prohibition against torture represent conduct rules that are not generally subject to direct enforcement by international tribunals. Just as common law courts look for objective indicators of disloyalty and lack of care

156. *See* text accompanying notes 109–114.

157. Committee Against Torture, General Comment 2, Implementation of article 2 by States Parties, § 25, U.N. Doc. CAT/C/GC/2/CRP. 1/Rev.4 (2007).

158. *Id.* § 21.

such as conflicts of interest, conduct inconsistent with fiduciary mandates, or the flagrant shirking of responsibilities, IHRL invites tribunals to look for objective evidence of human rights abuse in the form of state practices such as torture or CIDT before they will award remedies. The fact that the CAT does not invite searching scrutiny of a state's deliberations and motivations is hardly reflective of the torture prohibition's incompatibility with the fiduciary theory; it simply reflects the limits of courts' institutional competence to interrogate the deliberative processes and subjective motivations that inform a state's interrogation practices. Because Leib and Galoob consider only the negative obligations associated with human rights norms without taking into account those norms' positive dimensions, they erroneously dismiss human rights norms wholesale as beyond the pale of fiduciary law.

Other scholars have questioned whether "the exotic moral technology of fiduciary obligations" is truly necessary to justify human rights, suggesting that human rights "might be more parsimoniously explained simply by observing that the failure to secure such conditions might be one way for the state itself to instrumentalize or dominate its subjects."[159] What these scholars fail to appreciate is that the fiduciary theory's relational account of state sovereignty is necessary precisely to explain *why* the state is under a standing legal obligation to refrain from instrumentalizing or dominating its people: states are never entitled to instrumentalize or dominate their legal subjects because international law entrusts states with authority to exercise public powers in a fiduciary capacity only for and on behalf of individuals who are amenable to their jurisdiction. The state's sovereign authority is conditioned on its exercising public powers in a manner that satisfies the principles of integrity, formal moral equality, and solicitude. Accordingly, the obligation to refrain from instrumentalization and domination is not merely a free-floating moral obligation, but a legal constraint on the exercise of public powers that flows directly from the fiduciary character of a state's sovereign authority.

VII. CONCLUSION

Debates over human rights have been waged largely between foundationalist theorists who appeal to natural rights and proponents of practical theories who insist that IHRL must be understood on its own terms. Debates over jus cogens norms likewise turn on the question of their source, with implications for the further question of which norms properly count as peremptory. In the case of human rights, the fiduciary theory offers an attractive way forward by taking seriously, on the one hand, the foundational idea that agents must be regarded as possessing a special and equal moral status—that is, human dignity—and on the other, the practical idea that human rights law is the international community's best provisional estimate of the rights states must honor to regard the persons subject to their power as the bearers of human dignity. With respect to jus cogens, the fiduciary model's great attraction is its generation of principled criteria capable of identifying norms of peremptory status.

159. David Louis Attanasio, The State Obligation to Protect 228 (2015) (unpublished Ph.D. dissertation, University of California, Los Angeles) (on file with the author); *see also* Larry May, *Habeas Corpus as Jus Cogens in International Law*, 4 CRIM. L. & PHIL. 249, 251 (2010) (asking "why [we should] think that fiduciary as opposed to less strenuous duties [are] generated").

The lynchpin to the fiduciary theory is the idea that human rights and jus cogens cannot be understood or specified in the abstract; they arise only from a legal relationship in which public institutions hold administrative powers over vulnerable agents who, as private parties, are not entitled to exercise those powers. This relational aspect of the fiduciary theory is especially potent because it permits the theory to relativize particular international norms to the institutional circumstances of their application, but in a way that remains true to their spirit through a commitment to non-instrumentalization and non-domination. This same commitment calls for democratic deliberation, a requirement that reveals the fiduciary theory's allegiance to popular sovereignty, cultural sensitivity, and independent agency. Yet the fiduciary theory also provides concrete criteria to structure and constrain democratic deliberation, mitigating concerns that IHRL's interpretive dimensions may generate greater fragmentation.[160] Taken together, the various implications of the fiduciary principle comprise a unified theory that is capable of justifying international law's authority to confer public powers on states and state-like actors.

160. *See* Anne Peters, Constitutional Fragments: On the Interaction of Constitutionalization and Fragmentation in International Law, *at* http://cgc.wp.st-andrews.ac.uk/2015/04/14/cgc-working-paper-no-2-constitutional-fragments/ (last visited April 7, 2015) (suggesting that global constitutionalism discourse has contributed to international law's doctrinal fragmentation by promoting legal interpretivism, with an emphasis on systemic legitimacy and effectiveness, over legal formalism).

4

Emergencies

I. INTRODUCTION

At the heart of IHRL lies a practical challenge intertwined with a theoretical problem. The practical challenge is that many of the most grave and systematic human rights abuses occur during public emergencies, when states employ extraordinary powers to address threats to public order. In responding to this challenge, each of the leading international and regional covenants on civil and political rights has endeavored to regulate states' entry into and conduct within states of emergency. The "cornerstone[s]" of these covenants are their derogation clauses,[1] which permit states to restrict some human rights during emergencies—but only where strictly necessary to address threats to "the life of the nation"[2] or the "independence or security" of the state.[3] This derogation-centric approach enables IHRL to accommodate concerns for public necessity during emergencies, but it also presents a vexing theoretical problem: In what sense are human rights truly *rights* if they are subject to derogation during emergencies?

This chapter seeks to resolve this apparent paradox by demonstrating how the fiduciary conception of state sovereignty illuminates IHRL's normative foundations. In previous chapters, we have argued that human rights are best conceived in relational and legal terms as norms arising from a fiduciary relationship between states (or state-like actors) and persons subject to their power. States bear a fiduciary duty to guarantee their subjects' secure and equal freedom, a duty that flows from their institutional assumption of sovereign powers.[4] International law authorizes states to exercise sovereign powers on behalf of their people, but these powers

1. Jaime Oraá, Human Rights in States of Emergency in International Law 1 (1992).

2. Convention for the Protection of Human Rights and Fundamental Freedoms, art. 15.1, Nov. 4, 1950, 213 U.N.T.S. 221 [hereinafter European Convention]; International Covenant on Civil and Political Rights, art. 41, Dec. 16, 1966, 999 U.N.T.S. 171 [hereinafter ICCPR]; League of Arab States, Revised Arab Charter on Human Rights art. 4.1 (May 22, 2004), 12 Int'l Hum. Rts. Rep. 893 (2005) [hereinafter Arab Charter].

3. American Convention on Human Rights art. 27.1, Nov. 22, 1969, O.A.S.T.S. No. 36, 1144 U.N.T.S. 123 [hereinafter ACHR].

4. The fiduciary theory we develop here builds upon a long-standing tradition in Western legal and political theory of invoking "public trust" (*fides publica*, *fides*, or *Verfassungstreue*) as a constitutional constraint against the abuse of emergency powers. *See generally* Marc de Wilde, *Just Trust Us: A Short History of Emergency Powers and Constitutional Change*, 3 Comp. Leg. History

are subject to strict legal limitations flowing from the Kantian idea that agents are always to be treated as ends (the principle of non-instrumentalization) and the republican idea that persons are not to be subject to arbitrary power (the principle of non-domination). As discussed in the previous chapter, under the fiduciary theory's relational account, human rights are not timeless and absolute moral rights that individuals possess merely because they are human. Rather, human rights represent the normative consequences of a state's assumption of sovereign powers, and are thus constitutive of sovereignty's normative dimension.

The fiduciary theory of human rights provides a sound philosophical grounding for the central features of IHRL's derogation regime. According to the theory, states bear an obligation to safeguard their subjects' equal freedom during emergencies—even if this requires derogation from some human rights norms, such as the freedoms of expression, movement, and peaceable assembly. Nonperemptory human rights norms are subject to derogation in contexts where the strict observance of these norms would conflict with the state's overarching fiduciary obligation to guarantee their subjects' secure and equal freedom. But states must also refrain from taking measures in emergencies that would simply replace private domination with public domination. Thus, states may never derogate from peremptory norms, such as the prohibitions against genocide, prolonged arbitrary detention, and torture, because the violation of these norms could never be consistent with the state's obligation to guarantee the public's secure and equal freedom. International law recognizes these principles during emergencies—permitting derogation of some norms in some contexts—to ensure that persons are treated always as ends-in-themselves and not merely as means to the state's ends. States may employ emergency powers only where exigent circumstances imperil the state's ability to guarantee secure and equal freedom, and only where the particular measures employed are strictly necessary for this purpose. Thus framed, the fiduciary theory stakes out an intermediate position between the view that all human rights are absolute and timeless, on the one hand, and the equally popular Schmittian view, on the other hand, that states may abrogate human rights unilaterally in emergencies. The fiduciary theory also promises a charitable interpretation of international law's emergency constitution, in the sense that it allows human rights to provide baseline standards even when some of these rights are subject to derogation. It therefore stands in contrast to more "realist" views that view derogation as a dangerous and human-rights-threatening affirmation of the supremacy of state sovereignty over the individual.

At its core, the fiduciary theory is about the limits of legitimate state action. As such, it can provide guidance to international and regional tribunals charged with adjudicating those limits, even during emergencies. The fiduciary theory suggests that some judicial interpretations of international conventions unnecessarily restrict states' ability to safeguard legal order. For instance, the fiduciary theory challenges the standard developed by the European Court of Human Rights (ECHR) that a public emergency must "concern [a state's] entire population" to justify a state of emergency.[5] Under the fiduciary model, states would be permitted to derogate from

110 (2015) (tracing this tradition through the Roman Republic, medieval Europe, and Weimar Germany).

5. Lawless v. Ireland, 3 ECHR (1961) Series A, No. 3 (Court), 56 [hereinafter *Lawless* Court].

their human rights obligations where necessary to address localized instability that threatened the state's capacity to maintain legal order. Conversely, the fiduciary theory suggests that in some important respects international and regional tribunals have not gone far enough in limiting human rights derogation. Once a state of emergency has been declared, for example, the fiduciary theory's principles of non-instrumentalization and non-domination require states to provide or facilitate more robust public notification, justification, and contestation. The theory also dictates a more limited role for judicial deference to state decision-makers under the controversial "margin of appreciation" doctrine, and it offers a principled response to Carl Schmitt's argument that the rule of law cannot constrain state action during states of exception or emergency.[6] In these and other respects, the fiduciary theory more fully elucidates IHRL's proper content and consequences.

This chapter outlines the fiduciary theory's approach to public emergencies in several steps. In Part II, we lay out the central features of international law's emergency constitution as codified in human rights treaties and clarified in the jurisprudence of regional human rights tribunals. In Part III, we argue that the fiduciary theory's relational and deliberative conception of human rights explains why and under what conditions states are entitled to suspend certain human rights obligations during public emergencies. In Part IV, we outline Schmitt's challenge to the rule of IHRL, and in Part V we argue that the fiduciary theory defuses this challenge by affirming that states, as institutions constituted and regulated by international law, are required to exercise their sovereign power in a manner that is always consistent with the principles of formal legal equality, integrity, and solicitude. In Part VI, we explore how the fiduciary theory illuminates the role of courts and international institutions as facilitators of public justification and arbiters of legality during emergencies. Part VII addresses objections to the fiduciary theory's approach to public emergencies, and Part VIII offers a brief conclusion.

II. INTERNATIONAL LAW'S EMERGENCY CONSTITUTION

In common parlance, a "state of emergency" denotes a legal regime in which public institutions are vested with extraordinary powers to address existential threats to public order.[7] The contemporary state of emergency concept traces its historical origins to the Roman dictator, a temporary officer appointed to provide ad hoc leadership in a national emergency (*tumultus*) by repulsing attacks from abroad or quelling internal rebellion.[8] Over the past century, governments throughout the world have

6. *See* CARL SCHMITT, POLITICAL THEOLOGY: FOUR CHAPTERS ON THE CONCEPT OF SOVEREIGNTY (George Schwab transl. 2005) (rev'd ed. 1934).

7. ORAÁ, *supra* note 1, at 7; *see generally* OREN GROSS & FIONNUALA NÍ AOLÁIN, LAW IN TIMES OF CRISIS: EMERGENCY POWERS IN THEORY AND PRACTICE (2006).

8. *See* GIORGIO AGAMBEN, THE STATE OF EXCEPTION 41–42 (2005) (discussing the Roman dictatorship and defining *tumultus* as "the caesura by means of which, from the point of view of public law, exceptional measures may be taken" (quoting ADOLPH NISSEN, DAS IUSTITIUM: EINE STUDIE AUS DER ROMISCHEN RECHTSGESCHICHTE 76 (1877)). In Rome, the declaration of a *tumultus* "usually led to the proclamation of a *iustitium*"—the temporary cessation of public law. *Id.* at 41.

declared states of emergency in response to a variety of real and perceived crises, including not only the paradigmatic threats of foreign military intervention and insurrection, but also political unrest, general civil unrest, criminal or terrorist violence, labor strikes, economic emergencies, the collapse of public institutions, the spread of infectious diseases, and natural disasters.[9]

The suspension of legal order during emergencies, or the suspension of important aspects thereof, challenges states' commitment to the rule of law and often paves the way for systematic human rights violations. Although the rule of law has been defined variously, most scholars agree that the concept requires, at a minimum, public institutions that decide disputes impartially and non-arbitrarily according to preestablished legal principles.[10] Emergencies may compromise legal order by generating political pressures to augment executive power at the expense of legislative and judicial institutions. Some commentators lament that courts dial down the intensity of judicial review during emergencies in deference to the executive branch, enabling the executive to sidestep ordinary legal restraints.[11] As ordinary checks and balances of government are weakened, the executive's capacity to engage in human rights violations is magnified. Moreover, once legal restraints are relaxed or abandoned, emergency powers can become permanently entrenched, facilitating the further abuse of public powers long after the crisis has passed.[12]

Recognizing the dangers that accompany states of emergency, international law limits the circumstances under which states may legally derogate from their international obligations to respect, protect, and fulfill civil and political rights.[13] Each of the leading international and regional conventions on civil and political rights—the ICCPR,[14] African Charter on Human Rights,[15] American Convention on Human

9. *See, e.g.*, U.N. Treaty Collection Database: Status of Treaties, Ch. IV (ICCPR), http://treaties.un.org/Pages/ViewDetails.aspx?src=TREATY&mtdsg_no=IV-4&chapter=4&lang=en (last visited Nov. 12, 2009) [hereinafter ICCPR Derogation Notifications].

10. *See, e.g.*, T.R.S. Allan, Constitutional Justice: A Liberal Theory of the Rule of Law (2001); Lon Fuller, The Morality of Law (1964); Joseph Raz, *The Rule of Law and Its Virtue*, *in* The Authority of Law: Essays on Law and Morality 210 (1979); N.E. Simmonds, Law as a Moral Idea (2007); Andrei Marmor, *The Rule of Law and Its Limits*, 23 Law & Phil. 1 (2004).

11. *See, e.g.*, David Dyzenhaus, The Constitution of Law: Legality in a Time of Emergency (2006).

12. *See* Scott P. Sheeran, *Reconceptualizing States of Emergency Under International Human Rights Law: Theory, Legal Doctrine, and Politics*, 34 Mich. J. Int'l L. 491, 517–18 (2013) (discussing Egypt's thirty-year state of emergency).

13. Although public emergencies may also have profound consequences for economic, social, and cultural rights, the derogation and limitation clauses that constitute IHRL's emergency constitution focus exclusively upon civil and political rights. Accordingly, we also limit our discussion to civil and political rights, reserving for another day the fiduciary principle's application to emergency restrictions on economic, social, and cultural rights.

14. ICCPR, *supra* note 2.

15. The African Charter on Human Rights and Peoples' Rights, June 27, 1981, O.A.U. Doc. CAB/LEG/67/3 rev. 5, does not contain a derogation provision, but it has been suggested that a derogation clause would be superfluous because the Charter's broad individual duties permit

Rights (ACHR),[16] Arab Charter on Human Rights (Arab Charter),[17] and European Convention for the Protection of Human Rights and Fundamental Freedoms (European Convention)[18]—employs a two-stage inquiry to evaluate the legality of a state's derogation from general human rights standards: First, are circumstances sufficiently dire to justify initiating a state of emergency? Second, if a state of emergency is justified, what measures may a state employ to counter the emergency's threats to public order? International law addresses each of these inquiries independently through a two-tiered analysis that mirrors the law of armed conflict.[19] Just as international law distinguishes legal norms regulating the initiation of an armed conflict (*jus ad bellum*) from norms regulating the conduct of hostilities (*jus in bello*), so too it distinguishes norms regulating a state's initiation of a state of emergency from norms regulating a state's conduct within emergencies; for ease of exposition, we refer to these two bodies of law as "*jus ad tumultum*" for the former and "*jus in tumultu*" for the latter. Collectively, this law comprises the emergency constitution of international law.

Generally speaking, IHLR permits states to impose heightened restrictions on human rights during emergencies as necessary to preserve institutions that are essential to public order. Thus, the ICCPR, European Convention, and Arab Charter each allow states to derogate from certain human rights when national crises pose a demonstrable threat to "the life of the nation."[20] The ACHR similarly permits derogation where "war, public danger, or other emergency" threatens the "independence or security of a State Party."[21] Although these broad standards require further explication and therefore may be susceptible to abuse in the hands of opportunistic states, each contemplates that states of emergency will be legally permissible only where genuine public emergencies undermine the institutional prerequisites for the enjoyment of human rights by imperiling the "life," "independence," or "security of the state."

Among international and regional tribunals, the European Commission on Human Rights (European Commission) and the ECHR have been most active in clarifying the contours of *jus ad tumultum*. In *Lawless v. Ireland*,[22] the ECHR

restriction on human rights during emergencies. *See* Amrei Müller, *Limitations to and Derogations from Economic, Social, and Cultural Rights*, 9 Hum. Rts. L. Rev. 557, 594 (2009).

16. ACHR, *supra* note 3.

17. Arab Charter, *supra* note 2.

18. European Convention, *supra* note 2. Although the European Charter of Rights and Freedoms does not address emergencies expressly, it similarly provides that limitations are permissible only "[s]ubject to the principle of proportionality" and as "necessary [to] meet objectives of general interest recognised by the Union or the need to protect the rights and freedoms of others." E.U. Charter art. 52, ¶ 1.

19. *See* Agamben, *supra* note 8, at 42 ("The relation between *bellum* and *tumultus* is the same one that exists between war and military state of siege on the one hand and state of exception and political state of siege on the other.").

20. *See* ICCPR, *supra* note 2, art. 4.1; ECHR, *supra* note 2, art. 15.1; Arab Charter, *supra* note 2, art. 4.1.

21. ACHR, *supra* note 3, art. 27.1.

22. 1 ECHR (1960–61) Series B (Commission Report) [hereinafter *Lawless* Commission]; *Lawless* Court, *supra* note 5.

defined a "public emergency" as a "danger or crisis" that is (1) present or imminent, (2) exceptional, (3) concerns the entire population, and (4) constitutes a "threat to the organized life of the community."[23] Other international and regional bodies have followed the ECHR's lead when determining whether circumstances within a particular country are adequate to justify a state of emergency. For example, the Inter-American Commission on Human Rights (Inter-American Commission) has embraced the European Commission's formulation of the applicable legal standards, reasoning that an armed conflict would not support a state of emergency unless it was finite in duration and compromised "the continued viability of the organized community as a whole."[24]

To ensure that international law's restrictions on the commencement of states of emergency are taken seriously, each of the leading covenants on civil and political rights obligates states to notify the international community promptly—either directly or through an intermediary—when they suspend their human rights obligations during national crises.[25] Although none of these conventions requires states to notify their own people when they suspend their international human rights obligations, the U.N. Commission on Human Rights has suggested that states must exercise emergency powers in compliance with applicable requirements of municipal law, including requirements governing the declaration of a state of emergency.[26] Thus, each of the leading human rights conventions obligates states to establish the need for a state of emergency—based upon discrete substantive and procedural criteria—before proceeding to consider whether particular actions taken in response to an emergency are appropriate. In this manner, each convention seeks to safeguard human rights by limiting states' recourse to emergency powers.

Once a state demonstrates that an actual or imminent crisis satisfies the criteria for a state of emergency (*jus ad tumultum*), international law's focus shifts to the legality of a state's responsive measures (*jus in tumultu*). Under the ICCPR, European Convention, ACHR, and Arab Charter, national emergencies do not give states carte blanche to exercise public powers indiscriminately without regard to the humanitarian costs. Instead, each of these covenants regulates states' exercise

23. *Lawless* Court, *supra* note 5, at 56; *see also Lawless* Commission, *supra* note 22, § 90, at 82. Eight years later in the *Greek Case*, the European Court clarified that a national crisis would be sufficiently "exceptional" under the *Lawless* test if "the normal measures or restrictions, permitted by the Convention for the maintenance of public safety, health and order, are plainly inadequate." Denmark, Norway, Sweden, and the Netherlands v. Greece (the Greek Case) (Nov. 5, 1969), 1969 Y.B. Eur. Conv. on H.R. 1 (Eur. Comm'n on H.R.), at 70, ¶ 113 [hereinafter *Greek Case*].

24. *See* Judicial Guarantees in States of Emergency, 9 Inter-Am. Ct. H.R. (ser. A) at 40, OEA/ser.L./VI/111.9, doc. 13 (1987) (requiring finite duration); Claudio Grossman, *A Framework for the Examination of States of Emergency Under the American Convention on Human Rights*, 1 Am. U. J. Int'l L. & Pol'y 35, 45 (1986) (translating the Inter-American Commission's Report on Nicaragua, OEA/Ser.L/V/II.62, doc.10, rev.3 (Nov. 29, 1983), at 121–22 (original in Spanish)).

25. *See* ICCPR, *supra* note 2, art. 4; ECHR, *supra* note 2, art. 15(3); Arab Charter, *supra* note 2, art. 4.3; ACHR, *supra* note 3, art. 27.3.

26. *See* Comm'n on Human Rights, General Comment No. 29, States of Emergency (Article 4), UN Doc. CCPR/C/21/Rev.1/Add.11 (2001).

of emergency powers by imposing substantive and procedural limitations on state action within a state of emergency.

International law limits executive and legislative discretion within states of emergency by prohibiting states from employing emergency powers beyond the temporal and geographic scope specified in their notice of derogation. The ECHR affirmed this principle in *Sakik and Others v. Turkey*[27] when it considered Turkey's suspension of human rights protections in territories outside those identified in the state's derogation notice. The court explained that it "would be working against the object and purpose of [the European Convention's derogation provision] if, when assessing the territorial scope of the derogation concerned, it were to extend its effects to a part of Turkish territory not explicitly named in the notice of derogation."[28] Applying this principle, the court held that Turkey's derogation notice was inapplicable to the case at hand, and that the state's delay in presenting detainees before a judge in territories not covered by its derogation notice violated its commitments under the European Convention.[29]

Even within the scope of a state's formal derogation, states must tailor their responsive measures to minimize the potential impact on human rights. Some human rights such as the jus cogens prohibitions against torture, slavery, and the arbitrary deprivation of life or liberty are not derogable under any circumstances.[30] Other norms, such as the rights to freedom of movement, expression, and association, are subject to state derogation, but only "to the extent *strictly required* by the exigencies of the situation."[31] The influential *Siracusa Principles on the Limitation and Derogation Principles in the ICCPR* suggest that any measures a state undertakes to restrict or suspend human rights during emergencies must be supported by a valid state ground, a pressing public need, a legitimate aim, and proportionality.[32] States must strictly observe peremptory human rights norms during emergencies, and they may suspend nonperemptory human rights only if their responsive measures are consistent with the geographic and temporal scope of the derogation. Furthermore, any measures taken in response to an emergency must satisfy the substantive principle of proportionality, which requires states to use only those measures that minimally restrict the freedoms ordinarily protected by the suspended treaty rights.

27. Sakik & Others v. Turkey, App. No. 23878/94-23883/94, 26 Eur. H.R. Rep. 662 (1997).

28. *Id.* at 683; *see also* Abdulsamet Yaman v. Turkey, App. No. 32446/96, 40 Eur. H.R. Rep. 49 (2005), ¶¶ 68–69, at 12 (holding that Turkey abused its emergency powers by suspending human rights in territories beyond those identified in its formal notice of derogation).

29. *Sakik*, 26 Eur. H.R. Rep. at 683–85.

30. *See* European Convention, *supra* note 2, arts. 2–4, 7; ACHR, *supra* note 3, arts. 4, 5.2, 6, 9; ICCPR, *supra* note 2, arts. 6–8, 15; Arab Charter, *supra* note 2, art. 4.2.

31. European Convention, *supra* note 2, art. 15 (emphasis added); *see also* ACHR, *supra* note 3, art. 27 (providing that a state-party "may take measures derogating from its obligations under the present Convention to the extent and for the period of time strictly required by the exigencies of the situation"); Arab Charter, *supra* note 2, art. 4.1; ICCPR, *supra* note 2, art. 4.

32. *The Siracusa Principles on the Limitation and Derogation Provisions in the International Covenant on Civil and Political Rights*, 7 Hum. Rts. Q. 3, 4, ¶ 10 (1985) [hereinafter *Siracusa Principles*].

By prescribing principles and procedures to guide state action during national emergencies, international law's emergency constitution seeks to ensconce human rights firmly within the rule of law. Yet the current legal frameworks for *jus ad tumultum* arguably fail to satisfy the requirements of the rule of law in a variety of respects insofar as their constituent principles remain unclear, contradictory, and subject to inconsistent application. As we have seen, the ICCPR, European Convention, ACHR, and Arab Charter offer different accounts of the conditions that trigger states of emergency, and their use of vague formulations such as threats to the "life of the nation" provide insufficient guidance to state decision-makers. For example, although the ECHR has asserted that exigent circumstances must affect an entire national population to constitute a genuine "public emergency,"[33] state notices of derogation suggest that states believe localized instability within a particular region could also trigger a limited state of emergency.[34] Once courts move beyond *jus ad tumultum*, additional uncertainties and inconsistencies muddle international law's *jus in tumultu*. Human rights conventions contain competing catalogs of non-derogable norms that differ markedly from one another in length and content.[35] Moreover, none of the leading conventions specifies precisely how much deference courts should give states when derogating from their human rights obligations, leading to conflicting judicial practice.[36]

If international law's approach to states of emergency lacks coherence, the path forward must be cleared by international legal theory. A theory of human rights is needed to justify the emergency constitution's two-tiered structure, its categorical distinction between derogable and non-derogable human rights, its subjection of state emergency powers to external review, and the margin of appreciation (if any) that international tribunals would owe to states that derogate from their human rights obligations. A theory of human rights is necessary, as well, to address the Schmittian argument that sovereign discretion displaces legality during national crises.[37] Moreover, elucidating IHRL's theoretical basis and requirements is essential to clarify what counts as compliance with IHRL, which should in turn facilitate state accountability for violating human rights during emergencies.

33. *Lawless* Commission, 1 ECHR, Ser. B, § 90, at 82.

34. *See* ICCPR Derogation Notifications, *supra* note 9.

35. The Arab Charter and ACHR lead the field with sixteen and eleven articles, respectively, addressing peremptory norms. *See* ACHR, *supra* note 3, arts. 3–6, 9, 12, 17–20, 23; Arab Charter, *supra* note 2, arts. 5, 8–10, 13, 14, 15 ¶ 6, 15, 18–20, 22, 27–30. The European Convention identifies only four norms as non-derogable. European Convention, *supra* note 2, arts. 2–4, 7.

36. *See, e.g.*, Oren Gross, *Once More unto the Breach: The Systematic Failure of Applying the European Convention on Human Rights to Entrenched Emergencies*, 23 YALE J. INT'L L. 437 (1998); Oren Gross & Fionnuala Ni Aolain, *From Discretion to Scrutiny: Revisiting the Application of the Margin of Appreciation Doctrine in the Context of Article 14 of the European Convention on Human Rights*, 23 HUM. RTS. Q. 625 (2001).

37. *See* SCHMITT, *supra* note 6, at 17; Oren Gross, *Chaos and Rules: Should Responses to Violent Crises Always Be Constitutional?*, 112 YALE L.J. 1011 (2003).

III. FIDUCIARY STATES, HUMAN RIGHTS, AND EMERGENCIES

The fiduciary theory of human rights supports the central features of international law's emergency constitution and addresses confusion over the scope and application of human rights. Under the fiduciary theory, human rights come into focus as institutionally grounded legal constraints that arise from a state's assumption of sovereign powers. Because a state's fiduciary obligations are constitutive of its legal authority, public institutions cannot violate these obligations during emergencies without undercutting their claim to represent their people as a sovereign actor. The fiduciary theory furnishes substantive and procedural principles that can be used prospectively to clarify the two-tiered structure of international law's emergency constitution. Although the theory does not pretend to explain *all* the distinctive features of how human rights treaty derogations work in practice, it sets out normative presuppositions that explain the core of international law's emergency constitution. It also provides a critical perspective from which to evaluate this constitution's particular commitments and practices.

As noted in Chapter 3, the fiduciary theory explains why some human rights can be accepted as derogable during national crises while others cannot, and it offers principled criteria for distinguishing derogable rights from non-derogable rights. Under the fiduciary theory, human rights qualify as peremptory norms if a state's compliance with these norms is always necessary to accomplish the state's fiduciary mission of guaranteeing secure and equal freedom. Some international norms qualify as jus cogens on this account because states cannot violate these prohibitions without breaching their obligation to treat all persons as equal co-beneficiaries of state action. States must refrain from exploiting any person as a mere instrument of public policy through abusive practices such as genocide, crimes against humanity, summary executions, forced disappearances, prolonged arbitrary detention, torture, and cruel, inhuman, and degrading treatment. Such practices offend the fiduciary theory's criterion of legitimacy that requires all public acts to be interpretable as acts performed on behalf or in the name of every person subject to them. In addition, emergency measures must always take the form of general rules—not ad hoc commands—in order to satisfy the peremptory norm of non-discrimination. As human rights experts have recognized, this requirement of non-discrimination in emergencies constitutes a non-derogable "principle of legality" that prevents "arbitrary restrictions on human rights."[38] A state therefore may not subject persons residing lawfully within its borders to administrative detention without offering a particularized, non-discriminatory justification that satisfies the fiduciary principle. States cannot violate these norms under any circumstances without forfeiting their claim to possess sovereign authority because such practices always instrumentalize their victims and, as such, are never consistent with a regime of secure and equal freedom. In each of these respects, the fiduciary theory confirms the conventional wisdom that some measures a state might employ to restore public order are simply beyond the scope of state emergency powers under international law.

38. Bert Lockwood Jr. et al., *Working Paper for the Committee of Experts on Limitations Provisions*, 7 Hum. Rts. Q. 35, 44 (1985). Restrictions on human rights are "arbitrary" under the fiduciary theory if they violate the fiduciary principle by transgressing the standards of formal moral equality, integrity, or solicitude.

Not all human rights are peremptory, of course. Some international norms, such as the freedoms of expression, movement, and peaceable assembly, are widely accepted as human rights, yet do not qualify as jus cogens because the fiduciary principle permits—and may even require—the state to restrict their exercise in certain contexts. For instance, a state's fiduciary duty to guarantee secure and equal freedom for its people arguably entitles the state to enact laws that require manufacturers to place warnings on their products to notify the public of possible health risks and other dangers. Municipal courts have found that such laws infringe tobacco companies' freedom of expression; nonetheless, these laws have been upheld because the infringement is justifiable based on the health risks that these products pose.[39] Although such laws restrict free expression, they do not violate human rights on the fiduciary theory because they represent a necessary and proportional means to guarantee the public's security from unilaterally imposed risks. Unlike violations of peremptory norms, which are never consistent with a state's fiduciary duty to its subjects, a state fulfills its overarching fiduciary obligation when it adopts restrictions on human rights that are essential to establish a regime of secure and equal freedom. To satisfy the state's general obligation of solicitude, restrictions on liberties must be no more intrusive than strictly necessary. Accordingly, a state may not regulate private expression based solely upon the political, religious, or cultural viewpoint expressed, nor may it exercise permanent, plenary control over the content of private media and communications networks. The fiduciary theory thus furnishes a general framework for establishing the grounds on which nonperemptory human rights may be infringed: a state may adopt laws, policies, or practices that restrict the exercise of human rights only to the extent strictly necessary to satisfy its overarching fiduciary duty to guarantee secure and equal freedom.[40]

Although the schedules of peremptory and nonperemptory norms that appear in leading human rights conventions are generally (if not perfectly) consistent with the fiduciary theory, we argued in Chapter 3 that human rights do not derive their fundamental normative authority from state consent. Rather, the authority of human rights derives from their role as constitutive constraints emanating from the state's institutional assumption of sovereign powers. This is not to say that state consent and ratification of human rights conventions are irrelevant. Importantly, treaties signal the international community's best provisional estimate of the determinate content of particular human rights norms and the legal consequences of

39. *See, e.g.*, Canada (Attorney General) v. JTI-Macdonald Corp., 2007 SCC 30, [2007] 2 S.C.R. 610 (upholding legislation that requires tobacco manufacturers to include graphic product warnings notwithstanding that the legislation infringes the manufacturers' constitutionally protected right to freedom of expression); Commonwealth Brands, Inc. v. United States, 678 F. Supp. 2d. 512, 532 (W.D. Ky. 2010) (upholding detailed warning labels on cigarette packages as "sufficiently tailored" to the federal government's "substantial interest").

40. *See* ICCPR, *supra* note 2, art. 19 (noting that the right to freedom of expression is subject to legal restrictions in order to protect others' rights, national security, public order, and public health or morals); European Convention, *supra* note 2, art. 10.1 (same); ACHR, *supra* note 3, art 13.2 (same). In a similar vein, the ICESCR permits states to restrict economic, social, and cultural rights, provided that such restrictions are consistent with "limitations . . . determined by law," "compatible with the nature of these rights," and "solely for the purpose of promoting the general welfare in a democratic society." International Covenant on Economic, Social and Cultural Rights, art. 4, Dec. 16, 1966, S. Exec. Doc. D, 95-2 (1978), 993 U.N.T.S. 3.

their breach. Nonetheless, the basic normative authority of human rights remains traceable to the protection they afford against the threats of domination and instrumentalization engendered within the fiduciary relationship between public institutions and the persons subject to their powers.

Various legal and political theorists have struggled to explain why ordinary human rights are derogable during emergencies, because they have envisioned human rights as abstract, timeless, inalienable rights that all human beings possess solely by virtue of their shared humanity.[41] Once human rights are recast in relational terms under the fiduciary theory, however, these conceptual difficulties fade. The fiduciary theory posits that human rights are not abstract or timeless natural rights; instead, they are relational entitlements that reflect persons' moral capacity as self-determining agents to place public institutions under legal obligations. Because human rights derive from the fiduciary character of the state-subject relation, their scope and application are likewise defined relationally according to the state's fiduciary duties. By recasting human rights in relational terms, the fiduciary theory explains why nonperemptory human rights are properly characterized as "rights" while nonetheless being subject to derogation during emergencies.

Genuine public emergencies, such as foreign military aggression or civil war, raise special concerns for the state-subject fiduciary relation because they compromise the state's institutional capacity to guarantee secure and equal freedom. Where a public emergency renders a state unable to provide a credible check on privatized coercion, nationals and foreign nationals within the affected region may be vulnerable to physical violence and arbitrary deprivations of property. The fiduciary theory addresses the threats that arise within emergencies by authorizing the state to impose heightened restrictions on nonperemptory human rights—including, where applicable, derogations from human rights conventions—in order to restore a regime of secure and equal freedom. To satisfy the fiduciary principle, however, any such emergency measures must comport with the principle of formal moral equality, and must be strictly necessary to re-establish legal order.

For example, outside an emergency, the fiduciary theory would permit few restrictions on persons' freedom of movement as such broad restrictions are not necessary to guarantee secure and equal freedom. During a natural disaster or pandemic, however, the fiduciary principle might well authorize a state to restrict travel or impose a public curfew temporarily in order to preserve public safety and governmental services that are essential to legal order. Similarly, during a military insurrection, the fiduciary principle would authorize a state to employ administrative detention without prompt presentation to a judicial tribunal (a practice ordinarily prohibited under the ICCPR) if ordinary judicial administration had been interrupted. Even within an emergency, however, administrative detention must not be employed arbitrarily or for improper purposes. Nor can such practices be justified solely on the basis of protecting others' freedom. Under the fiduciary theory, an individual's detention must comport with a legal regime that treats all persons subject to the state's sovereign authority as equal co-beneficiaries and that aspires to provide equal freedom for all—including the detainee herself. The fiduciary

41. *See, e.g.*, JACK DONNELLY, INTERNATIONAL HUMAN RIGHTS 18 (1998); ALAN GEWIRTH, HUMAN RIGHTS: ESSAYS ON JUSTIFICATION AND APPLICATIONS 1 (1982).

theory thus frames IHRL's derogation regime as a principled effort to honor the equal freedom of nationals and foreign nationals by addressing the unique threats of domination and instrumentalization that arise when public emergencies temporarily overwhelm the state's capacity to guarantee secure and equal freedom. Viewed from this perspective, state derogation from human rights conventions during public emergencies does not constitute an exception to human rights norms so much as an extension of human rights' internal logic.[42]

The fiduciary theory thus provides a sound philosophical foundation for international law's two-tiered approach to states of emergency. Under the fiduciary theory, a state may not declare an emergency unless exigent circumstances frustrate the state's ability to provide secure and equal freedom through reliance on the laws, practices, or procedures that apply outside an emergency (*jus ad tumultum*). The fiduciary model thus offers an important interpretive gloss on derogation standards such as the treaty-based requirements that exigent circumstances threaten "the life of the nation"[43] or the "independence or security" of the state.[44] What is necessary to justify human rights derogation, under the fiduciary theory, is not an existential threat to the very survival of the state per se, but rather conditions that impair the state's capacity to guarantee fundamental security under the rule of law.[45] Once a state determines that this threshold has been crossed, and invokes emergency powers, the state must refrain from restricting human rights any further than strictly necessary to restore the state's ability to guarantee secure and equal freedom (*jus in tumultu*).

The process states employ when conducting this two-stage derogation analysis also has great significance under the fiduciary theory: public institutions must exercise their powers through a deliberative decision-making process that honors subjects' status as free and equal co-beneficiaries of legal order. Three principles of the fiduciary theory are particularly salient in the context of public emergencies: justification, notification, and contestation. When states decide to invoke emergency powers, they must provide an appropriate public *justification* for their derogation decisions, detailing the relevant factual circumstances and explaining why both the invocation of emergency powers generally and the specific responsive measures chosen are strictly necessary to address the public emergency. A state's entry into

42. The relational character of human rights norms also helps to explain why international human rights tribunals have been prepared to recognize "inherent limitations" on the application of human rights—limitations that do not appear in the express text of human rights treaties. *See, e.g.*, Pieter van Dijk et al., Theory and Practice of the European Convention on Human Rights 343–50 (4th ed. 2006) (discussing "inherent limitations" recognized by the ECHR and European Commission).

43. European Convention, *supra* note 2, art. 15.1; ICCPR, *supra* note 2, art. 41; Arab Charter, *supra* note 2, art. 4.1.

44. ACHR, *supra* note 3, art. 27.1.

45. This interpretive gloss helps to explain why international tribunals have not actually required states to demonstrate an existential threat to their own survival as a precondition for human rights derogation. *See* Thomas Poole, *The Law of Emergency and Reason of State*, *in* Human Rights in Emergencies (Evan J. Criddle ed., forthcoming 2016) (arguing that the "political emergency" paradigm, which demands an existential threat to the state's survival, does not accurately capture the nuances of most state responses to security threats).

a state of emergency and any laws, policies, or practices adopted in response to the crisis must be subject to public *notification*, ensuring that those whose rights are curtailed receive appropriate notice. Further, when public officials derogate from ordinary human rights, their decisions must be open to public *contestation* to ensure that emergency powers are not held or abused so as to dominate or instrumentalize the state's subjects. Observance of these principles demonstrates an appropriate respect for the individuals subject to emergency powers, mitigating concerns that those powers will be employed in a manner inconsistent with the fiduciary authorization of public power.[46] In the sections that follow, we consider further how these principles could be applied in practice to strengthen both tiers of international law's emergency constitution.

A. The Content and Consequences of *Jus ad Tumultum*

As we have seen, the leading conventions on civil and political rights limit emergency powers to crises threatening the "life of the nation" or the "independence or security" of the state. These conventions leave many important questions unanswered, however, because they do not fully elucidate the principles that govern states' entry into states of emergency. For example, how dire must a national crisis be before it can be considered to threaten the "life of the nation" or the "security of the state"? Must a state of emergency affect the entire territory of a member-state before international law will permit a state of emergency? May states derogate from their human rights obligations in order to take preemptive action against potential future threats?

The fiduciary theory offers a principled framework for clarifying these and other controversial aspects of *jus ad tumultum*. The starting point for this analysis is the state's overarching fiduciary obligation to furnish a regime of secure and equal freedom. A declaration of a state of emergency becomes necessary when exigent circumstances frustrate the state's ability to guarantee secure and equal freedom without temporarily employing laws, policies, or practices that would constitute a breach of its fiduciary duty under other circumstances. Although all exercises of coercive force by the state demand justification, the state bears a special burden to justify restrictions on personal freedoms when it asserts that exigent circumstances necessitate recourse to powers that would ordinarily violate the fiduciary principle.

The fiduciary theory confirms conventional wisdom regarding *jus ad tumultum* in some respects and disputes it in others. Recall that the ECHR established four criteria in *Lawless* for determining whether exigent circumstances justify a state of emergency: a "public emergency" must be (1) present or imminent, (2) exceptional, (3) concern the entire population, and (4) constitute a "threat to the organized life

46. In some settings, states may be forced to respond quickly to public emergencies, improvising on the fly without the benefit of robust public notification, justification, and contestation ex ante. This does not excuse a state, however, from offering reasoned justifications for its actions. Nor does it mean that a state may dispense with public contestation after emergency measures have been first deployed. Moreover, the fiduciary model suggests that states should use deliberative processes to develop response plans before emergencies arise to enhance their capacity to respect, protect, and fulfill human rights during emergencies.

of the community."[47] The fiduciary theory supports three of the *Lawless* criteria (subject to important clarifications), but rejects one criterion—the requirement that emergencies concern the entire population—as inconsistent with the state's obligation to guarantee secure and equal freedom for all subjects.

The fourth *Lawless* criterion fits comfortably within the fiduciary theory and provides a natural starting point for *jus ad tumultum* analysis. To justify the state's recourse to emergency powers, national crises must threaten "the organized life of the community" in the sense that they disrupt the state's ability to guarantee its subjects' secure and equal freedom. The fiduciary theory thus stakes out an intermediate position between the view that all credible threats to individual life and liberty justify recourse to emergency powers,[48] and the competing view that states may employ emergency powers only where the survival or independence of the political community as a whole is at stake.[49] A state's concern for its national security need not amount to a Sisyphean quest for absolute public safety at the expense of human rights; rather, a state satisfies its fiduciary obligation to secure legal order if it prohibits the illegitimate use of coercive force such that no private party or alien power may dominate or instrumentalize its subjects with impunity, and enforces the prohibition with proportionate means. The state's ability to discharge this fiduciary obligation may be compromised, as the *Siracusa Principles* suggest, in a civil war or natural disaster that threatens "the existence or basic functioning of [public] institutions indispensable to ensure and protect [human] rights."[50] Only such genuine public emergencies justify recourse to heightened human rights restrictions under international law's emergency constitution.

One important implication of the fourth *Lawless* criterion is that terrorist violence will rarely justify a state's recourse to emergency powers. Under the fiduciary theory, terrorist groups do not constitute full-fledged threats "to the organized life of the community" unless: (1) they have the capacity to launch an attack that would prevent the state from credibly guaranteeing secure and equal freedom (or such capacity is imminent), and (2) the state cannot address these threats without derogating from its human rights obligations. These standards might be satisfied if a state uncovers compelling evidence that a terrorist organization has obtained or will soon obtain a weapon of mass destruction capable of paralyzing essential public institutions. For example, suppose a state determines that a terrorist group has a chemical or biological weapon, which it intends to employ shortly against the national legislature, and which would plunge the country into political chaos. The state might justifiably impose random searches of commercial buildings, homes, and vehicles within the vicinity until the danger passes—even if these measures

47. *Lawless* Commission, 1 ECHR, Series B, § 90, at 82.

48. Eric A. Posner & Adrian Vermeule, Terror in the Balance: Security, Liberty, and the Courts 12 (2007).

49. *See* Joan F. Hartman, *Working Paper for the Committee of Experts on the Article 4 Derogation Provision*, 7 Hum. Rts. Q. 89, 91 (1985).

50. *The Siracusa Principles on the Limitation and Derogation Provisions in the International Covenant on Civil and Political Rights*, 7 Hum. Rts. Q. 3, 7 ¶ 39 (1985) [hereinafter *Siracusa Principles*].

arguably would require derogation from ICCPR Article 17.[51] Even under such extraordinary circumstances, however, the state would still bear the burden to show that it cannot adequately address the threat to legal order without derogating from its ordinary human rights obligations, and that the measures employed are the least intrusive available to address the threat. In contrast, threats of terrorism against civilian or nonessential governmental targets would not ordinarily justify recourse to emergency powers because such threats do not imperil the institutional prerequisites for legal order, and because random searches, which disproportionately burden the persons directly affected, are inconsistent with a regime of secure and equal freedom.

The fiduciary theory also supports the first *Lawless* criterion, which requires that a public emergency be "present or imminent." States may not employ emergency powers to address future threats to public order that are merely hypothetical or lack credible evidence. Hence, a state's mere "apprehension of potential danger" from terrorism, civic unrest, or economic turmoil would not justify emergency measures absent a plausible showing that such measures are strictly necessary to avert a present or imminent crisis that would disrupt legal order.[52] That this inquiry may turn on difficult questions of credibility and risk perception does not undermine its importance as a criterion in *jus ad tumultum* analysis; it simply underscores the state's fiduciary obligation to evaluate potential threats cautiously and deliberatively, with appropriate solicitude to those who would bear the burden of rights-infringing measures.

Consistent with *Lawless*'s second criterion, the fiduciary principle also precludes states from employing emergency powers unless "the normal measures or restrictions permitted by [international law] for the maintenance of public safety, health and order are plainly inadequate."[53] Emergency powers are "exceptional" in the sense that they are contingent upon the existence of exigent circumstances that frustrate the state's ability to satisfy its basic fiduciary obligation to provide legal order. That emergencies are "exceptional" is not to say, however, that they are necessarily short in duration, as some have insisted.[54] Under the fiduciary theory, a state may maintain a state of emergency as long as the crisis justifying emergency action persists—for decades, if necessary—provided that the state complies with *jus in tumultu* and abandons emergency powers immediately once the circumstances necessitating recourse to emergency powers have passed.[55] The fiduciary theory

51. *See* ICCPR, *supra* note 2, art. 17(1) ("No one shall be subject to arbitrary or unlawful interference with his privacy, family, home or correspondence . . . .").

52. *Cf. Siracusa Principles, supra* note 50, at 8, ¶¶ 40–41 (asserting that "[i]nternal conflict and unrest . . . cannot justify derogations" and that "[e]conomic difficulties per se cannot justify derogation measures.").

53. *Greek Case, supra* note 23, at 70, ¶ 113.

54. *See* Gross & Ni Aolain, *supra* note 36, at 644 ("Only a truly extraordinary crisis that lasts for a relatively brief period of time can be a derogation-justifying emergency.").

55. *See* Inter-Am. C.H.R., *Report on the Situation of Human Rights of a Segment of the Nicaraguan Population of Miskito Origin*, pt. II, subdiv. E, § 14, OEA/Ser.L/V.II.62 doc. 10, rev. 3 (Nov. 29, 1983); ACHR, *supra* note 3, art. 27, §§ 1, 3 (allowing for derogations for as long as necessary to address an emergency).

thus draws a distinction between permanent or institutionalized states of emergency, which are anathema to the fiduciary principle undergirding international law's emergency constitution, and entrenched emergencies, which may satisfy the fiduciary principle so long as they retain their conditional, "temporary" character.[56]

In each of the foregoing respects, the fiduciary theory offers a secure theoretical framework for the ECHR's approach to *jus ad tumultum*. But the fiduciary theory also challenges the status quo insofar as it rejects the court's assertion in *Lawless* that exigent circumstances must "concern" a country's "entire population" to justify the exercise of emergency powers.[57] The fiduciary principle dictates that a state's obligation to guarantee secure and equal freedom extends to all persons subject to the state's powers. To the extent that a state is unable to satisfy this fiduciary obligation in any isolated region—or for discrete groups within the country as a whole—the fiduciary principle authorizes the state to employ emergency powers to the extent strictly necessary to re-establish public order for those adversely affected. When addressing such geographically or demographically limited public emergencies, the state need not demonstrate that crisis conditions adversely affect the rest of the populace. For example, the Colombian government might reasonably resort to emergency measures to address threats posed by paramilitary insurgent groups, even if those groups' operations are confined to geographically limited regions of the country.[58] This approach to emergency powers arguably tracks the practice of international, regional, and municipal tribunals more closely with respect to localized emergencies than the canonical *Lawless* test.[59] Hence, the ECHR and other international and regional tribunals could easily abandon *Lawless*'s third requirement and embrace the fiduciary principle without disavowing their prior decisions.

One important implication of the fiduciary theory is that states may not exercise emergency powers pursuant to undeclared, de facto public emergencies. Commentators have observed that de facto emergencies have proliferated as states have endeavored to skirt international monitoring of their human rights compliance.[60] Under the fiduciary theory, however, states' obligation to treat their subjects always as self-determining agents entails a responsibility to notify the public

56. *See* U.N. Human Rights Committee, July 24, 2001, ICCPR art. 4, General Comment No 29, ¶ 2, U.N. Doc. CCPR/C/21/Rev.1/Add.11 (Aug. 31, 2001) ("Measures derogating from the principles of the Covenant must be of an exceptional and temporary nature.").

57. *See* J.E.S. Faucett, The Application of the European Convention on Human Rights 308 (2d ed. 1987) ("The emergency must be nation-wide in its effects, so that however severe the local impact of an emergency may be, it will not, in the absence of that condition, be a 'public emergency' . . . ."); Oraá, *supra* note 1, at 28–39 (asserting that a public emergency must affect the whole population, or at least the whole population within a limited area).

58. *See* ICCPR Derogation Notifications, *supra* note 9 Colombia (Apr. 11, 1984).

59. *See* Ronald St. J. Macdonald, *Derogations Under Article 15 of the European Convention on Human Rights*, 36 Columbia J. Transnat'l L. 225, 240–41 (1997) ("In fact, the manner in which the Convention has been applied in Northern Ireland and Turkey allows states to take measures in a severely affected area of the nation that would not be strictly necessary in other areas where the threat is less significant.").

60. *See* Gross & Ni Aiolain, *supra* note 7, at 305, 320–21.

regarding the state's use of emergency powers and the circumstances upon which the state relies to justify its emergency declaration.[61] This requirement that states proclaim a formal state of emergency "puts the citizenry on notice of the intent of the governing authorities and may provide a chance for public discussion and response, or at least fair warning of limitations" on the exercise of human rights.[62] The notice requirement ensures that the public has an opportunity to understand their legal rights and participate in shaping the state's response to the crisis at hand.

In sum, the fiduciary theory suggests that public emergencies may take a variety of forms, including not only traditional emergencies, such as armed conflicts and internal political unrest, but also other challenges to public order arising from grave financial distress, public health crises, and natural disasters. In each of these contexts, a state may derogate from its human rights obligations only if it can demonstrate that the crisis at hand overwhelms the capacity of public institutions to guarantee its subjects' secure and equal freedom through the application of generally applicable laws.

B. The Content and Consequences of *Jus in Tumultu*

The fiduciary theory also illuminates the content and consequences of *jus in tumultu*. When states restrict the exercise of human rights during emergencies, the fiduciary principle requires a reasoned public justification concerning the particular emergency measures employed. As Jerry Mashaw has observed, "[u]nreasoned coercion denies our moral agency and our political standing as citizens entitled to respect as ends in ourselves, not as mere means in the effectuation of state purposes."[63] Conversely, when states publicly justify their emergency measures, they respect persons subject to their power as self-determining agents who possess their own ends and purposes. The burden lies on states, therefore, to provide a "specific justification of each measure taken in response to an emergency, rather than an abstract assessment of the overall situation."[64] A state's failure to provide a reasoned justification for particular emergency measures renders those measures unlawful on their face, as the U.N. Human Rights Committee has recognized.[65]

61. Silva et al. v. Uruguay, Comm. No. 34/1978, Decision by Hum. Rts. Comm. Under Art. 5(4) of the Optional Protocol to the ICCPR, ¶ 8.3 (Apr. 8, 1981) (affirming that the state bears the burden to justify a state of emergency by "giv[ing] a sufficiently detailed account of the relevant facts" to "legitimize [its] departure from the normal legal regime prescribed by the Covenant").

62. Hartman, *supra* note 49, at 99.

63. Jerry L. Mashaw, *Reasoned Administration: The European Union, the United States, and the Project of Democratic Governance*, 76 Geo. Wash. L. Rev. 99, 104 (2007).

64. Hartman, *supra* note 49, at 106.

65. Silva et al. v. Uruguay, Comm. No. 34/1978, Decision by Hum. Rts. Comm. Under Art. 5(4) of the Optional Protocol to the ICCPR, ¶ 8.3 (Apr. 8, 1981) ("[I]f the respondeat Government does not furnish the required justification itself, as it is required to do under article 4(2) of the Optional Protocol and article 4(3) of the Covenant, the Human Rights Committee cannot conclude that valid reasons exist to legitimize a departure from the normal legal regime prescribed by the Covenant.").

The principal focus of justification at the *jus in tumultu* stage rests on the principle of necessity: states may restrict human rights only to the extent "strictly required" to restore public order.[66] Courts and legal scholars generally agree that the necessity principle requires states to identify the range of measures available to address an emergency and then to determine which of these measures are proportional to the desired end. The necessity principle does not mean, however, that states can take whatever steps they perceive are required to preserve human life, irrespective of the cost. Positing absolute human safety as the state's objective distorts necessity analysis, because human safety can never be fully secure, irrespective of how much energy the state devotes to this end. Instead, the fiduciary theory clarifies that the end against which emergency powers' necessity must be measured is the restoration of subjects' secure and equal freedom. General derogation clauses in human rights conventions must be understood, therefore, to permit restrictions on human rights only where a state's responsive measures are no more intrusive than strictly necessary. In assessing proportionality for these purposes, states should address the severity, duration, and scope of emergency measures, as well as consider the measures' compatibility with domestic law and other international obligations.[67]

Arguably a special justification is required if a state gives notice that it intends to derogate from treaty provisions that themselves contain limitation clauses, such as those addressing the rights to a public trial,[68] peaceable assembly,[69] and freedom of association.[70] The fiduciary theory allows states to employ limitation clauses during and outside states of emergency where such action is "necessary" to safeguard subjects against domination and instrumentalization. Such may be the case, as the ICCPR and other conventions recognize, where the state adopts non-discriminatory laws, policies, or practices to advance "national security or public safety, public order (*ordre public*), the protection of public health or morals or the protection of the rights and freedoms of others."[71] For example, ICCPR Article 14.1 arguably permits courts in the interest of "national security" to restrict the public's access to sensitive evidence introduced in terrorism trials,[72] but under the fiduciary theory basic elements of due process would have to remain in place because these are required as a matter of jus cogens. To the extent that such restrictions are necessary to safeguard public security, a state may justifiably adopt them pursuant to the limitation clause in Article 14.1 without filing a notice of derogation. However, it appears unlikely that the fiduciary principle would ever authorize a state to *derogate* from the right

66. *See* ICCPR, *supra* note 2, art. 4.1.

67. *See* Inter-Am. C.H.R., Advisory Opinion on Habeas Corpus in Emergency Situations, 27 I.L.M. 513, ¶ 39, at 522 (1988) (observing that emergency measures will have violated international law if they "lasted longer than the time limit specified, if they were manifestly irrational, unnecessary or disproportionate, or if, in adopting them, there was a misuse or abuse of power").

68. ICCPR, *supra* note 2, art. 14.1.

69. *Id.* art. 21.

70. *Id.* art. 22.

71. *Id.*

72. *Id.* art. 14.1.

to a public trial on "national security" grounds, as virtually any permissible restriction on this right could be justified based on the limitations clause of Article 14.1. The ultimate implication is that most permissible restrictions on human rights, such as restrictions under Article 14.1 and mandatory product warnings, will take the form of permanent limitations rather than temporary derogations. In practice, the fiduciary principle will rarely authorize a state to derogate from human rights treaty provisions that contain general limitation clauses.

Similarly, the fiduciary theory confirms the requirement that states must provide notice concerning their derogations from human rights conventions, but it suggests that this requirement exists primarily for the benefit of a state's subjects, not the international community per se. Traditionally, notification requirements have been understood primarily as devices to facilitate international monitoring; when states provide notice of derogation pursuant to their treaty commitments, international and regional tribunals and other states-parties are better equipped to check human rights abuses.[73] States have often ignored notification requirements during emergencies, however, viewing such provisions as mere procedural technicalities. The fiduciary theory, on the other hand, suggests that such notification requirements are central to the state-subject fiduciary relation: states must justify emergency measures publicly to honor their obligation to treat subjects as ends-in-themselves and not as mere means to the state's ends. Subjects must receive notice regarding the legal and practical consequences of public emergencies in order to appreciate how emergency measures will impact their rights and obligations.[74] The notice requirement also affirms the fiduciary character of state legal authority by empowering individuals to contest emergency measures. At a minimum, therefore, emergency proclamations must identify the circumstances constituting the public emergency, the particular rights suspended, the state's responsive measures, and the state's reasons for selecting those measures.[75] Whenever states derogate from their human rights commitments, public notice and justification are essential to secure individuals against domination and instrumentalization, and affirm a relationship in which the state serves as a fiduciary for those subject to its powers.

Just as the fiduciary theory supports public notification of emergency measures, it also dictates that individuals—rather than state-parties alone—have standing to contest violations of *jus ad tumultum* and *jus in tumultu* before independent human rights commissions, as well as through the political process and domestic judicial review. The principle of contestability in public emergencies derives from the

73. *See* ICCPR, Gen. Cmt. No. 29—States of Emergency (art. 4), ¶ 17, July 24, 2001 (asserting that the international notification regime is necessary to allow human rights bodies to discharge their functions, as well as to permit other states-parties to monitor compliance).

74. *See* Daniel O'Donnell, *Commentary by the Rapporteur on Derogation*, 7 HUM. RTS. Q. 23, 25 (1985) (noting the statement of ICCPR draftsman Rene Cassin that the "real purpose of Article 4 was to require States to take a decision in public when they were obliged to restrict such rights") (citing U.N. Doc. E/CN.4/SR 127, 14.6 (1949)).

75. *See* Silva et al. v. Uruguay, Comm. No. 34/1978, Decision by Hum. Rts. Comm. Under Art. 5(4) of the Optional Protocol to the ICCPR, ¶ 8.2 (Apr. 8, 1981); ICCPR General Comment No. 29: State of Emergency (Article 4), ¶ 17 ("[T]he notification by States parties should include full information about the measures taken and a clear explanation of the reasons for them, with full documentation attached regarding their law.").

republican principle of non-domination, securing persons against arbitrariness and state capture. Phillip Pettit describes the principle's application as follows:

> [I]f the state's power of interference is to be rendered non-arbitrary then whatever other devices are in place, people must be able to contest the decisions made by various arms of government. They must have access to the reasons supporting those decisions and they must be able to contest the soundness of those reasons or the degree of support they offer to the decisions made. Moreover they must be in a position, ideally, to expect that such contestations will be heard, will be impartially adjudicated and, if necessary, will be implemented against those in government. . . . It is only in the event of democracy having this deliberative cast that contestability, and ultimately non-arbitrariness, can be furthered.[76]

In short, states must afford the public an opportunity to contest emergency measures so as to ensure that all subjects have a voice and that all relevant interests are taken into account in the formulation and management of a state's response to an emergency. This opportunity for public contestation must remain open for the duration of an emergency to prevent temporary emergency measures from ossifying into permanent or institutionalized emergencies. Whenever states violate *jus ad tumultum* or *jus in tumultu*, persons adversely affected must have access to independent review to ensure that state emergency measures have an "objective justification" in international law's emergency constitution.[77] To the extent that oversight bodies such as the U.N. Human Rights Committee do not permit individuals to contest state emergency measures directly, their complaint procedures ought to be reformed to satisfy the fiduciary principle.

IV. CARL SCHMITT'S CHALLENGE

The principles of deliberative accountability contemplated in the ICCPR, European Convention, and other conventions essentially presuppose that international law can govern public emergencies. But what if law cannot deliver on this promise? What if law is incapable of guiding or constraining the sovereign during emergencies?

This is the central argument of Carl Schmitt's *Political Theology: Four Chapters on the Concept of Sovereignty*.[78] Schmitt announces at the outset that "[s]overeign is he

76. Philip Pettit, *Deliberative Democracy and the Discursive Dilemma*, 11 PHIL. ISSUES 268, 281–82 (2001).

77. Report of the Human Rights Committee, U.N. GAOR, 34th Sess., Supp. No. 40, at 20, U.N. Doc. A/34/40, ¶ 78 (1979).

78. *See* SCHMITT, *supra* note 6. Of course, Schmitt was not the first to suggest that executive power cannot reasonably be constrained by law during emergencies. *See, e.g.*, THE FEDERALIST No. 23, at 153 (Alexander Hamilton) (Clinton Rossiter ed., 1961) (observing that "it is impossible to foresee or to define the extent and variety of national emergencies, and the correspondent extent and variety of the means which may be necessary to satisfy them," and asserting that "for this reason no constitutional shackles can wisely be imposed on the power to which the care of it is committed").

who decides on the exception."[79] By this, Schmitt means that the sovereign is he who "decides whether there is an extreme emergency as well as what must be done to eliminate it."[80] Because "the precise details of an emergency cannot be anticipated, nor can one spell out . . . how it is to be eliminated," the power to decide on the exception "must necessarily be unlimited."[81] Schmitt's claim is based on the belief that the realm of the legal or juristic consists in exclusively two elements: general norms and particular decisions.[82] Legal norms, however, are not self-executing, and even if their meaning were transparent and agreed to by all, they can neither exhaustively anticipate the shape an emergency will take nor determine what must be done to eliminate it. Thus, Schmitt thought that the sovereign's power to decide on the exception cannot be checked by general norms. And because only decisions on the exception are capable of safeguarding the "normal" legal order, Schmitt could conclude that "[l]ike every other order, legal order rests on a decision and not a norm."[83] That is, even during normal times the sovereign retains an unlimited power to declare and deal with emergencies. By virtue of this power, the sovereign "stands outside the normally valid legal system," but also "belongs to it, for it is he who must decide whether the constitution needs to be suspended in its entirety."[84] Liberal legalists are therefore fooling themselves if they think that constitutional or other legal norms have purchase except at the discretion and sufferance of the sovereign.

Schmitt has had enormous influence on scholarship related to emergency powers.[85] To take one prominent example, Giorgio Agamben's *State of Exception* chronicles the reliance of earlier twentieth-century writers on Schmitt,[86] applies the German thinker's ideas to measures adopted by the Bush administration after 9/11,

79. SCHMITT, *supra* note 6, at 5.

80. *Id.* at 7.

81. *Id.* at 6–7.

82. *Id.* at 10. As Dyzenhaus points out, Schmitt's theory of sovereignty is tied closely to his understanding of "the political," a pre-juristic "moment" centered on the friend/enemy distinction. Enemies pose threats to the existence of political and legal order, and so, according to Schmitt, the sovereign must have unlimited power to identify and beat back those threats. *See* DYZENHAUS, *supra* note 11, at 34; CARL SCHMITT, THE CONCEPT OF THE POLITICAL 5 (1976). In the text we focus on Schmitt's claims about the nature of legal order. These claims pose an independent argument that cannot be dismissed on liberal grounds that the friend/enemy distinction is normatively irrelevant because inconsistent with the moral equality of individuals.

83. SCHMITT, *supra* note 6, at 10.

84. *Id.* at 7.

85. *See, e.g.*, AGAMBEN, *supra* note 8; GROSS & NÍ AOLÁIN, *supra* note 7 (drawing on Schmitt's work to develop a theory of sovereign prerogative to take extralegal action during emergencies); POSNER & VERMEULE, *supra* note 48, at 38–39 (identifying Schmitt as the "philosopher-jurist most often invoked in discussions of emergencies" and deploying Schmittian arguments to defend security-based restrictions on civil liberties); Austin Sarat, *Introduction: Toward New Conceptions of the Relationship of Law and Sovereignty Under Conditions of Emergency, in* SOVEREIGNTY, EMERGENCY, LEGALITY 1, 2 (Austin Sarat, ed. 2010).

86. *See, e.g.*, AGAMBEN, *supra* note 8, at 7–9 (discussing CARL J. FRIEDRICH, CONSTITUTIONAL GOVERNMENT AND DEMOCRACY (1950), and CLINTON ROSSITER, CONSTITUTIONAL DICTATORSHIP: CRISIS GOVERNMENT IN THE MODERN DEMOCRACIES (1948)).

and maintains that the state of exception "tends increasingly to appear as the dominant paradigm of government in contemporary politics."[87] As evidence of Schmitt's paradigm, Agamben points to the "military order" issued by President George W. Bush on November 13, 2001, authorizing inter alia "indefinite detention" of noncitizens suspected of terrorism and trial by military commissions.[88] Agamben observes that President Bush's order "radically erases any legal status of the individual. . . . Neither prisoners nor persons accused, but simply 'detainees,' they are the object of a pure de facto rule, of a detention that is indefinite not only in the temporal sense but in its very nature as well, since it is entirely removed from the law and judicial oversight."[89] The implication is that the U.S. president, like Schmitt's sovereign, has absolute and unfettered power to identify and confront perceived threats to national security.

Although Schmitt sought to contest the relevance of constitutionally entrenched limits on sovereign power within Germany during the interwar Weimar period, his theory also has obvious implications for IHRL. Like municipal constitutions, IHRL cannot anticipate the circumstances under which the sovereign might need to invoke emergency powers, nor can IHRL dictate in advance how those powers might properly be used. On a Schmittian construal, IHRL's accommodation of restrictions on (some) human rights during emergencies embodies an unstable compromise between liberal legalism and the absolute power held by the sovereign to deal with existential threats. This compromise is unstable because when push comes to shove, Schmitt's sovereign can simply ignore IHRL, as President Bush did when he authorized indefinite, summary detention of terrorism suspects after 9/11.[90] If Agamben is correct that Schmitt's conception of emergency powers has become the dominant national-security paradigm, disarming Schmitt's challenge may have profound consequences not only for international legal theory but also for the observance of human rights in practice.

V. THE FIDUCIARY THEORY'S RESPONSE

The fiduciary theory of human rights offers a potent response to Carl Schmitt's argument that the rule of law cannot constrain state discretion during emergencies. Specifically, the fiduciary theory draws on the principles of non-instrumentalization and non-domination to provide a seamless, normatively substantial account of IHRL's application during emergencies: states may derogate from their human rights commitments in emergencies only where such measures are strictly necessary to satisfy their overarching fiduciary obligation to guarantee secure and equal freedom. Such emergency measures preserve, rather than subvert, a legal order in which no person is subject to another's unilateral discretionary power. The fiduciary

87. *Id.* at 9.

88. *Id.* at 3 (discussing Military Order, Detention, Treatment, and Trial of Certain Non-Citizens in the War Against Terrorism, 66 Fed. Reg. 57,833, 57,834 (Nov. 13, 2001)).

89. *Id.* at 3–4.

90. *See* United Nations Economic and Social Council, Situation of Detainees at Guantánamo Bay, § 84 (Feb. 15, 2006), http://www.cbsnews.com/htdocs/pdf/ungitmo021506.pdf (last visited Mar. 16, 2010) (concluding that the United States had violated the ICCPR by denying

theory, we argue, disarms Schmitt's critique and contests neo-Schmittian accounts of emergency powers by explaining how derogation from certain human rights norms during emergencies may be consistent with a robust conception of legality rooted in the state-subject fiduciary relationship.

In contrast to the fiduciary theory, which places emergency powers within a rich body of substantive and procedural principles, Schmitt assumes that legal order consists of only norms and decisions. Schmitt can perhaps concede that the interpretation of norms (at least during normal times) may be guided by principles embedded within a legal tradition, much as inclusive legal positivists and incorporationists respond to Dworkin's hard cases by allowing moral principles to play a role in adjudication while denying that they are part of the concept of law. The more natural reading of Schmitt, however, is that he is an exclusive legal positivist. For exclusivists such as Raz, principles can temper decision-making, but they are always extralegal standards that judges may choose to apply (or not) at their discretion.[91] Similarly, on Schmitt's positivist legal theory the sovereign and his delegates may but are not required to use principles to inform the interpretation of norms. And if an emergency is declared, access to principles is cut off at the root because the norms that principles may influence are "destroyed in the exception."[92] Principles thus have no independent standing during normal times, and no standing at all during a state of exception.

In elaborating our preferred conception of the fiduciary theory above, we have relied on two theorists, Fuller and Kant, who vigorously dispute the idea that legal order is intelligible as such without recourse to principles. For Fuller those principles are found in his internal morality of law, whereas for Kant they are the constitutive normative elements of his regime of secure and equal freedom. As noted in Chapter 3, the intermediate regulative principles of the fiduciary model are ideals of non-instrumentalization and non-domination. Within the state-subject fiduciary relationship in particular, these normative precepts crystallize in principles such as integrity, formal equality, solicitude, and fundamental security under the rule of law. We have argued that these principles underpin human rights, but it is important to note that the principles intrinsic to the fiduciary model do much more than this: fiduciary principles also control exercises of discretionary power where there is no explicit norm in place to guide the power holder. As we shall see below, the fiduciary model's principled control of discretion enables it to answer Schmitt's challenge.

Dyzenhaus observes that for Schmitt the problem of the exception is akin to the problem of discretionary decision-making in ordinary cases; that is, decision-making within legal order when determinate legal rules do not supply an answer.[93] Similarly, for positivists such as Hart, Dyzenhaus says, "the moment of discretionary

Guantanamo detainees the opportunity to challenge "the legality of their detention before a judicial body," and that their continuing detention "amounts to arbitrary detention").

91. *See, e.g.*, Joseph Raz, Ethics in the Public Domain: Essays in the Morality of Law and Politics 195–237 (1994).

92. Schmitt, *supra* note 6, at 12.

93. Dyzenhaus, *supra* note 11, at 60–61.

judgment in a penumbral case is a kind of mini state of emergency of exception."[94] These moments pose a conundrum from the point of view of legality that resembles the puzzle posed by emergencies: in the absence of a controlling norm of positive law, on what basis can a judge (or anyone) second-guess the legality of an executive decision, especially if that decision is taken under valid statutory authority that confers an unqualified discretion?

Dyzenhaus's answer to both puzzles is common law constitutionalism: the theory that legal principles reside within the common law, are constitutive of legality, and inform (or should inform) statutory interpretation and exercises of discretion.[95] For Dyzenhaus, common law constitutionalism implies a joint commitment on the part of legislatures, executives, and judges to a "rule-of-law project."[96] The project consists in the legislature enacting laws capable of being interpreted by officials and judges in such a way that their implementation respects principles of due process, reasonableness, and equality, all of which is informed by the idea that "the legal subject has to be regarded as a bearer of human rights."[97] When either the legislature or the executive appear to lose their rule-of-law nerve, it falls to judges on review to keep the other branches within the project by imposing procedural safeguards or reading down legislation in accordance with common law values.

Dyzenhaus's reply to "Schmitt's challenge" begins with an admission that the judicial record in emergency situations is at best mixed: judges are often spineless and overly deferential to the executive. But sometimes they are not, and sometimes their decisions are of real benefit to detainees held indefinitely in legal black holes or "grey" holes, without due process or other rule-of-law safeguards. The mixed record thus shows that judges can play a meaningful role upholding the rule of law in the face of legislative or executive resistance. Even at the limit, where the resistance is extreme and reinforced by unambiguous legislation, the role of the judge in legal order is still to uphold the rule of law, so judges are duty-bound to decry its subversion. Contrary to Schmitt's claim that only a sovereign (executive) with unlimited power can declare and deal with emergencies, Dyzenhaus's discussion of national security cases arguably shows that if judges properly understand their role within legal order, they can regulate the use of emergency powers and publicly denounce attempts to evade the rule of law.

Not all are convinced that Dyzenhaus has met Schmitt's challenge. One of Dyzenhaus's critics, Thomas Poole, claims that Dyzenhaus fails to explain where common law values such as equality, fairness, and reasonableness come from, "save that they are inherent in the very notion of legality, which, given that this is precisely the subject in dispute, rather begs the question."[98] Moreover, Poole says, even as stated these values "do not offer a coherent blueprint for judicial decision

94. *Id.* at 60.

95. *Id.; see also* T.R.S. ALLAN, CONSTITUTIONAL JUSTICE: A LIBERAL THEORY OF THE RULE OF LAW (2003); David A. Strauss, *Common Law Constitutional Interpretation*, 63 U. CHI. L. REV. 877 (1996).

96. DYZENHAUS, *supra* note 11, at 3.

97. *Id.* at 12–13.

98. *Id.*

making."[99] Poole objects that "we are not told why these particular common law values should outweigh (always? generally?) other, countervailing values, such as security or even national preservation."[100] Part of the difficulty common law constitutionalists such as Dyzenhaus face, he says, is that the common law's normative content in the public sphere tends to be "soft-edged . . . as well as susceptible to change."[101]

The fiduciary theory offers a novel reply to Schmitt's challenge, which deepens the argument in favor of common law constitutionalism and furnishes the resources necessary to answer Poole's objections. Although our theory's ultimate prescriptions may be roughly similar to Dyzenhaus's and other common law constitutionalists', the fiduciary theory's novelty is the justification it offers for them, a justification that avoids or answers Poole's concerns. We shall also show that the fiduciary theory explains international law's unique de jure capacity to govern a sovereign's declaration of emergency and the measures adopted to deal with it, thus tying international law to common law constitutionalism within a seamless account of public law.

Consistent with common law constitutionalism, the fiduciary theory trades on the idea that sovereignty is constituted and regulated by international law, and this legal order is comprised of principles as well as norms and decisions. We have seen already that these include the principles of integrity, formal moral equality, and solicitude. These principles follow from application of the deeper normative principles of non-instrumentalization and non-domination to the fiduciary circumstances of the state and subject. These same principles guide the elaboration of the rule of law under the fiduciary theory, and explain why the fiduciary state owes its subjects a series of common law duties (duties owed without the prompt of a statute) when its administrative action touches them. These include duties of due process or procedural fairness, purposiveness in the sense of using entrusted powers exclusively for the purposes for which they are conferred (the duty of reasonableness in commonwealth jurisdictions), reason-giving, transparency, and proportionality. Legal principles such as these provide a bulwark against the possession and use of arbitrary power, and thereby embody in a more determinate form the requirements of non-instrumentalization and non-domination. The flagrant violation of any of them would offend the foundational idea that public decision-makers occupy a fiduciary position vis-à-vis the people they serve. Each principle is thus justified as a necessary and constituent part of the overarching fiduciary relationship.

The fiduciary theory's response to Schmitt's challenge, then, is to provide an account of how the principles and duties of common law constitutionalism play a constitutive role within legal order, which in turn explains how they are intrinsic to legality. The core principles and duties of common law constitutionalism are not merely artifacts of judicial practice; instead, they are intrinsic to legality itself because they constitute the normative dimension of the fiduciary relationship that

99. Thomas Poole, *Constitutional Exceptionalism and the Common Law*, 7 INT'L J. CONST. L. 247, 264 (2009); *see also* Adrian Vermeule, *Our Schmittian Administrative Law*, 122 HARV. L. REV. 1095, 1096 (2009) (dismissing attempts to extend the rule of law to all administrative action as "hopeless fantasy").

100. Poole, *supra* note 99, at 265.

101. *Id.* at 268.

makes legal order possible. The fiduciary theory thus offers a fresh account of common law constitutionalism in which the idea that principles are intrinsic to the common law is presented as the conclusion of the inquiry rather than as a premise or an article of faith.

With this principle-rich legal theory in place, we can see now how the fiduciary theory can disarm Schmitt's main argument that the sovereign must be able to decide on the exception because general norms cannot anticipate the unforeseeable in a time of crisis. Let us assume *arguendo* that, as Schmitt claims, general norms cannot anticipate the contingencies that may arise in emergencies. The point is irrelevant from the perspective of the fiduciary theory because legal principles immanent to the sovereign's fiduciary relationship to his subjects remain in place, and these supply standards that municipal judges and others can use to assess the legality of the sovereign's chosen measures. To put the point starkly, the sovereign may be able to declare martial law and suspend a variety of norms but, under the fiduciary theory, he cannot suspend the overarching fiduciary principle that authorizes him to establish legal order on behalf of his subjects. He cannot do so because that principle is triggered by his mere possession of sovereign powers. He may of course have the de facto means of violating the relevant legal principles and duties that attach to his office by dint of the fiduciary principle, but then he would be acting as an unauthorized usurper of public power rather than as a sovereign.

The fiduciary theory is particularly well-suited to the regulation of executive power in emergencies because it is premised on a normative structure in which the power-holder often holds discretionary power that affords a wide margin of appreciation. In some cases, the power is not controlled by specific norms apart from those derived from context-sensitive fiduciary principles. Perhaps the best example is the parent-child case. Parents must care for and manage their children, but how precisely this is to be done, within fiduciary limits, is determined by the parents. Another good example is someone who holds a power of attorney. As Pettit points out, when one person is entitled to interfere in my affairs but only on condition that she further my interests and take my opinions seriously, the power-holder "relates to me, not as a master, but more in the fashion of an agent who enjoys a power of attorney in my affairs."[102] Once again, the agent is not constrained by particular rules or norms, save those that proscribe self-dealing and others that flow from fiduciary principles. Like the parent and the agent with a power of attorney, the sovereign in an emergency enjoys a margin of appreciation but is nonetheless accountable to public, fiduciary standards.

We are now in a position to address Poole's objections to common law constitutionalism. As discussed above, the fiduciary theory offers a non-question-begging account of the source and basis of principles in legal order, including the principles and duties of common law constitutionalism. The thornier issue is whether the fiduciary theory and international law's emergency constitution can combine to provide meaningful guidance to policymakers and judges. It is important to recall at the outset that Poole's critique of common law constitutionalism on this issue is nuanced. Poole does not assert, as do some critical legal studies scholars,

102. Philip Pettit, Republicanism: A Theory of Freedom and Government 23 (1997).

that *all* legal decision-making is irremediably indeterminate.[103] He instead makes a more modest and more plausible point: decision-making in the public sphere is indeterminate, especially during emergencies, because the principles that govern it are "soft-edged." The hard/soft distinction is intended to distinguish law that can provide a "coherent blueprint for judicial decision making" from law that cannot.

An advantage of the fiduciary theory is that, like contract, it enjoys the relatively hard-edged normative structure of a capacious but specific class of private-law relationships, that is, the fiduciary relationship. It is no coincidence that the fiduciary theory's determinate legal principles such as fairness and reasonableness mirror those used by judges when they assess the legality of a private fiduciary's actions with respect to multiple beneficiaries. We have discussed above the fiduciary theory's capacity to justify and specify both peremptory and derogable norms of IHRL. We have also seen that the fiduciary theory supplies a robust set of legal principles to guide state decision-makers in deciding whether and how extensively to derogate from their treaty obligations during emergencies.

VI. THE ROLE OF COURTS AND INTERNATIONAL INSTITUTIONS

When courts and international institutions base their decisions upon general principles rather than discrete rules, their decisions may become ready targets for political contestation. In national security cases where the stakes are high, some might worry that the fiduciary theory calls upon courts and international institutions to second-guess a balance struck between liberty and security that only the democratically elected branches are entitled to make.[104] The fiduciary theory highlights three considerations that support a vigorous role for courts and international institutions during national emergencies. The first consideration concerns the function of courts and international institutions as facilitators of public justification, non-discrimination, and impartiality. The second addresses the legal limits of legislative and executive interest-balancing during extreme circumstances. The third explains how international law and its institutions are uniquely equipped to stand between the state and its subjects as arbiters of legality in times of emergency.

A. Calibrating Deference to National Authorities

How much weight should international institutions give to state assessments of the existence of a public emergency and the measures necessary to restore public order? Within the European human rights system, the ECHR has accorded an express

103. *See, e.g.*, Mark Tushnet, *Defending the Indeterminacy Thesis*, 16 Quinnipiac L. Rev. 339, 341 (1997); Mark Tushnet, *Critical Legal Studies: A Political History*, 100 Yale L.J. 1515, 1524 (1991).

104. *See, e.g.*, Secretary of State for the Home Department v. Rehman, [2002] 1 All E.R. 123, 142 (per Lord Hoffman); Posner & Vermeule, *supra* note 48; Eric A. Posner & Adrian Vermeule, *Crisis Governance in the Administrative State; 9/11 and the Financial Meltdown of 2008*, 76 U. Chi.

"margin of appreciation" to state assessments, holding that national authorities are often better placed to ascertain whether a public emergency exists "by reason of their direct and continuous contact with the pressing needs of the moment."[105] In *Ireland v. United Kingdom*, the ECHR explained that the European Convention contemplates "a wide margin of appreciation" to state decision-makers because "national authorities are in a better position than the international judge to decide both on the presence of . . . an emergency and on the nature and scope of the derogations necessary to avert it."[106] The margin of deference to national authorities is not based solely on functional considerations, however; it also reflects the fiduciary constitution of state sovereignty. As the ECHR has recognized, deference to national authorities is appropriate because international law entrusts states with "direct responsibility for establishing the balance between the taking of effective measures [to preserve the life of the nation] on the one hand, and respecting individual rights on the other."[107] The margin of appreciation doctrine acknowledges that under international law, states bear primary responsibility as fiduciaries for their people to adapt general human rights frameworks to the unique demands of particular public emergencies.

The fiduciary theory's account of the margin of appreciation doctrine marks a significant departure from other leading accounts. Some legal scholars argue that the primary purpose of the margin of appreciation doctrine is to accommodate moral pluralism through democratic policymaking.[108] Others assert that the court employs the margin of appreciation as an accommodation to principles of comity, reflecting the court's felt need "to avoid damaging confrontations between the Court and Contracting States over their respective spheres of authority."[109] Still other scholars contend that deference is warranted because national authorities are better positioned than international tribunals to evaluate what measures are necessary to

L. Rev. 1613, 1652 (2009) (arguing that emergencies relegate legislatures and judges to a "marginal, reactive, and essentially debilitated" role).

105. Brannigan & McBride v. United Kingdom, (1994) 17 E.H.R.R. 539, 556 (quoting *Ireland v. United Kingdom*).

106. 1 ECHR 15, ¶ 207 (1961).

107. *Brannigan & McBride*, 17 E.H.R.R., ¶ 59 (citing Ireland v. United Kingdom, Series A no. 25, p. 82, para. 214, and Klass and Others v. Germany, 6 Sept. 1978, Ser. A no. 28, at 23, para. 49); *cf.* Handyside v. United Kingdom, 24 Eur. Ct. H.R. (ser. A), at 22 (1976) (noting that the ECHR must not assume the role of national courts and legislatures when balancing conflicting interests); Belgian Linguistics Case, 6 Eur. Ct. H.R. (ser. A) at 34–35 (1968) (stating that the court must not supplant national authorities). Scholars have observed that the margin of appreciation doctrine has its genesis in continental administrative law—another field where discretionary power is entrusted to institutions for public purposes subject to obligations of reasoned justification. *See, e.g.,* Gross & Ní Aoláin, *supra* note 36, at 626.

108. *See, e.g.,* Eyal Benvenisti, *Margin of Appreciation, Consensus, and Universal Standards*, 31 N.Y.U. J. Int'l L. & Pol. 843, 844 (1999); Paul Mahoney, *Marvelous Richness of Diversity or Invidious Cultural Relativism?*, 19 Harv. Hum. Rts. L.J. 1 (1998).

109. R. St. J. MacDonald, *The Margin of Appreciation*, *in* The European System for the Protection of Human Rights 123 (R. St. J. MacDonald et al. eds., 1993); *see also* Yuval Shany, *Toward a General Margin of Appreciation Doctrine in International Law?*, 16 Eur. J. Int'l L. 907, 918 (2005).

address a public emergency.[110] Although these considerations all support deference to national authorities, none is sufficient on its own to justify the margin of appreciation doctrine. Deference to national authorities is justified only to the extent that international law entrusts states with primary responsibility to serve as fiduciaries for their people in deciding what measures are necessary to respect, protect, and fulfill human rights during emergencies.

Deference to states is not unlimited under the margin of appreciation doctrine. Consistent with the requirements of notice and justification from international law's emergency constitution, the fiduciary theory demands robust public justifications of derogations from human rights, all in the service of establishing what Etienne Mureinik called a "culture of justification."[111] This public justification requirement compels decision-makers to own their actions while providing a valuable record that can supply a basis for judicial review. It also invites individuals and groups to participate in decision-making processes that may result in the derogation of human rights. The point of the "culture of justification," then, is to hold power to account to the people, ensuring that the state takes seriously its obligation to respect individual dignity. Meaningful judicial review during emergencies is an essential safeguard for public justification and so fits congenially within the fiduciary model.

The ECHR has stressed that the ultimate "burden lies on [states] to justify their acts."[112] When states have not carried this burden—particularly in selecting measures responsive to public emergencies (*jus in tumultu*)[113]—the court has found them to have violated Article 4(3). For example, in *Brannigan & McBride v. United Kingdom*, the court held that the United Kingdom had abused its emergency powers by prolonging the detention and interrogation of two residents of Northern Ireland without an adequate justification.[114] Likewise, in *Aksoy v. Turkey*, the Court concluded that a two-week delay in presenting a citizen-detainee before a judge "exceeded the Government's margin of appreciation" because it "could not be said to be strictly required by the exigencies of the situation."[115] In this manner, the court has provided a meaningful check on state recourse to emergency powers.

The concept underlying the "margin of appreciation" doctrine is deference. As Dyzenhaus notes, deference can be understood in two ways, as either "deference as submission" or "deference as respect."[116] Whereas deference as submission requires

110. *Brannigan & McBride*, 17 E.H.R.R., ¶ 59. *But see* Gross & Ní Aoláin, *supra* note 36, at 638–38 (challenging the view that during emergencies national authorities are better positioned than international tribunals to evaluate the need for emergency measures).

111. *See* Etienne Mureinik, *Emerging from Emergency: Human Rights in South Africa*, 92 Mich. L. Rev. 1977, 1986 (1994).

112. Murray v. United Kingdom, 19 Eur. H.R. Rep 30, ¶ 38 (1994).

113. *See* Macdonald, *supra* note 59, at 258 (noting that the ECHR generally "undertake[s] more exacting scrutiny of measures the government chooses to take" in response to a perceived emergency).

114. 258 ECHR (1993) Ser. A.

115. 23 E.H.R.R. 553, 573 ¶ 183 (1997).

116. David Dyzenhaus, *The Politics of Deference: Judicial Review and Democracy*, *in* The Province of Administrative Law 278, 286 (Michael Taggart ed., 1997).

judges to submit without reflection "to the intention of the legislature, on a positivist understanding of intention," deference as respect "requires not submission but a respectful attention to the reasons offered or which could be offered in support of a decision, whether that decision be the statutory decision of the legislature, a judgment of another court, or the decision of an administrative agency."[117] In the context of emergency derogations, deference as respect provides a compelling framework for review because it recognizes the legitimate role states play as the primary guardians of human rights and, correspondingly, the subsidiary role of international institutions. Deference as respect also takes seriously the idea that national authorities may be in a "better position" to assess and respond to crises.

At the same time, deference as respect insists that states must offer reasoned justifications for declarations of emergency and derogation measures for those actions to be worthy of respect. Although states would receive a certain margin of appreciation, the scope of the margin would be circumscribed by the range of measures least restrictive of the derogated rights. States would bear the burden to show that the measures adopted were strictly necessary and proportionate, on an objectively defensible interpretation of the facts at the relevant time as they could best be known on a good faith basis. Truly egregious circumstances might warrant more restrictive measures, but those circumstances could not be invoked to violate jus cogens norms. And, as with the adoption of the least restrictive means, such measures would have to be objectively defensible and consistent with a rigorous principle of proportionality that would require the state to show that the measures adopted were strictly necessary. On the fiduciary theory, these requirements of reasoned justification are legal duties because they are essential safeguards to ensure that states deliver upon their obligation to guarantee secure and equal freedom for their people.

Two other limitations on the margin of appreciation doctrine flow from the fiduciary theory. First, states may not derogate from their human rights commitments in a manner that discriminates against a protected group.[118] When states suspend derogable human rights such as freedom of expression, movement, or association, their derogations must be facially neutral and must also reflect due regard for disparate impacts against vulnerable groups or individuals.[119]

Second, the margin of appreciation should not apply with the same force if there are other compelling reasons to conclude that national authorities are not prepared to serve as neutral arbiters for their people. For example, international courts need not cast a blind eye to evidence that national authorities have engaged in flagrant and systematic patterns of human rights abuse in the recent past. Similarly, international courts and commissions should give less deference to national authorities in contexts such as a domestic insurgency where national authorities' concerns for self-preservation may render them unreliable agents for their people. Although some deference to national authorities might still be warranted based on their greater familiarity with facts on the ground, international tribunals should

117. *Id.*

118. *See, e.g.*, ICCPR, *supra* note 2, art. 4.

119. *See* Ludovic Hennebel, *The Inter-American Court of Human Rights: The Ambassador of Universalism*, 2011 QUEBEC J. INT'L L. 57, 60 (observing that in the jurisprudence of the Inter-American Court of Human Rights, vulnerable groups that historically have been the subject

review the state's responsive measures closely to ensure that national authorities do not become effectively judge and party to the same cause. The more a public emergency threatens a government's survival, the greater the threat that a government's choice of responsive measures may be infected by institutional self-interest, thereby undermining the case for deference to the government's choice of responsive measures.

These dynamics of the fiduciary theory help to explain and justify differences in the application of the margin of appreciation doctrine between the European and Inter-American human rights systems. Unlike the ECHR, the Inter-American Commission and the Inter-American Court on Human Rights (Inter-American Court) have not applied the margin of appreciation doctrine consistently in their jurisprudence.[120] The Inter-American Court's reluctance to apply a deferential standard of review reflects the fact that the Inter-American Court began its work at a time when much of Latin America was ruled by oppressive military dictators, and the court's docket was flooded with cases involving torture, forced disappearances, and extrajudicial killing.[121] The Inter-American Court has frankly acknowledged that it views human rights derogation with a jaundiced eye:

> It cannot be denied that under certain circumstances the suspension of guarantees may be the only way to deal with emergency situations and, thereby, to preserve the highest values of a democratic society. The Court cannot, however, ignore the fact that abuses may result from the application of emergency measures not objectively justified in the light of the requirements prescribed in Article 27 [of the American Convention] and the principles contained in other relevant international instruments. This has, in fact, been the experience of our hemisphere.[122]

Given this sobering legacy of human rights abuse to suppress political dissent, it should come as no surprise that the Inter-American Court has declined to view states as faithful fiduciaries for their people. If national authorities use human rights

of discrimination such as children, women, indigenous groups, and disabled persons, receive "stronger protection").

120. *See* Andrew Legg, The Margin of Appreciation Doctrine in International Human Rights Law 31 (2012) (observing that the Inter-American Court lacks "a well-established doctrine of deference" and that "a number of cases seem to imply that there will be no deference to states").

121. *See, e.g.*, Gonzalo Candia, Comparing Diverse Approaches to the Margin of Appreciation: The Case of the European and the Inter-American Court of Human Rights, Pontificia Universidad Católica de Chile Law School, Working Paper No. 1 (2014); Pablo Contreras, *National Discretion and International Deference in the Restriction of Human Rights: A Comparison Between the Jurisprudence of the European and the Inter-American Court of Human Rights*, 11 Nw. J. Int'l Hum. Rts. 28, 28 (2012).

122. Habeas Corpus in Emergency Situations (Arts. 27(2) and 7(6) of the American Convention on Human Rights), Advisory Opinion OC-8/87, Jan. 30, 1987, Inter-Am. Ct. H.R. (Ser. A), No. 8, para. 20 (1987).

derogation for self-interested purposes, the legitimacy necessary to sustain a margin of appreciation cannot reasonably be sustained.[123]

The experience of the Inter-American Court thus illustrates why the margin of appreciation doctrine should not be treated as an all-or-nothing proposition. Although the fiduciary character of state sovereignty generally requires international tribunals to grant a healthy margin of appreciation to national authorities, it precludes deference where past oppression or conflicts of interest disqualify national authorities from serving as independent, rights-sensitive trustees for their people. Under the fiduciary theory, deference is also contingent on states providing reasoned justifications for their human rights derogations. When state derogations do not qualify for deference, international tribunals may be better qualified to decide whether measures taken in response to a public emergency are "strictly required by the exigencies of the situation."[124] In Chapter 8 we develop further the deferential standards appropriate when international courts must render judgment after a national court has spoken, and vice versa.

B. The Limits of Interest Balancing

A second consideration supporting a significant role for courts and international institutions during national crises concerns the types of measures that can be authorized by law to deal with emergencies. We have seen that, under the fiduciary theory, states cannot engage in policies that contravene jus cogens norms, such as the prohibition on arbitrary killing, because such actions are inconsistent with the state's overarching fiduciary obligation to guarantee secure and equal freedom. In other words, the fiduciary principle dictates that national law cannot authorize actions that violate jus cogens norms or make such actions the subject of a legal justification.

Some legal theorists argue that practices such as torture, discrimination, and prolonged arbitrary detention, which are morally repugnant during ordinary times, may be acceptable during emergencies, when necessary to prevent terrorist attacks that would significantly imperil human life.[125] In their view, rights-based theories of national security fail "to come to grips with the inevitability of tragic choices," which fall to the executive branch.[126] Drawing inspiration from Schmitt, they argue further that in principle, no human rights should be considered immune from derogation during emergencies, and that courts (and, by implication, international institutions) are ill-equipped to second-guess the executive's determination

123. Similarly, it has been suggested that the absence of a derogation provision in the African Charter on Human and Peoples Rights reflects a "historical legacy both in colonial and postcolonial societies" in which emergency powers were abused. *See* Frederick Cowell, *Sovereignty and the Question of Derogation: An Analysis of Article 15 of the ECHR and the Absence of a Derogation Clause in the ACHPR*, 1 Birbeck L. Rev. 135, 153 (2013).

124. ICCPR, *supra* note 2, art. 4(1).

125. *See, e.g.*, Posner & Vermeule, *supra* note 48, at 183–215; Richard A. Posner, Not a Suicide Pact: The Constitution in a Time of National Emergency 77–87 (2006); Alan Dershowitz, Shouting Fire: Civil Liberties in a Turbulent Age 477 (2002).

126. Posner & Vermeule, *supra* note 48, at 187.

that practices such as torture, discrimination, or prolonged arbitrary detention are necessary during emergencies. In the heat of a national security crisis, they argue, courts will wisely—and perhaps inevitably[127]—submit to the executive's determination that derogation from peremptory norms will advance the public interest.

Two post-9/11 cases originating in Germany illustrate a different approach to human rights during national emergencies. In both cases, the courts emphatically rejected the interest-balancing paradigm in favor of a rights-oriented approach that was broadly consistent with international law's emergency constitution. Moreover, both courts did so in contexts where the stakes for public security could scarcely have been higher.

In the first case, the German Federal Constitutional Court reviewed a statute enacted in the wake of the terrorist attacks of 9/11, which authorized the Federal Minister of Defense, in consultation with other officials, to order "direct use of force of arms" against a renegade aircraft, provided that "the [targeted] aircraft will be used against the lives of human beings and . . . the use of force of arms is the only way to prevent this."[128] A group of frequent flyers challenged the statute, arguing that they risked becoming the targets of military attack in the event of a renegade aircraft incident, and that this threat violated their "fundamental rights to human dignity and life" under the Basic Law by authorizing the military to treat them instrumentally as "mere objects of government actions."[129] The federal government staunchly defended the statute as a valid exercise of legislative power, insisting that targeting a renegade aircraft would not violate the right to life or human dignity if such action were necessary "in order to prevent an even greater wrong."[130] The court sided with the complainants. It observed that the right to life "demands of the state and its bodies to shield and to promote the life of every individual" rather than treat some persons as "mere objects of its rescue operation for the protection of others."[131] Hence, the military could not use force against a renegade aircraft when this would mean killing innocent passengers and crewmembers:

> By their killing being used as a means to save others, they are treated as objects and at the same time deprived of their rights; with their lives being disposed of unilaterally by the state, the persons on board the aircraft, who, as victims, are themselves in need of protection, are denied the value which is due to a human being for his or her own sake.[132]

127. *See* Bruce Ackerman, *The Emergency Constitution*, 113 Yale L.J. 1029 (2004); Posner & Vermeule, *supra* note 104.

128. Gesetz zur Neuregelung von Luftsicherheitsgesetz (*Aviation Security Act*) § 14(1) (BGBI, I) (Jan. 11, 2005).

129. Bundesverfassungsgericht [BVerfG] [Federal Constitutional Court] Feb. 15, 2006, 115 Entscheidungen des Bundesverfassungsgerichts [BVerfGE] 118, http://www.bverfg.de/entscheidungen/ rs20060215_1bvr035705.html (last visited Apr. 24, 2012), *English translation of press release available at* http://www.bverfg.de/en/press/bvg06-011en.html (last visited Apr. 24, 2012) [hereinafter *Aviation Security*].

130. *Id.* § 47.

131. *Id.* §§ 118, 122.

132. *Id.* § 122.

In effect, the court held that the federal government could not authorize its agents to privilege the lives of innocent persons on the ground over the lives of innocent passengers and crewmembers in the air. The assumption that passengers and crew of a renegade aircraft "are doomed anyway," the court reasoned, "cannot remove its nature of an infringement of their right to dignity" because "[h]uman life and human dignity enjoy the same constitutional protection regardless of the duration of the physical existence of the individual human being."[133] Thus, the Federal Constitutional Court declined to embrace the "necessary evil," concluding that the state could not invoke specific and urgent security concerns as a justification for granting its military a license to kill innocent civilians.

The Constitutional Court's judgment may appear overly indifferent to the consequences that follow from the use of a passenger plane as a weapon in a 9/11-style attack. Some might contend, as well, that the passengers in such a scenario are already effectively dead from the standpoint of the law's ability to provide for their security once the hijackers take control of the plane and exhibit a clear intent to use it as a weapon. Yet there is no avoiding the fact that if a Minister of Defense orders a hijacked airliner shot down, it is the shooting down of the airliner that will actually end the lives of innocent passengers.

Without attempting to resolve these challenging questions definitively, we foresee at least two approaches that the fiduciary theory might deploy to address these concerns. First, on Kant's strict account, which prohibits the taking of innocent life, the Minister of Defense would be barred from pleading self-defense (understood broadly to include defense of others) as a justification were he to order a passenger plane shot down, because the law cannot authorize either the legislation or the order based on saving the lives of others. Nor could the Minister plead necessity, under Kant's theory, because necessity operates only in those circumstances in which the law cannot give the wrongdoer a self-regarding reason for action. On Kant's theory, the Minister in a 9/11 scenario could not shoot down a hijacked plane filled with innocent passengers and plead necessity unless the plane threatened the Minister personally.

The second account, which we prefer, assumes that the innocent passengers are condemned to death, and that shooting down the plane can be excused on grounds of necessity that point to the lack of alternatives and the laudable objective of saving the lives of others. Importantly, however, so long as they are alive, the law must regard the innocent passengers as ends-in-themselves; it cannot authorize the Minister to kill them ex ante, nor can it let him plead justification after the fact (because justification implies authorization), as a purely consequentialist or cost/benefit theory might suggest. The result is that there can be no ex ante authorization to take innocent life, and so in principle a Minister who orders an airliner shot down could be brought before the courts and tried for first-degree murder. If prosecuted, he would carry the burden in the criminal proceeding of proving that the circumstances were such that to save life he had no option but to take (condemned) life.

Supporters of the interest-balancing model might reply to the renegade aircraft case, in part, by pointing out that it was decided in the abstract. Although the relevant legislation was passed in response to 9/11, the Constitutional Court decided the case

133. *Id.* § 130.

in a factual vacuum. As a result, the court did not need to grapple with an actual decision to shoot down a renegade aircraft that (let us assume) would have been destroyed by terrorists in any event and with a much greater loss of life. Furthermore, plausibly the court felt at liberty to stand fast on principle because it believed that, in a 9/11-type situation, the executive would order a renegade aircraft shot down in any event, with or without legal authority. Indeed, just two weeks after the Court handed down its decision, the Minister of Defense announced that he would do just this.[134] A proponent of balancing might therefore conclude that, in an actual emergency, Schmittian and consequentialist imperatives invariably (and appropriately) come to the fore, thus nullifying any meaningful application of the Court's judgment.

A second case, *Gäfgen v. Germany*, presses in the opposite direction. On September 27, 2002, Gäfgen, a lawyer living in Frankfurt am Main, lured an eleven-year-old child into his home and killed him, hiding the corpse under a jetty. Several days later, Gäfgen was arrested and taken to a police station where the Deputy Chief of the Frankfurt police ordered another officer to threaten Gäfgen with considerable pain and subject him to such pain in order to make him reveal the child's location. The Deputy Chief stated later that he believed the child's life was in danger, given lack of food and the frigid temperature outside. Subordinate department heads had previously and repeatedly opposed this measure, proposing instead further questioning and confronting Gäfgen with the child's family. Ultimately, the officer followed the Deputy Chief's order, threatening Gäfgen "with intolerable pain if he refused to disclose [the child]'s whereabouts"[135]—treatment that was to be administered by a person "specially trained for such purposes,"[136] who in fact was already en route via helicopter. Within ten minutes of receiving the threat, and fearing its imminent execution, Gäfgen informed the authorities of the child's whereabouts and later showed them where he had hidden the body.

Gäfgen challenged his subsequent conviction before the ECHR, arguing that admitting into evidence a confession obtained through threats of torture violated his rights under the European Convention, including Article 3, which provides that "[n]o one shall be subject to torture or to inhuman or degrading treatment or punishment."[137] Although the court recognized the "atmosphere of heightened tension and emotions" under which the interrogation of Gäfgen was conducted, and that the police officers had "acted in an attempt to save a child's life,"[138] it seized the opportunity to reaffirm that the prohibition against torture is absolute and admits of no exceptions:

> Torture, inhuman or degrading treatment cannot be inflicted even in circumstances where the life of an individual is at risk. No derogation is allowed even in the event of a public emergency threatening the life of the nation. . . . *The*

134. *Aufruf zum Verfassungsbruch?* (Call for violation of the constitution?), Frankfurter Allgemaine (Sept. 17, 2007), http://www.faz.net/aktuell/politik/inland/kritik-an-iunK-und-schaeuble-aufruf-zum-verfassungsbruch-1463080.html (last visited Nov. 25, 2015).

135. *Aviation Security, supra* note 129, § 94.

136. *Id.* § 15.

137. European Convention, *supra* note 2, art. 3.

138. *Aviation Security, supra* note 129, §§ 106–07.

> *philosophical basis underpinning the absolute nature of the right under Article 3 does not allow for any exceptions or justifying factors or balancing of interests,* irrespective of the conduct of the person concerned and the nature of the offence at issue.[139]

Applying this interpretation of the European Convention to the facts of the case, the court suggested that even when a child is kidnapped and thereby imperiled by an individual with information that can save the child's life, authorities are still not permitted to use torture, inhuman or degrading treatment—or even the mere *threat* of such treatment—to coerce life-saving information from a kidnapper.[140] If the threat of torture was "sufficiently real and immediate," as it was in Gäfgen's case, then the threat alone was a violation of the European Convention.[141] Although the court held unanimously that the prohibition on torture and threats of torture was absolute, ultimately it split 11–6 on the question whether evidence obtained through threat of torture must be excluded, with the majority declining to apply the "fruit of the poisonous tree" doctrine.

A Schmittian cynic might conclude that the majority's unwillingness to exclude Gäfgen's confession supports the view that, in emergencies, executive agents are free to call the shots with relative impunity. Yet two important aspects of this case resist this cynical interpretation. First, both the ECHR and the national courts below held that the Deputy Chief and the officer who threatened Gäfgen with torture and cruel, inhuman, and degrading treatment had broken the law; they did not defer to the government's position that the threats were legally justified.[142] Second, it is revealing that the Deputy Chief's subordinate department heads refused his repeated orders to threaten and, if necessary, torture Gäfgen. Instead of complying with those orders, they proposed legal alternatives. Although one can only speculate on the reasons the department heads may have given the Deputy Chief for their disobedience, it would be surprising if illegality did not figure among them. *Gäfgen* thus suggests that domestic and international law can guide executive decision-making during even the most pressing and time-sensitive crises, and that national courts and international bodies may play an important role in maintaining the fiduciary character of state sovereignty by affirming human rights protections—including the non-derogable character of jus cogens norms—during public emergencies.[143]

139. *Id.* § 107 (emphasis added).

140. *Id.* §§ 91, 108.

141. *Id.* § 91.

142. *Id.* §§ 47–48.

143. Thus far, we have addressed the suggestion that it may be permissible for a state to violate the security of some of its people to guarantee the security of others, a practice that we argue is fundamentally at odds with the fiduciary character of sovereignty. Some scholars have argued further that states may make trade-offs between their efforts to guarantee security, on the one hand, and their obligation to respect, protect, and fulfill the rule of law, on the other. *See, e.g.*, Posner & Vermeule, *supra* note 48, at 5 (describing this as the "tradeoff thesis"). This security/legality trade-off is particularly apparent, these scholars argue, in state policies and practices governing the prolonged detention of suspected terrorists without trial and laws that cast a vail of secrecy over the operations of national security agencies.

C. The Distinctive Role of International Law and Institutions

A third way in which the fiduciary theory supports a robust role for courts and international institutions in emergencies trades on international law's unique ability to govern *de jure* the claims of sovereign actors. In Chapter 2, we argued that international law is uniquely capable of distributing sovereignty to some legal actors (sovereign states) and not to others. In the words of Patrick Macklem, "international norms shape an international political reality into an international legal order by determining the legality of multiple claims of sovereign power."[144] By the same token, international law enjoys an equally disinterested third-party position with respect to assessments of whether state officials are acting in accordance with legal principles constitutive of their authority to exercise sovereign powers in times of crisis—principles associated with international law's emergency constitution and the fiduciary constitution of state sovereignty. Moreover, to the extent that international law seeks to support rather than supplant the fiduciary role of sovereign states, it does not threaten the legitimate margin of appreciation left to local decision-makers.[145]

This recasting of the relationship between international law and state sovereignty offers a compelling rejoinder to Schmitt. Recall that Schmitt's basic claim is that the exception "can at best be characterized as a case of extreme peril, a danger to the existence of the state," and that someone (or some institution) has to have final and unfettered decision-making power over questions of whether there is an "extreme emergency" and what is to be done about it.[146] When the sovereign declares an emergency and suspends legal order, "the state remains, whereas law recedes," but because "the exception is different from anarchy and chaos, order in the juristic sense still prevails even if it is not of the ordinary kind."[147] These qualifications demonstrate that Schmitt did not think that a declaration of emergency entails dissolution of all order and a retreat to a state of nature. But on Schmitt's construal of the exception, the sovereign and the people would confront one another in something like the state of nature in the following two senses: with legal order suspended there are no norms or standards available to assess the validity of the sovereign's actions, nor any persons or institutions entitled to assess or second-guess those actions. To show that Schmitt is mistaken requires demonstrating that

The same fiduciary principles of non-instrumentalization and non-domination that preclude states from engaging in practices such as torture and cruel, inhuman, and degrading treatment also dictate that states may not set aside the basic requirements of the rule of law by employing prolonged arbitrary detention. In particular, the fiduciary character of sovereignty places limits on a state's authority to detain suspected terrorists based on a secret record or to withdraw the protections of judicial review, as through the indefinite suspension of habeas corpus. We will have more to say about these lessons of the fiduciary theory in Chapter 6.

144. Patrick Macklem, *What Is International Human Rights Law? Three Applications of a Distributive Account*, 52 McGill L.J. 575, 587–88 (2007).

145. To close the fiduciary circle fully, we would need to show that international and regional institutions themselves stand in a fiduciary relationship to the states and individuals over whom they preside. We take up this question in Chapter 8.

146. Schmitt, *supra* note 6, at 6, 7.

147. *Id.*

there are grounds available for reviewing the sovereign's emergency declaration and chosen measures, and that there are institutions available with authority to invoke those grounds.

We have suggested already how to meet this challenge the fiduciary theory can strengthen Dyzenhaus's argument in favor of common law constitutionalism. International law's emergency constitution provides critical resources for assessing the validity of a sovereign's actions, while monitoring and judicial bodies such as the ECHR and national courts supply the requisite institutions. To the extent that the sovereign and the people confront one another in a state of nature during moments of crises, international law and its institutions can rescue them from this juristic anomie by standing as an impartial arbiter, much as Hobbes claimed that the judge and ultimately the sovereign was able to rescue individuals from the state of nature.[148] In short, the fiduciary theory shows that, pace Schmitt and Agamben, national crises need not result in a suspension of legal order. *Tumultum* need not lead to *iustitium*. Just as law can regulate states in times of war through doctrines of *jus ad bellum* and *jus in bello*, so too it can regulate states in times of emergency through doctrines of *jus ad tumultum* and *jus in tumultu*. Dyzenhaus is therefore right to conclude that derogation from human rights norms during a state of emergency need not be viewed as derogation from the rule of law, but rather as an extension of the same concept.[149]

VII. ON THE RELATIONSHIP BETWEEN LAW AND POWER

Although the fiduciary theory offers a robust framework for constraining executive power, attention to legal principles, norms, and institutions is obviously insufficient to guarantee in practice that states will not abuse their power during national crises. William Scheuerman has faulted the fiduciary theory for not engaging "the underlying empirical dynamics of emergency power, or the pathologies of a global arena plagued by stunning power inequalities."[150] Powerful political actors may seek to deploy the fiduciary principle as a shallow rhetorical trope—subverting the fiduciary theory's legal principles and prescriptions—much as they once deployed fiduciary concepts as an ideological justification for colonialist domination and exploitation. "Unless closer attention is paid to the political and social preconditions of a better global order," Scheuerman cautions, the fiduciary theory's "calls to reform judicial practice are likely to remain hortatory in character."[151]

We agree that the legal reform contemplated under the fiduciary theory will not be sufficient to safeguard humanity from oppression without significant political reform. As long as states have the power to disregard international human rights and

148. *See* Thomas Hobbes, Leviathan 23 (Edwin Curley ed., 1994) (1651).

149. David Dyzenhaus, *Schmitt v. Dicey: Are States of Emergency Inside or Outside the Legal Order?* 27 Cardozo L. Rev. 2005, 2038 (2006).

150. William E. Scheuerman, *Human Rights Lawyers v. Carl Schmitt*, *in* Human Rights in Emergencies (Evan J. Criddle ed., forthcoming 2016).

151. *Id.*

sidestep international law's emergency constitution with impunity,[152] the fiduciary theory's emancipatory vision of international legal order will prove illusory. To be credible in practice, the fiduciary theory may require institutional reforms designed to promote deliberative engagement at the national level between states and their people. Additionally, the international community may need to develop more robust judicial institutions and enforcement mechanisms to hold states accountable for abusing their peoples' human rights during national crises. Entrenched political resistance to such reforms at both the national and international levels suggests that the path forward is likely to be long and difficult.

Although we will not attempt to chart a detailed course for global political reform here,[153] the fiduciary theory is attentive to the role that power plays in global order. By clarifying when and to what extent states may derogate from their human rights commitments, the fiduciary theory makes it more difficult for states to manipulate ambiguities in derogation provisions to the detriment of international human rights. The fiduciary theory thus serves to strengthen the political legitimacy—and, hence, the political influence—of courts and international institutions as checks on states' exercise of emergency powers. The fiduciary theory may also serve to empower rights-conscious political and social movements in their efforts to hold states accountable through the "mobilization of shame."[154] Indeed, a significant virtue of the fiduciary theory is that it clarifies where political and social movements should concentrate their advocacy to foster a global legal order that respects human dignity. Although any theory of international law must grapple with the unruly character of global power politics, there is little reason to believe that the fiduciary theory fares especially poorly on this score or that it cannot be operationalized as well as any of its competitors to enhance respect for human rights in the rough and tumble world of global politics.

VIII. CONCLUSION

This chapter has argued that the fiduciary theory points to a unifying principle capable of justifying, on the one hand, a state's entitlement to declare states of emergency and derogate from ordinary human rights and, on the other, the norms and principles found in international law's emergency constitution: that is, the norms and principles of *jus ad tumultum* and *jus in tumultu*. This unifying principle is an overarching fiduciary duty, owed by states to persons amenable to their jurisdiction, to provide for their secure and equal freedom. On the basis of this duty, states can derogate from ordinary human rights if, and only if, they must do so to manage a crisis that threatens the secure and equal freedom of their people. To comply

152. *See* Fionnuala Ní Aoláin, *The Cloak and Dagger Game of Derogation, in* Human Rights in Emergencies (Evan J. Criddle ed., forthcoming 2016) (observing that states generally have used emergency powers after 9/11 without participating in the formal derogation procedures of IHRL).

153. The fiduciary theory we develop is ecumenical regarding the particular political institutions that might be necessary to guarantee secure and equal freedom for humanity.

154. *See* Robert F. Drinan, S.J., The Mobilization of Shame: A World View of Human Rights (2001).

with the same duty and therefore be lawful, derogations must conform to norms of notification, contestation, justification, and proportionality. Such derogations must be reviewable by municipal and international tribunals on objective grounds. States must comply with the core requirements of *jus ad tumultum* and *jus in tumultu* to ensure that their subjects are treated always as ends-in-themselves and not as mere means to the achievement of state objectives. The basic requirements of international law's emergency constitution are binding upon all states, as the Inter-American Court has recognized, irrespective of whether states are parties to the particular conventions in which these requirements find expression.[155] Whether or not states have ratified particular human rights conventions, the fiduciary principle dictates that they may not restrict peremptory human rights under any circumstances, and they may employ emergency powers to restrict other human rights only where such measures are strictly necessary to guarantee their subjects' secure and equal freedom.

Locating the state's authority to declare an emergency within the same conceptual framework as the norms that regulate the use of emergency powers is a significant theoretical accomplishment. By bringing together the two ways in which the sovereign decides on the exception within a single juridical frame of reference, the fiduciary theory shows that international law's two-tiered emergency constitution reflects a unified and credible conception of public law capable of governing states during times of crises. But the advantages of the fiduciary theory are practical as well as theoretical. The fiduciary theory lends clarity and precision to *jus ad tumultum* and *jus in tumultu*, and enriches the principles of contestation, justification, and proportionality found already in *jus in tumultu*, while strengthening the prohibition on derogation of peremptory norms.

Whereas Schmitt claims that during a state of exception "the state remains, whereas law recedes," under the fiduciary model the authority of the state to govern and represent its people during an emergency rests on its compliance with international law's emergency constitution. If this law recedes, so too does the authority of the state.

155. *E.g.*, Report of the Human Rights Committee to the General Assembly, U.N. GAOR, 39th Sess., Supp. No. 40, at 44–45 ¶¶ 95–99, U.N. Doc. A/39/40 (1984) (concluding that Chile, which was not a party to the ACHR, was bound by the *jus ad tumultum* principles expressed therein); ORAÁ, *supra* note 1, at 26 (noting that the Inter-American Commission has applied "[t]he same principles governing the assessment of the existence of a public emergency . . . to States non-parties to the Convention").

5

Armed Conflict

I. INTRODUCTION

In this chapter, we address states' legal obligations to their people and foreign nationals during armed conflict. Armed conflict poses a particularly important test for the fiduciary theory, because a state's fidelity to its own people may appear to preclude the state from assuming countervailing obligations toward the people of a hostile state. We argue that this view is mistaken. Although states bear fiduciary obligations primarily toward their own people, under the fiduciary theory they are also bound to respect the status and standing of foreign nationals as legal subjects of international law. International law's humanitarian limits on the use of force are best understood as legal duties that emanate from the fiduciary character of state sovereignty.

The international law of armed conflict has not always fit comfortably with a fiduciary conception of state sovereignty. Throughout the nineteenth century, war was widely accepted as a legitimate legal institution for resolving disputes between states. Legal positivists advanced a "contractual picture of war as a duel between two sides that were on a legal footing of full and complete equality."[1] International law regulated when and how states could engage in warfare, prohibiting some brutal and deceptive practices,[2] but the basic rules for the use of force were understood to derive their authority solely from state consent. As long as states respected the rules of the game, they remained at liberty to use warfare as an instrument of national policy, pursuing their own national self-interest without regard for the interests of foreign peoples.

The twentieth century marked a decisive departure from this permissive contractual paradigm. No longer would international law endorse recourse to war as a legitimate mechanism for settling international disputes. In the Pact of Paris of 1928, states renounced war "as an instrument of national policy."[3] Two decades later,

1. Stephen C. Neff, War and the Law of Nations: A General History 186 (2005); *see, e.g.*, 3 Robert Phillimore, Commentaries upon International Law pt. 9, chs. 1, 4 (1857) (characterizing "appeal to arms" as "the terrible litigation of States"); Hugo Grotius, De Juri Belli Ac Pacis bk. III, ch. 19, § 19 (F. Kelsey trans., 1925) (1625) (conceptualizing war as interstate litigation); Alberico Gentili, De Iure Belli Libri Tres bk. 2, ch. 1, at 132 (James Brown Scott transl., 1933) (1612) (same).

2. *E.g.*, Declaration of Paris, 16 Apr. 1856, 115 CTS 1; Geneva Convention (I) for the Amelioration of the Wounded, 22 Aug. 1864, 129 CTS 361.

3. Pact of Paris (Kellogg-Briand Treaty), 27 Aug. 1928, 94 LNTS 343, 188–89.

the U.N. Charter directed states to "refrain in their international relations from the threat or use of force against the territorial integrity or political independence of any state, or in any other manner inconsistent with the Purposes of the United Nations."[4] Together, these instruments established a baseline norm of peaceful relations among states, with disputes to be resolved through diplomacy, arbitration, or the intercession of international and regional institutions.

Accompanying this norm of peaceful relations was an equally profound shift in how international law framed states' authority to use force. As Stephen Neff has explained:

> What the world really witnessed after 1945 was less the abolition of war than its reconceptualization. . . . This process of reconceptualization or reassembly came about largely as a result of two major factors, both of them so far-reaching as justly to merit the label of "revolution." One was the "self-defence revolution" . . . . It marked the full emergence of self-defence to the front and centre of the international stage, as a kind of all-purpose justification for unilateral resorts to armed force. The other major factor undermining the abolition of war was what will be termed the "humanitarian revolution." This was a seismic shift in fundamental conceptions of the laws on the conduct of armed conflict: away from a focus on fairness and mutuality as between the warring states, to a primary concern with relieving the suffering of victims of war.[5]

These two developments in international law—the "self-defence revolution" and the "humanitarian revolution"—envision states' sovereign authority to use force as a fiduciary power to be exercised exclusively for the protection of humanity. Far from legitimating the use of force as a legally accepted institution for resolving grievances between states, the new international law on the use of force (*jus ad bellum*) outlaws aggressive warfare and enlists states as agents or trustees of international legal order. For example, Article 25 of the U.N. Charter contemplates that all U.N. member-states serve as agents of international legal order by requiring them "to accept and carry out" Security Council resolutions providing for coercive enforcement action[6]—including, potentially, the use of force—"to maintain or restore international peace and security."[7] Pending action from the Security Council, the Charter also entrusts states with responsibility to use force on their own independent initiative to protect their people from an "armed attack."[8] Although the Charter does not describe either compliance with Security Council resolutions or acts of "self-defense" as fiduciary obligations, we argue that a state's authority to use force abroad is a discretionary fiduciary power that is subject to fiduciary constraints.

4. U.N. Charter, art. 2(4).

5. NEFF, *supra* note 1, at 315.

6. Charter art. 25.

7. *Id.* art. 39.

8. *Id.* art. 51.

Coupled with the fiduciary character of contemporary *jus ad bellum* are other legal duties that govern the means and methods states employ when conducting hostilities (*jus in bello*). These duties constitute the law of armed conflict's "humanitarian revolution" and are embodied in international humanitarian law (IHL). Broadly speaking, IHL requires states and other actors to avoid taking actions that would inflict unnecessary suffering on civilians and combatants placed hors de combat. States also bear an affirmative responsibility to prevent and suppress jus cogens violations such as genocide, torture, and crimes against humanity.[9] Although many aspects of IHL are explicable from the perspective of the nineteenth-century contractual model, the contractual model cannot fully capture some core features of *jus in bello* today, including the peremptory character of some IHL norms. We argue that these peremptory duties to avoid unnecessary suffering emanate from the fiduciary character of state sovereignty, a conception of sovereignty that involves the state assuming the position of agent or trustee of international legal order.

In undertaking this brief review of the fiduciary theory's applications to armed conflict, we are forced of necessity to paint with a broad brush. Many important topics receive only passing treatment in the pages that follow. Other topics are omitted entirely, including preemptive self-defense, support for national liberation movements, treatment of private property during armed conflict, and threats posed by nuclear weapons and other dangerous technologies. Our purpose here is not to establish conclusively that the fiduciary theory can explain or justify the full corpus of contemporary *jus ad bellum* and *jus in bello*. Rather, this chapter focuses on developing two arguments. First, as an interpretive theory, the fiduciary theory is consistent with, and helps to explain and justify, core juridical features of the law of armed conflict as it has been progressively "reconceptualized" and "humanized" over the past century.[10] Second, as a prescriptive account of states' legal and moral obligations, the fiduciary theory offers resources for resolving some key theoretical puzzles in the law of armed conflict today, including the scope of state authority to use force against nonstate actors, and the proper relationship between IHL and IHRL across various arenas of conflict, including humanitarian intervention.

II. FIDUCIARY STATES' RESPONSIBILITY TO PROTECT

The idea that states bear a responsibility to defend their people from foreign aggression boasts a long pedigree in legal and political theory. Early luminaries such as Grotius, Wolff, and Vattel argued that a state's highest duty was to preserve itself and

9. *See, e.g.*, Convention on the Prevention and Punishment of the Crime of Genocide, art. II, Dec. 9, 1948, 102 Stat. 3045, 78 U.N.T.S. 277; Application of the Convention on the Prevention and Punishment of the Crime of Genocide (Bosn. & Herz. v. Serb. & Mont.), 2007 ICJ Rep. 169, ¶¶ 425–30 (Feb. 26, 2007); Eyal Benvenisti, *Sovereigns as Trustees of Humanity: On the Accountability of States to Foreign Stakeholders*, 107 Am. J. Int'l L. 295, 325 (2013); W. Michael Reisman, *Acting Before Victims Become Victims: Preventing and Arresting Mass Murder*, 40 Case W. Res. J. Int'l. L. 57 (2008).

10. Although we argue that the fiduciary theory offers a lucid interpretive theory of the increasing individualization of the law of armed conflict, this chapter does not attempt to rule out the possibility that other legal and ethical theories might lead to similar conclusions.

its people from external threats.[11] Pufendorf similarly characterized a state's interest in self-preservation as a trump that would support departures from the ordinary *jus ad bellum* constraints.[12] Although scholars in the seventeenth and eighteenth centuries engaged in spirited debates over the requirements for a just cause for war, many accepted the idea that states bore a responsibility to protect their people from attack, because they derived their sovereign authority from their people for whom they served as fiduciaries.[13]

In the twentieth century, the U.N. Charter framed *jus ad bellum* in terms consistent with the idea that states are responsible as fiduciaries to protect their people from threats arising abroad. The U.N. Charter provided that states could use force only as authorized by law, and only in a manner that was calculated to promote global security and human rights. In line with Kelsen's "*bellum justum* principle,"[14] U.N. member-states committed to refrain "from the threat or use of force against the territorial integrity or political independence of any state, or in any other manner inconsistent with the Purposes of the United Nations."[15] States would be permitted to use force against one another only under narrow conditions: (1) under the direction of the Security Council to address a "threat to the peace, breach of the peace, or act of aggression" (Articles 39 and 42); or (2) in response to "an armed attack" pursuant to "the inherent right of individual or collective self-defence" (Article 51).[16] In both contexts, the Charter anticipated that states would use force only for other-regarding purposes; namely, to protect their own people and "to maintain or restore international peace and security" for the collective benefit of humanity.

These formal limits on the use of force are consistent with a fiduciary conception of sovereignty. Some legal scholars characterize the event of an "armed attack" as returning states to a pre-Charter default position in which they may claim an "inherent right" to take whatever steps they deem necessary to guarantee their own national security.[17] The more plausible interpretation, however, is that the Charter incorporates self-defense into a comprehensive public-law framework that regulates

11. *See* GROTIUS, *supra* note 1, bk. III, ch. 3, at 625; CHRISTIAN WOLFF, JUS GENTIUM 22 (J. Scott ed., 1934); EMMERICH DE VATTEL, THE LAW OF NATIONS 161–63 (J. Chitty ed., 1883); *see generally* RICHARD TUCK, THE RIGHTS OF WAR AND PEACE 5, 78–79 (1999); Richard B. Lillich, *Lillich on the Forcible Protection of Nationals Abroad*, 77 INT'L L. STUD. 1, 1–5 (2002).

12. SAMUEL PUFENDORF, NATURE AND NATIONS 295–309 (Oldfather & Oldfather 1934).

13. *See* TUCK, *supra* note 11, at 18–19.

14. HANS KELSEN, PRINCIPLES OF INTERNATIONAL LAW 33–38 (1952).

15. U.N. Charter art. 2(4). The purposes of the United Nations, according to Article 1 of the Charter, include to promote international peace and security, and to promote "friendly relations based on respect for the principle of equal rights and self-determination of peoples." *Id.* art. 1(1)–(2); *see also* Covenant of the League of Nations art. X ("The Members of the League undertake to respect and preserve against external aggression the territorial integrity and political independence of all Members of the League . . . .").

16. D.W. BOWETT, SELF-DEFENSE IN INTERNATIONAL LAW 155 (1958) (suggesting that characterizing "the use or threat of force as either a delict, or a [U.N.-authorized] sanction, or self-defence" was "the greatest advance secured by the Charter").

17. U.N. Charter art. 51; *see, e.g.*, BOWETT, *supra* note 16, at 184–88.

when, how, and by whom force may be deployed for the protection of a state's people. By permitting self-defense only under specified conditions, Article 51 entrusts states with responsibility to vindicate their own people's interest in self-preservation (individual self-defense) or a foreign people's interest in self-preservation, with the other state's consent (collective self-defense). According to conventional wisdom, states may invoke a right to self-defense under Article 51 only in response to an actual or imminent attack ("if an armed attack occurs"), and only "until the Security Council has taken measures necessary to maintain international peace and security."[18] These features of the Charter contemplate that states will exercise the limited right of self-defense as fiduciaries for their people and agents of international legal order.

Significantly, although the Charter permits states to use force in self-defense, it does not require them to do so. States' fiduciary responsibility to defend their people finds clearest expression in another body of law, international human rights law (IHRL), which affirms states' positive duties to protect and fulfill human rights for their people. Under IHRL, states are not only *permitted* to use force, they bear a fiduciary *obligation* to protect their people from serious harm. An important aspect of this obligation is that states must use their diplomatic, economic, and military resources to discourage and repel foreign aggression, while also suppressing violence within their own borders. When states perpetrate or fail to prevent atrocities such as the genocide and ethnic cleansing that devastated Rwanda during the early 1990s and the Darfur region of Sudan in the early 2000s, they transgress their most basic fiduciary obligation to furnish a regime of secure and equal freedom for their people. States must also safeguard their citizens from other foreseeable catastrophes such as natural disasters and mass famines that would imperil the right to life and other fundamental human rights.[19] IHRL thus obligates states to take initiative to address the root causes of insecurity within their borders and, where appropriate, use force to prevent other states and nonstate actors from violating the human rights of their people.

Concerns about states' failure to satisfy these positive obligations have prompted many legal scholars and policymakers to embrace the idea that the international community collectively bears a "responsibility to protect" (R2P) human rights.[20] When states are unable or unwilling to satisfy their sovereign responsibility to

18. U.N. Charter art. 51. Most legal scholars agree that an armed attack must already be in process in a meaningful sense to justify self-defense, but that non-aggressor states need not wait until the blow has fallen before they mobilize their forces in self-defense and call for international assistance. *See, e.g.*, Christine Gray, International Law and the Use of Force 161 (3d ed. 2008); Yoram Dinstein, War, Aggression and Self-Defence 168 (3d ed. 2001). Some scholars argue, however, that states may engage in anticipatory self-defense to neutralize prospective threats even if an attack is not yet imminent. *See, e.g.*, Michael J. Glennon, *The Fog of Law: Self-Defense, Inherence, and Incoherence in Article 51 of the United Nations Charter*, 25 Harv. J. L. & Pub. Pol'y 539 (2002); George K. Walker, *Anticipatory Collective Self-Defense in the Charter Era: What the Treaties Have Said*, 31 Cornell Int'l L.J. 321 (1998).

19. The Responsibility To Protect, Report of the International Committee on Intervention and State Sovereignty viii (2001) [hereinafter ICISS Report].

20. Francis M. Deng et al., Sovereignty as Responsibility: Conflict Management in Africa xi (1996).

protect their people, the R2P principle suggests that the international community as a whole, acting as "the ultimate guarantor of the universal standards that safeguard the rights of all human beings," bears a subsidiary "responsibility to provide innocent victims of internal conflicts and gross violations of human rights with essential protection and assistance."[21] In 2001, the International Committee on Intervention and State Sovereignty, an expert body convened by the Canadian government to consider international responses to atrocities in Bosnia, Kosovo, and Rwanda, endorsed the R2P concept in a landmark report, arguing that "state authorities are responsible for the functions of protecting the safety and lives of citizens and promotion of their welfare" and bear responsibility "to their citizens internally and to the international community through the U.N."[22] Over time, the U.N. Security Council, U.N. General Assembly, and U.N. Secretariat have all accepted core elements of R2P, recognizing that both individual states and the international community as a whole bear overlapping responsibility for safeguarding human rights.[23]

We will have more to say later in this chapter about the circumstances in which humanitarian intervention by the international community may be consistent with the fiduciary theory of sovereignty. At this stage, we introduce the R2P principle simply to make a more general point about the fiduciary character of sovereignty within the Charter's collective security regime; namely, that R2P helps to explain how a state's positive fiduciary obligations to protect and fulfill human rights under IHRL interface with the formal limits of the state's authority to use force under *jus ad bellum*. When threats arise from sources within a state's borders, R2P affirms that the state enjoys a standing authorization under international law and bears primary responsibility to use force as necessary to protect its people, subject to constraints imposed by international *jus ad bellum* and *jus in bello*. Conversely, when a state faces attacks from a source outside its borders, it possesses no such general authorization to use force abroad; instead, the primary responsibility to prevent cross-border attacks rests with the states where the threats arise. In both contexts, if the state that bears the primary responsibility to protect fails to address a grave security threat

21. *Id.* at xii, xvii. Of course, determining precisely what steps states should take to fulfill their responsibility to protect is hardly a straightforward matter. Because the challenge of formulating a response to security threats such as genocide or crimes against humanity is an inescapably context-sensitive inquiry, international law cannot fully specify ex ante how states should fulfill their responsibility to protect. Consistent with the fiduciary character of state sovereignty, international law entrusts states with primary responsibility to exercise judgment in determining how to allocate their resources to protect their people.

22. ICISS Report, *supra* note 19, at 13, ¶ 2.15.

23. *See* Kofi Annan, *Two Concepts of Sovereignty*, THE ECONOMIST, Sept. 18, 1999, http://www.economist.com/node/324795; U.N. Secretary-General, *Implementing the Responsibility to Protect*, U.N. Doc. A/63/677 (Jan. 12, 2009); 2005 World Summit Outcome, G.A. Res. 60/1, A/RES/60/1, 24 Oct. 2005, ¶¶ 138–39 [hereinafter World Summit Outcome]; S.C. Res. 1973, S/Res/1973, Mar. 17, 2011, pmbl [hereinafter SCR 1973]; S.C. Res. 1970, S/Res/1970, Feb. 26, 2011. In contrast to the ICISS Report, the General Assembly's *World Summit Outcome* focuses more narrowly on the international community's responsibility to address mass atrocities such as "genocide, war crimes, ethnic cleansing and crimes against humanity." World Summit Outcome, *supra*, pmbl.

arising within its jurisdiction, the R2P principle confers authority on the international community as a whole to address the threats through institutions designated for this purpose under international law.[24] The R2P principle is thus a fiduciary principle that authorizes the international community to use force for international public purposes, but always subject to legal constraints that aim to prevent the use of force itself from morphing into a lawless violence that would undermine the R2P principle's authorization of force.

Ordinarily, the Security Council takes the lead in organizing the international community's collective response to aggression pursuant to Articles 41 and 42 of the U.N. Charter. In exceptional circumstances, however, Article 51 of the Charter also permits decentralized military action by individual states or groups of states, acting as temporary agents of necessity for the international community as a whole to defend a people against armed attacks. Put slightly differently, although both the Charter and the R2P principle affirm that states enjoy a broad authorization from international law to use force within their borders for the sake of protecting human rights, states' authority to use force abroad is far more limited. Generally speaking, for a state's extra-territorial use of force to be lawful, it must be accompanied by an ex ante international authorization from the target state or the Security Council—or perhaps in exceptional circumstances, by an ex post international ratification, though this is more controversial—so that the state's use of force, if lawful, is always intelligible as an action authorized by international law. The R2P concept thus supplies a unifying framework for *jus ad bellum* that complements IHRL and reinforces the fiduciary constitution of sovereignty under international law.

III. FIDUCIARY REALISM

The idea that states bear a responsibility to protect their people is an article of faith for political realists in international relations theory, who characterize the global arena as an existential contest between states for power and resources. According to Hans Morgenthau, an early champion of political realism, a state's only legitimate sovereign obligation is self-preservation. Because each state is morally bound to pursue this supreme interest as an expression of its undivided loyalty to its people, foreign nationals have no legitimate claim on a state's conscience: "[t]he individual may say for himself: '*Fiat justitia, pereat mundus* (Let justice be done, even if the world perisheth),' but the state has no right to say so in the name of those who are in its care."[25] A responsible state would therefore take all necessary steps to achieve security and prosperity for its people, without regard to the impact that its actions might have on foreign nationals. Far from constraining state power, Morgenthau's political realism envisions international law as "primarily a static social force"—one that both mirrors and cements global political ordering. Allen Buchanan has characterized this account of international relations as "fiduciary realism," because

24. *See* Anne Orford, International Authority and the Responsibility to Protect 25–26 (2011) (arguing that R2P is best understood as a power-conferring rule).

25. Hans J. Morgenthau & Kenneth W. Thompson, Politics Among Nations: The Struggle for Power and Peace 12 (6th ed. 1985).

Morgenthau's vision of international relations conceives of states as fiduciaries that wield power exclusively for the benefit of their own people.[26]

Most international lawyers today reject fiduciary realism as an impoverished account of states' moral obligations. As Buchanan has observed, Morgenthau's account fundamentally misconstrues how a state's duties to its own people interact with its other obligations under contemporary international law:

> Even though states have a fiduciary obligation to their own countrymen, it cannot be an absolute one. . . . When a person becomes an agent of some other individual or of a collectivity, she does not thereby wipe the moral slate clean. For example, a mother has fiduciary responsibility toward her child, but this does not justify her forcibly taking a kidney from another child to save her child's life. The most basic general obligations—including those that are correlates of human rights—are not swamped by any fiduciary obligation that a state official could have. One cannot contract out of one's basic moral obligations.[27]

Although Buchanan focuses on states' *moral* obligations to one another, the same logic supports a broader compass for states' *legal* obligations under a fiduciary theory of state sovereignty. The mere fact that a state stands in a fiduciary relationship with its people does not excuse the state from its legal duties to foreign states or foreign nationals. Although each state "has the right, and indeed the duty, to respond [to threats] in order to protect the life of its citizens," as the ICJ has affirmed, any "measures taken are bound nonetheless to remain in conformity with applicable international law."[28] D.W. Bowett likewise observes in his classic treatise on self-defense that:

> self-preservation and necessity . . . cannot, in purporting to illustrate the maxim "*Salus populi supema lex*," excuse all *prima facie* unlawful conduct against states . . . . That view, by which the whole of the duties of states are subordinated to the "right" of self-preservation or the "right" of necessity, is destructive of the entire legal order.[29]

There is no inherent inconsistency, in short, between a state bearing fiduciary obligations to its own people while simultaneously bearing legal duties to refrain from inflicting injury on foreign states and foreign nationals.

In the wake of the First and Second World Wars, the international community has decisively rejected fiduciary realism as a foundation for contemporary *jus ad bellum*. The U.N. Charter affirms that all uses of force are subject to international norms that states may not unilaterally abrogate, abridge, or modify to promote their

26. *See* Allen Buchanan, Justice, Legitimacy and Self-Determination 35–37 (2004) [hereinafter Buchanan, Justice]; Allen Buchanan, Human Rights, Legitimacy and the Use of Force 204–07 (2010).

27. Buchanan, Justice, *supra* note 26, at 36–37.

28. Legal Consequences of the Construction of a Wall in the Occupied Palestinian Territory, 2004 ICJ Rep. 131 (July 9), ¶ 141.

29. Bowett, *supra* note 16, at 10.

own national security. Looking beyond the Charter, principles of contemporary *jus ad bellum* also require states to take the interests of foreign nationals into account whenever they use force in self-defense. Under long-standing custom, states may resort to force in self-defense only if such action is strictly necessary to repel an actual or imminent armed attack, and only if the resulting harm to foreign nationals is "proportional, involving no more than the force reasonably required to cure the breach."[30] In deference to the principle of self-determination, the right of self-defense does not authorize a state that suffers an armed attack to assert control over foreign nationals or foreign territory unless absolutely necessary to avert an armed attack. International law thus requires states contemplating military action to take into account the interests of foreign nationals who may be impacted by their use of force.

These *jus ad bellum* constraints on a state's use of force confirm that fiduciary realism is inconsistent with contemporary international law. States are required to refrain from using force abroad even in settings where military action would clearly advance their fiduciary purpose to establish fundamental security under the rule of law. We argue that these constraints on the use of force are not merely consistent with the idea that states' bear fiduciary obligations to their own people: they also emanate from the fiduciary constitution of state sovereignty under international law. States must respect the security of foreign nationals abroad *because* they hold sovereign authority in a fiduciary capacity, not *in spite of* this fact.

IV. STATES AS FIDUCIARIES OF HUMANITY

In preceding chapters, we have argued that international law's entrustment of sovereign authority to states can be reconciled with the principle of self-determination only if states are required to use these powers for the benefit of their people. One prescriptive implication of this principle is that states must treat their people always as beneficiaries, not as mere objects that they may oppress or destroy at will. But states do not owe fiduciary duties solely to their own people; in a variety of respects, international law also enlists states as co-fiduciaries for humanity generally with responsibility to create and maintain an international legal order in which all human beings may enjoy secure and equal freedom. As Eyal Benvenisti has explained in a pathbreaking article on "Sovereigns as Trustees of Humanity," international law distributes sovereignty among states and entrusts states with shared responsibility to administer international legal order for the benefit of humanity as a whole.[31] Hence, although states' primary fiduciary obligation is to provide a regime of secure and equal freedom for their own people, they must also "take other-regarding considerations seriously into account" whenever their actions have the potential to impact the legitimate interests of foreign nationals.[32] Building upon Benvenisti's insight,

30. *See, e.g.*, Nicholas Rostow, *Nicaragua and the Law of Self-Defense Revisited*, 11 Yale J. Int'l L. 437, 453 (1987).

31. Benvenisti, *supra* note 9, at 300.

32. *Id.*; *see also* Ruti Teitel, Humanity's Law (2011) (arguing that "humanity" constitutes a cosmopolitan foundation for state obligations to foreign nationals); Vattel, *supra* note 11, bk. II, ch. 1, at 261 (characterizing state duties to care for foreign nationals abroad as "offices of humanity").

we argue that because international law entrusts states with sovereign authority as fiduciaries of humanity—and not merely to enable peoples of the world to pursue their own respective interests—states must always exercise their power over foreign nationals in a manner consonant with foreign nationals' status and standing as subjects of international legal order and bearers of human rights, rather than as mere objects of state coercion that they may injure or destroy arbitrarily.

At first blush, the idea that international law places states in a fiduciary relationship with enemy nationals may appear to pose overwhelming theoretical and practical difficulties. Skeptics may object that states' duty of loyalty to their own people necessarily precludes them from undertaking obligations to foreign nationals that would conflict with their primary duty of loyalty to their own subjects. The adversarial character of armed conflict may strike some as wholly antithetical to the concept of fiduciary obligation, which rests on principles of fidelity and trust. Thus, even if skeptics are prepared to concede that states bear duties to take the interests of foreign nationals into account in some fashion during armed conflict, they might still resist the idea that these duties have a fiduciary character.

The fiduciary character of some IHL obligations, however, cannot be so easily dismissed. For starters, the idea that a state's fiduciary relationship with its own people precludes it from assuming fiduciary obligations to others reflects a common misconception about the character of fiduciary loyalty. Although courts sometimes describe fiduciaries as being subject to a "rule of undivided loyalty" that cannot abide conflicts of interest between beneficiaries,[33] the truth is that many fiduciary relationships routinely feature divided loyalties. Fiduciaries are often retained for the purpose of mediating between the competing claims of beneficiaries with conflicting interests. To take but a few familiar examples, administrators of pension funds, receivers in bankruptcy, and corporate directors typically serve beneficiaries with conflicting interests (i.e., present and future pension beneficiaries, majority and minority shareholders, and investors in preferred and common shares). Although fiduciaries are not expected to treat different classes of beneficiaries exactly the same in all respects (e.g., preferred shareholders have a greater claim to assets and earnings than common shareholders), they are required to exercise their discretionary powers in a fair and impartial manner, giving "due regard" to the legitimate interests of vulnerable beneficiaries.[34] In Chapter 1, we explained that the state's fiduciary relationship with its own people bears a similar structure, insofar as a state's commission to establish a regime of secure and equal freedom for its people regularly requires the state to arbitrate between the rival claims of different groups and individuals within its polity. Consequently, the mere fact that states serve as fiduciaries primarily for their own people does not necessarily mean they may not assume fiduciary obligations toward others.

Still, the idea that states bear fiduciary obligations to the nationals of an enemy state with which they are engaged in hostilities will no doubt strike some readers as counterintuitive. Can foreign nationals be fairly categorized as both "enemies" and "beneficiaries" at the same time? Doesn't a state's obligation to protect its own

33. *See* Meinhard v. Salmon, 164 N.E. 545, 548 (N.Y. 1928).

34. *See* Jesse Dukeminier & Robert Sitkoff, Wills, Trusts & Estates 657–58 (9th 2013); Anupam Chander, *Minorities, Shareholder and Otherwise*, 113 Yale L.J. 119 (2003); Robert H. Sitkoff, *An Agency Costs Theory of Trust Law*, 89 Cornell L. Rev. 621, 651 (2004).

people preclude it from assuming fiduciary duties toward the people of an enemy state during time of war?

To understand why states at war bear fiduciary obligations to foreign nationals, we need to expand our frame of reference beyond the state-subject fiduciary relationship to account for the institutional role that states play in establishing and maintaining international legal order. Statehood actually entails two distinct fiduciary relationships, both of which are constitutive of states' institutional personality under international law: not only are states commissioned to serve as fiduciaries for their own people, but they are also entrusted with authority to serve as joint fiduciaries of international legal order generally for the purpose of establishing a regime of secure and equal freedom for humanity as a whole.

This global trusteeship dimension of state sovereignty has important implications for *jus ad bellum*. First, as joint fiduciaries of humanity, states are required to cooperate in efforts to defuse threats to international peace and security. As outlined in the U.N. Charter, states must endeavor to resolve international disputes through "peaceful means of their choice," such as "negotiation, enquiry, mediation, conciliation, arbitration, [or] judicial settlement."[35] Military aggression is categorically prohibited as a vehicle for settling international disputes.[36] When peaceful dispute resolution mechanisms prove unsuccessful, states are obligated to refer their dispute to the Security Council for the purpose of facilitating "a peaceful settlement."[37] Finally, the Charter requires all states to comply with Security Council resolutions that mandate steps for suppressing threats to human security, including the severance of diplomatic relations or economic sanctions against a state that threatens international peace and security,[38] or the deployment of "air, sea, or land forces" into conflict zones.[39] These features of the Charter's *jus ad bellum* regime reflect states' obligations as fiduciaries of humanity to cooperate in establishing an international regime of secure and equal freedom.

Second, as joint fiduciaries of humanity states must also moderate their responses to foreign aggression. Consistent with the customary *jus ad bellum* principles of necessity, imminence, and proportionality, states may use force in self-defense only if an attack is certainly pending, and only if a less harmful response such as diplomatic negotiation, retorsion, or countermeasures would be inadequate to counter the threat.[40] To be sure, the special fiduciary relationship that international law establishes between states and their own people on grounds of self-determination dictates that states bear only limited fiduciary obligations to the nationals of an aggressor state. States are not required to place foreign nationals on an equal footing with their own people, nor are they precluded from vigorously pursuing their own

35. U.N. Charter art. 33(1).

36. *Id.* art. 2(4).

37. *Id.* art. 37(1) & 38.

38. *Id.* art. 41.

39. *Id.* art. 42.

40. *See* William C. Banks & Evan J. Criddle, *Customary Constraints on the Use of Force: Article 51 with an American Accent*, 29 Leiden J. Int'l L. 67 (2016).

national self-defense in response to an "armed attack" from abroad.[41] Nonetheless, in deciding how to respond to an attack from abroad, states are not entitled to treat foreign nationals as mere objects of state coercion that they may injure or destroy arbitrarily. Rather, states bear a fiduciary obligation as joint fiduciaries of humanity to treat the people of an enemy state as persons whose interests in secure and equal freedom are entitled to respect.[42] These obligations are necessary corollaries of the fiduciary constitution of state sovereignty under international law because the entrustment of sovereign authority to states can be reconciled with the principles of non-instrumentalization and non-domination only if states are legally prohibited from visiting unnecessary suffering on foreign nationals.

V. INTERNATIONAL ARMED CONFLICT

When armed conflict breaks out between states, IHL prescribes rules that govern the conduct of hostilities (*jus in bello*). Among its other functions, IHL regulates which persons and property may be targeted during armed conflict, and it sets limits on the types of weapons and the degree of force that combatants may employ in pursuit of their military objectives. For example, under IHL's principle of distinction, states today are required to "distinguish between the civilian population and combatants and between civilian objects and military objectives," and they must take care to "direct their operations only against military objectives."[43] States may not target civilians who do not "take a direct part in hostilities,"[44] nor may they engage in "indiscriminate attacks" that "are of a nature to strike military objectives and civilians or civilian objects without distinction."[45] In addition, states may not "employ weapons" or "methods of warfare of a nature to cause superfluous injury or unnecessary suffering" or "widespread, long-term and severe damage to the natural environment."[46] International treaties identify some specific weapons that violate these requirements, including "dum-dum" bullets that expand upon impact, chemical and biological weapons, blinding laser weapons, and antipersonnel mines.[47] Even where

41. U.N. Charter art. 51.

42. *Cf.* TEITEL, *supra* note 32 (arguing that "humanity" constitutes a cosmopolitan foundation for state obligations to foreign nationals); VATTEL, *supra* note 11, bk. II, ch. 1, at 261 (characterizing state duties to care for foreign nationals abroad as "offices of humanity").

43. Additional Protocol I to the Geneva Conventions of August 12, 1949, Relating to the Protection of Victims of International Armed Conflicts art. 48, June 8, 1977, 1125 U.N.T.S. 3 [hereinafter API].

44. *Id.* art. 51(3).

45. *Id.* art. 51(4)(c); *see also id.* art. 54(1)–(2) (prohibiting the starvation of civilians and attacks on objects such as foodstuffs, crops, livestock, and drinking water, which are deemed indispensable to the survival of the civilian population).

46. *Id.* art. 35(2)–(3); *see also* The 1907 Hague Convention No. IV Respecting the Laws and Customs of War on Land art. 22, Oct. 18, 1907, 36 Stat. 2277, 205 Consol. T.S. 277; Legality of the Threat or Use of Nuclear Weapons, 1996 ICJ Rep. 226, 257 (advisory opinion).

47. *See, e.g., Declaration Concerning Expanding Bullets 1899,* 1 AM J. INT'L L. 157 (Supp. 1907); Protocol for the Prohibition of the Use in War of Asphyxiating, Poisonous or Other Gases, and of

states have not expressly outlawed particular weapons or techniques of warfare by treaty, they have recognized that "civilians and combatants remain under the protection and authority of the principles of international law derived from established custom, from the principles of humanity and from the dictates of public conscience."[48] These features of contemporary IHL aim to mitigate the horrors of war by limiting the means and manner in which states may use force during armed conflict.

Traditionally, these and other IHL rules have been conceptualized as contractual commitments grounded in principles of state consent and reciprocity. In the eighteenth century, the customs of war were viewed as a core feature of the "voluntary law of nations." Vattel characterized these rules as expressions of sovereigns' "great moderation and generosity,"[49] reflecting a spirit of chivalry, forbearance, and mutual respect, and an aversion toward "unbridled licentiousness."[50] Subsequent generations of international lawyers codified the customary law of war in instruments such as Francis Lieber's famous code for the Union army during the American Civil War, the Hague Conventions of 1899 and 1907, the Geneva Conventions of 1949, and the Genocide Convention. The international community thus endeavored "to revise the laws and general customs of war, either with the view of defining them more precisely or of laying down certain limits for the purpose of modifying their severity as far as possible."[51] The overarching purpose of these IHL conventions was 'humanitarian' in that they sought to reduce the human suffering associated with armed conflict. In regulating the use of force during armed conflict, however, these conventions focused primarily on minimizing human pain and property damage in the aggregate rather than ascribing rights to individuals as beneficiaries of international legal order.[52] True to the voluntarist spirit of nineteenth and early twentieth-century international legal positivism, IHL norms were framed as exceptions to the general principle of sovereign independence. As long as states honored their positive commitments to one another under the laws and customs of war, they remained free to use whatever means or methods they deemed necessary to achieve their military objectives.

Over the past several decades, international courts and legal theorists have challenged the conventional account of IHL as a set of contractual rules based on state

Bacteriological Methods of Warfare, June 17, 1925, 26 U.S.T. 571, 94 L.N.T.S. 65; Convention on the Prohibition of the Development, Production and Stockpiling of Bacteriological (Biological) and Toxin Weapons and on Their Destruction, Apr. 10, 1972, 26 U.S.T. 583; Convention on the Prohibition of the Development, Production, Stockpiling and Use of Chemical Weapons and on Their Destruction, *opened for signature* Jan. 13, 1993, S. Treaty Doc. No. 103–21, 1974 U.N.T.S. 317; Convention on the Prohibition of the Use, Stockpiling, Production and Transfer of Anti-personnel Mines and on Their Destruction, Sept. 18, 1997, 36 I.L.M. 1507 (1997).

48. API, *supra* note 43, art. 1(2).

49. Vattel, *supra* note 11, bk. III, ch. VIII, § 158.

50. *Id.* §§ 157–59, 191.

51. Convention (II) with Respect to the Laws and Customs of War on Land and its Annex: Regulations Concerning the Laws and Customs of War on Land, July 29, 1899, pmbl.

52. *See* David Luban, *Human Rights Thinking and the Laws of War*, *in* Theoretical Boundaries of Armed Conflicts and Human Rights (Jens Ohlin ed., forthcoming) (describing traditional IHL as "a form of negative benthamism").

consent and reciprocity. As the ICJ has recognized, some IHL rules that take "the overriding consideration of humanity" as their central concern, are now accepted as "intransgressible principles" of jus cogens.[53] For example, when attacks on military targets pose a risk of collateral civilian casualties, states must take "all reasonable precautions to avoid losses of civilian lives"[54] and ensure that unintended civilian casualties are not "excessive in relation to the concrete and direct military advantage related."[55] Under Common Article 3 of the Geneva Conventions, which governs non-international armed conflicts, and which we discuss further in the next chapter, states must refrain from violence, hostage taking, outrages against personal dignity, and withholding a fair trial from persons who have taken no active part in hostilities.[56] States are obligated to honor these peremptory norms even if they have not ratified the particular conventions in which the norms are expressed, and even if their enemies reject and systematically violate these norms. The peremptory and universal character of these rules suggests that IHL has evolved beyond its historical origins in inter-state commitments governed by principles of comity and reciprocity to reflect the fiduciary character of states' authority as joint fiduciaries of humanity. Although state consent might play a role in grounding and giving definition to IHL's "intransgressible principles," the traditional contract metaphor—which views states at war as independent actors entitled to pursue their own national self-interest, subject to only reciprocal obligations of mutual self-constraint—does not fit this new terrain of IHL.

Eric Posner and Alan Sykes argue that states have committed to comply with IHL's intransgressible humanitarian norms—even when their current adversaries do not—to encourage other states to respect these norms during future conflicts.[57] This explanation is superficially appealing, but it cannot fully explain why IHL retreated from the reciprocity principle in the first place. Requiring states to respect IHL norms even if their enemies refuse to reciprocate lowers the costs of IHL violations by preventing states from deterring rule-breaking by responding in kind to violations. Moreover, treating some IHL standards as peremptory norms systematically disadvantages law-abiding states relative to their adversaries by limiting their tactical options within a given conflict. These costs may be particularly high in asymmetrical conflicts, when states face nonstate insurgencies and guerilla movements that flagrantly and systematically violate the customary peremptory norms of non-international armed conflict. What is striking about IHL's intransgressible rules is precisely that international law requires states and other armed groups to observe these rules even when this demonstrably *undermines* their

53. Legality of the Threat or Use of Nuclear Weapons (advisory opinion), 1996 ICJ Rep. 226, 257 ¶ 79, 262 ¶ 95; *see also* API, *supra* note 39, art. 51; Int'l Comm. of the Red Cross, Customary International Humanitarian Law Rules 3–8, 37–45 (Jean-Marie Henckaerts & Louise Doswald-Beck eds., 2005) [hereinafter ICRC CIL Rules].

54. API, *supra* note 39, art. 57(4).

55. *Id.* art. 51(5)(b).

56. *See* Convention (III) relative to the Treatment of Prisoners of War art. 3, Aug. 12, 1949, 6 U.S.T. 3316, 75 U.N.T.S. 135.

57. *See* Eric A. Posner & Alan O. Sykes, Economic Foundations of International Law 194 (2013).

interests.[58] Clearly, something other than national self-regard and reciprocity must be at work here.

A more persuasive explanation for this phenomenon is that IHL has evolved to accommodate the fiduciary obligations associated with the possession of sovereignty. The utilitarian spirit of early IHL instruments—which sought to decrease the aggregate amount of human suffering caused by war—has been supplanted gradually by an "individual-rights perspective" informed by the idea that all human beings are entitled to be treated as beneficiaries of international legal order.[59] This approach arguably finds clearest expression in the jurisprudence of the International Criminal Tribunal for the Former Yugoslavia. According to the Trial Chamber's now-famous dictum in the *Furundžija* case:

> The essence of the whole corpus of international humanitarian law as well as human rights law lies in the protection of the human dignity of every person. . . . The general principle of respect for human dignity is . . . the very *raison d'être* of international humanitarian law and human rights law; indeed in modern times it has become of such paramount importance as to permeate the whole body of international law.[60]

Whether the Trial Chamber's dictum accurately describes IHL's original raison d'être may be fairly questioned.[61] There can be little doubt, however, that its vision of IHL captures the current thinking of many international tribunals, international legal scholars, and expert bodies such as the International Committee of the Red Cross (ICRC). This paradigm accords with the idea that states as fiduciaries of humanity must give respectful consideration to the interests of enemy combatants and civilians who may be affected by their use of force.

What legal obligations follow from the principle that states serve as fiduciaries of humanity during armed conflict? One possible response is that states' fiduciary obligations to foreign nationals are relatively modest: although states must consider foreign interests and solicit foreign input when their policies are likely to impact foreign stakeholders abroad, they are required to adjust their policies and practices

58. As noted in Chapter 1, nonstate entities that exercise de facto public powers also assume fiduciary obligations, including obligations associated with the proportional and discriminate use of force in non-international armed conflict. This is the case even if nonstate entities' individual members do not qualify for combatant immunity under international law and therefore could be prosecuted under national law for taking up arms against their government. In this chapter, however, we limit our focus to state obligations during armed conflict.

59. Theodor Meron, *The Humanization of Humanitarian Law*, 90 Am. J. Int'l L. 239, 240 (2000); *see also* Luban, *supra* note 52; David Luban, *Human Rights Pragmatism and Human Dignity*, *in* Philosophical Foundations of Human Rights 263 (Rowan Cruft et al. eds., 2015); Gabriella Blum, *The Individualization of War: From War to Policing in the Regulation of Armed Conflicts*, *in* Law and War (Austin Sarat et al. eds., 2014).

60. Prosecutor v. Furundžija, Judgment, Case No. IT-95-17/1-T, T.Ch. II, 10 Dec. 1998, ¶ 183; *see also* Charles Beitz, The Idea of Human Rights 14 (2009) (characterizing IHL as "the law of 'human rights in armed conflicts'" (quoting Sean MacBride)).

61. *See, e.g.*, Geoffrey Corn, *Mixing Apples and Hand Grenades: The Logical Limit of Applying Human Rights Norms to Armed Conflict*, 1 J. Int'l Hum. Studs. 52 (2010); Luban, *supra* note 52.

accordingly only when such adjustments would be costless for their own people. Benvenisti refers to this standard, which can be traced back to Grotius,[62] as the "restricted Pareto criterion."[63] Like Morgenthau's "fiduciary realism," the restricted Pareto criterion's parsimonious rendering of states' moral and legal obligations to foreign nationals is unconvincing because it assumes without proper justification that a state's fiduciary duty of loyalty to its own people invariably trumps its fiduciary obligations to foreign nationals. Strictly construed, this standard would allow belligerent states to commit atrocities such as war crimes and crimes against humanity so long as they could demonstrate that some benefit, however inconsequential, would accrue to their people.[64]

History is replete with examples of states deploying this logic of national self-interest to devastating results during armed conflict. During World War II, for example, the Allied powers concluded that carpet-bombing Dresden was necessary, in part, to hasten the war's conclusion and protect their own forces from a more costly effort to take the city. Today, an attack of this nature would be considered a war crime, despite the fact that the Allied powers likely would have suffered much higher casualties had they been forced to use more discriminating tactics such as introducing ground troops.[65] States must comply with peremptory "principles of international law derived from established custom, from the principles of humanity and from the dictates of public conscience" even if compliance would impose significant costs on their own people.[66] In times of war, as in peacetime, the fiduciary character of sovereignty requires states to temper their pursuit of national security in order to comply with jus cogens norms that are constitutive of their own sovereign authority as fiduciaries of humanity.

At a minimum, states' fiduciary obligations to foreign nationals require them to avoid gratuitous killing, injury, or destruction of property. The prescriptive implications of the fiduciary theory thus support incorporating a "least harmful means" requirement into IHL's principle of "proportionality in attack": if a state can accomplish its military objectives through multiple means that would cause differing degrees of harm to enemy nationals (e.g., capturing, incapacitating, or killing) without increasing the associated danger to friendly forces, states should employ the least harmful means available.[67] Consider, for example, the classic (if somewhat

62. *See* Hugo Grotius, Mare Liberum 38 (Ralph von Deman Magoffin trans., James Brown Scott ed., 1916) (1609).

63. *See* Benvenisti, *supra* note 9, at 320 (suggesting this standard as a framework for understanding states' obligations to provide assistance to foreign nationals abroad).

64. Significantly, Benvenisti does not advocate applying the restricted Pareto criterion to armed conflict.

65. *See* API, *supra* note 39, art. 51; Gabriella Blum, *The Laws of War and the "Lesser Evil,"* 35 Yale J. Int'l L. 1, 25 (2010).

66. API, *supra* note 39, art. 1(2).

67. The ICRC and at least one legal scholar argue that IHL already imposes a "capture rather than kill" requirement, *see* Int'l Comm. of the Red Cross, Interpretive Guidance on the Notion of Direct Participation in Hostilities Under International Humanitarian Law 78–82 (Nils Melzer ed., 2009) [hereinafter ICRC Guidance on Direct Participation]; Ryan Goodman, *The Power to Kill or Capture Enemy Combatants*, 24 Eur. J. Int'l L. 819 (2013); Ryan Goodman, *The Power to Kill or Capture Enemy Combatants: A Rejoinder*

fanciful) case of a soldier who has stripped naked to take a swim during an armed conflict. Conventional wisdom suggests that the naked soldier is a legitimate target under IHL who may be freely killed—even if he can be easily and safely captured.[68] The fiduciary theory, in contrast, supports calls for a blanket prohibition against the use of lethal force *in bello* if less harmful means can be used to neutralize a threat without substantial risk to friendly forces. To be sure, amidst the fog of war, states may be entitled to apply a strong presumption that enemy combatants who are not placed hors de combat by illness or injury cannot be captured safely during an active armed conflict.[69] Nonetheless, in settings where it is apparent that the threat posed by particular enemy combatants can be neutralized safely without recourse to lethal force, the fiduciary principle obligates states as fiduciaries of humanity to avoid unnecessary injury by employing the less harmful means.[70] As future advances in military technology expand the options for non-lethal weaponry, the least harmful means principle is likely to have greater salience and demand broader application.

Another implication of states' position as fiduciaries of humanity is that they must undertake a more robust proportionality inquiry than is currently accepted under IHL when they determine whether collateral harm to innocent civilians is justified by military necessity. Under contemporary *jus in bello*, states may conduct attacks that are "expected to cause incidental loss of civilian life, injury to civilians, damage to civilian objects, or a combination thereof," as long as this collateral harm

to Michael N. Schmitt, 24 Eur. J. Int'l L. 863 (2013); and some scholars have offered normative arguments in favor of a least-harmful-means requirement, *see, e.g.*, Larry May, Legitimating Leviathan: Hobbes on Law and International Affairs (2013) (arguing that Hobbes articulates a similar least-harmful-means test through a prohibition against cruelty or gratuitous harm); Gabriella Blum, *The Dispensable Lives of Soldiers*, 2 J. Leg. Analysis 115 (2010) (arguing prescriptively for a least-harmful-means test). Other scholars have challenged these arguments on positive and normative grounds. *See, e.g.*, Geoffrey S. Corn et al., *Belligerent Targeting and the Invalidity of a Least Harmful Means Rule*, 89 Int'l L. Studs. 536 (2013); Jens David Ohlin, *The Duty to Capture*, 97 Minn. L. Rev. 1268, 1272–73 (2013); Beth Van Schaack, *The Killing of Osama Bin Laden and Anwar Al-Aulaqi: Uncharted Legal Territory*, 14 Y.B. Int'l Humanitarian L. 255, 292 (2012); W. Hays Parks, *Part IX of the ICRC "Direct Participation in Hostilities" Study: No Mandate, No Expertise, and Legally Incorrect*, 42 NYU J. Int'l L & Pol. 794 (2010).

68. *See* Michael Walzer, Just and Unjust Wars 143 (4th ed. 2006); Blum, *supra* note 67, at 116–17; *cf.* Yoram Dinstein, The Conduct of Hostilities Under the Law of International Armed Conflict 29 (2d ed. 2010) ("A person who engages in military raids by night, while purporting to be an innocent civilian by day . . . can be lawfully targeted by the enemy.").

69. *Cf.* Corn et al., *supra* note 67, at 556. Consequently, application of the least harmful means approach, in practice, is likely to be restricted to exceptional circumstances that are remote from "hot" battlefields.

70. *See* ICRC Guidance on Direct Participation, *supra* note 67, at 78–79, 81 (identifying scenarios where using lethal force against civilians who participate directly in hostilities would not satisfy IHL's "guiding principle[]" of "humanity"); *cf.* Michael N. Schmitt, *Wound, Capture, or Kill: A Reply to Ryan Goodman's 'The Power to Kill or Capture Enemy Combatants,'* 24 Eur. J. Int'l L. 855, 860–61 (2013) (observing that "an individual [may have] effectively been captured without an affirmative act on either the captor's or prisoner's part," such that the use of lethal force would be "nothing but an execution").

is not manifestly "excessive in relation to the concrete and direct military advantage anticipated."[71] Some authorities suggest that under this standard "[m]ilitary necessity permits a belligerent, subject to the laws of war, to apply any amount and kind of force to compel the complete submission of the enemy with the least possible expenditure of time, life, and money."[72] As David Luban has observed, however, this rendering of military necessity would allow states in armed conflict to:

> use non-precisionguided bombs rather than more discriminating precision-guided munitions merely because they are cheaper, or merely because commanders do not want to wait for a shipment of [precision-guided missiles] to arrive, and describe the choice as military necessity; that is because there is always a remote probability that the extra money or time might spell the difference between victory and defeat.[73]

The fiduciary character of sovereignty requires a different approach: states must weigh the marginal military advantage they expect to gain from a given use of force against the anticipated civilian damage.[74] If an operation would not offer a substantial military advantage but would entail considerable injury to civilians, the state's claim to military necessity would fail under this approach.[75] A state that refused to follow this approach would transgress its obligations as a fiduciary of humanity by failing to treat the nationals of an enemy state as co-beneficiaries of an international legal system attuned to the status and standing of individuals as subjects of that system. The fiduciary character of sovereignty thus affirms that some uses of force are de jure impermissible within armed conflict—even if they would yield a distinct military advantage—because the advantage thus secured would be manifestly outweighed by the harm to foreign nationals.

Another reason that a state's fiduciary duty to respect the interests of foreign nationals cannot be defined solely by the restricted Pareto criterion relates to the diverse battlefields of twenty-first century conflicts. The restricted Pareto criterion is premised on the idea that the fiduciary relationship between a state and its own people is categorically different from a state's fiduciary-of-humanity relationship with

71. API, *supra* note 39, art. 51(5)(b).

72. United States v. List (Hostages Case) (American Military Tribunal, Nuremberg, 1948), 11 NMT 1230, 1253).

73. David Luban, *Military Necessity and the Cultures of Military Law,* 26 Leiden J. Int'l. L. 315, 343 (2013).

74. *See id.* at 341–47.

75. *See* Eyal Benvenisti, *Human Dignity in Combat: The Duty to Spare Enemy Civilians,* 39 Isr. L. Rev. 81, 83 (2006) [hereinafter Benvenisti, *Human Dignity in Combat*] ; Eyal Benvenisti, *How Should States as "Trustees of Humanity" Respond to an Armed Attack? Reflections in Light of the Gaza War 2014,* Global Trust: Sovereigns as Trustees of Humanity Blog, *available at* http://globaltrust.tau.ac.il/how-should-states-as-trustees-of-humanity-respond-to-an-armed-attack-reflections-in-light-of-the-gaza-war-2014/ (last visited Mar. 17, 2015); Luban, *Military Necessity, supra* note 73, at 343 ("Once civilian interests enter our moral deliberations—as they must— . . . what counts as military necessity must be determined by weighing military importance against civilian damage.").

enemy nationals. But many armed conflicts blur or efface this distinction, including internal armed conflicts, military occupations, and transnational counterterrorism operations. As Benvenisti has recognized, states may bear more robust *jus in bello* obligations in contexts such as internal armed conflict and occupation where they (or a host state that grants consent) have placed territory under their own authority.[76]

In the parts that follow, we examine each of these contexts in turn and consider how IHL should take into account the distinctive fiduciary relationships that arise in each. In particular, we argue that states must look to IHRL for the applicable legal standards for the use of force in internal armed conflict, occupation, transnational counterterrorist operations, and humanitarian intervention.

VI. INTERNAL ARMED CONFLICT

Since its inception, the law of armed conflict has focused primarily on conflicts between states, rather than conflicts between states and nonstate actors. As a result, contemporary IHL treaties offer a patchwork of regulations that do not provide a comprehensive legal regime for internal armed conflict. Additional Protocol I to the Geneva Conventions applies the full corpus of IHL safeguards to internal struggles against colonialism and apartheid, but not to other forms of domestic insurgency.[77] Additional Protocol II, which addresses "non-international armed conflicts," has a similarly limited field of application, addressing only conflicts with dissident armed groups "under responsible command" that "exercise . . . control over . . . territory" and are capable of conducting "sustained" military operations and complying with IHL.[78] With most insurgencies today being networked rather than hierarchical, intermittent rather than sustained, and itinerant rather than territorially entrenched, the practical effect of these conditions is to exclude many internal armed conflicts from the scope of most of the Geneva Conventions.[79] Only Common Article 3 of the Geneva Conventions, which extends a limited number of basic protections to "armed conflict not of an international character," applies directly to all internal armed conflicts.[80] Despite these limitations, commentary accompanying Additional Protocol II suggests that states must always respect IHL's "general principles relating to the protection of the civilian population which apply

76. *See* Benvenisti, *Human Dignity in Combat, supra* note 75, at 90; Eyal Benvenisti, *The Law on Asymmetric Warfare, in* Looking to the Future: Essays on International Law in Honor of W. Michael Reisman 931, 948–49 (2010) [hereinafter Benvenisti, *Asymmetric Warfare*].

77. API, *supra* note 39, art. 1(4).

78. Additional Protocol II to the Geneva Conventions of August 12, 1949, Relating to the Protection of Victims of Non-International Armed Conflicts art. 1(1), June 8, 1977, 1125 U.N.T.S. 609 [hereinafter APII].

79. *See* Leslie C. Green, The Contemporary Law of Armed Conflict 83 (3d ed. 2008) ("The definition of a non-international armed conflict in Protocol II . . . would exclude most revolutions and rebellions, and would probably not operate in a civil war until the rebels were well established and had set up some form of *de facto* government."). The United States is one of several states that have not ratified Additional Protocol II.

80. *See, e.g.*, Geneva Convention (III) Relative to the Treatment of Prisoners of War art. 3, Aug. 12, 1949, 6 U.S.T. 3316, 75 U.N.T.S. 135 [hereinafter GC3].

irrespective of whether the conflict is an international or an internal one," including "the principle of distinction and the principle of proportionality which only intervenes when it is not possible to ensure the total immunity of the population."[81] The conventional view among states today, therefore, is that IHL permits states to target civilian-insurgents "for such time as they take a direct part in hostilities,"[82] subject to the principles of distinction, necessity, and proportionality, which apply to all armed conflicts as a matter of customary international law.[83]

In addition to IHL's standards for the use of force, IHRL's prohibition against arbitrary deprivations of life arguably constrains how states may use force in internal armed conflict.[84] Under IHRL, states may use lethal force only to the extent "strictly necessary" to protect their people from potentially fatal injury.[85] Any operation undertaken by national authorities to promote national security must be "planned and controlled by the authorities so as to minimise, to the greatest extent possible, recourse to lethal force."[86]

Some IHL experts have argued that during internal armed conflict, IHL's traditional principles of distinction, necessity, and proportionality constitute a *lex specialis* regime for armed conflict that completely displaces human rights standards for the use of force.[87] Under the fiduciary theory's preferred approach to *jus in bello*, the

81. APII, *supra* note 78, at 1490, ¶ 4772.

82. API, *supra* note 39, art. 51(3); APII, *supra* note 78, art. 13(3).

83. *See*, e.g., Prosecutor v. Tadić, Case No. IT-94-1-l, Decision on the Defence Motion for Interlocutory Appeal on Jurisdiction, ¶¶ 119, 127 (Int'l Crim. Trib. for the Former Yugoslavia Oct. 2, 1995) (reasoning that principles of discrimination from the law of international armed conflict represented "customary rules" that would apply equally "in civil strife"); ICRC CIL Rules, *supra* note 53, at xxxv (asserting that "gaps in the regulation of the conduct of [non-international armed conflict] have largely been filled through State practice, which has led to the creation of rules parallel to those [governing international armed conflict], but applicable as customary law to non-international armed conflicts.").

84. *See, e.g.*, International Covenant on Civil and Political Rights art. 6(1), Dec. 16, 1966, S. Exec. Doc. E, 95-2 (1978), 999 U.N.T.S. 171 [hereinafter ICCPR]; Council of Europe, Convention for the Protection of Human Rights and Fundamental Freedoms art. 2(2), Nov. 4, 1950, E.T.S. No. 5, 213 U.N.T.S. 221 [hereinafter European Convention]; Organization of American States, American Convention on Human Rights art. 4, Nov. 22, 1969, O.A.S. Treaty Series No. 36, 1144 U.N.T.S. 123 [hereinafter American Convention].

85. U.N. Human Rights Council, Rep. of the Special Rapporteur on Extrajudicial, Summary or Arbitrary Executions, at 11, U.N. Doc. A/HRC/14/24/Add.6 (May 28, 2010) (prepared by Philip Alston) [hereinafter U.N. Report on Targeted Killing] ("Lethal force under human rights law is legal if it is strictly and directly necessary to save life."); International Human Rights Committee, Compilation of General Comments and General Recommendations Adopted by Human Rights Treaty Bodies, General Comment No. 6, HRI/GEN/1/Rev.7 (2004), ¶ 3 ("[T]he law must strictly control and limit the circumstances in which a person may be deprived of his life by [state] authorities.").

86. Isayeva v. Russia, 41 Eur. Ct. H.R. 847, ¶ 175 (2005).

87. *See, e.g.*, Corn, *supra* note 61, 57, 89. For a survey of several other possible paradigms for reconciling IHL and IHRL, see Marco Sassòli, *The Role of Human Rights and International Humanitarian Law in New Types of Armed Conflicts*, *in* International Humanitarian Law and International Human Rights Law 34, 69–78 (Orna Ben-Naftali ed., 2011).

distance between IHL and IHRL standards would narrow considerably, with IHL embracing a least-harmful-means test and a narrower interpretation of "military necessity." Nonetheless, to the extent that IHL and IHRL standards for the use of force currently diverge in important respects, the suggestion that IHRL norms do not apply at all during armed conflict merits further scrutiny.

Scholars who reject applying human rights standards to armed conflict tend to conceptualize armed conflict in terms that are reminiscent of Morgenthau's fiduciary realism. Naz Modirzadeh puts the matter thus:

> The logic behind the law [of armed conflict] is . . . apparent: this is not a long-term relationship, and the law does not provide the grounds for a good society or interactions based on trust and due process. Rather, this is a set of rules that restricts the military forces while they fight, while recognizing that they *will* fight, and that people (even those not involved in the fighting) will die in the process. The addition of human rights law to this clear and honest (albeit stark) framing of roles and relationships runs the risk of confusing all actors and (more important) raising expectations that can never be met.[88]

Under this view, human rights standards do not apply to internal armed conflict, because citizens who take up arms against their state rupture the bonds of mutual fidelity that form the legal and moral foundation of the state-citizen relationship. IHL norms alone govern internal armed conflict, the thinking goes, because these norms are properly attuned to the antagonistic relationship between foes at war, a relationship that is defined by enmity rather than trust.

The idea that international law frames the relationship between adversaries in armed conflict in terms of enmity rather than trust is only partly correct. During traditional international armed conflicts, warring states clearly do relate to one another as hostile adversaries rather than trusted partners. Unless a state takes steps to assert de facto jurisdiction over the people or territory of an enemy state,[89] its fiduciary obligations to enemy nationals are limited to its more general fiduciary obligations as a joint fiduciary of humanity. Nonetheless, the fiduciary model of state sovereignty underscores the fact that IHL's minimum standards for the use of force are, in fact, premised on a form of trust: states' shared commitment and responsibility as fiduciaries of humanity to respect the status of foreign nationals as co-beneficiaries and subjects of international legal order, even amidst the horrors of war. IHL thus rejects the notion that states at war are entitled to engage the nationals of an enemy state on the basis of enmity or indifference.

A more basic flaw in Modirzadeh's critique of human rights discourse is her assumption that internal armed conflict severs a state's robust fiduciary obligations toward domestic insurgents. Under the fiduciary theory, a state may not claim sovereign jurisdiction over people within its territory while simultaneously disavowing the fiduciary duties that are associated with this authority. Sovereignty and fiduciary constraint are inextricably linked; the former cannot be asserted or exercised

88. Naz K. Modirzadeh, *The Dark Side of Convergence*, 86 Int'l L. Studs. 349, 364 (2010).

89. We address these issues further *infra* in Section IX (occupation) and Chapter 6 (detention during armed conflict).

without triggering the latter, because the latter is a constitutive part of the former. Although international law entrusts each state with a standing authorization to use force internally to protect its people from grave harm, this authority is always subject to a concomitant fiduciary obligation to respect human rights standards for the use of force.[90]

Given these difficulties, it should come as no surprise that both the European Court of Human Rights (ECHR) and the Inter-American Court have soundly rejected the notion that IHRL norms do not apply during internal armed conflict. In a series of cases involving internal counterinsurgency (COIN) operations in Chechnya, Colombia, Guatemala, and Turkey, these tribunals have applied ordinary IHRL proportionality, notwithstanding the fact that the operations under review occurred within theaters of active armed conflict.[91] Illustrative of this approach is the ECHR's 2005 case, *Isayeva, Yusupova and Bazayeva v. Russia (Isayeva)*.[92] During Russia's October 2001 military campaign against insurgents in Chechnya, the Russian military established a temporary "humanitarian corridor" to facilitate the departure of civilians from Grozny, Chechnya's besieged capital. As civilian refugees were endeavoring to depart, Russian fighter planes fired missiles at a segment of the humanitarian corridor where militants were believed to be attempting to escape. Sixteen civilians were killed, including two ICRC workers.[93] In reviewing this episode for compliance with the European Convention on Human Rights (European Convention), the ECHR declined to apply IHL as the relevant *lex specialis*, and instead looked to IHRL for the applicable proportionality standard. The court stressed that Russia's "use of force" against Chechen insurgents "must be no more than 'absolutely necessary,'" and that the Russian military "must take appropriate care to ensure that any risk to life is minimised."[94] Although the court recognized that "the situation that existed in Chechnya at the relevant time called for exceptional measures," it nonetheless condemned the particular attack under review because Russia was unable to show that this measure was strictly necessary under the circumstances.[95]

90. APII, *supra* note 78, at pmbl (affirming that "international instruments relating to human rights offer a basic protection to the human person" that applies during internal armed conflict).

91. *See, e.g.*, Isayeva, Yusupova, and Bazayeva v. Russia, 41 Eur. H.R. Rep. 39 (2005) [hereinafter *Isayeva I*]; Isayeva v. Russia, 41 Eur. H.R. Rep. 38 (2005) [hereinafter *Isayeva II*]; Bámaca-Velásquez v. Guatemala, Merits and Judgment, Inter-Am Ct. H.R. (ser. C) No. 70, ¶ 209 (Nov. 25, 2000); Las Palmeras v. Colombia, Merits and Judgment, Inter-Am. Ct. H.R. (ser. C) No. 67 ¶ 33 (Feb. 4, 2000); Kaya v. Turkey (no. 22535/93), 2000-III, Eur. Ct. H.R. (2000).

92. *Isayeva I*, 41 Eur. H.R. Rep. 39, ¶ 13.

93. *Id.* ¶ 29.

94. *Id.* ¶¶ 167, 169, 171 (citing, *inter alia*, McCann and Others v. United Kingdom (ser. A) No. 324, 21 Eur. H.R. Rep. 39, 45–46, 57 (1995); *see also* McKerr v. United Kingdom, Eur. Ct. H.R. (2001), ¶ 110; Human Rights Committee, General Comment N)o. 6, ¶ 3 HRI/GEN/1/Rev.6 (1982) ¶ 129.

95. *Id.* ¶¶ 178–79. In the wake of *Isayeva* and similar decisions, many human rights scholars and treaty bodies have embraced the idea that IHRL's more restrictive standards apply alongside IHL standards during internal armed conflict and that these "spheres of law are complementary, not mutually exclusive." Human Rights Committee, General Comment No. 31, 26 May 2004, CCPR/C/21/Rev.1/Add.13, ¶ 11; *see also* Human Rights Committee, Aug. 4–5, 2003,

Isayeva thus illustrates how fiduciary principles can, and should, inform how states conduct military operations within their own borders to promote human rights for their people. Consistent with IHRL, the fiduciary theory bars states from using force unless such measures are "absolutely necessary" to protect life. To be sure, when domestic tensions erupt into internal armed conflict, states may have no alternative but to use lethal force if they wish to satisfy their responsibility to protect their own soldiers and civilians from deadly attacks. Whenever states use force within their own borders, however, their operations must be "planned and controlled by the authorities so as to minimise, to the greatest extent possible, recourse to lethal force."[96]

VII. ASYMMETRIC SELF-DEFENSE

The fiduciary character of sovereignty also offers insights for nontraditional battlefields such as transnational counterterrorism operations. Just as states bear obligations to respect human rights when they use force to quell domestic insurgencies, the fiduciary theory suggests that they must also observe IHRL constraints on the use of force when they use force against nonstate actors abroad with, or without, the host state's consent.

A. *Jus ad Bellum*

Questions regarding the application of IHL and IHRL to asymmetric self-defense have become increasingly important since the 9/11 terrorist attacks, as the United States and its allies have waged a global campaign to disrupt and dismantle the al-Qaeda terrorist network and other extremist groups that pose security threats. After invading Afghanistan in 2001, the United States soon broadened its counterterrorism operations to other states where al-Qaeda cells were believed to be operating. In December 2001, U.S.-led forces pursued Taliban insurgents beyond the borders of Afghanistan into the mountainous tribal regions of neighboring Pakistan. Subsequent operations targeted al-Qaeda-affiliated groups in Somalia and Yemen. Although it appears that the United States generally obtained other states' consent before using force within their territory, it did not follow this course in every case. Most prominently, in May 2011, U.S. special forces raided a compound in Abbottabad, Pakistan, killing al-Qaeda leader Osama Bin Laden without Pakistan's prior consent. Four months later, the United States conducted a drone and jet strike in Yemen to kill radical Islamic cleric Anwar Al-Awlaki, a U.S. citizen who had

Concluding Observations, ¶ 11, U.N. Doc. CCPR/CO/78/ISR (Aug. 21, 2003), http://www.unhchr.ch/tbs/doc.nsf/(Symbol)/CCPR.CO.78.ISR.En?OpenDocument (last visited Nov. 25, 2015); Christian Tomuschat, *Human Rights and International Humanitarian Law*, 21 Eur. J. Int'l L. 15, 20 (2010).

96. Isayeva v. Russia, 41 Eur. Ct. H.R. 847, ¶ 175 (2005); *see also* Khatsiyeva and Others v. Russia, App. No. 5108/02 Judgment, Jan. 17, 2008; David S. Koller, *The Moral Imperative: Toward a Human Rights-Based Law of War*, 46 Harv. Int'l L.J. 231, 260–61 (2005); Kenneth Watkin, *Controlling the Use of Force: A Role for Human Rights Norms in Contemporary Armed Conflict*, 98 Am. J. Int'l L. 1, 32 (2004).

allegedly participated in preparations for terrorist attacks against the United States. In August 2014, the United States joined NATO allies and other regional partners in targeting members of the so-called Islamic State of Iraq and the Levant (Islamic State), an extremist insurgent force that seeks to carve out a radical Islamic caliphate in the Middle East.[97] At the time of this writing, there is no end in sight to these targeted killing programs.

Although the 9/11 terrorist attacks and their aftermath have cast a fresh spotlight on the application of *jus ad bellum* principles to military operations against nonstate actors, the problem of asymmetrical self-defense is not new. Indeed, the classic nineteenth-century statement on preemptive self-defense, articulated by U.S. Secretary of State Daniel Webster during the *Caroline* affair of 1837, was prepared in response to the British government's use of force against nonstate actors in the United States. Concerned that an American ship was smuggling weapons across the Niagara River to Canadian rebels, British authorities had entered U.S. waters without the consent of the American government to neutralize the ongoing threat. Despite contesting the legality of this action, Webster agreed in principle that international law would permit cross-border military action where there was "a necessity of self-defence, instant, overwhelming, leaving no choice of means, and no moment for deliberation."[98] Under this influential *Caroline* doctrine, a vulnerable state's responsibility to protect its people, coupled with the absence of effective action from the host state, was understood to justify the use of force across international borders.

In the Charter era, it is far less clear whether states may use force in response to cross-border attacks by nonstate actors. Some authorities, principally in continental Europe, have concluded that only states are capable of conducting "armed attacks" within the meaning of Article 51, so the violent acts of nonstate actors can never trigger a right to self-defense under the Charter.[99] Although the ICJ has adopted a more nuanced approach to the issue, it too has held that Article 51 requires state action to justify the use of force in self-defense. According to the ICJ, attacks by nonstate actors must be "imputable to a foreign State"[100] based on a foreign state's effective control in order to trigger the right of self-defense under international law.[101] Moreover, even if nonstate actors are subject to a host state's effective control, the ICJ has reasoned that low-level violence, such as episodic rocket attacks or

97. *See* Joint Statement Issued by Partners at the Counter-ISIL Coalition Ministerial Meeting, Dec. 3, 2014, http://www.state.gov/r/pa/prs/ps/2014/12/234627.htm; Alissa J. Rubin et al., *U.S. Jets and Drones Attack Militants in Iraq, Hoping to Stop Advance*, N.Y. Times, Aug. 8, 2014, http://www.nytimes.com/2014/08/09/world/middleeast/iraq.html?_r=0.

98. Webster to Fox, 24 Apr. 1841, 29 BFSP at 1137–38, http://avalon.law.yale.edu/19th_century/br-1842d.asp.

99. *See, e.g.*, Antonio Cassese, *The International Community's "Legal" Response to Terrorism*, 38 Int'l & Comp. L.Q. 589, 597 (1989).

100. *See* Legal Consequences of the Construction on a Wall in the Occupied Palestinian Territory, Advisory Opinion, 2004 ICJ Rep. 136 (July 9) (*Palestinian Wall*); Case Concerning Armed Activities on the Territory of the Congo (Congo v. Uganda), 2005 ICJ Rep. 168, 223 (Dec. 19) (*Armed Activities*).

101. *See Armed Activities*, 2005 ICJ Rep. 201, ¶ 147; *Palestinian Wall*, 2004 ICJ Rep. 207, ¶ 139.

suicide bombings, does not meet the test of severity that distinguishes an "armed attack" from lesser violence under the Charter.[102] Thus, the ICJ has erected formidable hurdles to states' use of force against nonstate actors beyond their borders—hurdles that would preclude military action in contexts such as the *Caroline* affair and the Bin Laden operation.

Although the text of the Charter does not rule out the ICJ's approach to asymmetric self-defense, its reading of Article 51 is not compelled by the text itself,[103] and it has encountered stiff resistance in recent years from a growing number of states. In the 1970s and 1980s, the international community reacted with skepticism, if not outright hostility and condemnation, when states invoked Article 51 as a basis for cross-border military action in response to attacks by nonstate actors.[104] Beginning in the 1990s, however, a diverse collection of states have asserted the right to use force to defend their people against attacks from terrorist cells, paramilitary groups, and private militias outside their borders.[105] In the immediate aftermath of the 9/11 terrorist attacks, the Security Council appeared to take sides in this debate by describing these attacks as "a threat to international peace and security" that had triggered "the inherent right of individual or collective self-defence in accordance with the Charter."[106] More recently, the multinational coalition of states that is attempting to neutralize the Islamic State in Syria has relied on arguments based on individual or collective self-defense under Article 51—notwithstanding the fact that most have not sought Syria's approval for military intervention.[107] Although the ICJ has generally resisted these trends,[108] many governments and legal scholars now embrace the idea that states may use force in self-defense against dangerous nonstate actors outside their own borders without either Security Council authorization or the host state's consent, if the host state

102. *See* Case Concerning Military and Paramilitary Activities in and Against Nicaragua (Nicaragua v. United States), 1986 ICJ Rep. 14 (June 27), ¶¶ 191, 210–11, 247–49, Case Concerning Oil Platforms (Islamic Republic of Iran v. United States of America), 1986 ICJ Rep. 803 (Nov. 12), ¶¶ 51–64 (*Oil Platforms*); *cf.* Eritrea-Ethiopia Claims Commission, Partial Award, Jus ad Bellum, 19 Dec. 2005, ¶ 12.

103. *See Palestinian Wall*, 2004 ICJ Rep. 207, ¶ 3 (July 9) (Higgins, J., separate opinion) ("There is, with respect, nothing in the text of Article 51 that *thus* stipulates that self defense is available only when an armed attack is made by a State . . . .").

104. *See* Christian Tams, *The Use of Force Against Terrorists*, 20 Eur. J. Int'l L. 359, 367–68 (2009) (discussing criticism of "self-defence" operations undertaken by Israel, South Africa, and the United States).

105. *See* Theresa Rheingold, *State Weakness, Irregular Warfare, and the Right to Self-Defense Post 9/11*, 105 Am. J. Int'l L. 244, 285 (2011) (collecting examples); Tams, *supra* note 104 (same).

106. U.N. Sec. Council Res. 1368, SC/Res/1368 (Sept. 12, 2001).

107. *See, e.g.*, Letter from U.S. Special Representative to the United Nations Samantha J. Power to U.N. Secretary-General Ban Ki-moon, Sept. 23, 2014.

108. Some judges of the ICJ, however, have concluded that attacks by nonstate actors may trigger a right to self-defense. *See* Case Concerning Armed Activities on the Territory of the Congo (Congo v. Uganda), 2005 ICJ Rep. 168 (Dec. 19) (separate opinions of Judges Simma and Koojimans); *Palestinian Wall*, 2004 ICJ Rep. 207, ¶ 6.

allows its territory to be used as an operational command center or staging ground for cross-border attacks.[109]

At present, it is unclear how this debate over the legality of asymmetrical self-defense will be resolved. Should the ICJ's interpretation of Article 51 prevail, states could claim authority under international law to use force abroad without Security Council authorization or the other state's consent only if the armed attacks were conducted by a foreign state or by nonstate actors under the foreign state's control. Under this approach, states could continue to use force against nonstate actors within their own borders, consistent with IHRL, where absolutely necessary to protect their people. But they would have to seek the Security Council's approval for any cross-border military response to attacks committed by nonstate actors operating outside another state's control. The Security Council would therefore be solely responsible for deciding whether responsive military action would further the international legal system's overarching fiduciary purpose to establish a regime of secure and equal freedom.

If the ICJ's interpretation of Article 51 does not ultimately prevail, states could assert broader authority under international law to use force outside their borders without the Security Council's ex ante authorization. Even in this scenario, however, well-established principles of international law dictate that lawful cross-border military action would be exceptionally rare, and it would always be subject to scrutiny by the international community ex post. For example, the Charter provides that a threat to national security must cross the "armed attack" threshold to support self-defense. Sporadic incidents of low-intensity violence by nonstate actors do not suffice under this standard.[110] Customary principles of *jus ad bellum* such as necessity, imminence, and proportionality likewise limit the use of force abroad. Additionally, states may not use force against nonstate actors abroad if attacks can be averted through diplomacy, peaceful dispute-resolution mechanisms, non-forcible countermeasures such as economic sanctions, or appeals to either the Security Council or the host state.[111] Even if these requirements are satisfied, the fiduciary theory suggests

109. *See, e.g.*, Daniel Bethlehem, *Self-Defense Against an Imminent or Actual Armed Attack by Nonstate Actors*, 106 Am. J. Int'l L. 770, 774–77 (2012). Some authorities characterize the applicable legal standard for bypassing the host state's consent as an "unable or unwilling" test; others as an "aiding and abetting" requirement. *Compare* Elizabeth Wilmhurst, Chatham House Principles on Self-Defense 11–13 (Oct. 2005) (unable or unwilling), *and* Ashley Deeks, *"Unwilling or Unable": Toward a Normative Framework for Extraterritorial Self-Defense*, 52 Va. J. Int'l L. 483 (2012) (unable and unwilling), *with* Tams, *supra* note 104, at 385–86 (aiding and abetting); *and* Tom Ruys & Sten Verhoeven, *Attacks by Private Actors and the Right of Self-Defense*, 10 J. Conflict & Sec. L. 289, 312–17 (2005) (aiding and abetting). A few commentators have taken the more aggressive position that states may use force abroad in response to terrorist attacks irrespective of whether the host state is willing and able to neutralize the threat. *See, e.g.*, Jutta Brunnée & Stephen Toope, Legitimacy and Legality in International Law 296 (2010); Raphaël Van Steenberghe, *Self-Defence in Response to Attacks by Non-state Actors in the Light of Recent State Practice: A Step Forward?*, 23 Leiden J. Int'l L. 183, 184 (2010).

110. *See, e.g.*, *Armed Activities*, 2005 ICJ Rep. 168, at 223; Case Concerning Military and Paramilitary Activities in and Against Nicaragua (Nicaragua v. United States), 1986 ICJ Rep. 14, at 101–03.

111. *See* Report of the Secretary-General's High-Level Panel on Threats, Challenges and Change, A More Secure World: Our Shared Responsibility (2004).

that states as fiduciaries of humanity must refrain from using force against nonstate actors abroad if such action could foreseeably trigger an international armed conflict with the host state that would pose a disproportionate threat to international peace and security.[112] Thus, even if the ICJ eventually defers to countercurrents in state practice, states will rarely be justified in using force against nonstate actors abroad without the consent of either the Security Council or the host state, and when they purport to have an adequate justification for the use of force, they must still render an account ex post to the international community, taking into consideration the principles sketched above that limit the extraterritorial use of force.

B. *Jus in Bello*

As discussed previously, in the post-9/11 era states generally have conducted military operations against terrorists and paramilitary groups outside their borders with the consent of the host state. Under the fiduciary theory, states must adhere to IHRL standards for the use of force in these settings. As the ECHR has recognized, when a state exercises force abroad with

> the consent, invitation or acquiescence of the Government of that territory, it exercises all or some of the public powers normally to be exercised by that Government. Thus where, in accordance with custom, treaty or other agreement, authorities of the Contracting State carry out executive or judicial functions on the territory of another State, the Contracting State may be responsible for breaches of [human rights] thereby incurred, as long as the acts in question are attributable to it rather than to the territorial State.[113]

A state that uses force abroad with a host state's consent assumes the host state's fiduciary obligations to treat foreign nationals within that territory as equal beneficiaries of sovereign power. Under the fiduciary model, this obligation to respect and protect the human rights of foreign nationals flows from the host state's consensual delegation of sovereign authority to the intervening state.

These features of the fiduciary theory have far-reaching implications for transnational counterterrorism and COIN operations. For example, once the United States and its allies toppled the Taliban regime in Afghanistan and began conducting COIN operations at the behest of the new government, they also assumed a fiduciary obligation to respect IHRL rules for the use of force. Coalition forces were under an obligation, therefore, to take precautions to avoid or minimize injury to

112. As with any other exercise of individual or collective self-defense, a state's use of force against nonstate actors abroad is subject to ex post scrutiny by the broader international community to assess compliance with *jus ad bellum*. Although there is currently no formal institutional mechanism in place for international review of state decisions to use force (aside from the International Criminal Court's limited jurisdiction over the crime of aggression), international review may take the form of U.N. Security Council or General Assembly resolutions, investigations by independent international commissions, or decentralized responses by states and regional organizations.

113. Al-Skeini and Others v. United Kingdom, App. no. 55721/07, Eur. Ct. H.R. 7 July 2011, ¶ 135 (citing *inter alia* Bankovic v. Belgium, 2001-XII, Eur. Ct. H.R. 33, ¶ 71).

noncombatants who might be endangered by the coalition forces' military operations. Similarly, when conducting counterterrorist drone strikes in other countries with the express or tacit consent of the host government, the United States bears a fiduciary duty to take precautions to avoid any fatalities or other injuries that are not strictly necessary to protect the lives of friendly forces and civilians from terrorist attacks. These fiduciary obligations to respect human rights accompany the exercise of another state's delegated sovereign powers.

Human rights standards may also apply to the extent states use force in response to attacks from nonstate actors outside their borders without the host state's consent. When international law authorizes states to use force against nonstate actors abroad, a plausible implication of the fiduciary theory is that the intervening state wields public powers in the host state's place, effectively operating as a temporary agent of necessity under international law. The intervening state thus assumes the host state's fiduciary obligation to respect the IHRL "right to life," as enshrined in the ICCPR and regional human rights instruments.[114] Even in contexts where international *jus ad bellum* does not authorize states to use force against nonstate actors abroad, the fiduciary character of state sovereignty suggests that a state's unlawful exercise of military power activates a fiduciary obligation to satisfy human rights norms.[115] Some legal scholars have argued that applying IHRL standards to international COIN operations, as the fiduciary theory dictates, would be "operationally debilitating" for soldiers on the battlefield who must be "ready, willing, and able to kill on demand."[116] Developments in COIN theory over the past decade suggest, however, that this concern is somewhat overstated.[117] Military strategists have recognized that success in COIN operations generally requires support from the local populace and the international community. Achieving public support, in turn, depends on counterinsurgents' ability to minimize injury to both insurgents and innocent civilians alike.[118]

The United States' 2006 *Counterinsurgency Manual* explains, for example, that an "operation that kills five insurgents is counterproductive if collateral damage leads to the recruitment of fifty more insurgents."[119] Counterinsurgents should therefore "address lesser means of force when such use is likely to create the desired effects and joint forces can do so without endangering themselves, others, or mission

114. *See, e.g.*, ICCPR, *supra* note 84, art. 6(1); European Convention, *supra* note 84, art. 2(2); American Convention, *supra* note 84, art. 4.

115. *See* Benvenisti, *Asymmetric Warfare*, *supra* note 76, at 948–49.

116. Corn, *supra* note 61, at 83.

117. *See* Corn et al., *supra* note 67, at 612 (acknowledging that "[t]he inclusion of a least harmful means rule in contemporary counterinsurgency [rules of engagement] indicates that . . . soldiers can be trained to even more restrictive . . . standards").

118. *See* David Kilcullen, *Twenty-Eight Articles: Fundamentals of Company-Level Counterinsurgency* 5, http://smallwarsjournal.com/documents/28articles.pdf (last visited Nov. 25, 2015); Peter R. Mansoor & Mark S. Ulrich, *Linking Doctrine to Action: A New COIN Center-of-Gravity Analysis*, MIL. REV. 45, 46 (Sept.–Oct. 2007).

119. CHAIRMAN OF THE JOINT-CHIEFS OF STAFF, COUNTERINSURGENCY OPERATIONS, JOINT PUBLICATION 3-24, at III-17 (Oct. 5, 2009) [hereinafter U.S. COUNTERINSURGENCY MANUAL].

accomplishment."[120] To implement this civilian-centric approach, the United States experimented in Afghanistan with rules of engagement that were more protective of civilian life than IHL proportionality.[121] U.S. counterinsurgents were permitted to defend themselves from insurgent attack, but lethal force was reserved for circumstances where "no other options are available to effectively counter the threat"—a standard that mirrors IHRL.[122] Indeed, in some respects, these new COIN guidelines were even *more* attentive to the lives of insurgents than IHRL's strict standards. For instance, the *Counterinsurgency Manual* instructed counterinsurgents to refrain from using lethal force against insurgent fighters whenever innocent civilians were present (or it was unclear whether innocent civilians were present) in order to avoid even the slightest risk of civilian casualties.[123] These requirements to avoid civilian fatalities reflected the U.S. military's recognition that the success or failure of its mission could depend on whether its forces succeeded in using *less* force against insurgents and willingly accepting *greater* risks to their own soldiers.[124] Although it remains unclear to what extent this force-minimization paradigm will inform future COIN operations, the U.S. experience in Afghanistan illustrates how the strategic imperatives of COIN may support rules of engagement that are consistent with the fiduciary theory's prescriptions.

U.S. counterterrorism policy has also shifted toward IHRL standards for the use of force. As a formal matter, the United States has refused to accept the idea that its human rights obligations ever apply extraterritorially, much less that IHRL standards govern its drone strikes against suspected terrorists in the Middle East and North Africa.[125] As a matter of national policy, however, the United States has taken a more conciliatory approach. In a May 2013 press release, the White House stated that "[l]ethal force will be used [against terrorists abroad] only to prevent or stop attacks against U.S. persons, and even then, only when capture is not feasible and no other reasonable alternatives exist to address the threat effectively."[126] To justify lethal force, the target must "pose[] a continuing, imminent threat to U.S. persons."

120. *Id.* at III-18.

121. *See* Michael N. Schmitt, *Targeting and International Humanitarian Law in Afghanistan*, 39 Isr. Y.B. Hum. Rts. 307, 315–20 (2009) (discussing the "likely and identifiable threat" standard).

122. Int'l Security Assistance Force H.Q. Public Affairs, Press Release, *Gen. Petraeus Issues Updated Tactical Directive, Emphasizes "Disciplined Use of Force,"* http://www.dvidshub.net/news/53931/gen-petraeus-issues-updated-tactical-directive-emphasizes-disciplined-use-force (last visited Nov. 25, 2015) (providing excerpts from the classified tactical directive).

123. *Id.*

124. *See* U.S. Counterinsurgency Manual, *supra* note 119, at 48–49. *But see* U.S. Field Manual 3-24, Insurgencies and Countering Insurgencies 13-7 (May 13, 2014) (observing that rules of engagement in COIN operations would be "mission-specific").

125. *See* Beth Van Schaack, *The United States' Position on the Extraterritorial Application of Human Rights Obligations: Now Is the Time for Change*, 90 Int'l L. Studs. 20 (2014). *But see* Legal Consequences of the Construction of a Wall in the Occupied Palestinian Territory, Advisory Opinion, 2004 ICJ Rep. 136, 180 (July 9) (holding that the ICCPR "is applicable in respect of acts done by a State in the exercise of jurisdiction outside its territory").

126. The White House, Fact Sheet: U.S. Policy Standards and Procedures for the Use of Force in Counterterrorism Operations Outside the United States and Areas of Active Hostilities, May 23, 2013, http://www.whitehouse.gov/the-press-office/2013/05/23/

There must also be "[n]ear certainty that the terrorist target is present" and "that non-combatants will not be injured or killed."[127] Thus, it appears that policymakers in the United States have come to recognize that counterterrorism operations must satisfy IHRL's more stringent standards if they are to be accepted as legitimate by the international community.

VIII. OCCUPATION

Under the fiduciary theory, IHRL also supplies the applicable proportionality standard for states conducting military operations in contexts of belligerent occupation. International law requires an occupying power to maintain fundamental security under the rule of law within occupied territory as a temporary trustee for the state it has displaced.[128] With respect to property within occupied territory, the Hague Regulations provide that an occupying state "shall only be regarded as administrator and usufructuary of the public buildings, real property, forests and agricultural works belonging to the hostile State, and situated in the occupied territory." Although the occupying state may use public resources within occupied territory "according to the rules of usufruct," it must "protect the capital of these properties" as a fiduciary for eventual return to the displaced state.[129] The law of occupation also obligates an occupying power to afford "the civilian population" the "maximal safeguards feasible under the circumstances"[130] The occupying state must "assume active responsibility for the welfare of the population under its control," devoting special attention to particularly vulnerable groups such as foreign nationals, women, and children.[131] Specific responsibilities identified in the Geneva Conventions include requirements to maintain public schools,[132] ensure the delivery of food and medical

fact-sheet-us-policy-standards-and-procedures-use-force-counterterrorism (last visited Nov. 25, 2015).

127. *Id.* Critics have questioned whether the United States actually adheres to these standards in practice, and many have lamented the dearth of individualized procedural safeguards afforded to the targets of these operations (including U.S. nationals). *See, e.g.*, Philip Alston, *The CIA and Targeted Killings Beyond Borders*, 2 Harv. Nat'l Sec. L.J. 283 (2011).

128. *See* Ralph Wilde, International Territorial Administration: How Trusteeship and the Civilizing Mission Never Went Away 322–26 (2008) (discussing this trustee conception); Eyal Benvenisti, The International Law of Occupation 6 (2004) (observing that an "occupant's status is conceived to be that of a trustee"); Adam Roberts, *What Is Military Occupation?*, 55 Brit. Y.B. Int'l L. 249, 259 (1984) (stating that "the idea of 'trusteeship' is implicit in all occupation law . . . all occupants are in some vague and general sense trustees").

129. Hague Convention No. IV Respecting the Laws and Customs of War on Land art. 55, Oct. 18, 1907, 36 Stat. 2277.

130. Yoram Dinstein, The International Law of Belligerent Occupation 286 (2009); *see also* Legal Consequences of the Construction of a Wall in the Occupied Palestinian Territory (Palestinian Wall), Advisory Opinion, 2004 ICJ Rep. 136 (July 9), ¶¶ 107–12.

131. Meron, *supra* note 59, at 246.

132. *See* Geneva Convention (IV) Relative to the Protection of Civilian Persons in Time of War, art. 50, Aug. 12, 1949.

supplies,[133] maintain hospitals and other medical facilities,[134] and facilitate humanitarian relief.[135] Significantly, an occupying power must respect the human rights of the resident population and preserve public order regardless of whether the resident population has submitted peacefully to the occupation.[136] In each of these respects, international law tasks the occupying power with serving as a temporary fiduciary for the people of an occupied territory.[137]

A plausible implication of the fiduciary character of the law of occupation is that an occupying power must respect the "right to life" as defined by IHRL when it uses force within occupied territory. Once a state obtains effective control over foreign territory, as required to trigger the law of occupation, the fiduciary principle dictates that the occupying state must refrain from using lethal force against insurgents unless such measures are strictly necessary.

Over time, the ICJ and human rights bodies have embraced the idea that IHRL norms apply in contexts such as military occupation where states exercise de facto jurisdiction over foreign territory.[138] For example, in *Issa and Others v. Turkey*, the ECHR reviewed a Turkish military operation against Kurdish militants in northern Iraq.[139] The court reasoned that the European Convention applied

> where, as a consequence of military action—whether lawful or unlawful—[a] State in practice exercises effective control of an area situated outside its national territory. The obligation to secure, in such an area, the rights and freedoms set out in the Convention derives from the fact of such control, whether it be exercised directly, through its armed forces, or through a subordinate local administration.[140]

133. *Id.* art. 55.

134. *Id.* art. 56.

135. *Id.* art. 59.

136. This criterion is consistent with Dinstein's observation that under international law an occupying power's "jurisdictional rights . . . stem from effective control alone." DINSTEIN, *supra* note 130, at 35; *see also* Cordula Droege, *The Interplay Between International Humanitarian Law and International Human Rights Law in Situations of Armed Conflict*, 40 ISR. L. REV. 310, 334 (2007) ("International human rights bodies agree that where a state has effective control over a territory or over a person, their respective human rights treaties apply.").

137. *See, e.g.*, Martti Koskenniemi, *Occupied Zone—A Zone of Reasonableness*, 41 ISR. L. REV. 13, 17–18 (2008) (suggesting that the Israeli Supreme Court on various occasions has characterized its military as a "trustee of the Arab population"). For a dissenting view, see Modirzadeh, *supra* note 88.

138. *See Legal Consequences*, 2004 ICJ Rep. 136, ¶ 106; U.N. Human Rights Committee, General Comment No. 31, ¶ 10 (stating that the ICCPR applies "to anyone within the power or effective control of [a] State Party"); Committee Against Torture, General Comment 2, U.N. Doc. CAT/C/GC/2/CRP. 1/Rev.4 (Nov. 23, 2007), pt. IV (explaining that the Torture Convention extends to "all areas where the State party exercises, directly or indirectly, in whole or in part, de jure or de facto effective control, in accordance with international law"); Al-Skeini and Others v. United Kingdom, App. no. 55721/07, Eur. Ct. H.R. (July 7, 2011), ¶¶ 89, 133–42; Loizidou v. Turkey, 1996-IV Eur. Ct. H.R. 2216, 2235–36, ¶ 56.

139. Issa & Others v. Turkey, Nov. 16, 2004, Appl. No. 31821/96.

140. *Id.* ¶ 69.

In dicta, the court suggested that state responsibility might be triggered, as well, if a state claimed "authority" over territory (lawfully or unlawfully) in the absence of full "effective control."[141] Ultimately, the court concluded that even temporary de facto control of foreign territory by a state's military could be sufficient to trigger the state's obligation to respect human rights.

Several years later, the ECHR reaffirmed these principles in *Al-Skeini and Others v. United Kingdom*.[142] Several applicants brought claims against the United Kingdom based upon violent incidents between May and November 2003 in which their family members were killed by British troops in Iraq. The United Kingdom asserted that "[a]s an Occupying Power" it lacked the type of "effective control" over Iraq that would qualify as "jurisdiction" under the European Convention, because it "did not have sovereignty over Iraq and was not entitled to treat the area under its occupation as its own territory or as a colony subject to its complete power and authority."[143] The ECHR rejected this argument, considering it sufficient that "the United Kingdom (together with the United States) assumed in Iraq the exercise of some of the public powers normally to be exercised by a sovereign government," including "authority and control over individuals killed in the course of . . . security operations."[144] Although the court acknowledged that the deaths under review occurred at a time when "British soldiers and military police were the target of over a thousand attacks" from Iraqi insurgents, and thus the operational context could still qualify as an armed conflict, the court nonetheless affirmed that the European Convention's "right to life"—including the "general legal prohibition of arbitrary killing by agents of the State"—applied with full force to the occupation of Iraq.[145]

Additional support for this approach can be found in the Supreme Court of Israel's controversial 2005 decision, *Public Committee against Torture in Israel v. Israel* (*Targeted Killings*).[146] At issue in *Targeted Killings* was the Israeli military's practice of targeting suspected terrorists in the West Bank and the Gaza Strip with lethal force to prevent terrorist attacks in Israel. Between the start of the second intifada in February 2000 and the end of 2005, the Israeli military killed nearly 300 suspected terrorists and approximately 150 innocent civilians, while wounding hundreds of others, in military strikes designed to prevent future attacks in Israel.[147] At the request of two human rights groups, the Israeli Supreme Court, sitting as a High Court of Justice, agreed to review the military's targeted killing policy and issue an advisory opinion clarifying the legal standards applicable to lethal strikes in the West Bank and Gaza.

The court stressed at the outset of its opinion that Israel's targeted killing operations were conducted within the context of a long-standing occupation. The

141. *Id.* ¶ 72.

142. Application no. 55721/07, Eur. Ct. H.R., July 7, 2011.

143. *Id.* ¶ 114.

144. *Id.* ¶ 149.

145. *Id.* ¶¶ 161–63.

146. HCJ 769/02, The Public Committee Against Torture in Israel v. Government of Israel, Judgment of (Dec. 14, 2006) [hereinafter *Targeted Killings*].

147. *Id.* ¶ 2.

"normative system" applicable to this relational context "is complex," the court observed, because it implicates not only IHL, but also IHRL and "fundamental principles of Israeli public law, which every Israeli soldier 'carries in his pack' and which go along with him wherever he may turn."[148] Although the court characterized IHL as the relevant *lex specialis*,[149] its inquiry did not end with IHL's traditional standard that the use of force is permissible as long as it is not manifestly "excessive" in relation to the state's military objectives. Instead, it experimented with several different formulations of the proportionality principle. At one point, the court suggested that targeting terrorists would be permissible only if "innocent civilians nearby are not harmed," a standard even more restrictive than IHRL proportionality.[150] Almost in the same breath, however, the court reasoned that collateral damage to innocent civilians would be lawful if the military observed an appropriate "balance" between "military advantage" and "civilian damage" (roughly, IHL proportionality).[151] Ultimately, however, the court settled on the least harmful means test as the applicable legal standard for targeted killing: Israel could target terrorists in the West Bank and Gaza only where "there is no other less harmful means" to neutralize the threat.[152] Affirming that respect for human dignity "feeds the interpretation of international law,"[153] the court adopted constraints for targeted killing operations that resonated with the fiduciary constitution of sovereignty. The *Targeted Killings* case thus highlights the Supreme Court of Israel laying the groundwork for a context-sensitive approach to the use of force that seeks to honor human dignity within the unique security relationship between Israel and the Palestinian territories.

Although the *Targeted Killings* decision is not a model of clarity, the fiduciary theory suggests that the court was on the right track in requiring heightened solicitude to the security of Palestinians within the West Bank and Gaza.[154] As Yoram Dinstein has observed, Israel continues to exercise "diverse core ingredients of effective control" over the West Bank and Gaza, regulating aviation, maritime activities, and land borders,[155] as well as asserting authority to intervene militarily on a unilateral basis

148. *Id.* ¶ 18.

149. *Id.* ¶ 45. The U.S. Supreme Court reached a different conclusion in *Hamdan v. Rumsfeld*, 548 U.S. 557 (2006), holding that hostilities between state and nonstate actors did not constitute *international* armed conflict, *id.* at 629–31.

150. *Targeted Killings*, HCJ 769/02, ¶ 60.

151. *Id.*

152. *Id.* ¶ 60.

153. *Targeted Killings*, HCJ 769/02 (separate opinion of Vice President Rivlin), ¶ 4 (citing Benvenisti, *supra* note 75, at 88).

154. *See Targeted Killings*, HCJ 769/02, ¶ 44 (disclaiming any intent to articulate "a comprehensive doctrine of proportionality").

155. DINSTEIN, *supra* note 130, at 278; *see also* Ajuri v. IDF Commander of the West Bank, HCJ 7015/02, 56(6) PD 352, 358; *cf. Palestinian Wall*, 2004 ICJ Rep. at 178 (recognizing Israel as an occupying power in the West Bank). This conclusion is not universally accepted. *See* Nicholas Rostow, *Gaza, Iraq, Lebanon: Three Occupations Under International Law*, 37 ISR. Y.B. HUM. RTS. 205, 217–19 (2007).

to remove suspected militants to Israel for detention and trial.[156] Although Israel does not wield all of the public powers traditionally associated with sovereignty, its continued assertion of jurisdiction, including the right to intervene militarily in the West Bank and Gaza for security purposes, constitutes a form of discretionary power that triggers the fiduciary obligations associated with sovereignty.[157] The fiduciary theory suggests, therefore, that Israel's obligations are not exhausted by existing IHL standards; rather, Israel must respect the IHRL "right to life" in its targeted killing program, taking precautions to avoid any loss of life that is not strictly necessary to avoid grave harm to its people and residents of the Palestinian territories. This requirement of heightened solicitude to the interests of Palestinians in the West Bank and Gaza tracks Israel's continuing exercise of jurisdiction over these territories, and applies irrespective of whether this unique relationship formally qualifies as "occupation" under international law. Given the limited scope of Israel's authority to intervene in the West Bank and Gaza for national security purposes, the fiduciary principle does not require Israel to place the people of the West Bank and Gaza on an equal footing with its own people in all respects. Nonetheless, Israel does bear a fiduciary responsibility to respect and protect the human "right to life" for all people subject to its de facto jurisdiction—including those in the West Bank and Gaza whose safety is imperiled by targeted killing operations.

IX. HUMANITARIAN INTERVENTION

The contemporary international law of humanitarian intervention also reflects a fiduciary conception of international legal order. During international law's classical era, debates over the legality of humanitarian intervention were closely entwined with a fiduciary theory of state sovereignty. Influential scholars such as Vitoria, Grotius, Pufendorf, and Vattel defended humanitarian intervention on the ground that the law of nations would permit all states to intervene as fiduciary "guardians" for peoples who were unable legally or practically to cast off the yoke of a tyrannical ruler without foreign assistance.[158] Vitoria argued, for example, that Spanish rule in the Americas could be justified to protect indigenous people from the "tyrannical and oppressive acts" of their own rulers, including human sacrifice and cannibalism.[159] Grotius likewise contended that if monarchs "provoke[d] their people to despair and resistance by unheard of cruelties," they would thereby "lose the

156. Dinstein, *supra* note 130, at 279–80.

157. *See Palestinian Wall*, 2004 ICJ Rep. at 181 (emphasizing that Israel must honor the human rights set forth in the ICCPR "in light of the powers available to it" in the occupied territories); William A. Schabas, Lex Specialis? *Belt and Suspenders? The Parallel Operation of Human Rights Law and the Law of Armed Conflict, and the Conundrum of* Jus ad Bellum, 40 Isr. L. Rev. 592, 596–97, 611 (2007).

158. *See* Francisco de Vitoria, *On the Indians Lately Discovered* (1532), *in* Franciscus de Victoria, De Indis et de Ivre Belli Relectiones 115, 159 (Classics of International Law ed. 1917) (translation based on Boyer ed. 1557, Muñoz ed. 1565 & Simon ed. 1696); Pufendorf, *supra* note 12, bk. VIII, ch. 6, § 14; Vattel, *supra* note 11, ch. IV, § 56, ¶ 3.

159. Vitoria, *supra* note 158, at 159.

rights of independent sovereigns, and can no longer claim the privilege of the law of nations."[160] Although Grotius believed that subjects lacked legal capacity under the law of nations to rebel against their sovereigns,[161] other states could serve as surrogate guardians for the purpose of protecting a people's right to humane treatment.[162] In Grotius's view, the fiduciary structure of guardianship offered a legal framework for humanitarian intervention: whenever a state ruptured its own fiduciary relationship with its people through acts of intolerable cruelty, international law authorized other states to stand in as temporary surrogate guardians for the purpose of exercising an oppressed people's right of collective self-defense on their behalf.

Though perhaps well-intended, in practice this guardianship account of humanitarian intervention served as a pretext for colonialist domination. Robert Williams has shown that the guardianship account "provided Western legal discourse with its first secularly oriented, systematized elaboration of the superior rights of civilized Europeans to invade and conquer normatively divergent peoples."[163] By the middle of the sixteenth century, the Spanish crown formally embraced Vitoria's rendering of humanitarian guardianship, while largely ignoring its implications for the rights of indigenous peoples. Whereas Vitoria had stressed that Spain should seek every opportunity to promote security and individual rights in the New World through persuasion rather than the sword, Spanish statesmen employed Vitoria's guardianship theory primarily as a mandate for military conquest and imperialist exploitation.[164] Other colonial powers were also drawn to the concept of humanitarian guardianship and cited it regularly (albeit not uniformly) as justification for their own exercises in empire-building. For example, when King James I of England authorized the Virginia Company to establish what would become the Jamestown Colony, he emphasized its humanitarian purposes included to "bring the Infidels and Savages, living in those Parts, to human Civility, and to a settled and quiet Government."[165] Such was the power of the fiduciary theory of colonial governance that European nations would continue to characterize Western powers' authority over colonies and protectorates in these terms for over a century, as reflected in the 1884–1885 Berlin Africa Conference's affirmation of the "civilized"

160. *Id.* at bk. II, ch. XXV, pt. VIII(1); *cf.* John Locke, Second Treatise of Civil Government 35, § 65 (C.B. MacPherson ed. 1980) (1690) (arguing that parental "power so little belongs to the father by any peculiar right of nature, but only as he is guardian of his children, that when he quits his care of them, he loses his power over them, which goes along with their nourishment and education").

161. Grotius made allowance for individuals to exercise a limited right of resistance for self-preservation. *See* Grotius, *supra* note 1, at bk. I, ch. IV, pt. VII.

162. Grotius, *supra* note 1, at bk. II, ch. XXV, pt. VIII(2)–(3).

163. Robert A. Williams, Jr., The American Indian in Western Legal Thought: The Discourses of Conquest 106 (1990).

164. *Id.* at 93.

165. *Id.* at 201 (citing "The First Charter of Virginia," in *Documents of American History* 8–10 (H.S. Commager 8th ed. 1968)). In tension with the fiduciary theory was a competing vision of Native Americans as perpetual enemies (*perpetui inimici*) who could not be induced to civilized governance and must be destroyed. Robert A. Williams, Jr., Savage Anxieties 192–96 (2012).

world's continuing obligation "to watch over the preservation of the native tribes, and to care for the improvement of the condition of their moral and material well-being."[166] During the nineteenth century, European powers also claimed "an imperious humanitarian duty" to safeguard the peace and protect the vulnerable peoples of Greece, Syria, and Lebanon from the Ottoman Empire's "barbarous" aggression and oppression.[167] In each of these settings, conceptualizing intervention as a benevolent guardianship provided a formal legal framework that facilitated the subjection of "uncivilized" peoples to Western governance.

In the twentieth century, humanitarian intervention became subsumed within the Security Council's mandate "to maintain or restore international peace and security." The U.N. Charter did not expressly commit responsibility for preventing or suppressing human rights violations to the Security Council. Beginning in the early 1990s, however, the Security Council began to interpret its Chapter VII powers broadly to encompass humanitarian intervention. For example, in 1992 the Security Council endorsed a proposal from the Secretary-General "to establish a secure environment for humanitarian relief operations in Somalia" without Somalia's consent.[168] This proposal called for the United States to take the lead in organizing a multinational operation under "unified command and control" to establish security and address widespread famine throughout Somalia.[169] Subsequent years would witness the Security Council authorizing responses to humanitarian crises in Bosnia-Herzegovina, East Timor, and Sierra Leone.[170] During the 2011 Libyan revolution, the Security Council responded to war crimes and other human rights abuses by authorizing states to protect noncombatants and enforce a no-fly zone over Libya.[171] Although the Charter provides thin support for the idea that the international community may intervene in the internal affairs of particular states without a clear threat to international peace and security, over time states have generally accepted the Security Council's prerogative to authorize humanitarian intervention.

166. General Act of the Berlin Conference, Feb. 26, 1885, art. VI, 165 Consol. T.S. 485, *reprinted in* R.J. Gavin & J.A. Betley, The Scramble for Africa: Documents on the Berlin West African Conference and Related Subjects, 1884/1885, at 291 (1973); H. Duncan Hall, Mandates, Dependencies and Trusteeship 95 (1948).

167. Davide Rodogno, Against Massacre: Humanitarian Interventions in the Ottoman Empire, 1815–1914, at 12, 63–117 (2012); *see also* Neff, *supra* note 1, at 224 (quoting Note to the Porte, 8 Apr. 1830, *in* René Albrecht-Carrié (ed.), Concert of Europe, at 121–22 (1968)).

168. SCR 794, S/Res/794, Dec. 3, 1992, ¶ 7.

169. *Id.*

170. *See, e.g.*, SCR 754, S/Res/754, June 5, 1992 (authorizing the U.N. Protection Force (UNPROFOR) in the former Yugoslavia to take steps to ensure the delivery of humanitarian aid to Sarajevo); SCR 1240, S/Res/1240, Oct. 22, 1999 (establishing the U.N. Mission in Sierra Leone (UNAMSIL) to keep peace and ensure the delivery of humanitarian aid); SCR 1264, S/Res/1264, Sept. 15, 1999 (authorizing a multinational force to restore peace in East Timor). We discuss U.N. peacekeeping and its evolution in Chapter 8.

171. SCR 1973, *supra* note 23, at 37, ¶¶ 4, 8.

This move to coordinate international humanitarian intervention through the Security Council has been widely characterized as reflecting the international community's assumption of a collective responsibility to protect (R2P) peoples of the world from oppression when states flagrantly abuse their sovereign powers.[172] The fiduciary model of state sovereignty supports this account by underscoring states' shared responsibility as fiduciaries of humanity to establish a regime of secure and equal freedom for humanity. Under the fiduciary model, the international community's collective responsibility to protect derives from the individualized fiduciary responsibility that each state bears to contribute to the establishment of a just international order for the benefit of humanity. This responsibility is not a perfect legal duty, in the Kantian sense, because it is impossible to specify with precision what steps the international community must take to satisfy its collective responsibility to protect in any given crisis. Nor does the R2P principle specify which particular states, international institutions, or regional organizations should take the lead in conducting a particular humanitarian intervention.[173] Nonetheless, the fiduciary model supports the idea that international law confers authority upon the international community, acting collectively, to intervene in the jurisdiction of individual states as necessary to guarantee fundamental security under the rule of law.

The fiduciary model emphasizes that the direct legal and moral beneficiaries of humanitarian intervention are not states *ut singuli* or the international community collectively, but rather the people of a state that is unable or unwilling to respect, protect, and fulfill its people's human rights. Just as international law entrusts states with authority to wield public powers as fiduciaries on behalf of their people, international law entrusts the community of states collectively with authority to intervene on a people's behalf to prevent their state from abusing or neglecting its fiduciary obligations. The purpose of humanitarian intervention, in other words, is to provide a form of surrogate protection to people who would otherwise be subject to grave forms of instrumentalization or domination. Humanitarian intervention under the fiduciary model we propose thus mirrors Grotius's account of humanitarian intervention in crucial respects: whenever a state subjects its people to the threat of "grievous oppressions,"[174] international law authorizes the international community to appoint other states or regional organizations to serve as temporary fiduciaries for the purpose of guaranteeing an oppressed people's fundamental security under the rule of law.

Rather than exercise direct command and control over the forces that undertake humanitarian intervention, the Security Council has entrusted states and regional organizations with discretionary authority to conduct cross-border interventions to

172. *See, e.g.*, Catherine Powell, *Libya: Indicative of a Multilateral Constitutional Moment?*, 106 Am. J. Int'l L. 298 (2012).

173. Because individual states bear a fiduciary duty of loyalty primarily to their own people, they are not ordinarily obligated to risk the lives of their own soldiers to discharge the international community's collective responsibility to protect. *But see, e.g.*, Monika Hakimi, *Toward a Legal Theory of the Responsibility to Protect*, 39 Yale J. Int'l L. 247, 249–50 (2014) (arguing that some aspects of R2P may attach to specific states based on their past conduct or relationship with the imperiled people).

174. 2 Grotius, *supra* note 1, at ch. XXV, pt. VIII(2).

address humanitarian crises.[175] In its authorizing resolutions, the Security Council has imposed some meaningful constraints on intervening states' discretion, requiring them to pursue only prescribed humanitarian objectives, to develop and execute a coordinated strategy, and to respect the territorial integrity of other states. The Security Council has also reserved the right to supervise humanitarian intervention and, where necessary, modify or withdraw its mandate for humanitarian intervention if it determines that the mandate has been abused or is no longer warranted. However, because the Security Council has been unable ex ante to fully specify how states should conduct humanitarian intervention, intervening states have always enjoyed considerable discretion in practice to decide how they will use force to achieve their humanitarian missions. In each of these respects, humanitarian intervention in the Charter era bears the characteristic features of a fiduciary relationship. Through the Security Council, the international community entrusts states with discretionary authority to use force for and on behalf of foreign nationals, subject to public-regarding fiduciary duties.

The Security Council's 2011 resolution authorizing humanitarian intervention in Libya illustrates the fiduciary structure of humanitarian intervention. Although "reaffirming that parties to armed conflicts bear the primary responsibility to take all feasible steps to ensure the protection of civilians," the Security Council concluded that international intervention was warranted to address the "widespread and systematic attacks" against civilians in Libya, which the Security Council concluded "may amount to crimes against humanity."[176] "Expressing its determination to ensure the protection of civilians and civilian populated areas and the rapid and unimpeded passage of humanitarian assistance and the safety of humanitarian personnel," the Security Council demanded an immediate ceasefire, announced a "ban on all flights" in Libyan airspace, and authorized "Member States that have notified the Secretary-General, acting nationally or through regional organizations or arrangements, and acting in cooperation with the Secretary-General, to take all necessary measures . . . to protect civilians and civilian populated areas under threat of attack."[177] The authority entrusted to intervening states to use force was limited to a predefined purpose: to protect the human rights of the Libyan people and foreign nationals caught in the rising Libyan civil war. At the same time, the Security Council also limited the scope of state discretion by categorically excluding "a foreign occupation force of any form on any part of Libyan territory," reflecting the international community's "strong commitment to [Libya's] sovereignty, independence, territorial integrity and national unity."[178] Thus, although the Security Council gave a green light for humanitarian intervention in Libya, it permitted states to use force only as temporary fiduciaries for the Libyan people.

175. Although the U.N. Charter originally provided for states by "special agreement" to contribute "armed forces, assistance, and facilities" for a standing military force under the Security Council's command (art. 43), this provision never took effect because states declined to participate. As a result, the Security Council has been forced to rely upon states to commit their own forces to humanitarian interventions on a voluntary, ad hoc basis.

176. SCR 1973, *supra* note 171, pmbl.

177. *Id.* pmbl., ¶¶ 6 & 8.

178. *Id.* pmbl. & ¶ 4.

The fiduciary character of humanitarian intervention provides legal standards that regulate how states may conduct humanitarian intervention under international law. For example, the fiduciary principle of *integrity* dictates that states may not exploit human rights crises as an opportunity to destabilize another state or pursue their own economic advantage vis-à-vis another state. Under the principle of *impartiality*, intervening states must give due regard to the respective interests of foreign nationals with competing claims, seeking a fair balance to ensure that all people of a target state are respected as co-beneficiaries.[179] Perhaps most important, the fiduciary principle of *solicitude* requires an intervening state to give due and sensitive regard to the legitimate interests, values, and preferences of its foreign beneficiaries. This principle has begun to gain traction in other subfields of international law such as the law of diplomatic protection[180] and the rights of indigenous peoples,[181] and it has obvious resonance in the general principle of self-determination; nonetheless, it has yet to take hold fully in the international law and practice of humanitarian intervention. The principle of solicitude dictates further that, where possible, intervening states should consult with the oppressed groups they seek to protect, aiming to find consensus on the best approach for restoring human rights observance within a target state. If representatives of an oppressed group request the modification or discontinuation of armed intervention undertaken on their behalf, states that have undertaken intervention should make every effort to respect such a request, provided they can do so within the constraints of the Security Council's relevant resolutions. In each of these respects, the fiduciary obligations associated with humanitarian intervention offer a legal framework for safeguarding humanity from foreign domination.

Given the grave injustices that states have perpetrated against one another in the name of benevolent "guardianship," there is always a risk that military action undertaken in the name of "humanitarian intervention" may simply serve as a pretext for neocolonialist domination. International institutions such as the Security Council bear a particularly important responsibility to exercise vigilance against the abuse of power by intervening states. Unfortunately, flaws in the Security Council's decision-making structure have compromised its ability to perform this oversight

179. *See* Dukeminier & Sitkoff, *supra* note 34, at 657–58 (observing that the "duty of impartiality" in trust law is inaptly named because it does not require impartiality in the sense of equality, but rather a balancing by giving *due regard* to the beneficiaries' respective interests); Sitkoff, *supra* note 34, at 651 ("[B]alance is the overarching directive of the duty of impartiality.").

180. *See* Draft Articles on Diplomatic Protection with Commentaries, art. 19(b), *in* Rep. of the Int'l Law Comm'n, 58th Sess., May 1–June 9, July 3–Aug. 11, 2006, U.N. Doc. A/61/10; GAOR, 61st Sess., Supp. No. 10 (2006) (recommending that states asserting diplomatic protection claims "take into account, wherever feasible, the views of injured persons with regard to resort to diplomatic protection and the reparation to be sought").

181. *See* Declaration on the Rights of Indigenous Peoples art. 32, G.A. Res. 61/295, U.N. Doc. A/RES/61/295 (Sept. 13, 2007) ("States shall consult and cooperate in good faith with the indigenous peoples concerned through their own representative institutions in order to obtain their free and informed consent prior to the approval of any project affecting their lands or territories . . . ."); Case of the Saramaka People v. Suriname, Judgment, Inter-Am. Ct. H.R., Nov. 28, 2007 (Ser. C), No 172 (2007), ¶¶ 131–37 (emphasizing the need for good faith consultation with indigenous peoples and, for large scale projects, informed consent).

function effectively. Because U.N.-authorized interventions have always involved the Security Council's veto-wielding permanent members (the "P5"), the Security Council has been unable to check states that have abused or exceeded the scope of their entrusted authority. Once a P5 state has received a mandate for humanitarian intervention, this mandate is virtually impossible to withdraw through a new resolution. Critics of international military intervention have cited the United States' invasion of Iraq in 2003 and NATO airstrikes in Libya in 2011 as evidence that the P5 states are able to expand narrowly tailored resolutions into open-ended licenses for the use of force without meaningful accountability. This accountability deficit has made it more difficult for states advocating humanitarian intervention (chiefly, the United States and the United Kingdom) to persuade other P5 states (chiefly, China and Russia) to support Security Council resolutions authorizing intervention. The accountability deficit also provides fodder for critics who argue that the lofty rhetoric of "humanitarianism" merely serves as a pretext for great-power domination. In the long run, the Security Council will need to develop new and better ways to supervise humanitarian intervention—minimizing state abuse and facilitating better-executed interventions—if the fiduciary theory is to be credible in practice.

Pending more fundamental reform of the Security Council's decision-making structure, some relatively modest changes could significantly narrow the current accountability deficit. One commonsense reform, which Brazil has proposed in the wake of NATO's intervention in Libya, would be to establish standardized reporting and review procedures to enable the Security Council to continuously "monitor and assess the manner in which resolutions are implemented" and thereby provide for "the accountability of those to whom authority is granted to resort to force."[182] The Security Council could also establish its own independent monitoring body to investigate complaints that intervening states have exceeded their mandates.[183] Although such oversight procedures would require the Security Council to devote more resources to monitoring and could risk further politicizing humanitarian interventions,[184] the requirement that intervening states provide a regular accounting for their use of force is arguably a nonnegotiable requirement of the fiduciary character of their entrusted authority.

A second option for enhancing Security Council oversight would be to include a provision in future Security Council resolutions allowing the Security Council or a separate committee composed of Security Council members to narrow or withdraw mandates for humanitarian intervention by a simple majority or supermajority vote, reducing the threat of a P5 veto. This mechanism could deter states from undertaking humanitarian intervention in the first place by raising the possibility that the Security Council could seek to micromanage their military engagements or cancel a mission prematurely after an intervening state has already committed significant resources. On the other hand, allowing the Security Council to withdraw

182. Alex J. Bellamy, The Responsibility to Protect: A Defense 192 (2015) (quoting Letter from the Permanent Representative of Brazil, to the U.N. Secretary-General (Nov. 9, 2011)).

183. *See id.* at 201.

184. *Id.* at 199.

its mandate for humanitarian intervention by a majority vote would help to counter the threat of "mission creep" by enabling the Security Council to rein in intervening states that exceed the scope of their entrusted authority.[185]

Should this option prove impracticable, the Security Council could achieve a similar result by adding "sunset provisions"—clauses that provide a fixed expiration date—to resolutions that authorize humanitarian intervention.[186] In other settings, lawmakers have used sunset provisions to promote flexible and responsive governance,[187] and similar objectives could be achieved by requiring states to seek periodic reauthorization for humanitarian intervention. Although the duration of the sunset period would obviously have to be calibrated to the scope of the anticipated intervention, a presumptive sunset period in the range of sixty to ninety days would give intervening states sufficient scope for action to avert an impending humanitarian crisis (e.g., Kosovo, Libya), while preventing the exigencies of the moment from generating an open-ended mandate for a sustained foreign military presence in the target state. Requiring periodic Security Council reauthorization would compel intervening states to account for their performance, while also helping to ensure that their actions are consistent with fiduciary principles of integrity, impartiality, and solicitude. Should an intervening state abuse its discretion, the Security Council could decline to renew its authorization for the use of force, or it could issue a revised mandate that would define the humanitarian mission more precisely, or transfer responsibility for intervention to other states. The Security Council could also establish U.N.-sponsored institutions to facilitate deliberative engagement between intervening states and representatives of oppressed peoples. Although these are not the only conceivable mechanisms for enhancing international accountability for humanitarian intervention, they are suggestive of the kinds of sensible reforms that may help to address concerns about the fiduciary theory's potential for abuse.

Given the formidable political hurdles to Security Council authorization for humanitarian intervention, some scholars have suggested that international law should be construed to allow states to engage in humanitarian intervention without the Security Council's approval under certain circumstances.[188] For these advocates of decentralized humanitarian intervention, NATO's 1999 aerial bombardment of targets in Yugoslavia for the protection of Kosovo furnishes the controlling

185. As discussed in Chapter 8, regular accounting and a supermajority voting procedure have been built into the U.N. al-Qaeda targeted sanctions program, although the extent to which these measures legitimize the program is unclear.

186. *See id.* at 200 (observing that sunset clauses are "standard practice for UN peacekeeping operations").

187. *See* Rebecca M. Kysar, *The Sun Also Rises: The Political Economy of Sunset Provisions in the Tax Code*, 40 GA. L. REV. 335, 337 (2006).

188. *See, e.g.*, GEORGE P. FLETCHER & JENS DAVID OHLIN, DEFENDING HUMANITY: WHEN FORCE IS JUSTIFIED AND WHY (2008); FERNANDO R. TESÓN, HUMANITARIAN INTERVENTION: AN INQUIRY INTO LAW AND MORALITY (3d ed. 2005); Jens David Ohlin, *The Doctrine of Legitimate Defense*, 91 INT'L L. STUD. 119 (2015); W. Michael Reisman & Myers S. McDougal, *Humanitarian Intervention to Protect the Ibos*, *in* HUMANITARIAN INTERVENTION AND THE UNITED NATIONS 167 (1973).

precedent. Even if the Kosovo intervention cannot be squared with the Charter's formal requirements, some scholars argue that it should be construed as "legitimate" under international law in light of the urgent need to prevent ethnic cleansing and possible genocide or crimes against humanity.[189] However, most scholars reject the suggestion that the Kosovo model of humanitarian intervention without Security Council authorization has attracted sufficient support in state practice and *opinio juris* to generate customary international law.[190] And few accept the premise that under international law there can be such a thing as an "illegal but legitimate" use of force.[191]

By underscoring the bounded character of state authority under international law, the fiduciary model of state sovereignty lends support for the majority view that states may not engage in humanitarian intervention without obtaining the consent of the host state or international authorization. In their institutional role as fiduciaries for their own people, states are entrusted with authority to wield coercive power only (1) within their own borders, and (2) in exceptional cases outside their borders for the limited purpose of protecting their own nationals from imminent harm. As fiduciaries of humanity, states are also vested with jurisgenerative authority to collaborate in establishing international institutions through which the international community may exercise its collective authority to protect all humanity. However, because international authority for humanitarian intervention is vested solely in the collective judgment of the international community as a whole under the R2P principle, individual states lack authority to wield public power within the jurisdiction of another state without authorization from either the other state or the international community as a whole. Under current international law, the only institutional vehicle for obtaining the international community's collective approval for humanitarian intervention is Security Council authorization. Thus, insofar as the Charter and

189. *See, e.g.*, U.K. Permanent Representative to the United Nations, S/PV.3988, Mar. 24, 1999, at 12, *reprinted in* 70 BRIT. Y.B. INT'L L. 387, 571–601 (1999) (arguing that NATO action was "legal" because it was "justified as an exceptional measure to prevent [an imminent] humanitarian catastrophe").

190. *See, e.g.*, SIMON CHESTERMAN, JUST WAR OR JUST PEACE? HUMANITARIAN INTERVENTION AND INTERNATIONAL LAW (2001); Oona A. Hathaway et al., *Consent-Based Humanitarian Intervention: Giving Sovereign Responsibility Back to the Sovereign*, 46 CORNELL INT'L L.J. 499, 521–35 (2013); Saira Mohamed, *Restructuring the Debate on Unauthorized Humanitarian Intervention*, 88 N.C. L. REV. 1275, 1285–89 (2010); Louis Henkin, *Kosovo and the Limits of "Humanitarian Intervention,"* 93 AM. J. INT'L L. 824, 825 (1999); Bruno Simma, *NATO, the UN and the Use of Force: Legal Aspects*, 10 EUR. J. INT'L L. 1, 3 (1999). As one of us has argued elsewhere, the dismal historical record of unilateral humanitarian intervention counsels against abandoning a requirement of ex ante collective authorization. *See* Evan J. Criddle, *Three Grotian Theories of Humanitarian Intervention*, 16 THEORETICAL INQ. L. 473, 486–87 (2015) [hereinafter Criddle, *Grotian Theories*]. A stronger argument can be made that international law already entrusts individual states with authority to impose non-forcible countermeasures in response to human rights abuses abroad. *See* Evan J. Criddle, *Standing for Human Rights Abroad*, 100 CORNELL L. REV. 269 (2015) [hereinafter Criddle, *Standing*].

191. *See, e.g.*, Anthea Roberts, *Legality vs. Legitimacy: Can Uses of Force Be Illegal but Justified?*, *in* HUMAN RIGHTS, INTERVENTION, AND THE USE OF FORCE 179 (Philip Alston & Euan McDonald eds., 2008).

customary international law currently prohibit states and regional organizations from using force to conduct humanitarian intervention without Security Council authorization, these entities simply lack authority to enforce human rights beyond their borders unilaterally.

Nonetheless, we might reasonably ask how the international community should respond if political gridlock in the Security Council frustrates the purpose of international law's fiduciary constitution—establishing fundamental security under the rule of law. The fiduciary character of international legal order may be seriously undermined if the international community lacks the capacity in practice to protect humanity from grave and systematic human rights abuses. Alternative institutional mechanisms may be necessary at the international level, therefore, to compensate for the Security Council's weaknesses. Such mechanisms might include ex ante authorization by other international or regional bodies, or perhaps even ex post ratification by the Security Council, an international tribunal, or perhaps even by a supermajority of states in cases of extreme exigency.[192] Although we recognize that such alternative mechanisms for approving humanitarian intervention would carry their own risks, and we cannot work out the details of these alternatives here, our basic point is that a variety of institutional models for humanitarian intervention may be consistent with the fiduciary constitution of sovereignty. The idea is to construct a framework within which humanitarian intervention is never the unilateral act of an intervening state or even group of states, but rather authorized by international law, even if the relevant authorization comes only after the fact by way of ratification. At a minimum, more effective institutional mechanisms are needed at the international level to ensure that the international community can respond effectively when states flagrantly violate their fiduciary duties to their own people by engaging in grave human rights abuse.

Under the fiduciary theory, IHRL's more restrictive proportionality standard should apply when states conduct humanitarian intervention—even if states lack "effective control" over foreign territory. IHLR standards apply to humanitarian intervention, including internal armed conflict, occupation, and most counterterrorism and COIN operations, because international law entrusts states with authority to use force in a fiduciary capacity for the exclusive benefit of an oppressed people.

Although humanitarian intervention is, technically speaking, a subset of international armed conflict and therefore subject to the full corpus of IHL, the relationship between an intervening state and a foreign people is similar to the relationship between a state and its own people during internal armed conflict. During humanitarian intervention, international law temporarily shifts the sovereign responsibility to protect from a state that has engaged in systematic human rights abuse to other states that have been entrusted with authority to intervene by the Security Council. As surrogate sovereigns, intervening states assume fiduciary obligations to use their coercive powers for the benefit of an oppressed foreign people, and they must take care to avoid inflicting harm that is not strictly necessary to fulfill their

192. *See* David Dyzenhaus, *Hobbes on the International Rule of Law*, 28 Ethics & Int'l Affs. 53 (2014) (explaining how the international rule of law is possible even in a world without international institutions capable of authoritatively resolving interpretive disputes).

entrusted responsibility to guarantee basic security under the rule of law.[193] States that engage in humanitarian intervention therefore assume a fiduciary obligation to observe IHRL's strict-necessity standard for the use of force, treating the security of foreign nationals with the same solicitude that they accord to their own nationals. Merely satisfying IHL principles of distinction, necessity, and proportionality will not suffice.

From these observations, it follows that intervening states may assume human rights obligations toward foreign nationals even if they do not acquire full "effective control" over foreign territory. Consider the two most widely cited examples of multilateral humanitarian intervention from the past fifteen years: NATO's 1999 intervention in Kosovo and U.N.-authorized intervention during the 2011 Libya revolution. In both settings, states used air strikes to prevent human rights abuses without establishing "effective control" over the territory by "putting boots on the ground." The ECHR addressed this problem in the 2001 case *Bankovic and Others v. Belgium and 16 Other Contracting States*.[194] At issue in the case was a NATO air strike against television and radio production facilities in Belgrade that claimed the lives of sixteen civilians and seriously wounded sixteen others. Emphasizing the contractual character of the European Convention, the court held that the NATO strike did not take place within the "jurisdiction" of NATO states, and hence did not fall within the European Convention's scope, because the intervening states lacked "effective control of the relevant territory and its inhabitants."[195] The fiduciary theory, in contrast, would support an approach closer to the standard that the ECHR proposed several years later in its *Issa* dictum: whenever states assert authority to intervene abroad as a de facto surrogate sovereign to guarantee human rights—with or without the host state's consent—they assert a form of jurisdiction over foreign territory and assume a correlative obligation to use force in a manner that honors the IHRL right to life.[196] In particular, the fiduciary theory dictates that states must take all feasible precautions to avoid casualties, placing the lives of their own soldiers on an equal plane with the lives of foreign nationals whom they undertake to protect.[197] Within the context of humanitarian intervention, states may use force abroad only in a manner that treats the lives of foreign nationals with the same consideration they owe to their own people.

193. *See* Criddle, *Grotian Theories*, *supra* note 190; Criddle, *Standing*, *supra* note 190.

194. 2001-XII, Eur. Ct. H.R. 33, ¶¶ 9–11.

195. *Id.* ¶¶ 71, 80.

196. Issa & Others v. Turkey, Nov. 16, 2004, Appl. No. 31821/96, ¶ 72.

197. Whether NATO satisfied this standard in its Kosovo intervention is controversial. The Independent International Commission on Kosovo concluded that "NATO's overall record was unprecedented to the extent that it avoided civilian damage through the accuracy of its targeting." INDEPENDENT INTERNATIONAL COMMISSION ON KOSOVO, THE KOSOVO REPORT 181 (2000). But the Commission also expressed concern that NATO's rules of engagement, which set a 15,000-feet minimum altitude for aerial bombardment, might have impeded effective targeting in some settings. *Id.* At a minimum, the Commission suggested that the "high-altitude tactic . . . weaken[ed] the claim of humanitarianism to the extent that it appear[ed] to value the lives of the NATO combatants more than those of the civilian population of Kosovo and Serbia, and especially the lives of the Kosovar Albanians that it was acting to protect." *Id.; see also*

X. CONCLUSION

Over the course of the past century, the international law of armed conflict has undergone paradigm-shifting transformations aimed at protecting individuals from gratuitous and disproportionate violence. These transformations reflect and resonate with deeper shifts in international legal order. But the nature of these transformations remains poorly understood. In *Prosecutor v. Tadić*, the ICTY's Appeals Chamber suggested that IHL's humanitarian turn points to the waning influence of state sovereignty as an organizing principle for international law.[198] According to the Court, international law's traditional "[s]tate-sovereignty-oriented approach has been gradually supplanted by a human-being-oriented approach. Gradually the maxim of Roman law *hominum causa omne jus constitutum est* (all law is created for the benefit of human beings) has gained a foothold in the international community as well."[199]

The fiduciary theory supports the ICTY's relational account of the law of armed conflict, while clarifying how this law reflects a paradigm shift in state sovereignty itself. We have argued in this chapter that the much-celebrated "humanization" of international law does not reflect a "supplanting" of state sovereignty so much as a reframing of the concept. As fiduciaries under international law, states bear a responsibility to protect their people from domination and instrumentalization. But they also bear obligations to avoid imposing gratuitous or grossly disproportionate harm on foreign nationals based on their obligations as fiduciaries of humanity generally. And in a variety of settings, they bear obligations to respect, protect, and fulfill international human rights during armed conflict. Sovereignty and respect for human dignity thus constitute mutually reinforcing features of the relational character of state sovereignty.

Critics of the fiduciary theory of sovereignty might object that its approach to armed conflict conflates *lex lata* (law as it exists) and *lex ferenda* (law as it should be). The argument we have advanced in this chapter, however, is not that international law should set aside existing legal standards and manufacture new principles to govern the use of force from whole cloth. Rather, we have shown that the fiduciary theory's relational conception of sovereignty has already taken root in contemporary *jus ad bellum* and *jus in bello* with transformative implications for the legal norms that govern armed conflict. IHL has evolved gradually toward harmonization with the fiduciary conception of sovereignty by systematically proscribing arbitrary and unnecessary uses of force. The law of armed conflict thus rejects the maxim that *inter arma enim silent leges*, and it affirms that states must always respect the status and standing of their own people and foreign nationals as beneficiaries of international law's fiduciary constitution.

Richard A. Falk, *Kosovo, World Order, and the Future of International Law*, 93 Am. J. Int'l L. 847, 856 (1999) (observing that NATO's tactics shifted the risk of harm to civilians).

198. Prosecutor v. Tadić, Jurisdictional Appeal, Case No. IT-94-1-AR72, ¶ 97 (1995).

199. *Id.* Three years later, the ICTY returned to this theme in *Furundžija*, opining that the parallel development of IHL and IHRL are best conceived not as evidence of international law's irreparable fragmentation, but rather as mutually reinforcing components of a legal order that seeks to honor human dignity. *See* Prosecutor v. Furundžija, Judgment, Case No. IT-95-17/1-T, T.Ch. II, 10 Dec. 1998, ¶ 183.

6

Detaining Foreign Nationals

I. INTRODUCTION

In this chapter, we explore how the fiduciary role of states as joint fiduciaries of humanity supports cosmopolitan obligations owed to foreign detainees captured during armed conflict. The fiduciary theory explains key features of the law of armed conflict relating to detention. More broadly, the theory's account of cosmopolitan citizenship challenges the idea that national security concerns can ever justify exempting detention programs from independent scrutiny for compliance with due process, irrespective of where or on what grounds a state holds foreign nationals captive.

The idea of cosmopolitanism enjoys both a venerable history and a contemporary resurgence. The history dates back to Diogenes, who in 300 B.C. described himself as a "citizen of the world."[1] Stoics such as Cicero would later develop the idea of universal citizenship, but in a Janus-faced way that would foreshadow the promise and peril of international law generally.[2] On the one hand, Cicero believed that all humans shared a capacity for reason and susceptibility to universal law, so it was possible for all to be equal subjects under universal law.[3] But on the other hand, his cosmopolis was coextensive with the Roman Empire; those who did not accept membership in the empire, such as the German "barbarians," were excluded from universal citizenship.

In the modern period, the rise of the nation-state produced municipal law and the law of nations, which together left little room for the idea of universal citizenship. Theorists such as Grotius, Pufendorf, Vattel, and Wolff developed treatises on international law premised on the idea that states, like individuals in the state of nature, were subject to universal laws of nature.[4] For these writers, municipal law

1. Diogenes Laertius, The Lives of Eminent Philosophers (C.D. Yonge trans.), http://www.classicpersuasion.org/pw/diogenes/dldiogenes.htm (last visited Nov. 26, 2015).

2. *See* Garrett Wallace Brown, *Moving from Cosmopolitan Legal Theory to Legal Practice: Models of Cosmopolitan Law*, 28 Leg. Studs. 430, 432–34 (2008).

3. *See* Marcus Tullius Cicero, On the Commonwealth and on the Laws (1999).

4. *See* Hugo Grotius, The Rights of War and Peace (2005) (1625); Samuel Pufendorf, On the Law of Nature and of Nations (1703) (1672); Christian Wolff, The Law of Nations According to the Scientific Method (2014) (1749); Emmerich de Vattel,

governed interactions between citizens (domestic private law) as well as legal relations between citizens and their states (domestic public law). The law of nations or *ius gentium* governed inter-state relations. Kant, however, recognized that municipal law and the law of nations, taken together, left a crucial gap: neither of these legal regimes, as then understood, comprehended relations between states and citizens of other states, or foreign nationals.[5] Kant argued that a *ius cosmopoliticum* or "law of world citizenship" was necessary to supplement municipal law and the law of nations.[6]

Over the past few decades, cosmopolitanism has given rise to voluminous literatures in both political philosophy and legal scholarship. The political philosophy literature takes its motivation from the vast economic disparities that separate the global north from the global south.[7] Its central question is whether wealthy northern states and their members owe substantial duties to the disadvantaged in the south, duties that typically would involve restructuring international financial institutions and a far greater commitment of resources than is currently available through foreign aid. At the heart of the debate between cosmopolitans and their nationalist adversaries is the question of whether northern states and their citizens are entitled to treat their own interests as matters of exclusive or predominant moral concern, and if so, whether the priority of national allegiance contravenes the cosmopolitan agenda for global reform.[8]

Legal cosmopolitanism tends to be less ambitious in its normative prescriptions than its political-philosophy counterpart. Legal cosmopolitans typically draw on Kant's comparatively thin idea of cosmopolitan law rather than full-blown theories of justice. For example, Mark Walters points to the capacity of cosmopolitan law to fill the gap between municipal law and the law of nations in the context of non-nationals subject to executive power (typically the power to detain and deport).[9]

The Law of Nations, or the Principles of Natural Law Applied to the Conduct and to the Affairs of Nations and of Sovereigns (1834) (1758).

5. *See* Immanuel Kant, Perpetual Peace (2005) (1795).

6. *Id.* at 20.

7. *See, e.g.*, David Held, Democracy and the Global Order: From the Modern State to Cosmopolitan Governance (1995); Thomas Pogge, World Poverty and Human Rights: Cosmopolitan Responsibilities and Reforms (2002); Brian Barry, *Statism and Nationalism: A Cosmopolitan Critique*, *in* Global Justice 12–66 (Ian Shapiro & Lea Brilmayer eds., 1999); Charles R. Beitz, *Cosmopolitan Ideals and Nationalist Sentiment*, 80 J. Phil. 591 (1983); Martha C. Nussbaum, *Patriotism and Cosmopolitanism*, *in* For Love of Country: Debating the Limits of Patriotism 2–17 (Martha C. Nussbaum & Joshua Cohen eds., 1996); Peter Singer, *Famine, Affluence, and Morality*, 1 Phil. & Pub. Affs. 229 (1972).

8. *See, e.g.*, David Miller, On Nationality (1995) (defending nationalism); Held, *supra* note 7 (defending liberal cosmopolitanism); Kok-Chor Tan, Justice Without Borders: Cosmopolitanism, Nationalism, and Patriotism (2004) (defending liberal cosmopolitanism).

9. *See, e.g.*, Mark Walters, *The Common Law Constitution and Legal Cosmopolitanism*, *in* The Unity of Public Law 431 (David Dyzenhaus ed., 2004) (arguing that the common law of judicial review incorporates cosmopolitan values as part of its rule-of-law framework for principled statutory interpretation).

Garrett Brown fleshes out the duties of hospitality that Kant took to be constitutive of *ius cosmopoliticum*, noting that they embody five rights or freedoms: (i) the right to exit, enter, and travel within and between states; (ii) freedom from hostility and negligence that would harm one's body or property; (iii) freedom of speech; (iv) freedom to engage in commerce; and (v) freedom from false, misrepresented, extorted, or fraudulent contracts.[10] More generally, both international human rights law (IHRL) and international humanitarian law (IHL) embrace Kant's basic cosmopolitan claim that supranational law consists in more than just the law of nations. In both cases the duty-bearer is ordinarily the state, while the right-holder can be (and in the case of IHL typically is) a foreign national.

Drawing inspiration from the Kantian idea of cosmopolitan law, we begin in Part II by outlining the fiduciary theory's account of the duties owed by a detaining state to captured combatants or alleged terror suspects. We shall see that the detaining state-detainee relationship mirrors the parent-child relationship in important respects: in both cases the law, through the fiduciary principle, must set the terms of the relationship in order for it to be rightful.

In Part III we argue that the fiduciary model provides a lucid vantage point from which to explain and critically assess the law relating to foreign nationals detained during armed conflict. As an interpretive theory, the fiduciary model explains core features of the prisoner-of-war regime established in the Third Geneva Convention of 1949[11] and the 1977 Additional Protocols.[12] Specifically, the fiduciary theory explains the extensive protections afforded prisoners of war as an appropriate legal response to the necessarily intense and liberty-infringing power the detaining state exercises over prisoners. The protections themselves are explained as a compendium of rules that, within the restrictive confines of their application, generally aim to minimize the abuse of prisoners. As a prescriptive theory, the fiduciary model censures elements of the prison-of-war regime that facilitate instrumentalization or domination, such as the permissibility of forced labor.

Part IV turns to the war on terror and the status of detainees held potentially indefinitely without either a civilian trial or prisoner-of-war status. A number of these cases, discussed below, have reached the U.S. Supreme Court. The interpretive dimension of the fiduciary model explains due-process safeguards and the Court's grant of habeas corpus as the legal burden that arises from the detaining state's exercise of detention power. Where habeas corpus or robust procedural

10. *See* Brown, *supra* note 2, at 437.

11. Convention (III) Relative to the Treatment of Prisoners of War, 12 August 1949, 75 U.N.T.S. 135 [hereinafter Third Convention]; *see also* Convention (I) for the Amelioration of the Condition of the Wounded and Sick in Armed Forces in the Field, 12 August 1949, 75 U.N.T.S. 31; Convention (II) for the Amelioration of the Condition of the Wounded and Sick and Shipwrecked Members of the Armed Forces at Sea, 12 August 1949, 75 U.N.T.S. 85; Convention (IV) relative to the Protection of Civilian Persons in Time of War, 12 August 1949, 75 U.N.T.S. 287 [hereinafter Fourth Convention].

12. Protocol Additional to the Geneva Conventions of 12 August 1949, and Relating to the Protection of Victims of International Armed Conflicts, 8 June 1977, 1125 U.N.T.S. 3 [hereinafter API]; Protocol Additional to the Geneva Conventions of 12 August 1949, and relating to the Protection of Victims of Non-International Armed Conflicts, 8 June 1977, 1125 U.N.T.S. 609 [hereinafter APII].

safeguards are absent, as is the case of many detainees held by U.S. or Afghan forces at or near Bagram Air Base in Afghanistan (Bagram), the prescriptive side of the theory explains the wrongfulness of these "black holes"; detention under such conditions is wrongful because it constitutes domination of the detainee while treating her as a mere means of the detaining state's national security policy. Significantly, the fiduciary model supplies resources to guide policy on due process under non-ideal conditions, which in this case means real-world conditions in which war-on-terror detainees benefit from neither civilian trials nor prisoner-of-war status. The war-on-terror cases will thus show that the fiduciary theory is not pie-in-the-sky idealism, but instead offers a practical, theoretical framework capable of guiding balanced policy in circumstances where the detaining state refuses to grant civilian trials or recognize prisoner-of-war status.

Last, Part V addresses a hard case endemic to this real-world context: the detention of individuals on the basis of classified evidence they are barred from seeing and contesting. Here too, where the open-court principle of knowing the case to meet is plainly infringed, the fiduciary theory offers valuable insight, counseling the adoption of in situ substitute measures and habeas corpus review, both of which aim to minimize the risk of arbitrary detention.

II. A FIDUCIARY ACCOUNT OF COMBATANT DETENTION

We begin with the fiduciary model's general account of how states come to owe various legal duties to detained foreign nationals held extraterritorially. Some of these duties, such as those inscribed in the Geneva Conventions, are a matter of positive law. In these cases the interpretive question concerns the justification of the core duties of the positive law. In other cases, such as those involving war-on-terror detainees who are refused civilian trials and prisoner-of-war status, there is no clear positive law governing jurisdictional questions, such as the availability of habeas corpus review in U.S. courts. Nor in these cases, where civilian trials and the major part of the Geneva Conventions are deemed inapplicable, is there much positive law to go on with respect to the requirements of in situ due process. In this barren legal landscape, how can the fiduciary theory support a finding that due process and habeas corpus review is owed to foreign nationals detained extraterritorially?

As discussed in previous chapters, fiduciary obligations arise from the subjection of the beneficiary to the institutional, purposive, and other-regarding power of the fiduciary. A state's wartime detention power has each of these characteristics. It is institutional in the sense that it requires institutions to take effect, but also in the sense that it can take an institutional form without being intrinsically wrongful. The power is purposive in that it has national security as its aim. And it is other-regarding because it cannot be exercised for the private ends of the power-holder; the power can be exercised for public ends alone. This last feature of public fiduciary power may appear to pose a conundrum: if the state is a fiduciary of its people and acts as such when it detains foreign nationals extraterritorially on suspicion of terrorism, how can it also be said to act as a fiduciary of the detainee toward whom it owes no prior obligation?

The short answer is that the detaining state places itself in a fiduciary relationship with the detainee when it takes the suspect into its custody in the exercise of its detention power. The detaining state does not owe the detainee the various obligations that come with ordinary residence within the state, such as political and civil rights relating to voting, mobility, and assembly. But the detaining state, on the fiduciary theory, does owe the prisoner humane treatment and due process (understood broadly to include habeas corpus review). Only thus can the state avoid domination and instrumentalization of the detainee, and thereby keep its national security measures within the bounds of legality prescribed by the fiduciary theory. Put another way, under the fiduciary model international law authorizes the state to protect its people from harm through the use of a detention power, but only to the extent that the exercise of such power is consistent with the state's cosmopolitan duties of humane treatment and due process.

We can now resolve the apparent conundrum mentioned above. The purported conundrum trades on the private law understanding of fiduciary duty as a duty of loyalty. Were this the relevant duty, the fiduciary theory would face the irresoluble problem of conflicting loyalties that attends any attempt to serve two constituencies with single-minded loyalty. In this cosmopolitan public setting, however, the fiduciary theory reconciles the state's duty to protect its people from terrorism with its duties to the detainee by specifying the duties owed to the detainee as duties of humane treatment and due process. Compliance with these latter duties leaves the state with expansive discretionary power to protect its people from terrorism, but subject to limits flowing from the fiduciary character of the state's cosmopolitan power to detain.

The detention case closely resembles the parent-child case discussed in Chapter 1. As with the child, the detainee is at the de facto mercy of the detaining state and, for all practical purposes, is incapable of negotiating the terms of his detention with his captors. The detaining state, however, is not entitled to set unilaterally the terms of its relationship with the detainee. The fiduciary principle intercedes to set those terms by imposing legal duties on the detaining state. The duty of due process offers security against arbitrary and indefinite detention, while the duty of humane treatment protects the captive from abuse. On the fiduciary theory, international law authorizes belligerent states to capture and detain combatants temporarily, but always subject to duties of due process and humane treatment. At the most abstract and international level, the fiduciary principle authorizes states to act within lawful domestic, international, and cosmopolitan limits for the benefit of the people subject to their jurisdiction. The "lawful limits" aspect of the fiduciary authorization, in other words, applies to the state in its dealings with its own people, with other states, and with foreign nationals. Although the fiduciary principle does not bring a detained foreign national into a state's *demos*, it does bring the state and the detainee together in a rightful condition under *ius cosmopoliticum*.

It is worth emphasizing that under the fiduciary model, the detainee's nationality and the location of his internment is irrelevant. The lodestar of the fiduciary theory is the fiduciary relationship brought about by the detaining state's forcible custody of its captive. Because the fiduciary principle authorizes the exercise of sovereign power on behalf of every agent who is subject to it, it authorizes the exercise of such power on behalf of detained foreign nationals as well as citizens. But the authorization is constituted and conditioned by the requirements of IHRL and IHL. Thus, the fiduciary theory explains how detained foreign nationals, despite lacking recognition of prisoner-of-war status, are still entitled to humane treatment and meaningful due process.

Before turning to the war-on-terror cases, it is important for us to see that the international norm controlling the detention of combatants is that they are either to be granted prisoner-of-war status or treated as civilians subject to civilian trials. We turn now to the international legal framework from which this norm emerges–the Geneva Conventions.

III. THE GENEVA CONVENTIONS

In this part we discuss the history and justification of the Geneva Conventions, the detailed and comprehensive positive obligations they contain, and their scope, with particular attention to their application to detainees captured during the conflict in Afghanistan and the wider campaign against al-Qaeda.

A. History and Justification

The centerpiece of IHL's regime for the treatment of prisoners of war is the Third Geneva Convention of 1949, one of four conventions referred to collectively as the Geneva Conventions. The first two Conventions protect members of armed forces who fall sick or are wounded during active hostilities, while the fourth protects civilians. Two Additional Protocols were adopted in 1977 that extended the applicability of the provisions in the Geneva Conventions. The first, in part, establishes that struggles "against colonial domination and alien occupation and against racist regimes" will count as international conflicts such that the main body of Articles of the Geneva Conventions will apply to them.[13] The second Protocol develops Common Article 3 of the Geneva Conventions (an Article common to all four Conventions), which had been the only provision applicable to non-international armed conflicts such as civil wars.

The Geneva Conventions trace their origins to the Lieber Code, which arose in response to the savagery of the U.S. Civil War in 1863,[14] and to the Resolutions of the Geneva International Conference of the same year.[15] Like the Lieber Code, the 1863 Geneva Resolutions were inspired by collective moral condemnation of the needless death and suffering wrought by modern warfare, in this case the Battle of Solferino of 1859 that took place during the Second Italian War of Independence. Henry Dunant memorialized the battle and its aftermath, writing of "a hand-to-hand struggle in all its horror and frightfulness; Austrians and Allies trampling each other under foot, killing one another on piles of bleeding corpses, felling their

13. API, *supra* note 12, art. 1(4).

14. *See* John Fabian Witt, Lincoln's Code: The Laws of War in American History (2012); Richard Shelly Hartigan, Lieber's Code and the Law of War (1985).

15. Resolutions of the Geneva International Conference, Oct. 26–29, 1863, http://www.icrc.org/ihl.nsf/FULL/115?OpenDocument. The Resolutions founded the International Committee of the Red Cross (ICRC); *see also* Jean Pictet, Development and Principles of International Humanitarian Law 29–32 (1985) (tracing the modern laws of armed conflict to the Geneva Convention of August 22, 1864, which lay down initial guidelines for the care of wartime sick and wounded).

enemies with rifle butts, crushing skulls, ripping bellies open with sabre and bayonet . . . sheer butchery."[16]

The Geneva Conventions also responded to contemporary atrocity, and in particular to the horrors of war visited on civilians during the Second World War.[17] Since their adoption, 196 states have ratified the Geneva Conventions, such that they now enjoy near-universal international assent.[18] Theodor Meron, former president of the International Criminal Tribunal for the former Yugoslavia, aptly describes the Conventions as "the flagship of the post-World War II legal changes that shifted the paradigm of many aspects of IHL from an inter-State archetype to a homocentric system."[19] He rightly notes "the widespread recognition of the Geneva Conventions as customary law—and in some cases, as peremptory law."[20] Common Article 2 in effect commits the parties to acknowledge the customary status of the Conventions, as it affirms that the parties will remain bound by them "in their mutual relations" to one another even if an adversary in a conflict is not a party, and that parties become bound to nonparties if the latter simply "accepts and applies" the Convention's provisions.

In part, the Conventions codify the international community's attempt to eliminate cruelty and gratuitous suffering from the conduct of war, all the while assuming that armed conflict will occur from time to time. But they also go further, proscribing a wide range of limits on the means states may use to prosecute war. For example, under Article 17 of the Third Convention, prisoners of war, when questioned, are bound to give only their name, rank, date of birth, and military serial number. The same Article affirms that "[n]o physical or mental torture, nor any other form of coercion, may be inflicted on prisoners of war to secure from them information of any kind whatever."[21] Prisoners who refuse to answer "may not be threatened, insulted, or exposed to any unpleasant or disadvantageous treatment of any kind."[22] The Commentary on Article 17 of the ICRC explains that the raison d'être of these provisions is to give prisoners "protection against any inquisitorial practices," as the detaining state "may very naturally be tempted to obtain additional information from the prisoner . . . for this is obviously of interest from the military

16. Henry Dunant, A Memory of Solferino 19 (1986) (1862). Dunant played an instrumental role in bringing about the Geneva International Convention of 1863 and the ICRC. He was subsequently selected as co-winner of the first Nobel Peace Prize.

17. *See* Fourth Convention, *supra* note 11.

18. For a list of signatories, their ratifications, and reservations, see http://www.icrc.org/ihl.nsf/WebSign?ReadForm&id=375&ps=P (last visited Sept. 5, 2015). Protocols I and II have been ratified by 172 and 166 states respectively, but not by the United States.

19. Theodor Meron, *The Geneva Conventions and Public International Law*, 91 Int'l Rev. Red Cross 619 620 (2009).

20. *Id.* at 624 (citing, *inter alia, Military and Paramilitary Activities in and Against Nicaragua (Nicaragua v. U.S.)*, Jurisdiction and Admissibility, 1984 ICJ Rep. 392 (June 27); and *Case Concerning Armed Activities on the Territory of the Congo (Congo v. Uganda)*, 2005 ICJ Rep. 168, 223 (Dec. 19).

21. Third Convention, *supra* note 11, art. 17.

22. *Id.*

point of view."[23] The Commentary indicates that the drafters were particularly concerned with secret "interrogation camps" used during the Second World War.[24] Certain prisoners were sent to these camps before being sent to regular prisoner-of-war camps, and subjected to "great hardship" in order to obtain information from them.[25] Article 17 thus uses explicit language to ensure that the detaining state may not in any way mistreat prisoners, or threaten them with mistreatment, for the sake of acquiring information, including (but not limited to) actionable intelligence of military significance. This does not mean that detaining states cannot interrogate prisoners of war. The expectation is that they will, and as Stephen Ratner points out, the Conventions allow such tactics as "good cop-bad cop scenarios, repetitive or rapid questioning, silent periods, and playing to the detainee's ego."[26] But they do not allow threats, insults, punishments, cruel and degrading treatment, or torture.

In Chapter 4 we argued that the fiduciary theory offers an attractive alternative to the interest-balancing model that dominates the national security literature. The same argument applies here, and explains the absolute prohibition on coercive interrogation found in Article 17. Fiduciary states cannot coercively interrogate prisoners because to do so would treat them as mere means of the detaining state rather than as ends in themselves. Such action would run afoul of the principle of non-instrumentalization, and would exceed the scope of the state's right at international law to engage in armed conflict without incurring liability under *jus in bello*.[27] The interest-balancing model, on the other hand, is incapable of explaining the absolute bar against coercive interrogation, as that model prescribes a balancing of interests that the absolute bar prohibits.

An advocate of interest-balancing might try to defend the absolute bar indirectly, arguing that to permit torture at all would carry political and reputational costs in addition to immediate harm to its victims, and that in the long run these costs are likely to outweigh any gains. As mentioned in Chapter 4, however, this reply fails to explain the actual legal justification for the absolute prohibition, which throughout international conventions and judgments is consistently formulated as a rights-based justification grounded on the dignity of the victim. The fiduciary model, by contrast, explains this justification transparently as an instance of its principle of non-instrumentalization.

A similar worry afflicts the conventional humanitarian justification of the Geneva Conventions. According to this view, the Conventions are based on "respect for human personality."[28] This humanitarian basis explains the various substantive provisions within the Conventions that aim to mitigate the cruelty and

23. ICRC Commentary on Convention (III) Relative to the Treatment of Prisoners of War, 12 August 1949, art. 17, at 156 [hereinafter ICRC Commentary on Third Convention].

24. *Id.*

25. *Id.*

26. Stephen Ratner, *Geneva Conventions*, 165 Foreign Pol'y 26, 28 (2008).

27. *See* Chapter 5.

28. ICRC Commentary on Third Convention, *supra* note 23, art. 3, at 28. The ICRC here describes "respect for human personality" as "the basis on which all the Conventions rest." *Id.*

gratuitous suffering historically associated with armed conflict. As noted above, the Conventions arose within a tradition of humanitarian treaty-making that was driven by the international community's moral outrage over wartime atrocities. The tradition's impulse is to protect individuals from violence that serves no military purpose, but of course the difficult cases are the purported ticking time-bomb type scenarios. Here the prisoner poses no military threat, but she may have valuable information that could presumably save countless innocent lives. Why should the humanitarian impulse that underlies the Conventions not extend to the lives that could be saved through coercive interrogation? The fiduciary theory answers this vexing question by insisting that, even in cosmopolitan contexts involving foreign nationals, the fiduciary principle necessarily authorizes the possession and use of public power on behalf of every individual subject to it. This is the fiduciary theory's criterion of legitimacy, which itself is both a conceptual and normative criterion that illuminates the nature and scope of the fiduciary principle's authorization of public powers. It follows that intrinsically abusive actions cannot be authorized through law, as all exercises of public power must be intelligible, in part, as acts taken on behalf of each person subject to them.

The problem with the humanitarian justification of the Conventions is that it is an abstract philosophical and moral one that is indifferent to the institutional context of its application. Consequently, the humanitarian justification does not take into account constitutive limits that dictate the legal nature of authorization that public institutions enjoy.[29] Under the fiduciary theory, public institutions can act as such only to the extent that they respect legal limits inherent to, and therefore partially constitutive of, the fiduciary relationship that exists between public institutions and the persons subject to them. In the detention context, the constitutive fiduciary limits are requirements of humane treatment and due process; these limits partially make the state-detainee relationship a fiduciary one. The humanitarian justification admits no intrinsic and constitutive limits. Therefore, from the standpoint of the humanitarian justification and interest balancing, open-ended inquiries into the benefits to others of torturing a prisoner make good sense. Under the fiduciary theory, however, the only relevant considerations are those pertaining to the rightful scope and use of the detaining state's authority over captive prisoners. By circumscribing the operation of humanitarian concerns to the state-prisoner relationship, the fiduciary model explains the strict prohibition on mistreatment as a relational duty partially constitutive of the state's international legal authority to detain prisoners of war. Consequently, if a state violates this duty, it undermines its detention authority.

B. Positive Obligations

Just as striking as the absolute bar against coercive interrogation is the wide-ranging set of positive obligations the Third Convention imposes on detaining states from the moment of capture until the final release and repatriation of detainees. It is

29. For a similar distinction between philosophical and juridical justifications in the context of fiduciary relations, wherein the juridical justification alone takes seriously the legal normativity inherent to fiduciary relationships, see Paul B. Miller, *Justifying Fiduciary Duties*, 58 McGill L.J. 969 (2013); and Paul B. Miller, *Justifying Fiduciary Remedies*, 63 U. Toronto L.J. 570 (2013).

worth taking stock of a representative sample of these duties, as they place in sharp relief the degree to which the detention conditions of terror suspects held presently at Guantánamo and elsewhere depart from the Third Convention's standards, as discussed in the next section. Moreover, the comprehensive and generous nature of these duties lay the foundation for our argument below that detention of foreign nationals is properly within the jurisdiction of both IHL and IHRL.

Under the Convention, the general principle is that prisoners of war "must at all times be humanely treated" and "must at all times be protected, particularly against acts of violence or intimidation."[30] Apart from special considerations arising from rank and sex, prisoners are not to suffer adverse discrimination based on "race, nationality, religious belief or political opinions, or any other distinction founded on similar criteria."[31]

Upon capture, prisoners must be evacuated to camps situated away from combat and placed out of danger as soon as possible.[32] During evacuation, they are to be provided sustenance, clothing, and medical attention to ensure their safety.[33] Within a week of capture, "every prisoner of war shall be enabled to write direct to his family. . . . and to the Central Prisoners of War Agency provided for in Article 123."[34]

Once interned, the camps' locations and the identity of the camps' prisoners are to be made available to the "Protecting Powers," a neutral state (or states) charged with monitoring internment conditions.[35] Under Article 10, this external monitoring role can be delegated to a humanitarian organization such as the ICRC. The camps themselves must afford prisoners "every guarantee of hygiene and healthfulness."[36] They are to have "shelters against air bombardment and other hazards of war, to the same extent as the civilian population."[37] The prisoners' quarters are to be "as favorable as those for the forces of the Detaining Power who are billeted in the same area."[38] Food rations are to be "sufficient in quantity, quality and variety to keep prisoners of war in good health and to prevent loss of weight or the development of nutritional deficiencies."[39] Canteens are to be installed "where prisoners of war may procure foodstuffs, soap and tobacco and ordinary articles in daily use."[40] Every camp is to have an infirmary, and medical attention is to be provided to prisoners as needed, at the expense of the detaining state.[41] Seriously sick and wounded

30. Third Convention, *supra* note 11, art. 13.

31. *Id.* art. 16.

32. *Id.* art. 19.

33. *Id.* art. 20.

34. *Id.* art. 70.

35. *Id.* art. 23.

36. *Id.* art. 22.

37. *Id.* art. 23.

38. *Id.* art. 25.

39. *Id.* art. 26.

40. *Id.* art. 28.

41. *Id.* art. 30.

prisoners are to be returned to their countries of origin.[42] With respect to religious freedom, prisoners of war "shall enjoy complete latitude in the exercise of their religious duties," with adequate premises provided for this purpose.[43] Prisoners are also entitled to send and receive "not less than two letters and four cards monthly."[44] Additionally, they are entitled to receive "individual parcels or collective shipments" of personal, religious, sporting, cultural, musical, and other materials "allowing prisoners of war to pursue their studies or cultural activities."[45] The detaining state may compel prisoners who are not officers to do work "not military in character or purpose,"[46] for the same daily duration as "civilian workers in the district,"[47] and for a rate of pay set out in in the Convention.[48] The ICRC Commentary claims that the purpose of these provisions is to benefit the health, morale, and financial position of prisoners rather than support the economy of the detaining state.[49]

The ongoing relations between prisoners and camp officials are likewise heavily regulated. Prisoners are entitled to bring requests and complaints to the military authorities of the detaining state as well as to the Protecting Powers.[50] Senior officers are to be recognized as the prisoners' representatives, and where no officers are present, elections are to be held every six months to select representatives.[51] With respect to discipline, prisoners are to be "subject to the laws, regulations and orders in force in the armed forces of the Detaining Power,"[52] and "[i]n no circumstances whatever shall a prisoner of war be tried by a court of any kind which does not offer the essential guarantees of independence and impartiality."[53] Moreover, "[n]o moral or physical coercion may be exerted on a prisoner of war in order to induce him to admit himself guilty."[54] Regarding punishment, the Convention requires "the greatest leniency,"[55] and expressly forbids detaining states from using "[c]ollective punishment for individual acts, corporal punishment, imprisonment in premises without daylight and, in general, any form of torture or cruelty."[56] Finally, all prisoners of war are to be repatriated "without delay after the cessation of active hostilities."[57]

42. *Id.* art. 109.

43. *Id.* art. 34.

44. *Id.* art. 71.

45. *Id.* art. 72.

46. *Id.* arts. 49–50.

47. *Id.* art. 53.

48. *Id.* arts. 60–62.

49. ICRC Commentary on Third Convention, *supra* note 23, art. 49, at 260.

50. Third Convention, *supra* note 11, art. 78.

51. *Id.* art. 79.

52. *Id.* art. 82.

53. *Id.* art. 84.

54. *Id.* art. 99.

55. *Id.* art. 83.

56. *Id.* art. 87.

57. *Id.* art. 118.

In essence, the Third Convention provides for the establishment of temporary and dependent mini-states of a special kind: temporary because the camps are to close at the cessation of hostilities, dependent because they are wholly within the power of the detaining state, and of a special kind because they are premised on internment. The Convention's Articles impose a liberal constitution on these mini-states, complete with substantive guarantees with respect to housing, healthcare, food, religious freedom, cultural activities, communication with the outside world, the local administration of justice, and representation. These guarantees all reflect the idea that by bringing prisoners of war under their internment power, detaining states acquire obligations to ensure prisoner security and liberty within the fences of the camps.[58]

As an interpretive theory, the fiduciary model explains the duties imposed on the detaining state and their basis because the fiduciary model is premised on the idea that relationships of power and dependency are necessarily mediated by legal rules and principles that protect the vulnerable party from the arbitrary exercise of public power. As a prescriptive theory, the fiduciary model calls for the elimination of the provisions of the Convention that permit regulated but forced labor.[59] Although the ICRC interprets these provisions to aim at the well-being of prisoners, the same benefits could accrue if work opportunities were voluntary. Forced labor treats a person's body and labor as the means of another, and accordingly, is inconsistent with the fiduciary theory.

Although the Geneva Conventions are held out as pillars of IHL, the content of the Third Convention is essentially a bill of human rights designed to address threats to security and intra-internment liberty posed by wartime detention. Much as various provisions of the International Covenant on Civil and Political Rights[60] protect individuals against "standard threats"[61] of modern civilization (e.g., rights to due process within highly institutionalized criminal proceedings), the articles of the Third Convention are fashioned to protect prisoners against foreseeable threats arising from wartime detention, such as starvation, ill health, exposure, and arbitrary punishment. Put slightly differently, the concern of the Third Convention is not to govern the conduct of parties actively engaged in armed conflict, as is the concern of IHL generally, but rather to construct a temporary legal order for the

58. In many ways, the legal regime governing detention camps resembles the temporary authority international law provides to belligerent occupiers under the Hague Regulations of 1899 and 1907, and the Fourth Geneva Convention, where fiduciary principles of good governance are well recognized. *See, e.g.*, Fourth Convention, *supra* note 11, art. 55 ("To the fullest extent of the means available to it, the Occupying Power has the duty of ensuring the food and medical supplies of the population"); *id.* art. 56 ("To the fullest extent of the means available to it, the Occupying Power has the duty of ensuring and maintaining, with the cooperation of national and local authorities, the medical and hospital establishments and services, public health and hygiene in the occupied territory").

59. *See, e.g.*, Third Convention, *supra* note 23, arts. 49–57.

60. International Covenant on Civil and Political Rights, Dec. 16, 1966, S. Exec. Doc. E, 95–2 (1978), 999 UNTS 171.

61. For discussion of human rights as guarantees against "standard threats," see Henry Shue, Basic Rights (2d ed. 1996).

benefit of foreign nationals hors de combat and under the power of their state's adversary. The origin of the Convention's prisoner-of-war regimes is war, but the nature of those regimes reflects the requirements of IHRL more than *jus in bello*. It is not surprising, therefore, that the Inter-American Commission on Human Rights has found the Geneva Conventions and the 1977 Additional Protocols to be part of "an interrelated and mutually reinforcing regime of human rights protections."[62] ICRC Commentary on Protocols I and II acknowledges frankly that the guarantees of due process contained therein (Article 75 of Protocol I, Articles 4 and 6 of Protocol II) "reproduce, in some cases word for word, the corresponding provisions of the Covenant on Civil and Political Rights [*sic*]."[63] The Protocols can borrow liberally from IHRL on due process because in both cases the individual is vulnerable to the detention and disciplinary authority of a state. The fiduciary theory explains the thick human rights dimension of the Third Convention and its Additional Protocols as the constitution of the legal order the detaining state is duty-bound to provide as a consequence of its temporary but ongoing exercise of detention power.

C. The Question of Scope

The Geneva Conventions, however, were drafted primarily to regulate the fallout from armed conflicts between states with conventional armed forces. The principal beneficiaries of the Third Convention are captured "members of the armed forces of a Party to the conflict," as they will always count as prisoners of war.[64] Others, such as members of "other militias" and "other volunteer corps" not belonging to the armed forces of a party, may also acquire prisoner-of-war status, but only if (1) they can be said to "belong to a Party to the conflict," and (2) they are part of a command structure, have a "fixed distinctive sign recognizable at a distance" (such as a uniform), carry their arms openly, and conduct operations "in accordance with the laws and customs of war."[65] Consequently, irregular forces who do not wear uniforms or carry their arms openly are doubly excluded from prisoner-of-war status. If they are not fighting with a party to the conflict they cannot "belong to a Party to the conflict," and they fail to meet the substantive criteria of the Third Convention's Article 4(2). The exclusion of such forces from the main sweep of the Convention, and the proliferation of unconventional internal conflicts involving irregular forces, led eventually to some of the most controversial provisions of the Additional Protocols. One reason the United States declined to ratify the Additional Protocols was that, under Article 1(4) of Protocol I, insurgent fighters "would theoretically obtain prisoner-of-war status if captured, and thus immunity from prosecution for belligerent acts."[66]

62. Inter-American Commission on Human Rights, *Report on Terrorism and Human Rights*, Oct. 22, 2002, OEA/Ser L/V/II 116, Doc. 5, rev. 1 corr., ¶ 45.

63. ICRC Commentary on the Additional Protocols of 8 June 1977 to the Geneva Conventions of 12 August 1949, 879 (1987).

64. Third Convention, *supra* note 11, art. 4(1).

65. *Id.* art. 4(2).

66. Abraham D. Sofaer (Legal Adviser, U.S. Department of State), *The Rationale for the United States Decision*, 82 Am. J. Int'l L. 784, 785 (1988).

Decried as well were Protocol I's relaxation of the requirements from Article 4(2) of the Convention to carry arms openly, wear a distinctive sign, and comply with the laws and customs of war.[67]

Interestingly, at the Preliminary Conference of National Red Cross Societies in 1946, the ICRC proposed the adoption of an Article to be placed at the beginning of each Convention stating in effect that "[i]n the case of armed conflict within the borders of a State, the Convention shall also be applied by each of the adverse parties, unless one of them announces expressly its intention to the contrary."[68] The ICRC proposal met resistance from various states that would foreshadow U.S. concerns over the Additional Protocols. From the perspective of the fiduciary theory, the rejection of the ICRC proposal and the Additional Protocols is suspect, as the Protocols merely expand the scope of the Conventions, and the Conventions recognize the status and standing of civilians and fighters hors de combat as co-beneficiaries of IHL, and where appropriate their status as bearers of human rights (some non-derogable). Although insurgent combatants would enjoy immunity for belligerent acts conducted within the scope of *jus in bello*, they would not enjoy immunity from war crimes prosecution were they to breach the laws of war. Arguably, to deny such combatants prisoner-of-war status is to fetishize the incidents of conventional war (uniforms and carrying arms openly), as these incidents bear no relation to the foundational concern of the relevant Conventions, that is, the protection of civilians as well as wounded or captured fighters.[69]

Additionally, it is important to note that under Article 5 of the Third Convention, "should any doubt arise" as to whether captured fighters qualify as prisoners of war under Article 4, "such persons shall enjoy the protection of the present Convention until such time as their status has been determined by a competent tribunal." Thus, in the Vietnam War, U.S. Military Directives 381-46 and 20–5 provided for "Article 5 tribunals" to determine the prisoner-of-war status of captured enemy fighters, including irregular members of "secret" Viet Cong forces operating in government-of-Vietnam controlled areas.[70] Under Directive 381-46, the Article 5 tribunal was to classify these individuals as prisoners of war so long as they were not captured while engaged in acts of terrorism, sabotage, or spying. Directive 20–5 provided that the tribunals would be composed of "not less than 3 officers," with at least one being a judge advocate or other military lawyer familiar with the Geneva Conventions.[71] The detainee upon capture was deemed to have prisoner-of-war status, and would not "be deprived of his status as prisoner of war without having had an opportunity to present his case with the assistance of a qualified advocate or counsel."[72]

67. *Id.* at 786.

68. ICRC Commentary on Third Convention, *supra* note 23, art. 3, at 30.

69. *But see* Yvonne Chiu, *Uniform Exceptions and Rights Violations,* 36 Social Theory & Practice 44 (2010) (arguing for the requirement to wear uniforms as functionally necessary to preserve civilian immunity from acts of war).

70. Annex A of U.S. Military Directive No. 381-46 of December 27, 1967: Criteria for Classification and Disposition of Detainees, *reproduced in* 62 Am. J. Int'l L. 766 (1968); Directive Number 20–5 of March 15, 1968, *reproduced in* 62 Am. J. Int'l L. 768 (1968).

71. Directive Number 20-5, *supra* note 70, at 771.

72. *Id.*

Detainees were then either released, granted prisoner-of-war status, or surrendered to civilian authorities.

U.S. policy in Vietnam therefore made no allowance for the possibility of indefinite detention without either a civilian trial or recognition of prisoner-of-war status. This approach reflected the consistent position of the ICRC that under the Geneva Conventions one is either a civilian, and protected under the Fourth Convention, or a combatant, and protected under the Third.[73] As the ICRC Commentary put it in 1958, "[t]here is no intermediate status; nobody in the hands of the enemy can be outside the law."[74] U.S. policy in Vietnam was consonant with the fiduciary theory's principle of non-instrumentalization, as in the ordinary case both civilian trials and prisoner-of-war status are consistent with treating persons as ends in themselves rather than mere means.

In some cases, however, such as civil wars that are "not of an international character," only Common Article 3 applies.[75] The remainder of the Convention is inapplicable. Captured fighters cannot acquire prisoner-of-war status under Common Article 3, but it does establish a number of "minimum" guarantees that "each Party to the conflict shall be bound to apply."[76] The ICRC Commentary notes that this formulation marked "a step forward in international law," as it contemplates binding parties such as insurgents who do not yet exist and who may not possess international legal personality, suggesting again the customary nature of the Geneva Conventions.[77] Article 3(1) affirms a general principle that fighters "*hors de combat* by sickness, wounds, detention, or any other cause, shall in all circumstances be treated humanely," and without prejudicial discrimination.[78] The same provision prohibits several specific acts in relation to these persons:

> (a) violence to life and person, in particular murder of all kinds, mutilation, cruel treatment and torture;
> (b) taking of hostages;
> (c) outrages upon personal dignity, in particular, humiliating and degrading treatment;
> (d) the passing of sentences and the carrying out of executions without previous judgment pronounced by a regularly constituted court affording all the judicial guarantees which are recognized as indispensable by civilized peoples.[79]

73. *See* Barbara Falk, *The Global War on Terror and the Detention Debate: The Applicability of Geneva Convention III*, 3 J. Int'l L. & Int'l Rel. 31, 31 (2007) (discussing the ICRC position that there are no "gaps" in IHL).

74. ICRC Commentary: IV Geneva Convention Relative to the Protection of Civilian Persons in Time of War 41 (Jean Picket et al. eds., 1958) [hereinafter ICRC Commentary on Fourth Convention], *as cited in* Omar Akbar, *Losing Geneva in Guantanamo*, 89 Iowa L. Rev. 195, 215 (2003).

75. Third Convention, *supra* note 11, art. 3.

76. *Id.*

77. ICRC Commentary on Third Convention, *supra* note 23, art. 3, at 37.

78. Third Convention, *supra* note 11, art. 3(1).

79. *Id.*

Article 3(2) instructs that the wounded and sick shall be cared for, and authorizes the ICRC or another humanitarian organization to provide its services. Common Article 3 thus constitutes a "Convention in miniature" for non-international conflicts.[80]

Under the fiduciary theory, as we argued in Chapter 3, the prohibitions set out under Article 3(1)(a) and (c) are peremptory norms of jus cogens. The prohibition on taking hostages under 3(1)(b) arguably is as well, as doing so necessarily victimizes the hostages. So too is the core idea of due process contained in 3(1)(d), while its call for a "regularly constituted court affording all judicial guarantees" is a reasonable articulation of what due process means in these circumstances. To the extent the provisions of Article 3(1) belong within the family of jus cogens, they are customary and peremptory norms that can admit no derogation or infringement. In the next section we consider possibly the greatest challenge to the Geneva Conventions since their inception—the global war on terror and the U.S. administration's restrictive interpretation of them, including Common Article 3.

IV. BLACK HOLES

Shortly after 9/11, U.S. president George Bush signed a Military Order authorizing indefinite detention and trial by military commission of non-U.S. citizens suspected of terrorism.[81] Since then, the detention facilities at Guantánamo and Bagram have come to house several thousand detainees. The United States has held at least 780 terror suspects (107 as of November 26, 2015) at Guantánamo,[82] and several thousand have been held at Bagram.[83]

Colonel Lawrence Wilkerson, former Chief-of-Staff to U.S. secretary of state Colin Powell, claims that top administration officials, intelligence analysts, and lower-level interrogators knew early on that many of the Guantánamo detainees had no connection to terrorism.[84] According to Wilkerson, many detainees "clearly had no connection to al-Qaeda and the Taliban and were in the wrong place at the wrong time.

80. ICRC Commentary on Third Convention, *supra* note 23, art. 3, at 34.

81. Military Order of November 13, 2001, *Detention, Treatment, and Trial of Certain Non-citizens in the War Against Terrorism*, 66 Fed. Reg. 57,833 (Nov. 16, 2001).

82. *The Guantánamo Docket*, N.Y. Times, http://projects.nytimes.com/guantanamo (last visited Nov. 26, 2015).

83. *The Post-9/11 U.S. Military Prison Complex*, Sept 8, 2011, Human Rights First, http://www.humanrightsfirst.org/2011/09/08/the-post-911-u-s-military-prison-complex (last visited Nov. 26, 2015) (affirming that in 2011 the United States was holding 2,600 detainees indefinitely at Bagram). In 2013 the United States transferred authority over most detainees to the government of Afghanistan, but not before obtaining assurances that detainees designated by the United States would not be released. Rod Nordland et al., *Karzai Has Nothing but Praise for U.S. upon Bagram Prison Transfer*, N.Y. Times, Mar. 25, 2013, http://www.nytimes.com/2013/03/26/world/asia/us-cedes-control-almost-on-afghan-prisoners.html?ref=topics (last visited Nov. 26, 2015).

84. *See Most Guantanamo Detainees Are Innocent: Ex-Bush Official*, CBC News, Mar. 19, 2009, http://www.cbc.ca/news/world/story/2009/03/19/guantanamo-detainee-innocent.html (last visited Nov. 26, 2015).

Pakistanis turned many over for $5,000 a head."[85] A detailed 2006 report produced from U.S. government documents concludes that 86 percent of all detainees were turned over by Pakistan or the Afghan Northern Alliance at a time when the United States was offering large bounties for the capture of suspected enemy combatants, and that only 8 percent of all captured detainees were characterized as al-Qaeda fighters.[86] The significant likelihood that many war-on-terror detainees are innocent of any wrongdoing underscores the importance of developing a theory capable of explaining their cosmopolitan entitlement to humane treatment and due process.

Three aspects of the kind of detention practiced at Guantánamo and Bagram are of special concern: (1) detainees can be held indefinitely, (2) due process is compromised, and (3) harsh interrogation is common. The leading U.S. Supreme Court cases on detention at Guantánamo illuminate due process violations that detainees have suffered, but also suggest the availability of legal remedies, including those that can be grounded on Common Article 3. First, however, we begin with the coercive interrogation practices of the Bush administration, as the desire to use coercive methods motivated the administration's restrictive interpretation of the Geneva Conventions. The point throughout is to show, on the one hand, how the interpretive dimension of the fiduciary theory can explain judicial recognition of rights to due process, humane treatment, habeas corpus review, and a generous reading of Common Article 3, while suggesting, on the other hand, that the prescriptive dimension of the fiduciary theory supports meaningful due process and humane treatment independently of current positive law.

A. Enhanced-Interrogation Techniques

American personnel have used "enhanced-interrogation techniques" at both Guantánamo and Bagram, as well as at Abu Ghraib prison in Iraq and a number of secret "black sites" in foreign jurisdictions such as Afghanistan, Taiwan, and Poland.[87] The Bush administration authorized these methods in 2002.[88] In a secret memo dated August 1, 2002, John Yoo, a legal advisor in the Justice Department's Office of Legal Counsel, and Jay Bybee, head of the office, concluded that the use of waterboarding, sleep deprivation, enforced stress postures, and other measures did not constitute torture (as proscribed by U.S. domestic law and the Convention Against Torture[89]), and were a lawful exercise of the president's

85. *Id.*

86. Mark Denbeaux et al., Report on Guantanamo Detainees: A Profile of 517 Detainees Through Analysis of Department of Defense Data (2006), http://law.shu.edu/publications/guantanamoReports/guantanamo_report_final_2_08_06.pdf (last visited Nov. 26, 2015).

87. *See generally CIA Interrogations*, N.Y. Times, http://topics.nytimes.com/top/reference/timestopics/organizations/c/central_intelligence_agency/cia_interrogations/index.html (last visited Nov. 26, 2015).

88. *See Senate Report: Rice, Cheney OK'd Use of Waterboarding*, CNN, Apr. 23, 2009, http://www.cnn.com/2009/POLITICS/04/23/cheney.rice.waterboarding/ (last visited Nov. 26, 2015).

89. Convention Against Torture and Other Cruel, Inhuman or Degrading Treatment or Punishment, Dec. 10, 1984, 1465 U.N.T.S. 85, 113; S. Treaty Doc. No. 100–20 (1988).

Commander-in-Chief power.[90] The memo asserted that "[p]hysical pain amounting to torture must be equivalent in intensity to the pain accompanying serious physical injury, such as organ failure, impairment of bodily function, or even death."[91] Khalid Shaikh Mohammed, the self-described mastermind of the 9/11 attacks, was waterboarded 183 times in March 2003.[92] Although this memo was rescinded in 2004, subsequent Justice Department memos, written in 2005, defended the use of enhanced-interrogation techniques in combination with one another.[93] Furthermore, prisoner abuse both predated and exceeded the scope of the Bush administration's authorization. Harsh interrogation and sleep deprivation were used routinely at Bagram and Guantánamo before the Yoo/Bybee memo. Notably, two Afghan men (one considered innocent by his interrogators) died at Bagram in December 2002 from severe beatings while shackled to the ceiling.[94]

As discussed in Chapter 3, states are under a peremptory duty of jus cogens not to torture or subject persons to cruel, inhuman, or degrading treatment. In that chapter we argued that any use of physical or mental violence that treats a person as a mere means to the state's ends qualifies as cruel, inhuman, or degrading treatment. Thus, enhanced-interrogation techniques such as waterboarding, hanging by the wrists, and prolonged sleep deprivation all qualify as such treatment, and under the fiduciary theory are strictly prohibited. But such techniques also count as torture, we argued, because torture (unlike cruel, inhuman, and degrading treatment simpliciter) involves the conscription of the subject against her will through the illicit use of violence. Rather than focus on the severity or intensity of pain and suffering, the fiduciary theory's test for torture asks whether the intent of the infliction of harm is to break the subject's will and force her to participate in the furtherance of an end she does not share. Under the fiduciary theory, this is the special wrong of torture.[95]

90. U.S. Dep't of Justice, Office of Legal Counsel, Memorandum for Alberto R. Gonzales, Standards of Conduct for Interrogation under 18 U.S.C. §§ 2340–2340A (Aug. 1, 2002), http://www.justice.gov/sites/default/files/olc/legacy/2010/08/05/memo-gonzales-aug2002.pdf (last visited Nov. 26, 2015).

91. *Id.* at 1.

92. *See Khalid Shaikh Mohammed (Guantánamo 9/11 Attacks Trial)*, N.Y. Times, http://topics.nytimes.com/top/reference/timestopics/people/m/khalid_shaikh_mohammed/index.html (last visited Nov. 26, 2015) Former vice president Richard Cheney infamously described waterboarding as a "no-brainer." Dan Egan, *Cheney's Remarks Fuel Torture Debate*, Wash. Post, Oct 27, 2006, http://www.washingtonpost.com/wp-dyn/content/article/2006/10/26/AR2006102601521.html (last visited Nov. 26, 2015).

93. For a catalog of memoranda from the Bush era defending harsh interrogation, see *Justice Department Memos on Interrogation Techniques*, N.Y. Times, *available at* http://documents.nytimes.com/justice-department-memos-on-interrogation-techniques#p=1 (last visited Nov. 26, 2015). On his second full day in office in 2009, President Obama instructed officials not to rely on any Justice Department opinions on interrogation issued since 2001.

94. *See "Enduring Freedom": Abuses by U.S. Forces in Afghanistan*, Human Rights Watch, March 2004, 43–44, https://www.hrw.org/reports/2004/afghanistan0304/afghanistan0304.pdf (last visited Nov. 26, 2015).

95. William Hayden, former Director of the U.S. Central Intelligence Agency (CIA) under the Bush administration, has admitted that enhanced-interrogation techniques were specifically designed to break the will of detainees, though he refuses to acknowledge that these techniques

B. Avoiding Geneva

From the beginning, in addition to enhanced-interrogation techniques, detainees at Bagram and Guantánamo have been refused civilian trials and prisoner-of-war status. The avouched motivation of setting up a detention facility at Guantánamo Bay, rather than bringing suspects back to the United States for trial, was precisely to avoid the jurisdiction of U.S. courts and the U.S. criminal justice system, including the right of habeas corpus.[96] The intent of the Bush administration from the outset, in other words, was to devise a space between domestic and international law in which the detainees would find themselves without legal rights and without a forum in which to assert them. Detainees were classified as unlawful or enemy combatants rather than prisoners of war, and were held without trial while military commissions were established to try them (or some of them) for war crimes.[97] Avoiding the prisoner-of-war classification was important to the administration because, as discussed already, Article 17 of the Third Convention expressly provides that prisoners of war who refuse to answer questions may not be coerced in any way.

The administration's legal argument for denying Taliban and al-Qaeda fighters prisoner-of-war status is set out concisely in a White House statement of February 7, 2002, the relevant portion of which is as follows:

> Afghanistan is a party to the Geneva Convention. Although the United States does not recognize the Taliban as a legitimate Afghani government, the President determined that the Taliban members are covered under the treaty because Afghanistan is a party to the Convention.
>
> Under Article 4 of the Geneva Convention, however, Taliban detainees are not entitled to POW status. . . .
>
> The Taliban have not effectively distinguished themselves from the civilian population of Afghanistan. Moreover, they have not conducted their operations in accordance with the laws and customs of war. Instead, they have knowingly adopted and provided support to the unlawful terrorist objectives of the al Qaeda.
>
> Al Qaeda is an international terrorist group and cannot be considered a state party to the Geneva Convention. Its members, therefore, are not covered by the Geneva Convention, and are not entitled to POW status under the treaty.[98]

constituted torture. *See* William Saletan, *The Case for Torture*, SLATE, Jan. 30, 2013, http://www.slate.com/articles/health_and_science/human_nature/2013/01/the_case_for_torture_ex_cia_officials_explain_enhanced_interrogations.html (last visited Nov. 26, 2015).

96. *See* Rasul v. Bush, 542 U.S. 466 (2004) (summarizing the U.S. government's position on habeas corpus for the U.S. military installation at Guantánamo Bay).

97. George W. Bush, Memorandum on Humane Treatment of Taliban and Al Qaeda Detainees (Feb. 7, 2002), http://www.pegc.us/archive/White_House/bush_memo_20020207_ed.pdf (last visited Nov. 26, 2015). For discussion of the early-2002 memoranda that culminated in the memorandum cited here of February 7, 2002, and the decision to deny captured al-Qaeda and Taliban fighters prisoner-of-war status, see Falk, *supra* note 73.

98. White House Press Secretary Announcement of President Bush's Determination re Legal Status of Taliban and Al Qaeda Detainees (Feb. 7, 2002), http://www.state.gov/s/l/38727.htm. For early discussion of the administration's determination, see Sean D. Murphy, *Decision Not to*

The administration thus did away with the individualized Article 5 tribunal process in favor of collective assessments of guilt by association. The ICRC quickly rebuked the U.S. government, stating that the organization "stands by its position that people in a situation of international conflict are considered prisoners of war unless a competent tribunal decides otherwise."[99]

There are grounds for doubting the merits of the Bush administration's interpretation of the Third Convention. In the case of al Qaeda, its fighters could be understood to "belong to a Party to the conflict" (i.e., the Taliban), in the sense of fighting with the Taliban but not being part of their armed forces, as provided for in Article 4(2). And as Omar Akbar points out, it is "conceivable that Al Qaeda soldiers fighting in Afghanistan did fulfill [the four requirements of Article 4(2)],"[100] pointing to the need for an Article 5 tribunal process to decide individual cases on their merits. Furthermore, under Article 4(6), "[i]nhabitants of a non-occupied territory, who on the approach of the enemy spontaneously take up arms to resist the invading forces" need only "carry arms openly and respect the laws and customs of war" to qualify for prisoner-of-war status.[101] No distinctive sign, such as a uniform, is required. Nor is affiliation with any other entity. Arguably, some members of al-Qaeda may have satisfied these requirements.

The argument for recognizing at least some of the Taliban is even easier to make. The administration acknowledged that the Convention applied to Taliban fighters, but only as "other militias and members of other volunteer corps" under Article 4(2). Taliban soldiers could have been viewed as "[m]embers of the armed forces of a Party to the conflict" under Article 4(1), as the Taliban was the government at the time. But even setting this aside, it is probable that some of the Taliban soldiers complied with the four conditions of Article 4(2). Without an Article 5 tribunal process in place, however, individual cases could not be adjudicated.

As for Common Article 3, the administration determined that the conflict with the Taliban was of an international character, so Common Article 3 did not apply to its soldiers. Al-Qaeda fighters could not benefit from Common Article 3, according to the administration, because, as noted above, it had determined that the Third Convention did not apply to them. The United States has also declined to recognize al-Qaeda members as civilians protected under the Fourth Convention, which provides that "[p]ersons protected by the Convention are those who, at a given moment and in any manner whatsoever, find themselves, in case of a conflict or occupation, in the hands of a Party to the conflict or Occupying Power of which they are not nationals."[102] A person does not qualify for protection under the Fourth Convention

Regard Persons Detained in Afghanistan as POWs, 96 Am. J. Int'l L. 475, 478 (2002) (describing the government's position on the detainees' prisoner-of-war status).

99. *See U.S. POW Decision Criticized*, Wash. Post, Feb. 9, 2002, at A22. *But see* Geoffrey Corn, Eric Talbot Jensen & Sean Watts, *Understanding the Distinct Function of the Combatant Status Review Tribunals: A Response to Blocher*, 116 Yale L.J. Pocket Part 327 (2007) (arguing that the executive has unilateral authority to determine whether classes of fighters are eligible for prisoner-of-war status).

100. Akbar, *supra* note 74, at 216.

101. Third Convention, *supra* note 11, art. 4(6).

102. Fourth Convention, *supra* note 11, art. 4.

if she is protected under one of the other three, so prisoners of war and persons protected under Common Article 3 are not protected under the Fourth Convention. But detained persons determined to be civilians by an Article 5 tribunal, such as those found innocent by such tribunals in Vietnam, would be protected under the Fourth Convention.

The English Court of Appeal noted that war-on-terror detainees, who included several British citizens, were in a "legal black hole": their human rights were in jeopardy of being violated, but neither domestic nor international law seemed to offer protection.[103] As a consequence, detainees faced a substantial risk of perpetual detention. They had no means of compelling the U.S. administration to arraign them for trial. Nor did they have any practical assurance of eventual release, as there was no foreseeable circumstance in which the two sides of the conflict would declare an end to hostilities.[104]

A black hole is a particularly egregious case of domination because the detainee is in the power and at the mercy of a hostile captor who is at liberty to treat the detainee in any way imaginable. It is no exaggeration to characterize the legal and practical status of the black-hole detainee as a form of status akin to that of a slave. In both cases, the fate of the vulnerable rests wholly in the discretion of the powerful, who themselves enjoy immunity vis-à-vis the detainee or slave. As Giorgio Agamben writes, the black-hole regime established by the Bush administration "radically erases any legal status of the individual. . . . Neither prisoners nor persons accused, but simply 'detainees,' they are the object of a pure de facto rule, of a detention that is indefinite not only in the temporal sense but in its very nature as well, since it is entirely removed from the law and from judicial oversight."[105] With the aim of safeguarding national security, the Bush administration removed detainees from Afghanistan and transferred them to Guantánamo Bay, thereby placing them outside the reach of domestic courts and IHL. This black-hole detention regime constitutes severe domination, and because non-domination is an organizing principle of the fiduciary theory, such black-hole regimes are anathema to it.

In addition to enhanced-interrogation techniques, the black-hole regime has led to a lack of due process at Guantánamo, Bagram, and secret "black sites."[106] A series of U.S. cases to which we now turn consider the procedural deficiencies of extraterritorial detention and the availability of habeas corpus review.

103. R (Abassi & Another) v. Sec'y of State for Foreign & Commonwealth Affairs & Another, [2002] EWCA Civ. 1316, ¶ 64.

104. Hamdi v. Rumsfeld, 542 U.S. 507, 540 (2004).

105. Giorgio Agamben, The State of Exception 3–4 (Kevin Attell trans., 2005) (2003).

106. *See* U.N. Economic and Social Council, Situation of Detainees at Guantánamo Bay § 84 (Feb. 15, 2006), http://www.cbsnews.com/htdocs/pdf/ungitmo021506.pdf (concluding that the United States had violated the International Covenant on Civil and Political Rights by denying Guantánamo detainees the opportunity to challenge "the legality of their detention before a judicial body" and that their continuing detention "amounts to arbitrary detention"). At the "black sites" there was no due process at all, as the detentions were carried out in secret by the CIA and without judicial or international oversight from bodies such as the ICRC. The black

C. From De Facto Power to Law

In the years since the U.S.-led invasion of Afghanistan in 2001, a number of U.S. Supreme Court decisions have rebuked the Bush administration for its initial detention scheme at Guantánamo. This jurisprudence is relevant from the perspective of international law because there is an important sense in which all municipal courts are also international courts; in the ordinary case, international law expects individuals to exhaust domestic avenues of redress before seeking relief internationally.[107] Moreover, U.S. courts often have access to classified national security materials, giving them a privileged epistemic vantage point from which to render judgment.

In 2004, a 6–3 majority in *Rasul* held that the United States had "exclusive jurisdiction and control" over the Guantánamo territory where the detainees were held, and that as a consequence, U.S. courts had jurisdiction to hear habeas corpus challenges of foreign nationals.[108] At issue was the jurisdictional reach of the federal habeas corpus statute.[109] Justice John Paul Stevens, writing for the majority, held that because "the statute draws no distinction between Americans and aliens held in federal custody, there is little reason to think that Congress intended the geographical coverage of the statute to vary depending on the detainee's citizenship."[110] In *Hamdi*, decided the same year, Justice Sandra Day O'Connor, for a plurality, held that "a citizen-detainee seeking to challenge his classification as an enemy combatant must receive notice of the factual basis for his classification, and a fair opportunity to rebut the Government's factual assertions before a neutral decisionmaker."[111]

The fiduciary theory explains and lends coherence to *Rasul* and *Hamdi* because de facto sovereign control over a territory, under the fiduciary model, generates a fiduciary relationship between the de facto sovereign and the people subject to its power. This fiduciary relationship in turn yields public law obligations such as due process. The fiduciary model also explains Justice Stevens's principle of statutory interpretation from *Rasul*, according to which nationals and foreign nationals are to be treated as equals before the law unless the governing statute plainly says otherwise. As discussed in Chapter 3, the fiduciary model affirms a default position of equality before the law. In the context of statutory interpretation, this principle implies that individuals, regardless of nationality, are to be regarded as equals before the law in the absence of clear statutory language to the contrary.

sites essentially brought back the secret "interrogation camps" from the Second World War that the authors of the Geneva Conventions had attempted to outlaw.

107. For an in-depth exploration of the principle, see Chittharanjan Felix Amerasinghe, Local Remedies in International Law (2004).

108. Rasul v. Bush, 542 U.S. 466 (2004). The territory is leased from Cuba on terms that Cuba retains no rights as a sovereign unless the parties agree to a modification of the lease or the United States abandons the territory.

109. 28 U.S.C. §§ 2241, 2243 (2008).

110. *Rasul*, 542 U.S. at 481.

111. Hamdi v. Rumsfeld, 542 U.S. 507, 533 (2004).

Two years later, in *Hamdan v. Rumsfeld*, a majority of the Supreme Court held that the procedure adopted by a military commission to try Salim Hamdan, a Yemeni national, was unlawful.[112] In an opinion authored by Justice Stevens, the Supreme Court noted that although the accused was entitled to civilian counsel, neither the accused nor his civilian counsel were permitted to attend closed-door sessions in which classified evidence was disclosed. The accused's military-appointed counsel could attend such sessions, but could also be prohibited, at the presiding officer's discretion, from revealing to her client the allegations and evidence discussed in the closed-door sessions. Another "striking feature" of the commission's rules, the Court observed, was that "they permit the admission of *any* evidence that, in the opinion of the presiding officer, 'would have probative value to a reasonable person,'" including hearsay testimony and evidence obtained through coercion.[113] The Court concluded that these procedures were inconsistent with statutory authority that required compliance with the law of war.[114]

According to the Court, ordinary courts-martial procedures, as mandated by Article 36 of the U.S. Uniform Code of Military Justice (UCMJ), supplied the relevant procedural requirements under the law of war.[115] The Bush administration did not dispute that the order establishing the military commission "deviates in many respects" from the rules of courts-martial.[116] The Court emphasized, in particular, the military commission's failure to satisfy "one of the most fundamental protections afforded . . . by the UCMJ itself: the right to be present."[117] Accordingly, the military commission's procedures were not in compliance with the relevant law of war, and were thus illegal under U.S. law.

The court in *Hamdan* also held that the military commission's procedures were inconsistent with statutory authority because they did not meet the requirements of Common Article 3. Like the UCMJ, Common Article 3 applied to Hamdan's military commission because it was part of the law of war, and so constituted one of the conditions on which Congress had granted the president authority to establish military commissions.[118] The Court reasoned that Common Article 3 applied, in part, because its scope included "[p]ersons taking no active part in the hostilities, including members of the armed forces who have laid down their arms and those

112. Hamdan v. Rumsfeld, 548 U.S. 557 (2006). A military commission later found Hamdan guilty of "providing military support for terrorism," but this conviction was overturned on appeal by the U.S. Court of Appeals in 2012. *See* Hamdan v. United States, 696 F.3d 1238 (D.C. Cir. 2012) (holding that "material support for terrorism" was not a crime under international law at the time Hamdan was convicted). *But see* Al Bahlul v. United States, 767 F.3d 1 (2014) (en banc) (concluding that U.S. law authorized retroactive prosecution for "material support for terrorism").

113. *Hamdan*, 548 U.S. at 614 (emphasis in original).

114. *Id.* at 592–93.

115. *Id.* at 620–25 (citing Article 36 of the UCMJ).

116. *Id.* at 624.

117. *Id.*

118. *Id.* at 628–33.

placed *hors de combat* by ... detention."[119] Justice Stevens noted that Common Article 3(1)(d) required that Hamdan be tried by "a regularly constituted court, affording all the judicial guarantees which are recognized as indispensable by civilized peoples."[120] The Court ultimately held, therefore, that Article 3(1)(d) "must be understood to incorporate at least the barest of those trial protections that have been recognized by customary international law," and that these include the right to be present at one's trial and privy to the evidence.[121]

The fiduciary model explains these various due-process safeguards as markers of cosmopolitan legality—that is, as incidents of a cosmopolitan legal order that distinguish a lawfully compliant regime from one that is legally suspect. The noncompliant regime is suspect because the lack of due process subjects the detainee to the will of his captors rather than to legal rules and standards under which the detainee has a fair opportunity to challenge her detention. Although the military commission procedure under review in *Hamdan* had some due process, and so is perhaps more a gray hole than a black hole, its denial of a fair hearing through closed-door sessions nonetheless constitutes domination, as the detainee is ultimately left vulnerable to the unchecked will of the administration. And as David Dyzenhaus suggests, gray holes are really "disguised black holes," and perhaps even more wrongful because they present a charade of legality as the genuine article in order to garner legitimacy.[122]

The Bush administration and Congress responded to *Hamdan* by rewriting the law through the Military Commissions Act of 2006 (MCA).[123] The MCA contained a privative clause that purported to oust judicial review of detention via habeas corpus. It stipulated further that "combatant status review tribunals" (CSRTs) would be responsible for reviewing the designation of detainees as enemy combatants. The Bush administration had created CSRTs previously in 2004, after *Hamdi* and *Rasul*, and they were later entrenched in the Detainee Treatment Act of 2005 (DTA).[124] The DTA gave the Court of Appeals for the District of Columbia Circuit (D.C. Circuit) a limited authority to review CSRT determinations. The Court of Appeals' review authority was limited to review of the CSRT's use of standards and procedures supplied by the Department of Defense.

In *Boumediene v. Bush*, decided in 2008, Justice Anthony Kennedy wrote the opinion for a 5–4 majority striking down as unconstitutional the privative clause of the MCA that purported to oust habeas corpus review, as applied to Guantánamo detainees.[125] The majority found that the impugned legislation infringed Article One, Section 9 of the U.S. Constitution, which provides that "[t]he Privilege of the

119. *Id.* at 629–30 (citing Article 3(1)). The court also concluded that Common Article 3 applied because the United States' conflict with al-Qaeda was "not of an international character." *Id.* at 630–31.

120. *Id.* at 630 (citing Article 3(1)(d)).

121. *Id.* at 633.

122. DAVID DYZENHAUS, THE CONSTITUTION OF LAW: LEGALITY IN A TIME OF EMERGENCY 3 (2006).

123. 10 U.S.C. § 948a *et seq.* (Supp. 2007).

124. 119 Stat. 2739.

125. 553 U.S. 723 (2008).

Writ of Habeas Corpus shall not be suspended, unless when in Cases of Rebellion or Invasion the public Safety may require it."[126] Importantly, the majority accepted the government's position that Cuba, and not the United States, retained de jure sovereignty over Guantánamo Bay, but insisted that de jure sovereignty, although a relevant consideration, is not "the touchstone of habeas corpus jurisdiction."[127] Instead, as in *Rasul*, the United States' more than 100-year possession of de facto sovereignty over the territory was crucial to the inquiry. After reviewing the history of the territory at Guantánamo Bay, the Court concluded:

> The necessary implication of the [government's] argument is that by surrendering formal sovereignty over an unincorporated territory to a third party, while at the same time entering into a lease that grants total control over the territory back to the United States, it would be possible for the political branches to govern without legal constraint. Our basic charter cannot be contracted away like this.[128]

At the heart of Justice Kennedy's opinion in *Boumediene* is the idea that de facto sovereign power denotes legal responsibility, and that responsibility in turn requires accountability. The content of responsibility in this context is humane treatment and due process tailored to accommodate legitimate national security concerns. The mechanism for securing accountability is habeas corpus review. All of this is explained by the fiduciary model, which affirms as a first principle that the possession and exercise of de facto sovereign power triggers public fiduciary duties owed to those subject to the power. In the case of extraterritorial detention of foreign nationals, the requirements of the fiduciary model are all the more stringent because the risks to the detainee of instrumentalization and domination are so severe.[129]

In *Boumediene*, the government had argued that the CSRT process was an adequate substitute for habeas corpus. However, Justice Kennedy noted that at the CSRT stage, unchallengeable hearsay evidence is admissible, and the detainee "does not have the assistance of counsel and may not be aware of the most critical allegations that the Government relied upon to order his detention."[130] Furthermore, the Court held that the Court of Appeals' limited review authority was inadequate because it was unclear whether the Court of Appeals could consider challenges to the president's detention authority, contest the CSRTs' findings of fact, and request an order of release.[131] Most important, the detainee "would have no opportunity to present evidence discovered after the CSRT proceedings concluded."[132] In sum,

126. U.S. Const. art. I, § 9.

127. Boumediene v. Bush, 553 U.S. 723, 755 (2008).

128. *Id.* at 765.

129. In the corporate law context, corporate directors owe heightened fiduciary duties to minority shareholders given the risk to them of exploitation by majority shareholders. *See* Anupam Chander, *Minorities, Shareholders and Otherwise*, 113 YALE L.J, 119 (2003).

130. *Boumediene*, 553 U.S. at 783–84.

131. *Id.* at 786.

132. *Id.* at 789.

the *Boumediene* majority found that full habeas corpus review must remain in place for detainees at Guantánamo because the CSRT procedures and limited appellate review failed to provide an adequate substitute that could ensure a fair hearing.

President Obama halted trial by military commissions when he first came into office in 2009, but rescinded his order in March 2011.[133] At the time of this writing, trials by military commission are planned with revamped procedures that will allegedly give detainees greater access to classified information, impose some restrictions on hearsay evidence, and exclude statements made during coercive interrogation.[134] In May 2012, military commission proceedings commenced against Khalid Shaikh Mohammed and four other men detained at Guantánamo and accused of conspiring in the 9/11 attacks. However, as this book goes to press their trials had not yet commenced due to delays arising from litigation over various procedural matters, such as the confidentiality of attorney-client communications.[135] If and when the 9/11 trials do commence, it is unclear whether the reformed procedures will provide meaningful due process,[136] but detainees can still access habeas corpus review.

Most of the current detainees at Guantánamo have not been nor are likely to be tried by military commissions, but rather will have their cases heard by Periodic Review Boards (PRBs). These parole-style proceedings were also authorized by President Obama in March 2011,[137] although the first hearing was not held until late 2013.[138] PRBs hear cases where the government does not have enough evidence or a legal basis for prosecution, but believes the detainee is too dangerous to release. PRBs can clear a detainee for release, but they cannot actually grant a release, which requires negotiation with a third-party receiving state and a decision to release from the U.S. government. Because they are strictly administrative procedures, PRB hearings do not substitute for habeas review in federal court.

A crucial question left unanswered by *Boumediene* was whether its habeas corpus ruling would apply to detainees held at Bagram or other detention centers in or near

133. *See Obama Orders Resumption of Military Commissions at Guantanamo*, CNN, Mar. 8, 2011, *at* http://www.cnn.com/2011/POLITICS/03/07/obama.guantanamo/.

134. *See Military Commissions*, N.Y. TIMES, http://topics.nytimes.com/top/reference/timestopics/subjects/d/detainees/military_commissions/index.html (last visited Nov. 26, 2015).

135. *See Guantánamo Detainee's Request Delays Progress Toward 9/11 Trial*, N.Y. TIMES, Oct. 19, 2015, http://www.nytimes.com/2015/10/20/us/politics/guantanamo-detainees-request-delays-progress-toward-9-11-trial.html (last visited Nov. 26, 2015).

136. *See The Road We Need Not Have Travelled*, N.Y. TIMES, Apr. 7, 2012, http://www.nytimes.com/2012/04/08/opinion/sunday/the-road-we-need-not-have-traveled.html (last visited Nov. 26, 2015) (characterizing the revamped military tribunal process as "still profoundly flawed").

137. U.S. Dep't of Defense, Periodic Review Board Secretariat, *About the Periodic Review Board*, http://www.prs.mil/AboutthePRB.aspx (last visited Dec. 2, 2015); *see also Dispatches: Opaque as Ever at Guantánamo*, HUMAN RIGHTS WATCH, Jan. 28, 2014, https://www.hrw.org/news/2014/01/28/dispatches-opaque-ever-guantanamo (last visited Nov. 26, 2015) (noting that media access to PRB hearings is very limited).

138. *See Pentagon Prepares Review Panels for 71 Guantánamo Detainees*, MIAMI HERALD, July 21, 2013, http://www.miamiherald.com/news/nation-world/article1953426.html (last visited Nov. 26, 2015).

a theater of war. In 2010, the D.C. Circuit reversed a lower court ruling, holding in *Al Maqaleh v. Gates* that three non-Afghan, Bagram detainees could not bring habeas corpus challenges in U.S. courts.[139] The three detainees had been captured outside Afghanistan and transported to Bagram. The Court of Appeals held that although they benefitted from fewer procedural protections than detainees at Guantánamo, the United States did not intend to occupy the Bagram base and hold the detainees permanently, and Afghanistan remained a theater of war. Ultimately, the Court of Appeals deemed the relevant territory to be under neither the de jure nor de facto sovereignty of the United States, and dismissed the detainees' habeas corpus petitions. Although the Court found that the procedural infirmities at Bagram were worse than at Guantánamo, the lack of de facto sovereignty over Afghan territory, as well as the ongoing war, led the Court to deny admitting the habeas corpus petitions. In short, the Court held that de facto territorial sovereignty must be established for habeas corpus jurisdiction to attach to detained foreign nationals within that territory.[140]

Under the fiduciary theory, the relationship between territory and persons is just the reverse. It is first and foremost the exercise of de facto sovereign power over *persons* that attracts the jurisdiction of competent judicial oversight. State authority and state duty are fundamentally personal rather than territorial in nature. This is because the fiduciary principle authorizes state power on behalf of all persons who are de facto subject to it, and independently of where, geographically, the individual happens to be. Of course, de facto territorial sovereignty is ordinarily sufficient to trigger a state-subject fiduciary relationship, because if an individual is within territory under the state's control, the individual (ordinarily) is subject to the state's power. But de facto territorial sovereignty is not a necessary condition of a state-subject relationship. It is, rather, a generally reliable proxy for it. Just as a parent need not own her home to be held accountable to her child, a state need not have de jure or de facto territorial sovereignty over a prison under its administration to be held to account for its treatment of the prisoners therein. The state's possession and exercise of its detention power, within the prison's walls, is enough.

Interestingly, the Court of Appeals rested the burden of its judgment not so much on the lack of de facto territorial sovereignty, but rather on the fact that Afghanistan remains a theater of war. The Court cited obiter dictum in *Boumediene* that "if the detention facility [at Guantánamo] were located in a theatre of war, arguments that issuing the writ [of habeas corpus] would be 'impractical or anomalous' would have more weight."[141] The alleged worry, going back to *Johnson v. Eisentrager*,[142] is that military commanders in the field would be hampered in their wartime mission if members of an enemy force could call them into civil court. In a conventional war with a foreseeable end, and in which detainees are eventually treated as either civilians or prisoners of war, this argument may have some merit. But in an asymmetrical war

139. 605 F.3d 84, 99 (D.C. Cir. 2010).

140. Two years later, in October 2012, the District Court for the District of Columbia dismissed a subsequent attempt to bring a habeas corpus challenge from the same petitioners, relying on *Al Maqaleh*. *See* Memorandum Opinion, Al Maqaleh v. Gates 24 (D.D.C. Oct. 19, 2012).

141. *Al Maqaleh*, 605 F.3d at 23 (citing *Boumediene*).

142. 339 U.S. 763, 779 (1950).

with no foreseeable end, in which scores of detainees are turned over for bounties, and in which all detainees are refused civilian trials and prisoner-of-war status, it is unpersuasive. In the Afghan war, and in the war on terror generally, the protection of civilian or prisoner-of-war status is absent, while the risk of arbitrary and indefinite detention is severe.

We turn now to the due-process requirements of the fiduciary theory in relation to a hard case that arises frequently in the national security detention context: when, if ever, a state may detain an individual on the basis of classified evidence he does not know and has no opportunity to contest. In *Boumediene,* the Court found that the habeas petitioner must be given a "meaningful review,"[143] but left the details of how this was to be accomplished to the lower courts.

V. THE PROBLEM OF CLASSIFIED EVIDENCE

As discussed in Chapter 3, the fiduciary theory classifies the core of due process as a peremptory norm, while recognizing that it is flexible enough to adapt to different contexts. A state transgresses its general fiduciary duties of impartiality and solicitude when it deprives detainees of life or liberty without employing decision-making procedures that are sufficiently robust to minimize the risk of a biased, arbitrary, or otherwise unfair hearing. In the war-on-terror detention context, these procedures would include a right to counsel and an impartial decision-maker. In addition, as Justice Stevens noted in *Hamdan,* elaborating on Common Article 3, due process "must be understood to incorporate at least the barest of those trial protections that have been recognized by customary international law," including the right to be present at one's trial and disclosure of the evidence on which one may be detained.[144] Recall that in *Boumediene* Justice Kennedy, too, complained that under the CSRT process the detainee "may not be aware of the most critical allegations that the Government relied upon to order his detention."[145] Yet neither justice went so far as to say that the only choice facing an administration whose case rests on classified materials is to reveal those materials to the detainee or order her release. The troubling, unresolved issue is how a detainee is supposed to receive a fair hearing if she does not have access to sensitive information on which her continued detention depends. As noted, the Court in *Boumediene* held that the habeas petitioner must receive a "meaningful review,"[146] but did not explain how this is to occur when the detainee is deprived of knowledge of the case to meet.

The fiduciary theory commends a way forward based on the successful practice of experienced legal institutions. The best solution in terms of diminishing the risk of arbitrary detention is a criminal trial by a municipal court with the usual guarantees of due process. From 2001 through 2013, nearly 500 terror suspects were tried and

143. Boumediene v. Bush, 553 U.S. 723, 783 (2008).

144. Hamdan v. Rumsfeld, 548 U.S. 557, 633 (2006).

145. *Boumediene,* 553 U.S. at 729.

146. *Id.* at 783.

convicted in U.S. federal court.[147] On the assumption, however, that some long-term extraterritorial detention on national security grounds is likely to continue into the future, plausibly the best mechanism available to ensure due process is habeas corpus. In 2010, various former U.S. federal court judges wrote a detailed report confirming the practicability of bringing Guantánamo cases before federal court.[148] At the time the report was written, sixteen habeas petitions had been granted whereas fourteen had been denied. In their report, the judges discuss the habeas process, including the legal standard for detention, the rules of discovery, the burden of proof, release orders and, of particular interest, the process for dealing with classified information.

The process for managing classified materials at both the discovery and the merits stages is guided by the lower courts' experience with the interpretation and application of the Classified Information Procedures Act (CIPA).[149] The procedure itself has been implemented through judicially crafted case management orders (CMOs) that establish a framework for habeas discovery and merits hearings.[150] In *Al Odah v. United States*,[151] the D.C. Circuit Court of Appeals used the CIPA by "analogy to criminal proceedings," ruling inter alia that alternatives to the disclosure of sensitive information under CIPA could be used in the habeas context.[152] One alternative is to limit disclosure of classified information to security-cleared counsel. All counsel for Guantánamo detainees must receive a security clearance from the FBI, and they must agree in writing to comply with a Protective Order that bars counsel from disclosing classified information to any detainee, including his or her client.[153] Importantly, *Al Odah* established that habeas courts are entitled to order the government to grant the petitioner's counsel access to any classified material on which it will rely that is "helpful to the petitioner's habeas case," so as "to facilitate meaningful review."[154]

147. Human Rights Watch, *Fact Sheet: Trying Terror Suspects in Federal Courts*, https://www humanrightsfirst.org/wp-content/uploads/pdf/USLS-Fact-Sheet-Courts.pdf (last visited Nov. 26, 2015).

148. Human Rights First, *Habeas Works: Federal Courts' Proven Capacity to Handle Guantánamo Cases* (June 2010), https://www.humanrightsfirst.org/wp-content/uploads/pdf/Habeas-Works-final-web.pdf (last visited Nov. 26, 2015) [hereinafter *Habeas Works*]. *But see* Stephen I. Vladeck, *The D.C. Circuit After* Boumediene, 41 Seton Hall L. Rev. 1451, 1456 (2011) (arguing that Judges Brown, Kavanagh, Randolph, and Silberman of the D.C. Circuit "are effectively fighting a rear-guard action" against Supreme Court jurisprudence from the detention cases, while "their colleagues coalesce around substantive and procedural rules materially consistent with what little guidance the Supreme Court has provided").

149. 18 U.S.C. app. III (2006).

150. *See In re* Guantanamo Bay Detainee Litig., No 08-0442, 2008 WL 5245890 (D.D.C. Dec. 16, 2008) (the fountainhead case management order drafted by former chief judge Thomas Hogan).

151. 559 F.3d 539 (D.C. Cir. 2009).

152. *Id.* at 547.

153. *Habeas Works*, *supra* note 148, at 17.

154. *Al Odah*, 559 F.3d at 544, 549.

In the criminal law context, CIPA authorizes the government to produce various substitutes for classified evidence, such as redacted versions of classified documents, a summary of the information contained in the classified materials, or a substitute statement that admits "relevant facts that the classified information would tend to prove."[155] But the substitute must "provide the defendant with substantially the same ability to make his defense as would disclosure of the specific classified information."[156] If an adequate substitute is unavailable, the government can prosecute a different charge that does not rely on the classified information, seek a delay to gather more evidence, wait until the sensitivity of the classified information has diminished, or dismiss the charge.[157]

The prescriptive side of the fiduciary theory advises a similar substitution regime in the habeas context.[158] At present, the petitioner is entitled to only an unclassified, redacted statement of the government's record.[159] In *Boumediene*, this meant that the petitioner received a fifty-three-page brief, of which forty-eight pages were wholly redacted and the remaining pages were partially blacked out.[160] This was the only evidence Boumediene and the other petitioners saw. The difficulty with limiting the petitioner's access to relevant information so severely is that it restricts his ability to participate in his own defense. Because the petitioner's counsel cannot communicate the content of classified information to her client, she cannot ask her client for testimony that might challenge or explain the government's assertions. A CIPA-like requirement of substitute information may help to ameliorate this problem. It is worth noting that the MCA, like CIPA, authorizes substitutions of classified evidence at military tribunal hearings.[161]

155. CIPA, *supra* note 149, § 6.

156. *Id.*

157. *See* SERRIN TURNER & STEPHEN J. SCHULHOFER, THE SECRECY PROBLEM IN TERRORISM TRIALS 33–35 (2005).

158. *See* Sarah Lorr, *Reconciling Classified Evidence and a Petitioner's Right to a "Meaningful Review" at Guantanamo Bay: A Legislative Solution*, 77 FORDHAM L. REV. 2665 (2009) (arguing for enactment of CIPA-like legislation to govern habeas corpus review of terror suspect cases). In presenting CIPA-style substitution procedures as an alternative approach, we do not intend to endorse all features of the CIPA framework. For challenging critiques of CIPA, see Dana Carver Boehm, *Guantanamo Bay and the Conflict of Ethical Lawyering*, 117 PENN ST. L. REV. 283, 338–40 (2012); Ellen Yaroshefsky, *Secret Evidence Is Slowly Eroding the Adversary System: CIPA and FISA in the Courts*, 34 HOFSTRA L. REV. 1063, 1070–76 (2006).

159. *See, e.g.*, Boumediene v. Bush, No. 04-1166, at 3 (D.D.C. Oct 27, 2008) (order governing procedures).

160. Amended Factual Return for Petitioners, Boumediene v. Bush, 579 F. Supp. 2d 191 (No. 04-1166) (D.C. 2008).

161. *See* U.S. Department of Defense, Manual for Military Commissions, pt. 3, rule 505(h)(4) (2007) (providing the standard for disclosure of classified information or a substitute or summary of such information). In practice, the MCA procedure has been much criticized, including by those responsible for prosecution. At least six officers of the Judge Advocate General's Corp have resigned or requested transfer, citing due process concerns. *See* Josh Meyer, *For Lawyer, Trial Was Tribulation; Guantanamo Prosecutor Who Quit Had "Grave Misgivings" About Fairness*, L.A. TIMES, Oct. 12, 2008, http://articles.latimes.com/2008/oct/12/nation/na-gitmo12 (last visited Nov. 26, 2015).

Of course, counsel access to sensitive evidence and substitute information are not equivalent to a fully open and transparent hearing. Even taken together, these measures may not be enough to constitute a fair hearing, depending on the need for detainee input. But as noted above, the government has various alternatives apart from dismissing all charges or revealing classified material. Moreover, if the only plausible case for detention against a suspect relies on classified evidence, and that evidence cannot be challenged effectively because the detainee is denied access to it, the court is entitled to grant the habeas petition on the grounds that the government has not met its burden. In *Boumediene*, the government's case against five of the six petitioners rested on a single classified document from an "unnamed source."[162] Judge Leon of the D.C. District Court granted the petitions of these five detainees, finding that to "rest [continued detention] on so *thin* a reed would be inconsistent with this Court's obligation . . . to protect petitioners from the risk of erroneous detention."[163] The interpretive side of the fiduciary theory explains Judge Leon's holding as an appropriate exercise of judicial authority designed to counteract the elements of domination and instrumentalization implicit in arbitrary detention.

The judge-made CMOs mentioned above, which formulate the legal standards and discovery procedures of habeas review, may also be viewed in this light. To the extent that these orders implement the "meaningful review" standard articulated in *Boumediene*, they are explicable as legal bulwarks against an otherwise unchecked executive power that threatens detainees with domination and instrumentalization. Their due-process content embodies the public fiduciary duty of the detaining state to take reasonable measures to avoid indefinite, arbitrary detention of foreign nationals. In the absence of legislation such as CIPA, CMOs thus embody legal principles that the fiduciary model explains as institutional and constitutive requirements of cosmopolitan legal order.

Nonetheless, as noted previously, in Bagram and elsewhere foreign-national detainees have been held without prisoner-of-war status, without civilian trials, and without the benefit of habeas review. In such cases, the fiduciary model recommends first-instance procedures that are substantially similar to those discussed above. The main point, as Judge Leon put it, is to protect detainees "from the risk of erroneous detention."

The fiduciary model also requires that at some point there be an end to the detention if the state declines to try the accused. Ideally, domestic and international lawmakers would set a maximum number of years, but courts can lead the way by releasing detainees held for extended periods without trial.[164] The point of a

162. Boumediene v. Bush, 579 F. Supp. 2d 191, 197 (D.D.C. 2008).

163. *Id.* (citing *Hamdi*).

164. *Cf.* Zadvydas v. United States, 533 U.S. 678, 691 (2001) (holding that "[i]n cases in which preventive detention is of potentially *indefinite* duration," under U.S. legislation "the dangerousness rationale [must] be accompanied by some other special circumstance, such as mental illness, that helps to create the danger," and requiring release of two deportable foreign nationals, who had been convicted of crimes in the United States and could not be returned to their home countries). *But see* Kiyemba v. Obama, 555 F.3d 1022, 1026–29 (D.C. Cir. 2009) (distinguishing *Zadvydas* on the ground that the due process clause does not apply extraterritorially to Guantánamo Bay), *vacated and remanded on other grounds in* Kiyemba v. Obama, 559 U.S. 131 (2010).

maximum is to let the detainee know where she stands, and to recognize her status and standing as a subject of international legal order who cannot be deprived of her liberty forever without trial. This may mean that, like in the criminal context when the state abandons a prosecution for lack of evidence, persons who have committed wrongs and may commit them again will go free. It may also mean that long-term detainees held at Guantánamo that no other state will take must be released into the United States, possibly subject to strict conditions that themselves could be subject to judicial oversight. Ultimately, holding individuals indefinitely without trial treats them as objects rather than subjects, and is inconsistent with the fiduciary theory's criterion of legitimacy, according to which all individuals under a sovereign power are necessarily co-beneficiaries of it.

An objector might contend that the fiduciary model is too apologetic for states engaged in long-term, extraterritorial detention of terror suspects. After all, it seems to follow that if a detaining state conforms to the substantive requirements of due process, then under the fiduciary model the state is entitled to detain the individual for a certain (though not indefinite) period of time in compliance with its duty to its nationals to provide for their security.

We have called into question already the U.S. refusal to recognize, on the basis of Article 5 tribunal hearings, the possible prisoner-of-war status of individuals captured as part of the war on terror. But an advantage of the fiduciary model is that a detaining state can be held accountable on the basis of due process norms even if courts cannot second-guess a government's blanket refusal to recognize the possibility of prisoner-of-war status within the war on terror. Under the fiduciary theory, these norms are derived from inquiry into the institutional protections that must be in place to reduce the threats of domination and instrumentalization that arise from the state's exercise of detention power. Recognition of such norms does not legitimate war-on-terror detention without trial, nor does it dispute the long-standing ICRC position that, even in the war on terror, the Geneva Conventions necessarily require a civilian trial or prisoner-of-war status. All that the fiduciary theory necessarily implies is that there is a firm juridical basis for the application of due process norms whenever a state detains terror suspects without a civilian trial or prisoner-of-war status. The theory is thus well-suited to the non-ideal conditions of war-on-terror detention.

It is a further and complicated question whether a detaining state that complies with due process norms can be said to have authority, as a matter of international law, to detain a foreign national. We speculate that if a competent international body were to determine that the Geneva Conventions did not apply in a given case (i.e., there is no legal requirement of either prisoner-of-war status or a civilian trial), and a state complied with meaningful due process in its humane detention of a belligerent combatant, then in principle the state would have international legal authority to detain the individual for a limited period of time, subject to periodic and independent review. If, however, the Geneva Conventions apply but the detaining state ignores them while providing meaningful due process, then the state would lack international authority to detain, but by hypothesis the wrongfulness of the detention would not be aggravated by breaches of due process. The main point, nonetheless, is that whatever detention authority the detaining state could conceivably have would be subverted by a failure to guarantee meaningful due process.

VI. CONCLUSION

Detention is a direct infringement of a person's liberty. Since at least the time of the Magna Carta, detention has required special justification. The fiduciary theory explains the detention power of states at war as a power derived from the state's fiduciary duty to protect its nationals, but one that is simultaneously circumscribed by the obligations of the Geneva Conventions. These obligations are explained as the legal effects of the state's use of its detention power. Conversely, the fiduciary theory condemns the legal black holes of the war on terror as a form of subjugation akin to slavery. More productively, the fiduciary theory also explains the requirements of due process and humane treatment as elements of cosmopolitan law applicable to all states. These elements safeguard foreign nationals from domination and instrumentalization, making a cosmopolitan legal order possible.

In short, the fiduciary theory's relational nature and sensitivity to power allows it to explain the rights of due process and humane treatment recognized in the Geneva Conventions and the Guantánamo cases, while also offering practical prescriptions in favor of such rights, possibly in modified form, for other war-on-terror detention contexts. In explaining the Geneva Conventions and the Guantánamo cases, the interpretive side of the fiduciary theory calls on its criterion of legitimacy to make sense of the detaining state's cosmopolitan duties of due process and humane treatment. This criterion allows the prescriptive side to draw out the implication that, to recall the words of the ICRC, no one "in the hands of the enemy can be outside the law."[165]

165. ICRC Commentary on Fourth Convention, *supra* note 74, at 41.

7

The Right to Refuge

I. INTRODUCTION

In the previous chapter we discussed the fiduciary theory's cosmopolitan implications in circumstances in which states detain foreign nationals in the course of an armed conflict. Those implications arise, we argued, from the state's ongoing assertion of liberty-depriving control over detainees. In this chapter, we discuss the theory's implications in the refugee context in which foreign nationals petition a state (the "receiving" or "host" state) for asylum. In these circumstances, the state typically does nothing to put itself into contact with the asylum seeker; it is the refugee claimant who ordinarily arrives at the border of the receiving state in search of safe harbor. Thus, unlike in the detention context, the state's duties to the claimant cannot rely on any particular liability-incurring action it has undertaken. Of course, many states have ratified the 1951 Convention Relating to the Status of Refugees (Refugee Convention)[1] and the 1967 Protocol Relating to the Status of Refugees (Protocol),[2] and have thereby acquired various treaty-based duties to asylum seekers, most notably the duty of non-refoulement, an obligation to refrain from expelling or returning asylum seekers to places of danger. But it is within the state's prerogative to ratify these instruments or not, just as it is within the state's prerogative to withdraw from them. Generally, then, an unwilling state does nothing obvious to incur an international legal obligation to take in refugees. To make matters more difficult still, under the Westphalian conception of sovereignty, the state has exclusive jurisdiction over its territory and questions of entry, with the result that, under this conception, the state has unfettered discretion to decide whether to admit foreign nationals into its territory. Both the classical conception of sovereignty and the relative passivity of the receiving state pose significant challenges to any attempt to explain or defend the rights enjoyed by refugees under international law.

1. Convention Relating to the Status of Refugees, July 28, 1951, 189 U.N.T.S. 150, *entered into force* Oct. 4, 1954 [hereinafter Refugee Convention].

2. Protocol Relating to the Status of Refugees, Jan. 31, 1967, 606 U.N.T.S. 267, *entered into force* Oct. 4, 1967 [hereinafter Protocol]. As of February 2015, there were 145 parties to the Convention and 146 to the Protocol.

Bearing these and other challenges in mind, we argue that the fiduciary theory of sovereignty explains the duty of non-refoulement as a peremptory norm of international law. As a prescriptive theory, the fiduciary approach mandates non-absolute, defeasible rights of asylum and eventual permanent residence, including the option of naturalized citizenship. Collectively, these norms confer on asylum seekers an entitlement to enter and remain within a receiving state (subject to some qualification), even if the state is not a party to the Refugee Convention and its Protocol, or any other treaty with relevantly similar provisions. The rights of refugees, then, ultimately crystallize as a right of potentially permanent residence in a host state, with the possibility of eventual citizenship. This right of refuge flows, we claim, from the intersection of the state's position as a joint fiduciary of the earth's surface on behalf of humanity, on the one hand, and its position as a local fiduciary that international law entrusts with sovereignty over the people within a certain territory, on the other. The state acquires a cosmopolitan duty to grant refuge when an individual fleeing irresoluble threats to her human rights appears at its border.

When judged against the current state of international refugee law (IRL), advocacy of a universal right of refuge is an admittedly strong prescriptive claim.[3] As we shall see, the Convention and the Protocol do not provide a right of asylum—much less permanent status—but rather the weaker duty of non-refoulement. We begin with a discussion of the development and practice of IRL, which is grounded mainly in the Convention and its Protocol, certain provisions of other international conventions, and regional agreements. As an interpretive theory, the fiduciary account of sovereignty explains many of the central features of this regime beyond its explanation of the conventional duty of non-refoulement, including: the customary and jus cogens status of the duty of non-refoulement, IRL's self-understanding as a system of surrogate protection, the Refugee Convention's principles of non-discrimination and non-penalization for unauthorized entry, the doctrine of alienage according to which IRL applies only to persons outside their countries of origin or habitual residence, the connection of IRL to de jure and de facto statelessness, and, the availability of international identity and travel documents. Some of the fiduciary theory's prescriptions, in addition to a general right of refuge, include: eliminating the Refugee Convention's limited grounds of persecution and focusing instead on the individual's vulnerability to human rights abuses under conditions of impunity, condemnation of current interdiction and other non-entrée practices, significant constraints on burden-sharing arrangements that involve forcible transfers of asylum seekers or refugee "warehousing" in camps, a duty of justification owed to any person denied asylum, and, independent and international review of any municipal decision to deny asylum. Moreover, the fiduciary theory clarifies one of IRL's most contested and important concepts—persecution—which is central to the definition of "refugee" found in the Refugee Convention but is itself undefined.

We develop these arguments in three stages. In Part II, we sketch the history and main features of IRL. In Part III, we discuss humanitarian, human rights, and territorial accounts of refugee law, and their respective shortcomings. In Part IV, we

3. *See, e.g.*, Kay Hailbronner, *Nonrefoulement and "Humanitarian" Refugees: Customary International Law or Wishful Legal Thinking?*, 26 VA. J. INT'L L. 857, 858 (1985) (describing a universal customary norm of even the duty of non-refoulement as "wishful legal thinking").

develop the interpretive and prescriptive aspects of the fiduciary theory of IRL. The fiduciary theory borrows important ideas from human rights and territorial accounts of refugee law, and combines these with the claim that local fiduciary states are also, necessarily, joint fiduciaries of the earth's surface on behalf of humanity. As such, receiving states must open their borders to persons who have fled persecution in their home state. Although our argument in this chapter focuses on providing a coherent jurisprudential framework for refugee protection, the arguments we develop have broader implications for transnational migration, highlighting states' obligations to treat foreign nationals in a manner consonant with their status and standing as beneficiaries of international legal order.[4]

II. THE DEVELOPMENT OF INTERNATIONAL REFUGEE LAW

Numerous religious and cultural traditions contain teachings and historical practices that call for the protection of asylum seekers. As Khadija Elmadmad observes, the founders of Judaism, Islam, and Christianity—Moses, Muhammad, and Jesus Christ—all "experienced exile and sought asylum in foreign communities."[5] In ancient Israel, six Levitical cities of refuge provided asylum to individuals who had committed unintentional homicide and who were sought by blood avengers of the victim.[6] In Europe, from the fourth century through the eighteenth century, the Catholic Church provided sanctuary for individuals fleeing civil authority, beginning with runaway and abused slaves, but extending the practice eventually to citizens accused of criminal wrongdoing.[7] Islamic migration law (*hijrah*) maintains that "any person (even a non-Muslim) fleeing and seeking protection has the right to enter an Islamic community and ask for protection (*aman*)."[8] When asylum seekers request protection from Muslim authorities or even Muslim individuals living in *dar al-Isla* (the world where Islamic law applies), those authorities and individuals are duty-bound to provide it.[9] The idea of granting protection to asylum seekers, then, has a rich history in non-European as well as Western legal traditions.

4. One of us has argued elsewhere that states' position as fiduciaries of humanity entails an obligation to justify excluding peaceful but non-necessitous migrants, as well as refugees, from their territory. *See* Evan Fox-Decent, *Constitutional Legitimacy Unbound, in* PHILOSOPHICAL FOUNDATIONS OF CONSTITUTIONAL LAW 119 (David Dyzenhaus & Malcolm Thorburn eds., 2016).

5. Khadija Elmadmad, *Asylum in Islam and Modern Refugee Law,* 27 REFUGEE SURVEY Q. 51, 53 (2008).

6. Deuteronomy 4:41–43; Joshua 20:7; *see also* Haim Herman Cohn, *City of Refuge,* in ENCYCLOPAEDIA JUDAICA (1972). During that period, blood vengeance for unintentional homicide was legally permitted.

7. *See* HILARY CUNNINGHAM, GOD AND CAESAR AT THE RIO GRANDE: SANCTUARY AND THE POLITICS OF RELIGION 72–83 (1995); George Cyprian Alston, *Sanctuary, in* 13 THE CATHOLIC ENCYCLOPEDIA (1912), http://www.newadvent.org/cathen/13430a.htm (last visited Nov. 27, 2015).

8. Elmadmad, *supra* note 5, at 54.

9. *Id.; see also* G.M. Arnaout, Asylum in the Arab-Islamic Tradition (Office of the U.N. High Comm'r for Refugees, Int'l Inst. of Humanitarian L. 1987).

Refugees first became a concern of modern international law in the years following the First World War.[10] In response to the plight of some 800,000 Russians who fled the Bolshevik regime, the League of Nations created in 1921 the office of the High Commissioner for Russian Refugees, appointing Fridtjof Nansen as High Commissioner.[11] In addition to a humanitarian crisis calling for "immediate relief measures,"[12] the Russian exiles were in a position of de jure statelessness. Lenin had stripped them of their citizenship, leaving them with no means to identify themselves or travel between states. Moreover, their host countries, for the most part, were unwilling to naturalize them.[13] In 1922, at Nansen's urging, the governing Council of the League of Nations authorized host countries to issue international identity and travel documents to the refugees. These would later become known as "Nansen passports."[14] Over the next thirteen years, Nansen passports would be granted to stateless persons of Armenian, Turkish, Assyrian, Assyro-Chaldaean, Syrian, Kurdish, and Saar origin. In 1926, at a time when Nansen passports were available to persons of Russian and Armenian origin only, a League of Nations Inter-Governmental Conference defined a refugee as simply any person of Russian or Armenian origin who did not enjoy the protection of the government of the USSR or the Turkish Republic, respectively, and who had not acquired another nationality.[15] Initially, Nansen passports were valid for one year only, and not for return to the issuing country unless specifically authorized. But in 1926, twenty-three countries agreed to permit refugees to return to the issuing country.[16] The point of the Nansen passport was to give the stateless a way of identifying themselves so they could enjoy freedom of movement between states as well as protection and civil rights in whichever state they happened to reside.[17]

In 1928, the Assembly of the League authorized the High Commissioner, through his representatives in the different host countries, to exercise consular functions on behalf of refugees. The 1928 Assembly also approved granting refugees civil rights relating to property and work and familial relations akin to the rights held by nationals, and it asked states to refrain from expelling refugees without assurance

10. *See* Louise W. Holborn, *The Legal Status of Political Refugees, 1920–1938*, 32 Am. J. Int'l L. 680 (1938) (chronicling interwar efforts to meet refugee crises).

11. U.N. Ad Hoc Committee on Refugees and Stateless Persons, A Study of Statelessness, United Nations, August 1949, Lake Success—New York, Aug. 1, 1949, E/1112, E/1112/Add.1, http://www.refworld.org/docid/3ae68c2d0.html (last visited Nov. 27, 2015) [hereinafter *Study of Statelessness*]; James Hathaway, *A Reconsideration of the Underlying Premise of Refugee Law*, 31 Harv. Int'l L. J. 129, 137–39 (1990) (arguing that although there was no individualized screening of refugees in the interwar period, refugee law still "constituted a largely humanitarian exception to the protectionist norm" privileging state sovereignty).

12. Holborn, *supra* note 10, at 681.

13. *Id.* at 682–83.

14. *Id.* at 684.

15. Arrangement Relating to the Issue of Identity Certificates to Russian and Armenian Refugees, May 12, 1926, League of Nations Treaty Series, No. 2004, LXXXIX, at 47.

16. Holborn, *supra* note 10, at 685–86.

17. Norman Bentwich, *The League of Nations and Refugees*, 16 Brit. Y.B. Int'l L. 114 (1935).

that the refugees would be received by another country. Norman Bentwich summarized nicely the underlying motivation of this request: "[t]he tossing of the human victim from state to state, interrupted by periods of imprisonment which the victim served for having been compelled to trespass the frontiers, was a standing injustice; and the aim of the *voeu* of the Assembly was that the refugee should not be turned into an outcast."[18] The Assembly's resolutions, however, were not legally binding; states could legally adopt them or not at will.

The League Assembly in 1930 assigned the legal protection of refugees (the problem of statelessness) to the League's Secretary-General, whereas substantive humanitarian work concerning the settlement and welfare of refugees was entrusted to the international Nansen Office.[19] In 1933, a conference of the Inter-Governmental Advisory Commission for Refugees drafted a convention that aimed to make binding the League's existing recommendations. The League Assembly established in 1938 a High Commissioner's Office responsible for all international work concerning "Nansen" refugees, as well as other refugees coming from Germany, and later from the Sudetenland and Austria.

From a contemporary perspective, two aspects of the interwar regime are particularly striking. The first is that refugees who poured out of Russia, Turkey, and elsewhere were not subject to an individualized screening process aimed at determining whether particular asylum seekers merited international protection. It was enough that they were stateless and from a country of origin known to be hostile to them. The second and related aspect is the centrality of statelessness to the interwar international framework and response to refugee crises. Beneficiaries of Nansen passports were de jure stateless and considered refugees because they had lost their original citizenship. But as indicated by the League of Nations' 1926 definition of refugee and a subsequent U.N. report on statelessness from 1949, persons were considered de facto stateless and therefore also refugees if they "left the country of which they were nationals" and no longer enjoyed "the protection and assistance of their national authorities."[20] As Louise Holborn commented in 1938, the position of the de jure and de facto stateless "in practice" was "identical."[21] Nansen passports, then, provided refugees with a form of cosmopolitan citizenship to help them overcome the challenges of both de jure and de facto statelessness. Right from the beginning, IRL conceived of itself as imbued with the mission of providing surrogate legal status and protection to individuals fleeing persecution. Presupposed by IRL was the crucial idea that international law was juridically capable of authorizing national and international actors alike to provide refugees with surrogate legal status and protection.[22]

18. *Id.* at 117.

19. *Study of Statelessness, supra* note 11, at 26–28. The Nansen Office closed on December 31, 1938.

20. *Id.* at 7.

21. Holborn, *supra* note 10, at 681.

22. As elaborated in Part IV below, the fiduciary theory offers an account of international law's juridical capacity to provide this surrogate legal status and protection.

The year 1938 marked a watershed for IRL, for in that year the seeds were sown for the kind of individualized refugee status determination that would be taken up in the Refugee Convention.[23] The United States organized the Evian Conference that led to the creation of the Inter-Governmental Committee for Refugees, an organization that would operate from 1938 until 1947.[24] Although its initial mandate was to provide protection to German refugees, its terms of reference were eventually extended to "all persons . . . who, as a result of events in Europe, have had to leave, or may have to leave, their countries of residence because of the danger to their lives or liberties on account of their race, religion or political beliefs."[25] The Committee assisted refugees from Germany, Austria, and Spain as well as others who were stateless, and assumed the work of the League of Nations' High Commissioner's Office when it was wound up at the end of 1946.[26]

In the aftermath of the Second World War, the U.N. Relief and Rehabilitation Administration (UNRRA) was tasked with repatriating millions of persons displaced by the Nazis and their allies. These individuals fell under the protection of UNRAA and were not liable to repatriation if they could establish "concrete evidence" of persecution.[27] The General Assembly of the United Nations subsequently referred the problem to the U.N.'s Economic and Social Council.[28] The Council's deliberations were guided by two principles: first, that "the problem is international in scope and nature," and second, that "no refugees or displaced persons who have . . . expressed valid objections to returning to their countries of origin . . . shall be compelled to return to their country of origin."[29] When the United Nations established the International Refugee Organization (IRO) in 1946, it conducted refugee status determinations on the basis of whether asylum seekers could demonstrate "valid objections" to return.[30] Anticipating the definition of refugee that would emerge in the Refugee Convention a few years later, the IRO's Constitution stipulated that "valid objections" would include "persecution, or fear, based on reasonable grounds of persecution because of race, religion, nationality or political opinions."[31] The United Nations High Commissioner for Refugees (UNHCR) replaced the IRO in 1951.[32] Its enabling statute entrenched further the definitional refugee criteria

23. *See* Hathaway, *Reconsideration, supra* note 11, at 137–43 (characterizing refuge law from 1920 to 1938 as "humanitarianism qualified," and from 1938 to 1950 as "human rights protection qualified").

24. Study of Statelessness, *supra* note 11, at 29–30.

25. *Id.*

26. *Id.* at 30.

27. UNRRA European Region Order 40(I), July 3, 1946, *cited in* Hathaway, *Reconsideration, supra* note 11, at 139.

28. G.A. Res. 8(1), U.N. G.A.O.R., (Feb. 12, 1946).

29. *Id.*

30. United Nations, Constitution of the International Refugee Organization, Dec. 15, 1946, 18 U.N.T.S. 3, Annex 1(C)1.

31. *Id.* Annex 1(C)1(a)(i).

32. *See* G.A. Res. 319 (IV), U.N. G.A.O.R. (Dec. 3, 1949) (decision to establish UNHCR); G.A. Res. 428 (V), U.N. G.A.O.R., Dec. 14, 1950 (Annex) (Statute of the Office of the UNHCR).

found in the IRO's Constitution.[33] It was the 1951 Refugee Convention, however, that would make the individualized approach to refugee status determination an enduring fixture of IRL.

The drafting of the Refugee Convention was significantly influenced by three factors: the presence of massive numbers of European refugees and displaced persons in the aftermath of World War II; the start of the Cold War, during which the Soviet bloc largely boycotted discussions and western-European views dominated; and, to a much lesser extent, the rise of the human rights movement.[34] While Article 14(1) of the 1948 Universal Declaration of Human Rights (UDHR) provides that "[e]veryone has the right to seek and to enjoy in other countries asylum from persecution,"[35] an earlier version of Article 14(1) had provided "the right to seek and *be granted* . . . asylum" rather than "the right to seek and to enjoy . . . asylum."[36] Hersch Lauterpacht considered the final formulation of Article 14(1) as "artificial to the point of flippancy."[37] Commenting on the lack of an express guarantee of an individual right to asylum in Article 14(1), Paul Weis, former Director of the Legal Office of the UNHCR, remarked that "the right of asylum was generally understood [by traditional international law] to be the right of a sovereign state to grant asylum and refuse extradition."[38] That is, in the exercise of its sovereign rights, one state would not wrong another if it granted asylum to an individual.

Negotiation of the Refugee Convention was likewise influenced by the statist view of asylum as well as western-European concerns that a universal right to asylum would expose receiving states to unforeseeable burdens.[39] Furthermore, at the time, states such as the United States, Canada, and Australia restricted migration to Europeans, and some participants at the foundational Conference of Plenipotentiaries expressed ethnocentric worries about the possible origins of future would-be refugees.[40] These factors, combined with the pressing refugee crisis

33. *Id.* at II(6)(A)(ii) (extending the competence of the UNHCR to persons unable or unwilling to seek the protection of their country of nationality "owing to well-founded fear of being persecuted for reasons of race, religion, nationality or political opinion").

34. *See* Joan Fitzpatrick, *Revitalizing the 1951 Refugee Convention*, 9 HARV. HUM. RTS. J. 229, 232–33. (1996); Hathaway, *Reconsideration, supra* note 11.

35. Universal Declaration of Human Rights, Dec. 10, 1948, 217 A (III), art. 14(1) [hereinafter UDHR].

36. As cited in Paul Weis, *Territorial Asylum*, 6 INDIAN J. INT'L L. 173, 179 (1966) (emphasis added in original).

37. Hersch Lauterpacht, *The Universal Declaration of Human Rights*, 25 BRIT. Y.B. INT'L L. 354, 374 (1948).

38. Weis, *supra* note 36, at 179 (noting that this statist understanding reflected the views of Pufendorf and Vattel, views that would initially prevail in international law over the position of Grotius, Suarez, and Wolf that placed the right of asylum with the individual on humanitarian grounds derived from the idea of a community of states or *civitas maxima*).

39. *See* Statement of Mr. van Heuven Goedhart, High Commissioner for Refugees, U.N. Conference of Plenipotentiaries on the Status of Refugees and Stateless Persons, at 12, U.N. Doc. A/CONF.2/SR.21 (1951).

40. *See* Statement of Mr. Rochefort of France, U.N. Conference of Plenipotentiaries on the Status of Refugees and Stateless Persons, at 11, U.N. Doc., A/CONF.2/SR. 19 (1951) (observing

in Europe, led to the adoption of a regime enshrined within the Convention that falls well short of a general and universal right of refuge.

Nonetheless, the influence of the budding human rights movement is discernible in the Refugee Convention's principles of non-discrimination and non-penalization. Under Article 3, States are instructed to apply the Convention "without discrimination as to race, religion, or country of origin."[41] And under Article 31, states are barred from penalizing asylum seekers who have entered the state without authorization, so long as those persons "present themselves without delay to the authorities and show good cause for their illegal entry or presence."[42] We argue in Part IV that IRL, properly understood, serves the human rights of foreign nationals by reconstituting—rather than merely limiting—state sovereignty.

Notably, however, the Refugee Convention does not provide a right of asylum.[43] Article 33(1), which is widely regarded as the cornerstone of the Convention, provides the more limited duty of non-refoulement: states may not "expel or return ('refouler') a refugee in any manner whatsoever to the frontiers of territories where his life or freedom would be threatened on account of his race, religion, nationality, membership in a particular social group or political opinion."[44] The benefit of Article 33(1), however, is denied to any person "whom there are reasonable grounds for regarding as a danger to the security of the country in which he is, or who, having been convicted by a final judgment of a particularly serious crime, constitutes a danger to the community of that country."[45] Other possible claimants to refugee status are barred by the Refugee Convention's Article 1(F) "exclusion clauses," which exclude persons from claiming refugee status if they have engaged in crimes against peace, war crimes, crimes against humanity, serious nonpolitical crimes, or acts "contrary to the purposes and principles of the United Nations."[46]

Furthermore, Article 33 places no bar on a potential receiving state closing its borders to claimants proceeding to it from safe third countries. Nor does Article 33 expressly prohibit states from interdicting possible claimants on the high seas[47] or in

that "neither the total number of refugees, nor their distribution by nationality of origin, was yet known").

41. Refugee Convention, *supra* note 1, art. 3.

42. *Id.* art. 31.

43. Guy S. Goodwin-Gill & Jane McAdam, The Refugee in International Law 370 (3d ed. 2007) (affirming that a general and universal right to asylum was too controversial for states to reach agreement on it).

44. Refugee Convention, *supra* note 1, art. 33(1).

45. *Id.* art. 32(2).

46. *Id.* art. 1(F).

47. This has led to a divergence of views about whether interdiction on the high seas qualifies as refoulement under the Refugee Convention and related human rights agreements. Some national authorities have taken the position that such measures do not violate Article 33. *See, e.g.,* Sale v. Haitian Ctrs. Council, 509 U.S. 155 (1993); Paul Power, *YLS Symposium: "Stopping the Boats"—Australia's Appalling Example to the World,* Opinio Juris, Mar. 12, 2014, *available at* http://opiniojuris.org/2014/03/12/yls-sale-symposium-stopping-boats-australias-appalling-example-world/ (last visited Nov. 27, 2015). Conversely, the U.N. High Commissioner for

foreign jurisdictions[48] so as to prevent them from reaching the host state to make a claim, or from using carrier sanctions and visa requirements for the same purpose.[49] This is a significant omission, as Article 16 of the Convention gives refugees "free access to the courts of law on the territory of all Contracting States," whereas Article 32 permits expulsion of refugees only for reasons of public order and national security "in accordance with due process of law."[50] States typically allow inland claimants to challenge adverse refugee status determinations and deportation orders,[51] so interdiction and other non-entrée policies have the effect of depriving asylum seekers of international due process rights they would otherwise enjoy.

Perhaps most significant, Article 33(1) reiterates the restrictive civil and political grounds of persecution found in Article 1, which sets out the Refugee Convention's formal definition of a refugee. Under Article 1, a person is considered a refugee if, and only if, she is outside his country of nationality or habitual residence and "owing to a well-founded fear of being persecuted for reasons of race, religion, nationality, membership of a particular social group or political opinion . . . is unable or unwilling to avail himself of the protection of that country."[52] Thus, persons are excluded who face even lethal risks arising from natural disasters, disease, and socioeconomic causes. Others, such as women, sexual minorities, and labor activists, have to show that their persecution is worthy of recognition under the Convention framework because it stems from their "membership of a particular social group." Article 1 also restricts the temporal scope of the Convention to "events occurring before 1 January 1951," and provides as well that the parties are entitled to interpret this clause to mean "events occurring *in Europe* before 1 January 1951," thus attributing a geographic as well as a temporal limitation to the Convention.[53] The

Refugees, the European Court of Human Rights, and the Inter-American Commission on Human Rights have taken the position that interdiction on the high seas for purpose of summarily returning claimants to foreign jurisdictions may constitute refoulement under the Refugee Convention and human rights agreements. *See* Hirsi Jamaa v. Italy, 55 Eur. Ct. Hum. Rts. 627 (2012); Center for Human Rights v. United States, Inter-Am. Comm'n H.R., Report No. 51/96, OEA/Ser.L/VII.95, doc. 7, rev. at 550 (1997); U.N. High Commissioner for Refugees, UNHCR Note on the Principle of Non-refoulement (Nov. 1997), http://www.refworld.org/docid/438c6d972.html (last visited Nov. 27, 2015).

48. *See* Regina (European Roma Rights) v. Immigration Officer at Prague Airport, [2005] 2 A.C. 1 (H.L. 2004) (holding that the Refugee Convention does not prohibit the United Kingdom from preventing individuals in a foreign jurisdiction from traveling to the United Kingdom). *But see* G.A. Res 2312 (XXII), 22 U.N. G.A.O.R. Supp. (No. 16) at 81, U.N. Doc. A/6716 (1967) (calling on states to apply non-refoulement to include nonrejection at their frontier).

49. *See* David A. Martin et al., Forced Migration: Law and Policy 592–94 (2007).

50. Refugee Convention, *supra* note 1, arts. 16, 32.

51. *See, e.g.*, Minister of State for Immigration and Ethnic Affairs v. Teoh, (1995) 183 C.L.R. 273, 128 A.L.R. 353 (H.C.A.); Baker v. Canada (Minister of Citizenship and Immigration), [1999] 2 S.C.R. 817 (leading cases from Australia and Canada quashing deportation orders with reference to the Convention on the Rights of the Child, Nov. 20, 1989, 1577 U.N.T.S. 3, *entered into force* Sept. 2, 1990 [hereinafter CRC]).

52. Refugee Convention, *supra* note 1, art. 1(A)(2).

53. *Id.* art. 1(B)(I)(a) (emphasis added).

1967 Protocol removed the Convention's temporal and geographic restrictions,[54] but kept in place the Convention's restrictive definition of refugee, and, like the Convention, declined to entrench a right to asylum.

A further limitation of the Refugee Convention is its neglect of stateless persons. During the Convention's ideologically fueled negotiations, the views of the U.S. and French delegations prevailed over those of the Soviet Union, with the result that only persons fearing persecution would be recognized as refugees and protected under the Convention.[55] Stateless persons as such would not come to be protected by international law post–World War II until 1960, when the Convention Relating to the Status of Stateless Persons came into force.[56] The Stateless Persons Convention and its companion accord, the 1961 Convention on the Reduction of Statelessness,[57] comprise the heart of the current international legal regime on statelessness.[58] These Conventions attempt to give effect to Article 15 of the UDHR, which asserts that "[e]veryone has the right to a nationality" and that "[n]o one shall be arbitrarily deprived of his nationality nor denied the right to change his nationality."[59]

Generally, the Stateless Persons Convention offers protection to the stateless, whereas the 1961 Convention addresses the causes of statelessness. Article 1 of the Stateless Persons Convention defines a stateless person in strictly de jure terms: "the term 'stateless person' means a person who is not considered as a national by any State under the operation of its law."[60] A consequence of this definition is that if someone is legally recognized as a citizen of a state, but cannot obtain her state's protection or assistance or other benefits of citizenship, she falls outside the ambit of the Convention. In other words, the Stateless Persons Convention protects the

54. *See* Protocol, *supra* note 2, arts. 1(2) and 1(3).

55. *See* Statement of Mr. Henkin of the U.S., U.N. ESCOR Ad Hoc Committee on Statelessness and Related Problems, Summary Record of Second Meeting 6, U.N. Doc. E/AV.32/SR.2 (1950) ("The applicability of the draft convention should . . . be limited to refugees. It should not be based upon a confusion between the humanitarian problems of the refugees and the primarily legal problems of stateless persons . . . .").

56. Convention Relating to the Status of Stateless Persons, Sept. 23 1954, 360 U.N.T.S. 177, *entered into force* June 6, 1960) [hereinafter Stateless Persons Convention]. As of December 15, 2014, there were eighty-four state parties.

57. Convention on the Reduction of Statelessness, Aug. 30, 1961, 989 U.N.T.S. 175, *entered into force* Dec. 13, 1975 [hereinafter 1961 Convention]. As of December 15, 2014, there were fifty-five signatories.

58. Other international instruments also address statelessness: the International Covenant on Civil and Political Rights art. 24(3), Dec. 16, 1966, 999 U.N.T.S. 171, *entered into force* Mar. 26, 1976 ("[e]very child has the right to acquire a nationality") [hereinafter ICCPR]; the CRC, *supra* note 41, art. 7 (children "shall have the right from birth to a name, [and] the right to acquire a nationality"); Convention on the Elimination of All Forms of Discrimination Against Women art. 9(1), Dec. 18, 1979, 1249 U.N.T.S. 13, *entered into force* Sept. 3, 1981 ("neither marriage to an alien nor change of nationality by the husband during marriage shall . . . render [a woman] stateless"). In both the ICCPR and the CRC, the relevant right is a "right to acquire a nationality" rather than simply a right to a nationality.

59. UDHR, *supra* note 35, art. 15.

60. Stateless Persons Conventions, *supra* note 56, art. 1.

de jure but not the de facto stateless.[61] Articles 27 and 28 of the Stateless Persons Convention operate as modern-day Nansen passports, requiring states to grant identity papers and travel documents to stateless individuals in their territory.[62] Article 31 prohibits states from expelling "a stateless person lawfully in their territory save on grounds of national security or public order."[63] And Article 32 directs that states shall "as far as possible facilitate the assimilation and naturalization of stateless persons."[64] There are parallel provisions on expulsion, naturalization, and identity and travel documents in the Refugee Convention.[65]

The 1961 Convention on the Reduction of Statelessness requires states to grant nationality to persons born in its territory who would otherwise be stateless (Article 1), and likewise requires states to grant citizenship to anyone born outside its territory to a national of the state, if the person in question would otherwise be stateless (Article 4).[66] The UNHCR helpfully characterizes the intended relationship between the two Conventions on statelessness and state sovereignty: "while States maintain the right to elaborate the content of their nationality laws, they must do so in compliance with international norms relating to nationality, including the principle that statelessness should be avoided."[67] Neither Convention, however, gives adult stateless persons the unqualified "right to a nationality" announced by Article 15 of the UDHR.

More important still, in practice states determine questions of nationality unilaterally, and with nothing like the international scrutiny that attends matters involving refugee law. The Stateless Persons Convention and the 1961 Convention enjoy much more limited ratification than the Refugee Convention and its Protocol,[68] and none of the U.N. human rights treaty bodies is responsible for monitoring compliance with the accords on statelessness.[69] Furthermore, the Stateless Persons Convention did not establish a supervisory body. And although Article 11 of the 1961 Convention did envision a body to which persons claiming the benefit of that Convention could apply, it has never come into existence. The U.N. General Assembly in 1974 designated the UNHCR to play the role

61. *See* Allison Bartlett, *An Endless Quest for a Home: The Gap in Protection Between Stateless Persons and Refugees*, 33 Immigr. & Nat'lity L. Rev. 445, 450 (2012) (discussing the lack of international protection for the de facto stateless).

62. Stateless Persons Convention, *supra* note 56, arts. 27, 29.

63. *Id.* art. 31.

64. *Id.* art. 32.

65. Refugee Convention, *supra* note 1, arts. 28 (identity papers), 29 (travel documents), 32 (expulsion) & 34 (naturalization).

66. 1961 Convention, *supra* note 57, arts. 1, 4.

67. U.N. High Commissioner for Refugees, Introductory Note, Text of the 1961 Convention on the Reduction of Statelessness 3 (2014), http://www.unhcr.org/3bbb286d8.html (last visited Nov. 26, 2015).

68. *See supra* notes 2, 56, 57.

69. *See* David Weissbrodt & Clay Collins, *The Human Rights of Stateless Persons*, 28 Hum. Rts. Q. 245, 272–75 (2006) (noting that U.N. monitoring bodies have only infrequently reprimanded states for failure to comply with international norms related to statelessness).

envisioned by Article 11,[70] but the UNHCR's mandate is limited by the scope of the 1961 Convention, which seeks to prevent the growth of statelessness rather than provide remedies to those who suffer it.

One of the consequences of modern international law's relative neglect of statelessness is a lack of reliable information concerning the magnitude of the problem, including even knowledge of whether the number of de jure stateless persons is growing or declining.[71] Most estimates place that number at 12 million,[72] while statelessness continues to compromise the freedom and human rights of its victims. As Chief Justice Earl Warren once put it, "[c]itizenship is man's basic right, for it is nothing less than the right to have rights. Remove this priceless possession and there remains a stateless person, disgraced and degraded in the eyes of his countrymen."[73] Few states freely admit stateless persons into their territory, leading to innumerable cases of prolonged or indefinite detention as the fate of the stateless detainee is decided.[74] The lack of status and identity documents typical of persons without citizenship limits their rights to employment, medical care, property, education, social benefits, travel, marriage, registering the births of their children, and legal protection.[75] Scores of stateless persons are thereby forced into beggary and unsafe sex work, while others become "victims of bonded labor or human trafficking."[76] The vulnerability of the de facto stateless is especially severe. They fall outside the scope of the Stateless Persons Convention, and infringements of their economic and social human rights resulting from de facto statelessness—for example, rights to housing, healthcare, employment, and social security—place them outside the ambit of the Refugee Convention. As numerous commentators have noted, this constitutes a serious "gap" in the international legal regime pertaining to persons in need of protection, as does, more generally, the differential treatment of stateless persons relative to refugees.[77] In Part IV, we suggest the fiduciary theory supplies a congenial model through which to understand and help close the gap.

70. G.A. Res. 3274 (XXIX), U.N. G.A.O.R., Dec. 10, 1974; G.A. Res. 31/36, U.N. G.A.O.R., Nov. 30, 1976.

71. *See Imagine This: You Have No Country, No Country Will Claim You*, DIPNOTE—U.S. DEPARTMENT OF STATE OFFICIAL BLOG (Sept. 16, 2008), https://blogs.state.gov/stories/2008/09/16/imagine-you-have-no-country-no-country-will-claim-you (last visited Nov. 27, 2015).

72. *See, e.g.*, Jay Milbrandt, *Stateless*, 20 CARDOZO J. INT'L & COMP. L. 75, 76 (2011).

73. Perez v. Brownell, 356 U.S. 44, 64 (1958) (Warren, J., dissenting). Hannah Arendt observes in *Eichmann in Jerusalem* that prior to the "Final Solution," the Nazi regime deliberately rendered all Jews in its territory stateless, making it impossible for other countries to inquire into the fate of the Nazis' victims, and enabling the Nazi regime to confiscate their victims' property. HANNAH ARENDT, EICHMANN IN JERUSALEM 115 (1963).

74. Weissbrodt & Collins, *supra* note 69 at 267–68 (chronicling mass detention of stateless Rohingya in Malaysia, and frequent detention elsewhere of stateless asylum seekers).

75. *See id.* at 266; Milbrandt, *supra* note 72, at 92–95.

76. Millbrandt, *supra* note 72, at 92–93.

77. *See* Bartlett, *supra* note 61 (noting the gap in the quality of protection between refugees and stateless persons). *But see* Niraj Nathwani, *The Purpose of Asylum*, 12 INT'L J. REF. L. 354, 363 (2000) (arguing that stateless persons do not "regularly" face persecution in their home state and therefore "statelessness does not raise the issue of non-refoulement").

In the years since the drafting of the accords on stateless persons and refugees, various human rights instruments have been ratified that include provisions protective of asylum seekers. The Convention Against Torture and Other Cruel, Inhuman, or Degrading Treatment or Punishment (CAT),[78] for example, provides that "[n]o State Party shall expel, return ('refouler') or extradite a person to another State where there are substantial grounds for believing that he would be in danger of being subjected to torture."[79] The inquiry mandated by the CAT does not concern itself with the grounds of persecution if a person faces a serious risk of torture; the test is simply whether there are "substantial grounds for believing" that an individual may be tortured if deported to another state.

The formulations of regional human rights instruments have also provided more robust protection of refugees than the Refugee Convention. Article 12(3) of the African (Banjul) Charter on Human and Peoples' Rights provides that "[e]very individual shall have the right, when persecuted, to seek and obtain asylum in other countries in accordance with the law of those countries and international conventions."[80] The Organization of African Unity's Convention Governing the Specific Aspects of Refugee Problems in Africa explicitly expands on the grounds of the Refugee Convention to include certain general country conditions rather than individualized persecution: that is, "external aggression, occupation, foreign domination, or events seriously disturbing public order."[81] Similarly, the American Declaration of the Rights and Duties of Man declares a "right of asylum" under Article 27, and affirms that "[e]very person has the right, in case of pursuit not resulting from ordinary crimes, to seek and receive asylum in foreign territory, in accordance with the laws of each country and with international agreements."[82] And like the Organization of African Unity Convention (OAU Convention), the influential 1984 Cartagena Declaration on Refugees calls for an expansive conception of refugee that includes those fleeing "generalized violence, foreign aggression, internal conflicts, massive violation of human rights or other circumstances which

78. Convention Against Torture and Other Cruel, Inhuman or Degrading Treatment or Punishment, Dec. 10, 1984, S. Treaty Doc. No. 100–20 (1988), 1465 U.N.T.S. 85 [hereinafter CAT].

79. *Id.* art. 3(1).

80. African (Banjul) Charter on Human and Peoples' Rights art. 12(3), *adopted* June 27, 1981, OAU Doc. CAN/LEG/67/3 rev.5, 21 I.L.M 58 (1982), *entered into force* Oct. 21, 1986 [hereinafter African Charter].

81. Organization of African Unity (OAU), Convention Governing the Specific Aspects of Refugee Problems in Africa art. 1(2), Sept. 10, 1969, 1001 U.N.T.S. 45, *entered into force* June 20, 1974 [hereinafter OAU Convention]; *see also* Andrew E. Shacknove, *Who Is a Refugee?*, 95 Ethics 274, 276 (1985) (defending the OAU definition on the basis that disintegration of public order as well as persecution threatens "the normal bond between the citizen and the state" and therefore is of proper concern to refugee law).

82. American Declaration of the Rights and Duties of Man, O.A.S. Res. XXX, art. 27, adopted by the Ninth International Conference of American States, OEA/Ser.L.V/II.82 doc.6 rev.1 at 17 (1948), *reprinted in* Basic Documents Pertaining to Human Rights in the Inter-American System (1992) [hereinafter American Declaration].

have seriously disturbed public order."[83] Moreover, both the OAU Convention and the Cartagena Declaration insist that any repatriation must be voluntary.[84] In sum, the African Charter and the American Declaration provide a straightforward right of asylum, whereas the OAU Convention and the Cartagena Declaration affirm that dangerous country conditions alone are a sufficient ground of refugee status, and that refugees themselves are the ultimate authorities over the question of their repatriation. The more extensive protections found in these regional agreements and the CAT confirm the widely held view that the Refugee Convention's internal limitations arose from political compromise rather than intrinsic or unavoidable requirements of refugee law.

Among the most important features of the Convention framework is a delegation to states of responsibility for first-instance refugee status determination; that is, determination of whether an individual claimant meets the eligibility and definition requirements for refugee status and is not subject to the exclusionary provisions of Articles 1 and 33.[85] Whereas international offices and commissioners had previously been charged with refugee protection by various international accords, under the Convention it is states themselves who assume this authority. Although the UNHCR sometimes provides refugee protection services directly—so much so that some have called the UNHCR a "surrogate state"[86] when it plays this role—the UNHCR nonetheless operates "under a wholly recommendatory and non-binding legal mandate."[87] State assumption of refugee protection is reflected in Article 13 of the ICCPR, which provides that an "alien lawfully in the territory of a State Party to the present Covenant may be expelled therefrom only in pursuance of a decision reached in accordance with law and shall . . . be allowed to submit the reasons against his expulsion and to have his case reviewed by . . . the competent authority."[88] The Convention, however, is silent on the nature of the procedure states may use to determine refugee status, leading to state practices that "vary widely."[89]

83. Cartagena Declaration on Refugees ¶ 3, Nov. 22, 1984, Annual Report of the Inter-American Commission on Human Rights, OAS Doc. OEA/Ser.L/V/II.66/doc.10, rev. 1, at 190–93 (1984–1985) [hereinafter Cartagena Declaration].

84. *Id.* ¶ 12; OAU Convention, *supra* note 81, art. 5.

85. Hathaway, *supra* note 11, at 166–68 (citing inter alia the Refuge Convention's *travaux préparatoires* and the UNHCR's lack of authority to conduct independent refugee status determinations).

86. *See, e.g.*, Amy Slaughter & Jeff Crisp, *A Surrogate State? The Role of UNHCR in Protracted Refugee Situations*, *in* UNITED NATIONS, PROTRACTED REFUGEE SITUATIONS 123 (Gil Loescher et al. eds., 2008) (characterizing the United Nations as a "surrogate state" when it carries out refugee protection services); Michael Kagan, *The UN "Surrogate State" and the Foundation of Refugee Policy in the Middle East*, 18 U.C. DAVIS J. INT'L L. & POL'Y 307, 309 (2012) (defending the "UN surrogate state" in the Middle East as sometimes offering "a more viable political foundation for refugee protection than conventional notions of state responsibility.")

87. Jack I. Garvey, *Toward a Reformulation of IRL*, 26 HARV. INT'L L.J. 483, 488 (1985).

88. ICCPR, *supra* note 58, art. 13.

89. Patricia Hyndman, *Refugees Under International Law with a Reference to the Concept of Asylum*, 60 AUSTL. L.J. 148, 151 (1986).

We turn now to consider three leading theoretical approaches to refugee law. All have significant drawbacks. They either remain within the shadow of the Westphalian conception of sovereignty and therefore can produce only an unstable compromise with it, or they rely on a commitment to humanitarianism that is incapable of explaining the legal significance of claims to asylum.

III. HUMANITARIANISM, HUMAN RIGHTS, AND TERRITORY

The main theories of refugee law draw on humanitarianism, the human rights of vulnerable individuals, or the systemic effects of international law's exhaustive division of the world's limited surface into territorially sovereign self-governing states.[90] Many scholars combine these elements,[91] but for the sake of clarity we focus on a selection of theories in which one or the other of these elements plays an especially salient role.

The Preamble of the Refugee Convention explicitly recognizes "the social and humanitarian nature of the problem of refugees."[92] Even staunch advocates of state rights to unilateral border control tend to make an exception for refugees on humanitarian grounds. Donald Galloway, for example, criticizes Joseph Carens's argument for open borders, but insists that liberal states must let in refugees because everyone owes others duties of mutual aid when the cost is not "excessive."[93] Likewise, Michael Walzer famously defends closed borders, but allows that the just state must take in refugees—if doing so does not undermine a community's shared culture—on the basis of a humanitarian duty of mutual aid.[94] Catherine Dauvergne argues persuasively that there is a "liberal consensus over the mutual-aid principle," and that one of the consequences of this consensus is that "humanitarian scenarios are the core of theoretical concern with migration."[95]

One of the most careful theorists in this liberal school is Matthew Gibney. He defends a "principle of humanitarianism" akin to Galloway's idea of mutual aid in order to reconcile "the competing claims of citizens and refugees" with the "real-world forces"

90. Joseph Carens identifies three kinds of (nonexclusive) moral justifications capable of supporting a duty to accept refugees: the receiving state has played some causal role in producing the relevant refugee claimants (e.g., the United States in Vietnam), humanitarian concerns, and "the responsibility to make some provision for the foreseeable failures of [the modern state system]." Joseph H. Carens, The Ethics of Immigration 195–96 (2013). The latter two justifications overlap with the leading accounts from the legal literature discussed in the text below.

91. *See, e.g.*, Matthias Kumm, *Constitutionalism and the Cosmopolitan State* (NYU Public Law and Legal Theory Working Paper No. 423, 2013) (arguing that territorial sovereignty is subject to a Lockean proviso and must yield if an asylum seeker does not have access to another territory where her human rights would not be violated).

92. Refugee Convention, *supra* note 1, pmbl.

93. Donald Galloway, *Liberalism, Globalism, and Immigration*, 18 Queen's L.J. 266, 287 (1993).

94. Michael Walzer, Spheres of Justice: A Defense of Pluralism and Equality 48–51 (1983).

95. Catherine Dauvergne, *Amorality and Humanitarianism in Immigration Law*, 37 Osgoode Hall L.J. 597, 616 (1999).

that are likely to hinder the adoption of more just refugee policies.[96] Gibney suggests that an ideal state would strive "to create a national community consistent with liberal egalitarian principles" but would also take seriously the idea the liberal principles "can only be maintained in communities where relations among citizens are characterized by solidarity and trust."[97] Under ideal theory, he claims, states would "accept as many refugees as they can without undermining the provision of collective or public goods among their members."[98] Nonetheless, refugee policy, Gibney contends, must contend with unavoidable "real-world forces" such as the possibility of political backlash. For policy to be feasible under real-world or non-ideal conditions, it must call on non-ideal rather than ideal theory. Under Gibney's preferred non-ideal theory, states can reasonably be expected to comply with a less-demanding principle of humanitarianism, as the burden it places on the receiving state, unlike ideal theory, is "relatively minor."[99]

Gibney takes it as a virtue of his theory that "humanitarianism does not explicitly specify the kinds of assistance morally required to be given to strangers in need," and that this indeterminacy means that states can pursue alternatives to resettlement.[100] He rightly asserts that "there is nothing inherent in humanitarianism that justifies privileging the claims of needy people on the grounds of proximity . . . it is owed to all human beings on the basis of need alone."[101] And so he draws the logical conclusion that states can opt out of taking in refugees so long as they do their humanitarian duty to outsiders in some other way.

Whatever the merits of Gibney's account as a moral-political theory directed toward questions of global justice and humanitarian relief, as a *legal* theory that purports to explain a right to asylum or even the weaker duty of non-refoulement, it is unconvincing. The fundamental problem is that law tracks rights rather than need. If a claimant has a *right* to refuge or non-refoulement, then in principle she and she alone may waive it. But if the asylum seeker has merely a need to find refuge or avoid refoulement—a need that triggers only an indeterminate humanitarian duty—and the receiving state may satisfy its humanitarian duty in another way, then she enjoys no legal guarantee of refuge or non-refoulement. The needful but right-barren claimant would be at the mercy of humanitarian policy decisions she has no legal standing to challenge. To put the point more starkly still, receiving states might at any time decide they could do more to alleviate need in some way other than by taking in refugees, and simply abolish the practice with no compromise to the humanitarian principle. While humanitarianism may motivate recalcitrant states to do their refugee-law duty, its thoroughgoing indeterminacy renders it incapable of explaining or justifying the idea that they have a legal duty to refugees at all.[102]

96. Matthew J. Gibney, *Liberal Democratic States and Responsibilities to Refugees*, 93 Am. Pol. Sci. Rev. 169, 169–70 (1999).

97. *Id.* at 173–74.

98. *Id.* at 174.

99. *Id.* at 178.

100. *Id.*

101. *Id.* at 179.

102. For extended discussion of the ways in which liberal humanitarianism resists justice claims, see Dauvergne, *supra* note 95.

Gibney's humanitarianism, without more, subverts rather than supports the right of a refugee to claim asylum or non-refoulement.

Another familiar approach assimilates IRL to international human rights law (IHRL). This view is also reflected in the Convention's Preamble, which cites the UDHR and affirms "its profound concern" that refugees enjoy "the widest possible exercise of these fundamental rights and freedoms."[103] As noted above, Article 14(1) of the UDHR foreshadowed the duty of non-refoulement of the Refugee Convention, and refugee protections are found in the CAT and various other human rights instruments. Commentators have long observed that the "refugee protection regime . . . has its origins in general principles of human rights."[104] Others still, such as G.J.L. Coles, former Senior Legal Adviser to the UNHCR, argue for a "human rights approach" that locates the fundamental problem in the adverse conditions of the individual's home country, conditions that compel her to flee and thereby deny her freedom of movement—that is, she is not free to remain in or return to her country of origin.[105] Coles's "basic solution" is to prevent or remedy the refugee-producing conditions within home states, though he recognizes the need for a fallback or "contingent" solution involving external settlement when the "basic solution" is unavailable.[106] Challenging the refugee literature's focus on admission to a host country, Coles insists that "[t]he refugee issue should be presented, therefore, as basically *not* one of admission to a receiving country . . . but as essentially that of the adverse conditions within the country of origin which are producing the trans-frontier movement."[107]

Building on Coles's work, James Hathaway and Alexander Neve boldly claim that "refugee protection is not about immigration" but rather "is intended to be a situation-specific human rights remedy: when the violence or other human rights abuse that induced flight comes to an end, so does refugee status."[108] Hathaway and Neve defend an international regime of temporary protection and equitable sharing of the refugee-receiving burden, but stress that because it is a human rights regime, it

103. Refugee Convention, *supra* note 1, pmbl.

104. E. Feller, *International Refugee Protection 50 Years On: The Protection Challenges of the Past, Present and Future,* 83 Int'l Rev. Red Cross 581, 582 (2001); *see also* Alice Edwards, *Human Rights, Refugees, and the Right "to Enjoy" Asylum,* 17 Int'l J. Refugee L. 293 (2005); Brian Gorlick, *Human Rights and Refugees: Enhancing Protection Through International Human Rights Law,* 69 Nordic J. Int'l L. 117 (2000).

105. G.J.L. Coles, *The Human Rights Approach to the Solution of the Refugee Problem: A Theoretical and Practical Enquiry, in* Human Rights and the Protection of Refugees Under International Law 195, 197 (Alan Nash ed., 1988).

106. *Id.* at 201.

107. G.J.L. Coles, Placing the Refugee Issues on the New International Agenda (unpublished manuscript, 1990), *as cited in* James L. Hathaway, *Reconceiving Refugee Law as Human Rights Protection,* 4 J. Refugee Studs. 113, 117 (1991).

108. James C. Hathaway & R. Alexander Neve, *Making IRL Relevant Again: A Proposal for Collectivized and Solution-Oriented Protection,* 10 Harv. Hum. Rts. J. 115, 117 (1997); *see also* Hathaway, *supra* note 107; James C. Hathaway, *Why Refugee Law Still Matters,* 8 Melb. J. Int'l L. 89 (2007) (reaffirming his and Neve's collectivized solution).

cannot compromise "the critical right to seek asylum."[109] Like Gibney, their project is intended to respond to the reluctance of Northern states to accept non-European refugees in the post–Cold War era, and the proliferation of interdiction practices intended to thwart refugees from arriving at their borders. Because the Hathaway/Neve proposal is framed by human rights, it is not susceptible to the criticism that in principle states could meet their cosmopolitan duties while overtly disregarding the international legal rights of refugees.

Hathaway and Neve propose a multilateral system to be supervised by "a revamped UNHCR" in which refugees have prompt access to temporary protection.[110] That protection is intended to end, however, with "the repatriation of most, if not all, refugees."[111] They argue that because "refugees are admitted on the basis of necessity, it cannot legitimately be asserted that they should routinely be entitled to stay in the host state once the harm in their own country has been brought to an end."[112] Under the burden-sharing component of their proposal, "[e]ach participating state would contribute by providing temporary protection, receiving refugees whose special needs make temporary protection inappropriate, resettling those refugees who cannot return home at the end of the period of temporary protection, funding the protection system, or through a combination of these roles."[113] States from the global north and south "will cooperate in a manner akin to participation in an insurance scheme" by forming "interest-convergence groups" with "[a]greements in place that authorize the asylum seeker to be sent to a safe country in his or her region for refugee status determination."[114] Hathaway and Neve acknowledge that the result of their proposal "would clearly be an increase in the number of refugees protected in the South,"[115] as northern countries would recognize that it is in their self-interest to pay southern states to provide temporary protection and resettlement in order to meet northern policy goals presently sought through costly non-entrée measures.

Critics of the Hathway/Neve proposal question it on many fronts. Deborah Anker, Joan Fitzpatrick, and Andrew Shacknove point to a lack of empirical evidence to suggest that regional and collectivized burden-sharing would better protect refugees than the present universal and decentralized system.[116] They doubt that northern states will divert to southern countries savings realized from reduced refugee status determination procedures or diminished non-entrée policies.[117] They

109. Hathaway & Neve, *supra* note 108, at 118. For a similar burden-sharing proposal that envisions creating a market with refugee quotas traded within groups of states, see Peter H. Shuck, *Refugee Burden-Sharing: A Modest Proposal*, 22 Yale J. Int'l L. 243 (1997).

110. Hathaway & Neve, *supra* note 108, at 103.

111. *Id.* at 140.

112. *Id.*

113. *Id.* at 145.

114. *Id.* at 143, 146.

115. *Id.* at 147.

116. Deborah Anker, Joan Fitzpatrick & Andrew Shacknove, *Crisis and Cure: A Reply to Hathway/Neve and Shuck*, 11 Harv. Hum. Rts. J. 295, 300–01 (1998).

117. *Id.* at 301–02.

point out that it is "the exception rather than the rule that the causes of flight can be resolved within the approximately five-year period that defines the outer bounds of a temporary protection system meeting basic standards of humane treatment."[118] They also observe that the Hathway/Neve proposal would largely remove asylum seekers' access to courts, while at the same time their "commodification" would make involuntary transferees to temporary protection areas in the south vulnerable to unsafe refoulement and poor conditions, especially if northern states failed to deliver the financial support promised under a burden-sharing agreement.[119]

Gregor Noll credibly suggests that the burden-sharing regime envisioned by Hathaway and Neve would impair the refugee's right to leave any country. States could be convinced to pool the resources otherwise dedicated to non-entrée policies and refugee status determination, Noll claims, only if they were confident that they would not have to contend with spontaneous arrivals in the way they do now; if this were not the case, states would be saddled with the costs of an ambitious collective scheme *and* those associated with spontaneous arrivals and refugee claims.[120] As a consequence, once the assignment of responsibility for temporary protection is made—for example, by transferring a refugee who arrived at a northern country to a target country in the south—migration "would need to be subjected to complete control."[121] If the assigned refugee attempted to leave the target country and enter another country participating in the burden-sharing regime, this other country would have to return her to the target country in order to maintain the integrity of the regime and its resource allocation compromise. Alternatively, the target state itself could preserve the regime's integrity by preventing the refugee from leaving in the first place. In both cases, the refugee's right under international law to leave any country in which she finds herself would be infringed or at least significantly restricted.[122]

In addition to the practical and legal concerns raised by Hathaway and Neve's critics, there is a deeper theoretical problem with their proposal, at least to the extent it purports to be a human rights account and justification of refugee law and not merely "a radical reconfiguration of the international refugee regime."[123] Importantly, they do not explain why a non-signatory to the Refugee Convention might owe a legal duty of non-refoulement to asylum seekers based on customary international law or jus cogens—plausible and universalizing bases of the duty of non-refoulement we discuss in Part IV—nor why a recalcitrant state might have a legal duty to participate in a

118. *Id.* at 302.

119. *Id.* at 305–06; *see also* Carens, *supra* note 90 at 216–17 (affirming that "any attempt to separate the place where a person files a claim for asylum from the place where she receives asylum is likely in practice to undermine existing protections for refugees without delivering the promised benefits").

120. Gregor Noll, *Why Refugees Still Matter: A Response to James Hathaway*, 8 Melb. J. Int'l L. 536, 538 (2007).

121. *Id.*

122. *Id.* at 540 (listing provisions from the UDHR (Article 13(2)), ICCPR (Article 12), and other instruments that enshrine the right to leave).

123. Anker et al., *supra* note 116, at 295.

burden-sharing regime. They do not offer such explanations as their account of IRL is wholly conventional, derived as it is from the Convention framework.[124] Their approach could be explained as a response to "real-world forces," as countries unwilling to ratify the Convention and its Protocol are unlikely to comply with a duty of non-refoulement except to the extent it is in their interest to do so. Hathaway elsewhere characterizes refugee law itself as essentially a state-centric "means of reconciling the commitment of states to discretionary control over immigration to the reality of coerced international movements of persons between states."[125] But from the standpoint of articulating a human rights justification of refugee law, these practical considerations are beside the point. If the ultimate justification of refugee law is that it provides an international remedy for human rights abuses when a domestic remedy is unavailable, and if at least some human rights are legally salient independently of treaties or conventions, then it is doubtful that the proper reach of refugee law is limited to the signatories of the Refugee Convention, or that IRL's content is necessarily limited to the Convention's requirements, much less a minimalist interpretation of those requirements.

Hathaway and Neve are driven to a conventional account of refugee law because, like Gibney, they want their proposal to be amenable to "the perceived self-interest of states."[126] To this end, they take on board a Westphalian conception of sovereignty under which the primary (if not sole) source of international legal obligation is found in conventions ratified by sovereign states, including the Refugee Convention. Arguably, their commitment to this exclusionary conception of sovereignty leads them to conclude that refugees "admitted on the basis of necessity" should not "routinely be entitled to stay in the host state," as on the Westphalian conception the grant of permanent residence to a foreign national lies within the unfettered prerogative of the state.[127] Although Hathaway and Neve purport to advance a human rights approach to refugee protection, the conventional and Westphalian aspects of their theory leave it ill-equipped to account for the customary and peremptory nature of the duty of non-refoulement.

As for a right to asylum with the option of permanent settlement in the host state, Hathaway strenuously denies that such a right exists—"refugee law does not require states to admit refugees as permanent immigrants"—and he decries the contrary view as "erroneously insisting on an absolutist linkage between refugee status and a right of permanent immigration."[128] His critics reply that the "fundamental premise

124. There is no reference to customary international law or jus cogens in any of the Hathaway papers cited in this chapter.

125. Hathaway, *supra* note 107, at 114.

126. *Id.*

127. The basis on which an individual is admitted to a state may have nothing to do with the considerations that are relevant to assessing whether she is entitled to stay. An individual may enter on a tourist visa, stay for a number of years, and in that time marry a citizen. International law protects family life and would "routinely" protect her against deportation. *See* Dalia v. France, App. No. 26102/95, 33 Eur. H.R. Rep. 625, 641–46 (1999) (Eur. Ct. H.R.) (judgment of Feb. 19, 1998) (concluding that under Article 8 of the European Convention on Human Rights a deportation must pass a test of proportionality, taking into account any interference the deportation would have on the alien's family life).

128. Hathaway, *supra* note 108, at 96, *citing* Anker et al., *supra* note 116, at 302–03.

of the Refugee Convention . . . was a right to personal protection and the chance to rebuild a life with dignity,"[129] and that the duty of non-refoulement must be interpreted in light of the paucity of cases in which a dangerous home country becomes safe for return within a reasonable period of time. In Part IV, we suggest that the OAU Convention offers a congenial halfway house between an "absolutist . . . right of permanent immigration" and no right whatsoever to asylum with the possibility of permanent status.

A non-minimalist interpretation of the duty of non-refoulement is further suggested by the prevailing practice in northern countries of giving successful asylum seekers the option of permanent residence.[130] A plausible explanation of this practice is that it is a generous way to comply with the Refugee Convention's duty of non-*refoulement*, a mode of compliance that ultimately reflects a human rights-based duty to provide refuge to necessitous claimants. This explanation of the practice implicitly acknowledges a feature of non-voluntary or "mandated repatriation" that Hathaway and Neve play down: mandated repatriation of asylum seekers is always coercive repatriation; it always depends on the state's use or threat of violence.[131] A right to remain avoids subjecting the successful asylum seeker to an invasively coercive deportation regime, a form of subjection that remains invasive and coercive even if the danger in the home country has subsided within a reasonable period of time.[132] Although the moral cost of deportation cannot by itself supply a right to remain without eviscerating the general right to exclude presently enjoyed by states at international law, it can inform a liberal interpretation of the duty of non-refoulement, as the duty is already an exception to the general right to exclude. Although the Refugee Convention does not expressly enshrine a right to asylum,[133]

129. Anker et al., *supra* note 116, at 306.

130. *See* Hathaway & Neve, *supra* note 108, at 119 ("Northern states, in law or in practice, have historically afforded refugees permanent status."). In the United States, a refugee must be returned to the custody of the Department of Homeland Security for inspection and examination, and upon a successful inspection and examination, this person is to be regarded as lawfully admitted for permanent residence under the Immigration and Nationality Act, 8 U.S.C. 1159 § 209. In the European Union, third-country nationals to whom international protection has been granted who have resided legally and continuously in a member-state for five years will receive long-term resident status under Council Directive 2003/109/EC of 25 November 2003 concerning the status of third-country nationals who are long-term residents, OJ L 16, 23.1.2004, at 44, arts. 4(1) & 4(1a.).

131. Hathaway & Neve, *supra* note 107, at 186 (calling for "mandated repatriation" where voluntary repatriation to a newly stable country fails, but insisting that coercive repatriation is to be "minimally violative of the dignity of the returnees").

132. As noted above, one of us has argued elsewhere that states owe a duty of justification to any peaceful migrant they wish to exclude from their territory. *See* Fox-Decent, *supra* note 4. In this chapter, we assume the standard view that states have a general right to exclude foreign nationals other than persons in need of protection, a view that nonetheless can be qualified to grant successful refugee claimants a right to remain.

133. To ground the right to remain in the Convention would require something like a "living tree" approach under which the original meaning intended by a text's framers is liable to displacement over time, taking into consideration the underlying purpose of the positive law, changing interpretive values, and the way in which the relevant text is interpreted and applied

the moral cost of deportation combines with the northern practice of permanent settlement to suggest that the non-derogable human right to non-refoulement entails a (non-absolute) right to asylum with the option of permanent residence.

Before we turn to our positive view, however, one last theoretical approach to refugee protection deserves attention. Under this approach, the earth's surface is analogized to a state of nature over which multiple states have claimed exclusionary property-like rights to discrete territories that collectively encompass the entirety of earth's habitable surface. Kant adopted such a view, affirming that as a matter of cosmopolitan right states owe a duty of hospitality to foreign nationals; outsiders are entitled to enter a state's territory for a "visitation" by virtue of "their common possession of the surface of the earth."[134] Kant thought that generally an outsider cannot demand to be a permanent "guest," but the state's right to exclude the foreigner could not cause "his death."[135] Arthur Ripstein interprets Kant to be claiming that the state's right to exclude has an "internal limit": the would-be entrant must have somewhere safe to go.[136] If you were an outsider seeking entry and had nowhere else to go, an unqualified right to exclude would make your very existence "subject to the choice of another," and thus, Ripstein says, "the officials have to let you stay, simply in your capacity as a citizen of the world."[137]

In a subsequent footnote Ripstein elaborates on Kant's approach, and defends safe third country provisions as "neither irrational nor illusory."[138] The implication is that the refugee generally has a right of non-refoulement, but he acquires a right to remain only if remaining in the host state is the only way to respect his right of non-refoulement; that is, there is nowhere else at all the receiving state can send him without putting him in harm's way. On Ripstein's construal of Kant, the host state would be entitled to remove asylum seekers to safe third countries for refugee status determination, or to other states participating in burden-sharing arrangements, as the asylum seeker's sole claim to enter the receiving state is that he has nowhere else to go. In principle, and as with the Hathaway/Neve proposal, refugee claimants could be sent to distant holding areas that, within their confines, minimally

in practice. *See* Henrietta Muir Edwards & Others v. The Attorney General of Canada, [1929] UKPC 86, [1930] A.C. 124 (Oct. 18, 1929), P.C. (on appeal from Canada), per Viscount Sankey (affirming that "persons" within the British North America Act include women, in part because the Act "planted in Canada is a living tree capable of growth and expansion within its natural limits"). We cannot enter the debate between originalists or textualists and their rivals here, but note in passing that the fiduciary theory of IRL developed in Part IV would support the purposive interpretation of the duty of non-refoulement suggested above.

134. Immanuel Kant, Perpetual Peace: A Philosophical Sketch 138 (Campbell Smith transl., 1917) (1795).

135. *Id.* at 137.

136. Arthur Ripstein, Force and Freedom: Kant's Legal and Political Philosophy 298 (2009). For a Lockean view to much the same effect, see Kumm, *supra* note 91.

137. Ripstein, *supra* note 136, at 298; *see also* Garrett W. Brown, *The Laws of Hospitality, Asylum Seekers and Cosmopolitan Right: A Kantian Response to Jacques Derrida*, 9 Eur. J. Pol. Theory 308, 317 (2010) (arguing inter alia that Kant made asylum available for persons fleeing a wide range of "inhospitable conduct").

138. Ripstein, *supra* note 136, at 298 n.48.

respected the bulk of the refugees' human rights. But because every state would be entitled to remove asylum seekers to such areas, either on their initial arrival for status determination or after subsequent migration, the asylum seekers' right of exit, as Noll foresees, could become illusory; protection could become imprisonment. Indeed, as any decision by a refugee to leave a temporary protection area would be wholly dominated by the right of states to send the refugee back, the refugee has no genuine right of exit. Interned refugees would find themselves much like serfs of the Middle Ages who, as Kant claimed, were mere "possessors only of what is the property of another, and therefore deprived of all freedom."[139] With no right of exit, propertyless serfs were subject to a regime in which rather than owning land themselves, the land's master, in a sense, owned them.[140]

This is essentially what one finds in the refugee camps along the Thai border that have held roughly 120,000 Burmese for more than thirty years, and in which human rights abuses are endemic.[141] The UNHCR estimates that over 6.4 million persons were in protracted refugee situations of this kind at the end of 2012.[142] The practitioners' term of art used to describe these situations is "refugee warehousing."[143] This is ultimately the danger posed by cutting down the right of refuge to a minimal right of non-refoulement. Kant's account of refugee law, on Ripstein's interpretation, is problematic because it is consistent with the universalization of refugee warehousing.

There are, nonetheless, important insights to be gleaned from both the human rights and territorial approaches to IRL. The human rights approach draws our attention to the underlying problem refugee law aims to address, whereas accounts focusing on the systemic effects of states' exclusionary claims to territory make explicit the possibility of an asylum seeker finding himself with nowhere to exist lawfully without the protection of refugee law. We draw on these insights as we elaborate now a fiduciary account of IRL.

IV. A FIDUCIARY INTERPRETATION OF INTERNATIONAL REFUGEE LAW

As signaled in the introduction to this chapter, our theory of refugee law is structured by the state's occupation of dual but complementary fiduciary positions. One is local, the other global. The local position is the trustee-like role and status of the state we

139. Immanuel Kant, The Metaphysics of Morals [6:324] 134 (Mary Gregor transl., 1991) (1797). We thank Jacob Weinrib for pointing us to this passage.

140. Of course, this is generally true of persons seeking to migrate for any reason, given the right of states to exclude outsiders, but the "serfdom" of interned refugees is particularly pronounced, as they are barred from appealing to the threat of persecution to exit internment in order to start a new life in a new place.

141. For insightful discussion of this and other protracted refugee situations, see Anna Lise Purkey, A Dignified Life: Legal Empowerment in Protracted Refugee Situations (DCL dissertation, McGill Faculty of Law, 2015).

142. UN High Commissioner for Refugees, UNHCR Statistical Yearbook 2012, at 23 (12th ed. 2013), http://www.unhcr.org/52a7213b9.html (last visited Nov. 26, 2015).

143. *See* Merrill Smith, *Warehousing Refugees: A Denial of Rights, a Waste of Humanity, in* U.S. Committee for Refugees, World Refugee Survey 38 (2004).

have elaborated throughout this book; that is, the state as a public fiduciary entrusted and authorized by international law with sovereignty over a given territory and the people subject to its jurisdiction. As discussed in the last chapter, "people" in this context includes foreign nationals as well as citizens, and so asylum seekers appearing at the border are beneficiaries of the legal order governed by the receiving state.

The second fiduciary position occupied by the receiving state—the "global" position—is that of a joint fiduciary of the earth's surface, a position of joint stewardship held with all other states on behalf of humanity.[144] Eyal Benvenisti characterizes the state in this position as "a trustee of humanity,"[145] with the result that the state is under an "obligation not to deny entry to migrants and refugees without taking into account the asylum seekers' individual concerns and without at least providing justification for their exclusion."[146] The argument for joint stewardship proceeds from the normative consequences of a particular kind of spillover effect produced by states' possession of sovereign power. An indispensable cosmopolitan premise of this argument is that states are not entitled to set policies unilaterally that have spillover effects prejudicial to the rights or justice claims of foreign nationals, such as policies related to carbon emissions or the development of a dangerous nuclear facility near the border of a neighboring state.[147] As Matthias Kumm rightly asserts, international law must settle these contested matters because "any claim by one state to be able to resolve these issues authoritatively and unilaterally amounts to a form of domination."[148] When national exercises of sovereign power produce

144. *See* Evan Fox-Decent, *From Fiduciary States to Joint Trusteeship of the Atmosphere: The Right to a Healthy Environment Through a Fiduciary Prism*, *in* FIDUCIARY DUTY AND THE ATMOSPHERIC TRUST 253 (Ken Coghill, Charles Sampford & Tim Smith eds., 2012) (arguing that states are joint trustees of the atmosphere on behalf of humanity).

145. Eyal Benvenisti, *Sovereigns as Trustees of Humanity: On the Accountability of States to Foreign Stakeholders*, 107 AM. J. INT'L L. 295 (2013).

146. *Id.* at 311. We owe a considerable debt to Benvenisti, who in the article cited here draws on historical and contemporary sources of international law to argue that in a globalized and interdependent world such as ours, it is plausible and desirable to view sovereigns as trustees of humanity. However, Benvenisti stops short of characterizing international legal order itself as fiduciary in nature, and he declines to offer a general account of trusteeship from which the trustee-like position of states might be inferred. Consequently, his account of state duties to foreign nationals, which trades largely on an extension of the state's human-rights obligations so as to encompass foreign nationals, is hard-pressed to explain why we should think that such duties arise from the state's position as a trustee of humanity, rather than from merely the personhood of foreign nationals as bearers of human rights, as the orthodox view of human rights would have it. In Chapters 3 and 4 we tried to fill this gap. In Chapter 8 we argue that international legal order itself is fiduciary in nature, and therefore one cannot explain state duties to foreign nationals without taking into account the fiduciary constitution of international legal order.

147. *See* Kumm, *supra* note 91, at 18; Matthias Kumm, *The Cosmopolitan Turn in Constitutionalism: On the Relationship Between Constitutionalism in and Beyond the State*, *in* RULING THE WORLD? INTERNATIONAL LAW, GLOBAL GOVERNANCE, CONSTITUTIONALISM 258 (J.L. Dunoff & J.P. Trachtman eds., 2009); Matthias Kumm, *The Cosmopolitan Turn in Constitutionalism: An Integrated Conception of Public Law*, 20 IND. J. GLOBAL LEGAL STUDS. 605 (2013).

148. Kumm, *supra* note 91, at 9.

"justice-sensitive externalities" touching foreign nationals, national sovereigns must resort to international law, for "[i]t is the point and purpose of international law to authoritatively resolve these concerns by way of a procedure that involves the fair participation of relevantly effected stakeholders."[149] In sum, the sovereignty to govern domestically enjoyed by fiduciary states is properly subject to international law whenever its exercise would create justice-sensitive spillover effects affecting extraterritorial non-nationals. In cases that affect humanity generally, such as the regulation of carbon emissions, the "people" subject to the local state's sovereign power is humanity at large. And so the class of beneficiaries in this iteration of the state-subject fiduciary relationship is humanity itself.

The next step in this argument is to apply the spillover principle sketched above to the case of borders and the right to exclude that comes with territorial sovereignty. Kumm observes that borders present a "structural" justice-sensitive externality, one that arises as a consequence of international law's organization of the world into multiple territorially sovereign states.[150] As noted above, the central insight from the territorial model of refugee law is that worldwide territorial sovereignty raises the specter of a refugee with no place to exist lawfully. At the limit, in a case where the refugee was forcibly removed from her home state and denied a right of asylum by all others, the territorial jurisdiction exercised over the earth's surface by sovereign states would convert her very physical existence into an illegality: her body occupies space and must exist somewhere, but she herself (on the present assumption) has no right to be anywhere. And so her mere and unavoidable presence anywhere would constitute a permanent trespass.[151] Benvenisti compellingly argues that "the dramatic consequences of states universally acting to exclude entry" must be addressed "with certain limitations on the sovereign's right to exclude."[152]

The "dramatic consequences" to which Benvenisti refers are structural spillover effects arising from international law's distribution of territorial sovereignty to states. Under the fiduciary model, that distribution can be legitimate only if the fiduciary principle's authorization of territorial sovereignty through international law can be understood to be made on behalf of every person subject to it (the fiduciary theory's criterion of legitimacy), which is to say, on behalf of humanity.[153] For this to be possible, international law must legally guarantee that every individual, come what may, has a fair opportunity to pursue his or her life *somewhere* in a regime of secure and equal freedom. Ordinarily, this opportunity is provided in the first instance through the state's grant of citizenship to individuals either born within its territory (*jus soli*) or born to citizens of the state (*jus sanguinis*). Under international

149. *Id.* at 9–10.

150. Id. at 15–17.

151. *See* Ripstein, *supra* note 136, at 279–80 (arguing that if all land were privately held and the landless were denied permission to be anywhere, "they would do wrong simply by being wherever they happened to be").

152. Benvenisti, *supra* note 145, at 311.

153. *Cf.* Patrick Macklem, *What Is International Human Rights Law? Three Applications of a Distributive Account*, 52 McGill L.J. 575 (2007) (arguing that international human rights law is best conceptualized as a remedial response to the injustices created by international law's distribution of sovereignty to states).

law, states must provide at least one of these paths to citizenship.[154] But if an individual is forced to flee or is stripped of citizenship and deported from her home state, international law must step in to provide the refugee somewhere she can live in secure and equal freedom. It is only with this guarantee of surrogate protection in place that all individuals can be regarded as equal beneficiaries of international legal order. Without the availability of surrogate protection, international law could not be said to guarantee to every individual, come what may, a fair opportunity to live a life of dignity somewhere. International law would lose its clam to universal legal authority with respect to territory—as well as its legitimacy—because it could not be said to authorize territorial sovereignty on behalf of every person subject to it; refugees and the stateless would be excluded.[155]

A plausible way to avoid this result is to conceive of states, at the global level, as joint fiduciaries of the earth's surface on behalf of humanity. Under this conception, the fiduciary principle authorizes joint stewardship of the earth's surface, but requires as a condition of its authorization that states participate in a collective regime of surrogate protection in the service of exiled outsiders. Significantly, IRL conceives of itself as a regime of surrogate protection,[156] and so the fiduciary theory supplies an account of refugee law's self-understanding. International law supplies the legal framework for a regime of surrogate protection by carving out an exception to territorial sovereignty in favor of refugees. The fiduciary model explains the refugee's standing to make a claim on this exception by positing states as joint fiduciaries of the earth's surface on behalf of humanity, and in particular on behalf of asylum seekers entitled to resort to surrogate protection. Properly understood, the fiduciary theory in this context does not place limits on otherwise unbridled sovereign power, as this approach asserts that there simply is no de jure sovereign power to unilaterally exclude asylum seekers. Rather, the fiduciary model reconceives sovereignty in a manner that makes its territorial dimension consistent with the universal entitlement of every member of humanity to have his or her physical existence not treated as a wrong.

In addition to its accounts of the refugee's special standing and IRL's self-understanding, the fiduciary model explains central doctrinal features of refugee law. First, there is an emerging consensus that the duty of non-refoulement found in the Refugee Convention is a customary and peremptory norm of international law, binding all states whether or not they have ratified the Convention. The duty is widely recognized as a customary norm because states generally, at least since

154. *See supra* notes 56–64.

155. Carens proposes the following criterion to test the moral legitimacy of any approach to refugees: "What would this [approach] have meant if we had applied it to Jews fleeing Hitler [in the late 1930s]?" Carens, *supra* note 90 at 194. Carens notes that at the 1938 Evian Conference discussed at note 24 of this chapter, over thirty states participated, but only the Dominican Republic agreed to take in more refugees. *Id.* at 192. As will become evident, the fiduciary account would have required states to take in persecuted Jews in the late 1930s, and offer them the possibility of permanent residence and eventually citizenship.

156. *See, e.g.*, Canada (Attorney General) v. Ward [1993] 2 SCR 689, at 709 (referring to the international refugee regime as one of "surrogate or substitute protection") (citing James Hathaway, The Law of Refugee Status 135 (1991)) [hereinafter *Ward*].

the end of the Cold War, do not forcibly repatriate refugees, and they do not do so in part because they believe themselves to be under a legal obligation not to do so.[157] Acknowledgement of the jus cogens status of the duty can be found in various Conclusions of the Executive Committee of the UNHCR,[158] the Cartagena Declaration,[159] and the work of publicists.[160]

The fiduciary theory explains the customary nature of the norm by reference to the local and global fiduciary positions of states vis-à-vis asylum seekers. As all states occupy these fiduciary positions, all are subject to a duty of non-refoulement regardless of whether they have ratified the Convention. As noted already, it is only through subjection to such a duty that states could be understood to assert exhaustive territorial sovereignty on behalf of everyone subject to it, which is to say, on behalf of humanity. With this universal duty in place, it becomes possible for international law to confer on states authoritative and collective territorial sovereignty over the earth's surface, as in principle the conferral is made in the name of every individual subject to it, where every individual is presumed to have the right to exist lawfully somewhere without fear of abuse. The authority and legitimacy of the *actual* distribution of sovereignty to particular states *within* this collective conferral of territorial sovereignty is, of course, quite another matter. For this reason, under the fiduciary model, the universal subjection of states to a duty of non-refoulement is a necessary but not sufficient condition of the all-things-considered authority and legitimacy of international law's present distribution of sovereignty. Likewise, we assume that subjection of states to a duty of non-refoulement is merely a necessary condition of the authority of international law to distribute to states collective territorial sovereignty over the earth's surface. But this is enough: that the duty is a necessary condition of international law's authority in this respect entails that it is an obligatory adjunct to international law's conferral on states of exhaustive territorial sovereignty over the earth's surface.

The argument for recognition of the jus cogens status of the duty of non-refoulement follows a parallel trajectory, except rather than addressing the duty's universally obligatory nature, the argument addresses the duty's paramountcy. The issue is whether the customary or conventional norm of non-refoulement can admit

157. *See* Jean Allain, *The Jus Cogens Nature of Non-refoulement*, 13 Int'l J. Refugee L. 533, 538 (2001), *citing* G.S. Goodwin-Gil, The Refugee in International Law 166–67 (2d ed. 1996); Elihu Lauterpacht & Daniel Bethlehem, *The Scope and Content of the Principle of Non-refoulement: Opinion, in* Refugee Protection in International Law: UNHCR Global Consultations on International Protection 87, 158 (Erika Feller et al. eds., 2003).

158. *See, e.g.*, Executive Committee Conclusion No. 79, General Conclusion on International Protection, 1996 ("[T]he principle of *non-refoulement* is not subject to derogation.").

159. *See* Cartagena Declaration, *supra* note 83, ¶ 5 ("This principle [of non-refoulement] ... should be acknowledged and observed as a rule of jus cogens."). For discussion of state practice in Latin America confirming the peremptory status of non-refoulement, see Arthur Helton & Eliana Jacobs, *What Is Forced Migration*, 13 Geo. Imm. L.J. 526 (1999).

160. *See, e.g.*, Harold Hongju Koh, *The Haitian Centers Council Case: Reflections on Refoulement and Haitian Centers Council*, 35 Harv. Int'l L.J. 30 (1994); Alice Farmer, *Non-refoulement and Jus Cogens: Limiting Anti-Terror Measures That Threaten Refugee Protection*, 32 Geo. Imm. L.J. 1 (2008).

of limitation or derogation, either through state practice or treaty-making. In some cases—such as refoulement to a place where the individual would face a substantial risk of torture[161]—the jus cogens status of the prohibition on refoulement can be explained by the peremptory quality of a particular human right, such as the right to security against torture. Because states may not under any circumstances commit acts of torture or be accomplices to the same, a receiving state may not under any circumstances deport an individual to a country where he faces a substantial risk of torture, as to do so would make the deporting state an accomplice. The strict prohibitions on arbitrary killing, genocide, and other norms of jus cogens discussed in Chapter 3 can likewise explain a peremptory bar on *refoulement* when the home state is systematically violating such norms or is unable or unwilling to prevent third parties from doing so. But what if the persecution that awaits the asylum seeker is less severe and not proscribed by a peremptory norm, such as persecution where the abuse inflicted is a denial of access to public services such as education or healthcare?

In some of these cases, the jus cogens norm prohibiting arbitrary discrimination can do the work. The Refugee Convention requires an asylum seeker to show that the persecution she fears is causally linked to at least one of the Convention grounds of persecution. In many instances, the persecution will consist in arbitrary discrimination based on race, religion, nationality, or membership of a particular social group.[162] Because the fiduciary theory qualifies the prohibition on arbitrary discrimination as jus cogens, in these cases it can explain the peremptory nature of non-refoulement by reference to the peremptory status of the prohibition on arbitrary discrimination, an international norm the deporting state would offend were it to refoule an individual to suffer arbitrary discrimination. In other cases, however, it may not be easy to characterize the persecution as a form of discrimination. The victim may be persecuted not because she belongs to a particular race, religion, nationality, or other minority group, but because she has criticized a government or third party, and now has a well-founded fear of persecution based on political opinion.[163] To explain these and other cases, we need a more general account of the peremptory status of the duty of non-refoulement.

The general account offered by the fiduciary theory draws on the principle of non-domination, and looks not to the severity or form of the abuse that could be suffered by a returned claimant, but rather to the absence of protection and the

161. *See* CAT, *supra* note 78, art. 3(1) ("No State Party shall expel, return ('refouler') or extradite a person to another State where there are substantial grounds for believing that he would be in danger of being subjected to torture.").

162. *See, e.g.*, Islam v. Secretary of State for the Home Department; R v. Immigration Appeal Tribunal and Another Ex Parte Shah, [1999] 2 All ER 545, at 562 (Lord Hoffman) ("[T]he concept of discrimination in matters affecting human rights and freedoms is central to an understanding of the Convention . . . in the context of a human rights instrument, discrimination means making distinctions which principles of fundamental human rights regard as inconsistent with the right of every human being to equal treatment and respect.").

163. *See, e.g.*, *Ward*, *supra* note 156, ¶ 88 (finding that the applicant "was the target of a highly individualized form of persecution and does not fear persecution because of his group characteristics").

implicit ongoing threat of abuse. If a government or third party persecutes an individual with impunity, the individual lives under conditions of indefinite domination, as the persecutor may abuse her at any time, for any reason, and she will have no recourse. There is a good sense in which impunity is domination institutionalized, as it denotes a lawless institutional condition under which individuals can suffer human rights abuses without hope of a domestic remedy. These conditions of lawlessness combine with a credible threat of persecution to explain the peremptory status of the duty of non-refoulement. But for impunity, the claimant would be expected to seek domestic redress to acts or threats of persecution. Where impunity is the norm, however, redress within the home state is unavailable, and so the host state may not under any circumstances return the claimant to it. To do so would deny the individual the chance to live in a regime of secure and equal freedom. As such, persecution coupled with impunity satisfies the criteria for jus cogens.[164]

A consequence of viewing the duty of non-refoulement as peremptory is that it raises doubts about the lawfulness of returning individuals to places of danger if they are found to fall within the exclusion clauses of Article 1(F) of the Refugee Convention, or within the restrictions of Article 33(2).[165] In our view, the customary nature and peremptory status of the norm governing non-refoulement implies that individuals falling within Articles 1(F) and 33(2) cannot be sent to places where they face a substantial threat of persecution. This result follows directly from the supremacy of jus cogens norms over conflicting provisions of international treaties, as discussed in Chapter 3.

The discussion above also raises the question of just what counts—or should count—as persecution from the perspective of IRL, as well as the related question of who is to count as a refugee. As noted in the introduction to this chapter, the term "persecution" is not defined in the Refugee Convention or its Protocol. The influential UNHCR Handbook claims that "serious violations of human rights," including threats to life or freedom based on Convention grounds, constitute persecution, and that "[w]hether other prejudicial actions or threats would amount to persecution will depend on the circumstances of each case."[166] Similarly, Hathaway characterizes persecution as "sustained or systematic violations of basic human rights demonstrative of a failure of state protection."[167] On the fiduciary model, persecution consists in threats to violate human rights or to engage in acts directly abusive of them with respect to which there is no effective domestic form of redress. This conception of persecution shares with Hathaway's the idea that an absence or failure of state protection is partially constitutive of persecution. And it uses human rights as the standard for determining whether a given harm (or threat of harm) is also a violation of a person's rights and therefore potentially, within the meaning of IRL, persecution. This conception of persecution can explain the Refugee Convention

164. *See supra* Chapter 3.

165. *See supra* notes 45 & 46.

166. U.N. High Commissioner for Refugees, Handbook and Guidelines on Procedures and Criteria for Determining Refugee Status under the 1951 Convention and the 1967 Protocol Relating to the Status of Refugees, Dec. 2011, HCR/1P/4/ENG/REV. 3, ¶¶ 51–52.

167. Hathaway, *supra* note 108, at 104–05.

grounds (political opinion aside) as markers of suspect discriminatory conduct that at a certain point or threshold becomes persecutory. What is that threshold?

Hathaway refers to violations of "basic human rights." On the fiduciary view, there is no reason in principle to close off the list of relevant human rights to those considered "basic" (usually a shorthand for civil and political rights, or more narrowly still, rights protective of life, liberty, and security of the person). The crucial issue is not whether a right is enshrined under the ICCPR or the International Covenant on Economic, Social and Cultural Rights (ICESCR),[168] but rather whether its deprivation in a context of significant impunity leads to the conclusion that the individual is thereby denied a fair opportunity to live a dignified life of secure and equal freedom. By this measure, in a home state marked by significant impunity, any violation of the right to life, liberty, or security of the person is likely to be enough to count as persecution. But persistent violations of other rights, such as the right to join a trade union and the right to family life—economic and social rights protected under Articles 8 and 10 respectively of the ICESCR[169]—may likewise count as persecution. Sustained violations of these rights also deny possible aspects of a dignified life of equal freedom that no person can reasonably be forced to live without. Last, and despite the fiduciary theory's capacity to explain most of the Convention grounds of persecution by reference to the prohibition on arbitrary discrimination, the fiduciary view would ultimately eschew reference to grounds of persecution as an independent requirement of protection.[170] The motivation for the violation of a human right is irrelevant to the fact that deliberate rights violations carry with them a denial of equal freedom regardless of their motive.[171] If this denial transpires within a context of significant impunity, then the exiled individual, under the fiduciary theory, should be entitled to international protection.

The fiduciary model would likewise support the expansive definitions of refugee from the Cartagena Declaration and OAU Convention.[172] Recall that the OAU Convention incorporates the definition from Article 1 of the Refugee Convention, and then adds that persons will also be deemed refugees if they are compelled to flee "owing to external aggression, occupation, foreign domination or events seriously disturbing public order."[173] As Shacknove comments, the OAU definition recognizes that the "normal social bond" between state and citizen may be broken

168. International Covenant on Economic, Social and Cultural Rights, Dec. 16, 1966, 993 U.N.T.S. 3, *entered into force* Jan. 3, 1976 [hereinafter ICESCR].

169. *Id.* arts. 8 & 10.

170. *But see* INS v. Elias-Zacarias, 502 U.S. 478 (1992) (holding that persecution must be tied to a protected ground for an individual to count as a refugee under U.S. immigration law, which mirrors the definitional requirements of the Refugee Convention).

171. *Cf.* U.N. High Commissioner for Refugees, UNHCR Guidance Note on Refugee Claims Relating to Sexual Orientation and Gender Identity at 14, ¶ 28 (Nov. 21, 2008), http://www.refworld.org/cgi-bin/texis/vtx/rwmain?docid=48abd5660 (last visited Nov. 27, 2015) ("[T]he motivation need not be one of enmity, malignity or other antipathy towards the victim on the part of the persecutor, if the applicant experiences the abuse as harm.").

172. *See supra* notes 81 & 83.

173. OAU Convention, *supra* note 81, art. 1(2).

in a number of ways.[174] It may be destroyed by a predatory government, but it may also be broken by social collapse and disintegration, such as the conditions that obtain within a failed state, "where a government (or society) has, for all practical purposes, ceased to exist."[175] Asylum seekers who flee a catastrophic natural disaster, economic meltdown, or civil strife may qualify as bona fide refugees under this approach, if emergency conditions prevent a state from guaranteeing basic public order. In each of these cases, there is "an absence of state protection [of the citizen's basic needs] which constitutes the full and complete negation of society and the basis of refugeehood."[176] Translated into the theoretical framework of the fiduciary model, the claim would be that the absence of secure and equal freedom within one's home state constitutes "the basis of refugeehood," and that intractably dangerous conditions can be produced by the collapse of public institutions as well as by persecution. Whereas persecution denotes tyranny and oppression through the violence made possible by centrally organized institutions, in circumstances of collapse, individuals are thrown into a state of nature and are ever subject to decentralized but ubiquitous private forms of domination and abuse.

One place the fiduciary theory would part from Shacknove as well as Gibney, however, is with respect to their claim that alienage—being outside one's country of nationality or habitual residence, as required by the Refugee Convention—is morally irrelevant to the question of who counts as a person in need of protection from the perspective of IRL. As we have seen, Gibney dismisses alienage because it is irrelevant to his humanitarian principle: whether we should help some needy people rather than others, on humanitarian grounds, depends on the cost to us, the benefit our help would provide, and the relative intensity of the claimant's need. The physical location of the needy claimant, on this view, is irrelevant. For Shacknove, alienage, like persecution, is "a subset of a broader category: the physical access of the international community to the unprotected person."[177] Refugees must be "within the reach of the international community," but this does not necessarily mean they must be outside their home country.[178] Shacknove's position is reinforced by the plight of internally displaced persons (IDPs), who generally resemble refugees except for not having crossed an international border.[179] The close resemblance of IDPs to refugees may make the latter's sole access to the protection of IRL seem arbitrary.

On the fiduciary view, IRL's alienage condition is explained as a function of international law's distribution of sovereign responsibility among states. As long as an asylum seeker remains within her home country, international law does

174. Shacknove, *supra* note 81, at 277.

175. *Id.*

176. *Id.*

177. *Id.*

178. *Id.* at 82.

179. The Internal Displacement Monitoring Centre reports 38 million IDPs displaced by conflict as of January 2015. *See* Internal Displacement Monitoring Center, *available at* http://www.internal-displacement.org (last visited June 16, 2015).

not ordinarily obligate other states to offer their territory as a place of refuge.[180] Instead, international law obligates the asylum seeker's home state to abandon its threatening conduct and establish a regime of secure and equal freedom so that all of its people find a safe haven within its borders. This is not to say that international law provides no means to provide relief to IDPs. The UNHCR and numerous international organizations provide ongoing assistance to IDPs,[181] and situation-specific humanitarian aid (e.g., responses to natural disasters) is always possible with the home state's consent. But if the home state does not consent, then the international community would have to determine whether humanitarian intervention over the objections of the home state is morally desirable and legally possible—that is, whether intervention is worthwhile given the costs that attend the threat or use of force, and whether the home state's claim to non-interference can be set aside lawfully. The principles appropriate to this task are those governing humanitarian intervention, as discussed in Chapter 5. The principles related to the cosmopolitan rights of asylum seekers—principles that govern relations between asylum seekers and receiving states—are simply not applicable to the question of whether humanitarian intervention in a given case is legally and morally justifiable. This does not mean that IDPs have a lesser claim to international protection than refugees; in some cases, such as the threat of imminent genocide, humanitarian intervention through the U.N. Charter system may be morally obligatory as well as legally permissible. The point is that even if humanitarian relief or intervention took the form of rescuing IDPs from terrible home states and seeking resettlement for them in other states, until they actually cross an international border they pose no challenge to the territorial sovereignty of another state, and so the principles constitutive of IRL are not engaged. As long as IDPs remain within their home state—possibly in need of rescue and, let us assume, certainly in need of humanitarian relief—a failure to protect on the part of the international community is better characterized as a failure to extend humanitarian assistance rather than a failure of refugee law.[182]

180. Arguably, states may bear more robust duties to accept asylum seekers abroad under the fiduciary theory if their actions have contributed directly to the circumstances that give rise to the threat of persecution.

181. These organizations cooperate through the Global Protection Cluster Working Group, an umbrella organization dedicated to the protection of IDPs in which the UNHCR plays a coordinating role. *See* Global Protection Cluster, Handbook for the Protection of Internally Displaced Persons, http://www.unhcr.org/50f94dcc9.html (last visited Jan. 27, 2015).

182. *Cf.* Matthew Lister, *Who Are Refugees?* 32 Law & Phil. 645, 657 (2013). Lister critiques Shacknove's rejection of alienage as a condition of refugeehood, in part, on the grounds that to be of practical use Shacknove's proposal must be capable of regulating international action to rescue persons at risk within their home states, and this in turn would require "something that we do not have, namely, a well worked-out and agreed upon account of when and how so-called 'humanitarian intervention' is required." In our view, it is a category error to conflate refugee law with humanitarian intervention or relief, as the norms governing each are distinct, as are the parties to the relationships governed by those norms (asylum seeker versus receiving state in the case of refugee law; international community versus home state in the case of humanitarian relief or intervention).

An advantage of this understanding of alienage is that it helps explains IRL as a distinctive legal institution while leaving room for better-suited practices—humanitarian relief and intervention—to attend the needs of IDPs.[183] A further advantage of this approach is that it mitigates the concern of theorists such as Gibney, Hathaway, Neve, and Lister that an expansive understanding of refugee-hood may lead, as Lister puts it, to "strained resources, an unwillingness of the populations of host countries to recognize the privileged position of refugees, and a backlash against the asylum process in general."[184] Lister defends the Refugee Convention definition, in part, due to "the costs, both monetary and humanitarian, of physically relocating hundreds of millions of [severely impoverished] people."[185] In the course of his defense of the Convention standard, he challenges Shacknove, Michael Dummett, and Stephen Perry, among others, who all argue for a broader refugee definition.[186] Our account charts a middle course. On the one hand, by questioning the relevance of the Convention grounds and favoring a generous human rights approach to refugee status determination, the fiduciary model counsels a more liberal approach than the Refugee Convention and Lister. But on the other, by adhering to the doctrine of alienage as a precondition of a claim to asylum within an international legal order carved into territorial states, the fiduciary theory takes on board a key element of the Convention definition and narrows the range of potential claimants, reducing the threat of "strained resources" and backlash.

At the same time, the fiduciary character of sovereignty supports construing the alienage requirement restrictively to allow individuals fleeing persecution to assert asylum claims at international borders.[187] This approach follows naturally from the coercive character of state immigration controls, along with the fiduciary character of the non-refoulement principle as a constraint on state coercion. As discussed in previous chapters, whenever states exercise sovereign authority over foreign nationals they bear fiduciary obligations to treat foreign nationals with due care and solicitude as beneficiaries of international legal order. States may not exercise their coercive powers in a manner that is indifferent to the security and liberty of foreign nationals. Accordingly, when states encounter foreign asylum seekers at their borders, the fiduciary character of their sovereign authority prohibits them from

183. *See* Thomas Pogge, *Migration and Poverty*, *in* CITIZENSHIP AND EXCLUSION 12 (Veit Bader ed., 1997) (arguing that providing aid to the global poor in their home countries is likely to do more good overall than granting them refuge).

184. Lister, *supra* note 182, at 655.

185. *Id.* at 660 n.51.

186. *See* MICHAEL DUMMETT, ON IMMIGRATION AND REFUGEES 37 (2001) (identifying a denial of the "minimal conditions for a decent human life" as the basis of refugee status); Stephen Perry, *Immigration, Justice, and Culture*, *in* JUSTICE IN IMMIGRATION 104 (Warren Schwartz ed., 1995) (arguing for refugee status of persons lacking protection "whether or not they are outside [their home country] and whether or not they are actually persecuted.").

187. *See* JAMES C. HATHAWAY, THE RIGHTS OF REFUGEES UNDER INTERNATIONAL LAW 301 (2005) ("[W]here there is a real risk that rejection [at the border] will expose the refugee 'in any manner whatsoever' to the risk of being persecuted for a Convention ground, Art. 33 amounts to a de facto duty to admit the refugee, since admission is normally the only means of avoiding the alternative, impermissible consequence of exposure to risk.").

driving the asylum seeker back to a jurisdiction where "her life or freedom would be threatened."[188] Those who flee persecution in their home country become "refugees" entitled to the protection of non-refoulement as soon as their flight brings them into direct contact with the security forces of another state—whether this occurs within the other state's territory, at a land border, on the high seas, or in airspace outside the home state's territorial jurisdiction.[189] In each of these settings, the fiduciary character of sovereignty bars states from using their immigration authority in a manner that would treat foreign nationals with hostility or indifference.

The fiduciary theory's account of non-refoulement lends clarity to other core features of IRL. For example, the fiduciary theory supports the view that states may not use interdiction to prevent refugees at sea from reaching their shores. A state that prevents refugees on the high seas from accessing its territory violates the principle of non-refoulement—even if the refugees might potentially find protection elsewhere—because if every state were to follow suit, refugees would have nowhere to go. They would be rendered permanent exiles adrift on the oceans with no safe harbor to welcome them. To guard against this possibility, the fiduciary theory prohibits states from interfering with refugees' travel on the high seas. These features of the fiduciary theory link IRL back to its origins as a safeguard against de jure and de facto statelessness.

Some might worry still that a liberal human rights approach to refugeehood will open migratory floodgates to northern countries, threatening an influx that would jeopardize the cultural and economic integrity of some receiving states, leading in turn to a backlash against the asylum process. And independently of these hypothetical concerns, IRL needs to take account of actual situations of mass influx, such as the rapid migration of nearly 3 million Syrians to Lebanon and Turkey as of June 2015,[190] or the forced migration of Somalis to Kenya over the past two decades, with more than 426,000 currently registered with the UNHCR in Kenya, most of whom remain "warehoused" in suffocating camps at Dadaab.[191] As discussed, refugees enjoy a peremptory right of non-refoulement to a place of danger, even under exigent circumstances. To deny them this entitlement would be inconsistent with their status as equal subjects and beneficiaries of international legal order, as refoulement

188. Refugee Convention, *supra* note 1, art. 33(1).

189. The principle of non-refoulement would also preclude a state from sending its security forces into a foreign state (with or without the consent of the foreign state) to intercept and repel asylum seekers who seek to reach its borders.

190. *See* U.N. High Commissioner for Refugees, *Syria Regional Response: Inter-agency Information Sharing Portal, available at* http://data.unhcr.org/syrianrefugees/country.php?id=224 (Turkey), *and* http://data.unhcr.org/syrianrefugees/country.php?id=122 (Lebanon) (last visited June 16, 2015). By April 2014, Syrian refugees constituted one-quarter of Lebanon's resident population, leading to "serious economic shocks" and straining the country's "health, education, electricity, and water and sanitation" infrastructure. U.N. High Commissioner for Refugees, *Syrian Refugees in Lebanon Surpass One Million*, Apr. 3, 2014, http://www.unhcr.org/533c15179.html (last visited Nov. 27, 2015).

191. *See* U.N. High Commissioner for Refugees, *Refugees in the Horn of Africa: Somali Displacement Crisis*, http://data.unhcr.org/horn-of-africa/country.php?id=110 (last visited Jan. 29, 2015) (reporting 339,050 Somali individuals in Dadaab as of December 31, 2014).

deliberately places them at risk while treating their very physical existence as an illegality. But read narrowly, compliance with the duty of non-refoulement is consistent with temporary protection and refugee warehousing that in practice often morphs into multi-decade protracted refugee situations in which rights violations are virtually unavoidable. How, then, might international law contend with the problem of mass influx, where we assume that rapid and massive involuntary migration really does pose a serious threat to the receiving state's public order, health and welfare programs, protection of minorities, economic stability, and/or cultural and religious character? If it is possible to set out the barebones of an international legal framework for these kinds of crises, we may then be able to look to that framework as a guide to the rights of refugees arriving at the borders of northern counties where the issue of mass influx does not ordinarily arise (and if it did, there would be a framework available to deal with it).

Adequately elaborated, Article 2 on "Asylum" of the OAU Convention supplies an apposite if skeletal legal framework for contending with mass influx. Article 2(1) provides that "Member States of the OAU shall use their best endeavours consistent with their respective legislations to receive refugees and secure the settlement of those refugees who, for well-founded reasons, are unable or unwilling to return to their country of origin or nationality."[192] The reference to "best endeavours" and "respective legislations" may appear to subordinate the international imperative to receive and settle refugees to the limitations imposed by municipal law. The remaining paragraphs of Article 2, however, suggest that the better reading is that there is a best-efforts duty to receive and settle refugees through a grant of asylum, and that this duty is to be complied with through the application and rule of domestic law.

Article 2(2) explicitly refers to a "grant of asylum," whereas Article 2(3) imposes a strict duty of non-refoulement on the Member States, with no reference to "best endeavours" or "respective legislations."[193] The African Charter, Article 12(3), reinforces the OAU Convention by providing a right "to seek and obtain asylum."[194] More significant still, Article 2(4) of the OAU Convention provides that if "a Member State finds difficulty in continuing to grant asylum to refugees, such Member State may appeal directly to other Member States and through the OAU, and such Member States shall . . . take appropriate measures to lighten the burden of the Member State granting asylum."[195] This provision presupposes throughout that the distressed Member State is granting asylum to arriving refugees, consistent with its duty to receive and settle refugees under Article 2(1). But importantly, the receiving state is not left to shoulder the burden alone: other Member States are required to provide assistance, which may include burden-sharing through resettlement of refugees comprising a mass influx.[196]

In the case of a mass influx that truly threatens to overwhelm a host country, international financial aid, humanitarian assistance, and possibly burden-sharing

192. OAU Convention, *supra* note 81, art. 2(1).

193. *Id.* arts. 2(2)–(3).

194. African Charter, *supra* note 80, art. 12(3).

195. OAU Convention, *supra* note 81, art. 2(4).

196. *Id.* art. 2(5).

may be appropriate, because the alternative is to compel the receiving state to risk suffering public disorder and even the collapse of its public institutions, depending on the circumstances.[197] When a mass influx occurs, there are two constituencies with a claim to international protection: the refugees comprising the influx, and the receiving country (or countries) into which they are migrating. The key to understanding Article 2 in this context is seeing the way it articulates the relationship among refugees, the host country, other Member States, and the international community. The receiving country has a duty to grant asylum to refugees, but if it encounters "difficulty" in doing so, it is entitled to petition other states for assistance, directly and through the OAU (now the African Union), and those states are required to "take appropriate measures to lighten the burden of the Member State granting asylum."[198] If a receiving state seeks assistance from another Member State and is refused, under Article 9 the receiving state is invited to refer the dispute to the Commission of Mediation, Conciliation and Arbitration of the OAU (Commission).[199] Thus, in principle, the African Union hovers in the background with international authority to influence or even adjudicate questions of humanitarian assistance and burden-sharing.[200] In summary, Member States are under a best-efforts obligation to grant asylum in the case of mass influx, they are entitled to relief if under distress, and the measure of relief to which they are ultimately entitled is in theory reviewable by an international body.

The fiduciary theory explains the right of asylum implicit in the OAU Convention and affirmed in the African Charter as a context-sensitive compromise between, on the one hand, the individual's right to pursue his or her life somewhere in a regime of secure and equal freedom, and, on the other, the right of a receiving state not to be overwhelmed by a mass influx. As noted above, on a strict and narrow reading of non-refoulement, states could transfer asylum seekers indefinitely to successive temporary protection areas, or to one safe state after another, keeping them in constant and indefinite limbo, though not in fear of persecution. Further, if asylum seekers are denied permanent legal status in the country where they have taken refuge, they may be denied the opportunity to pursue education, develop marketable skills, and reunite with family members.

Hathaway and Neve themselves insist that permanent resettlement must be granted to those "unable to return home at the end of a reasonable period of temporary protection."[201] They offer five years as an "outside time limit," warning against "warehousing" and noting that with prolonged temporary status "[e]ntire

197. *See, e.g.*, DUMMETT, *supra* note 186, at 14, 25 (affirming the right of a receiving state "not to be submerged" while extending refugee status to individuals fleeing poverty of the global south).

198. *See* OAU Convention, *supra* note 81, art. 2(4).

199. *Id.* art. 9.

200. Although the Commission in practice never became operational—thus the "in principle" qualification—it still remains on the books as part of the OAU Convention structure, and was at least intended at some point to play a third-party role in dispute resolution. *See* Makane Moïse Mbengue, *African Perspectives on Inter-state Litigation*, *in* LITIGATING INTERNATIONAL LAW DISPUTES: WEIGHING THE OPTIONS 166, 177 (Natalie Klein ed., 2005).

201. Hathaway & Neve, *supra* note 107, at 192.

generations of refugee children may grow up in uncertainty and despair."[202] The problem Hathaway and Neve face, however, is that from the perspective of their narrow and Convention-circumscribed interpretation of IRL, any claim to permanent status after a "reasonable period" is ad hoc and without a legal basis. If the threat of persecution subsides after seven or eight years, but for whatever reason the asylum seeker has yet to obtain permanent status, then the legal basis on which she could seek to remain within the host state, under Hathaway and Neve's assumptions, is far from clear. Tellingly, Hathaway and Neve decline to offer a single legal justification for their position in favor of eventual permanent status.

Under the fiduciary theory, the threat of human rights abuses in a refugee's home country triggers the receiving state's duty of non-refoulement, but that threat alone does not exhaust the reasons for complying with the duty. Those reasons are derived from the individual's right to live somewhere in a regime of secure and equal freedom. When an individual is forced to flee her own state, under the Refugee Convention she is entitled to seek international protection in any state she enters, and without penalty for unauthorized entry. As a joint fiduciary of the earth's surface on behalf of humanity, the receiving state must let her in and, ordinarily, grant her asylum. The receiving state must do so because, as a fiduciary of humanity, it cannot treat the asylum seeker's claim to asylum with hostility or indifference, as it would do were it to adopt blanket non-entrée policies such as interdiction or safe third country agreements that provide for refugees' removal without their consent. As a fiduciary of the refugee as well as her people, in the typical case not involving mass influx the host state cannot decide for the asylum seeker that she must pursue her life somewhere else.

There may, of course, be exceptions to the rule, even in the absence of mass influx. When a person in need of protection has entered a foreign state on account of a crisis or natural disaster of foreseeably short duration, then limiting his stay to a temporary period may be justifiable.[203] But when a refugee flees persecution—a distinctively human phenomenon—only rarely will the endpoint of the threat of persecution be reasonably foreseeable. Hathaway and Neve's critics plausibly observe that it is uncommon for the causes of flight to be resolved within five years.[204] Accordingly, refugees generally ought to know from the outset that with continued residence in the host country, and favorable refugee status determination, they are on a path to permanent status within a reasonable period, and eventually citizenship, should they wish it. Without such an arrangement in place, the exiled refugee lives within a safe state, but remains effectively stateless, always liable to expulsion, never able to plan his life, and ultimately in a condition, as Walzer puts it, of "infinite danger."[205] A path to permanent status is mandated by the fiduciary theory's principle of non-domination, which in turn suggests a demanding interpretation of

202. *Id.* at 132, 181–82.

203. For example, foreign nationals fleeing natural disasters may avail themselves of Temporary Protected Status in the United States for a period of six to eighteen months. *See* Immigration and Nationality Act, 8 U.S.C. § 244 (2006).

204. *See* Anker et al., *supra* note 116, at 302.

205. Walzer, *supra* note 94, at 32.

the directive from Article 34 of the Refugee Convention that receiving states must facilitate naturalization "as far as possible."[206]

Unlike the right of non-refoulement, however, under the fiduciary theory the right to asylum and eventual permanent status is not peremptory. There may be circumstances, such as mass influx, in which a host state cannot reasonably be asked to grant asylum or permanent status to needy claimants. In these cases, the fiduciary theory would insist, with Benvenisti, that the overwhelmed state must provide a justification to needy claimants whose applications for asylum it rejects. Furthermore, and now borrowing from the model from the OAU Convention, the fiduciary theory would invite distressed host states to appeal to other states for relief, directly or through a revamped UNHCR. The UNHCR could be authorized to express views on the nature and extent of the relief owed, and could be empowered to act as a nonbinding arbitrator in the event of a dispute between distressed receiving states and others.

The fiduciary theory would also extend the OAU Convention model to give refugees standing under international law to challenge judicially denials of asylum or applications for permanent status. Northern states generally permit judicial review of denied claims for refugee status, as these decisions determine whether the duty of non-refoulement applies, and many likewise feature review of decisions to reject a claim for asylum or permanent status following a *positive* determination that the individual has a well-founded fear of persecution and merits refugee status.[207] Independent national courts could wear international hats for this purpose, thereby serving as an independent and impartial assessor of the host state's justification of its rejection of a needy claimant's request for asylum.[208] The fiduciary theory also suggests that in some settings a failure to secure asylum at the national level should be subject to review by international bodies such as the U.N. Human Rights Committee or the Committee Against Torture.[209] The overarching point is to avoid domination of the asylum seeker by the host state, while likewise avoiding the domination of the host state by asylum seekers who unintentionally but collectively may comprise a threatening mass influx. In principle, domination in this context can be overcome by resort to transnational norms and international institutions that stand between the parties as impartial adjudicators, much as cosmopolitans like Kumm envision the role of international law generally.

Thus, the fiduciary character of states' obligations to refugees challenges current state practices in a variety of respects, requiring states to expand their domestic

206. Refugee Convention, *supra* note 1, art. 34.

207. *See, e.g.*, Ward, *supra* note 156 (deploying the Refugee Convention to interpret Canadian law on refugee status determination); Huang v. INS, 436 F.3d 89 (2d Cir. 2006) (holding that U.S. courts have jurisdiction to review the discretionary denial of an asylum petition even if the petitioner has been granted withholding of removal).

208. We will have more to say about this in the next chapter, which is a development of George Scelle's idea of *dédoublement fonctionnel* or "role splitting." *See* GEORGE SCELLE, MANUEL DE DROIT INTERNATIONAL PUBLIC 15–24 (1948).

209. *See, e.g.*, Agiza v. Sweden, Communication No. 233/2003, U.N. Doc. CAT/C/34/D/233/2003, ¶¶ 13.1–13.8 (2005) (concluding that Sweden violated its non-refoulement obligations under the CAT by returning an asylum seeker to Egypt).

criteria for refugee status and to refrain from returning refugees interdicted on the high seas, all the while permitting robust judicial review of refugee status determinations. Some legal scholars and policymakers are likely to object that these requirements, like other progressive implications of the fiduciary theory, are politically unsustainable because they cut too deeply against the grain of state interests.[210] Even if some national authorities might be prepared to accept the fiduciary theory's account of states' obligations to refugees, they may not have the political capital necessary to fully implement these obligations.[211] Yet it is precisely because the national political landscape is often so inhospitable for refugee protection that international norms and institutions are necessary to illuminate the legal framework necessary for refugees to enjoy secure and equal freedom. Just as human rights norms are designed to protect minorities within a state from domination at the hands of a politically empowered majority, IRL norms are necessary to ensure that refugees may obtain refuge from persecution notwithstanding entrenched political opposition from the receiving state's citizenry. And just as international human rights tribunals have a special role to play in protecting minorities within a state from domination, robust review from international institutions (including national courts, operating as quasi-international tribunals) is essential to affirm the cosmopolitan right to refuge within a state-dominated system that all too often treats refugees with indifference, if not outright hostility.[212] Like other power-regulating features of international law's fiduciary constitution, IRL's peremptory non-refoulement norm is constitutive of state authority, and therefore operates outside the domain of state consent, guaranteeing that states respect all individuals subject to their jurisdiction as beneficiaries of the international system.

V. CONCLUSION

We have argued that prevailing conceptions of IRL either fail to treat the claims of refugees as legal claims (humanitarianism), or they fail to articulate a stable and legitimate legal framework through which the competing claims of sovereign states and asylum seekers might be authoritatively resolved (human rights and territorial approaches). By conceiving of states as local and global fiduciaries whose relations to asylum seekers are necessarily mediated by international law, the fiduciary

210. *See, e.g.*, David A. Martin, *The Need for Balance*, 98 AM. SOC'Y INT'L L. PROC. 252, 255 (2004) ("By skewing the balance in the name of human rights, [public officials sympathetic to the plight of refugees] risk triggering an overreaction in the name of control.").

211. *See* Erwin Chemerinsky, *Losing Faith: America Without Judicial Review*, 98 MICH. L. REV. 1416 (2000) (observing "that the political process has no incentive to protect aliens from discrimination, but it has great incentive to impose burdens on aliens who cannot vote and thereby to benefit the citizens who do"); David A. Martin, *Interdiction, Intervention, and the New Frontiers of Refugee Law and Policy*, 33 VA. J. INT'L L. 473, 474 (1993) ("A central feature, then, of the policy context for refugee law and refugee assistance, for as far as the eye can see, is this: we can expect sustained resistance to offering refuge to large numbers of threatened people.").

212. *See* David Cole, *Enemy Aliens*, 54 STAN. L. REV. 953, 981 (2002) ("As a group that is subject to government regulation but denied a vote, aliens are without a meaningful voice in the political bargains struck by our representative system.").

theory explains the cosmopolitan obligations of states to asylum seekers under IRL as correlates of the entitlement of every member of humanity to secure and equal freedom. Under this theory, the provision of asylum to refugees is the juridical price of statehood. And although the right to asylum is not absolute, for the state to deny asylum to needy claimants, it must be prepared to submit such decisions to independent and international review.

The central place of international institutions in this framework raises the question of their relationship to sovereign states and the people living in them. In the next chapter we attempt to close the fiduciary circle by arguing that international institutions too are fiduciaries of humanity.

8

International Institutions as Fiduciaries of Humanity

I. INTRODUCTION

In the preceding chapters we elaborated a model of international law that is structured and animated by the idea that the state is a fiduciary of the nationals and non-nationals subject to its power. In the last chapter in particular, we drew on Benvenisti's claim that states are trustees of humanity to help explain and critique international refugee law (IRL).[1] In this chapter, we consider international institutions and their relation to the entities or persons subject to them. We argue that international institutions, like states, are fiduciaries of humanity.[2]

International organizations (IOs) are the paradigmatic example of international institutions, and are generally understood to be entities established by agreement under international law having at least one organ with a will of its own.[3] There are some 500 to 700 IOs operating in the world today.[4] They take many forms and assume many roles. Some IOs, such as the United Nations (U.N.) and the World Trade Organization (WTO), have a universal mandate. Others, such as the European Union (EU), the Organization of American States, and the African Union, have a regional mandate. The aforementioned organizations are all formal and umbrella-like IOs in that they establish an international legal system that contains other specialized international institutions or organs with relatively specific functions. Their founding treaty sets out their organs and competences. Ordinarily,

1. Eyal Benvenisti, *Sovereigns as Trustees of Humanity: On the Accountability of States to Foreign Stakeholders*, 107 AM. J. INT'L L. 295 (2013).

2. Benvenisti has argued similarly that international institutions bear "trusteeship obligations," which include rule of law requirements and human rights obligations. *See* EYAL BENVENISTI, THE LAW OF GLOBAL GOVERNANCE 117–44 (2014).

3. HENRY G. SCHERMERS & NIELS M. BLOKKER, INTERNATIONAL INSTITUTIONAL LAW 37 (5th rev'd ed. 2011); *see also* MATTHIAS RUFFERT & CHRISTIAN WALTER, INSTITUTIONALISED INTERNATIONAL LAW 9 (2015) (defining an IO as "an association of two or more subjects of public international law (mostly States) based on an international treaty, that is vested with [*sic*] own bodies and designed to fulfill tasks of common interest.").

4. SCHERMERS & BLOKKER, *supra* note 3, at 37.

these organizations have a plenary body, an executive body or council, an administrative secretariat, and sometimes a dispute resolution entity or court.[5] In the case of the United Nations, for example, the principal organs are the plenary General Assembly, the U.N. Security Council and the Economic and Social Council (both executive entities), the U.N. Secretariat, and the International Court of Justice (ICJ). Other IOs and treaty bodies, such as the International Labour Organization (ILO), U.N. human rights monitoring bodies, the European Court of Human Rights (ECHR), and the WTO's Appellate Body, are established by multilateral treaties or by the founding treaty of the umbrella organization to which they belong (e.g., the ICJ was established by Chapter XIV of the U.N. Charter).[6] In yet other cases, states may choose to cooperate through non-treaty based or soft law organizations, such as the General Agreement on Tariffs and Trade (GATT) that preceded the WTO, and the Organization for Security and Cooperation in Europe (OSCE).[7]

In this chapter, we deploy a capacious understanding of "international institution" in which the key consideration is whether an entity recognized under international law has authority to make, interpret, implement, apply, or enforce some range of international or transnational norms. Under this classification scheme, IOs count as international institutions, as do treaty bodies such as those tasked with monitoring U.N. human rights treaties, organs such as the Security Council, and soft law organizations such as the OSCE.[8] The idea is to capture all those supranational institutions that international legal subjects (mainly states) have created to establish and govern humanity's international, transnational, and cosmopolitan legal order.

As the growing literature on globalization and transnational law rightly adverts, IOs are not the only legal actors engaged in the administration of inter- or transnational matters. Benedict Kinsbury, Nico Krisch, and Richard Stewart point to four additional kinds of global administration.[9] The first involves informal transnational networks between national regulatory officials, such as the Basel Committee that

5. *See* Geir Ulfstein, *Institutions and Competences, in* Jan Klabbers, Ann Peters & Geir Ulfstein, The Constitutionalization of International Law 46–48 (2009).

6. U.N. Charter ch. XIV, arts. 92–96. Schermers and Blokker point out that the United Nations has numerous specialized agencies, such as the U.N. Industrial Development Organization (UNIDO) and the U.N. Conference on Trade and Development (UNCTAD), which in practice have enjoyed functional autonomy independently of whether they eventually became autonomous IOs, as was the case with UNIDO in 1986. Schermers & Blokker, *supra* note 3, at 41–42.

7. *See* Ulfstein, *supra* note 5, at 51–55. There are various ways of classifying IOs. Schermers and Blokker distinguish between universal and closed organizations (e.g., the United Nations versus the European Union, the OECD, the Commonwealth, etc.); intergovernmental versus supranational organizations (decision-making power rests with national governments versus decision-making rests with the IO); and special organizations versus general organizations (organizations created to perform a specific function versus IOs that are not limited by subject matter, such as the United Nations, European Union, OAS, and AU). Schermers & Blokker, *supra* note 3, at 50–59.

8. *See, e.g.*, Ulfstein, *supra* note 5, at 46–55 (distinguishing formal IOs from treaty bodies and soft law organizations).

9. Benedict Kingsbury, Nico Krisch & Richard Stewart, *The Emergence of Global Administrative Law*, 68 Law & Contemp. Probs. 15, 20–23 (2005).

regulates banking. The second consists in "distributed administration" in which domestic agencies take decisions on issues of foreign or global concern, such as those concerning greenhouse gas emissions.[10] The third is "hybrid intergovernmental-private administration," such as the Codex Alimentarius Commission, which adopts food safety standards with the participation of governmental and nongovernmental actors.[11] And finally, there are strictly private bodies carrying out globalized public functions, such as the International Organization for Standardization (ISO), which has adopted over 19,500 product harmonization standards. The idea that these bodies hold any form of public authority is highly controversial, given that their formal membership is private. Nonetheless, we suggest that the fiduciary theory might be able to explain the limited form of public authority that the ISO and its standards appear to possess. If the argument succeeds, it could offer a blueprint for explaining the (limited) public authority of other transnational global entities.

International institutions are frequently classified and discussed in terms of their functions. Indeed, functionalism is generally considered "the leading approach to international organizations."[12] Functionalists look to an organization's founding document to distill its main functions, and then proceed to delineate the scope of its powers based on those functions. Most notably, the ICJ, in the *Reparations for Injuries Case*,[13] developed the doctrine of implied powers under which the scope of an institution's powers and authorized activity may extend further than the powers and activities expressly authorized in its constituent document. The guiding interpretive principle is whether the alleged implied power is necessary for the organization to fulfill its function (or functions). As Jan Klabbers notes, however, the function of an IO "is very much in the eye of the beholder,"[14] and more worrying still, functionalism offers little insight into the question of the organization's accountability. Typically, the delineation of an institution's function would not specify to whom the institution is accountable, the standards or principles under which its actions may be properly assessed, or the institutions and remedial means through which it may be held to account.

International law has replied to the accountability deficit of functionalism through various attempts to bring its institutions within the constraints of international legal order. In 1986, the United Nations sponsored a conference in Vienna

10. *Id.* at 21–22.

11. *Id.* at 22.

12. Jan Klabbers, *International Institutions, in* The Cambridge Companion to International Law 230 (John Crawford & Marti Koskenniemi eds., 2012) (citing M. Virally, *La notion de fonction dans la théorie de l'organisation internationale, in* Mélange offerts à Charles Rousseau: La Communauté Internationale 277–300 (S. Bastid et al. eds., 1974)); *see also* Schermers & Blokker, *supra* note 3, at 50 (affirming that for purposes of classification and comparative study, Virally's idea of function continues to provide "the most fundamental" and "most useful" criterion).

13. Reparations for Injuries Suffered in the Service of the United Nations, Advisory Opinion, 1949 ICJ Rep. 174, 180–85 (affirming that the United Nation's rights and duties "depend upon its purposes and functions as specified or implied in its constituent documents and developed in practice."). We discuss this case in Part III.

14. Klabbers, *supra* note 12, at 231.

that led to the Vienna Convention on the Law of Treaties between States and International Organizations or between International Organizations (VCLT-IO).[15] The VCLT-IO is essentially a carbon copy of the Vienna Convention on the Law of Treaties (VCLT),[16] suitably adjusted to include IOs as parties. The Preamble of the VCLT-IO affirms the functionalist implied powers doctrine, justifying the treaty-making capacity of IOs on the grounds that this capacity "is necessary for the exercise of their functions and the fulfillment of their purposes."[17] But as with states under the VCLT, the treaty-making powers of IOs under the VCLT-IO are limited by legal principles codified in the VCLT-IO. IOs cannot bind other parties whose purported consent was given in error (Article 48) or as a result of fraud (Article 49), corruption (Article 50), or coercion (Articles 51 & 52).[18] Nor can IOs make valid treaties that conflict with peremptory or jus cogens norms of international law (Article 53).[19] The VCLT-IO, however, has yet to attract the requisite number of state parties to come into force.[20]

In 2011, the International Law Commission (ILC) adopted Draft Articles on the Responsibility of International Organizations.[21] The draft articles affirm that IOs are responsible for internationally wrongful acts (Article 3), and that this responsibility arises when an IO commits an act attributable to it that constitutes a breach of one of its international obligations (Article 4). Nonetheless, although Article 26 and Chapter III attribute responsibility to IOs for violations of peremptory norms, the draft articles provide merely that the "characterization of an act of an international organization as internationally wrongful will be governed by international law" (Article 5).[22] There is no discussion of whether or how treaty law or customary law might govern IOs or ground a determination that an act is "internationally wrongful."

More promising than these relatively austere and inchoate measures of positive law, publicists have observed that the accountability of international institutions may be framed and addressed through four contemporary approaches to international accountability: global or transnational constitutionalism,[23] global

15. Vienna Convention on the Law of Treaties Between States and International Organizations or Between International Organizations, 25 I.L.M. 543 (1986), Doc. A/CONF.129/15 (Vienna, Mar. 21, 1986) [hereinafter VCLT-IO].

16. Vienna Convention on the Law of Treaties, May 23, 1969, 1155 U.N.T.S. 331 [hereinafter VCLT].

17. VCLT-IO, *supra* note 15, pmbl.

18. *Id.* arts. 48–52.

19. *Id.* art. 53. See Chapter 3 for discussion of jus cogens.

20. The VCLT-IO has not attracted thirty-five state parties, as required by its "Entry into Force" provision, Article 85. As of July 25, 2015, thirty-one states and twelve IOs had ratified or acceded to the treaty: https://treaties.un.org/pages/ViewDetails.aspx?src=TREATY&mtdsg_no=XXIII-3&chapter=23&lang=en (last visited July 25, 2015).

21. Draft Articles on the Responsibility of International Organizations, 2 Y.B. Int'l L. Comm'n, 2011, pt. 2.

22. *Id.* art. 5.

23. *See, e.g.*, Jean Cohen, Globalization and Sovereignty: Rethinking Legality, Legitimacy and Constitutionalism (2012); Klabbers et al., *supra* note 5; Martti

administrative law,[24] international institutional law,[25] and a hybrid theory (though structured mainly by international institutional law) that its advocates call simply a "public law approach."[26] Constitutionalists typically invest their preferred conception of international legal order and its organizations with constitutional ideals of democracy, human rights, and the rule of law.[27] Global administrative lawyers look to domestic administrative law to borrow principles of due process, public participation in rulemaking, transparency, and reason-giving.[28] International institutional lawyers focus on the relatively similar rules and principles that govern the legal status, structure, and operation of IOs; that is, rules related to membership, legal personality, attribution of powers, representation of members, decision-making, finance, dispute-settlement, and external relations, as well as internal and external supervision.[29]

The public law approach aims to bring the "sensibility" of constitutionalism and the "insights of administrative legal thinking" into contact with international institutional law, but with a normative orientation that expressly envisions a "move beyond mere functionalism."[30] The ambition of the public law approach is to lend a legal framework to global governance by conceiving of all instances of international public authority as "the legal capacity to *determine* others and to reduce their freedom; i.e., to unilaterally shape their legal or factual situation."[31] Capacity is understood broadly to apply to both binding and non-binding decisions, regulations, standards, and so forth.[32] Binding decisions change the legal position of the subject,

Koskenniemi, *Constitutionalism as Mindset: Reflections on Kantian Themes about International Law and Globalization*, 8 J. THEORETICAL INQUIRIES L. 22 (2007); Matthias Kumm, *The Legitimacy of International Law: A Constitutionalist Framework Analysis*, 15 EUR. J. INT'L L. 907 (2006); Anne Peters, *Contemporary Constitutionalism: The Function and Potential of Fundamental Norms and Structures*, 19 LEIDEN J. INT'L L. 579 (2006).

24. *See, e.g.*, Kingsbury et al., *supra* note 9; Sabino Cassese, *Administrative Law Without the State? The Challenge of Global Regulation*, 37 N.Y.U. J. INT'L L. & POL. 663 (2005); Daniel Esty, *Good Governance at the Supranational Scale: Globalizing Administrative Law*, 115 YALE L.J. 1490 (2006).

25. *See, e.g.*, JOSÉ E. ALVAREZ, INTERNATIONAL ORGANIZATIONS AS LAW-MAKERS (2005); JAN KLABBERS, AN INTRODUCTION TO INTERNATIONAL INSTITUTIONAL LAW (2002); NIGEL D. WHITE, THE LAW OF INTERNATIONAL ORGANIZATIONS (2D ED. 2005); SCHERMERS & BLOKKER, *supra* note 3.

26. *See, e.g.*, Armin von Bogdandy, Philipp Dann & Matthias Goldman, *Developing the Publicness of Public International Law: Towards a Legal Framework for Global Governance Activities, in* THE EXERCISE OF PUBLIC AUTHORITY BY INTERNATIONAL INSTITUTIONS: ADVANCING INTERNATIONAL INSTITUTIONAL LAW 21 (Armin von Bogdandy, Rüdiger Wolfrim, Jochen von Bernstorff, Philipp Dann & Matthias Goldman eds., 2010).

27. *See, e.g.*, Kumm, *supra* note 23.

28. *See, e.g.*, Kingsbury et al., *supra* note 9.

29. *See, e.g.*, SCHERMERS & BLOKKER, *supra* note 3; RUFFERT & WALTER, *supra* note 3.

30. von Bogdandy et al., *supra* note 26, at 6, 11.

31. *Id.* (emphasis in original).

32. *Id.* at 11–16.

whereas a non-binding decision simply "*conditions* another subject" by giving her an incentive to comply.[33]

Like the public law theory, we wish to harness the insights of both constitutionalists and global administrative lawyers, all the while remaining faithful to the core structural features of international institutional law. Furthermore, as with the public law approach, we agree that the authority of international institutions holds the key to understanding the nature and effects of the legal framework they lend to global governance. Where we diverge from the public law approach, however, is in our account of public international authority. Under the fiduciary model, we argue, international public authority consists in the legal power to make, interpret, and apply authoritatively international norms. This legal power is held in trust by international institutions on behalf of humanity. Accordingly, international institutions must exercise their legal power in a manner that serves humanity. In practice, this means that for a purported exercise of international legal power to be authoritative as an actual exercise of legal power, it must satisfy the fiduciary theory's criterion of legitimacy: that is, it must be intelligible as an action taken on behalf of, or in the name of, every person subject to the relevant institution's jurisdiction. The basis of this authority is the institution's subjection to and compliance with the requirements of the trust-like or fiduciary position in which it stands vis-à-vis its legal subjects.

The basic argument for viewing international institutions as fiduciaries of humanity is the same as the foundational argument for viewing states as fiduciaries: the relationship between international institutions and those subject to their power—states, nonstate entities, and individuals—satisfies the constitutive criteria of fiduciary relationships, as elaborated in Chapter 1. Like domestic legal institutions, international institutions possess discretionary and administrative powers that are other-regarding, purposive, and institutional in nature. Moreover, the persons subject to those powers are not entitled to exercise them unilaterally or in their individual capacity. For them to do so would ordinarily indicate capture, just as a private party exercising a putatively public power in the domestic sphere would signal corruption.

Of course, states commonly make international law through treaty-making, and customary international law emerges from state practice. Decentralized lawmaking of this kind, however, is always a collective endeavor. Just as no individual private party is entitled to make national law, no individual state is entitled to announce unilaterally a treaty or custom binding on others.

Once international legal authority is entrusted to an international institution—be it an adjudicative, administrative, rule-making, or enforcement authority—that authority constitutes legal power that is always other-regarding, purposive, and institutional in nature, in the senses explained in Chapter 1. As a consequence, states and others subject to international authority are in a public fiduciary relationship with the institutions that possess this authority, and those institutions themselves may properly be called fiduciaries of humanity. By this we do not mean that every international institution has a universal mandate (they do not), but rather that any international legal subject within the scope of an international institution's

33. *Id.* at 12 (emphasis in original).

mandate may be thought of as a beneficiary entitled to impartial and solicitous regard irrespective of nationality.

International institutions stand in a position of stewardship to humanity that assumes both indirect and direct forms. Institutions are *indirect* or second-order fiduciaries of humanity when they stand as lawgiving fiduciaries of an international legal order within which states are both agents and subjects. States are agents of international legal order because they enjoy delegated authority from international law to govern and represent their people. But they are also its subjects because they remain highly significant bearers of international rights and duties. When international institutions construct and oversee an international legal order that enables states to interact rightfully among themselves and with their own nationals and foreign nationals, they act as second-order or indirect fiduciaries of humanity. What unites this class of stewardship is that even after international institutions have spoken, individuals and substate actors are still ultimately subject to the legal authority of states. In Part II of this chapter, we elaborate some of the ways international institutions function as indirect fiduciaries of humanity.

International institutions are *direct* or first-order fiduciaries of humanity when they themselves interact directly with groups of individuals. For example, when the U.N. High Commissioner for Refugees (UNHCR) provides protection to refugees or internally displaced persons, it is acting as a first-order or direct fiduciary of humanity. Likewise, when the United Nations conducts international territorial administration, as it did in Kosovo and East Timor (now Timor-Leste), it does so as a direct fiduciary of humanity. More controversially, when the U.N. Security Council adopts measures to promote peace and security under Chapter VII, including its more recent targeted sanctions program, it too must be viewed as at least purporting to act as a direct fiduciary of humanity. In Part III, we discuss these and other cases in which international institutions serve as direct fiduciaries of humanity, and the implications that follow from their status as fiduciaries.

In Parts IV and V, we suggest that viewing international institutions as fiduciaries of humanity helps to resolve the following puzzles regarding their legal authority and obligations:

a) Do international institutions owe individuals subject to their authority human rights obligations, notwithstanding that international institutions are not states and therefore are not parties to human rights treaties?

b) What is the basis of the authority of international courts that at times interpret international law in ways states would never have anticipated when they created them, and whose rulings, ordinarily, are not enforced through the threat or use of force?

c) What is the basis of the legal authority possessed by the informal transnational entities identified by global administrative lawyers—transnational networks, "distributed administration," hybrid public-private bodies, private bodies exercising global functions—and what is the basis of global administrative law's procedural obligations?

d) What is the nature of the relationship between international and national authorities tasked with interpreting and applying international norms to the same or similar cases? Under what circumstances, if any, should a state defer to an international body's determination? And conversely, under what circumstances should an international authority defer to a national-level decision?

We can of course provide only an outline of a reply to these questions, which implicate perennial debates over monism and dualism, and the relationship between international and domestic law.

In Part VI we conclude and briefly sketch some future directions of inquiry where the fiduciary theory promises to supply a helpful and illuminating framework. These areas of future interest include climate change, the international legal status and rights of indigenous people, global economic justice through the prism of the emerging right to development, and the fiduciary theory's relation to global democracy and the idea of an unbounded demos. Our ultimate conclusion is that international legal order is fiduciary in nature from top to bottom, and across all dimensions in which public power is held and exercised. The fiduciary constitution of state sovereignty is thus a reflection at the state level of the fundamental nature of international legal order itself.

II. INTERNATIONAL INSTITUTIONS AS INDIRECT FIDUCIARIES OF HUMANITY

Under the fiduciary theory, the primary function of international institutions is to serve as indirect fiduciaries for humanity. In contrast to the direct fiduciary relationship between a state and its people, the fiduciary relationship between international institutions and particular human beings is ordinarily indirect in the sense that it is filtered through the state-centric international system. International institutions do not generally exercise power directly over human beings, though in Part III we discuss some of the contexts in which they do. Instead, their predominant purpose is to facilitate and supervise an international legal order that benefits all humanity by ensuring that states fulfill their basic fiduciary responsibilities. As indirect fiduciaries of humanity, international institutions make international legal order possible by subjecting both inter-state relations and state-individual relations to the rule of law. International law subjects transnational relations to the rule of law through two intertwined institutional devices: empowerment and constraint.

A. Empowerment

International institutions *empower* states by conferring on them—and not others—legal capacity to provide a territorially bounded regime of secure and equal freedom for every person subject to their jurisdiction. IOs also provide practical guidance and material resources to help states discharge their responsibilities more effectively. For example, the U.N. Development Programme (UNDP) works in more than 170 countries and territories to help national authorities to develop effective strategies for eliminating poverty and to create effective institutions for sustainable and equitable economic growth, good governance, peacebuilding, disaster risk reduction, and climate change resilience.[34] These efforts to enhance states' capacity to protect and serve

34. *See* United Nations Development Programme, *A World of Development Experience*, http://www.undp.org/content/undp/en/home/operations/about_us.html (last visited Apr. 15, 2015).

their people resonate with a central "pillar" of R2P discourse: the idea that the international community as a whole bears a responsibility to equip states to protect their people effectively from grave threats such as genocide, war crimes, and crimes against humanity.[35] As U.N. Secretary-General Ban Ki-moon observed in a 2009 report:

> What is most needed, from the perspective of the responsibility to protect, are assistance programmes that are carefully targeted to build specific capacities within societies that would make them less likely to travel the path to crimes relating to the responsibility to protect. . . . Experience and common sense suggest that many of the elements of what is commonly accepted as good governance—the rule of law, a competent and independent judiciary, human rights, security sector reform, a robust civil society, an independent press and a political culture that favours tolerance, dialogue and mobility over the rigidities and injustices of identity politics—tend to serve objectives relating to the responsibility to protect as well.[36]

According to this vision, the interests of humanity are most likely to be served when international institutions take proactive measures to strengthen states' capacity to protect and care for their people's equal freedom. By promoting "good governance" at the domestic level, international bodies reinforce international law's fiduciary constitution for humanity's ultimate benefit.

International institutions also empower states by enabling them collectively to exercise regulatory power outside the limits of their respective sovereign jurisdictions. As discussed in Chapter 2, a defining feature of sovereignty's distributive dimension is that international law grants states only limited authority over persons and territory outside their borders. Accordingly, states lack authority to protect their people unilaterally from serious threats such as those posed by transnational criminal networks, global financial instability, and climate change. States also depend on international cooperation to facilitate the transfer of people, goods, information, financial capital, and other critical resources across international borders for the benefit of their people. Sovereignty's distributive dimension thus leaves states with little choice but to work together to develop collaborative solutions to global challenges.

International institutions commonly promote international cooperation by facilitating international lawmaking. The United Nations frequently sponsors conferences, committees, and working groups to generate new multilateral treaties and customary norms for humanity's benefit. In the field of human rights, for example, the United Nations played a leading role in developing the three foundational texts of the so-called "International Bill of Rights"—the UDHR, the ICCPR with its optional protocols, and the ICESCR.[37] The ILC likewise prepares draft

35. *See* Implementing the Responsibility to Protect: Report of the Secretary-General, A/63/677, Jan. 12, 2009, http://www.un.org/en/ga/search/view_doc.asp?symbol=A/63/677 (last visited Apr. 15, 2015) [hereinafter Secretary-General Report]; 2005 World Summit Outcome, G.A. Res. 60/1, ¶¶ 138–39, U.N.Doc. A/RES/60/1 (Sept. 16, 2005).

36. Secretary-General Report, *supra* note 35, ¶ 44.

37. *See generally* Mary Ann Glendon, A World Made New: Eleanor Roosevelt and the Universal Declaration of Human Rights (2001).

conventions, draft articles, statements of principles, and other materials to promote the codification and progressive development of international law.[38] Although General Assembly resolutions are not binding of their own force and are not generally considered sufficient to generate customary obligations,[39] international deliberations in the General Assembly have hastened the emergence of new customary norms in a variety of contexts.[40] States have also entrusted independent lawmaking authority to some international bodies such as the Security Council,[41] the Council of the International Civil Aviation Organization (ICAO),[42] and the International Atomic Energy Agency (IAEA).[43] The treaties that constitute the European Union likewise authorize the European Parliament and the Council of the European Union to promulgate regulations and directives that are legally binding for all EU member-states.[44] By establishing international institutions such as these, states have been able to resolve various coordination and collective action problems, thus strengthening their capacity to protect the interests of their peoples.

B. Constraint

The second primary function of international institutions as indirect fiduciaries of humanity is to *constrain* states for the benefit of humanity. When states create IOs such as the ICAO, the IAEA, or the European Union, they simultaneously commit themselves to international obligations that limit their unilateral discretionary power. International institutions make these commitments credible by monitoring state practice and holding states accountable for noncompliance. International institutions also ensure that states respect peremptory norms such as the prohibitions against torture, military aggression, and refugee refoulement. International law thus entrusts international bodies, as indirect fiduciaries of humanity, with responsibility to ensure that states honor their fiduciary obligations.

38. *See* Laurence R. Helfer & Timothy Meyer, *The Evolution of Codification: A Principal-Agent Theory of the International Law Community's Influence, in* CUSTOM'S FUTURE: INTERNATIONAL LAW IN A CHANGING WORLD (Curtis Bradley ed., forthcoming); Jacob Katz Cogan, *The Changing Form of the International Law Commission's Work, in* EVOLUTIONS IN THE LAW OF INTERNATIONAL ORGANIZATIONS 275, 278–79 (Robert Virzo & Ivan Ingravallo eds., 2015).

39. *See* Legality of the Threat or Use of Nuclear Weapons, Advisory Opinion, 1996 ICJ Rep. 226, ¶ 71 (July 8) (concluding that General Assembly resolutions "fall short of establishing the existence of an *opinio juris* on the illegality of the use of [nuclear] weapons"); INTERNATIONAL LAW ASSOCIATION, COMMITTEE ON THE FORMATION OF CUSTOMARY (GENERAL) INTERNATIONAL LAW, STATEMENT OF PRINCIPLES APPLICABLE TO THE FORMATION OF GENERAL CUSTOMARY INTERNATIONAL LAW 56 (2000) [hereinafter ILA STUDY].

40. ILA STUDY, *supra* note 39, at 57–65.

41. *See* U.N. Charter arts. 25, 39–42, 48.

42. *See* Convention on International Civil Aviation arts. 37, 54(l) & annex 2, 15 U.N.T.S. 295 (Apr. 4, 1947) (as amended); *see generally* ALVAREZ, *supra* note 25, at 111 (2005).

43. *See* Statute of the International Atomic Energy Agency arts. 3(a)(5), 9 & 12, 276 U.N.T.S. 3 (July 29, 1957).

44. Treaty of Lisbon Amending the Treaty on the European Union and the Treaty Establishing the European Community, art. 15, 2007/C 306/1.

Many international institutions are charged with monitoring state practice to hold states accountable for their international obligations. In the field of human rights, for example, the General Assembly has tasked the U.N. Human Rights Council with establishing general standards for human rights compliance, reviewing states' human rights practices, and issuing recommendations for improvement. Treaty bodies such as the U.N. Human Rights Committee and the U.N. Committee Against Torture (UNCAT) perform similar oversight functions for states that are parties to their constitutive agreements. Regional institutions such as the African Commission on Human and Peoples Rights and the Inter-American Commission on Human Rights also monitor state compliance with regional human rights agreements. In matters of collective security, the Security Council and the General Assembly actively track states' compliance with *jus ad bellum*, alongside regional organizations such as the African Union, the European Union, and the Organization of American States. The UNHCR monitors states' treatment of refugees, internally displaced persons, and other vulnerable groups. Nongovernmental organizations (NGOs) such as the International Committee of the Red Cross (with its affiliated national societies) and news organizations such as Al Jazeera, the British Broadcasting Corporation, and the New York Times also provide complimentary reporting on states' adherence to their commitments under international law. Although persuasion and public shaming by IOs and NGOs may be insufficient to ensure that states will always satisfy their international obligations, they do provide a form of international accountability that may discourage states from violating international norms. At the very least, IO and NGO monitoring of state actors makes it possible for civil society to hold state actors to account politically, and contributes generally to the development of law that Etienne Mureinik described as "a culture of justification."[45]

International oversight sometimes is supported with concrete "carrots" and "sticks." The IAEA owes much of its success in promoting nuclear nonproliferation to the (usually implicit) threat of Security Council-authorized economic sanctions or military action against nonconforming states. In contrast, Security Council enforcement of international human rights law (IHRL), international humanitarian law (IHL), and IRL is inconsistent, at best, and tends to arise only in response to the most widespread and systematic violations of jus cogens. Because most other international institutions do not command coercive powers that are comparable to the Security Council, they often struggle to persuade states to bring their domestic laws, policies, and practices into conformity with their international legal obligations. Yet, as we will discuss in Part IV, there is a relatively high level of compliance with the rulings of international courts, notwithstanding the general lack of coercive enforcement. Following Oona Hathaway and Scott Shapiro, we suggest that this compliance may be largely attributable to international law's use of outcasting as a sanction—that is, the international community's withdrawal of the benefits

45. *See* David Dyzenhaus, *Law as Justification: Etienne Mureinik's Conception of Legal Culture*, 14 S. Afr. J. Hum. Rts 11 (1998), citing *inter alia* Etienne Mureinik, *A Bridge to Where? Introducing the Interim Bill of Rights*, 10 S. Afr. J. Hum. Rts. 31, 34 (1994) (affirming that South Africa's new Constitution "must lead to a culture of justification—a culture in which every exercise of power is expected to be justified.").

of international cooperation.[46] Ultimately, however, we suggest in Part IV that the force of international law must be explained by what David Dyzenhaus calls "the compulsion of legality,"[47] which is the compulsion of all public legal actors to show that their actions have legal warrant.

Under the fiduciary theory, the relatively weak enforcement mechanisms available to most international authorities—particularly in the fields of IHRL, IHL, and IRL—is cause for concern. To be sure, international oversight may reinforce international law's fiduciary constitution even if an institution's findings and recommendations are not backed by the threat of coercive force or some form of outcasting. For international bodies to serve as effective indirect fiduciaries of humanity, however, international oversight must be sufficiently robust to ensure that states are unable to violate their international obligations with impunity. At a minimum, this means that adequate means of monitoring and reporting must be available so that wrongdoing can be brought to the attention of the international community for review and possible sanction.

Empowering international institutions to enforce states' fiduciary obligations carries its own set of risks, given the possibility that these institutions may not operate in practice as independent, impartial, and credible fiduciaries for humanity. Some legal scholars have argued, for example, that international financial institutions such as the International Monetary Fund, the World Bank, and the WTO serve the interests of wealthy states by forcing developing countries to organize their economic life in a manner that makes them more vulnerable to exploitation.[48] According to these scholars, international financial institutions represent "a modern, more subtle version" of nineteenth-century capitulations and twentieth-century trusteeships, perpetuating Western colonialism by other means.[49] At the opposite end of the ideological spectrum, some observers in the global north have faulted international institutions for catering disproportionately to the political agendas of the global south. For example, before the U.N. Commission on Human Rights was dissolved in 2006, it was widely panned for the "selectivity and politicization" of its investigations,[50] which tended to focus disproportionately on certain disfavored states (e.g., Israel) to the neglect of other states with deplorable human

46. Oona A. Hathaway & Scott J. Shapiro, *Outcasting: Enforcement in Domestic and International Law*, 121 Yale L.J. 252 (2011).

47. David Dyzenhaus, *The Compulsion of Legality*, *in* Emergencies and the Limits of Legality 33 (Victor V. Ramraj ed., 2009).

48. *See, e.g.*, B.S. Chimni, *International Institutions Today: An Imperial Global State in the Making*, 15 Eur. J. Int'l L. 1 (2004); Antony Anghie, *Colonialism and the Birth of International Institutions: Sovereignty, Economy, and the Mandate System of the League of Nations*, 34 NYU J. Int'l L & Pol. 513, 624–25 (2002); Antony Anghie, *Time Present and Time Past: Globalization, International Finance Institutions, and the Third World*, 32 NYU J. Int'l L. & Pol. 243 (2000).

49. Alvarez, *supra* note 25, at 242.

50. Rosa Freedman, The United Nations Human Rights Council: A Critique and Early Assessment 1, 28–33 (2013); *see also* Report of the Secretary-General to the General Assembly, In Larger Freedom: Towards Development, Security and Human Rights for All, Mar. 21, 2005, U.N. Doc. A/59/2005, http://www.unmillenniumproject.org/documents/Inlargerfreedom.pdf (last visited Apr. 17. 2015) (observing that "the Commission's

rights records (e.g., Sudan, Zimbabwe, Democratic Republic of Congo).[51] To make matters worse, states with poor human rights practices regularly secured election to the Commission, as epitomized by Libya assuming the Commission's chair in 2003.[52] Although it would be a mistake to tar all international bodies with the broad brush of political bias, the persistent criticism of international financial institutions and human rights bodies underscores the very real threat that international institutions may breach their fiduciary obligations as indirect fiduciaries of humanity by using their entrusted powers to advance narrow state, regional, or private interests.

The fiduciary theory suggests that these concerns about accountability deserve to be taken seriously to ensure that international oversight does not unduly compromise states' ability to protect and care for their people. Fortunately, contemporary practice offers a variety of models for holding international institutions accountable for their performance as indirect fiduciaries of humanity. In a recent series of lectures on the "law of global governance," Benvenisti identifies three general approaches to accountability for international institutions: (1) "internal review mechanisms established as part of the institution"; (2) "'peer review,' namely the review of one global body by another"; and (3) "national review, where a domestic court or another state agency reviews a decision by a global governance body."[53] The international community has experimented with each of these three approaches across a variety of settings.

As mentioned above, the General Assembly's decision to disband its Commission on Human Rights in favor of a new and improved Human Rights Council offers a striking example of "internal review" in action. IOs also use internal administrative review to correct their mistakes, as when the World Bank Inspection Panel investigates complaints that the Bank has not followed its own internal policies and procedures.[54] International "peer review" often involves external review by an independent international tribunal. For example, many international actors have selected the International Labour Organization Administrative Tribunal (ILOAT) as the designated forum for resolving labor disputes with their employees.[55] National and regional authorities tend to follow a more ad hoc approach in their review of international decision-making. When an international institution is alleged to have exceeded its entrusted authority, states may seek to amend, terminate, or withdraw from its constitutive treaty; withhold promised funding; or provide domestic legal

capacity to perform its tasks has been increasingly undermined by its declining credibility and professionalism").

51. Freedman, *supra* note 50, at 26–28, 30–31. The subsequent Human Rights Council was designed specifically to address the Commission's most glaring defects. *See* G.A. Res. 60/251, Human Rights Council, ¶¶ 1, 4, A/RES/60/251 (Apr. 3, 2006), http://www2.ohchr.org/english/bodies/hrcouncil/docs/A.RES.60.251_En.pdf (last visited Apr. 17, 2015). It has been the target of similar criticism, however, during its first decade in operation. *See* Freedman, *supra* note 50, at 55, 297–99.

52. Freedman, *supra* note 50, at 18–26.

53. Benvenisti, *supra* note 3, at 253.

54. *Id.* at 256.

55. *Id.* at 253–56.

safeguards against its decisions.[56] A striking example of the last option is the celebrated judgment of the European Court of Justice (ECJ) in *Kadi and Al Barakaat v. Council of the European Union*,[57] where the Grand Chamber declared invalid a regulation of the European Council (EC) implementing the Security Council's antiterrorism sanctions program on the ground that the EC regulation (and, implicitly, the Security Council program itself) violated the European Convention on Human Rights' "principle of effective judicial protection."[58] Such accountability measures at the international, regional, and domestic levels provide checks against IOs overstepping their authority.

In furnishing these examples, we do not intend to convey the impression that the international community has solved the riddle of institutional accountability at the international level. Accountability for international institutions, like state accountability, remains very much a work in progress. Nonetheless, the examples provided do suggest that the international community has a variety of credible options for maintaining and improving the accountability of international institutions. The challenge is to craft legal frameworks based on internal review, external review, and national/regional review that enhance international accountability without undermining the effectiveness of international institutions as fiduciaries of international legal order. We will have more to say on the relationship between international and national authorities in Part V.

C. International Adjudication

International courts and tribunals are among the most significant institutions for delivering accountability through legality at the international level. When the Cold War ended in 1989, there were six permanent and functioning international courts. Now there are some twenty-four such courts that collectively have handed down over 37,000 binding legal judgments, 91 percent of those since the end of the Cold War.[59] Like other IOs, they have all been created by states through a founding treaty, and vary considerably in their subject matter and geographic jurisdiction. The ICJ,

56. *See* Benvenisti, *supra* note 3, at 272–73.

57. Joined Cases C-402/05 P and C-415/05 P, Kadi & Al Barakaat v. Council of the European Union, 2008 ECR I-6351 (*Kadi*). We discuss the present targeted sanctions program in Part III.

58. *See id.*

59. Karen Alter, The New Terrain of International Law: Courts, Politics, Rights 68 (2014) [hereinafter, Alter, The New Terrain]; Karen J. Alter, *The Multiple Roles of International Courts and Tribunals: Enforcement, Dispute Settlement, Constitutional and Administrative Review*, *in* International Law and International Relations: Synthesizing Insights from Interdisciplinary Scholarship 345, 346 (Jeffrey L. Dunoff & Mark A. Pollack eds., 2013) [hereinafter Alter, *Multiple Roles*]. For a full catalog of the twenty-four international courts referencing their subject matter and geographic jurisdiction, see Alter, *Multiple Roles, supra*, at 347. The summary that follows in the text of the jurisdictions and roles of international courts is taken from Alter's careful and comprehensive discussion, *id.*, and does not include the review mechanisms under the International Centre for the Settlement of Disputes (ICSID), the Southern Common Market Dispute Settlement Permanent Review Tribunal (MERCOSUR), or the arbitral panels under the North American Free Trade Agreement (NAFTA).

the Appellate Body of the WTO, the International Criminal Court (ICC), and the International Tribunal of the Law of the Sea (ITLOS) have global mandates. The remainder are regional bodies in Africa (9), Europe (6), Latin America (4), and Asia (1). Eighteen international courts have jurisdiction to hear economic disputes (e.g., WTO, ECJ, Andean Tribunal of Justice (ATJ), Economic Community of West African States Court of Justice (ECOWAS)). Nine have a general jurisdiction to hear any issue if the complainant has standing (e.g., ICJ, Benelux Court of Justice (BCJ), Caribbean Court of Justice (CCJ), Court of Justice of the East African Community (EACJ)). Five courts hear human rights cases (ECHR, Inter-American Court of Human Rights (IACtHR), CCJ, African Court of Peoples and Human Rights, ECOWAS). Three hear war crimes cases (ICC, International Criminal Tribunal for the Former Yugoslavia (ICTY), International Criminal Tribunal for Rwanda (ICTR)).[60]

Of the twenty-four international courts, twenty-one have at least partial compulsory jurisdiction, sixteen permit international institutions to commence proceedings, and fourteen allow private actors to initiate legal action. As Karen Alter aptly summarizes, "the lion's share of all international legal rulings [today] are issued in cases instigated by supranational commissions and prosecutors or private litigants with the plaintiff seeking to have state or international actions reviewed and international legal rules enforced."[61] The compulsory jurisdiction of international courts, however, is contingent on states ratifying treaties that place them under the authority of these courts. In principle, states may denounce these treaties at any time and withdraw from the relevant international regime, thereby ending the international court's jurisdiction over them. In practice, however, defections are relatively rare. No state has ever exited the WTO, and the economic and diplomatic costs of doing so would be severe. Venezuela denounced the American Convention on Human Rights in 2012, formally withdrawing from the jurisdiction of the IACtHR and the complaint procedure of the Inter-American Commission of Human Rights.[62] The denunciation came after more than a decade of criticism from the Commission and numerous embarrassing rebukes at the IACtHR, and was met with worldwide condemnation.[63]

Alter contends that international courts have four principal roles, and that all international courts—with the exception of the criminal courts—assume more than one such role: oversight of compliance with international law,[64]

60. We exclude for these purposes the so-called "hybrid courts" established within national jurisdictions with international assistance for the purpose of trying international crimes.

61. ALTER, THE NEW TERRAIN, *supra* note 59, at 68.

62. *See* Diego Gérman Méjia-Lemos, *Venezuela's Denunciation of the American Convention*, 17 ASIL INSIGHTS (Jan. 9, 2013), *at* http://www.asil.org/insights/volume/17/issue/1/venezuelas-denunciation-american-convention-human-rights (last visited Oct. 3, 2015).

63. *See, e.g.,* International Justice Resource Center, Venezuela Denounces American Convention on Human Rights as IACHR Faces Reform (Sept. 19, 2012), http://www.ijrcenter.org/2012/09/19/venezuela-denounces-american-convention-on-human-rights-as-iachr-faces-reform/ (last visited Oct. 3, 2015).

64. Alter somewhat infelicitously refers to oversight as "enforcement," a characterization that is in tension with her recognition that international courts, like national courts, have no direct

administrative review, constitutional review, and dispute resolution. Nineteen courts are empowered to oversee state compliance with international law, and in many cases order remedies for individual victims (e.g., ECJ, WTO, EACJ, ECHR, IACtHR, ICC). Twelve courts hear challenges to the decisions of international and national administrative actors tasked with implementing international regulations, mainly in the sphere of trade and commerce (e.g., BCJ, ATJ, CCJ, EAC, ECOWAS). Ten courts have a form of strong constitutional review authority in that they have formal authority to review the validity of international legislative enactments. These courts operate chiefly within common market systems where supranational political bodies are empowered to enact policies directly binding on member states. Their constitutional review power is typically grounded on norms from trade agreements and international human rights law that are treated as a form of "higher order law" (e.g., ECJ, ECHR, ATJ, CCJ, EACJ, ECOWAS).[65] Eighteen courts have a dispute settlement role, usually as part of a general jurisdiction or a more limited jurisdiction over economic matters (e.g., ICJ, WTO, ECJ, ATJ, EACJ).[66]

There is a lively debate in international relations scholarship over whether international courts are best understood as delegated agents of the states that create them or trustees of the law they administer. Advocates of the principal-agent theory argue that states would not delegate authority to international courts if it did not serve their interests to do so, and that states to a greater or lesser extent control courts through judicial appointment and institutional budgeting processes, the threat of noncompliance, and ultimately the threat of exit from the relevant treaty system.[67] Defenders of the trustee theory claim that it best explains the activity of international courts because, like trustees, judges are appointed on the basis of their personal and professional reputation, they are authorized to make decisions on the basis of their best judgment rather than their principal's wishes, and they make these decisions on behalf of one or more third-party beneficiaries (e.g., the parties to an international suit, and the broader publics subject to their jurisdiction) rather than a principal or settlor.[68] For present purposes, the most salient aspect of this debate is that both sides agree that international courts are fiduciaries of one kind or another, but dispute the character of the court's fiduciary office, and to whom

enforcement mechanisms of their own. *See* Alter, *Multiple Roles, supra* note 59, at 350 ("[N]o court actually enforces its rulings or the remedies judges create.").

65. *Id.* at 353.

66. *Id.* at 356.

67. *See, e.g.*, Geoffrey Garrett, *The Politics of Legal Integration in the European Union*, 49 Int'l Org. 171 (1995); Paul B. Stephan, *Courts, Tribunals and Legal Unification—The Agency Problem*, 3 Chi. J. Int'l L. 333 (2002).

68. *See, e.g.*, Alec Stone Sweet, The Judicial Construction of Europe (2004); Karen J. Alter, *Agents or Trustees? International Courts in Their Political Context*, 14 Eur. J. Int'l Rel. 33 (2008); Ingo Venzke, *Understanding the Authority of International Courts and Tribunals: On Delegation and Discursive Construction*, 14 J. Theoretical Inquiries 381, 390–92 (2013) (discussing the agent/trustee distinction from a conceptual perspective that treats delegation of authority as merely a "starting point.").

fiduciary duties are owed.[69] We suggest in Part IV that although the principal-agent theory may have some explanatory appeal from a descriptive and rational actor point of view, the trustee theory offers better resources for explaining the nature of the authority of international courts.

The challenge of justifying the authority of international courts is particularly acute. As Andreas Føllesdal points out, critics' concerns over unelected judges trampling the wishes of democratic legislatures arguably apply with equal or greater force to international judges, who are further removed from local democratic decision-making.[70] Like constitutional courts in national legal orders, international courts are often tasked with interpreting and applying open-textured norms to unforeseen circumstances. When they interpret international law so as to apply it to cases that were not plausibly in the contemplation of the states that created them, they engage in robust judicial lawmaking that frequently meets resistance at the national level.[71] It is hard to see how this authority could be derived from an initial delegation that never envisioned such lawmaking, and that is usually exercised in the wake of national courts and executives having rejected the claim sought.

For example, the IACtHR has delivered a series of judgments that vindicates indigenous peoples' communal right to territory, and even a right to have the state obtain indigenous consent if a proposed project is so massive in scale that it would threaten their way of life.[72] The requirement of consent in effect gives indigenous peoples a veto and co-legislative power over large-scale projects. These judgments rest largely on a novel interpretation of Article 21 of the American Convention on Human Rights, which on its face enshrines an individualized rather than collective right to property—"[e]veryone has the right to the use and enjoyment of *his* property"—and does so with the following qualification: "The law may subordinate such use and enjoyment to the interest of society."[73] One need not have any sympathy for

69. The debate parallels the controversy in corporate law over the nature of the firm—that is, whether officers and directors are agents who owe fiduciary duties to the corporation and its shareholders alone, or whether they are trustees of a broader constituency that includes employees and other stakeholders as well as the corporation. *See* Adolph A. Berle, *Corporate Powers as Powers in Trust*, 44 Harv. L. Rev. 1049 (1931) (defending the shareholder primacy theory); E. Merrick Dodd, *For Whom Are Corporate Managers Trustees?*, 45 Harv. L. Rev. 1145 (1932) (defending the stakeholder theory).

70. Andreas Føllesdal, *The Legitimacy Deficits of the Human Rights Judiciary: Elements and Implications of a Normative Theory*, 14 Theoretical Inquiries L. 339, 344 (2013) (*citing* Richard Bellamy, Political Constitutionalism: A Republican Defense of the Constitutionality of Democracy (2007); and Jeremy Waldron, *The Core of the Case against Judicial Review*, 115 Yale L.J. 1346 (2006)).

71. *See* Machiko Kanetake & André Nollkaemper, *The International Rule of Law in the Cycle of Contestation and Deference*, *in* The Rule of Law at the National and International Levels: Contestations and Deference (Machiko Kanetake & André Nollkaemper eds., 2016) (discussing *inter alia* cases of national-level resistance to international judgments).

72. *See* Saramaka People v. Suriname, Preliminary Objections, Merits, Reparations, and Costs, Judgment, Inter-Am. Ct. H.R. (ser. C) No. 172 (Nov. 28, 2007) [hereinafter *Saramaka People*].

73. American Convention on Human Rights art. 21(1), Nov. 21, 1969, 1144 U.N.T.S. 143 (emphasis added).

originalism to recognize that the IACtHR's jurisprudence on indigenous peoples marks a significant departure from the plain meaning of Article 21 and the intent of the Convention's drafters in 1969. It is unlikely that any state at that time would have accepted protection of ancestral claims to territory, much less the sharing of sovereign power. The court's practical authority thus requires a justification that looks beyond the state parties' initial delegation of judicial power to the court. In Part IV, we argue that delegation explains the founding *origin* and *authorization* of international courts, but not the *nature* of their ongoing *authority.*

* * *

International institutions serve humanity indirectly by helping to develop and sustain an international legal system in which states are encouraged to promote human security, economic development, environmental conservation, and other important shared interests. International actors thus help to ameliorate the distributive consequences of international law's state-centric system, with humanity as the ultimate beneficiary.[74] There are, however, circumstances in which international institutions do assume direct authority over individuals, sometimes with virtually all the public powers of a sovereign state. We discuss several of these cases now.

III. INTERNATIONAL INSTITUTIONS AS DIRECT FIDUCIARIES OF HUMANITY

Although the international legal system continues to feature states as its primary agents and subjects, increasingly international institutions themselves are playing direct roles in the protection and governance of vulnerable persons. In this section, we canvas a number of contexts in which this occurs. The first is peacekeeping, the traditional form of which arguably has elements of both indirect and direct stewardship, whereas more recent cases involve far greater direct stewardship. Peacekeeping has undergone significant change since the end of the Cold War, and now includes multisectoral institutional strengthening ("multidimensional" peacekeeping) as well as the use of force to protect civilians against armed groups ("robust" peacekeeping). Our second example of direct stewardship is comprehensive territorial administration and state-building, as occurred in Kosovo and East Timor. The third context is where international institutions exercise legal authority over particular individuals or classes of individuals. In the first two cases we discuss under this heading—persons in need of UNHCR protection, and injured U.N. personnel—the relevant IOs provide surrogate protection to the vulnerable. The third case in this group is much more controversial, and is in a sense the mirror image of the other two: the Security Council's targeted sanctions program that blacklists individuals suspected of terrorism. In this case, the Security Council purports to restrict the rights and liberty of individuals for the sake of international peace and security.

74. For careful development of the idea that IHRL is best explained as international law's attempt to mitigate the adverse effects of its distribution of sovereignty to states in order to structure global politics into an international legal order, see PATRICK MACKLEM, THE SOVEREIGNTY OF HUMAN RIGHTS (2015).

A. Peacekeeping

Since U.N. peacekeeping began in 1948 with the deployment of military observers to the Middle East to monitor the Armistice Agreement between Israel and its neighbors, there have been sixty-nine U.N. peacekeeping operations, fifty-six of them since 1988.[75] Until the end of the Cold War, international peacekeeping consisted mainly in the United Nations assembling military observers from member-states and deploying them to monitor and observe a ceasefire, typically through the use of buffer zones.[76] For example, in 1964 the Security Council established the U.N. Peacekeeping Force in Cyprus (UNFICYP), an operation that to this day supervises ceasefire lines and maintains a buffer zone between Greek Cypriot and Turkish Cypriot communities.[77] Three guiding principles—the "holy trinity"—emerged from the practice of traditional peacekeeping: consent of the parties, impartiality, and minimum use of force.[78] Notably, impartiality tended to be paired with or simply understood as neutrality.[79] Although neutrality shares with impartiality the concern that an arbitrator of a dispute must not show favor to one side or the other, in practice neutrality is understood to demand passivity by requiring peacekeepers to refrain from taking any action that could be perceived as either assistance or hostility toward one of the parties.[80]

In the context of traditional inter-state peacekeeping, passive neutrality may be adequate to the mission's principal role of observing and facilitating a ceasefire through buffer zones and observation posts. The fiduciary theory explains traditional peacekeeping generally, and neutrality specifically, by conceiving of the United Nations as a fiduciary of humanity's interest in peace and security. The

75. *See* United Nations, United Nations Peacekeeping: History of Peacekeeping, http://www.un.org/en/peacekeeping/operations/history.shtml (last visited Aug. 4, 2015) [hereinafter UN Peacekeeping].

76. The exception was the large-scale armed ONUC mission to the Congo (1960–1964), which resembled the complex and robust U.N. operations in the Congo of recent years. *See infra* text accompanying notes 91–95.

77. *See* United Nations, UNFICYP: United Nations Peacekeeping Force in Cyprus, http://www.un.org/en/peacekeeping/missions/unficyp/ (last visited June 12, 2015). For balanced assessment of the challenges and successes of UNFICYP, see Norrie MacQueen, *Judging Peacekeeping Operations: Three Perspectives on U.N. Operations*, 12 J. Int'l Peacekeeping 1, 12–14 (2008). Similar operations include those undertaken in Egypt (UNEF I), India/Pakistan (UNMOGIP)), Israel/Syria (UNDOF), Lebanon (UNIFIL), Yemen (UNYOM), and West New Guinea (UNSF). *See* UN Peacekeeping, *supra* note 75.

78. *See, e.g.*, Daniel H. Levine, *Peacekeeper Impartiality: Standards, Processes, and Operations*, 15 J. Int'l Peacekeeping 422, 423 (2011) (elaborating seven plausible standards for impartiality).

79. *See* Dominick Donald, *Neutral Is Not Impartial: The Confusing Legacy of Traditional Peace Operations Thinking*, 29 Armed Forces & Soc'y 415 (2003) (distinguishing impartiality from neutrality, and chronicling peacekeeping's unstable—and sometimes confused or unknowing—ambivalence toward these principles).

80. *Id.* at 429 (offering the embarrassing example of "the bamboo pole incident," where a convoy with the Head of Mission of the U.N. Transitional Authority in Cambodia (UNTAC), fearing the appearance of partiality, turned back when confronted by a few youthful guerillas and a single bamboo-pole barricade).

parties themselves are juridically incapable of playing this role, as they are parties to the dispute and therefore cannot have standing inter se to oversee the dispute's resolution and ongoing pacification.[81] Traditional peacekeepers are therefore direct fiduciaries of humanity inasmuch as they occupy an international public role the parties themselves cannot legitimately occupy. But because states are ultimately responsible for keeping the peace, and because the principal beneficiaries of peace are the state's people, there is also an important sense in which traditional peacekeepers are indirect fiduciaries of humanity. The direct and indirect stewardship of peacekeepers is not surprising, as making and keeping peace is a joint endeavor undertaken by both the international community and belligerent states.

The end of the Cold War saw a significant rise in the number of peacekeeping operations, and a dramatic transformation in the mandates of many of them. Rather than separate once-warring parties with a buffer zone, so-called multidimensional peacekeeping operations became deeply enmeshed in intrastate and comprehensive peace processes, often at the conclusion of a civil war. In Guatemala, for instance, from 1994 to 1996 the United Nations brokered an end to the country's thirty-six-year civil war. The peace accords arising from those negotiations consisted of ten separate agreements with commitments related to human rights, a ceasefire, reintegration of rebel forces, constitutional and electoral reform, police and armed forces reform, justice sector reform, indigenous peoples, resettlement of refugees, socioeconomic and land policy, and a truth and reconciliation commission.[82] Although the principal mandate of the U.N. Verification Mission in Guatemala (MINUGUA) was verification of the parties' compliance with the accords, MINUGUA was also tasked with reforming and strengthening state institutions, as well as capacity building with aboriginal peoples, NGOs, universities, municipalities, and other civil society actors.[83] From the time the insurgents turned over their arms in 1996, the mission was commonly referred to as one of peacebuilding rather than peacekeeping.[84]

In this kind of context, impartiality cannot mean passive neutrality, as the United Nations is explicitly undertaking an active role to promote a peace process. Instead, impartiality is more plausibly construed as even-handedness toward the parties

81. Thomas Hobbes, Leviathan with Selected Variants from the Latin Edition of 1668 ch 5, ¶ 3, 23 (Edwin Curley ed., 1994) (arguing that parties to a dispute must appoint an arbitrator or judge if their dispute is to be settled justly).

82. For all accords of the Guatemalan peace process, see United States Institute of Peace, Peace Agreements: Guatemala, http://www.usip.org/publications/peace-agreements-guatemala (last visited Aug. 6, 2015). Other multidimensional missions have included those deployed to El Salvador (ONUSAL), Haiti (UNSMIH, UNTMIH, MIPONUH), Angola (UNAVEM I, II, III; MONOA), Cambodia (UNTAC), Mozambique (ONUMOZ), Namibia (UNTAG), Burundi (ONUB), Côte d'Ivoire (UNOCI), Liberia (UNMIL), and Sierra Leone (UNAMSIL).

83. *See, e.g.*, MINUGUA: Renewal of Mandate Report, A/55/389, Sept, 14, 2000. The report notes that the parties asked MINUGUA to verify implementation of all the accords, and that in addition its functions comprise "good offices, advisory and support services, and public information" with a "special focus on socioeconomic issues, rural development, strengthening of civilian power and various forums for increased citizen participation." *Id.* ¶¶ 6, 9.

84. *Id.* ¶ 4 ("The peace agreements provided the framework for the peacebuilding process in Guatemala, within which MINUGUA received a mandate aimed at supporting this process.").

while endeavoring to fulfill the peacebuilding aspects of the mission's mandate. In the case of MINUGUA, this involved an effort to support human rights through verification of the human rights accord, all the while supporting reforms conducive to democracy and the rule of law, as articulated in the various peace agreements. Peacebuilding is thus a particularly poignant example of how the ideals of global constitutionalism can inform and guide an intrastate peace process. The fiduciary theory explains the ideals of constitutionalism and peacebuilding as constitutive features of the regime of secure and equal freedom that states have an overarching fiduciary duty to provide. The project of realizing human rights, democracy, and the rule of law makes good on the promise of the fiduciary theory's guiding principles of non-domination and non-instrumentalization, and therefore the constitutionalist peacebuilding project is both explained and prescribed by the theory.

To the extent multidimensional U.N. missions promote human rights through on-the-ground verification of a state's human rights commitments, they act as indirect fiduciaries of humanity, because states are still the primary duty-bearers responsible for the respect and protection of human rights. But in another sense U.N. missions are closer to direct fiduciaries, as they operate within the state's territory during a time of tension and rebuilding, for the benefit of its people, as essentially ombudspersons. The same may be said of international efforts to reform and strengthen democratic institutions as part of a comprehensive peace process. As with traditional peacekeeping, multidimensional operations exhibit both direct and indirect forms of stewardship.

An even more dramatic departure from traditional peacekeeping has come to prominence more recently.[85] In the wake of the debacles in Rwanda and Srebrenica in the 1990s, where U.N. peacekeeping forces were deployed when the tragedies occurred,[86] the United Nations underwent a period of extensive soul-searching.[87] The United Nations commissioned a Report to the Secretary-General in the case of Srebenica,[88] an Independent Inquiry in the case of Rwanda,[89] and a comprehensive report on U.N. peacekeeping operations (the "Brahimi Report").[90] One of the results of this reflection was the development of "robust" peacekeeping, a form of peacekeeping that takes seriously the protection of vulnerable civilians. The Security Council resolution authorizing UNAMSIL in Sierra Leone, for example,

85. For a comprehensive account, see SIOBHÁN WILLS, PROTECTING CIVILIANS: THE OBLIGATIONS OF PEACEKEEPERS (2009).

86. *See* FRED GRÜNFELD & ANKE HUIJBOOM, THE FAILURE TO PREVENT GENOCIDE IN RWANDA: THE ROLE OF BYSTANDERS (2007); DAVID ROHDE, ENDGAME: THE BETRAYAL AND FALL OF SREBRENICA, EUROPE'S WORST MASSACRE SINCE WORLD WAR II (1998).

87. For discussion of this soul-searching and its consequences, see Frédéric Mégret, *Between R2P and the ICC: "Robust Peacekeeping" and the Quest for Civilian Protection*, 26 CRIM. L. FORUM 101 (2015).

88. U.N. General Assembly, Report of the Secretary-General Pursuant to General Assembly Resolution 53/35: The Fall of Srebrenica, A/54/549. Nov. 15, 1999.

89. U.N. Security Council, Report of the Independent Inquiry into the Actions of the United Nations During the 1994 Genocide in Rwanda, S/1999/1257, Dec. 16, 1999.

90. U.N. General Assembly & Security Council, Report of the Panel on United Nations Peace Operations, A/55/305–S/2000/809, Aug. 21, 2000.

provided in part that the operation was to "afford protection to civilians under immanent threat of physical violence."[91] The mandates of U.N. operations in the Congo, Côte d'Ivoire, Darfur, South Sudan, and Liberia expressly enjoin peacekeepers to use "all necessary means" for this purpose.[92] As Frédéric Mégret puts it, robust peacekeeping "emerged as an attempt to bridge the gap between peacekeeping and peace enforcement (the elusive 'Chapter VI ½'), which claimed to safeguard the fundamental commitment to impartiality of the former whilst not risking the UN's soul by failing to engage the latter."[93] In recent years, U.N. peacekeepers in the Congo have frequently engaged M23 rebels, a militia force with a lengthy history of war crimes and atrocities.[94] On March 28, 2013, the Security Council authorized its first-ever explicitly offensive "Intervention Brigade" to deploy to the Congo under MONUSCO.[95] The Security Council resolution instructs the Brigade to "carry out targeted offensive operations . . . in a robust, highly mobile and versatile manner and in strict compliance with international law . . . to prevent the expansion of all armed groups, neutralize these groups, and to disarm them."[96]

The demands of robust peacekeeping have led to an outright rejection of passive neutrality as an interpretation of peacekeeper impartiality. The U.N. Capstone Doctrine affirms a principled approach to impartiality consistent with the practice of robust peacekeeping:

> Impartiality is crucial to maintaining the consent and cooperation of the main parties, but should not be confused with neutrality or inactivity. . . . The need for even-handedness towards the parties should not become an excuse for inaction in the face of behavior that clearly works against the peace process. Just as a good referee is impartial, but will penalize infractions, so a peacekeeper operation should not condone actions by parties that violate the undertakings of the peace process or the international norms and principles that a United Nations peacekeeping operation upholds.[97]

In short, peacekeepers are to pursue their mandate and promote the peace process as even-handed referees who favor neither side,[98] but who nonetheless operate with

91. S.C. Res. 1289, ¶10(e), S/RES/1289, Feb. 7, 2000. Other missions with similar protection-of-civilian mandates include Burundi (ONUB), Côte d'Ivoire (UNOCI), the Congo (MONUC, MONUSCO), Darfar (UNAMID), South Sudan (UNMISS) and Liberia (UNMIL).

92. *See, e.g.*, S.C. Res. 1649, ¶ 11, S/RES/1649, Dec. 21, 2005 (instructing MUNOC in the Congo to "use all necessary means, within its capabilities.").

93. Mégret, *supra* note 87, at 110.

94. *See Q & A: Who Are DR Congo's M23 rebels?*, Al Jazeera, Nov. 5, 2013, http://www.aljazeera.com/news/africa/2013/08/201382411593336904.html (last visited Aug. 7, 2015).

95. U.N. Security Council Res. 2089, ¶ 9, S/Res/2089 (Jan. 24, 2013).

96. *Id.* ¶ 12(b).

97. United Nations Department of Peacekeeping Operations and Department of Field Support, Principles and Guidelines 33 (2008).

98. *See* Levine, *supra* note 78, at 439–43 (defending promotion of the peace process as the appropriate standard for impartiality).

a commitment to the rules of the game: most notably, the terms of the ceasefire or peace accords as articulated in the mission's mandate, the principles and objectives of the peace process, IHL, and the protection of civilians if the norms of IHL do not apply (e.g., there is no conflict triggering IHL).

Robust peacekeeping may set back the interests of one side or the other, and this may pose serious political and practical difficulties in the field, as the United Nations attempts to maintain the appearance of an independent mediator.[99] But in principle, so long as impartiality is understood to bear on the *rights* of civilians and the parties, rather than on their *interests*, and so long as peacekeepers do not themselves benefit from their operations and are careful to conduct themselves even-handedly, they can be seen to occupy a fiduciary position analogous to that of a judge. The good judge is impartial if she treats the parties as equals and even-handedly, notwithstanding that her ruling may advance or set back their interests.

Commentators have been quick to link robust peacekeeping to R2P.[100] Both seek to protect civilians from atrocities their own states are either unable or unwilling to prevent, while at the same time locating primary responsibility for civilian protection with the state.[101] It is only when the state proves unwilling or unable to protect that the international community—under R2P and peacekeeping equally—acquires a "residual responsibility" to protect.[102] R2P is in principle wider than robust peacekeeping because it contemplates "collective action" without state consent through the Security Council under Chapter VII (i.e., peace enforcement).[103] But more significant for present purposes, both R2P and robust peacekeeping assume a conception of sovereignty as responsibility,[104] wherein sovereignty itself imposes on the state primary responsibility to protect its people.[105] This is of a piece with the fiduciary theory: responsibility is the normative consequence of the fiduciary relationship between states and their people, a relationship which in turn explains and helps specify the conditions under which sovereign rights may be held and exercised.

Under the fiduciary theory, robust peacekeepers are direct fiduciaries of humanity because they themselves provide protection and security to vulnerable civilians,

99. *See, e.g.*, Mégret, *supra* note 87, at 114–16 (chronicling, *inter alia*, the trade-offs and challenges that may arise as the United Nations tries to act as an independent broker between two belligerents while using force against one).

100. *See, e.g.*, Mégret, *supra* note 87, at 145–46 ("R2P and the ICC further entrench an anti-atrocity norm in international society that significantly raises expectations in terms of what peace operations are expected to do.").

101. *See* Sabine Hassler, *Peacekeeping and the Responsibility to Protect*, 14 J. Int'l Peacekeeping 134, 143 (2011).

102. Report of the International Commission on Intervention and State Sovereignty, The Responsibility to Protect 17 (International Development Research Centre for ICISS, Dec. 2001) [hereinafter ICISS Report].

103. World Summit Outcome Document ¶ 139, A/60/L.1 (Sept. 20, 2005).

104. Francis M. Deng, *Frontiers of Sovereignty: A Framework of Protection, Assistance, and Development for the Internally Displaced*, 8 Leiden J. Int'l L. 249 (1995).

105. ICISS Report, *supra* note 102, at xi ("State sovereignty implies responsibility, and the primary responsibility for the protection of its people lies with the state itself.").

their principal beneficiaries. Typically, these peacekeeping forces will work with the armed forces of the local state,[106] and to that extent they usually also act as indirect fiduciaries. But their distinctiveness lies in the direct and armed surrogate protection they provide when the local state is unable or unwilling to guarantee the security of its people. Moreover, their in-principle availability to deploy anywhere in the world where civilians are at risk reveals the literal sense in which they are fiduciaries of humanity at large. And finally, the fiduciary theory explains the protection-of-civilians conception of impartiality because, as discussed in Chapter 3, its principle of formal moral equality is precisely a principle of even-handedness that allows for differential treatment if circumstances so warrant. As long as peacekeepers provide protection to civilians even-handedly, they conform to the principled understanding of impartiality shared by peacekeeping and the fiduciary theory.

B. State-Building and International Territorial Administration

As discussed above, multidimensional peacekeeping operations typically have a significant peacebuilding component.[107] In some cases, such as MINUGUA, the peacebuilding mission is comprehensive in that it proceeds from an ambitious peace process that envisions reform and institutional-strengthening across many sectors. In these kinds of operations, the peacebuilding mission is fundamentally facilitative: the overarching modus operandi is to strengthen national democracy, respect for human rights, and the rule of law by involving national state and nonstate actors from the beginning. Crucially, the local government retains sovereign authority throughout. In state-building operations involving international territorial or transitional administration, however, the international authority *is* the government, or at least significant parts of it. As Simon Chesterman notes, *state-building* includes "quasi-governmental activities such as electoral assistance, human rights and rule of law technical assistance, security sector reform, and certain forms of development assistance," whereas *transitional administration* refers to operations "in which these ends have been pursued by assuming some or all of the powers of the state on a temporary basis."[108]

106. *See, e.g., Congolese Troops Prepare for Offensive Against Rebels*, ALJAZEERA, Jan. 31, 2015, http://www.aljazeera.com/news/africa/2015/01/congolese-troops-prepare-offensive-rebels-150131083433354.html (last visited Aug. 7, 2015) (reporting that the United Nations would provide Congolese troops support with helicopter gunships).

107. *See* Dieter Fleck, *The Responsibility to Rebuild and Its Potential for Law-Creation: Good Governance, Accountability, and Judicial Control*, 16 J. INT'L PEACEKEEPING 84 (2012) (arguing that of R2P's three pillars—prevent, react, and rebuild—it is "rebuild" that holds the promise of greatest innovation, as it is least controlled by existing international law).

108. SIMON CHESTERMAN, YOU, THE PEOPLE: THE UNITED NATIONS, TRANSITIONAL ADMINISTRATION, AND STATE-BUILDING 5 (2005). Commentators categorize various kinds of state-building/transitional administration in different ways. Jarat Chopra, for instance, divides transitional administration into *governorship* (the United Nations assumes directly governmental powers), *control* (U.N. personnel occupy controlling positions in existing state institutions), *partnership* (United Nations is an equal partner within state institutions), and *assistance* (assistance to functioning state administration). Jarat Chopra, *Introducing Peace-Maintenance*, *in* THE POLITICS OF PEACE-MAINTENANCE 1, 13–14 (Jarat Chopra ed., 1998).

In Namibia in 1989 (United Nations Traditional Assistance Group, or UNTAG) and Cambodia in 1993 (United Nations Transitional Authority in Cambodia, or UNTAC), for example, the United Nations supervised elections but also assumed various governmental functions. UNTAC's mandate included "military arrangements, civil administration, the maintenance of law and order, the repatriation and resettlement of the Cambodian refugees and displaced persons and the rehabilitation of essential Cambodian infrastructure during the transitional period."[109] UNTAC was regarded as an exemplar of the kind of massive civil reconstruction that the post–Cold War United Nations could fruitfully undertake.[110] In the case of UNTAG in Namibia and that state's decolonization process, the United Nations supplied, inter alia, a police force, support for refugee repatriation, legislative reform, and a military component responsible for monitoring the ceasefire.[111] In these and other cases,[112] the United Nations has acted as a direct fiduciary of the people subject to the various aspects of its local governing authority.

In 1999, the United Nations launched comprehensive state-building operations in East Timor (UNTAET) and Kosovo (UNMIK). In both cases, the United Nations took on the role of territorial administrator, and found itself acting as "both state and state builder."[113] In East Timor, for example, the Security Council granted to UNTAET "overall responsibility for the administration of East Timor" and sovereign-like powers "to exercise all legislative and executive authority, including the administration of justice."[114] Mégret and Hoffman provide a vivid account of the wide range of functions assumed by the United Nations in Kosovo and East Timor:

> From security provision *lato sensu* and the organization of elections, to such unlikely tasks for the United Nations as creating an army, the collection of taxes, national budgeting, the maintenance of civil and commercial registers, border and customs control, accreditation of foreign legations and representations, issuing of ID cards, travel documents, registration plates and stamps, prisons, currency, radio frequency management, down to the question of what flags get to appear on public buildings or the regulations of road traffic, the United Nations is involved in nearly every aspect of public administration.[115]

109. United Nations, Cambodia—UNTAC, http://www.un.org/en/peacekeeping/missions/past/untacmandate.html (last visited Aug. 15, 2015); *see also* S.C. Res. 745, S/Res/745, Feb. 28, 1992 (establishing UNTAC).

110. *See* Michael W. Doyle, U.N. Peacekeeping in Cambodia: UNTAC's Civil Mandate (1995).

111. United Nations, Namibia—UNTAG, http://www.un.org/en/peacekeeping/missions/past/untagFT.htm (last visited Aug. 15, 2015); *see also* S.C. Res. 632, S/Res/632, (Feb. 16, 1989) (establishing UNTAG).

112. Other places where the United Nations provided at least partial local administration include Bosnia and Herzegovina from 1995–2002 (UNMIBH), Somalia from 1993 to 1995 (UNOSAM II), and Eastern Slavonia from 1996–1998 (UNTAES).

113. James Cotton, *Against the Grain: The East Timor Intervention*, 43 Survival 127, 139 (2001).

114. S.C. Res. 1272, S/Res/1272 (Oct. 25, 1999) (establishing UNTAET).

115. Frédéric Mégret & Florian Hoffman, *The U.N. as a Human Rights Violator? Some Reflections on the United Nations Changing Human Rights Responsibilities*, 25 Hum. Rts. Q. 314, 329 (2003).

Mégret and Hoffman note as well that far from being relegated to a limited caretaker role,

> UNMIK and UNTAET were involved in efforts to trigger reconciliation processes; attempts to organize both national and local democracy; economic, justice, law, education, pension, health, and land reform; the launching of a policy of environment protection; legislation over matters of public mores; the drafting of a constitutional framework; or the negotiation of complex treaties over natural resources that will affect the long term prospects of the territories.[116]

Mégret and Hoffman refer to Kosovo and East Timor under U.N. rule as "The New Protectorates."[117] Ralph Wilde helpfully compares and contrasts these instances of international territorial administration with governance under the League of Nations' Mandate System and the United Nations Trusteeship Council.[118] We will turn to some of these scholars' insights below, when we take up the question of the applicability of human rights norms to international institutions. For now, we simply note that administration of the kind carried out by UNMIK and UNTAET represents a high-water mark of an IO serving as a direct fiduciary of humanity. In these cases, the United Nations stands in a comprehensive sovereign relation to the individuals within the relevant territory, a relation in which the international administration claims authority to announce and enforce law on behalf of both humanity at large and the people immediately subject to its jurisdiction.

C. International Institutions and Individuals

Peacekeeping, peacebuilding, state-building, and territorial administration all involve an international commitment to create or protect legal order within one or more states. There are numerous other contexts in which the international community's mandate is far less comprehensive, and is particularized to individuals in specific contexts. In these cases, international institutions assert direct legal authority over individuals, or purport to have authority to represent them. Here, too, international institutions act as direct fiduciaries of humanity and the individuals subject to their jurisdiction. To illustrate, we briefly discuss three such cases: UNHCR governance of protracted refugee situations, the United Nation's authority to represent its staff in legal proceedings, and the Security Council's targeted sanctions program. In the first two cases, the United Nations provides a form of surrogate protection to

116. *Id.* at 330.

117. *Id.* at 327.

118. Ralph Wilde, International Territorial Administration: How Trusteeship and the Civilizing Mission Never Went Away (2008); Ralph Wilde, *Understanding the International Territorial Administration Accountability Deficit: Trusteeship and the Legitimacy of International Organizations* 12 J. Int'l Peacekeeping 93 (2008) [hereinafter Wilde, *Accountability Deficit*]; Ralph Wilde, *Representing International Territorial Administration: A Critique of Some Approaches*, 15 Eur. J. Int'l L. 71 (2004); *see also* Carsten Stahn, *Governance Beyond the State: Issues of Legitimacy in International Territorial Administration*, 2 Int'l Org. L. Rev. 9 (2005).

individuals, whereas in the last the United Nations itself sanctions terror suspects on grounds of international peace and security.

1. UNHCR and Protracted Refugee Situations

As discussed in Chapter 7, the UNHCR was established to replace the International Refugee Organization at roughly the same time the 1951 Refugee Convention was drafted. And, like the Refugee Convention, the enabling statute of the UNHCR firmly entrenched an individualized protection regime limited to persons with a well-founded fear of persecution based on civil or political grounds.[119] Permanent solutions are to be sought by "assisting Governments and ... private organizations to facilitate the voluntary repatriation of such refugees, or their assimilation within new national communities."[120] As reiterated in scores of General Assembly resolutions,[121] durable solutions for persons in need of protection—resettlement to a third country, voluntary repatriation, and local integration—are primarily the responsibility of states. Nonetheless, the UNHCR now conceives of its broader mission as encompassing some 33.9 million persons of concern "who lack the full protection of their state."[122] These "persons of concern" include internally displaced persons at risk from armed conflict (IDPs), stateless individuals, people displaced in urban areas, and individuals displaced by natural disasters and climate change.

As noted in Chapter 7, more than 6 million individuals now live in "protracted refugee situations," and in many of these situations the UNHCR operates medium and long-term camps as a kind of "surrogate state."[123] Amy Slaughter and Jeff Crisp observe that tasks typically assumed by the UNHCR include

> registering refugees and providing them with personal documentation; ensuring that they have access to shelter, food, water, health care and education; administering and managing the camps where they are usually accommodated; and establishing policing and justice mechanisms that enable refugees to benefit from some approximation to the rule of law.[124]

119. G.A. Res. 428 (V), at II(6)(A)(ii) (Dec. 14, 1950) (Annex) (Statute of the Office of the UNHCR).

120. *Id.*

121. *See, e.g.,* G.A. Res., Res/68/141 (Jan. 28, 2014) ("*The General Assembly ... Re-emphasizes* that the protection of refugees is primarily the responsibility of States.").

122. U.N. High Commissioner for Refugees, The State of the World's Refugees: In Search of Solidarity 2 (2012).

123. *See, e.g.,* Amy Slaughter & Jeff Crisp, *A Surrogate State? The Role of UNHCR in Protracted Refugee Situations, in* Protracted Refugee Situations: Political, Human Rights and Security Implications 123, 124 (Gil Loescher et al. eds., 2008) (noting that host country involvement is generally restricted to admission and recognition of refugees, respect for the principle of non-refoulement and the provision of security).

124. *Id.; see also* Ralph Wilde, *From Danzig to East Timor and Beyond: The Role of International Territorial Administration,* 95 Am. J. Int'l L. 583, 584 (2001) (describing camps as "small cities where education, medical services, and basic infrastructure are provided by a network of international agencies under the control of UNHCR.").

Jacob Stevens offers a less sanguine account:

> The camps are, in the first instance, a legal anomaly. Although they are on the territory of the host country, that country attempts to absolve itself of responsibility by handing control of the camps over to 'humanitarian' organizations. That initial abdication of duty creates a legal void that makes it hard to prevent violence, corruption and neglect; however good the intentions of the majority of UNHCR workers may be, there is no structural solution to the abuses of a minority. Once they are beyond the rule of law, refugee camps become "total institutions" like prisons and mental hospitals, where the agency workers can exercise their powers unchecked.[125]

In these circumstances, where the UNHCR operates as a "de facto sovereign,"[126] it also serves as a direct fiduciary of the individuals subject to its rule inside the camps, and that stewardship, we argue in Part IV, entails that the UNHCR is never "beyond the rule of law," even if in practice "agency workers can exercise their powers unchecked."

2. International Representation of Personnel

Another way the United Nations exercises legal authority on behalf of individuals is by representing them in legal proceedings. In the *Reparations for Injuries Case,* the ICJ held unanimously that in the event an agent of the United Nations on assignment suffered injury for which a state was responsible, the United Nations was entitled to bring an international claim for reparations for damage caused to the organization itself.[127] An 11–4 majority reached the same conclusion regarding the United Nation's standing to bring a claim for reparations on behalf of the injured individual or his or her survivors.[128] The decision is remarkable because the U.N. Charter and the ICJ Statute are silent on the question of the United Nation's capacity to bring claims for reparations. The conventional rule under international law was that only states could make claims against states. Through a purposive analysis, the ICJ reasoned that the United Nations could not maintain its independence when it carried out the various functions assigned it by the Charter—including "the maintenance of international peace and security"—without international legal personality, and thus concluded that the United Nations is "an international person."[129] Having found that the United Nations possessed legal personality separate

125. Jacob Stevens, *Prisons of the Stateless: The Derelictions of UNHCR,* 42 New Left Rev. 53 (2006) (drawing on Barbara Harrell-Bond, Imposing Aid: Emergency Assistance to Refugees (1986), and Barbara Harrell-Bond, Rights in Exile (2005)).

126. Ralph Wilde, Quis Custodiet Ipsos Custodes?: *Why and How UNHCR Governance of "Development" Refugee Camps Should be Subject to International Human Rights Law,* 1 Yale Hum. Rts. Dev. L.J. 107, 113 (1998).

127. Reparations for Injuries Suffered in the Service of the United Nations, Advisory Opinion, 1949 ICJ Rep. 174, 178–81 (Apr. 11).

128. *Id.* at 181–84.

129. *Id.* at 179.

from its members, the Court inferred that it had capacity to seek redress for damage resulting from a member-state's breach of its international obligations. Similarly, the majority held that for the United Nations to be able to function effectively and independently in "disturbed parts of the world," where its agents face "unusual dangers," it must be able to provide its agents with legal protection, including redress for injuries suffered.[130]

The principle at the heart of the ICJ's judgment is institutional independence. If an injured U.N. agent had to rely on the protection of his state rather than the United Nations, his independence might be compromised. Thus, the court held, to "ensure the independence of the agent, and, consequently, the independent action of the Organization itself, it is essential that in performing his duties he need not have to rely on any other protection than that of the Organization."[131] This reasoning embodies a core fiduciary doctrine that prohibits conflicts between one's duty as a fiduciary and one's interest (the "no conflicts rule"). Were a U.N. agent compelled to rely on her own state for protection, her personal interest in protection could conflict with her duty to the United Nations, comprising both her independence and the United Nation's. The ICJ underlined the importance of avoiding this conflict:

> it is essential that—whether the agent belongs to a powerful or to a weak State; to one more affected or less affected by the complications of international life; to one in sympathy or not in sympathy with the mission of the agent—he should know that in the performance of his duties he is under the protection of the Organization.[132]

As Thomas Franck points out, with this decision "the judges had deliberately broken the exclusive fiduciary relationship between a citizen and his state in those cases where the citizen is working for the international organization."[133] In these circumstances, the international organization steps into the fiduciary role "to protect [its agents] and safeguard their interests," in part through its capacity to represent them and seek reparations for damages on the international plane.[134] In sum, the international reparations case reveals the presence of two salient fiduciary relationships: the U.N.-humanity relation, and the U.N.-agent relation. The overarching fiduciary requirement of institutional independence arising from the former entails not only that the United Nations must have legal capacity to represent its injured agents, but that the United Nations, in taking up the stewardship role vis-à-vis its agents, is thereby under a fiduciary duty to exercise its representational capacity so as to ensure their protection. It is only the presence of this ongoing duty that ensures the independence of the agent, and thus, ultimately, the independence of the organization. For this reason, the United Nation's fiduciary duty to the agent

130. *Id.* at 183.

131. *Id.*

132. *Id.* 183–84.

133. Thomas Franck, Nation Against Nation: What Happened to the U.N. Dream and What the U.S. Can Do About It 99 (1985).

134. *Id.*

is also a duty to humanity at large, as the organization cannot claim to speak for humanity if it lacks independence.

A sceptic might concede that where international institutions protect vulnerable individuals who states are unable or unwilling to protect, the fiduciary model may appear to explain the relevant international institution's responsibilities. In these cases, the international institution has stepped into a protective and, in some instances, quasi-sovereign role. But, the sceptic might continue, if an international institution targets individuals for sanction rather than protection, and does so in a way that violates their human rights, then there is no plausible sense in which that institution can be said to stand as a fiduciary of the very individuals it both sanctions and wrongs. This being so, the fiduciary theory is implausible to the extent it makes the universalist and comprehensive claim that international institutions are fiduciaries, collectively, of every individual subject to every form or kind of international legal authority. We disagree. The sceptic's provocative argument falsely assumes that a public fiduciary cannot, under limited and legally prescribed circumstances, set back the interests of a beneficiary, and likewise falsely assumes that an abuse of power necessarily impeaches the power's fiduciary character and the possible legitimacy of its possession. We use the Security Council's controversial targeted sanctions regime to elaborate on this reply.

3. U.N. Targeted Sanctions Program

In 1999 the Security Council, acting under Chapter VII of the U.N. Charter, adopted Resolution 1267.[135] Resolution 1267 and numerous others that followed require all states to impose various sanctions on individuals or entities associated with al Qaeda, the Taliban, or Osama bin Laden.[136] States are directed to impose an assets freeze, a travel ban, and an arms embargo on individuals designated as having an association with a terrorist organization. Resolution 1267 established a committee to make these designations consisting of all Security Council members—the "1267 Committee." The Committee was charged with considering states' requests to add or remove names from its "Consolidated List," and keeping the list updated.[137]

The justification for this regime emerged from criticism that comprehensive sanctions against states, such as those imposed against Iraq in the 1990s, had adverse humanitarian consequences on innocent civilians within them, while leaving the actual wrongdoers unaffected.[138] Targeted sanctions, on the other hand, are

135. S.C. Res. 1267, S/RES/1267 (Oct. 15, 1999).

136. For discussion of the resolutions subsequent to Resolution 1267 but prior to Kadi, see Christopher Michaelson, *Kadi and Al Barakaat v Council of the European Union and Commission of the European Communities: The Incompatibility of the United Nations Security Council 1267 Sanctions Regime with European Due Process Guarantees*, 10 Melb. J. Int'l L. 329 (2009). For ease of exposition, we will refer to "individuals and entities" subject to targeted sanctions as simply "individuals."

137. *Id.* at 331.

138. *See, e.g.*, Global Policy Forum, Iraq Sanctions: Humanitarian Implications and Options for the Future (Aug. 6, 2002), https://www.globalpolicy.org/component/content/article/170-sanctions/41947-iraq-sanctions.html (last visited Sept. 8, 2015).

intended to apply to the very individuals responsible for international wrongdoing, and to do so in a way that suppresses the opportunity for such wrongdoing.

After the events of September 11, 2001, the work of the 1267 Committee achieved new salience. That Committee's work was folded into a wider Security Council antiterrorist initiative that culminated in Resolution 1373, also adopted under Chapter VII.[139] This resolution called on all states to take far-reaching measures to prevent and suppress terrorism, including the criminalization of activities alleged to support terror groups, and the freezing of assets of individuals and entities alleged to finance terror organizations. As numerous commentators have pointed out, Resolution 1373 marked a significant shift in the Security Council's use of Chapter VII measures.[140] Whereas previously those measures generally had been used to address discrete conflicts or emergencies, they since have been used to establish binding norms of indefinite duration applicable to all states, in relation to issues of indefinite duration (the global antiterror campaign), and whose ultimate targets are not states but individuals and nonstate entities.

Measures adopted in Security Council resolutions under Chapter VII purport to be binding on all states to which they are directed. Under Article 25 of the U.N. Charter, "[m]embers of the United Nations agree to accept and carry out the decisions of the Security Council."[141] More specifically still, under Article 41 of Chapter VII, the Security Council is empowered to "call upon the Members of the United Nations to apply such measures" as it determines necessary "to give effect to its decisions."[142] And under Article 103, the obligations of member-states under the Charter prevail over obligations "under any other international agreement."[143]

With its Chapter VII mandate in hand, the 1267 Committee placed individuals on its Consolidated List without notice, without giving them an opportunity to know or reply to the case against them, and without an independent (much less judicial) review mechanism. Initially, any individual who wished to contest her designation had to ask her state to make a request to the 1267 Committee. In 2007, a "focal point" was established that let named individuals seek delisting directly from the Committee.[144] The focal point, however, did not provide notice of Committee deliberations on initial designations, nor did it disclose the reasons for designation, offer an opportunity to be heard in the review process, or provide an independent review mechanism.[145] Just as significant, delisting remained possible only with the

139. S.C. Res. 1373, S/RES/1373 (Sept. 28, 2001).

140. *See, e.g.*, COHEN, *supra* note 23, at 272–77; David Dyzenhaus, *The Rule of (Administrative) Law in International Law*, 68 LAW & CONTEMP. PROBS. 127 (2005); Paul Szasz, *The Security Council Starts Legislating*, 96 AM. J. INT'L L. 901 (2002).

141. U.N. Charter art. 25.

142. U.N. Charter art. 41; *see also* U.N. Charter art. 49 ("The Members of the United Nations shall join in affording mutual assistance in carrying out the measures decided upon by the Security Council.").

143. U.N. Charter art. 103.

144. S.C. Res. 1730, S/RES/1730 (Dec. 19, 2006).

145. *See* Chia Lehnardt, *European Court Rules on U.N. and EU Terrorist Suspect Blacklists*, 11 ASIL INSIGHTS (Jan. 2007), http://www.asil.org/insights/volume/11/issue/1/european-court-rules-un-and-eu-terrorist-suspect-blacklists (last visited Sept. 8, 2015).

unanimous consent of the 1267 Committee members, usually including the original designating member, or at least the permanent Security Council members.[146]

In 2009, after the ECJ Grand Chamber in *Kadi* implicitly determined that the sanctions regime violated due process and would not apply to members of the European Union, the Security Council established an Ombudsperson empowered to receive delisting requests directly from named individuals.[147] The Ombudsperson was not authorized to delist individuals, but rather communicated the grounds of designation—less confidential information—to the petitioner, received submissions from the petitioner (typically meeting with him or her), and then made a recommendation to the 1267 Committee in the form of a comprehensive report.[148]

During the Ombudsperson's first eighteen months, delisting remained possible only with the unanimous approval of the Committee. In mid-2011, the Security Council split the 1267 Committee into two: the "1988 Committee" that designates persons allegedly associated with the Taliban, and the "1267/1989 Committee" or "Al Qaida Sanctions Committee" that designates persons allegedly associated with al Qaeda.[149] Only the latter remained subject to the Ombudsperson's mandate. However, within that narrower mandate, the Security Council strengthened the Ombudsperson's review capacity.[150] Since then, a recommendation to delist becomes effective unless the Al Qaida Sanctions Committee unanimously rejects it. If there is no consensus within the Committee, delisting can be avoided only through an overriding vote of nine out of fifteen members of the Security Council, a vote that can be vetoed by any of the five permanent members. In practice, the Committee has always followed the Ombudsperson's recommendation.[151] Reasons are given to the petitioner, but not the Ombudsperson's comprehensive report (not even with confidential information redacted), and the public receives only a cursory summary available on the Al Qaida Sanctions Committee website.[152] In 2014, the Security Council allowed designating states and states of residence or nationality of named persons to request the Ombudsperson's relevant comprehensive reports (with confidential information redacted).[153]

In her final report to the Security Council in July 2015, the first Ombudsperson advised that in her five-year term, the Ombudsperson process had received sixty-four applications (half without legal representation), and had "fully completed"

146. *Id.*

147. S.C. Res. 1904, Annex II, ¶¶ 20–21, S/RES/1904 (Dec. 17, 2009).

148. *See* Report of the Office of the Ombudsperson Pursuant to Security Council Resolution 2161, S/2015/533 (July 13, 2015) [hereinafter July 2015 Ombudsperson Report]; Juliane Kokott & Christoph Sobotta, *The Kadi Case—Constitutional Core Values and International Law—Finding the Balance?*, 23 Eur. J. Int'l L. 1015 (2012).

149. S.C. Res. 1988, S/RES/1988 (June 17, 2011); S.C. Res. 1989, S/Res/1989 (June 17, 2011).

150. S.C. Res. 1989, ¶¶ 22–23, S/RES/1989 (June 17, 2011); S.C. Res. 2161, Annex II, S/RES/2161 (June 17, 2014) (providing fixed-time phases for information gathering, dialogue, and committee discussion and decision).

151. July 2015 Ombudsperson Report, *supra* note 148, ¶ 31.

152. S.C. Res. 2083, Annex II, at 19, ¶ 15, S/RES/2083 (Dec. 17, 2012).

153. July 2015 Ombudsperson Report, *supra* note 148, ¶ 38, *citing* S.C. Res. 2161 (2014).

fifty-six cases, delisting thirty-nine individuals and twenty-eight entities, removing one entity as an alias of a listed entity, and refusing seven delisting requests.[154] Yet the Ombudsperson faces two significant institutional limitations that limit the extent to which the office can serve as an effective review mechanism.

The first is that the Ombudsperson's mandate extends only to persons designated by the Al Qaida Sanctions Committee, wholly excluding individuals named under other targeted regimes, such as those relating to the Taliban, Somalia,[155] Côte d'Ivoire,[156] and the Congo.[157] Furthermore, the Ombudsperson observes that in one case a person delisted through the Ombudsperson process was listed the very same day under another regime, where the infringements of due process noted in *Kadi* still prevail.[158] The possibility of relisting in this fashion underscores the distance between the Ombudsperson process and effective judicial protection. In the latter but not the former, the doctrines of res judicata, issue estoppel, and abuse of process (or in a criminal process, double jeopardy) would ordinarily block subjecting the individual to a liability that had previously been determined to lack a factual foundation.

The second structural limitation that afflicts the Ombudsperson concerns the office's lack of independence.[159] There is as yet no independent Office of the Ombudsperson. Instead, the Ombudsperson and her colleagues are employed as consultants, and subject to a periodic certification requirement that involves "an evaluation with reference to undefined 'conditions' by unidentified officials within the division of the United Nations responsible for supporting and assisting the Security Council and the Al Qaida Sanctions Committee."[160] Budgeting, resource allocation, and staffing are managed by political affairs officers within the Security Council Subsidiary Organs Branch, who are in a position to direct Ombudsperson staff. Because the Office of the Ombudsperson does not exist as an independent institution, it receives no independent budget. The funds provided can be cut at any time for a failure to meet the above-mentioned "undefined" certification requirement. Furthermore, the U.N.'s Security Council Affairs Division, within the Department of Political Affairs, has administrative responsibility for the Ombudsperson. As the Ombudsperson remarks, "it is difficult to envisage a worse placement of these

154. *Id.* ¶¶ 6, 27–28.

155. S.C. Res. 1844, S/RES/1844 (Nov. 20, 2008).

156. S.C. Res. 1572, S/RES/1572 (Nov. 15, 2004).

157. S.C. Res. 1596, S/RES/1596 (Apr. 18, 2005).

158. Briefing of the Ombudsperson at the Security Council's Open Debate on "Working Methods of the Security Council" (S/2014/725) (Oct. 23, 2014), https://www.un.org/sc/suborg/sites/www.un.org.sc.suborg/files/scbriefing23oct2014.pdf (last visited Mar. 17, 2016) (complaining, *inter alia*, against the Ombudsperson's narrow mandate, the 1267/1989 Committee's reluctance to provide adequate reasons, and her office's lack of independence).

159. *See* July 2015 Ombudsperson Report, *supra* note 148, ¶¶ 55–72; Improving Fair and Clear Procedures for a More Effective United Nations Sanctions System: Input paper by the Group of Like-Minded States on Targeted Sanctions, U.N. Doc. S/2014/286 (Apr. 17, 2014). The subsequent discussion in the text is taken from these sources.

160. July 2015 Ombudsperson Report, *supra* note 148, ¶ 62.

functions than in the branch/division/department which provides direct support on sanctions-related matters to the bodies from which independence is essential."[161]

Under the fiduciary model, the move away from comprehensive sanctions regimes is welcome, given the cost they impose on innocent civilians and the instrumentalization of those civilians for the sake of policy objectives. The goal of the targeted sanction regimes—international peace and security—is likewise amenable to the fiduciary theory: the Security Council acts as a direct fiduciary of humanity to the extent it makes this its goal, as international peace and security are fundamental ends humanity shares. The question, of course, is whether the means are appropriate, given the consequences to listed individuals. Apart from the regime overseen by the Al Qaida Sanctions Committee, all the rest are plainly offside the prescriptions of the fiduciary model, as they infringe the rights of individuals without even the rudiments of due process, which we argued in Chapter 3 is a norm of jus cogens. The people listed under these regimes are in deep black holes.

The situation for individuals designated by the Al Qaida Sanctions Committee is markedly better given the intervention of the Ombudsperson, but here too, from the perspective of the fiduciary model, there is significant cause for concern. Because the Ombudsperson lacks independence, her office operates under conditions of domination. The Ombudsperson offers examples of U.N. administrators interfering with her office's discharge of its mandate, including the temporary blocking of travel to meet with a petitioner.[162] The real issue from the point of view of the principle of non-domination, however, is that the Office could be eliminated through administrative or budgetary measures at any time, and for any reason. Moreover, even if U.N. political officials never interfered with the Office, their structural domination of it compromises its freedom and autonomy, because at any time interference with impunity is possible. Because the Office is a public office whose only purpose is to safeguard the freedom and security of individuals who are designated or who could be designated, a compromise of the Office's freedom is also a compromise of the freedom of its beneficiaries. As there is no restriction on who may be designated, the unfreedom caused by the Ombudsperson's lack of independence is ultimately suffered by humanity at large.

The legitimacy of targeted sanctions, from a legal point of view, could be improved by providing for the Ombudsperson's independence within the U.N. system and widening the Office's mandate to include all targeted sanctions regimes. However, even with these improvements, there is good reason for national and regional courts to continue to stand ready to provide independent review. Because the Ombudsperson is not formally empowered to make delisting decisions, she herself cannot invalidate an individual's designation. Although the Committee has thus far gone along with her recommendations, it may not do so in the future, or the Security Council itself may vote to reject a particular recommendation. As with the Ombudsperson's lack of institutional independence, the Ombudsperson's review authority is held and exercised at the discretion of the Security Council, and could be overridden and even eliminated at any time. Here too the problem of domination surfaces, while the credibility of the threat of arbitrary interference is brought home

161. *Id.* at 70.

162. *Id.* at 67.

by the case of relisting. Jean Cohen's piercing remarks, made prior to the revamp of the Ombudsperson process in 2011, remain applicable today:

> This, then, is the underside of the "individualization" of international law so celebrated by globalists. For here the direct link between public (or global) law and the individual involves a global enforcement model that undermines instead of securing their basic constitutional and/or human rights.[163]

So long as relisting an individual to a black hole remains available and the Ombudsperson lacks independence, the Security Council's targeted sanctions program falls well short of the requirements of office that attend an international fiduciary of humanity. As discussed in Chapter 6 in relation to detained terror suspects, the possession and exercise of legal power by all public fiduciaries must be intelligible as an authority held and exercised on behalf of every person subject to it, including those whose interests are set back, such as terror suspects detained without the benefit of a criminal trial or prisoner-of-war status. The same principle—the fiduciary theory's criterion of legitimacy—applies to individuals designated under the targeted sanctions program.

* * *

We have argued that international institutions act as direct fiduciaries of humanity when they engage in peacekeeping, state-building, and international territorial administration, as well as when they administer camps for refugees and displaced persons with nowhere else to go. In these cases, international institutions act in a surrogate or quasi-sovereign capacity, providing and securing legal order for people directly subject to either their authority or the authority of a state emerging from crisis. We have also argued that international institutions act as direct fiduciaries of humanity when they undertake to represent individuals on the international plane, and that their capacity and obligation to do so is essential to their own independence. Finally, we have suggested that in principle the Security Council can act as a direct fiduciary of humanity through the use of its Chapter VII powers, but that its targeted sanctions program fails to live up to the demands of this stewardship. In this section and the previous, we have attempted to show that in a wide range of contexts international institutions can be plausibly understood to serve as direct or indirect fiduciaries of humanity. Viewing international institutions in this light helps explain the independence they actually enjoy, while also prescribing independence as an institutional feature they must enjoy to be properly constituted as supranational legal institutions.

IV. THE AUTHORITY AND OBLIGATIONS OF INTERNATIONAL INSTITUTIONS

We now draw on the idea of international institutions as fiduciaries of humanity to address various puzzles surrounding the legal authority international institutions typically assert, the obligations they may possess, and the relationship between international and domestic legal institutions. To recap briefly: under the fiduciary

163. Cohen, *supra* note 23, 274 (critiquing the U.N. targeted sanctions program).

theory, the principal role of international law and its institutions is to establish an international legal order within which states are both empowered and constrained to interact on terms of equal freedom with their nationals, foreign nationals, and other states. If a state respects the sovereignty of other states and complies with the core requirements of international law in its dealings with its nationals and foreign nationals, its actions will be considered authorized under international law, and its institutional autonomy will be protected as a mechanism for advancing the collective self-determination of peoples. In this context, international institutions act as indirect fiduciaries of humanity charged with the construction and maintenance of international legal order. An important subsidiary role of international law and its institutions, however, is to provide surrogate protection to vulnerable persons where state protection is either unavailable or inadequate. In this context, international institutions assume public powers that are functionally equivalent to those possessed by domestic public authorities, and thereby serve as direct fiduciaries of humanity. The questions and issues we consider now apply to all international institutions that serve as direct fiduciaries of humanity, indirect fiduciaries of humanity, or both.

A. Human Rights Obligations of International Institutions

If an individual acting in a private capacity kills another person without legal justification or excuse (e.g., self-defense or necessity), and the state has done all that it reasonably could to protect the victim, this arbitrary taking of life would constitute wrongful homicide under the state's criminal law, but under international law it would not ordinarily count as a human rights violation. Conventionally, only state parties that have consented to human rights treaties are understood to have justiciable international obligations to respect the human rights norms enshrined in those treaties. And as Klabbers observes, it is not obvious that incorporating human rights norms within customary international law can supply an adequate basis for holding international institutions to legal obligations flowing from human rights law:

> It remains unclear why, for example, in the absence of a clear consensual link, the World Bank and the International Monetary Fund (IMF) would be legally bound to respect human rights, as is regularly claimed. One answer refers to customary international law (including human rights law), but this is only plausible if a double standard is accepted regarding the basis of obligation in international law (states would need to express consent; but organisations would be bound without their consent); this though is not easy to reconcile with the conception that organisations are independent actors in their own right, with a legal personality separate from that of their member states.[164]

Despite this worry, numerous commentators have found principled grounds for asserting that international institutions are, in at least some contexts, "bound by international human rights norms not only as protector and promoter, but also as

164. Klabbers, *supra* note 12, at 235.

a potential guarantor."[165] Mégret and Hoffman, as well as Wilde, point to the cases of international territorial administration, UNHCR-administered refugee camps, and U.N. prisons as instances where the United Nations is either territorially sovereign or "exercises the equivalent of sovereign control over certain persons through the exercise of select functions of sovereignty."[166] For Mégret and Hoffman, in these cases the key to establishing the United Nation's obligation to respect and guarantee human rights "*tout court*" is recognition that "control" over a population flowing from the United Nation's assumption of sovereignty (or parts of it) is "the wedging criterion for ultimate human rights responsibility."[167] Their argument, in a nutshell, is that if an international institution assumes the domestic authority of a state (or significant aspects of it), then there is no reason in principle that the international institution should not be held to the same human rights standards to which states are held.

Like Mégret and Hoffman, Wilde explains resistance to viewing the United Nations as a human rights duty-bearer as "intrinsically linked to the UN's identity as the champion of human rights," while noting that the Ombudsperson in Kosovo had found that UNMIK discharged its mandate "in a manner that is undemocratic, violative of human rights, and above the law."[168] Wilde argues that although the U.N. missions in Kosovo and East Timor had all the hallmarks of international trusteeship under the mothballed U.N. Trusteeship System, this model and the U.N. Trusteeship Council were not deployed due to the United Nation's self-image as "the champion of human rights" and a perceived tension between trusteeship per se and self-determination.[169] Rejection of the trusteeship model, Wilde contends, explains the inadequacy of the "accountability structures" that governed UNMIK and UNTAET, notwithstanding "the widely-held assumption" that if "the UN is acting as a government, then it should be subject to the same checks and balances as any other government."[170]

The fiduciary theory explains this "widely-held assumption," and does so in a way that answers Klabbers's concern about states and IOs acquiring human rights obligations through different sources (treaty-making versus customary international law). As discussed in Chapter 3, under the fiduciary theory states and state-like entities acquire human rights obligations as a consequence of the public power they hold and exercise over private parties who themselves, as private parties, are not entitled to exercise public power. On this understanding, when states enter into human rights treaties, they become liable for the specific content of the obligations contained in those treaties, and subject to any external review or dispute resolution mechanisms contained therein. But, by dint of their fiduciary relationship to the people subject to their authority, states were already under a relational legal obligation to respect the human rights of the citizens and noncitizens amenable to their

165. Mégret & Hoffman, *supra* note 115, at 339.

166. *Id.* at 339–40; *see also* Wilde, *supra* notes 118, 122 & 124.

167. Mégret & Hoffman, *supra* note 115, at 341.

168. Wilde, *Accountability Deficit, supra* note 118, at 110, 93.

169. *Id.* at 103–10.

170. *Id.* at 94.

jurisdiction. In the case of peremptory human rights norms, states may not pursue policies that infringe these norms. Although most human rights are not peremptory and therefore are subject to limitation, in these cases the limitation must be publicly justifiable under a principle of proportionality.

Rather than force the human rights obligations of international institutions into a procrustean bed of treaty-making or customary international law, the fiduciary theory imputes human rights obligations to them on the same grounds as it attributes those obligations to states: in both cases, human rights norms arise as a consequence of the direct stewardship that states and international institutions assert over the persons subject to their authority. Moreover, the sovereign authority exercised by an international institution need not be plenary or state-like in all dimensions. It may be limited to governance of a refugee camp or a prison, but so long as the power asserted purports to be public in nature and authoritative, the people subject to it are entitled to the benefit of human rights protection that is responsive to the public nature of the power held over them.

The ultimate source of these norms can be considered a general and overarching fiduciary principle of international law. We can see this by analogy to how the common law operates in common law jurisdictions. In common law countries, statutes and constitutions are frequently said to codify the principles and values of the common law.[171] If there is no statutory or written constitutional provision applicable to a given case, or if there are gaps in the positive law or its meaning is unclear, the common law either governs itself or serves as a guide to interpret the positive law.[172] In the international sphere, the fiduciary principle plays a similar role: it subjects international public authorities to human rights obligations, and serves as well as a guide to the content of open-textured obligations codified in treaties.

B. The Authority of International Courts

Standard accounts of the legitimacy of international courts point to their consent-based foundation and the role they typically play in solving international coordination and collective action problems so as to facilitate international cooperation.[173] As Allen Buchanan and Robert Keohane rightly point out, however, state consent simpliciter is insufficient for legitimacy (and arguably is not even a necessary condition of it) because some states are undemocratic and systematically violate the

171. *See, e.g.*, Mark Walters, *Written and Unwritten Constitutionalism*, *in* Expounding the Constitution: Essays in Constitutional Theory 245 (Grant Huscroft ed., 2008); James R. Stoner, Jr., Common-Law Liberty: Rethinking American Constitutionalism (2003).

172. For discussion of recent developments of the common law/positive law relationship regarding human rights in the United Kingdom, see Richard Clayton, *The Empire Strikes Back*, 2015 Pub. L. 2.

173. *See, e.g.*, Føllesdal, *supra* note 70, at 341–42. We use "authority" and "legitimacy" in a conceptual and normative sense to refer to an entitlement to hold and exercise legal power. These terms are sometimes used sociologically to refer to whether or not their addressees happen to recognize or accept an authority (acceptance is usually taken as a necessary and/or sufficient basis of "legitimacy"), whereas we are referring to the justifiable grounds on which a purported authority is a genuine and legitimate authority.

rights of their people ("wicked states"), and therefore "[s]tate consent in these cases cannot transfer legitimacy for the simple reason that there is no legitimacy to transfer."[174] Moreover, even if the relevant consent is limited to consent supplied by rights-respecting democracies ("decent states"), the putative consent of a decent but weaker state to a judicialized regime such as the WTO "is hardly voluntary, since the state would suffer serious costs by not participating."[175]

Consent-based views are also hard-pressed to explain the authority of international courts over both foreign nationals and individuals from wicked states. If the relevant consent is restricted to the kind supplied by decent states, it is unclear how we can explain the legitimacy of international courts vis-à-vis the people of wicked states, as decent states do not speak for the people of wicked states when they consent to the creation of international courts. This problem of standing can be generalized to all circumstances involving foreign nationals of states that have not ratified a court-creating treaty. Even if a state is a decent state, it arguably lacks standing to authorize an international court to render judgment on behalf of foreign nationals.[176] And yet, cosmopolitan contexts involving detained terror suspects and refugees seem to be where international law and its courts may have a particularly strong claim to legitimacy. The fiduciary theory explains why this is so, notwithstanding the standing problem that attends consent-based views.

Under the fiduciary theory's conception of international adjudicative authority, international courts are never mere delegates of the states that create them, but rather are trustees of the law they administer on behalf of humanity. International courts cannot be simple agents or delegates of states because, pace Buchanan and Keohane, states themselves do not possess the kind of international adjudicative authority possessed by international courts. States are of course public bodies with adjudicative authority of their own. Moreover, consistent with the principle of *dédoublement fonctionnel* ("role splitting") developed by George Scelle,[177] international law sometimes authorizes states to exercise first-instance supranational adjudicative authority, such as when international law authorizes states to make refugee

174. Allen Buchanan & Robert O. Keohane, *The Legitimacy of Global Governance Institutions*, 20 Ethics & Int'l Aff. 405, 414 (2006). Buchanan and Keohane discuss a legitimacy standard appropriate to global governance institutions, such as the United Nations and the WTO, but their discussion is equally relevant to international courts, including of course those within global governance institutions, such as the ICJ and the WTO's Appellate Body.

175. *Id.* at 414. This is the international equivalent of Hume's "poor peasant," the person too poor or disadvantaged to exit an oppressive regime, and whose continued residency in it cannot reasonably be viewed as consent. David Hume, *Of the Original Contract* (1748), *in* Social Contract, Essays by Locke, Hume and Rousseau (Sir Ernest Baker ed., 2013).

176. One might think that foreign nationals are akin to third-party beneficiaries of treaties between states, especially human rights treaties that speak capaciously about the rights of every human being. Still, even if states have duties to foreign nationals on this basis, it is not obvious that states have the representative legal capacity to authorize an international court to assume jurisdiction over foreign nationals whom no state party to the treaty has standing to represent.

177. *See, e.g.*, George Scelle, Manuel de Droit International Public 15–24 (1948); Antonio Cassese, *Remarks on Scelle's Theory of "Role Splitting"* (dédoublement fonctionnel) *in International Law*, 1 Eur. J. Int'l L. 210 (1990).

status determinations subject to judicial review at the national level. In these cases, the national court may be thought to act in an international capacity, with its determination subject to review at the international level.

In international law, then, states are somewhat akin to municipalities in domestic law: in both instances, the relevant legal authority exercises delegated legal power that is subject to independent review. The analogy is not perfect, because unlike municipalities, states have a general authority to delegate to international legal actors certain functions, including, for example, refugee status determination by the UNHCR. Nonetheless, neither municipalities in domestic legal order nor states in international legal order possess independent adjudicative authority over legal disputes in which they themselves are parties. With respect to inter-state disputes, only international courts can possess independent and first-instance adjudicative authority. In cases involving disputes of international concern between states and nationals or non-nationals, domestic courts can wear international hats at first instance. In doing so, however, they acknowledge the primacy of international law, a primacy that is reflected by the possible subjection of national level judicial decisions involving international norms to review at the international level. It follows that states cannot transfer or delegate international adjudicative authority to international courts, as they themselves have no such power to transfer. How does this international public power come into being?

When states ratify a multilateral treaty that creates an international court, they succeed in doing so only because a power-conferring rule of public international law has delegated treaty-making power to them; namely, the pacta sunt servanda rule.[178] As discussed in Chapter 3, pacta sunt servanda empowers states to adopt through treaty any legal obligation consistent with the peremptory norms of international law. States can therefore give laws to themselves collectively by binding themselves to treaty provisions the ultimate interpretation and application of which is entrusted to international courts. But consistent with the principle of sovereign equality, states at no time enjoy adjudicative authority over other states, and the treaty-making authority they possess to create international courts is itself provided by pacta sunt servanda. States, therefore, do not transfer international adjudicative authority to international courts—they have no such authority to transfer—but rather agree omnilaterally to be bound by the determinations of such courts.[179] The origin of the legal authority of international courts—their founding authorization—thus flows from the legal authority invested by pacta sunt servanda in the omnilateral agreement of states to be bound by the determinations of these courts. But for the reasons given by Buchanan and Keohane, this account of the consent-based origin and legal authorization of international courts cannot explain their ongoing authority and legitimacy.[180]

178. Jan Klabbers, The Concept of Treaty in International Law 38–40 (1996). The rule is now enshrined in Article 26 of the VCLT, *supra* note 16 ("Every treaty in force is binding upon the parties to it and must be performed by them in good faith.").

179. The authorization analysis here follows loosely Hobbes's account of sovereignty by institution, as well as his commitment to the idea that public authority can only be held and exercised by public institutions. *See* Hobbes, *supra* note 81, chs. 17 & 28.

180. We would make one modification to the argument against deriving legitimacy from state consent simpliciter. On the fiduciary view, the problem is not, as Buchanan and Keohane would

The fiduciary view of the constitution and legitimacy of international adjudicative authority rests on a fundamental distinction between the origin and authorization of institutions, on the one hand, and their nature and authority, on the other. The nature of an institution is distinct from its origin. Consider the case of trustees. A court may appoint a trustee to act as a receiver in a bankruptcy, a private settlor may appoint a trustee to manage a trust's assets, or a public trustee may be appointed under a statute to act for someone incapacitated. In each of these cases, the origin of the trustee's office is different, but the nature his office remains basically the same. In every case the trustee is managing the affairs or interests of other people and is subject to a common set of fiduciary obligations. The origin or source of the trustee's mandate does not determine the nature of the legal power she holds to discharge it.

A similar distinction attends the authorization and authority of an institution. Consider the parent-child case and the institution of parental authority. In the standard case, parents gain legal authority over their children when the children are born to them and registered as theirs, or through a legally regulated adoption process. Procreation and adoption are triggering events that ultimately result in the state authorizing parents to have ongoing and exclusive custody of their underage children. The authorization comes with many strings related to the child's health and welfare, and may be suspended temporarily or terminated permanently in an extreme case. But to understand the nature of parental authority and its appropriate limits, we need to consider the legally salient features of the relationship between parents and children. In Chapter 1 we suggested that those include the child's legal incapacity and her status as a legal person. Parental authority over children must account for both of these features, and does so through its incorporation of a fiduciary obligation to exercise power over children in what the parent reasonably perceives as the child's best interest. On our view, the parent's fiduciary obligation and his or her discretionary power are constitutive of parental authority. But even if one has a different view of parental authority, on any plausible conception the authority relation between parent and child is interpersonal, and so to understand it we must inquire into the nature of that interpersonal relationship, an inquiry that is distinct from the question of how a parent's legal authority over a child comes into existence through a public process of authorization.

Likewise, to understand the authority of international courts, we need to inquire into their relationship to the public amenable to their jurisdiction, including the parties who come before them. Within this context, we need to consider the things they can do with their legal power that states or others cannot do, and we need to explain how the possession and exercise of this power denotes a relationship of legal authority between international courts and their legal subjects. Ultimately, the nature and legitimacy of international adjudicative authority, we contend, is found

have it, that wicked states cannot transfer legitimacy to the international level due to their lack of legitimacy: neither decent nor wicked states have the kind of authority held by international courts, so neither can transfer it to them, and authority is the subject matter of the legitimacy inquiry. The problem is that the representatives of wicked states lack standing to represent their people internationally, and so they cannot participate in a treaty process that might create an international court as legitimate representatives of their state's people.

in the remedy it provides to the problem of unilateralism, which arises whenever one state acts against another, or against groups or individuals, according to only its assessment of the legality of its action. The remedy to unilateralism provided by international courts lies in their legal power to interpret and apply international law as an independent third party, their adherence to legal principles of adjudication such as impartiality, and their fiduciary duty to everyone subject to their jurisdiction to respect these legal principles.

Unilateralism is problematic from a legal point of view for two main reasons.[181] First, it invariably denotes the subjection of one party to the will of another who has no authority to represent or speak for the subjugated party. Ordinarily, the strong will dominate the weak. But the threat of unilateralism remains even if the two contending parties negotiate in good faith and are guided in their deliberations by all the relevant moral considerations. The governing law may be susceptible to more than one reasonable interpretation, and the imposition of one reasonable interpretation rather than another by a party without authority to speak for both remains an imposition of that party's will. Second, unilateralism implicitly denies the legal equality of the parties to a dispute. Where one party asserts its will over another, the former arrogates to itself, and to itself alone, authority to resolve the dispute. The unilateralist becomes judge and party of the same cause, implicitly denying the equal standing of his or her adversary. As we now explain, in the international context, submission of the dispute to an independent and impartial international court removes this threat.

When an international court is seized of a matter, both parties are subject to the court's public authority rather than the will of other party. On the fiduciary view, international law authorizes the court to resolve the parties' dispute within a legal framework that treats them as equals under the law. Courts are trustees of this framework on behalf of all who are amenable to their jurisdiction—potentially, all of humanity. Accordingly, they owe standing duties to all potential litigants to maintain the integrity of their institution by steadfastly striving to bring it into "the deepest possible conformity" with the anti-unilateralist purpose for which it was instituted.[182] When parties come before international courts, the overarching duty of these courts is to exercise their adjudicative power in a manner consistent with their institution's constitutive principles. These principles include a duty of impartiality or even-handedness, a duty to respect the norms of due process or natural justice, and a duty to interpret and apply the law in a manner that is reasonable, taking into account all the relevant factual considerations as well as all relevant legal norms, doctrines, and jurisprudence.[183]

181. *See* Evan Fox-Decent, *Unseating Unilateralism*, *in* PRIVATE LAW AND THE RULE OF LAW 116 (Lisa Austin & Dennis Klimchuk eds., 2014) (developing the problematic nature of unilateralism, and arguing that Hobbes's legal theory supplies an antidote).

182. For a Kantian view that distinguishes sharply a principle of authority from a principle of justice, and that attributes to the principle of justice a duty on the part of public institutions "to bring legal order into the deepest possible conformity with the independence [equal freedom] of all who are bound by it," see Jacob Weinrib, *Authority, Justice, and Public Law: A Unified Theory*, 64 U. TORONTO L.J. 703, 716 (2014). In our view, the duty is constitutive of authority, the proper possession and exercise of which produces justice.

183. For reflections on national judges' fiduciary obligations, see Ethan J. Leib, David L. Ponet & Michael Serota, *A Fiduciary Theory of Judging*, 101 CALIF. L. REV. 699 (2013).

The legal power of international courts to issue rulings of an authoritative nature, then, is not explained by the process of treaty-making and authorization through which courts come into existence. This process explains a court's subject-matter jurisdiction, and specifies the parties over whom it has jurisdiction. In other words, the authorization process explains what we referred to in Chapter 2 as international law's *distributive* dimension in this sphere; that is, how international law distributes to some bodies but not others adjudicative authority over certain international subject matters and parties. But the consent that underwrites that process does not explain the *constitutive* and *regulative* dimensions of a court's authority. The constitutive aspect of an international court's authority consists in its public status as an independent and impartial adjudicator that is duty-bound to abide by the procedural and substantive requirements of its office. These procedural and substantive requirements, in turn, are the regulative aspect of an international court's authority; they govern the court's exercise of its legal power. When courts comply with these constitutive and regulative requirements in the execution of their mandates, they undo unilateralism and exercise legitimate authority over the parties subject to them.

Once we disentangle the source or origin of an international court's authority from inquiry into its nature, and thereby distinguish the distributive process of its authorization from the constitution and regulation of its authority per se, we can respond to concerns about courts exercising authority ultra vires their authorization, such as the IACtHR grounding indigenous land rights on a right to property. The general mandate given to international courts through the authorization process is to resolve cases submitted to them in accordance with their independent and impartial interpretation of the relevant law. The court's authority as an impartial third-party adjudicator entitles it to interpret the law as it thinks best as a trustee of international legal order. This is just what it means for a court to have final interpretive authority over the contested meaning of open-textured legal terms. While *travaux préparatoires* and other preliminary discussions explain how the parties came to agreement and provided for the court's *authorization*, they are not determinative of the court's *authority*.

In any international legal dispute, the interests of the losing side may be set back, or its hopes for gain frustrated. The unsuccessful litigant may contest the merits of the decision, and claim the court erred. But if the court abides by the constitutional requirements of its office in the discharge of its duty, then the court, like any authority, is allowed to err without losing its authority. The defeated party cannot challenge the authority and legitimacy of the court's ruling without at the same time asserting for itself a unilateral and impermissible right to rule. And because, we have assumed, the court has complied with the legal and constitutive requirements of its office, the court's ruling is intelligible as a ruling made on behalf of both parties, because compliance with those requirements is precisely the court's performance of the overarching fiduciary duty it owes as a judicial trustee of international legal order. The good judicial trustee therefore satisfies the fiduciary theory's criterion of legitimacy.

Some might argue that if the court's jurisdiction depends on the consent of the parties, as is the case with the ICJ, then mere access to adjudication is not enough to dispel unilateralism. Others might similarly claim that unilateralism remains even if the court has compulsory jurisdiction, because states can in principle opt out by denouncing the relevant jurisdiction-conferring treaty. Yet others might suggest that even if international courts had fully compulsory jurisdiction, the problem of unilateralism remains so long as international legal order lacks a global executive capable of enforcing international judgments through the threat or use of force: without such an executive in place, the winner of an international legal dispute is left to rely on the goodwill of the losing side, and therefore has no assurance its rights will ultimately be vindicated.[184] In other words, one might think that courts can resolve the threat of unilateralism in relation to international law's indeterminacy, but still worry that the threat remains due to the relative absence of executive enforcement and assurance. The alleged lack of coercive sanctions at the international level is a standard reference point in scholarly discussions of whether international law is really law.[185]

We can offer only a few passing comments on this difficult topic, which is an instance of the question of whether the threat or use of force is a necessary feature of the concept of law. Hobbes's views, perhaps surprisingly, are instructive. Hobbes is well known for his claim that only the authorization of a robust sovereign can bring people out of the state of nature and prevent a slide back into it, as "covenants without the sword are but words."[186] In *Leviathan*, however, he defines law as the command "of him whose command is addressed to one formerly obliged to obey him,"[187] making no reference to coercion. He also insists that "the ground of these rights [of the sovereign] have the rather need to be taught diligently, and truly taught; because they cannot be maintained by any civil law, or terror of legal punishment."[188] In *Behemoth*, his history of the English Civil War, Hobbes writes: "If men know not their duty, what is there that can force them to obey the laws? An army, you will say. But what shall force the army?"[189] On the one hand, Hobbes insists that we must institute a sovereign with a sword to enforce justice, but on the other, he concedes that sovereign authority ultimately rests on a duty to obey that cannot be coerced. We can resolve this tension, and doing so will pave the way for explaining how international law is possible without reliance on the threat or use of sanctions.

Hobbes's sword-wielding sovereign is necessary to the construction of legal order between private parties. The fundamental juridical problem Hobbes seeks to resolve with a strong sovereign is not that people will behave opportunistically and breach their legal obligations without the fear of sanction to keep them in line. The juridical problem is that without reliable assurance that others will perform, there

184. *See, e.g.*, Arthur Ripstein, Force and Freedom: Kant's Legal and Political Philosophy 159–68 (2009) (defending executive enforcement power as necessary to provide assurance without which equal rights to things are neither possible nor secure).

185. *See, e.g.*, H.L.A. Hart, The Concept of Law ch. X (2d ed. 1994); Hathaway & Shapiro, *supra* note 46; John R. Bolton, *Is There Really "Law" in International Affairs?*, 10 Transnat'l L. & Contemp. Probs. 1 (2000).

186. Hobbes, *supra* note 81, at 106 (ch. 18, ¶ 2).

187. *Id.* at 173 (ch. 16, ¶ 2).

188. *Id.* at 220 (ch. 30, ¶ 4).

189. Thomas Hobbes, Behemoth or the Long Parliament 29 (London: Cass 1681) (1668).

can be no legal obligations to perform at all. A fixed point in Hobbes's account of legal order is that no person can be under an obligation to "make himself a prey to others."[190] Without a sovereign in place to motivate performance with the threat of sanction, the first-performer of a covenant would "make himself a prey to others," as he would be subject to the unilateral will of the party that has yet to perform. As a consequence, there can be no legal obligation to perform without a sovereign to provide assurance.[191] Public coercive assurance, then, is a necessary condition of legal obligation between private parties.

As Hobbes's comments on the need for civic education make clear, however, he plainly thought that the threat of coercion alone could not maintain legal order. For Hobbes, the maintenance of legal order relies on the willingness of actors to do their duty for the sake of the moral and prudential reasons that justify legal order and an ongoing commitment to it. For private parties, the reasons are both prudential and moral: private parties have prudential reasons to avoid the state of nature, and the means of doing so require them to regard others as their equals, which arguably involves a moral commitment to equality.[192] But in the case of public actors, the reasons for the performance of duty can only be moral, because public actors as such have no self-regarding or private interest: their mandate is to act solely in the public interest. With this in mind, we are now in a position to offer an answer to Hobbes's question, "But what shall force the army?"

By "the army," Hobbes is referring to the sovereign's executive enforcement authority, and is implicitly making three related points. The first and most obvious is that there is no one available to coerce the army's compliance, as the army itself possesses decisive coercive power (if some other body had this power, then that body would be "the army"). The second is that in principle the army cannot legitimately be compelled to act for private or prudential motives because the army is a public body: to motivate the army by appealing to the self-interest of its leaders would corrupt and denature the army as a public institution, in effect transforming it into a private mercenary force. Finally, and more constructively, the only legitimate ground on which the army as such can be compelled to act is through an appeal to its commitment to its role in the lawgiving enterprise. At the national level, then, legal order depends ultimately on the willingness of public actors to abide by the duties that are constitutive of their offices. In the extreme case, should "the army" lose faith in the grounds or legitimacy of its sovereign's authority, as occurred with various Eastern Bloc regimes and during the "Arab Spring" of 2010 through 2012, even the most authoritarian municipal order is prone to collapse.

190. Hobbes, *supra* note 81, at 99 (ch. 15 ¶ 36).

191. Hobbes thought that second-performers in the state of nature have a *moral* duty to perform, but it is a case of the exception proving the rule, as second-performers have assurance of the other side's cooperation by dint of the other side having performed already. *Id.* at 86 (ch. 14, ¶ 27). As a general matter, Hobbes thought that the duty to abide by moral principles or "laws of nature" are always binding on conscience, but are binding on action only if one can perform under conditions of security, when one cannot be made "a prey to others." *Id.* at 99 (ch. 15, ¶ 36).

192. Hobbes's ninth law of nature is that "*every man acknowledge* [every] *other for his equal by nature*" (emphasis in original). *Id.* at 97 (ch. 15, ¶ 21).

In light of public authority's dependence on the commitment of its agents, the stability of well-ordered societies may seem surprising. Even more surprising, from this perspective, is the degree of state compliance with the rulings of international courts. There are, of course, well-known examples of states rejecting such rulings.[193] The IACtHR in particular has faced considerable national opposition to its decisions, most notably with Venezuela announcing its withdrawal from the court's jurisdiction in 2012, as mentioned above.[194] But in the main, compliance with international court decisions is "quite high:" 65 to 75 percent of ICJ decisions and 88 percent of WTO rulings have led to full or partial compliance.[195] The dramatic increase in the sheer number of international courts and international rulings since the end of the Cold War further attests to the widespread commitment of states and others to the international law project.

International courts in the first instance rely on states themselves to comply with adverse rulings. When states resist doing so, international institutions can attempt to enlist various means available at international law to enforce compliance, including the authorization of states to use sanctions or countermeasures such as asset freezes, trade embargos, and investment restrictions.[196] They can also enlist the international community to shame the wrongdoing state, as occurred over decades in the case of Apartheid South Africa. In cases of collective self-defense or international peace and security, such as the Korean War, the Security Council may call on member-states to use physical force.[197] Oona Hathaway and Scott Shapiro make a compelling case, however, that international law's "primary mode of law enforcement" is through *outcasting* rather than the use of force.[198]

Outcasting does not involve the threat or use of physical force, but rather denies the recalcitrant party the benefits of international cooperation or membership in a supranational organization. When the World Health Organization suspends members who fail to meet their financial obligations to the organization, it engages in *internal* outcasting; in this case, a form of banishment.[199] But the more prevalent form of outcasting at international law is decentralized and *external* in nature. This type of outcasting occurs when the WTO's Dispute Settlement Body authorizes

193. Iran infamously dismissed the ICJ judgments dealing with the U.S. embassy staff taken hostage in 1979. *See* United States Diplomatic and Consular Staff in Tehran (U.S. v. Iran), Provisional Measures, 1979 ICJ Rep. 7 (Dec. 15); United States Diplomatic and Consular Staff in Tehran (U.S. v. Iran), 1980 ICJ Rep. 3 (May 24). Of equal note, the U.S. government rejected the rulings of the ICJ condemning U.S. military action against Nicaragua and support of the Contras. *See* Military and Paramilitary Activities in and Against Nicaragua (Nicaragua v. U.S.), Jurisdiction and Admissibility, 1984 ICJ Rep. 392 (Nov. 26); Military and Paramilitary Activities in and Against Nicaragua (Nicaragua v U.S.), 1986 ICJ Rep. 14 (June 27).

194. See Alexandra Huneeus, *Courts Resisting Courts: Lessons from the Inter-American Court's Struggle to Enforce Human Rights*, 44 CORNELL INT'L L.J. 493 (2011).

195. Alter, *supra* note 68, at 58.

196. *See* Evan Criddle, *Standing for Human Rights Abroad*, 100 CORNELL L. REV. 269 (2015).

197. *See* S.C. Res. 83, S/RES/83 (June 27, 1950).

198. Hathaway & Shapiro, *supra* note 46, at 308.

199. *Id.* at 306.

the aggrieved state party to adopt countermeasures; states, not the WTO, impose the sanction to enforce the WTO's ruling.[200] Another example can be seen in the enforcement mechanism of ECHR decisions. If a state party refuses to comply with the Court's ruling, the Council of Europe's Committee of Ministers is authorized to suspend or revoke the scofflaw state's membership in the Council of Europe.[201] To the extent that the threat or use of outcasting is effective—and in the case of the WTO and the ECHR it appears to be much so—the threat of unilateralism with respect to the problem of assurance at the international level is significantly diminished.

Nonetheless, as Hathaway and Shapiro acknowledge, outcasting has various limitations.[202] It depends crucially on states receiving benefits from international cooperation or membership in transnational organizations or networks. States that are not enmeshed within a particular web of international cooperation have nothing to lose by being excluded from it, or they may view the loss as worth the gain accruing from a breach of their international obligations. States that withdraw from international society, such as North Korea, are unlikely to care much about outcasting because they themselves are voluntary outcasts. More significant from the point of view of the authority and legitimacy of international courts, outcasting structurally favors the strong over the weak, as weaker states have much more to lose by cutting ties to a stronger or even hegemonic state. For example, in 2007, Antigua won a case against the United States at the WTO, authorizing Antigua to disregard trade obligations to the United States so as to benefit Antigua $21 million a year.[203] With the United States accounting for 58.2 percent of Antigua's imports, and providing to Antigua regional military security, Antigua ultimately declined to exercise its remedial right against the United States.[204] As Hathaway and Shapiro have observed, Antigua confronted "the reality that [it] has far more to lose from cutting itself off from the United States than it has to gain."[205]

There is much to praise about the outcasting account of enforcement of international law, not the least of which is the powerful explanation it offers of the considerable extent to which states comply with international judgments. In our view, however, outcasting is just part—though an important part—of a wider phenomenon attending the nexus of obligation and compliance at international law, one that explains state compliance in cases in which it is not in the state's interest to comply,

200. *Id.* at 307.

201. *Id.* at 338. Hathaway and Shapiro refer to this as "cross-countermeasures," as the countermeasures are brought by third parties, and they note that the penalty need not be proportional to the harm done and is mandatory—"once a state is cast out of the Council, Council members cannot treat it as if it were a party." *Id.* at 337–38.

202. *Id.* at 339–44.

203. World Trade Organization, United States-Measure Affecting the Cross-Border Supply of Gambling and Betting Services (Current Status Summary) (Feb. 24, 2010). http://www.wto.org/english/tratop_e/dispu_e/cases_e/ds285_e.htm (last visited Oct. 15, 2015).

204. Hathaway & Shapiro, *supra* note 46, at 341–42.

205. *Id.* at 342.

even taking into account the costs of being outcast. This wider phenomenon is what David Dyzenhaus refers to as "the compulsion of legality."[206] The compulsion of legality is found in the public obligation of states, as national and international legal actors, "to justify all acts of state as having a legal warrant, the authority of law."[207] The compulsion of legality arises from a formal commitment to the normativity of law, and this entails "that jurists proceed as if law's claim to authority can be vindicated."[208] Thus, the lawyers supporting the Bush administration with memoranda on torture and the Geneva Conventions, discussed in Chapter 6, did not argue that the U.S. administration had extralegal authority to flout international law; rather, they argued that enhanced interrogation tactics were not torture and therefore were legal under international law, and that the Geneva Conventions did not apply.

The compulsion of legality, of course, provides no assurance against an executive determined to breach its international legal obligations, or (what is more likely) to interpret them in an unreasonable manner. But, as Dyzenhaus rightly observes, the compulsion of legality is a necessary condition of constitutional democracy because it embodies the rule of law, which itself "presupposes one kind of political accountability, the requirement that all acts of public power count as such only if they can trace their authority to a legal warrant."[209] So although the compulsion operates within the realm of legality rather than representative government, it nonetheless "arises out of the normative commitments to democracy."[210] The overarching authority of international courts, then, consists in their legal power to specify authoritatively whether under international law the public justifications that national or supranational bodies offer for their actions provide an adequate legal warrant, and thereby live up to their commitments to both the rule of law and democracy. In a democracy, what will ultimately "force the army," if anything, is its public subjection to the compulsion of legality and its unwillingness to reject openly the legal basis of its legal and political authority. Outcasting can helpfully enforce an international determination that a state is in breach, but it is only the compulsion of legality that comprehensively explains how international rulings can retain their legal authority and provide a basis for compliance when outcasting or coercive enforcement are unavailable. Thus, even if a state subject to an adverse ruling continues to unilaterally impose its will on others, the international judgment provides an authoritative legal basis to call into question the legitimacy of the state's actions, and ultimately its standing as a public authority. In this way, international courts contribute to Mureinik's conception of law as a "culture of justification."

206. Dyzenhaus, *supra* note 47, at 34.

207. *Id.*

208. *Id.* at 39. Some scholars have explored already how a formal or objective compulsion of legality in international law contributes to a "socialization" or "acculturation" of states that is driven by IHRL, driving up the cost of noncompliance with human rights norms, and thereby creating an internalized or subjective compulsion to comply. *See, e.g.*, Ryan Goodman & Derek Jinks, Socializing States: Promoting Human Rights Through International Law (2013).

209. Dyzenhaus, *supra* note 47, at 49.

210. *Id.* at 50.

International courts also provide the paradigmatic institutional framework for what might be thought of as an arbitral conception of authority. We suggest now that, mutatis mutandis, this arbitral conception can account for the putative legal authority held and exercised by transnational institutions or networks, as well as their obligations to respect the rules, standards, and principles of global administrative law.

C. The Authority and Obligations of Transnational Institutions

Attention to informal global governance networks fruitfully extends the horizon of public international law, with the promise of extending the accountability and legitimacy that international legality makes possible. Global administrative lawyers identify transnational intergovernmental networks, "distributed administration" across states, and hybrid public-private bodies as important sites of global governance not directed by a formal IO. We will focus, however, on private entities exercising global regulatory functions. From the point of view of establishing the public authority of a transnational entity, the case of private entities is arguably the most challenging. By dint of the sheer fact that they are private, how can they be understood to exercise any form of transnational legal authority? Moreover, how can they properly be understood to be subject to procedural and public law-like obligations similar to those from administrative law when, once again, they are formally private rather than public entities? On the one hand, for such an institution to claim legal authority without a formal legal source supporting its claim may appear to be a bald assertion, while on the other, the procedural safeguards offered voluntarily by a private entity risk being discounted as self-serving measures aimed at bootstrapping its claim to transnational regulatory authority. As Klabbers remarks, "at the end of the day global administrative law cannot entirely escape from the question of where its principles and standards derive their legally binding force from: the global administrative law project, for all its merits, still requires a plausible sources chapter."[211] Although we cannot hope to provide that chapter here, we will sketch a framework from which it might be developed, using global administrative law's most difficult case, the private global regulatory entity. We hasten to forewarn that the kind of legal authority attributable to such entities, on our telling, is of a limited and non-binding nature.

Global administrative lawyers delineate global administrative action as "rule-making, adjudications, and other decisions that are neither treaty-making nor simple dispute settlements between parties."[212] This "global administrative space," they claim, is populated by individuals, firms, and NGOs, as well as states, all of which are subject to international and transnational regulatory regimes such as "the OECD networks and committees, the administration and the committees of the WTO, the committees of the G-7/G-8, structures of antitrust cooperation, and financial regulation performed by, among others, the IMF, the Basel Committee and the Financial Action Task Force."[213] But global administration is sometimes undertaken by private bodies, such as the ISO.

211. Jan Klabbers, *Setting the Scene, in* KLABBERS, PETERS & ULFSTEIN, *supra* note 5, at 28.

212. Kingsbury et al., *supra* note 9, at 17.

213. *Id.* at 18–19.

Founded in 1947, the ISO is now a network of national standard bodies from 162 countries, with permanent headquarters in Geneva.[214] It has adopted more than 19,500 commercial standards that harmonize product and business process rules globally. In its own words, "ISO International Standards impact everyone, everywhere."[215] The ISO develops standards when it receives a request from industry or another stakeholder, such as a consumer group. The ISO then consults experts who are grouped into over 250 technical committees comprised of industry representatives, academics, NGOs, government representatives, and consumer associations. The technical committee develops a draft standard that is then shared with ISO members for comment and a preliminary vote. The draft is revised in light of comments. A final draft of the standard is submitted to members for a vote, which then produces an ISO standard if two-thirds vote in favor and not more than one-quarter vote against the proposed standard. As a rule, the ISO attempts to establish standards on the basis of consensus rather than a supermajority vote.

The relatively open consultation and participation procedures of the ISO have developed organically as the organization has grown. The fiduciary theory supplies a helpful analogy to explain why these procedures, or ones much like them, are legally obligatory. This is a particularly tall order because the ISO's standards are used on a voluntary basis. The ISO has no formal legal authority to impose its standards on recalcitrant firms. As it has no legal power to impose its standards, one can reasonably doubt whether the ISO, as a private entity, can be said to owe its stakeholders administrative law-like obligations regarding the development and dissemination of its standards. The fiduciary theory may even appear to support this conclusion, as most fiduciary relations involve legal powers, and fiduciary obligations are typically understood as constraints on the fiduciary's exercise of a legal power.

Some fiduciary relations, however, involve factual rather than legal powers. The classic case is the financial adviser-client relationship. Financial advisers give advice to their clients, but ordinarily do not have discretionary legal power to invest their clients' assets. Advisers have factual power to influence their clients' decisions, but not legal power to actually make those decisions for them. Nonetheless, in light of the client's dependence on the financial adviser's advice, and the fundamental purpose for which the client and the adviser interact (the provision of impartial advice to the client), courts have found that advisers have a fiduciary obligation to disclose any conflict of interest they may have in relation to investment advice they give to their clients.[216] In this relation of dependence and vulnerability, the adviser has factual discretionary power over her client's interest in pursuing the most profitable investments on the basis of impartial financial advice. In principle, the adviser's discretionary power is other-regarding (it concerns the client only and is to be exercised for the client's benefit), purposeful (it is oriented exclusively toward giving the client impartial financial advice), and institutional (it can be exercised within a lawful relation in which the client is not instrumentalized). In the standard case, the

214. For details of the ISO's standard-development process, see the ISO's webpage: http://www.iso.org/iso/home.htm (last visited Dec. 16, 2015).

215. *Id.* http://www.iso.org/iso/home/about.htm (last visited Dec. 16, 2015).

216. *See, e.g.*, Hodgkinson v. Simms, [1994] 3 SCR 377; SEC v. Capital Gains Research Bureau, 375 U.S. 180 (1963).

client entrusts the adviser with factual discretionary power over him because the client lacks the specialized knowledge possessed by the adviser and thus, practically speaking, commits his investment decisions to the adviser's discretionary judgment. Thus, on our account of fiduciary relations set out in Chapter 1, the adviser and her client stand in a fiduciary relation, and therefore the adviser owes the client a fiduciary duty that controls the adviser's exercise of factual discretionary power in relation to her client.

A similar account can be given of the ISO's relation to its stakeholders and the wider public affected by the adoption of its standards. The ISO's rulemaking power is other-regarding (it concerns only the interest of its stakeholders and the wider public in having sound industrial standards), purposeful (it is oriented toward the development of sound industrial standards), and lawfully institutional (it comprehends the development of standards within an institutional context that is transparent, inclusive, and responsive, and avoids—or can avoid—instrumentalizing anyone). The stakeholders most affected by the development of a standard entrust its development to the ISO, and ordinarily the ISO accepts this charge. Notwithstanding the private constitution of its organization, the ISO's mission is avowedly public in nature, as it involves resolving transnational coordination problems over standards that potentially impact "everyone, everywhere." In undertaking a public mission, then, the ISO enters into a public fiduciary relation with stakeholders and the wider public affected by its development of a new standard. The ISO's overarching fiduciary duty is to develop such standards impartially, through the use of a transparent, responsive, and participatory institutional framework. Opportunities for stakeholder participation and responsiveness within the ISO process are similar to the opportunities for participation and responsiveness embedded in notice-and comment procedures governing rulemaking in some national jurisdictions.[217] In effect, notice-and-comment procedures are to rulemaking what due process is to adjudication.[218] In both national and transnational contexts, subjection to a notice-and-comment duty allows the relevant rulemaking entity to claim credibly that it speaks on behalf of those affected by its determinations. The legitimate rulemaking of the ISO is necessarily regulated by such a duty because it is only through this regulation that the ISO can be understood to develop standards on behalf of all who are affected by them. In other words, the ISO's subjection to duty allows it to satisfy the fiduciary theory's criterion of legitimacy. The legal source and basis of the ISO's administrative law-like obligations, then, is its public fiduciary relationship to stakeholders and the affected public.

Consistent with the arbitral conception of authority discussed above, the ISO's legal authority to develop standards is constituted in part by its subjection to a fiduciary duty to exercise its rulemaking power impartially and within a transparent,

217. *See* 5 U.S.C. § 553 (providing for general notice-and-comment procedures); U.S. Dep't of Justice, Attorney General's Manual on the Administrative Procedure Act 26 (1947) ("In general, the purpose of [notice-and-comment rulemaking] is to guarantee to the public an opportunity to participate in the rule making process.").

218. *See* Evan J. Criddle, *When Delegation Begets Domination: Due Process of Administrative Lawmaking*, 46 Ga. L. Rev. 117, 191–93 (2011) (characterizing notice-and-comment procedures and due process as complementary checks against domination).

participatory, and responsive institutional framework. The key difference between the financial adviser's power and the ISO's is that one is public in nature whereas the other is not. By "public" we mean that the ISO's power is constituted to resolve a certain kind of coordination problem, and that to act consistently with its fiduciary duty, the ISO must take into account all potentially affected parties, including stakeholders with divergent interests. The public nature of the ISO's rulemaking power triggers a *public*—not private—fiduciary obligation, and subjection to this public fiduciary duty lends the *exercise* of the ISO's rulemaking power a limited and very particular kind of legal authority.

Because, strictly speaking, subscription to its standards is voluntary, the ISO does not have authority to impose duties on firms to adopt its standards. The content of its authority, rather, derives from its rulemaking capacity to resolve coordination problems between firms through the development of standards. Firms are under a liability to lose the benefits of cooperation if they choose to behave as voluntary outcasts by declining to use ISO standards. To the extent this loss of benefits entails a change in the firm's legal position (e.g., through the loss of property or contractual entitlements that depend on the firm's adoption of an ISO standard), the liability is legal and not merely factual or prudential.

Although it is true that a firm's rejection of ISO standards would be a sufficient cause of the firm's loss of benefits, that hypothetical causal story must be interpreted within the context of the ISO's dominance of the transnational standard-setting domain. Most transnational firms, to conduct business at all, must work with other firms and suppliers, many of which will themselves work with still other firms and suppliers, and so on. The transnational commercial domain is thus a complex sphere populated by interdependent actors who are often divided by numerous degrees of separation. The ascendant position of the ISO in this domain entails that in practice a transnational firm—an entity created for the purpose of lawfully maximizing profit—could not be a transnational firm without adopting ISO standards. There is, in practice, no exit from the ISO regime that is consistent with a transnational firm being a transnational firm; that is., an entity dedicated to maximizing profit lawfully.[219] In a good sense, then, the "choice" of a firm to adopt ISO standards is existential: to be a transnational firm capable of engaging in commerce, ISO standards must be used for the production and distribution of goods, and those standards therefore are partially constitutive of the legal framework of transnational commerce. It follows that the liability of firms to the exercise of the ISO's rulemaking power is a legal liability of a very comprehensive kind, for the firms' very ability to operate within the legal framework of transnational commerce (i.e., their ability to buy and sell goods transnationally) depends on their adoption of ISO standards. The ISO, we suggest, achieves legal authority to subject firms to this liability through the dutiful exercise of its rulemaking power. The ISO's subjection to and compliance with its fiduciary duty to stakeholders and others, then, is constitutive of its rulemaking authority.

We have not yet, however, addressed the *distributive* dimension of the ISO's authority. Why does the ISO, as opposed to some other entity, get to set international

219. For the classical statement on the practical implications of a lack of exit, see ALBERT O. HIRSCHMAN, EXIT, VOICE, AND LOYALTY (1970).

industrial standards? In our view, the ISO can be conceived as the authorized occupant of a public office notwithstanding its private constitution. There are precedents for this idea in both international law and legal theory. As discussed in Chapter 5, in cases of belligerent occupation, international law will confer on the (illegitimate) occupier a temporary authority to establish and maintain legal order. In the absence of the rightful sovereign, the occupier is recognized to have a mandate to rule. Arguably closer still to the case of the ISO is Hobbes's treatment of the so-called "right of zeal" from scriptural Judaic Law.[220] Hobbes recounts the case of Phinehas's killing of Zimri and Cozbi, an Isrealite and Midianite who married, contrary to Moses's command. Although Phinehas executed Zimri and Cozbi as a private party without affording them the benefit of a hearing or trial, Hobbes claims that the execution could be understood as lawful "upon a subsequent ratification."[221] In the same paragraph he extrapolates that the "presumption of a future ratification is sometimes necessary . . . as in a sudden rebellion any man that can suppress it by his own power . . . without express law or commission, may lawfully do it, and provide to have it ratified or pardoned whilst it is in doing or after it is done."[222] When the actions of a private party serve a public purpose, the possibility of their contemporaneous or subsequent public ratification entails that in these circumstances a private actor may be understood to hold a public office or warrant that authorizes her acts.

In the case of the ISO, it is significant that its standards are recognized ex post as authoritative in decisions of international regulatory organizations such as the WTO.[223] This recognition by international public institutions is arguably a form of public ratification of the ISO's standards and standard-setting process. As such, it can explain how international law distributes to the ISO legal authority to set transnational standards, notwithstanding their non-binding nature and the ISO's private constitution. This is not to say that the ISO has a monopoly on standard-setting. In principle, any number of transnational standard-setters could develop standards and enjoy public ratification. The fiduciary theory's distributive criterion in this area is not externally constrained by the territorial limits of the earth's surface, as it is in the case of its distribution of territorial sovereignty to states. Thus, a plurality of private-*cum*-public institutions with overlapping mandates is fully conceivable. Generally, we might imagine the norms and standards of private global regulators to comprise a form of non-binding transnational common law or *lex mercatoria*. Entry into this pantheon would be guided by the fiduciary principle's criterion of legitimacy, which always asks whether a norm, standard or body of soft law that purports to be made on behalf of everyone subject to it has in fact been so made.

We cannot explore the extent to which this analysis is more widely applicable to the myriad informal transnational networks and institutions that govern "global

220. Hobbes, *supra* note 81, at 492 (Review & Conclusion, ¶ 10).

221. *Id.* at 493 (Review & Conclusion, ¶ 11).

222. *Id.* at 493–94 (Review & Conclusion, ¶ 11). For elaboration of this idea in relation to the criminal law doctrine of self-defense, see Malcolm Thorburn, *Justifications, Powers and Authority*, 117 Yale L.J. 1070 (2008). Where violence can be fairly characterized as self-defense, the public warrant model authorizes the assaulted party to act as a public official would be entitled to act were she present and available to stop the assault.

223. Kingsbury et al., *supra* note 9, at 23.

administrative space."[224] The prospects for such research are rich and exciting, however, because establishing the legal authority and administrative law-like obligations of private bodies is arguably among the most challenging theoretical puzzles confronting the global administrative law project. Global administrative lawyers tend to focus their attention on how global governance can be made accountable so as to address the "real democracy or legitimacy deficits in global administrative governance."[225] The fiduciary theory takes these insights on board, and contributes to them by providing to global administrative law a distinctively legal blueprint for a "plausible sources chapter."

In the next section, we discuss various domestic implications of international law under the fiduciary theory, as well as the theory's prescriptions regarding the relationship between international and domestic institutions in various contexts.

V. THE RELATIONSHIP BETWEEN INTERNATIONAL AND DOMESTIC INSTITUTIONS

In international law and legal scholarship today, there is a rough divide between global constitutionalists and pluralists. Constitutionalists view international law (or significant sectors of it) as a form of higher law that is integrated with and hierarchically superior to domestic law.[226] Pluralists defend the autonomy of municipal law on the grounds that it gives best expression to a people's right to collective self-determination.[227] Various publicists seek to reconcile constitutionalism with pluralism, or at least establish a détente in which neither dominates the other.[228] The dispute between constitutionalists and pluralists parallels the venerable debate between monists and dualists. Monists see international and national law as part of a single legal system, whereas dualists see the two kinds of law as distinctive and operating on different planes, with the result that for dualists international norms must be legislatively implemented into municipal law to have domestic effect.

224. We acknowledge that the Lockean account of fiduciary authority outlined in Chapter 1 may provide a more direct justification of the public authority of private global entities than our Kantian/Hobbesian account. Recall that for Locke, private parties in the state of nature have natural public powers (i.e., rights of redress and punishment), and so it could be argued that private bodies operating transnationally (and without subjection to a common authority) already have an inherent measure of public authority. We cannot pursue this here. In our view, on balance the Kantian/Hobbesian approach is preferable because its sharp public/private distinction allows it to explain comprehensively the anti-unilateralist structure and ethos of international law.

225. Kingsbury et al., *supra* note 9, at 31.

226. *See, e.g.*, BARDO FASSBENDER, THE UNITED NATIONS CHARTER AS THE CONSTITUTION OF THE INTERNATIONAL COMMUNITY (2009); Stephen Gardbaum, *Human Rights as International Constitutional Rights*, 19 EUR. J. INT'L. L. 749 (2009); Anne Peters, *Are We Moving Towards Constitutionalization of the World Community?*, *in* REALIZING UTOPIA: THE FUTURE OF INTERNATIONAL LAW 118 (Antonio Cassese ed., 2012).

227. *See, e.g.*, NICO KRISCH, BEYOND CONSTITUTIONALISM: THE PLURALIST STRUCTURE OF POSTNATIONAL LAW (2012); BRADLEY ROTH: SOVEREIGN EQUALITY AND MORAL DISAGREEMENT: PREMISES OF A PLURALIST INTERNATIONAL LEGAL ORDER (2011).

228. *See, e.g.*, COHEN, *supra* note 23; Kumm, *supra* note 23; Neil Walker, *Our Constitutional Unsettlement*, 2014 PUB. L. 529 (2014); Eyal Benvenisti & Alon Harel, *Embracing the Tension*

Commonwealth countries are dualist in orientation, whereas some European states such as the Netherlands adopt a monist approach.[229]

The fiduciary theory counsels a context-sensitive approach under which states owe a certain measure of deference to the determination of an international decision-maker. The measure of deference owed operates on a continuum that runs from ordinary deference through heightened deference to stringent deference. The kind of deference due in a given case is guided by the nature of the parties to the dispute, the identification of which provides a helpful starting point for answering the fundamental question of whether one of the parties, such as a state, has standing to rule on the relevant matter vis-à-vis *the other party*. As noted in Chapter 6, Kant identified three parties implicated by the combination of municipal law, the law of nations, and cosmopolitan law: states, nationals, and non-nationals. One of the burdens of this chapter has been to show that international institutions serving as direct fiduciaries of humanity are like states in that both are agents and subjects of international law. In practice, then, we can identify four legal relationships of interest to our inquiry into the relative authority of international institutions vis-à-vis domestic institutions tasked with interpreting international law: states versus states, states versus international institutions (as direct fiduciaries of humanity), states versus nationals, and states versus non-nationals.[230]

A. Inter-State Disputes

In the case of inter-state disputes, neither party has standing to resolve the matter, as neither can do so without engaging in unilateralism against the other state. In this context, the fiduciary theory supports a robust constitutionalist approach in which international law and the determinations of its institutions are treated as authoritative. The same reasoning applies to disputes involving states and international institutions acting as surrogate states, in a quasi-sovereign capacity, or in some other manner as direct fiduciaries of humanity. Where international institutions are acting as direct fiduciaries of humanity, they, like states, are akin to municipalities or administrative agencies within national legal orders whose actions are subject to independent review. The *Reparations for Injuries Case* supplies a nice example. In that case, the U.N. Secretariat was not entitled to announce unilaterally that

Between National and International Human Rights Law: The Case for Parity (GlobalTrust Working Paper Apr. 4, 2015), http://globaltrust.tau.ac.il/publications (last visited Oct. 25, 2015).

229. *See, e.g.*, 1 William R. Anson, The Law and Custom of the Constitution 65–66 (4th ed. 1935) (affirming that in the United Kingdom a treaty cannot amend municipal law without explicit legislative endorsement); André Nollkaemper, *The Application of Treaties in the Netherlands*, *in* The Role of Domestic Courts in Treaty Enforcement: A Comparative Study 326 (David Sloss ed., 2009) (discussing the Netherlands' monism and its lack of the dualist requirement of legislative implementation).

230. There may also be conflicts between international institutions, between international institutions and nationals or non-nationals, between nationals, between non-nationals, and between nationals and non-nationals. We set these conflicts aside for now, as they do not bring into relief directly the issue of the legal authority of international institutions relative to national institutions, nor illuminate how best to understand the relationship between public institutions at the national and international levels.

member-states were liable for injuries suffered by U.N. personnel stationed on their territory. The matter had to be adjudicated by the ICJ. That the U.N. Secretariat is an international body was of no relevance because the Secretariat lacked prima facie authority to determine liability for breaches of international obligations. Furthermore, even if the Secretariat did possess such authority as a general matter, it could not exercise its purported authority in this case because for the Secretariat to do so would have made it judge and party to the same cause.

In these sorts of cases as well as pure inter-state disputes, the appropriate attitude of state or state-like parties subject to international courts is stringent deference. As a general matter, only evidence of bad faith or corruption on the part of the international arbiter would clearly justify a national body's rejection of an international ruling. Moreover, even a legitimate rejection of an international ruling would not empower one state to resolve its dispute with another state, as the problem of unilateralism would again arise. To respect the internal requirements of international legal order with respect to inter-state and similar disputes, the parties must follow Hobbes's admonition and "set up for right reason the reason of some arbitrator, or judge, to whose sentence they will both stand, or their controversy must either come to blows, or be undecided, for want of a right reason constituted by Nature."[231] When national courts purport to act as international courts in situ (a possibility we discuss next section), international courts should take the reasons for their rulings into account, but cannot defer to their outcomes. In inter-state disputes there may be two national courts arriving at different outcomes, and so to defer to the determination of one would be to let that court's will prevail over the other. An international court has to render its own judgment impartially. This may appear to confirm one national-level ruling while denying the other. However, so long as the international court treats the parties before it impartially, its judgment cannot be fairly characterized as deference to the ruling of one or the other national courts.

The *Western Sahara Case*[232] illustrates the role international courts can play as impartial arbiters of inter-state disputes. At issue before the ICJ were competing claims to sovereignty over the Spanish Sahara (now Western Sahara) during its decolonization. Spain quit the territory before organizing a referendum. The claimants at the ICJ were Morocco, which adjoins Western Sahara to the north, and Mauritania, which adjoins it to the south and east. Importantly, however, a U.N. mission found in 1975 that "the majority" of the local Sahrawi population was "manifestly in favour of independence" from Spain, Morocco, and Mauritania.[233] Although the ICJ found that there were historical "legal ties" between Western Sahara and both Morocco and Mauritania, it also found that there was no "tie of territorial sovereignty between the territory of Western Sahara" and either of the claimants.[234] The court thus concluded that there was no international legal impediment to the decolonization of Western Sahara in accordance with "the principle of

231. Hobbes, *supra* note 81, at 23 (ch. 5, ¶ 3).

232. Western Sahara, Advisory Opinion, 1975 ICJ Rep. 12 (Oct. 16).

233. *See* Report of the United Nations Mission to Spanish Sahara, U.N. GAOR, 30th Sess., Supp. No. 23, at 66, U.N. Doc A/10023/Rev. 1 (1975).

234. *Id.* at 68.

self-determination through the free and genuine expression of the will of the peoples of the Territory."[235] The case is instructive because both parties before the court had arguable claims about which reasonable disagreement was possible, and which called for an independent assessment. It is also instructive because it shows that the Court can take account of the interests of nonparticipants—"the peoples of the Territory"—so as to guide the distribution of sovereignty as a fiduciary of humanity.

B. Disputes between States and Their Nationals

At the other pole of the deference continuum is a dispute between a state and one or more of its citizens. In this context, the state enjoys delegated authority from international law to govern its citizens autonomously, thus allowing for their collective self-determination. Moreover, many states have independent judiciaries. When these judiciaries take account of international law in their rulings, and in particular IHRL, they embody Scelle's idea of *dédoublement fonctionelle* by acting as international as well as national courts, thereby providing a first-instance opportunity for independent international review.[236] In virtue of states' delegated authority to govern their people, the democratic value of self-rule, and the possibility of national courts wearing international hats, on the fiduciary view international institutions owe ordinary deference to the determinations of national public actors.

By "ordinary deference" we mean what David Dyzenhaus calls "deference as respect," which requires "not submission but respectful attention to the reasons offered or which could be offered in support of a decision."[237] On this conception, deference, like respect, is earned. Deference is not given blindly but rather is earned when the decision-maker provides a public justification that shows—or with friendly amendments could show—that the decision under review has legal warrant, and therefore authority of law.[238] Within this conception, we would expect deference to be modulated and adjusted to take account of various contextual factors, as occurs in many national jurisdictions when judges review administrative action.[239] For example, ordinarily we would expect less deference with respect to

235. *Id.*

236. *See, e.g.,* Gérard V. La Forest, *The Expanding Role of the Supreme Court of Canada in International Law Issues,* 34 Canadian Y.B. Int'l L. 89, 100 (1996) (a Supreme Court of Canada justice observing that international human rights norms "are applied consistently, with an international vision and on the basis of international experience. Thus our courts—and many other national courts—are truly becoming international courts in many areas involving the rule of law.").

237. David Dyzenhaus, *The Politics of Deference: Judicial Review and Democracy, in* The Province of Administrative Law 286 (Michael Taggart ed., 1997).

238. By "earned" we do not mean what U.S. scholars sometimes intend when they speak of "earned deference" implying no deference at all, where the reviewing court is understood to exercise independent judgment that need not take into account the reasons offered for an administrative decision. *See, e.g.,* Kristin E. Hickman & Matthew D. Krueger, *In Search of the Modern Skidmore Standard,* 107 Colum. L. Rev. 1235 (2007).

239. *See, e.g.,* Dunsmuir v. New Brunswick, [2008] 1 SCR (calibrating deference based on the nature of the issue (legal, factual, or mixed), relative expertise, the nature of the decision (legal

national interpretations of a norm of jus cogens than we would with respect to human rights norms subject to restriction or progressive realization, such as social and economic rights. Likewise, we would expect less deference to be accorded legal as opposed to factual determinations, where the national authority can usually be presumed to have best access to the available evidence. And, we would expect less deference with respect to executive or administrative decisions than might be accorded to the rulings of independent judiciaries that made credible efforts to act as in situ international courts by taking international law into account.

Importantly, the idea of deference as respect implies that international courts have an obligation to amend if possible the reasons national actors offer for their decisions, so as to respect the lawgiving authority of the national decision-maker. As discussed in Chapter 4, international courts typically grant national bodies a "margin of appreciation" when assessing the international legality of their actions or decisions.[240] When international courts deploy the margin of appreciation doctrine to take seriously the "reasons offered or which could be offered" by a national authority, they affirm the legitimacy of states as international public actors by exhibiting deferential respect for state efforts to reconcile the demands of international legality with their people's preferred means of self-determination. Likewise, when national authorities take international law seriously, they show respect for the wider international legal system that distributes sovereignty to them. In the state-citizen context, deference is a two-way street, governing international as well as national decision-making.

Particularly hard cases arise when a democratic regime and its independent judiciary come to one view on the interpretation of a contested legal norm of international concern, an international court subsequently reaches a contrary conclusion, and then the apex court at the national level must give judgment in another proceeding in which the legal meaning of the contested norm is at stake. *R v. Horncastle and Others*[241] is one such case. The U.K. Supreme Court (UKSC) had to rule on whether the admission of evidence from witnesses not available for cross-examination (i.e., hearsay) was consistent with the right to a fair trial guaranteed under Article 6 of the European Convention on Human Rights. Earlier the same year, the Fourth Section Chamber of the ECHR had ruled against the United Kingdom in a similar case, *Al-Khawaja and Tahery v UK*.[242] In that case, the ECHR had held that a conviction based "solely or to a decisive degree" on hearsay evidence violates Article 6, notwithstanding counterbalancing factors within the national legal system that protect the accused and favor admission of the relevant hearsay (the "sole or decisive rule").[243] In *Horncastle*, a unanimous UKSC held that this was a "rare" occasion where the

interpretation or discretionary), the purpose of the statute and the relevant provision within it, and the presence or absence of a privative clause).

240. *See* Brannigan & McBride v. United Kingdom, (1994) 17 E.H.R.R. 539, 556 (quoting *Ireland v. United Kingdom*); Ireland v. United Kingdom, 1 ECHR 15, ¶ 207 (1961).

241. [2009] UKSC 14 (Dec. 9, 2009).

242. Al-Khawaja & Tahery v. United Kingdom, App nos 26766/05 and 22228/06, [2009] 49 EHRR 1 (ECHR, Jan. 20. 2009).

243. *Id.* ¶¶ 36 (citing Lucà v. Italy, no. 33354/96, ECHR 2001-II, § 40), 41–48.

court had "concerns as to whether a decision of the Strasbourg Court sufficiently appreciates or accommodates particular aspects of our domestic process. In such circumstances, it is open to this court to decline to follow the Strasbourg decision, giving reasons for adopting this course."[244]

In an exhaustive seventy-five-page judgment that canvassed the principles and rules on hearsay from the United Kingdom and the ECHR, as well as numerous common law and civilian jurisdictions, the UKSC found that it was not obligated to apply the sole or decisive rule if the hearsay evidence was reliable and the principle of a fair trial was not compromised.[245] The UKSC was encouraged by the ECHR's past practice of concerning itself with the fairness of the trial as a whole rather than the admissibility of certain evidence, and the fact that the Grand Chamber of the ECHR had deliberately stayed its appeal hearing of *Al-Khawaja* until after the UKSC had the opportunity to give judgment in *Horncastle*.[246] The UKSC expressed the hope that its decision would "give the Strasbourg Court the opportunity to reconsider the particular aspect of the decision that is in issue, so that there takes place what may prove to be a valuable dialogue between this court and the Strasbourg Court."[247]

That hope was fulfilled when the Grand Chamber, in a judgment as exhaustive as *Horncastle*, subsequently upheld the UKSC's determination that exceptions to the sole and decisive rule were permissible if, on the facts of a given case, safeguards from the national legal system ensure that the admission of hearsay does not compromise the fairness of the trial.[248] The Grand Chamber agreed that an exception to the sole and decisive rule was justified in Al-Khawaja's case, but disagreed with the UKSC's failure to apply the rule in Tahery's case, concluding ultimately that in this instance there had been a violation of Article 6.[249]

The Grand Chamber's temporary stay of its hearing is a vivid depiction of how international courts can attend to Alexander Bickel's "passive virtues" so as to let national courts adjust and apply international norms to the particular contexts of their national legal systems.[250] The interplay between *Horncastle* and *Al-Khawaja* is also a testament to how international courts can apply the margin of appreciation doctrine in conformity with deference as respect by attending carefully to the reasons offered in support of a national level decision, even if there is a difference in opinion regarding a case's final disposition. More generally still, the interplay of the two cases suggests that international and national law can share a constitutionalist sensibility without effacing important differences that exist at the national level. We venture that if a reconciliation of constitutionalism and pluralism is at all possible, that possibility will depend on the kind of commitment displayed by the reason-giving of

244. *Horncastle*, [2009] UKSC ¶ 11.

245. *Id.* ¶ 108.

246. *Id.* ¶¶ 87, 9.

247. *Id.* ¶ 11.

248. Case of Al-Khawaja & Tahery v. United Kingdom, 26766/05 [2011] ECHR 2127 (Dec. 15, 2011, Grand Chamber), ¶¶ 146–151.

249. *Id.* ¶¶ 153–65.

250. Alexander Bickel, The Least Dangerous Branch: The Supreme Court at the Bar of Politics (2d ed. 1986).

the UKSC and the ECHR's Grand Chamber, which is a shared commitment to the compulsion of legality and the idea of law as a public culture of justification.

C. Disputes between States and Foreign Nationals

The final kind of interaction we will briefly discuss involves states exercising public power over foreign nationals. In this context, the appropriate standard of review for international entities to adopt when they review decisions of national actors is ordinary deference or deference as respect, for the reasons given above. Deference as respect affirms the legitimacy of national bodies authorized to make decisions on matters of international concern such as IHRL, but nonetheless requires that deference be earned through the production of an adequate justification. However, when *national* entities deliberate over whether to apply an international determination to a given case involving a foreign national, we contend that heightened rather than ordinary deference is owed.

Heightened deference falls between ordinary and stringent deference. Its content approximates the deferential standard of review under the U.S. *Chevron* doctrine,[251] or alternatively, the deferential standard set out by the House of Lords in *Associated Provincial Picture Houses Ltd. v. Wednesbury Corporation*.[252] The basic idea is that in this context national bodies should defer to the international level regarding the interpretation and application of an international norm even if they disagree strongly with the merits of the international decision, as long as some reasonable justification is offered, or could be offered, in defence of the international disposition. There is no bright line separating ordinary from heightened deference, as in both cases the justification of the decision is paramount. These different standards of deference are positioned relative to each other on a continuum rather than a spectrum. The distinction between ordinary and heightened deference, then, is a matter of degree, and will invariably rely on the practical judgment of those who apply it and their commitment to legality. The distinction nonetheless appropriately marks, we argue now, the conceptually and normatively superior authority of international institutions in relation to disputes involving states and foreign nationals.

International law delegates to states lawgiving authority over persons within their territory, whether they are nationals or non-nationals. Foreign nationals, however, are generally unlike nationals in two important respects: they are not members of the state's political community and therefore they are not generally entitled to vote in national elections and referenda, and they are liable to expulsion from the state's territory.[253] In practice, state sovereignty as an expression of its people's right

251. Chevron U.S.A., Inc. v. Natural Res. Defense Council, Inc., 467 U.S. 837 (1984).

252. [1948] 1 KB 223.

253. A distinguishing hallmark of citizenship is that it carries an unqualified right to enter and remain in the state of which one is a citizen. Even refugees are potentially subject to deportation if the host state concludes that the conditions justifying refugee status in the home state no longer exist. *See* Convention Relating to the Status of Refugees art. 1.C (5), July 28, 1951, 189 U.N.T.S. 150 (permitting removal if "[the refugee] can no longer, because the circumstances in connection with which he has been recognized as a refugee have ceased to exist, continue to refuse to avail himself of the protection of the country of his nationality").

of self-determination has been interpreted to imply that states can determine unilaterally whether a foreign national can enter its territory (refugees excepted), and the terms and conditions on which she may remain. Ordinarily, therefore, a foreign national residing within another state's territory lacks the franchise and is perennially liable to deportation.

When a state and a foreign national come into dispute, both of these differences support recognition of the standing of international institutions to resolve the matter. Because non-nationals generally cannot vote, the state's authority to govern them cannot flow from its internal democratic credentials; the foreign national is simply not part of the relevant demos. As a consequence, the state's laws are not laws that the foreign national can be said to have authored jointly with members of the local political community, and so *her* subjection to them is not an instance of her and others giving laws to themselves. Nor can the state's authority over foreign nationals within its territory flow from its legal capacity under international law to serve as its people's vehicle for self-determination. The foreign national is not one of the state's people, in the relevant sense,[254] and "peoples" under international law are the collective entities to which the right of self-determination applies.[255]

On the fiduciary view, when international law authorizes states to govern a particular territory, it does so on behalf of humanity at large as well as the nationals of the polity within that territory. As Benvenisti puts it capaciously, from the perspective of viewing sovereigns as trustees of humanity, "the entire system of state sovereignty is subject to the duty to protect human rights."[256] Patrick Macklem offers a kindred analysis, arguing that human rights "require the international legal order to attend to pathologies of its own making" by imposing "obligations on sovereign and other legal actors to exercise the authority they receive from international law in ways that respect the rights of all."[257] On our preferred formulation, human rights do not simply limit or mitigate the effects of sovereignty: the duty to respect human rights is itself part of the structure of state sovereignty. Accordingly, international law's authorization of state sovereignty in relation to foreign nationals is not a prerogative power that entitles states to treat foreign nationals howsoever they wish, but rather a limited power to govern them, the very scope of which is partially defined by the duty to respect and protect their human rights.

254. We assume for these purposes that a state does not arbitrarily deny citizenship to individuals within its territory in a manner that would transgress the "right to nationality." *See* Universal Declaration of Human Rights art. 15 ("Everyone has a right to a nationality."); Convention on the Rights of the Child art. 7.1, G.A. Res. 44/25, U.N. GAOR, 44th Sess., U.N. Doc. A/RES/44/25 (1989) ("The child . . . shall have . . . the right to acquire a nationality . . . ."); Peter J. Spiro, *A New International Law of Citizenship*, 105 Am. J. Int'l L. 694, 695 (2011) (identifying developments in state practice that "point to the emergence of norms that require the extension of territorial birthright citizenship in some cases and that limit discretion concerning naturalization thresholds," but concluding that "these trends qualify as no more than the softest kind of law").

255. *See, e.g.*, International Covenant on Civil and Political Rights art. 1, Dec. 16, 1966, S. Treaty Doc. No. 95-20, 6 I.L.M. 368 (1967), 999 U.N.T.S. 171 ("All peoples have the right of self-determination.").

256. Benvenisti, *supra* note 1, at 307.

257. Macklem, *supra* note 74, at 1.

When a dispute arises between a foreign national and a state with an independent judiciary, the state's judiciary may be understood to adjudicate at first instance as an international court in situ. The national court, on this view, is authorized by international law to resolve the dispute between the state and the foreign national, taking into account the relevant international law. The authorization consists in international law's delegation of sovereign powers to the state with respect to nationals and non-nationals within its territory, a delegation that includes judicial powers. Once local avenues for redress are exhausted, however, and the matter proceeds to the international level, a ruling at that level ought to be treated with heightened deference by the national level. One reason for heightened deference is that the ultimate source of national-level authority over foreign nationals is international rather than national law. States cannot credibly give themselves authority over foreign nationals without bootstrapping, whereas international law can give states such authority, because in this context international law alone can speak for foreign nationals. It does so by positing states as fiduciaries of humanity as well as their people. A related and equally important reason for heightened deference is that, in the standard case, international bodies will have the greatest claim to legitimacy because, in principle, they are wholly independent and impartial, having no allegiance to either side.

Importantly, however, although the deference owed by national actors to the international level is heightened, it is not absolute or even stringent, in the sense discussed above. Were international legal order a monist "utopia of legality"[258] in which international law was simply a further avenue of appeal within a single global legal system, something like stringent deference might be appropriate. But international legal order remains fundamentally constituted and structured by states that enjoy primary jurisdiction to articulate and implement the means of their people's self-determination. International law's constitution of sovereignty limits the things sovereigns can do in their people's name, but it nonetheless grants to sovereign states a comprehensive plenary power so that their people can enjoy to the fullest extent possible their right of self-determination. No international institution—not even the Security Council under Chapter VII, nor an international territorial administration—has this kind of mandate.[259] Thus, when international institutions issue rulings or non-binding opinions in relation to state action over foreign nationals, they stand in a relation to the state much like commonwealth courts stand in relation to administrative agencies or municipalities whose actions are subject to national courts' review. In the domestic case, the reviewing court has jurisdiction to pronounce on the legality of the executive body's action. Ordinarily, reviewing courts do not have first-instance decision-making authority. Thus, the standard remedy at administrative law is that the frontline decision is vacated and sent back to the decision-maker for redetermination, taking into account the court's judgment.

258. Lars Vinx, Hans Kelsen's Pure Theory of Law: Legality and Legitimacy 25 (2007) (arguing that Kelsen's political writing and views on international law can be read in conjunction with his legal-theoretical works as theorizing a "utopia of legality" in which legality achieves legitimacy).

259. The institutions of the European Union come closest, but even its regulations with direct effect do not purport to arise from a plenary regulation-making power intended to provide fully and capaciously for the self-determination of the distinctive peoples of member states.

Although it would be more efficient for a reviewing court to make an order tantamount to the decision it believes would be correct or reasonable, the court would offend the rule of law were it to do so, as such an order is not authorized by law.

The same is generally true of international courts and other bodies that give judgments or opinions on matters of international concern in cases involving states and foreign nationals. Although various international institutions have authority to rule on these matters, they do not typically have primary jurisdiction to govern within a state; only the state has this jurisdiction. Moreover, the state has a responsibility to its people and their right of self-determination, and is entitled to make their legitimate interests its predominant—but not exclusive—moral concern. Although international law constitutes and regulates the exercise of sovereign powers, it cannot extinguish those powers without doing violence to the right of self-determination of the people in whose name sovereignty is held. The Security Council targeted sanctions program is a sober reminder that realizing international law's best ambitions is a joint endeavor, and one for which national institutions appropriately bear final responsibility with respect to the people subject to them. In our view, the most that can reasonably be asked of international law is that it draw on the compulsion of legality so as to place recalcitrant states under a particularly heavy justificatory burden when confronted with an adverse international ruling in a case involving a foreign national. Even in the wholesale absence of sanctions to enforce such a ruling, the fiduciary model helps to illuminate that if a state disregards a reasonable determination from the international level, it demonstrates indifference to the ultimate international basis of its authority over foreign nationals. Such a state rules over foreign nationals without authority of law.

Recent litigation over the Vienna Convention on Consular Relations (VCCR)[260] illustrates the tensions that can arise when international and domestic institutions exercise concurrent jurisdiction over disputes between states and foreign nationals. Between 1998 and 2009, the ICJ considered three cases—*Breard*, *LaGrand*, and *Avena*[261]—in which foreign nationals residing in the United States had been placed on death row without receiving timely notice of their right to consular assistance as guaranteed in Article 36 of the VCCR. In all three cases, state-level courts in the United States deemed the defendants to have waived their VCCR rights under generally applicable procedural default rules by failing to assert these rights in a timely manner before the trial court.[262] The ICJ issued provisional measures in all three cases, emphasizing that the "United States should take all measures at its disposal to ensure that [the defendants are] not executed pending the [Court's] final decision."[263] And in two of the cases, the ICJ proceeded to render a final judgment,

260. Vienna Convention on Consular Relations art. 36, Apr. 24, 1963, 21 U.S.T. 77.

261. *See* Case Concerning Avena and Other Mexican Nationals (Mex. v. U.S.), 2004 ICJ Rep. 12 (Mar. 31); LaGrand Case (Germ. v. U.S.), 2001 ICJ Rep. 466 (June 27); Case Concerning the Vienna Convention on Consular Relations (Paraguay v. U.S.), 1998 ICJ Rep. 248 (Apr. 9) [hereinafter *Breard*].

262. The ICJ determined that the VCCR "creates individual rights for the detained person in addition to the rights accorded the sending State." *LaGrand*, 2001 ICJ Rep. at 497, ¶ 89; *see also id.* at 494, ¶ 77.

263. *See* Case Concerning Avena and Other Mexican Nationals (Mex. v. U.S.), Provisional Measures, 2003 ICJ Rep. 77, 91–92, ¶ 59 (Feb. 5); LaGrand Case (Germ. v. U.S.), Provisional Measures, 1999 ICJ Rep. 9, 16, ¶ 29 (Mar. 3); *Breard*, 1998 ICJ Rep. at 258, ¶ 41.

concluding that the United States had failed to provide an effective remedy for VCCR violations and therefore was obligated to supply a mechanism for judicial reconsideration.[264] Nonetheless, in all of these cases state officials declined to fashion a remedy for the breaches identified by the ICJ, and individuals covered by the ICJ's judgments were promptly executed.[265]

Although the U.S. Supreme Court affirmed that the ICJ's judgments were binding on the United States as a matter of international law[266] and federal officials in the United States encouraged state officials to comply with these judgments,[267] many state officials greeted the ICJ's decisions with indifference, if not outright derision. Although some state courts accorded "respectful consideration" to the ICJ's decisions,[268] others dismissed the ICJ's legal conclusions as non-binding under domestic law without considering whether these conclusions might nonetheless merit a measure of deference.[269] Several state governors publicly repudiated the idea that they should exercise their clemency power to vacate or commute sentences that were based on procedurally defaulted VCCR objections. For example, following the ICJ's provisional measures in *Breard*, then-governor George W. Bush scoffed at legal objections to executions pending in Texas, asserting that the state was not bound by the ICJ's judgments because it was "not a signatory to the [VCCR]."[270] To the extent that state-level officials in the United States casually disregarded the ICJ's

264. *See Avena*, 2004 ICJ Rep. at 50, ¶ 90 & 65–66, ¶¶ 138–41; *LaGrand*, 2001 ICJ Rep. at 497–98 ¶ 91, 514 ¶ 127(7). Following the ICJ decisions, the Inter-American Commission adopted a report concluding that the United States' failure to provide timely notice of VCCR rights also violated the rights to due process and a fair trial under the American Convention on Human Rights. *See* Tamayo v. United States, Case 12.873, Inter-Am. Comm'n H.R., Report No. 44/14, OEA/Ser.L/V/II.151, doc. 9, at 27–28, ¶ 142 (2014).

265. *See* Jeffrey L. Dunoff et al., International Law: Norms, Actors, Process 235–37, 247 (4th ed. 2015).

266. Medellín v. Texas, 552 U.S. 491, 504 (2008) ("No one disputes that the *Avena* decision—a decision that flows from the treaties through which the United States submitted to ICJ jurisdiction with respect to Vienna Convention disputes—constitutes an international law obligation on the part of the United States.").

267. *See* Dunoff et al., *supra* note 265, at 235, 247; *cf. Medellín*, 552 U.S. at 523–32 (concluding that the U.S. president lacks authority to direct state officials to comply with the ICJ's VCCR judgments).

268. *Breard*, 523 U.S. at 375; *see, e.g.*, Com. v. Gautreaux, 941 N.E.2d 616, 621–26 (Mass. 2011); Torres v. Oklahoma, No. PCD-04-442 (Okla. Crim. App. May 13, 2004) (Chapel, J., concurring), 43 I.L.M. 1227 (2004); *cf.* Contreras v. State, 324 S.W.3d 789, 792–93 (Tex. App. Eastland 2010) (acknowledging that ICJ decisions merit respectful consideration, but concluding that they are not relevant to due process analysis under domestic law).

269. *See, e.g.*, Valle v. State, 70 So. 3d 530 (Fla. 2011); People v. Najera, 864 N.E.2d 324 (Ill. 2d Dist. 2007); State v. Sanchez-Llamas, 108 P.3d 573 (Or. 2005). The U.S. Supreme Court has held that the VCCR does not generate "self-executing" obligations under U.S. law. *See* Sanchez–Llamas v. Oregon, 548 U.S. 331 (2006).

270. Andreas L. Paulus, *From Neglect to Defiance? The United States and International Adjudication*, 15 Eur. J. Int'l L. 783, 809 (2004) (citing President George W. Bush, Address on National Public Radio, Dec. 9, 1998); *see also id.* (quoting former Texas governor Rick Perry's assertion that "the International Court of Justice does not have jurisdiction in Texas").

authoritative interpretations of the VCCR, they essentially asserted a prerogative to decide unilaterally which procedures they would apply when prosecuting foreign nationals. Having demonstrated indifference to the ultimate international basis of their authority over foreign nationals, these officials on our view lacked authority to punish foreign nationals within their jurisdiction.

In specifying a range of deferential attitudes appropriate to different contexts, we have deliberately avoided the theoretically complex question of whether national actors owe international institutions a (defeasible) duty to obey. We do not need to resolve this question because the central concept of deference on which we rely is adequate to our purpose and felicitously capacious. Deference is arguably the attitude appropriate for someone subject to a legitimate authority whose directives do imply a duty to obey.[271] But deference is also the attitude appropriate for an authority that must take into account the determination of another authority with whom it is not itself in a relationship of authority. As noted already, this is frequently the attitude of national courts toward the decisions of expert administrative agencies. Deference also animates private international law, where the guiding relational norm is horizontal comity rather than vertical authority.[272] We think that inquiry into the relationship between public international law and national law has much to gain from private international law, and in particular, from its principles governing how norms and legal determinations from one legal system can be respectfully interpreted and applied in another. Our conclusion is that the fiduciary theory's nuanced guidance on the relationship between international and national institutions is applicable to global constitutionalists and pluralists alike. Whether the relation between contending authorities is understood as hierarchical (and constitutionalist/monist), horizontal (and pluralist/dualist), or mixed, the compulsion of legality requires both international and national actors to accord a context-sensitive measure of deference to the justifications offered in support of the other authority's decisions.

In the next and final section, we point to a few areas of future research where the fiduciary theory promises to offer insights, and then offer a few concluding remarks.

VI. CONCLUSION AND FUTURE DIRECTIONS

Over the course of this book, we have discussed the lessons the fiduciary theory holds for international law's understanding of sovereignty, the formation of states, human rights, jus cogens, emergencies, the laws of war, extraterritorial detention, refugee law, and international institutions. Although we believe this array of subjects provides a representative sample of international law's historical and contemporary concerns, it by no means exhausts the avenues of inquiry where the fiduciary theory could be expected to make a significant contribution. These fields include climate change, indigenous rights and sovereignty, global economic justice, and

271. *See, e.g.*, Philip Soper, The Ethics of Deference: Learning from Law's Morals (2002) (explicating the duty to obey the law as a duty to defer).

272. For penetrating discussion, see Timothy Endicott, *Comity among Authorities*, 68 Current Legal Probs. 1 (2015) (affirming that comity can be explained as a horizontal analog of subsidiarity).

global or transnational democracy. Although we cannot do justice to these topics here, our brief concluding observations serve to illustrate how the fiduciary theory may shape international law's future development.

Climate change is a pressing concern of all humanity. One of the signal conceptual challenges faced by scholars working in this area, from a legal point of view, is to explain how states can owe extraterritorial legal duties to foreign nationals affected by their domestic policies. The development of the fiduciary model in Chapter 7 offers a framework to explain such duties. Recall that in Chapter 7 we suggested that states can be viewed collectively as joint fiduciaries of the earth's surface on behalf of humanity, thus explaining the wrong of statelessness and the right of refugees to refuge and (we argue) asylum: every member of humanity has a presumptive right against all states to exist legally somewhere, a right that would be imperiled if states could close their borders to the stateless or refugees. With respect to climate change, the model could be expanded to envision states as co-fiduciaries of the entirety of the earth and its atmosphere on behalf of humanity. As co-fiduciaries, states would have duties to safeguard the environment from degradation, and might further be imagined to have obligations to engage in good faith multilateral negotiations aimed at addressing climate change. The emerging right to a healthy environment could thus be seen to arise from the collective imposition of a system of state sovereignty over the earth and its inhabitants. Conceptualizing states as co-fiduciaries of humanity confronts head-on the familiar view that sovereign states are entitled to craft environmental policy with regard for only their own people's interests. The co-fiduciary approach thereby helps to bring such matters under international law's compulsion of legality.[273]

At the time of this writing, states from around the world were meeting in Paris to negotiate and draft an agreement that aims to address climate change at the global level. These negotiations resulted in the Paris Agreement,[274] which was adopted by 195 countries and folded into the United Nations Framework Convention on Climate Change.[275] The centerpiece of the Paris Agreement is a commitment by all countries to develop and continually update "nationally determined contributions" (NDCs) to mitigate climate change.[276] Sensitive to the concerns of developing countries, the preamble underscores the principle of "equity and common but differentiated responsibilities and respective capabilities."[277] NDCs are to be submitted to the United Nations every five years and used as public metrics to gauge state parties' compliance with their ongoing commitments.[278] Although the success of

273. For pioneering work in this direction, see Mary Christina Wood, Nature's Trust: Environmental Law for a New Ecological Age (2014).

274. Conference of the Parties to the United Nations Framework Convention on Climate Change, Adoption of the Paris Agreement, Annex, Dec. 12, 2015, FCCC/CP/2015/L.9/Rev.1 [hereinafter Paris Agreement].

275. United Nations Framework Convention on Climate Change, May 9, 1992, 1771 U.N.T.S. 107 (entered into force Mar. 21, 1994).

276. Paris Agreement, *supra* note 274, arts. 3, 4.

277. *Id.* pmbl.

278. *Id.* art. 4, ¶ 9.

the plan will depend on the willingness of countries to develop and adhere to meaningful NDCs, the obligation of states to do so is explained by the idea that states, severally and jointly, are fiduciaries of humanity.

Another place where the fiduciary theory might be put to good use concerns indigenous peoples. As noted in Chapters 1 and 2, legal scholars such as Antony Anghie and Martti Koskenniemi rightly decry the way European powers came to invest sovereignty with Eurocentric meaning so as to carry imperial projects into indigenous lands and over indigenous peoples.[279] Worse yet from the standpoint of defending a contemporary fiduciary theory of international law, for centuries colonialism was justified through the use of guardianship and trust-like concepts.[280] Be that as it may, over the past three decades international law has made significant strides in recognizing indigenous rights and, arguably, indigenous sovereignty. The most controversial development in this field has been recognition by international law of a duty on the part of states to obtain indigenous consent whenever states contemplate development of large-scale projects on indigenous peoples' ancestral lands.[281] The duty is truly revolutionary because it gives indigenous peoples a veto over state action, in effect recognizing in them co-legislative power over the project subject to their consent. The implication is that indigenous peoples are now recognized by international law, to a limited extent, as sovereign legal actors *within* sovereign states. Just as the recognition of human rights expanded the subjects of international law to include individuals, the recognition of indigenous sovereignty promises to expand the sovereign legal actors of international law to include indigenous peoples. Because nonstate entities can hold public authority under the fiduciary theory, the theory promises to explain this pluralist reconfiguration of international law's understanding of sovereignty as a progressive development of the right of a people to self-determination.

The fiduciary model can also contribute usefully to debates on the relationship between international law and global economic justice. International law facilitates international trade and commerce through the global integration of markets, institutions such as the WTO and the IMF, and bilateral or multilateral trade agreements (e.g., NAFTA). But international law also addresses global poverty, in large part through the deployment of intrastate and inter-state rights frameworks. The intrastate framework consists mainly of economic, social, and cultural human rights guaranteed in international instruments such as the International Covenant on Economic, Social and Cultural Rights.[282] The barebones of the inter-state framework is also present in this Covenant, which calls on states to "take steps, individually and *through international assistance and co-operation*" to "achieve progressively the

279. *See* ANTONY ANGHIE, IMPERIALISM, SOVEREIGNTY AND THE MAKING OF INTERNATIONAL LAW (2005); MARTTI KOSKENNIEMI, THE GENTLE CIVILIZER OF NATIONS: THE RISE AND FALL OF INTERNATIONAL LAW 1870–1960 (2002).

280. *See, e.g.*, Andrew Fitzmaurice, *Sovereign Trusteeship and Empire*, 16 THEORETICAL INQUIRIES L. 447 (2015).

281. *See Saramaka People*, *supra* note 72.

282. International Covenant on Economic, Social and Cultural Rights, Dec. 16, 1966, S. Treaty Doc. No. 95-19, 6 I.L.M. 360 (1967), 993 U.N.T.S. 3.

full realization of the rights recognized in the present Covenant."[283] The heart of the inter-state legal framework for addressing global poverty, however, is the 1986 U.N. General Assembly Declaration on the Right to Development.[284] The Declaration makes specific reference to the need for "more rapid development of developing countries," and specifies that states have a duty "to formulate international development policies with a view to facilitating the full realization of the right to development."[285]

Macklem persuasively suggests that we can understand the emerging right to development as international law's attempt to mitigate its own contribution to disparities in wealth between developed and developing countries. International law has made this ignoble contribution to global inequality by extending "legal validity to processes of economic globalization and integration" that generally favor developed countries, by fencing in resource-poor states with territorial borders, and by having established inequitable rules governing decolonization that left many colonized peoples irremediably dispossessed of much of their national patrimony by the time they achieved statehood.[286] This reasoning is congenial to the fiduciary theory because both approaches look explicitly to the consequences of subjection to public authority to explain the duties of public authorities. The fiduciary theory develops Macklem's insights by offering a distinctive account of *why* an impoverished people's subjection to the adverse effects of international legal order generates a positive and extraterritorial duty owed collectively by developed states: as fiduciaries of humanity that enjoy international legal authority, developed states must take into account the adverse effects on foreign nationals of the structure and operation of the very international legal order that grants them their authority. Although states can favor their people, for them to do so in a way that takes unfair advantage of arbitrary benefits flowing from the structure and operation of international law would be for them to engage, as fiduciaries of humanity, in a form of self-dealing.

Additionally, the fiduciary model supplies resources to extend the content of the duty correlative to the right to development beyond what may be required for the sake of mitigation, as the fiduciary of humanity's ultimate duty is to bring international legal order into the deepest possible conformity with the secure and equal freedom of every person subject to it. Redistributions of wealth guided by mitigation alone may or may not be enough to satisfy this duty, depending on the facts of a given case. For example, suppose a country such as Thailand were to suffer a natural catastrophe such as a severe and widespread earthquake that devastated its public infrastructure, commercial operations, housing, and so forth. Suppose as well that only a long-term and robust development plan supported by the international community could bring Thailand back to something like the level of development it enjoyed before the disaster. The fiduciary view can explain an international obligation derived from the right to development, because the right flows from the very condition of being subject to an international legal order in which states are viewed

283. *Id.* art. 2(1) (emphasis added).

284. U.N. Doc. A/RES/41/128 (1986) (passed by a vote of 146 to 1 (U.S. voting against), with 8 abstentions).

285. *Id.* art. 4.

286. Macklem, *supra* note 74, at 187.

as fiduciaries of humanity that bear a collective (if secondary) responsibility for humanity as well as their people. Much as R2P provides that the international community bears a secondary responsibility for the peoples of wicked states, the right to development, under the fiduciary theory, provides that the international community bears a secondary obligation to support the development of impoverished states through appropriate international institutions, even when the cause of underdevelopment is natural. The mitigation theory is challenged by these sorts of cases, where the cause of the development crisis and its attendant poverty is not attributable to the operation or structure of international legal order.[287]

The fiduciary theory may also have valuable pointers for developing connections between international law and global or transnational democracy. As global administrative lawyers and others have noted, a major criticism of globalization generally and transnational networks in particular is a lack of democratic legitimacy. In practice, the connection between states and their people is highly attenuated in international affairs. NGOs and other stakeholders can sometimes participate in global governance institutions, but their standing to do so is typically precarious and dependent on the goodwill of the dominant states and major IOs involved in the regulation of a particular matter. So, for example, the WTO's Dispute Resolution Body's practice is to accept amicus curiae briefs (sometimes unsolicited) from NGOs, academics, and other third parties, but there is nothing in the WTO's Dispute Settlement Understanding (the rules that govern dispute settlement) or the Working Procedures for appellate review that address the issue.[288] Although stakeholder participation such as this may contribute to the accountability and democratic legitimacy of global bodies, what is missing is a general account of how third parties could be understood to have legal standing to participate in networks or institutions of which they are not formally members.

There are structural similarities between the fiduciary conception of international legal order and transnational democracy that may pave the way toward such an account. Under both fiduciary and democratic principles, for public authority to be legitimate it must be cognizable as an authority that acts on behalf of every person subject to it. Thus, we have seen time and again that under the fiduciary theory, states must respect the human rights of foreign nationals as well as nationals subject to their authority. Likewise, under democratic theory, public authority must act with equal regard for all who are part of the relevant demos; in principle, office holders are not entitled to favor those who voted for them. Democratic theory and the fiduciary theory, in other words, share the same criterion of legitimacy.

When democratic theory of the kind sketched above is combined with the fiduciary theory, we have a democratic and juridical basis for explaining the standing of stakeholders to participate in the institutions of global governance. The possession

287. One reply would be to argue that in practice the structure and operation of international law *always* plays a role in how a natural disaster is addressed, but note that this still leaves the mitigation theory without a *positive* standard of adequacy with which to measure the success or failure of development efforts.

288. WTO Webpage, *Participation in Dispute Settlement Proceedings: Amicus Curiae Submissions*, https://www.wto.org/english/tratop_e/dispu_e/disp_settlement_cbt_e/c9s3p1_e.htm (last visited Nov. 4, 2015).

and exercise of transnational public authority must be justifiable to all who are subject to it such that the authority in question is capable of being understood to act in their name. The fiduciary theory makes this justification possible in part by holding global institutions to various substantive standards, such as those imposed by human rights and international institutional law. But the fiduciary model also makes the justification of authority possible by dovetailing with democratic theory through the requirement that global institutions take seriously the participatory and deliberative procedures of global administrative law. Although it would be utopian to think that global democracy could soon resemble national-level democracy, global institutions' claim to legitimacy arguably rests on their commitment to take seriously the deliberative possibilities of an unbounded demos, beginning with a generous approach to the standing of those most affected by the institutions' policies. On this point, fiduciary and democratic theory are as one.

* * *

Because the fiduciary theory is fundamentally a legal and relational one of what it means for institutions to hold and exercise authority on behalf of others, it offers the possibility of explaining the authority and obligations of any and all institutions that purport to hold public authority. States, international institutions, and transnational networks all fall within the scope of this wide compass. Over the course of this book, we have endeavored to develop a model for thinking about international law and its institutions through a reconceptualization of sovereignty that is interpretively powerful and normatively persuasive. The fiduciary theory is interpretively powerful because it offers an explanation of various spheres of international law that are either under-theorized or highly contested, such as jus cogens, the salience of international law in emergencies, the laws of war applicable to asymmetrical conflict, and the rights of refugees and other foreign nationals subject to the authority of states or international institutions. But its greater interpretative contribution lies in the unified framework it lends to the thought of Francis Deng and others that sovereignty is first and foremost a responsibility owed in equal measure to everyone subject to it.

The normative appeal of the theory lies in its account of what this responsibility entails and the structure of international legal order it demands. On our view, the fiduciary state is under an obligation to guarantee for nationals and non-nationals a regime of secure and equal freedom. This implies a commitment to legal institutions that protect individuals from domination and instrumentalization, as exemplified by the commitment to human rights under the rule of law. At the national level the fiduciary theory seeks to secure people from the threat of unilateralism and abuses of public power. These same principles apply to inter-state and transnational relations as well as cosmopolitan contexts involving states and foreign nationals. In all of these settings, the fiduciary view prescribes an international legal order capable of liberating humanity from the threat of unilateralism. The fiduciary theory of international law is thus a theory of equal and universal freedom.

Index